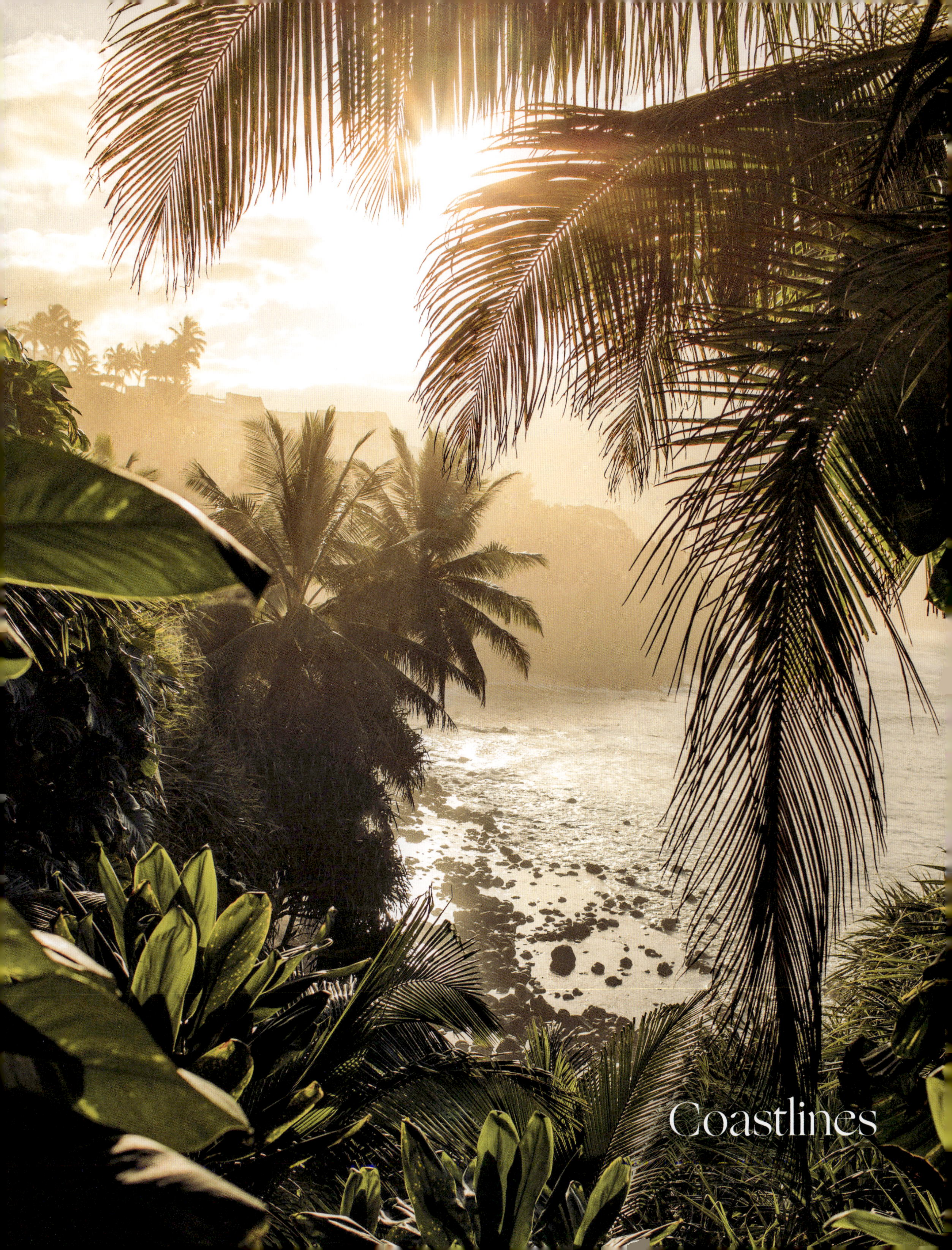
Coastlines

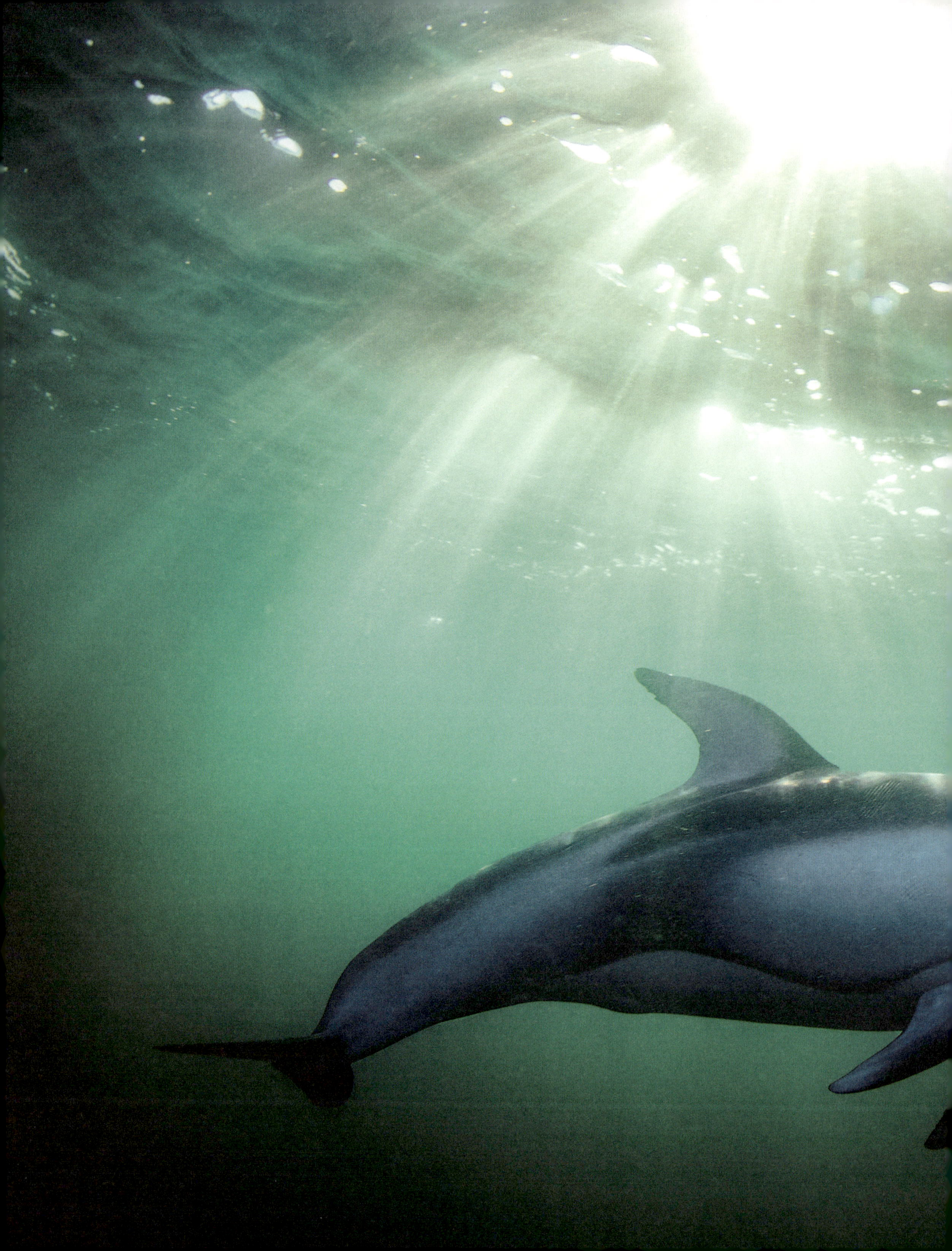

Coastlines

AT THE WATER'S EDGE

EMILY NATHAN

TEN SPEED PRESS
California | New York

contents

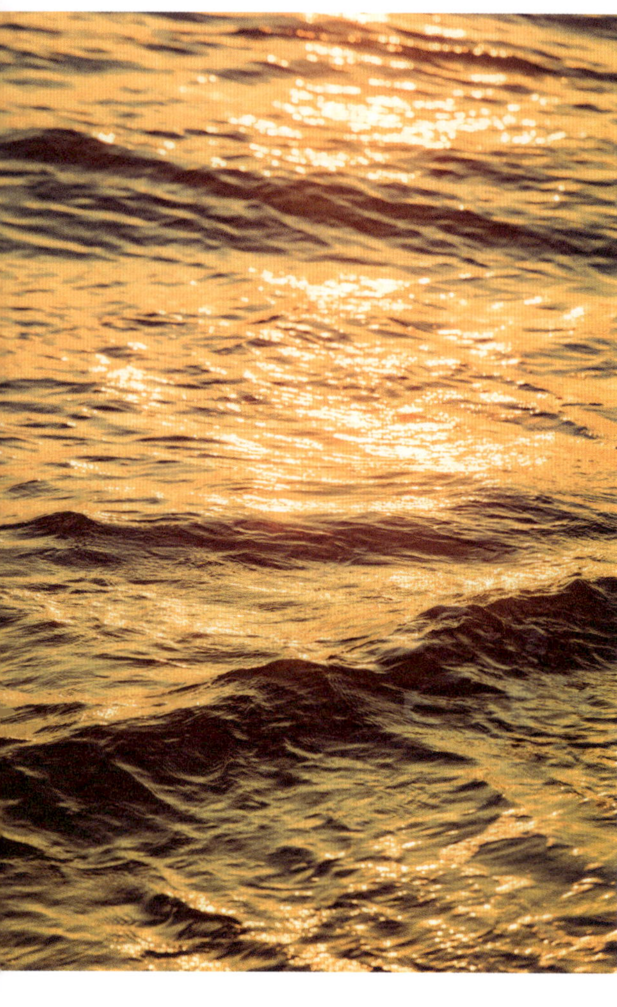

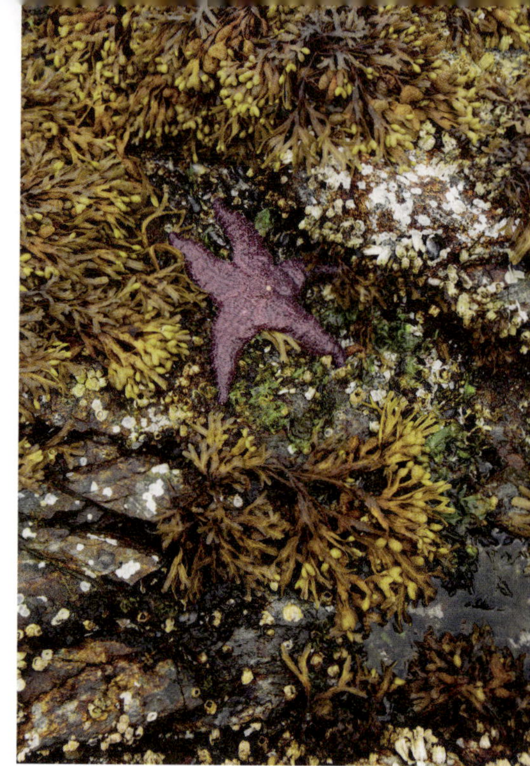

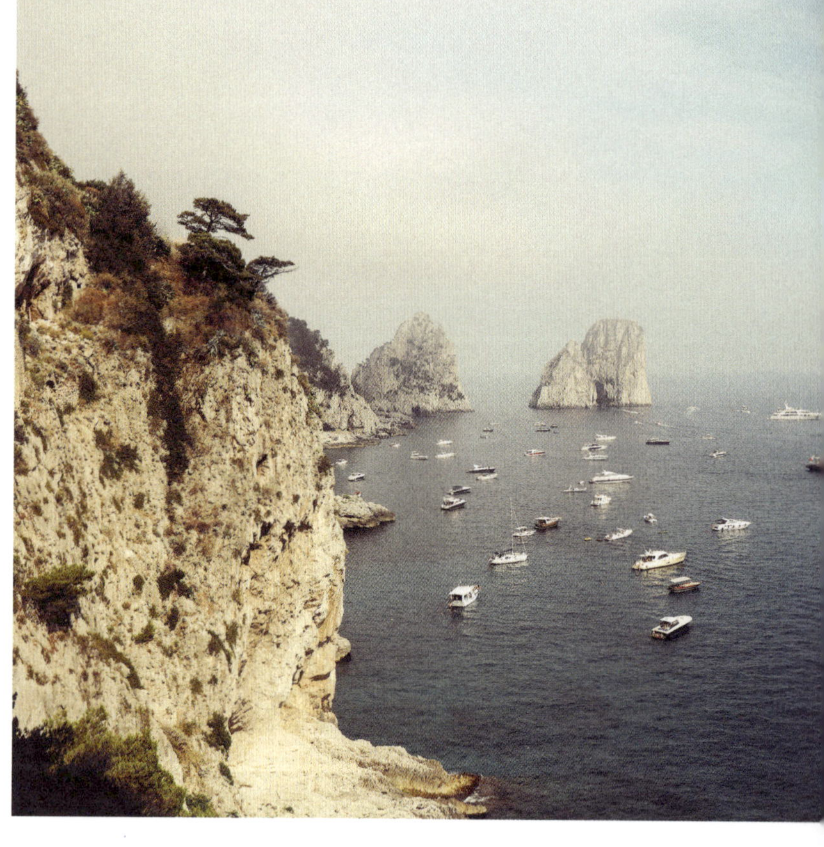

← **i: Princeville, Kaua'i, Hawai'i, United States**

Stefan Elmer

← **ii: Tofino, British Columbia, Canada**

Jeremy Koreski

↑ **Herradura Bay, Costa Rica**

Gabriela Herman

↗ **Nelson Island, British Columbia, Canada**

Grant Harder

→ **Capri, Italy**

Lucy Laucht

Water is the source of all life. Constantly cycling from the earth to the sky and back, water both energizes and calms us. Nowhere is that energy more apparent than on our coasts, where the sea is continuously in motion. We come to the ocean as we come to the stars: for forgiveness, for healing, for love, and for joy. We come to spend time with our loved ones and to spend time with our own thoughts. A reset that reminds us of our own elemental and magnetic nature happens when we submerge ourselves in the ocean. We too are moved by the moon, made up of water, and filled with life. From the moment our feet touch the water from the shore, especially after a long journey, we feel that we have arrived home.

We crave the coasts from the deepest part of our beings. We are soothed by the sound of the water, calmed by watching the waves roll in and out. We pine for the smell of salt in the air. For those of us who live near the sea, we find relief when we make our way to the shore and take a break from our work and commitments. Those of us who live far from the water dream of it and long for the next trip that will take us to a coast. Next to the ocean, we take comfort in how small we and our worries can seem.

For photographers and artists, inspiration arrives with the shifting tides, weather, and light on the coast. My first job was teaching sailing at a summer camp, and the best part was that my office was essentially on the water. My view changed daily: the water's surface calm and blue on a clear day, or black, with wind whipping up white caps on another. Some of the first pictures I took as an artist were made right there as I tried my best to capture the shifting moods. Photographers are drawn to water for reasons similar to those that draw us to faces, for the unending variety and curiosities that we can find there.

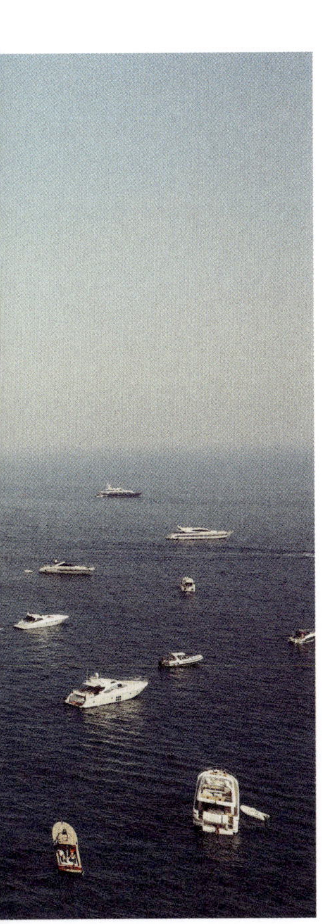

When my online travel magazine *Tiny Atlas Quarterly* brought a group of photographers to Tahiti and Mo'orea—a trip organized for people who love travel and photography and sought a taste of adventure the *Tiny Atlas* way—everyone who came with us was blown away by the lush, wild beauty that surrounded us. While there, we were fortunate to connect with Liz Clark, a native Californian, and her Tahitian partner, Tahui, who lived anchored off a tiny atoll in French Polynesia. Liz is a sailor, writer, surfer, and environmental activist, and she took our group to a special surf break to experience the beauty of her community on the water. She introduced each person who paddled out to all the other surfers (not something that usually happens in a surf lineup). At the end of our brief time on the islands, filled with gratitude for this experience, Tyson Wheatley, one of the photographers on the trip, asked Liz how we could help raise awareness for that beautiful and fragile ecosystem.

Liz explained what she does; how she tries to make her readers and the people who follow her on social media fall in love with the ocean. To her, this is a way she can inspire people to feel a personal responsibility to protect it. She's inspired me to make changes and choices in my own life that are better for the planet and the sea. We cannot rejoice in the gifts of the oceans without acknowledging how humanity is taking its toll on them. Rising sea levels, erosion, and many other issues that result from our choices and lifestyles threaten not only our way of life and survival, but the life and survival of all who call the ocean and its coastlines home. While these problems can seem insurmountable, each of us can choose to take responsibility for the oceans and waterways we love, and we can work to mitigate the damage that has been done. With the knowledge we have gained, we can all make a difference by making better choices.

This book is a celebration of the beauty and power of the world's oceans, and the "How You Can Help" section of each chapter offers a first step for anyone wanting to elevate their love for the ocean into practical steps to protect it. Seeing and experiencing that beauty—in person and in photos—helps us understand and appreciate the majesty of our most important resource and, in turn, to care for it. In her book *On Photography*, Susan Sontag wrote, "The most grandiose result of the photographic enterprise is to give us the sense that we can hold the whole world in our heads—as an anthology of images. To collect photographs is to collect the world." The images in this book are sourced from seashores around the world from more than one hundred professional and amateur photographers. Their images present a patchwork that weaves together a story of our coastlines today, and reminds us of our deep connection to the water.

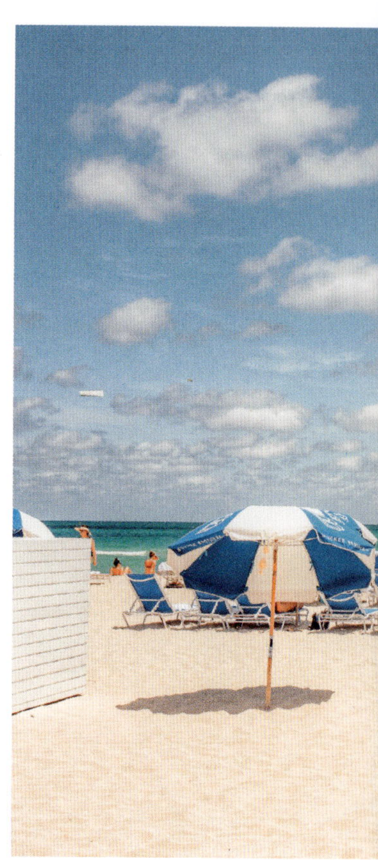

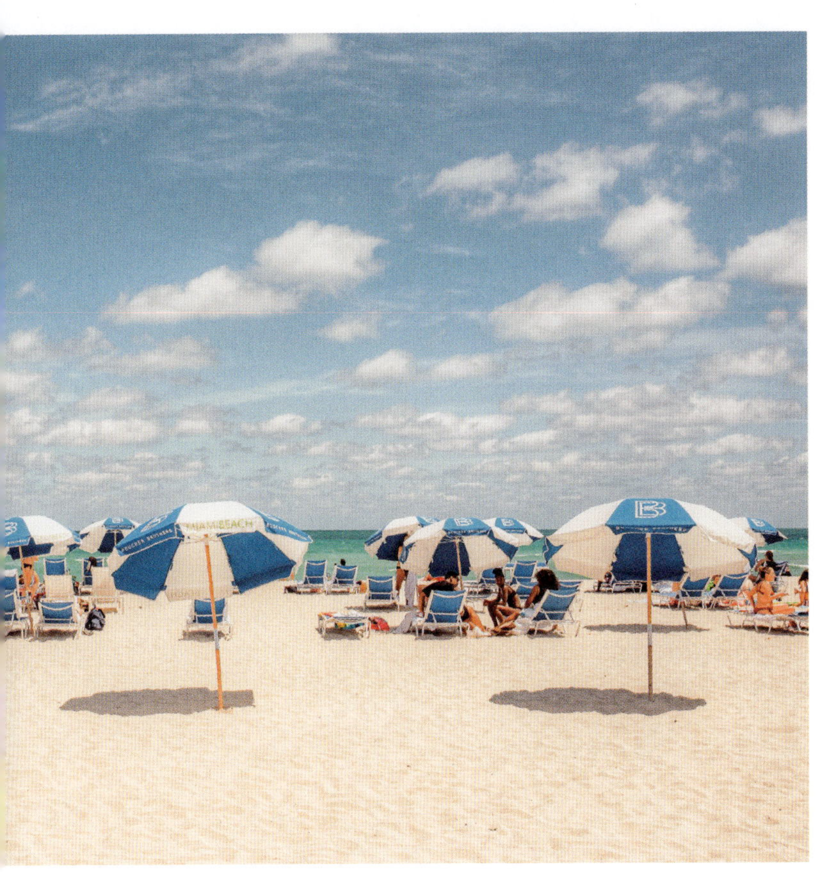

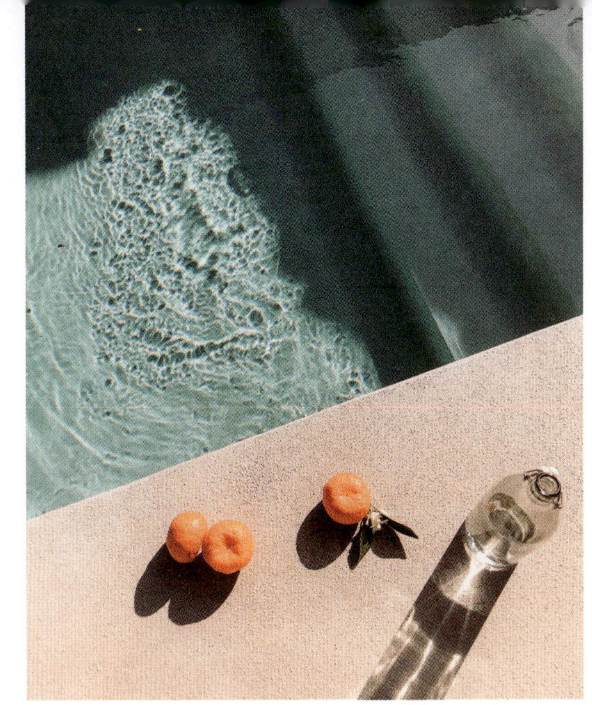

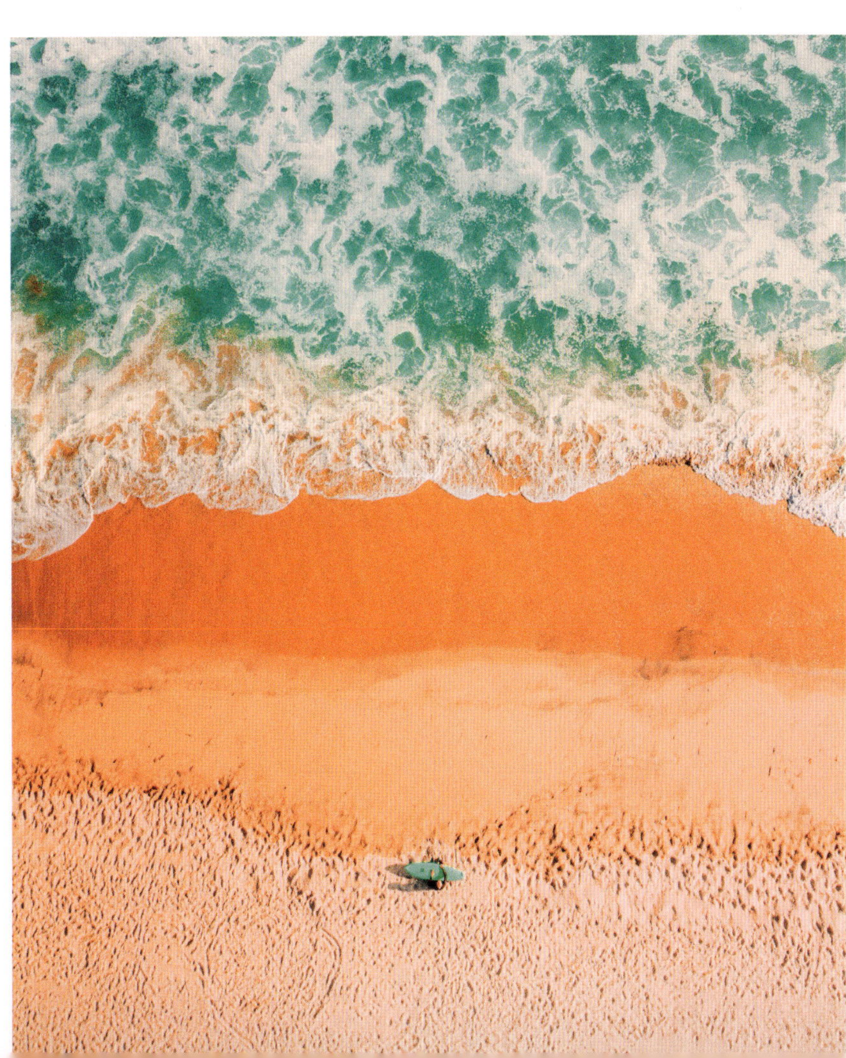

↑
**Miami Beach,
Florida, United States**

Marcus Lloyd

↗
Lisbon, Portugal

Carley Rudd

→
**Balboa Beach,
California,
United States**

Dirk Dallas

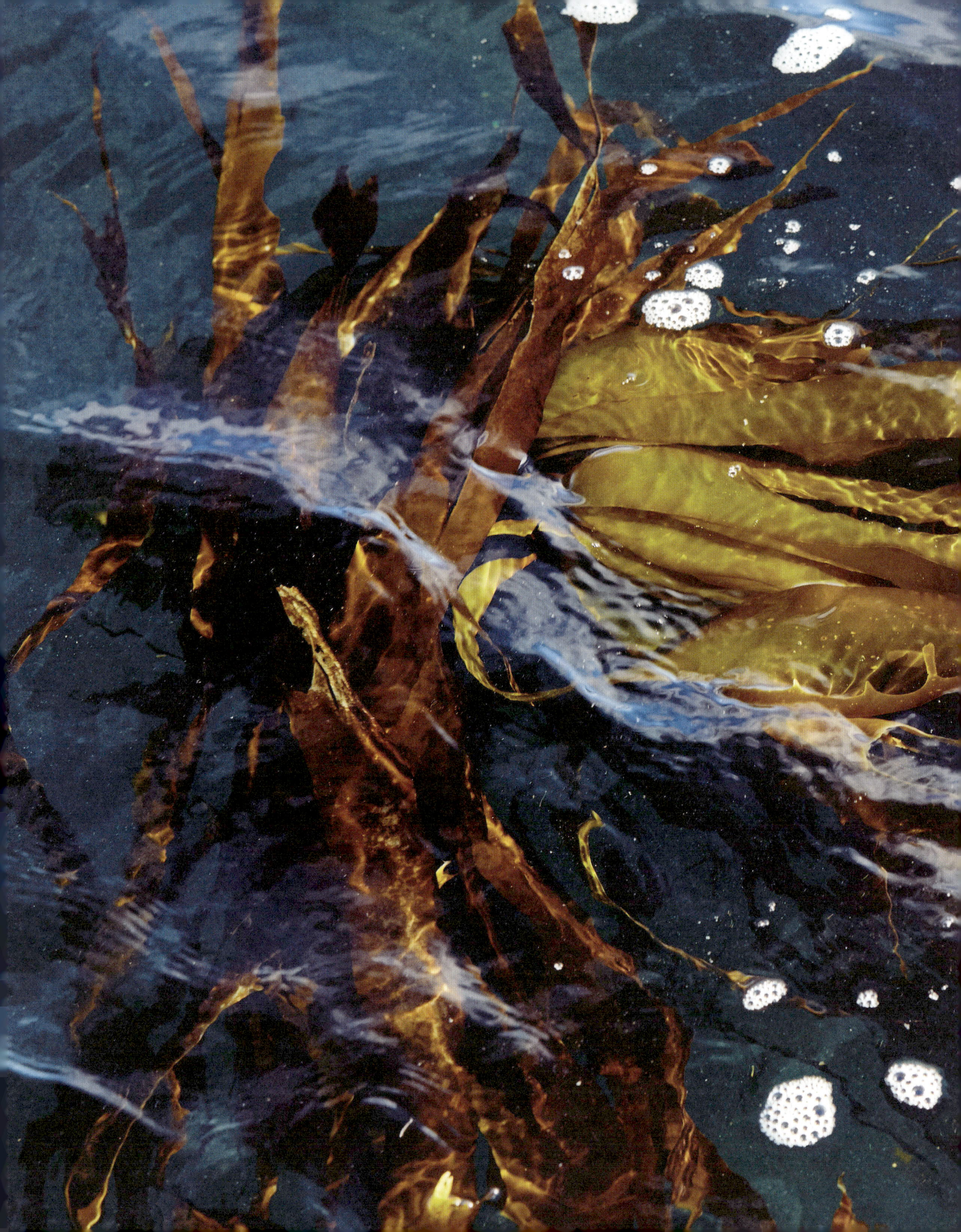

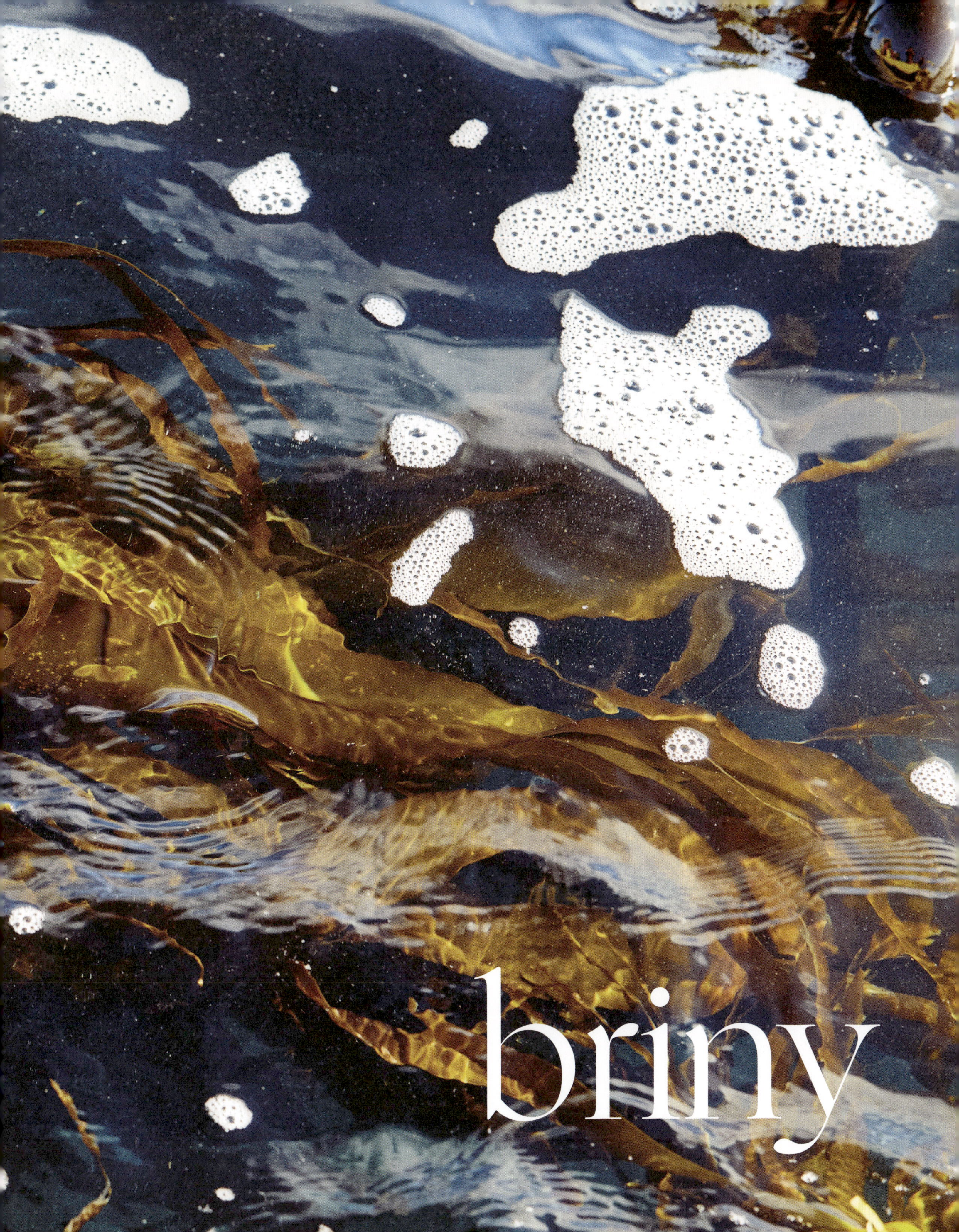
briny

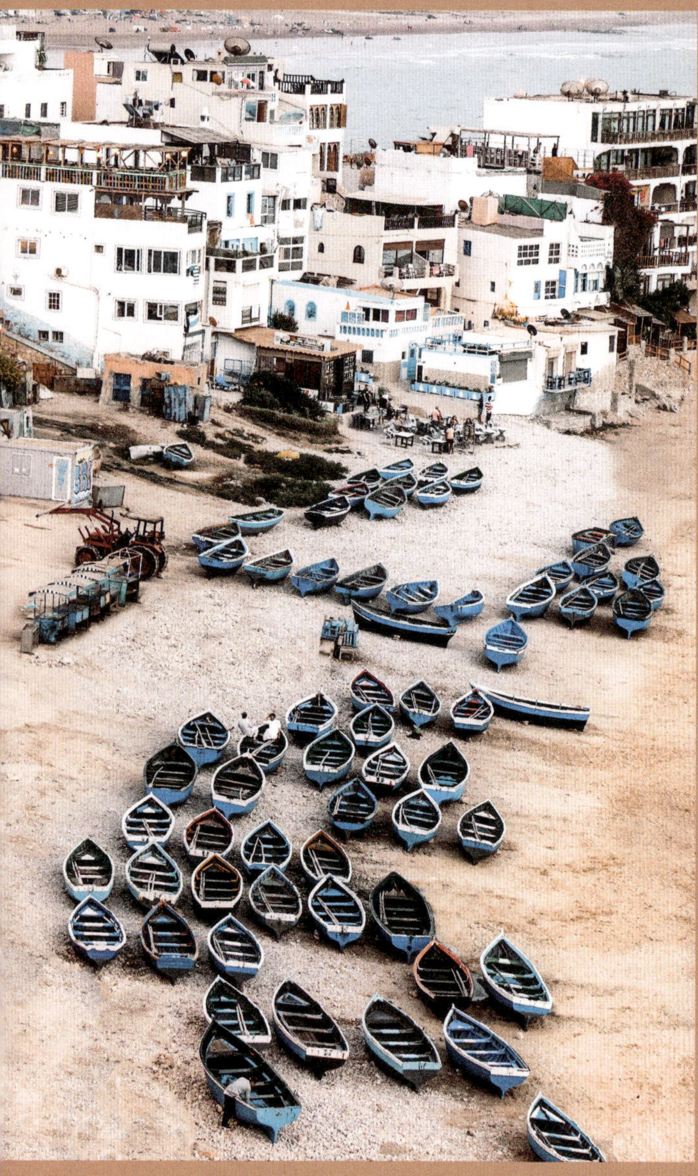

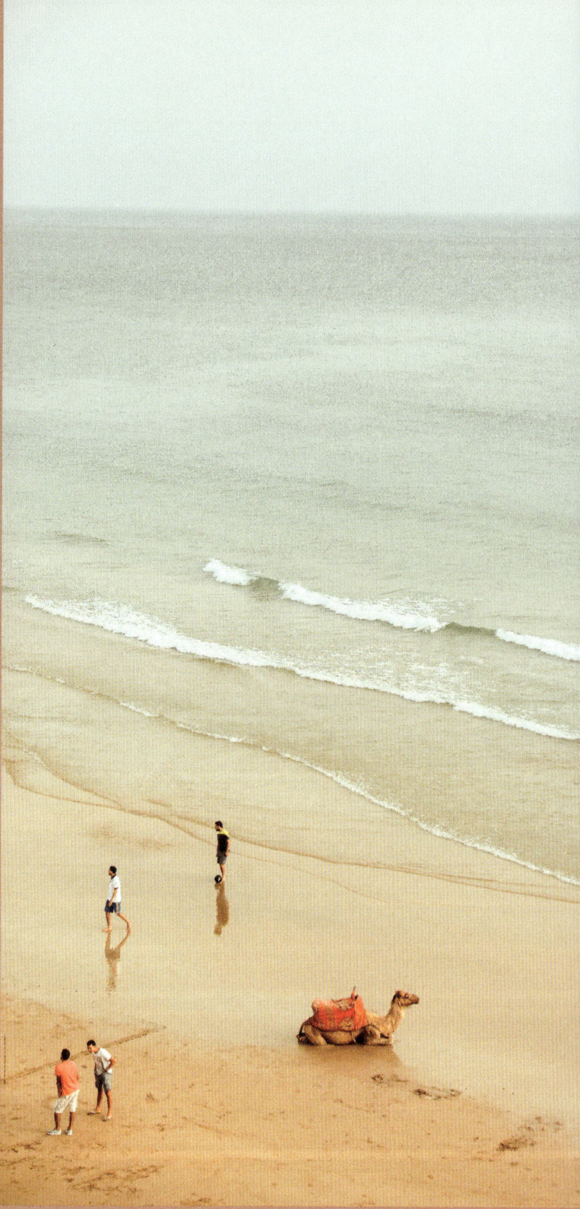

The clear, cold waters of Clayoquot Sound off Vancouver Island's west side are a pristine marine refuge, along the temperate rain forest of the Pacific Rim National Park Reserve.

**Tofino,
British Columbia,
Canada**

Nicole Franzen

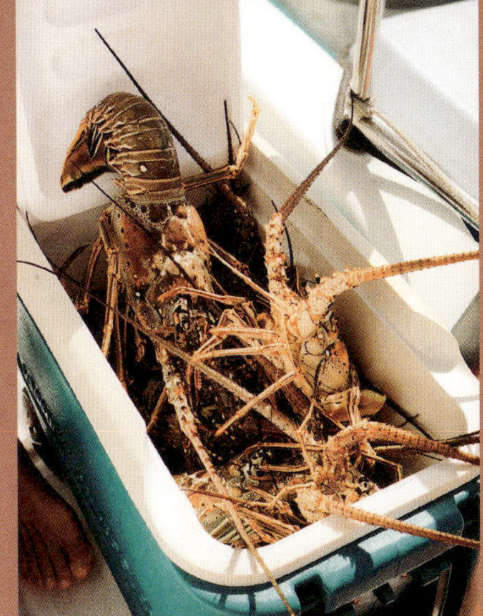

AS WE APPROACH THE COASTLINE, we smell its flavor. Brine. Water heavy with salt. The signifying essence of the sea. We taste it in everything we consume from the ocean and feel it on our skin as we pack up our things for the day and head home. Humans have always been sustained by the ocean's bounty and beauty. The ways we experience, catch, and savor the sea are varied, but the "where" of that place is always apparent in what we taste as well as what we see.

Place is encoded in the brine that nourishes Tomales Bay oysters in Northern California and distinguishes them from the Miyagi oysters raised in the cooler waters at the base of the Olympic Mountains in Washington State. Regional sea greens, such as crunchy saltwort (or sea beans) and delicate roasted nori sheets wrapped around fresh fish, are known the world over for their sought-after and prized flavors and textures. The taste of the sweet "crayfish" lobsters found in the warm waters of the Caribbean contrasts with the firm, salty lobster from the cold waters of the Northern Atlantic and reveals the distinctive characteristics determined by place. Deep sentimental attachments develop to the smell and taste of each person's favorite stretch of coastline, anchoring us in the places we love and providing the opportunity for delight when sampling the bounty from new locations.

Similarly, the diverse fishing vessels used around the world inform those who see them about the culture of their home ports as well as the character of the seas they ride. The ultramarine blue fishing boats on the coast of Morocco at Essaouira are often simple wide rowboats, offering an easy ride on the gentle waters of the harbor. They're striking in their cerulean color, painted with a natural dye made from the shells of a local mollusk. The varied hues of ocean water signal the type of sea life found there. On the cold, lucid navy waters of Tofino, British Columbia (seen on pages 4 and 5), humpback and gray whales can be seen in the spring while riding over whitecaps and shifting tides.

I vividly remember the first time I tasted sea urchin, on the docks of a fish market in Puerto Montt, Chile, when I was a college student. The pungent ocean flavor found in this orange delicacy was a shock to the tongue, and each time I taste sea urchin to this day, I recall that first taste at that crowded Chilean pier. The images in this chapter are meant to be a visceral reminder of the smell and taste of the sea.

↑
**Canarreos Archipelago,
Caribbean Sea, Cuba**
Michaela Trimble

↖
**Taghazout, Souss-Mazza,
Morocco**
Giane Portella

←
**Taghazout, Souss-Mazza,
Morocco**
Katie McKnoulty

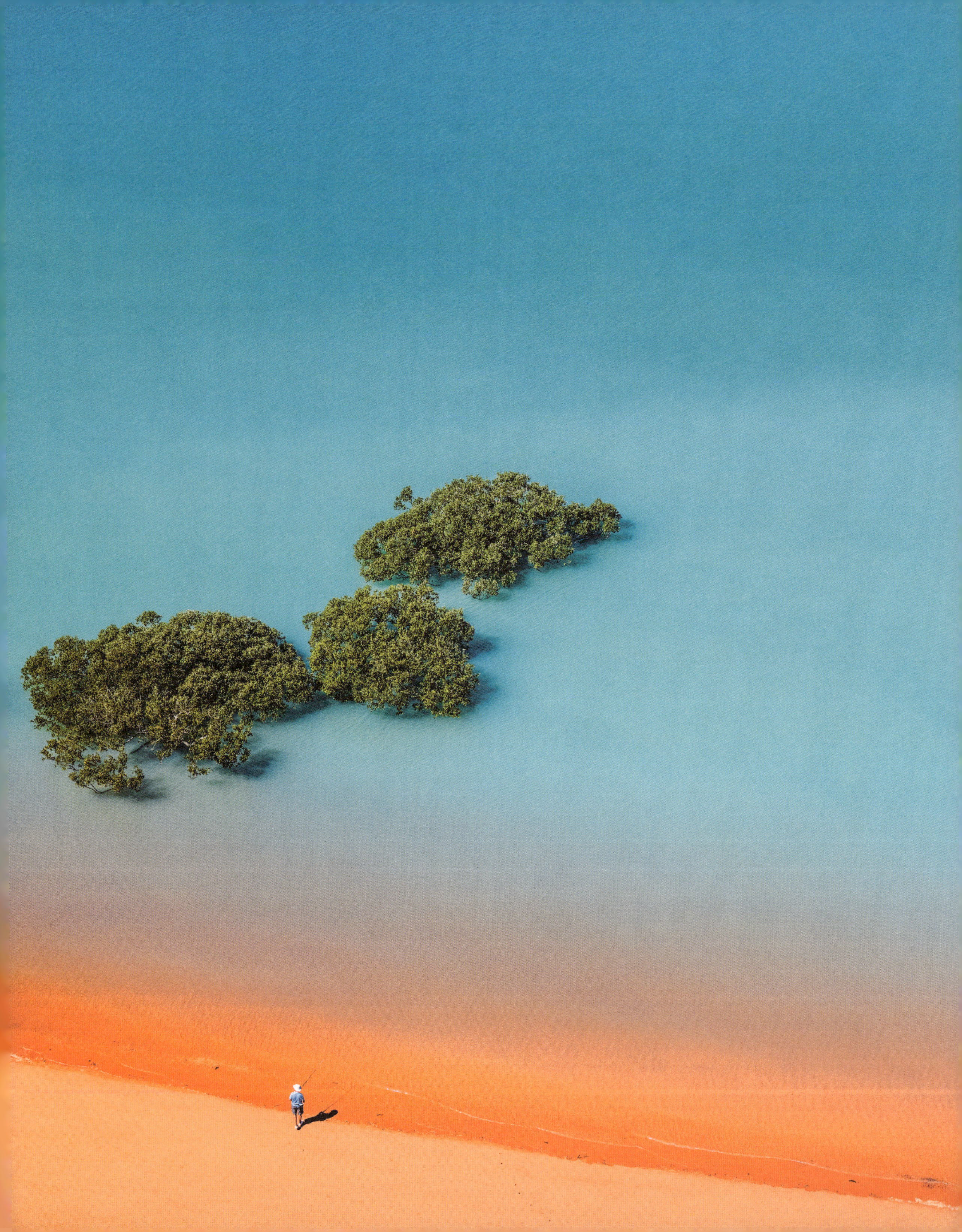

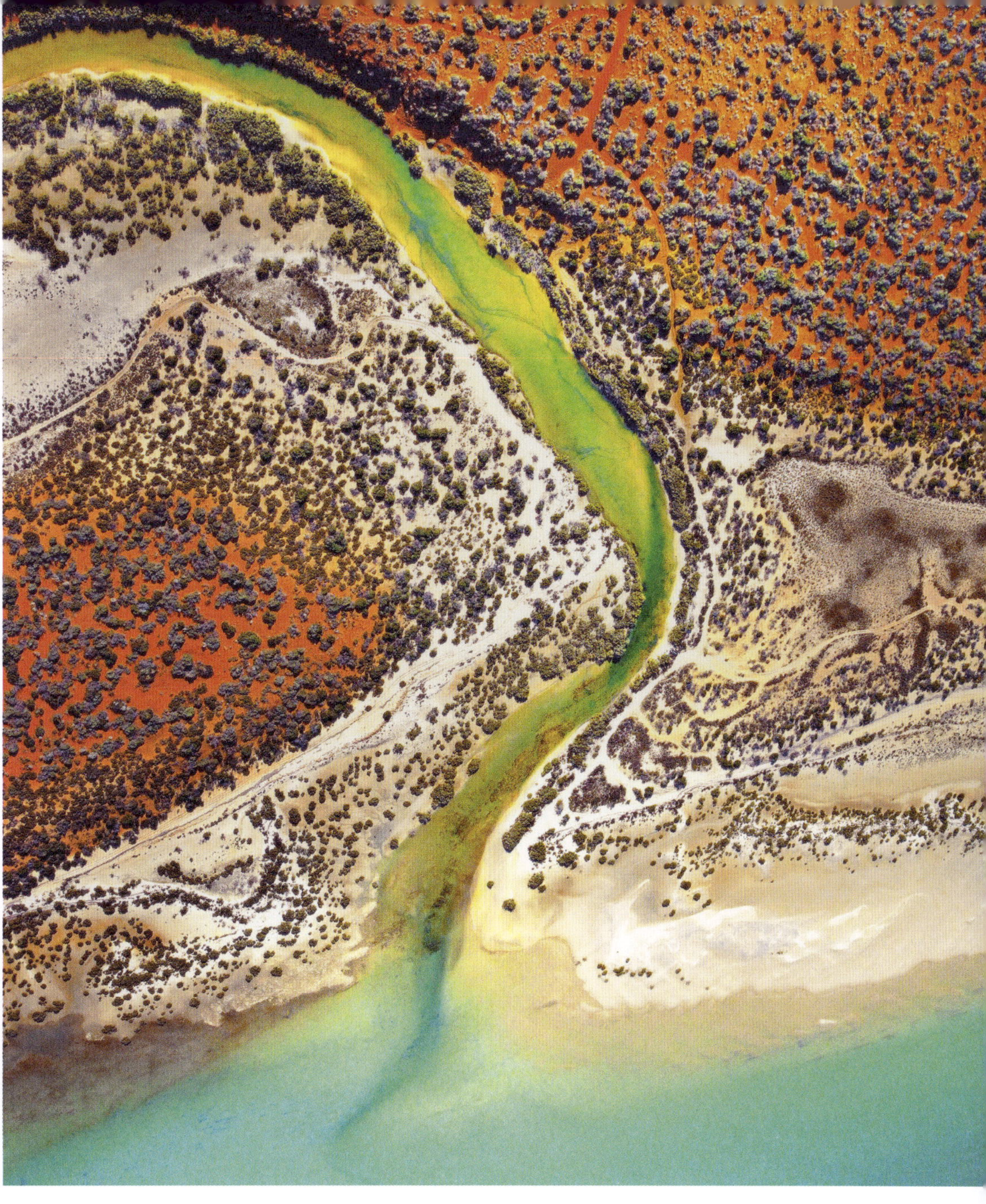

AT THE EDGE of the northernmost province of Western Australia (two and a half hours north by plane from Perth), past the gorges and through the semiarid savannah of the Kimberley, you can find the red sand beach of Roebuck Bay on the estuary side of the Dampier Peninsula. The bright red color of the sand (called pindan) strikes a sharp contrast to the aqua waters of the Indian Ocean lapping its shore.

**Broome,
Western Australia**

Michael Goetze and
Jampal Williamson

**Shark Bay,
Western Australia**

Jarrad Parker

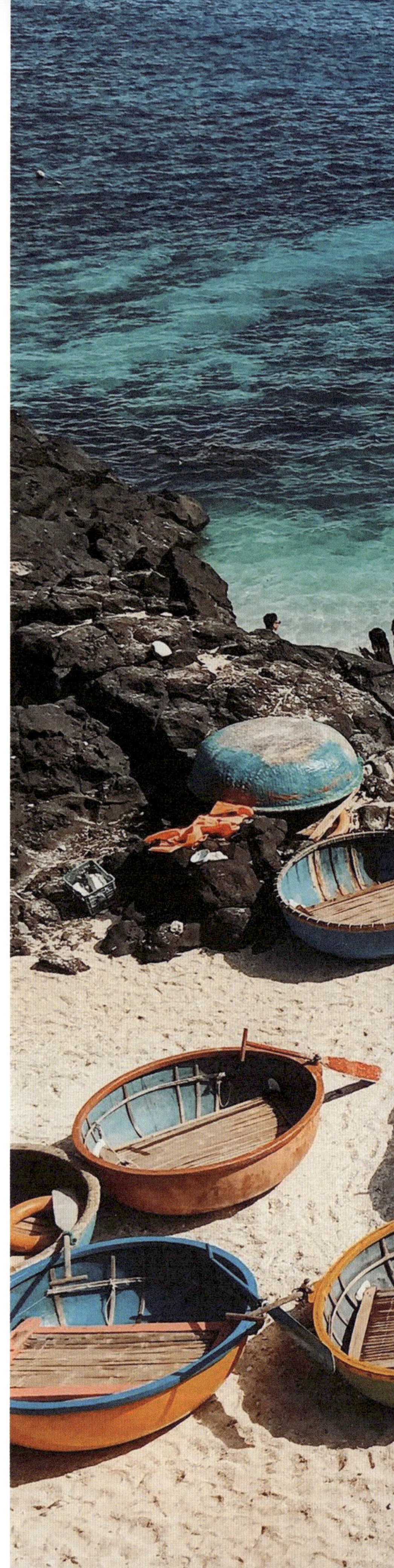

LÝ SƠN IS the only island in Quảng Ngãi Province. From the mountain peaks above its beaches—which are remnants of a volcanic caldera—you can see wide green fields of garlic, as well as black volcanic rocks, white sand, and colorful fishing boats in contrast with the vivid blue water. The cuisine is locally famous for king crab and a prized variety of mild garlic. To get there, drive two and a half hours south from Hôi An (or take a train north from Hanoi) along the east coast of Vietnam to the fishing village of Sa Kỳ. From there, you take a half-hour speedboat ride to this tiny gem of an island, which is also called Cù Lao Ré.

**Lý Sơn Island, Quảng
Ngãi Province, Vietnam**
Dug Tùng Đàm

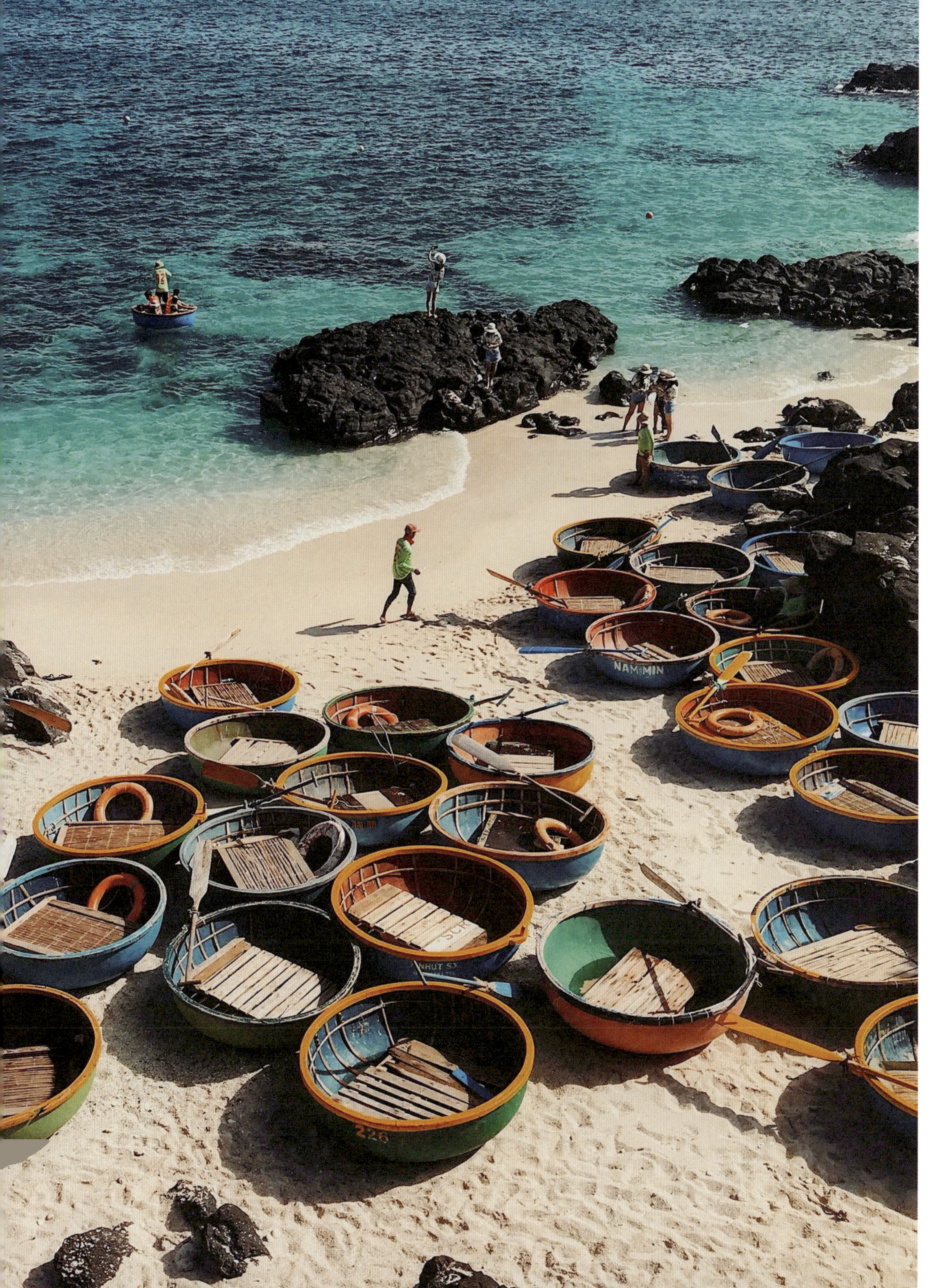

Andros, Greece
Lavinia Cernau

Sidi Kaouki, Essaouira Province, Morocco
Raquel Guiu Grigelmo

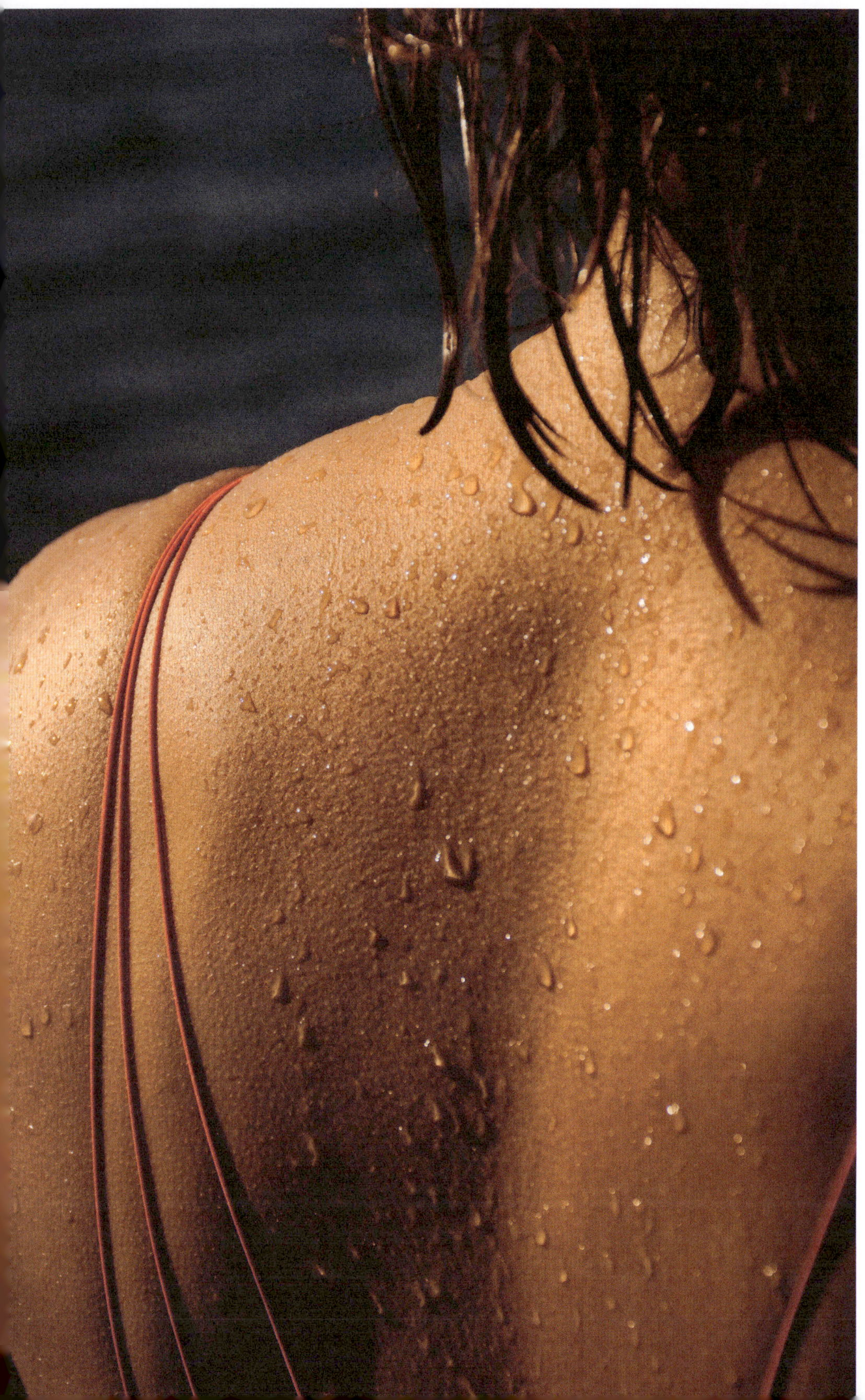

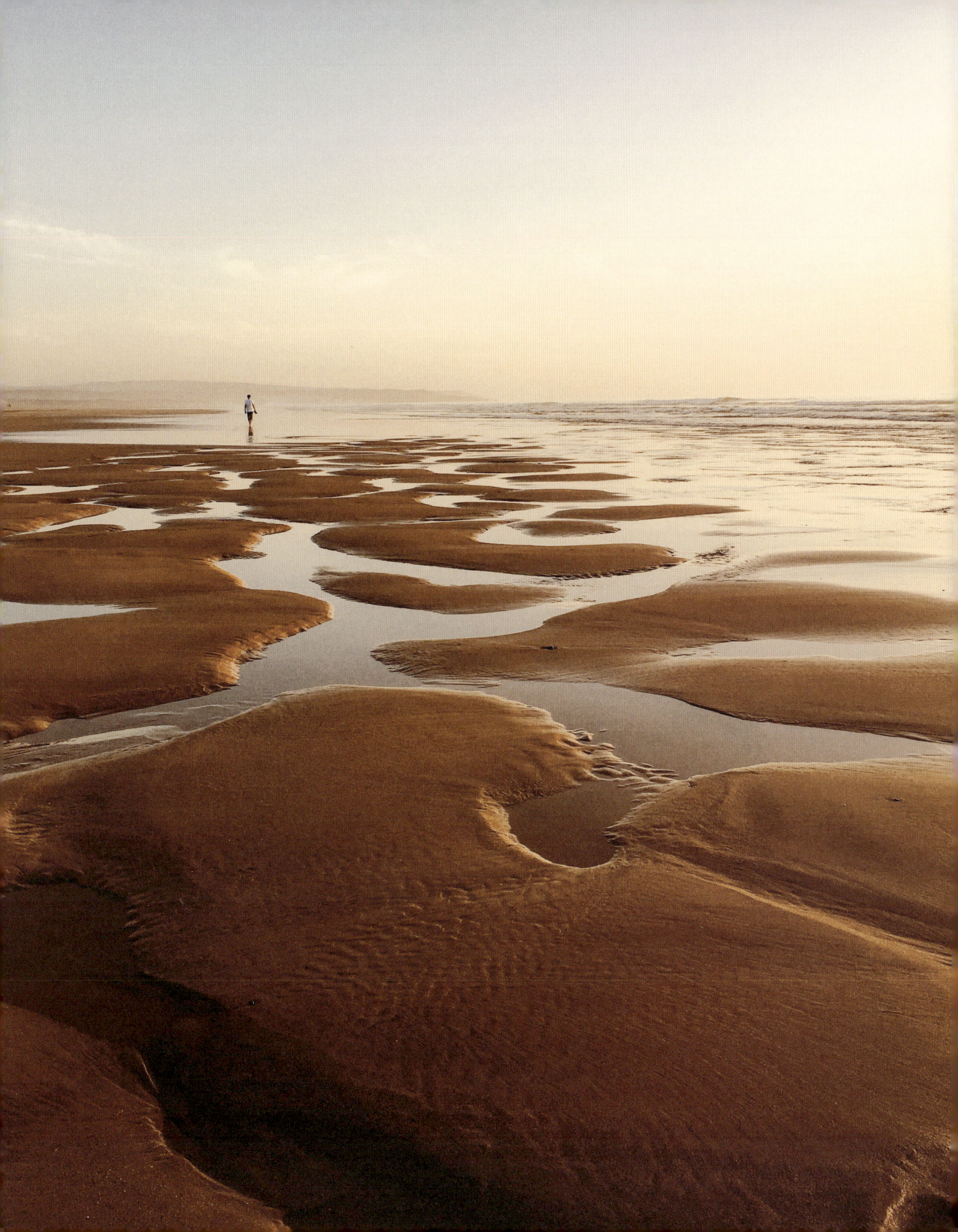

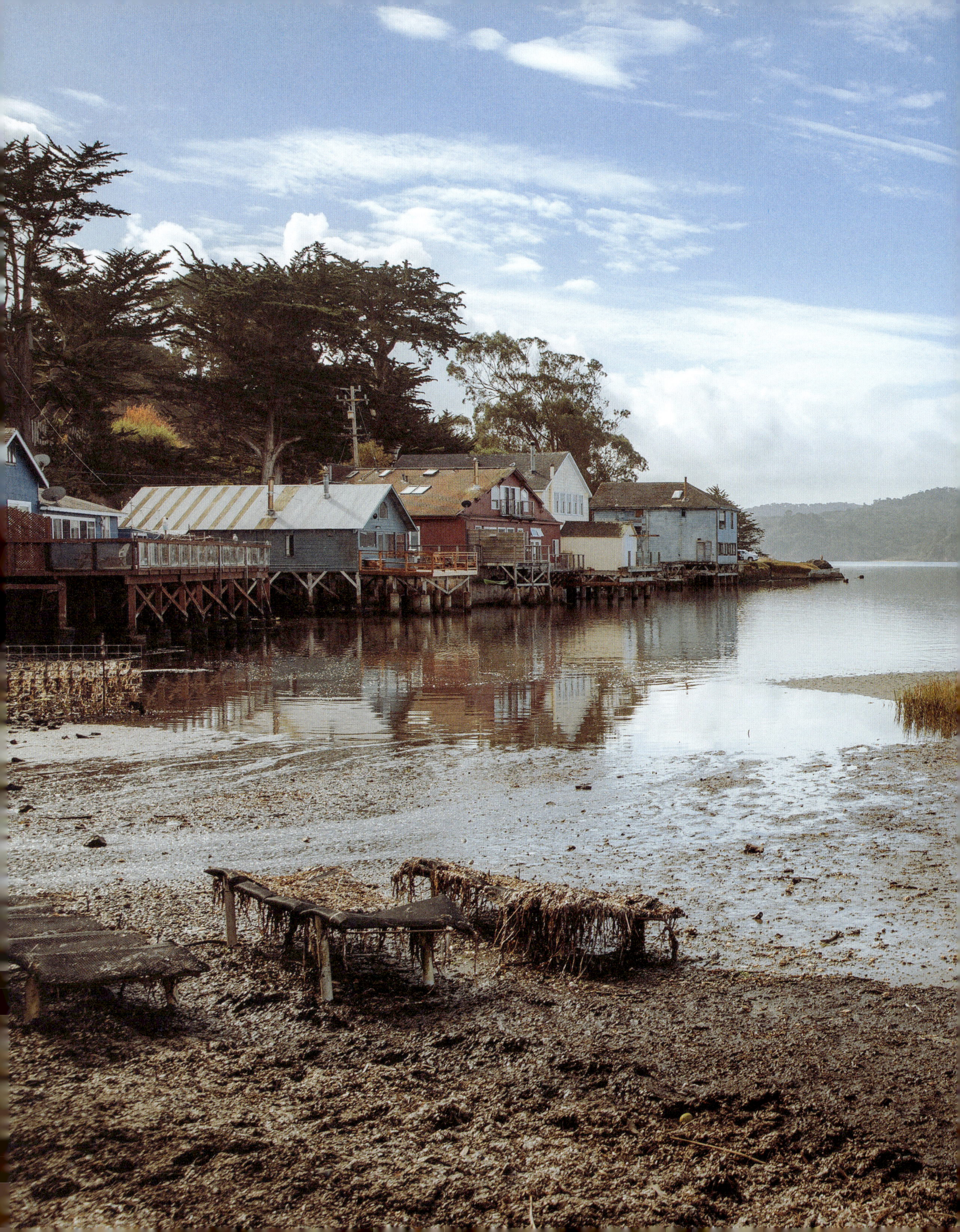

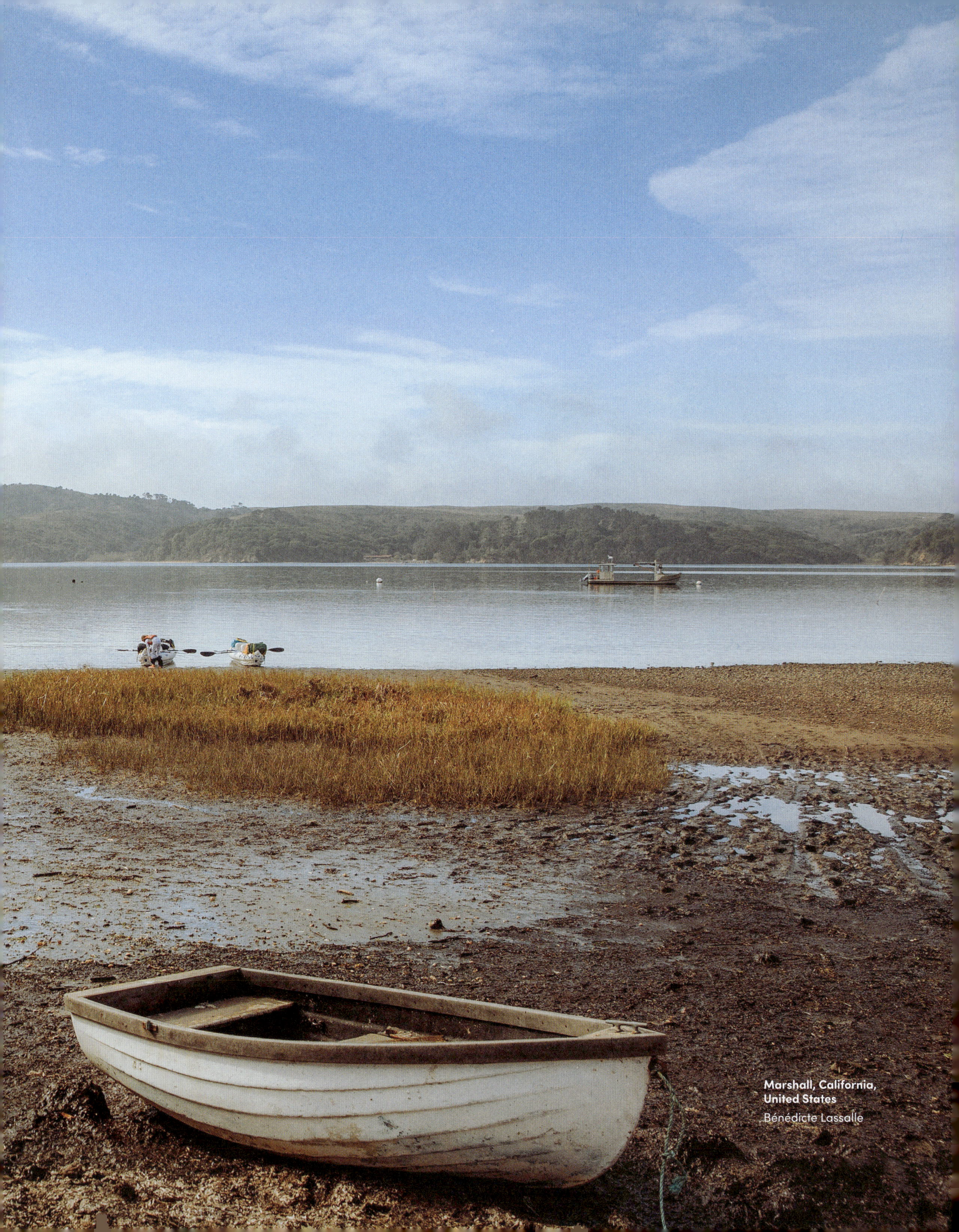

Marshall, California,
United States
Bénédicte Lassalle

Bridgetown,
Saint Michael,
Barbados

Will Adler

Santa Barbara,
California,
United States

Will Adler

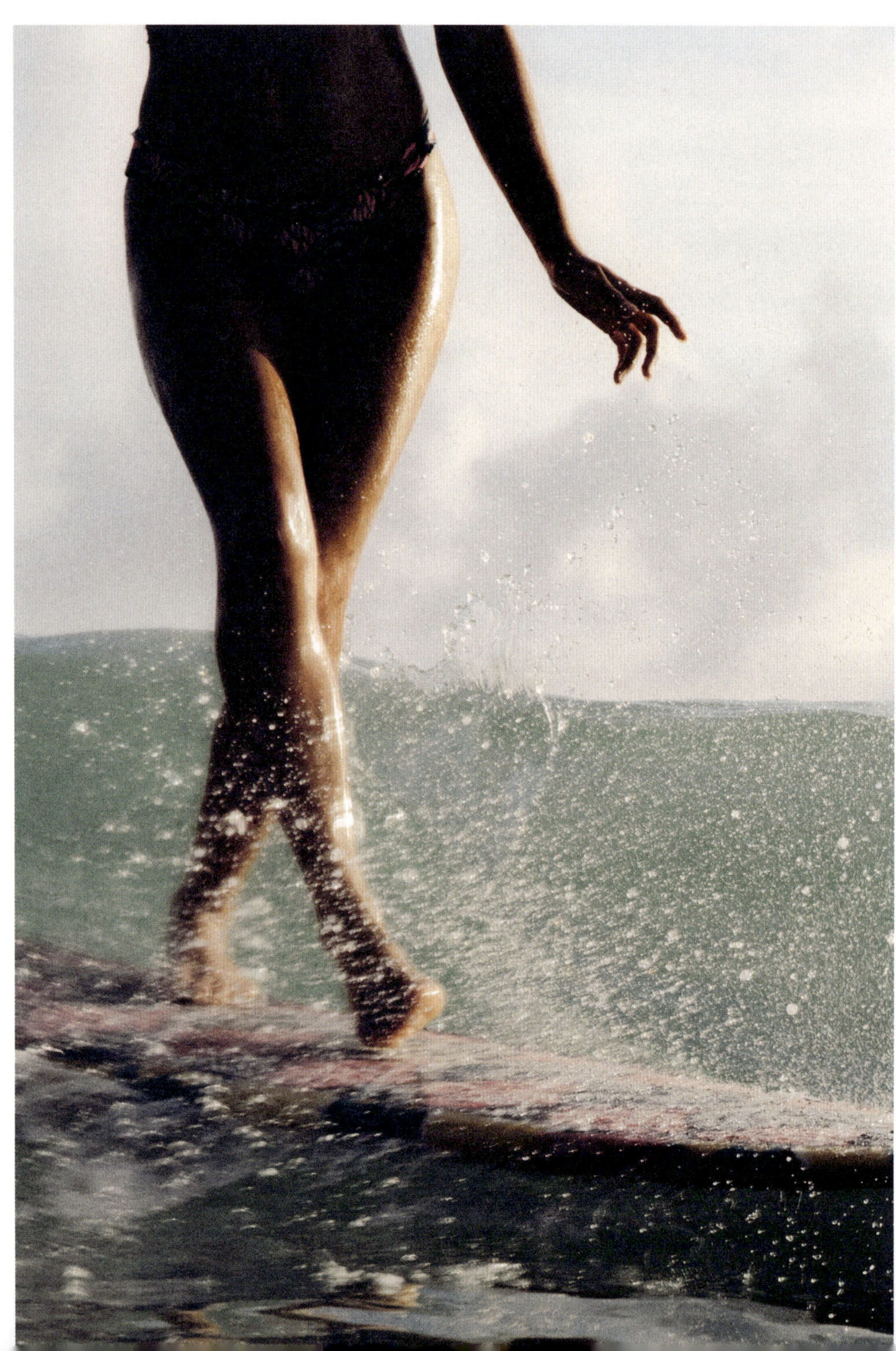

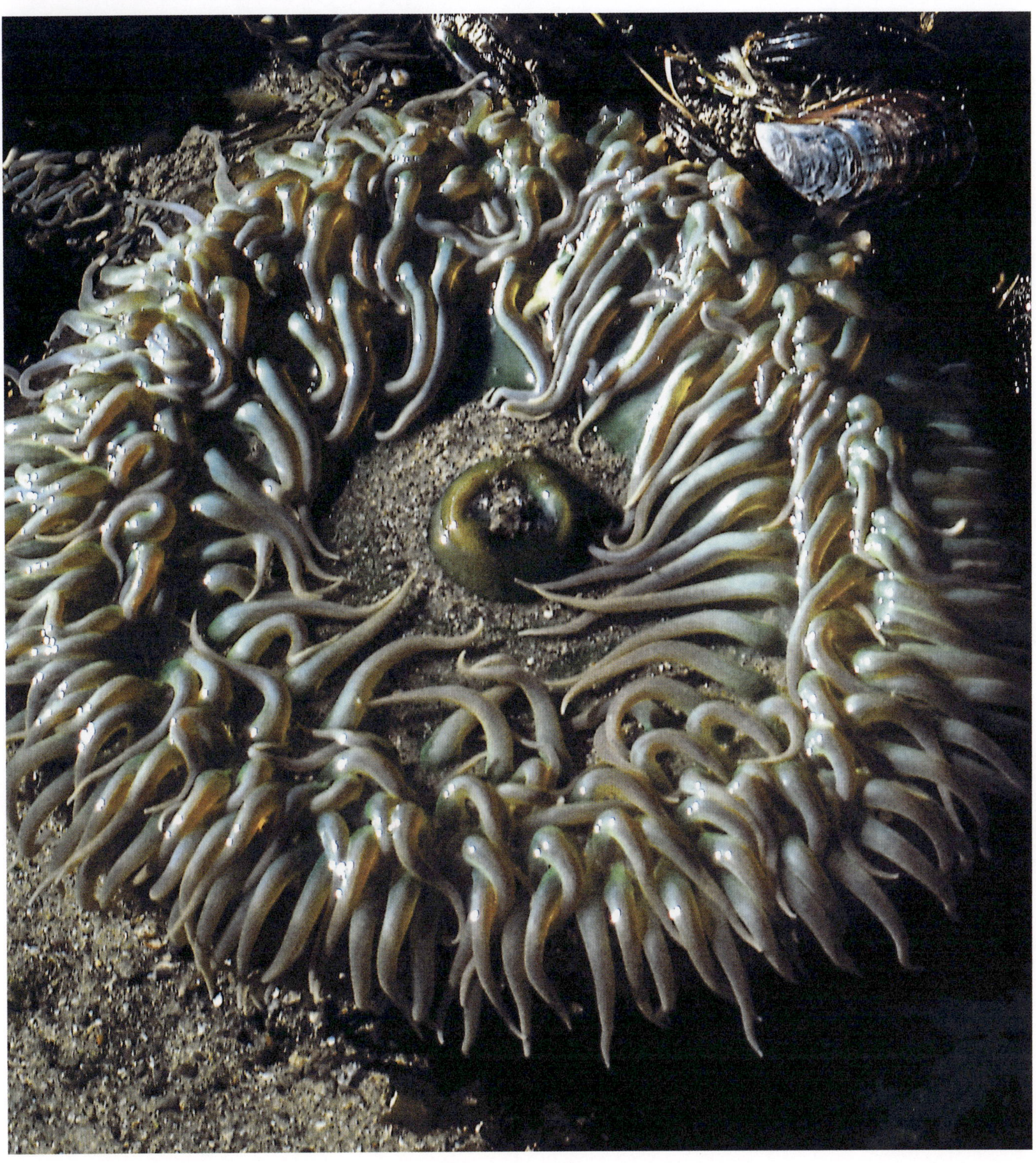

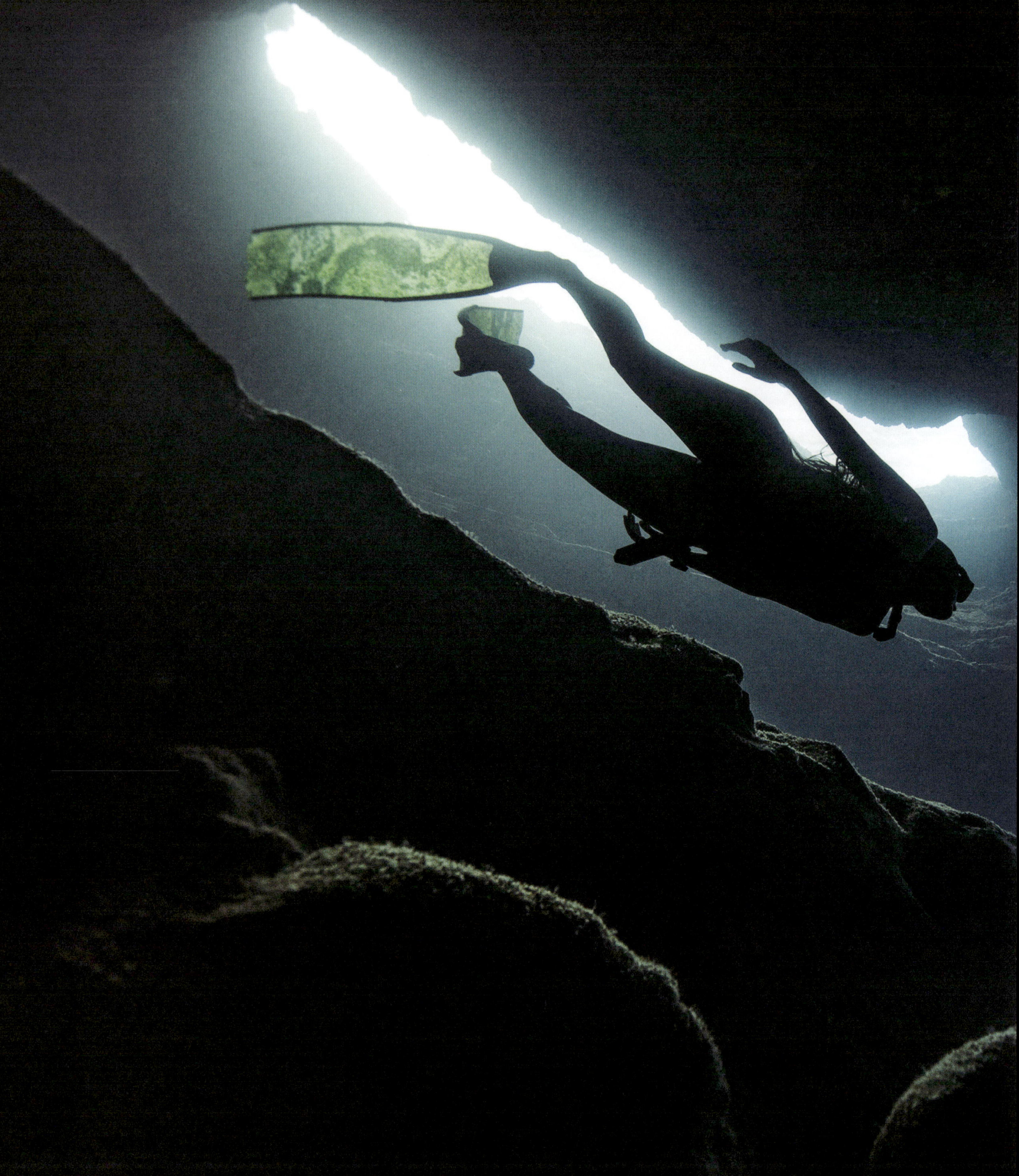

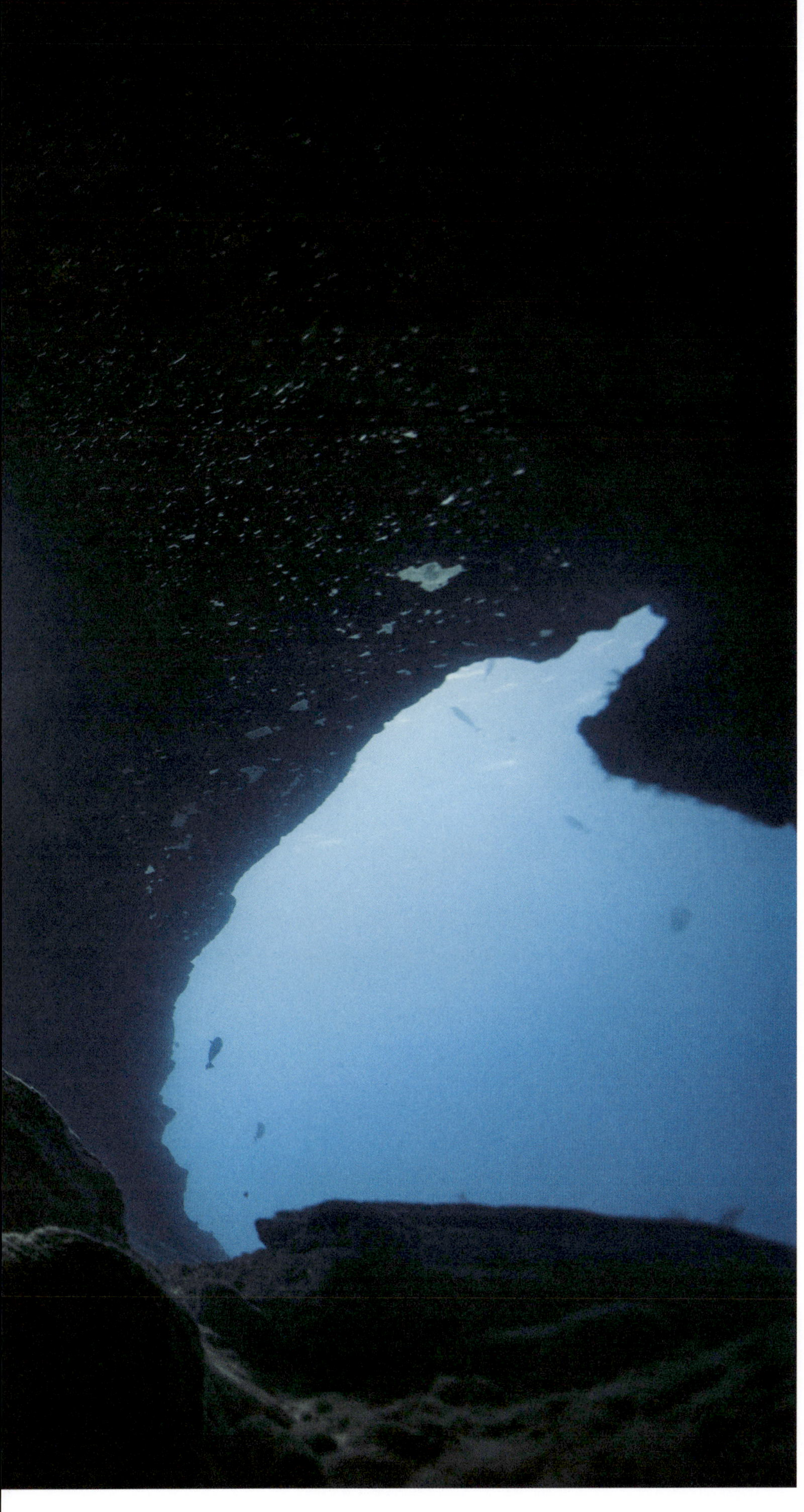

**Ni'ihau, Hawai'i,
United States**
Justin Bastien

san juan

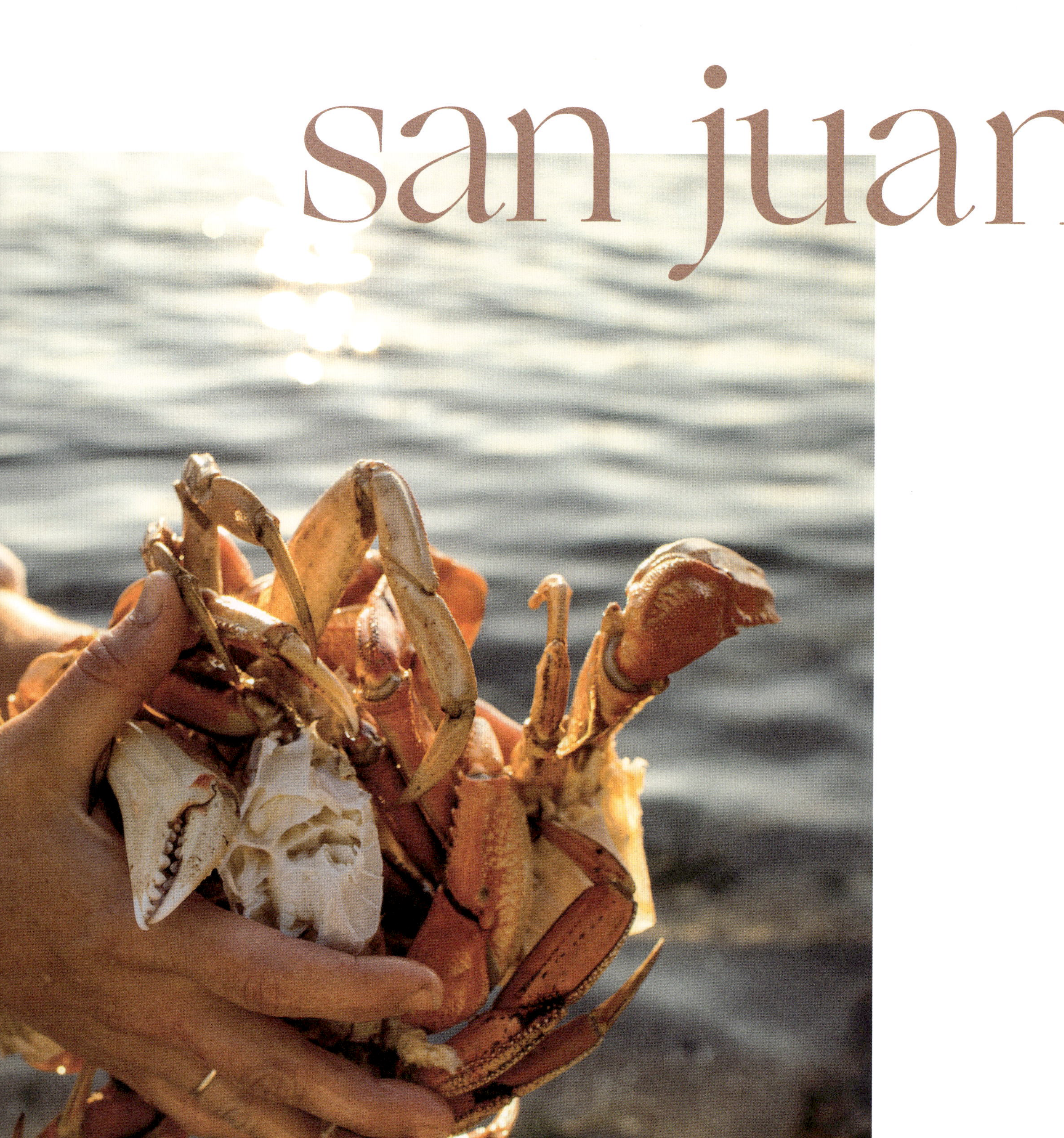

islands

UNITED STATES

THE SAN JUANS ARE a quiet place. Forming an archipelago in the cold waters of the Pacific Northwest about a two-hour drive from Seattle (or a twenty-minute drive from Bellingham), they serve as an escape for weekend visitors, especially in the drier summer months when days are often filled with sunshine that lasts until 10 p.m. The islands are close enough to a major metropolis to feel accessible to the year-round residents but just the right distance away to appeal to any travelers seeking an escape.

Only a handful of the larger islands have regular car-ferry service; the smaller islands and islets that orbit the larger ones are best experienced by marine craft or seaplanes. Travelers arrive via kayaks, canoes, paddleboards, sailboats, and motored vessels of all kinds to uninhabited islets for an afternoon of fishing or overnight camping. Entire islands, like Clark Island, which is a short boat ride from the car-ferry–serviced Lummi Island, are designated as state parks and offer campsites (complete with bathrooms and cook stations) perched on low bluffs overlooking the water.

The area has been the home of the Salish tribes for thousands of years, and the waters of the Salish Sea, which surround the San Juans, are cold, deep, and nutrient rich. The area is also home to endangered orca whales and other marine mammals, hundreds of bird and fish species, and thousands of kinds of invertebrates including colorful anemones, sea urchins, mussels, and oysters. Reefnet fishing, which uses nets to hoist fish from the sea, has traditionally been used to catch wild Pacific salmon along the coastal waters surrounding Lummi Island. This method of fishing was developed by native people in the region and is still in use today, most notably in a collaborative effort between the Lummi Nation tribe and the local fishery Lummi Island Wild. After the nets are lifted from the water, spotters standing on high ladders identify and remove any bycatch before harvesting their take. Electric motors running on batteries fueled by solar power are used to raise and lower the nets, and the result is deliciously clean-tasting local wild-caught salmon.

Activities on the islands center around being outside in nature: hiking, gardening, and enjoying the water. Many artists have made their way to the islands, and galleries sit alongside sustainable restaurants and breweries on Lopez, Orcas, Lummi, and San Juan Island. The emerging food scene focuses on the abundant sea life and wide variety of foraged edible plants and locally grown produce. In the San Juans, summer days are spent riding bikes, beachcombing for shells and smooth granite stones, and hiking through coastal forests to lookouts over nearby islands.

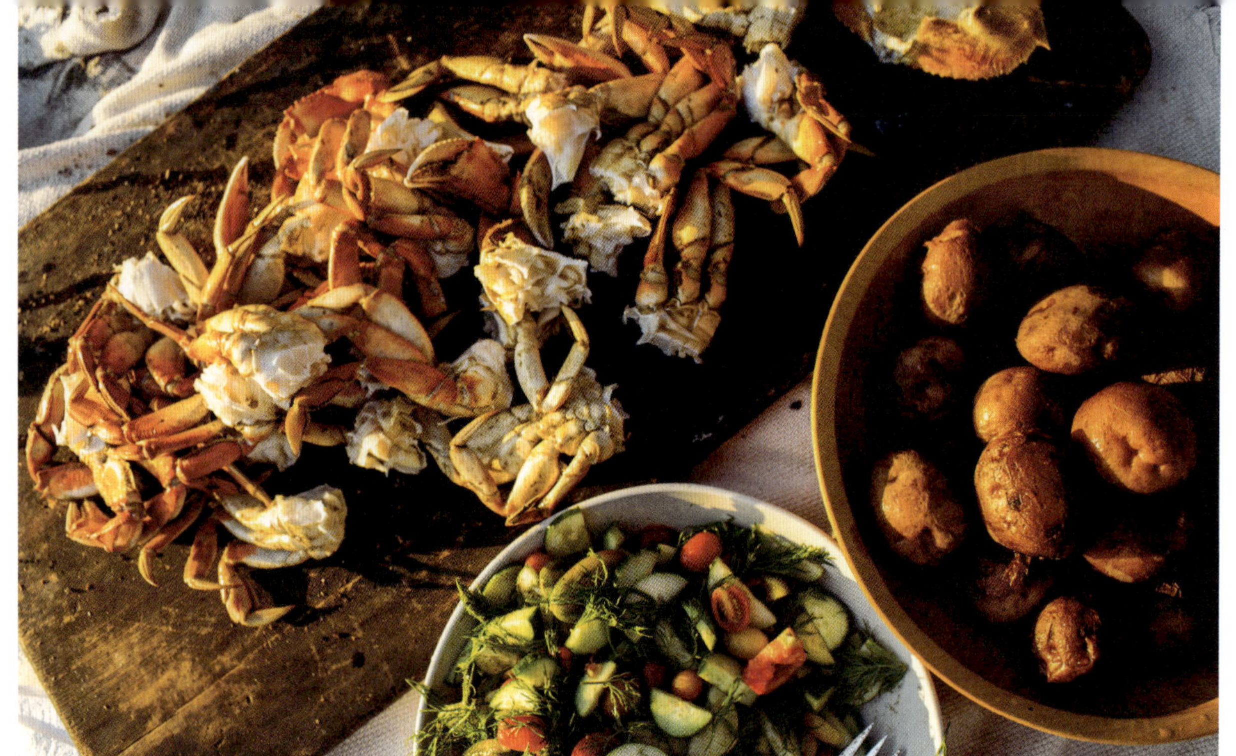

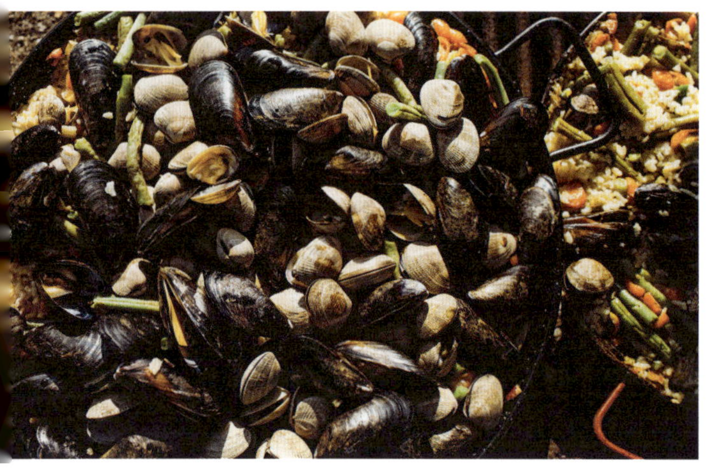

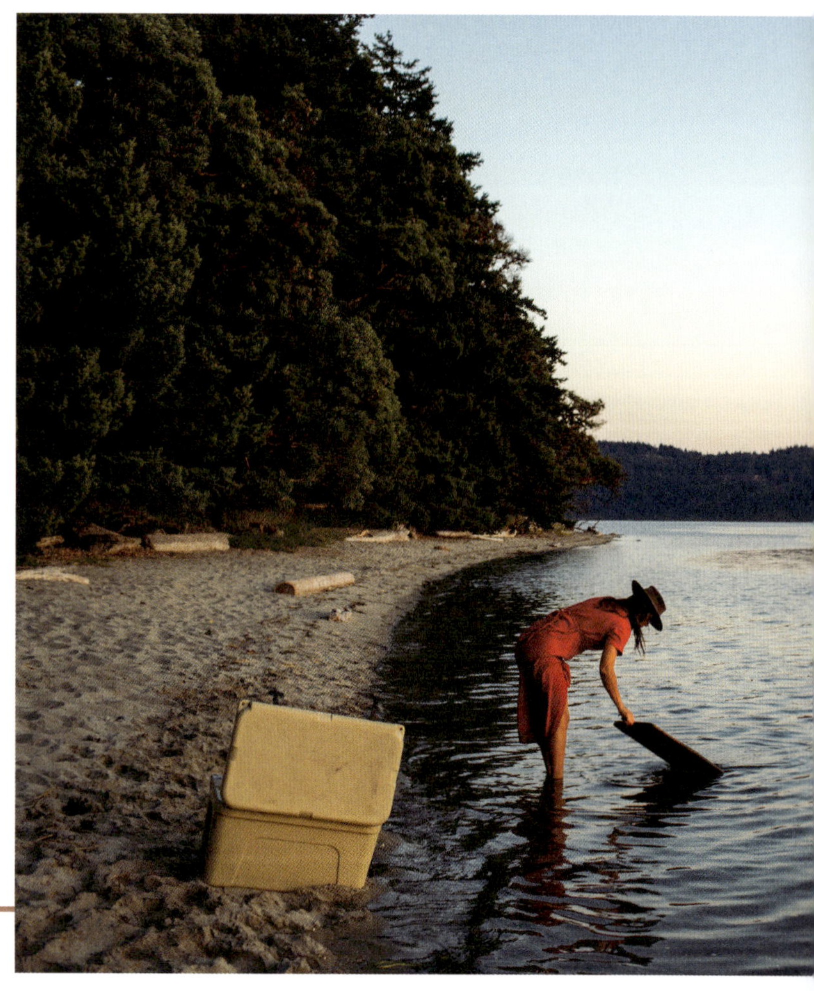

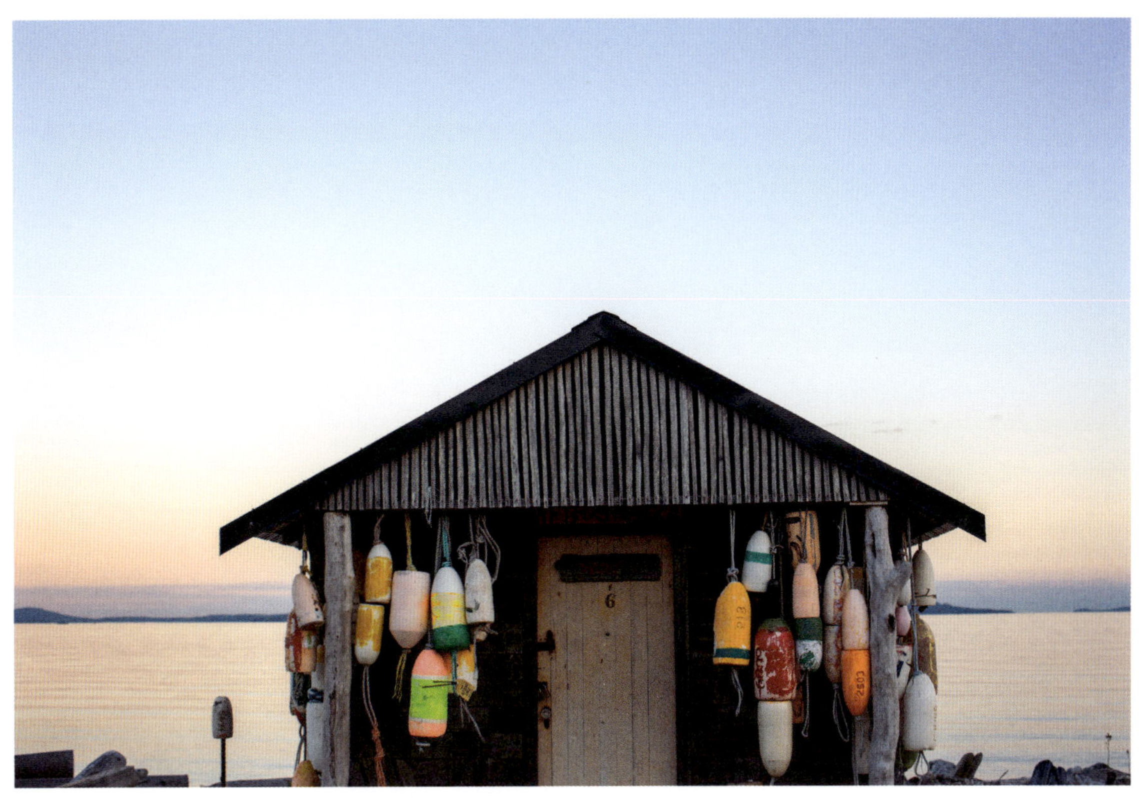

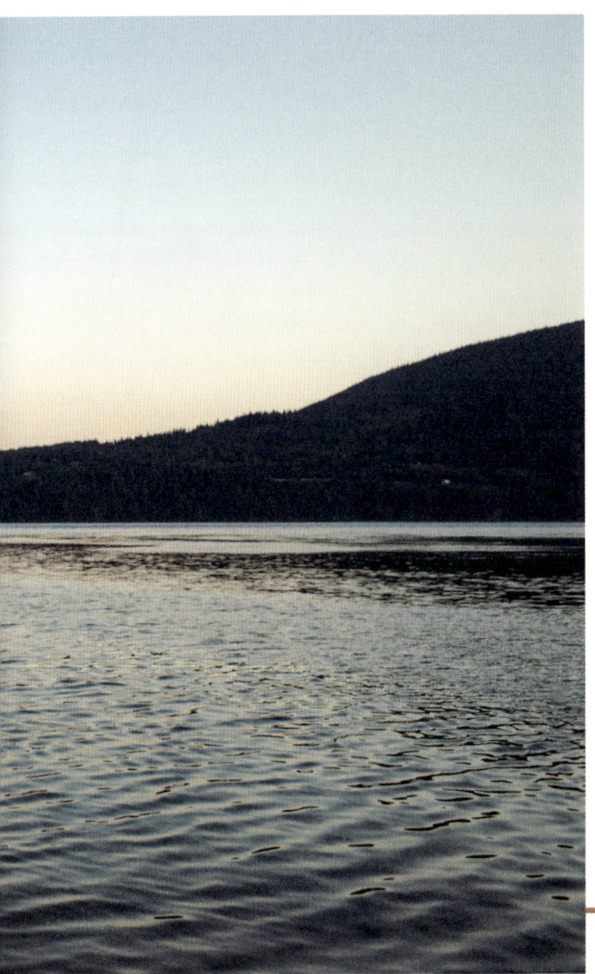

SAN JUAN ISLANDS, UNITED STATES

Photographs by Emily Nathan

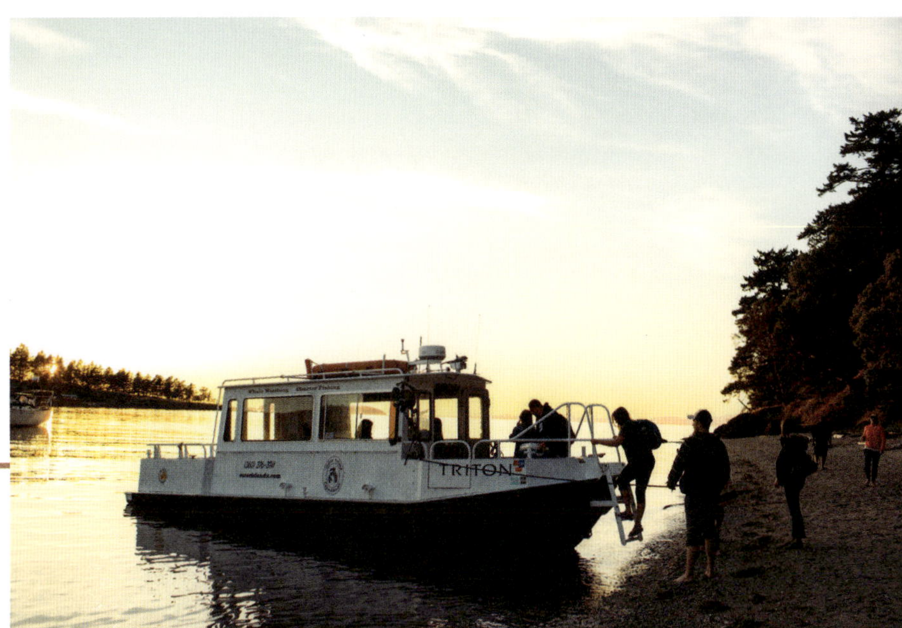

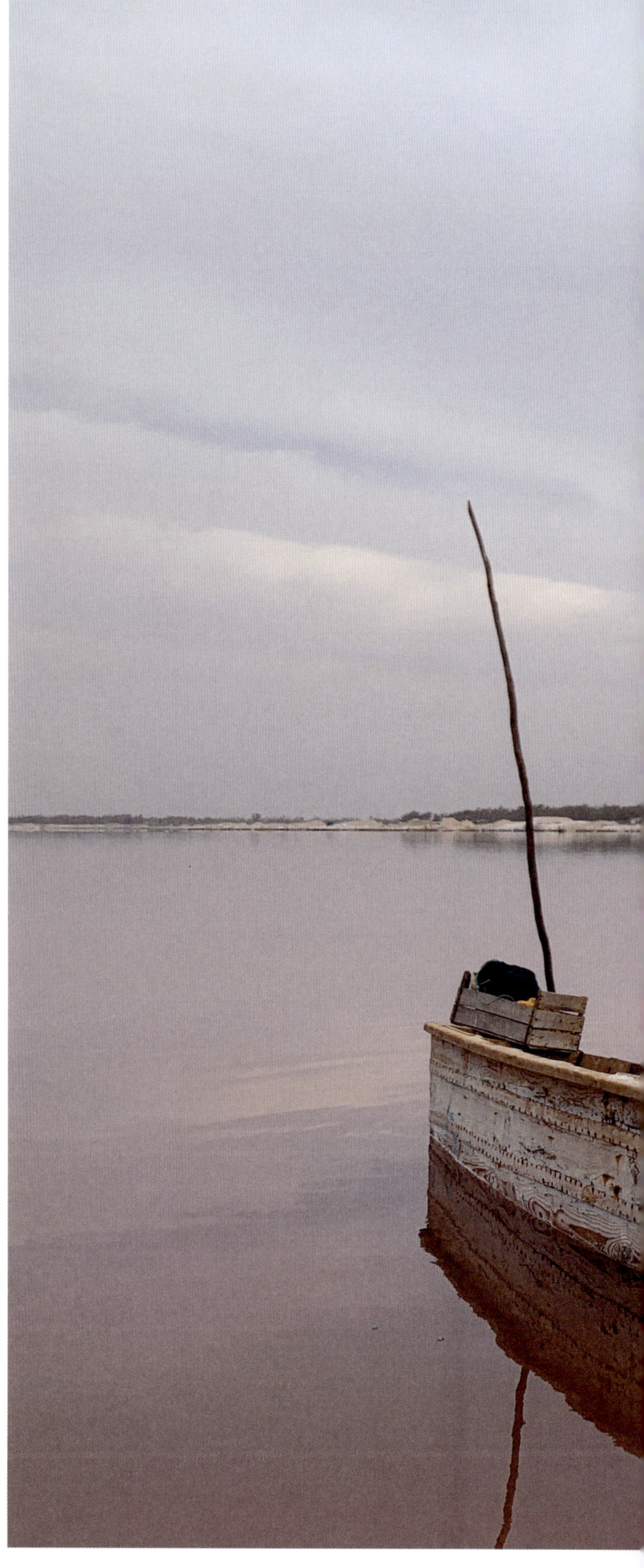

LAKE RETBA, KNOWN locally as Lac Rose, is a UNESCO World Heritage Site north of the Cap-Vert peninsula less than a half-hour drive from the Senegalese capital Dakar. This salt lake is separated from the sea by a narrow stretch of coastal dunes with a subterranean ingress of salt water. The salt is harvested by hand and piled into baskets by thousands of workers, who come to the lake from various nations in West Africa to work. The colors of Lac Rose are especially vivid during the dry season from November to June. Some fish do manage to live in the extremely salty lake, but they grow to a fraction of their normal size due to the high saline content of the water. The algae, which give the lake its color, are generally harmless to people who swim and work in the lake, but those who work in the water coat themselves with shea butter to protect against the drying effect of the salt and sun on their skin.

**Lac Rose, Dakar
Region, Senegal**
Ame Igharo

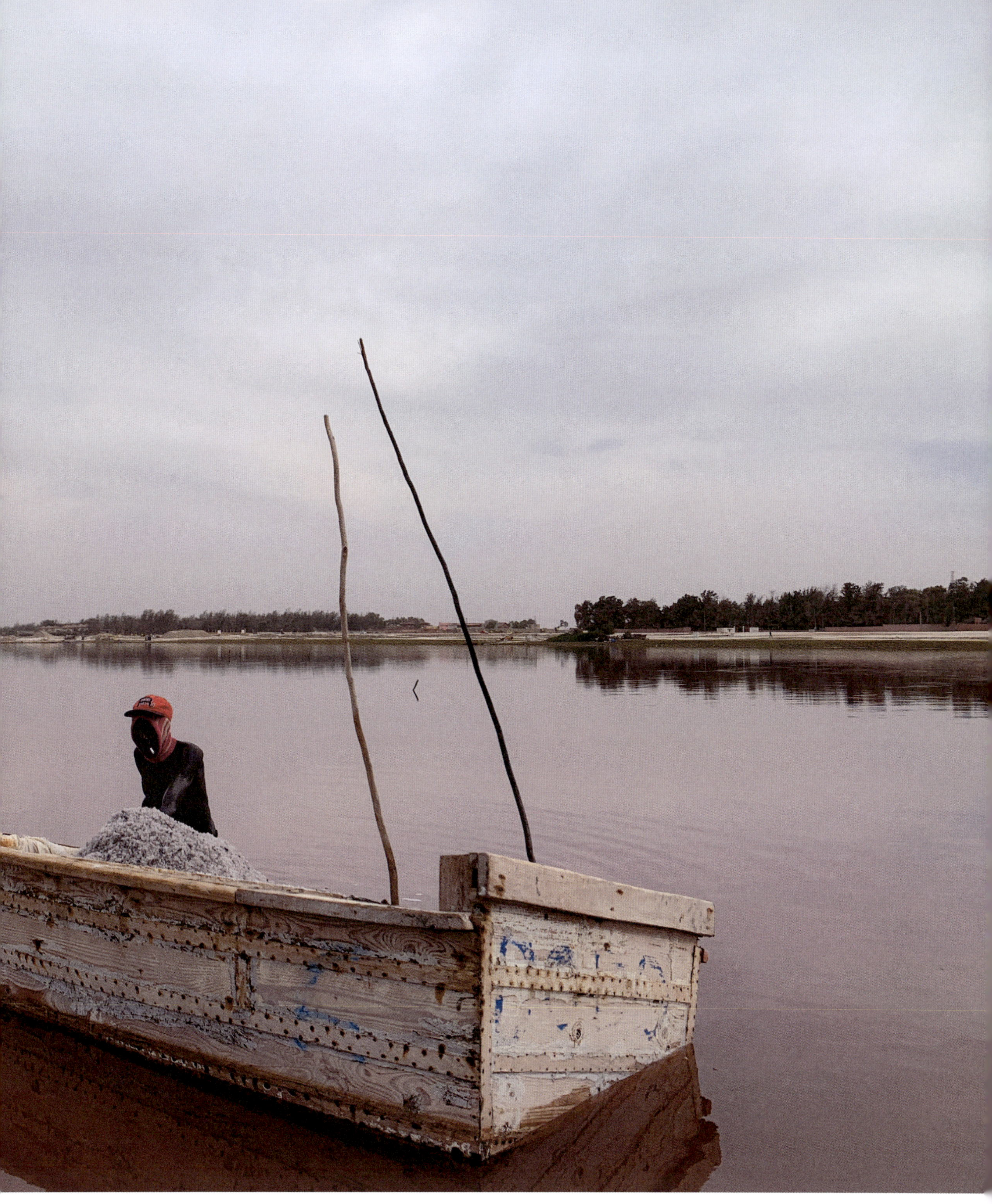

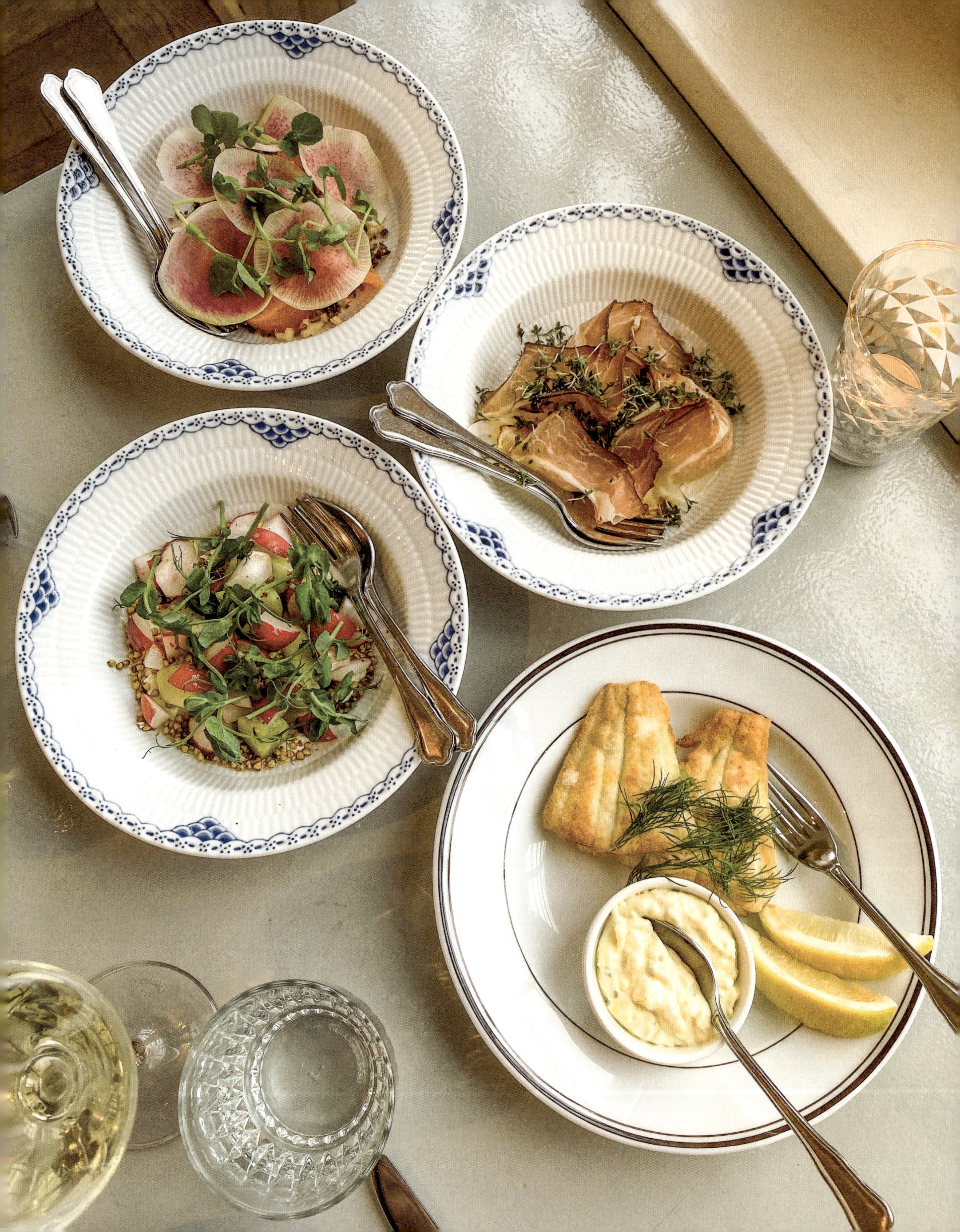

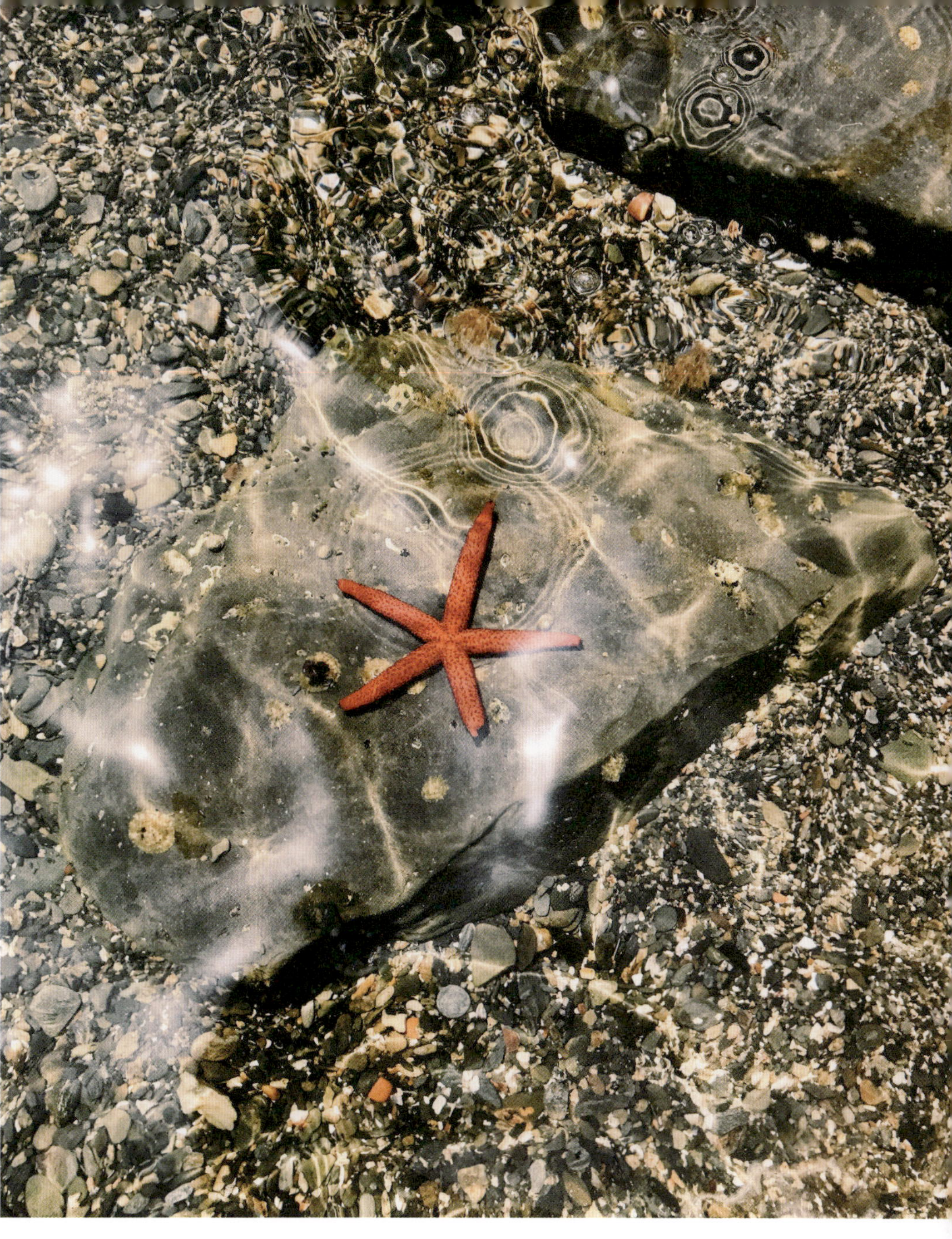

LOCAL AND INTERNATIONAL tourists alike make the short drive from Copenhagen to the resort town of Tisvilde to experience classic Danish summer vibes: green lawns, whitewashed houses, and laid-back time at the beach. Rental homes and a few hotels dot the cliffside beaches. On a cliff above the Kattegat Sea, Helenekilde Badehotel is a rustic escape (originally built in 1896 as a private home) that serves delicious understated cuisine focused on fresh catch from the sea and local vegetables.

Tisvilde, North Zealand, Denmark
Emily Nathan

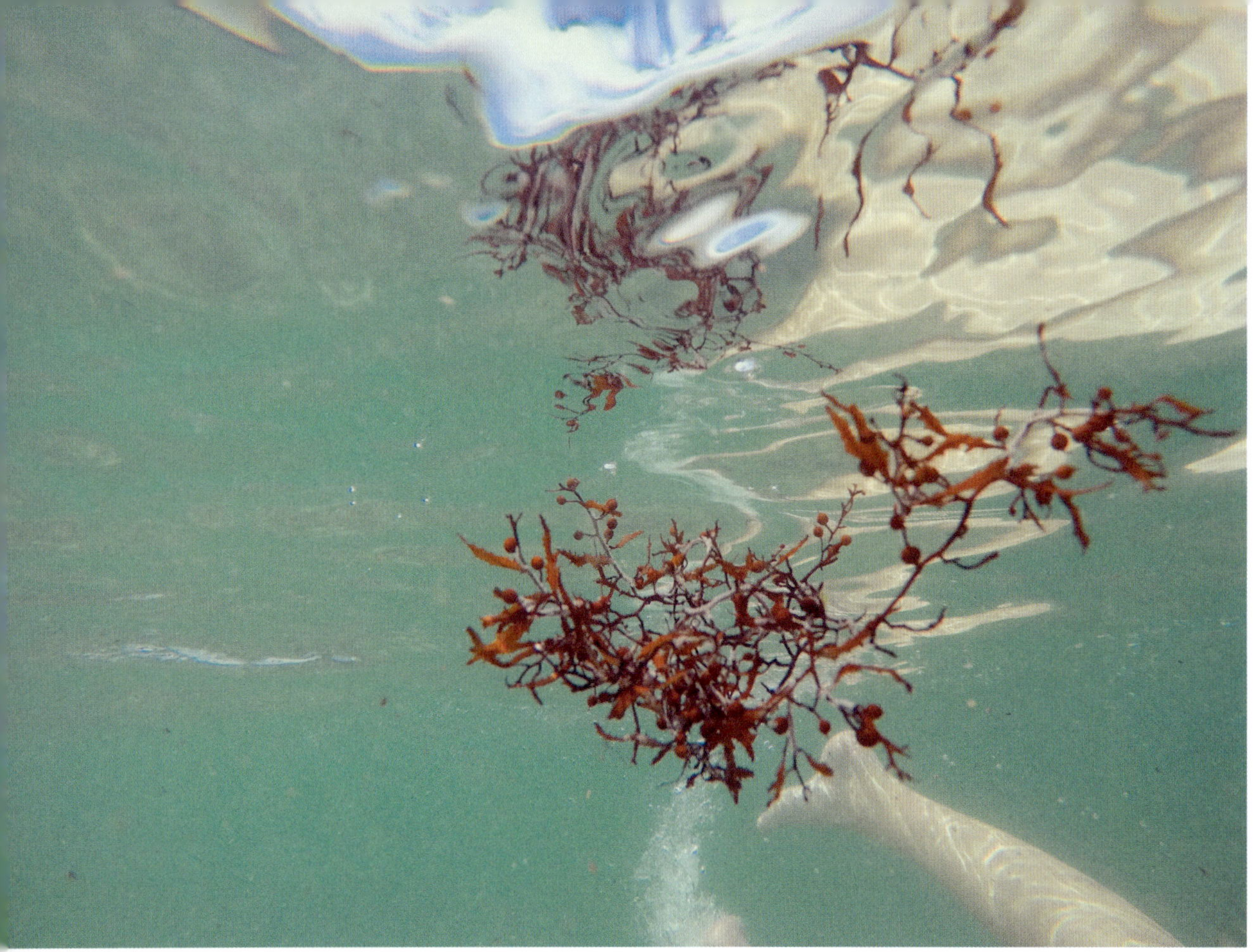

**Red Reef Park,
Boca Raton, Florida,
United States**

Cynthia Monaghan

ABOUT AN HOUR and a half south of Sydney, the Figure Eight Pools are a collection of naturally occurring baths in the Royal National Park near Burning Palms Beach. The pools are visible only for a few hours of the day and require a 3.7-mile hike down through steep cliffs and forest where the trail meets the Coast Track. To enter the pools, visitors need to plan the hike perfectly to have enough time to explore before high tide, when massive waves can crash over the pools and make them hazardous.

**Figure Eight Pools,
Royal National Park,
New South Wales,
Australia**

Courtney Kinnare

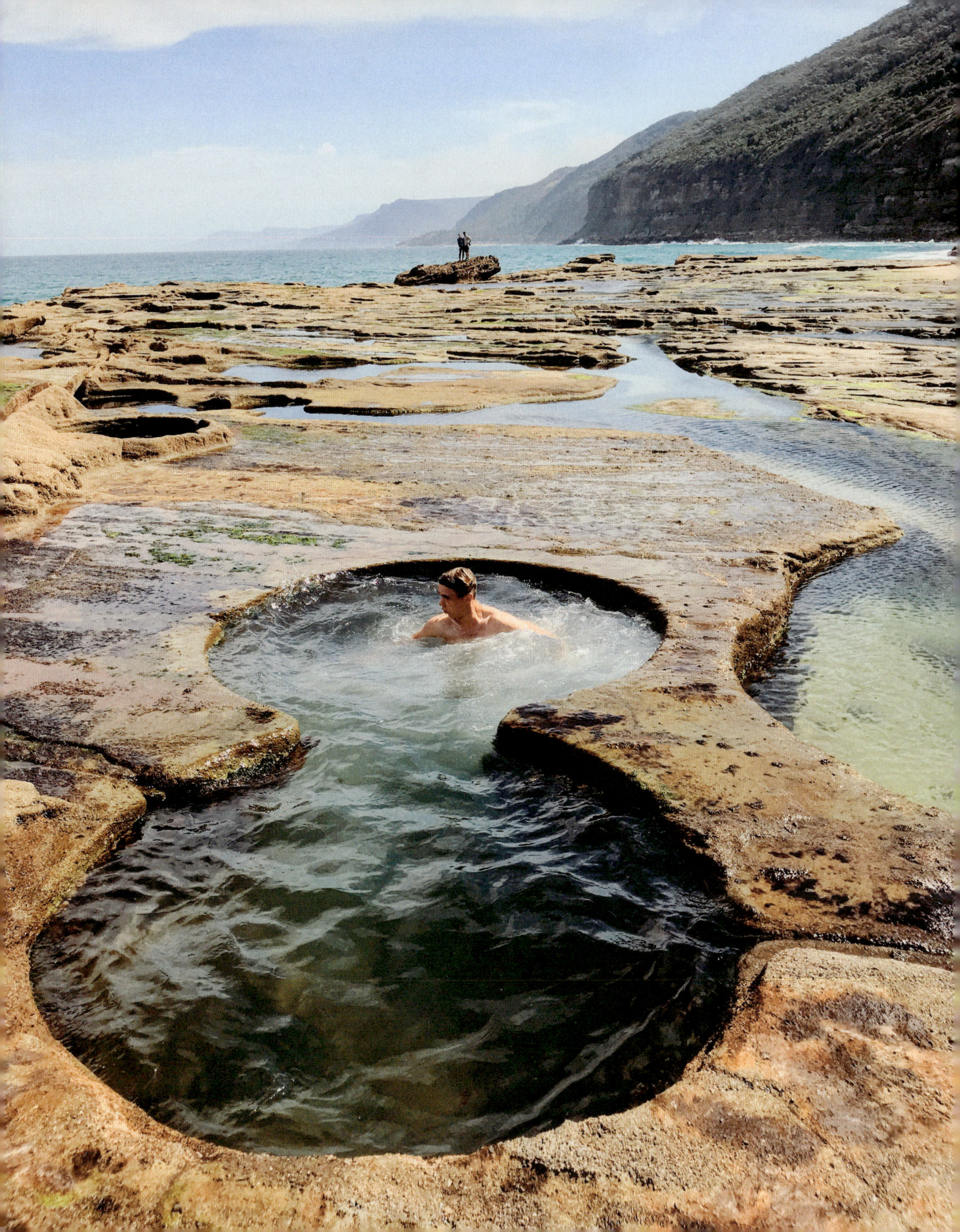

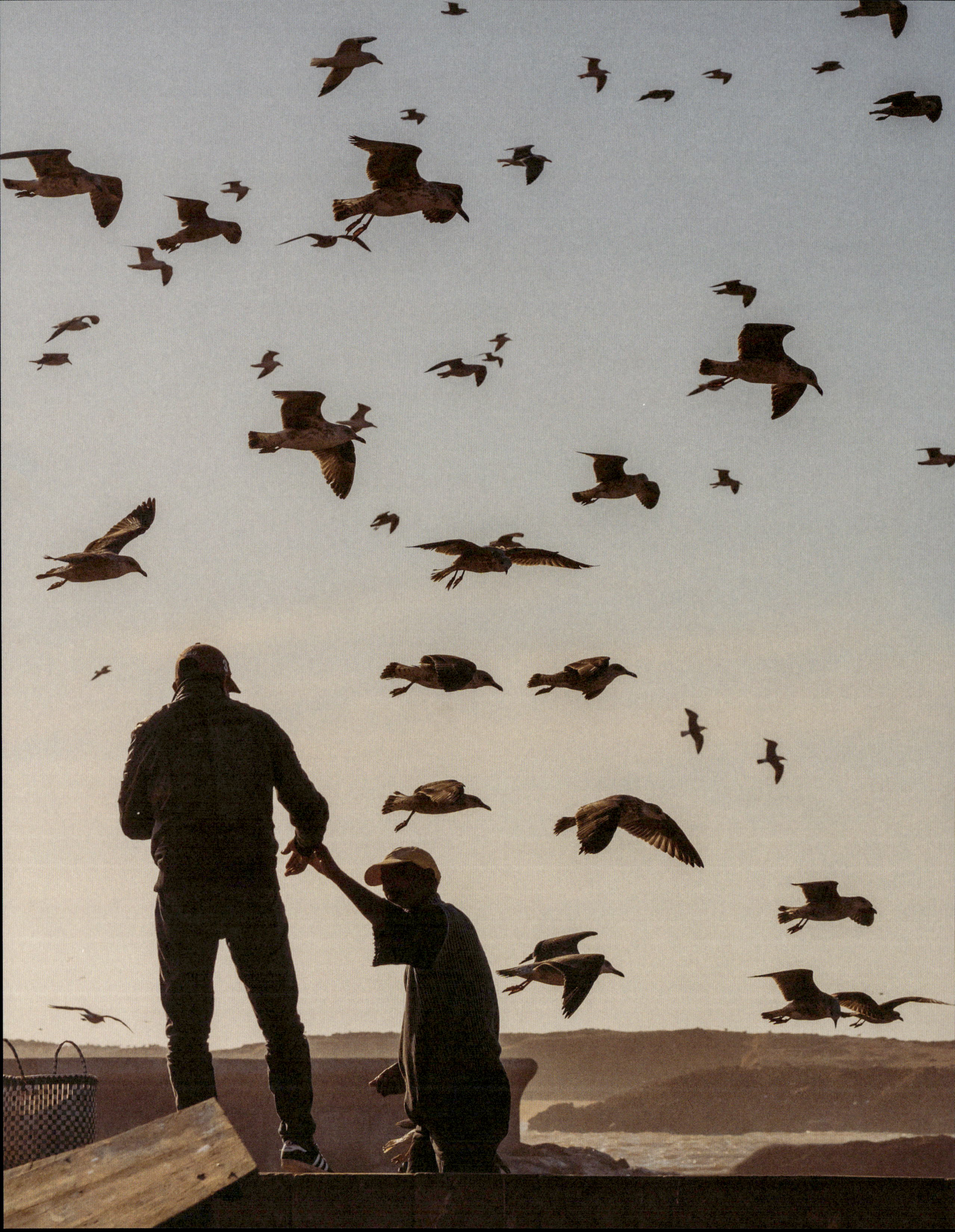

← **Essaouira, Essaouira Province, Morocco**

Erika Hobart

↓ **Santa Barbara, California, United States**

Ryan Tatar

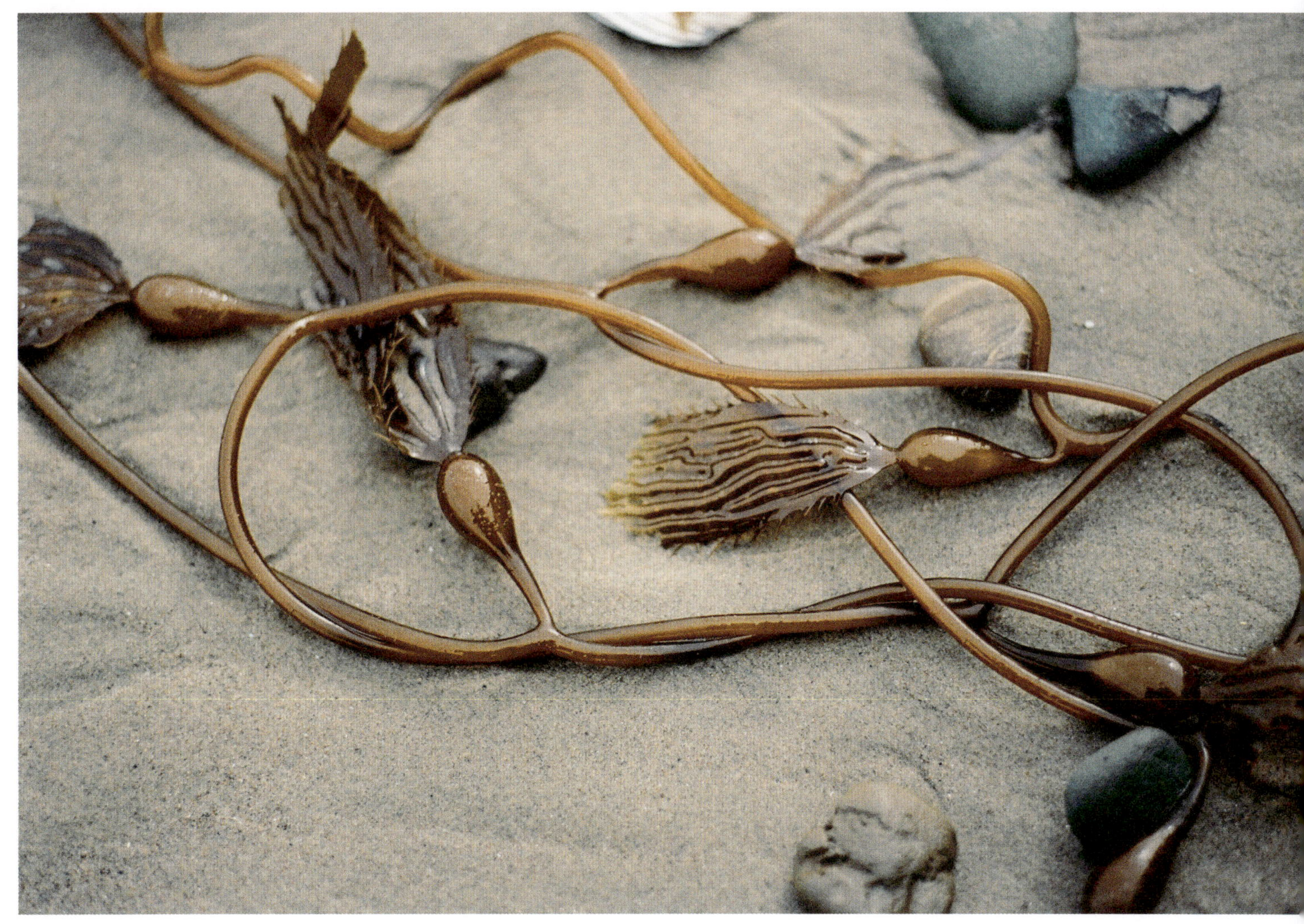

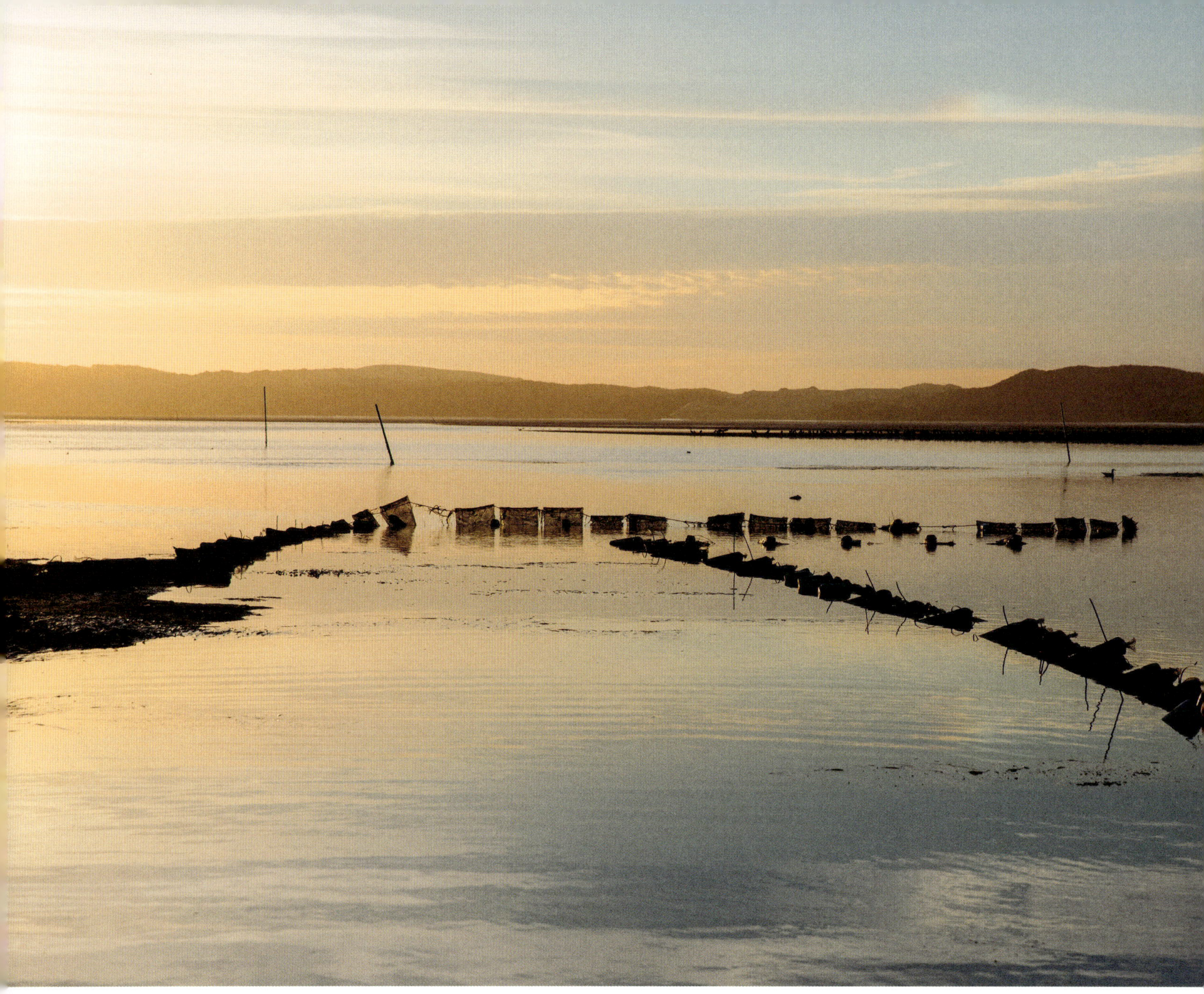

MORRO BAY ESTUARY, on the Central California coast nearly
halfway between Los Angeles and San Francisco, is home
to Pacific Gold oysters, which are grown in an intertidal farm
that uses floating long-line and tide-tumbled bag culture.
From filtering water to acting as an artificial nursery reef, oyster
farming is considered extremely sustainable and beneficial to
the health of the bay. The changing tide of the bay tumbles the
oysters, which helps form deeply cupped, uniformly shaped shells.

**Morro Bay, California,
United States**
Christa Renee

**Ston, Dalmatia,
Croatia**
Kristin O'Connell

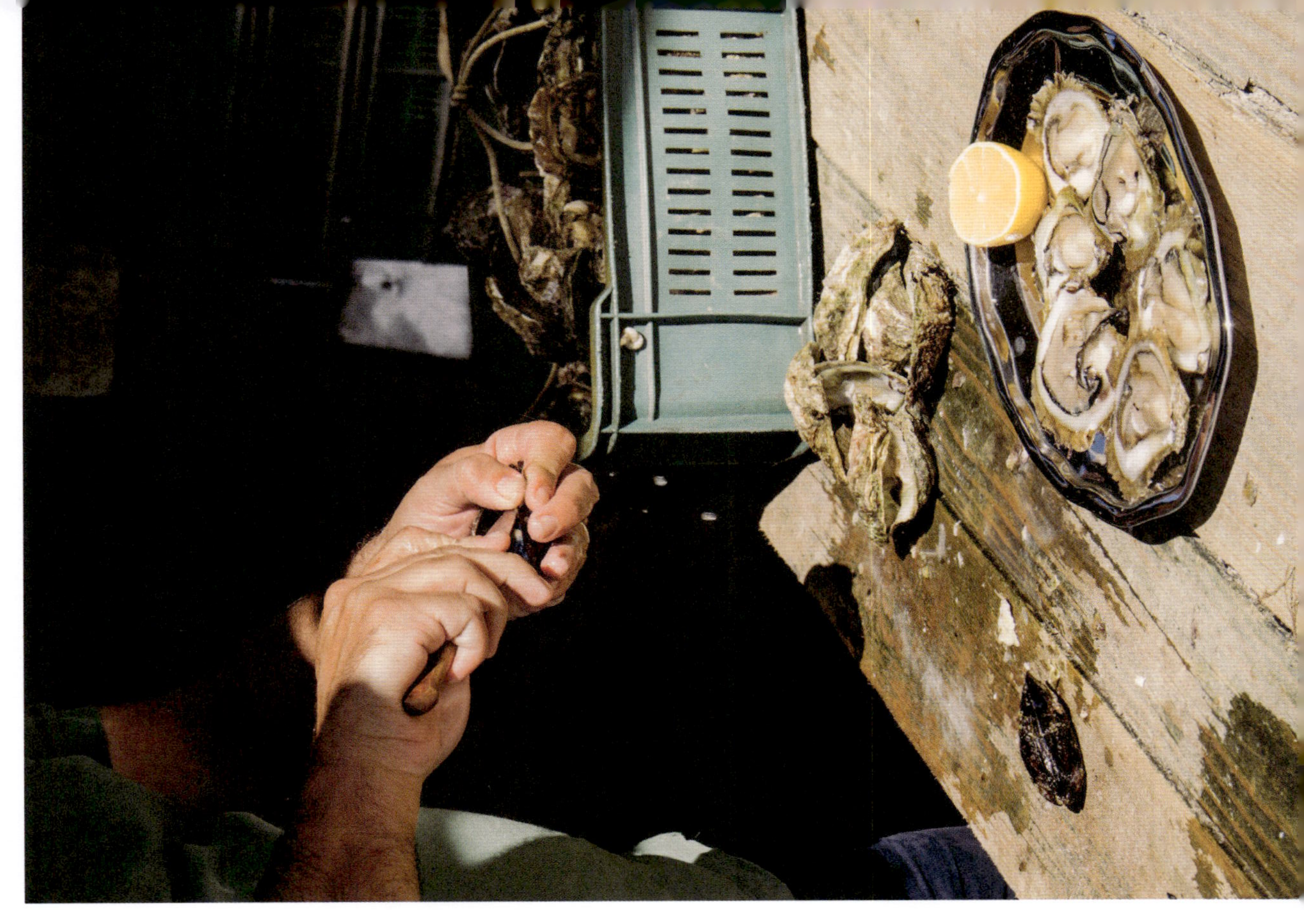

AROUND SIX HOURS from Perth along the Indian Ocean Drive, the wild and shifting shades of Hutt Lagoon are a delightful rarity. The bubble-gum pink hue is a result of extreme levels of salinity that create a fine habitat for *Dunaliella salina* algae. The lagoon is located between the fishing village of Gregory and the town of Kalbarri on Western Australia's Coral Coast and is spectacular to photograph from a scenic flight. The surreal pink stands in vivid contrast to the clear blues of the Indian Ocean that borders the lagoon. The lagoon is also home to the world's largest microalgae plant and is a supplier of commercial brine shrimp used as feed for farmed shrimp and fish.

Hutt Lagoon, Gregory, Western Australia
Jarrad Parker

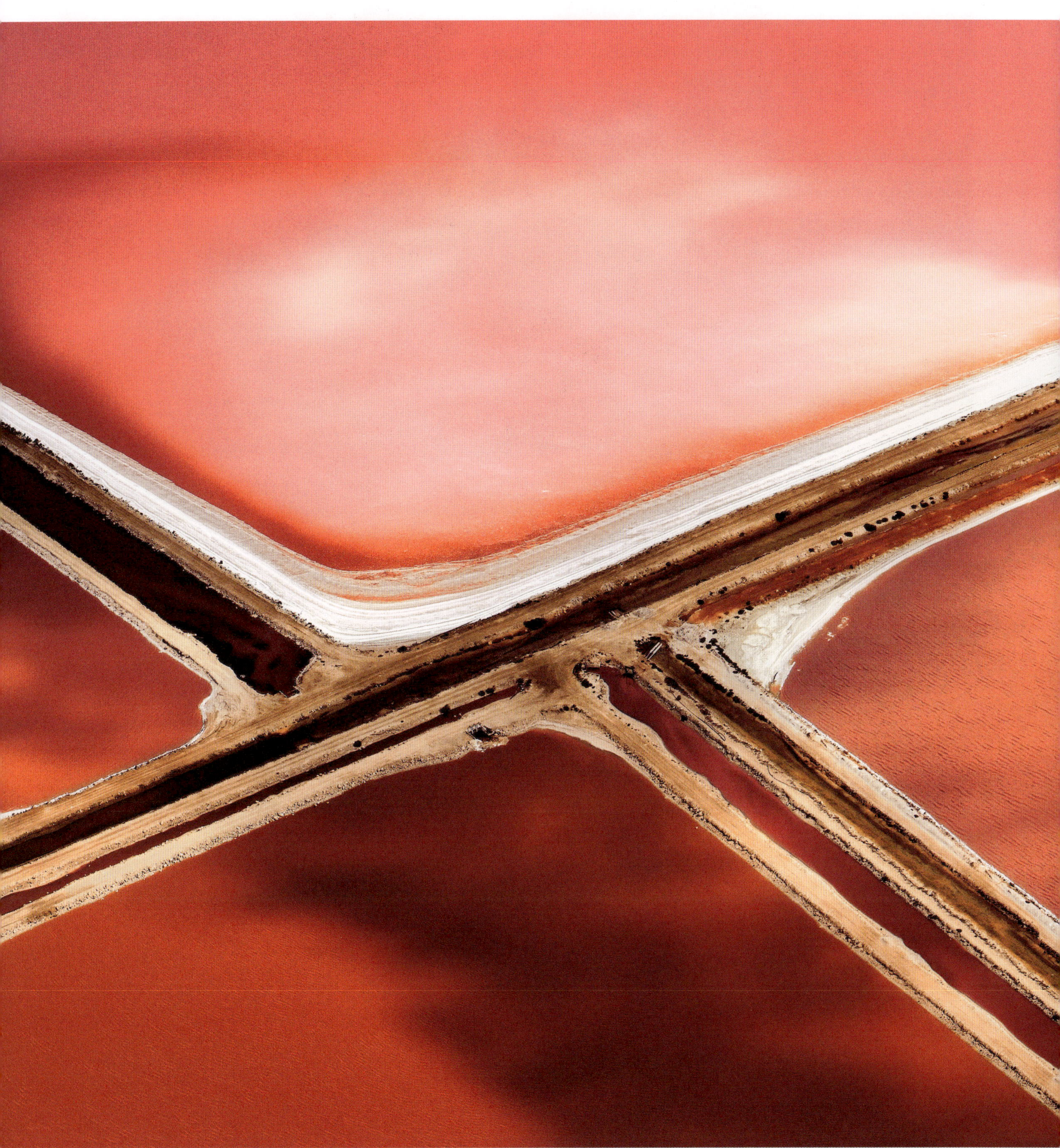

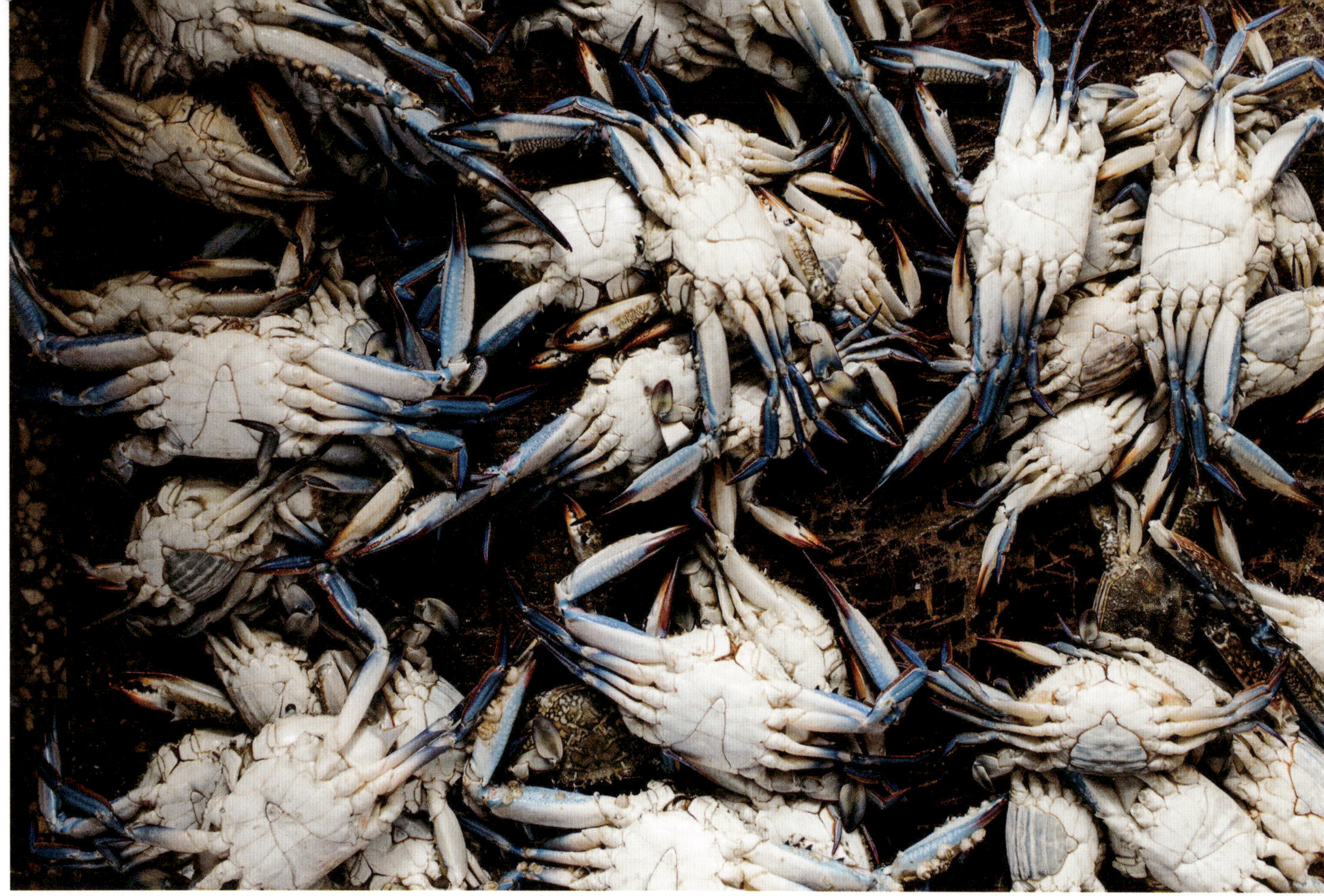

↑
STONE TOWN (also known in Swahili as Mji Mkongwe), which is the name of the old town of Zanzibar City, sits on the western shore of Zanzibar's main island, Unguja; it is surrounded on three sides with soft sand beaches that bustle with tourists, fisherman, hotels, and restaurants. Visitors can access the town via regular ferry service that takes roughly two hours from Tanzania's capital, Dar es Salaam, or via less predictable flights into the small regional airport. Stone Town is a port famous for its position in the spice trade and notorious for its slave trade. Today, visitors wander through the narrow streets, seeking out the food markets and shops selling local designers' handiwork. The island features a mix of cultural influences from other African nations, as well as Oman, India, and elsewhere.

**Stone Town,
Zanzibar City,
Tanzania**

Sam Vox

→
Andros, Greece

Nicole Franzen

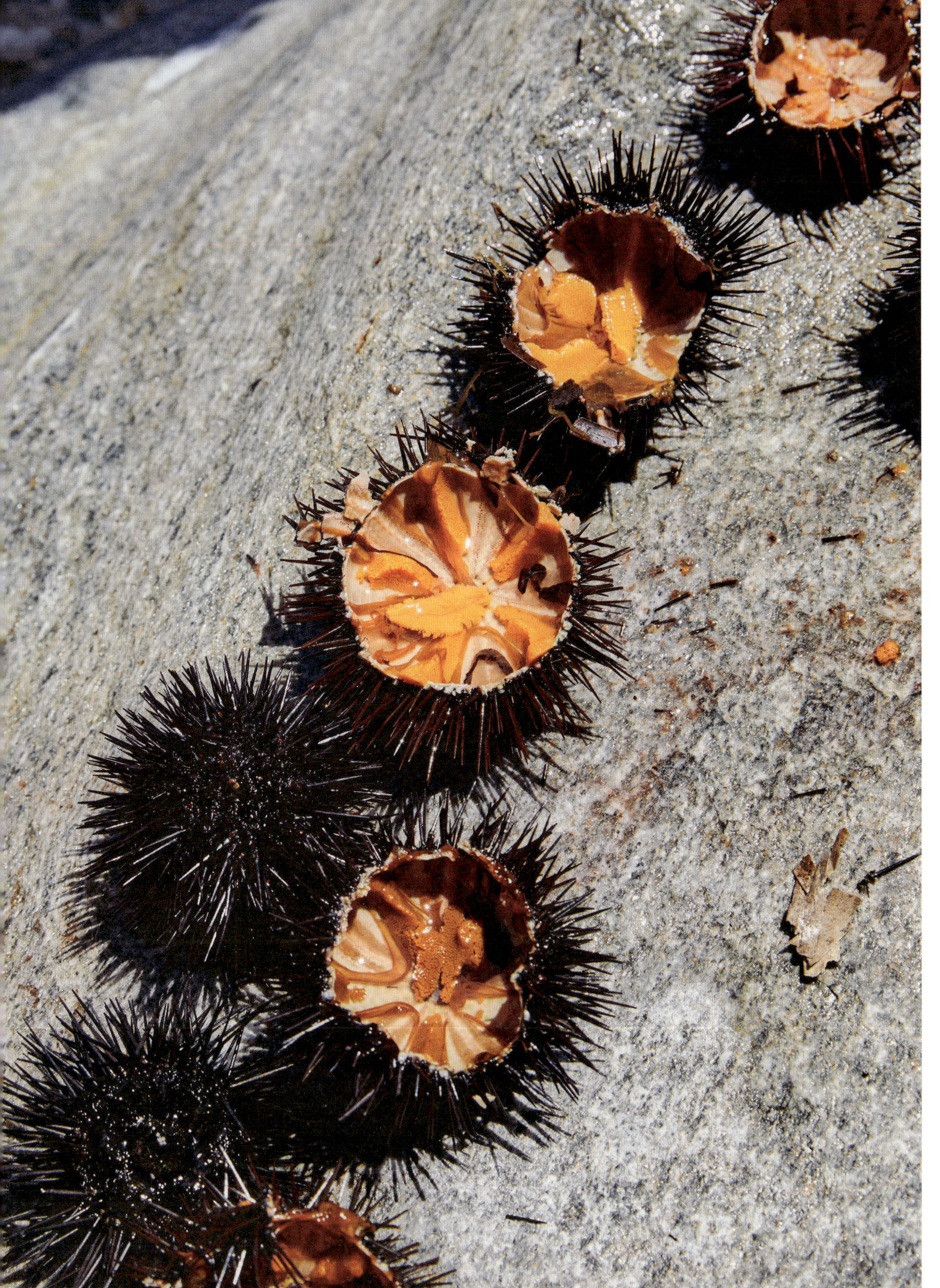

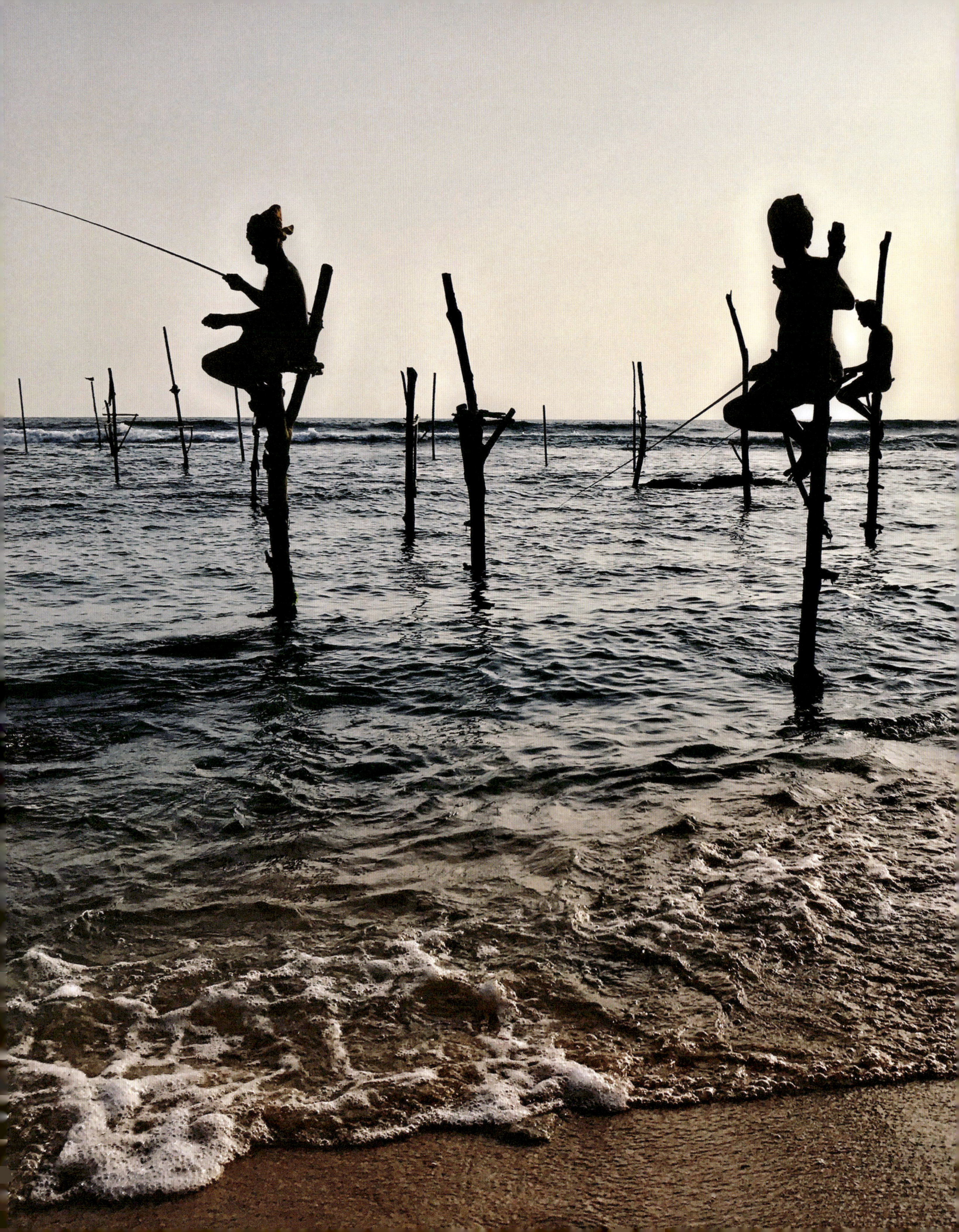

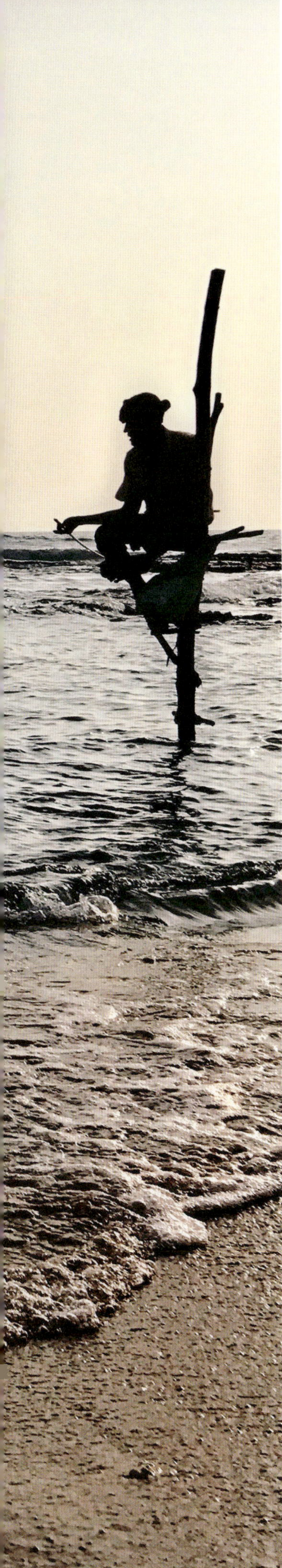

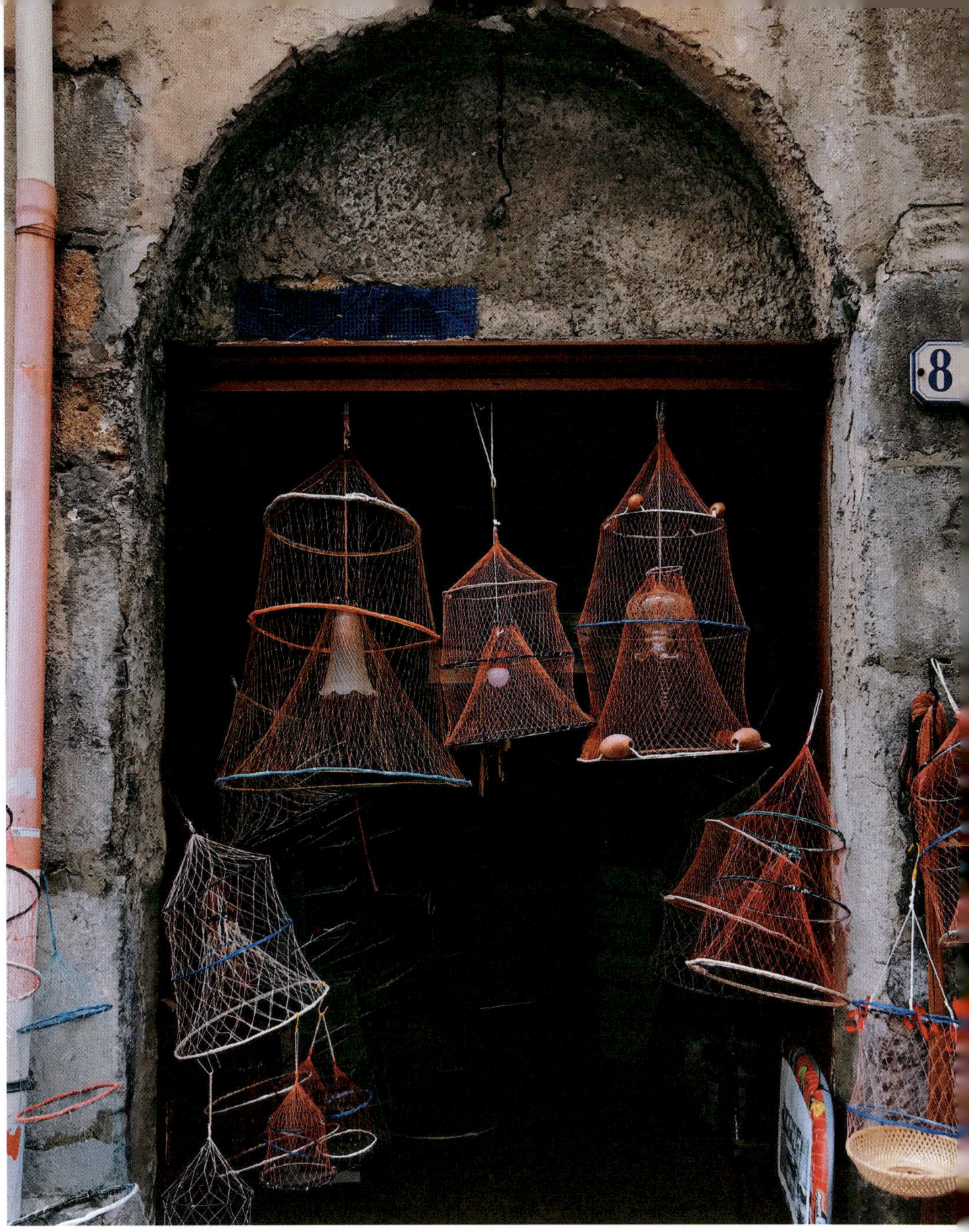

SOUTH OF THE Sri Lankan town of Galle, you can see traditional stilt fisherman hovering above the reef on large poles fitted with small handmade seats. The fishermen first hike into the jungle to source and trim the slender branches they use as fishing poles, each one selected for its desired bend. Many of the fisherman also make their own hooks from lead, cutting and polishing them to a bright silver finish to attract fish.

Koggala, Sri Lanka
Gemma Cagnacci

Cefalù, Sicily, Italy
Gemma Cagnacci

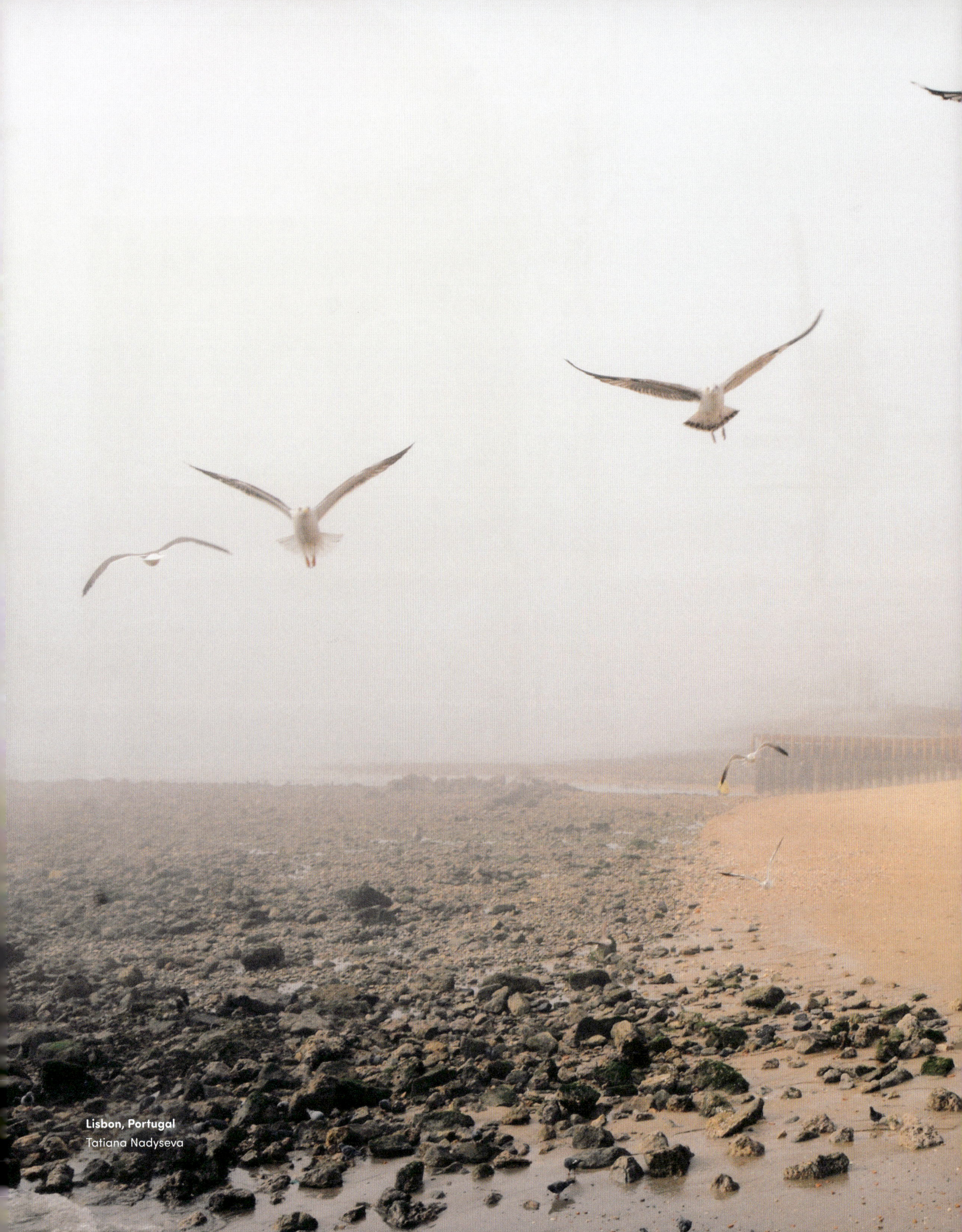

Lisbon, Portugal
Tatiana Nadyseva

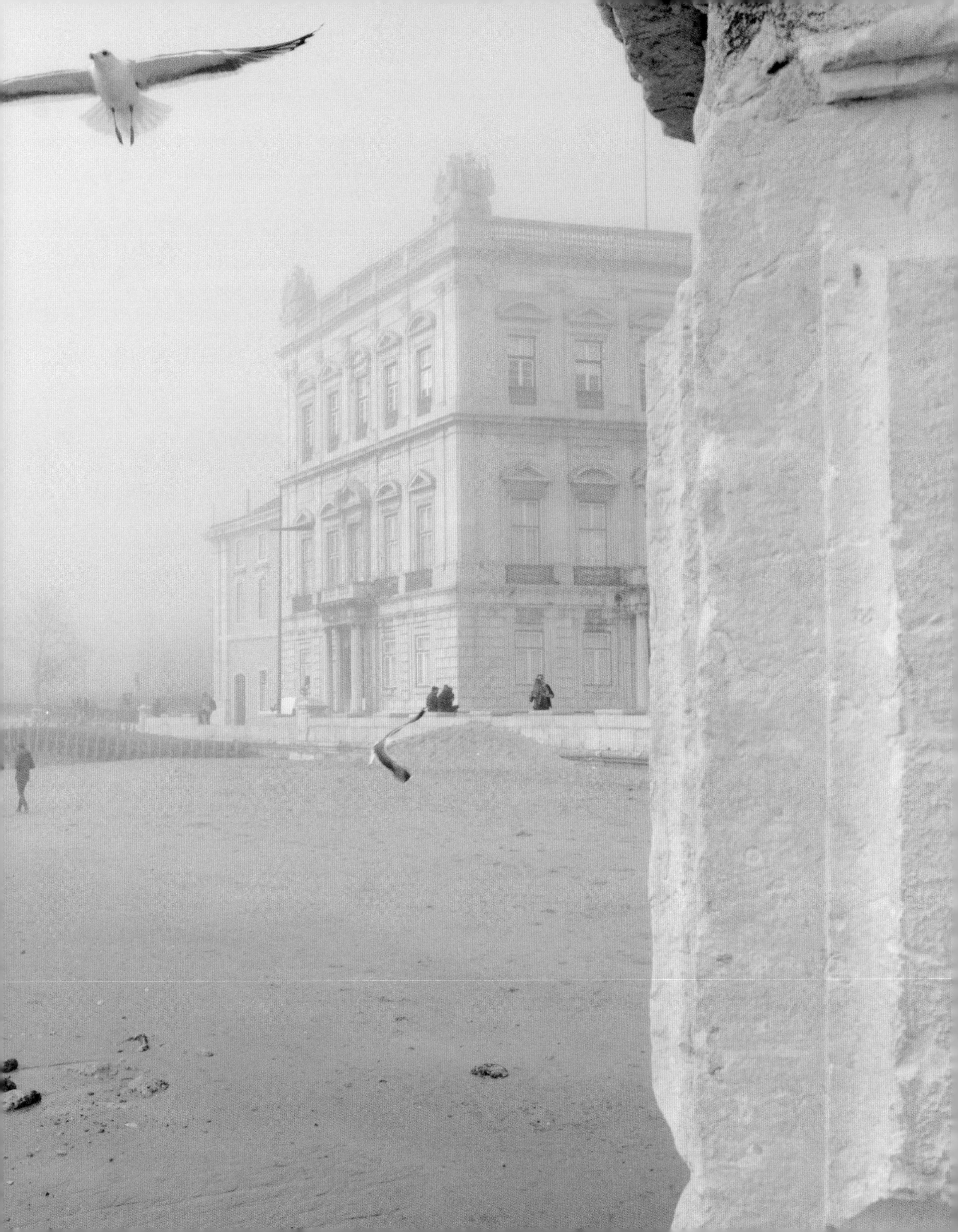

Travelers visiting the idyllic tropical island of Bali are often alarmed by the plastic pollution. Because of Bali's position in the Indonesian Throughflow (the world's largest ocean current, which moves vast volumes of water through the Indonesian archipelago) and poor waste management, its tropical beaches collect an enormous amount of plastics. Although plastics are the most common ocean pollutant (and particularly harmful since they break down into small particles that marine animals may mistake for food), much of the waste we produce on land eventually makes its way to the oceans, adversely affecting almost all animal species globally. Fortunately, thanks to initiatives by local conservation groups, Bali is now working to reduce its 33,000 tons of annual plastic waste by banning single-use plastics and imposing a tax on tourists to help raise funds to combat this problem.

Even sparsely populated communities feel the effects of plastics in our oceans. On the coast of the Scottish Highlands, massive quantities of fishing debris wash up on the shores as a result of dramatic winter storms and ocean currents. Some fishing debris found in northwest Scotland originated in Atlantic Canada in the 1980s. Discarded nets, ropes, traps, and other fishing gear are the single biggest contributor to plastics in the ocean and to pollution on our coastlines. All plastic is detrimental to marine environments, but abandoned fishing gear can be especially dangerous, since nets, traps, and ropes often entangle fish, coral reefs, turtles, and even whales. Plastics often take hundreds of years to decompose. The inherent interconnectedness of our oceans means that every choice matters, as each action we take has truly global consequences.

**Barra de Potosi,
Guerrero, Mexico**
Meg Haywood Sullivan

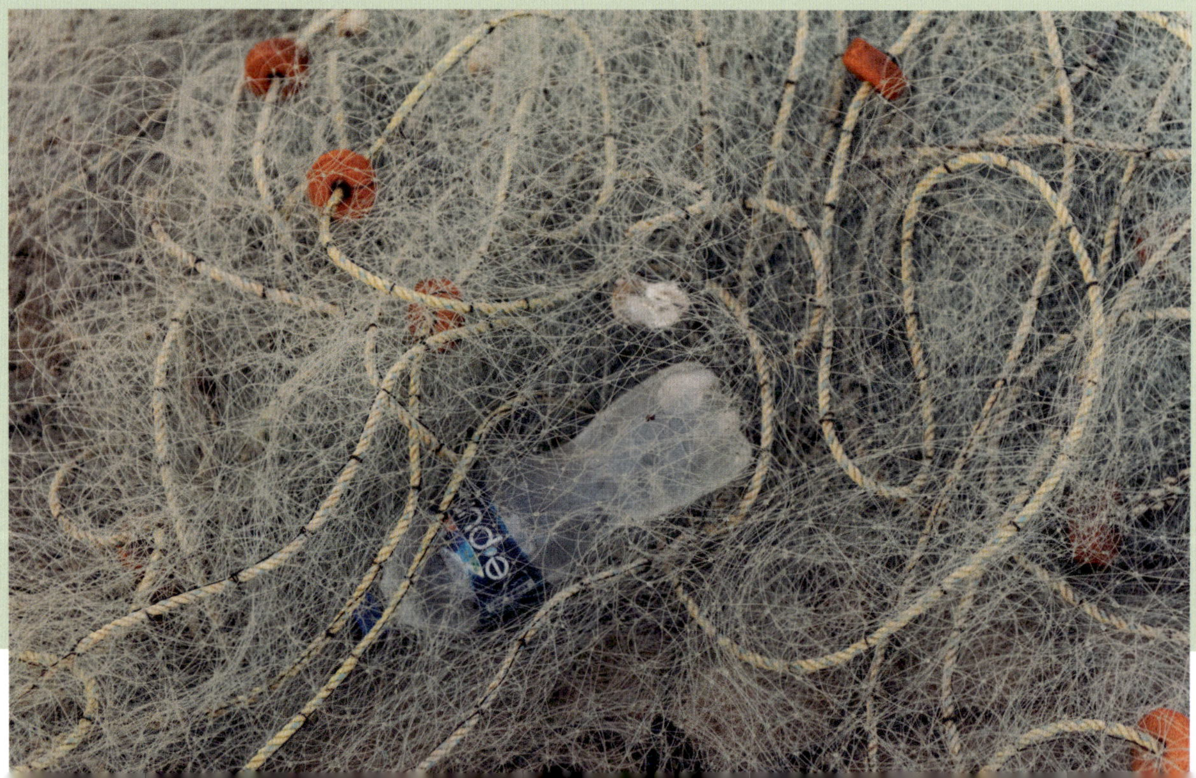

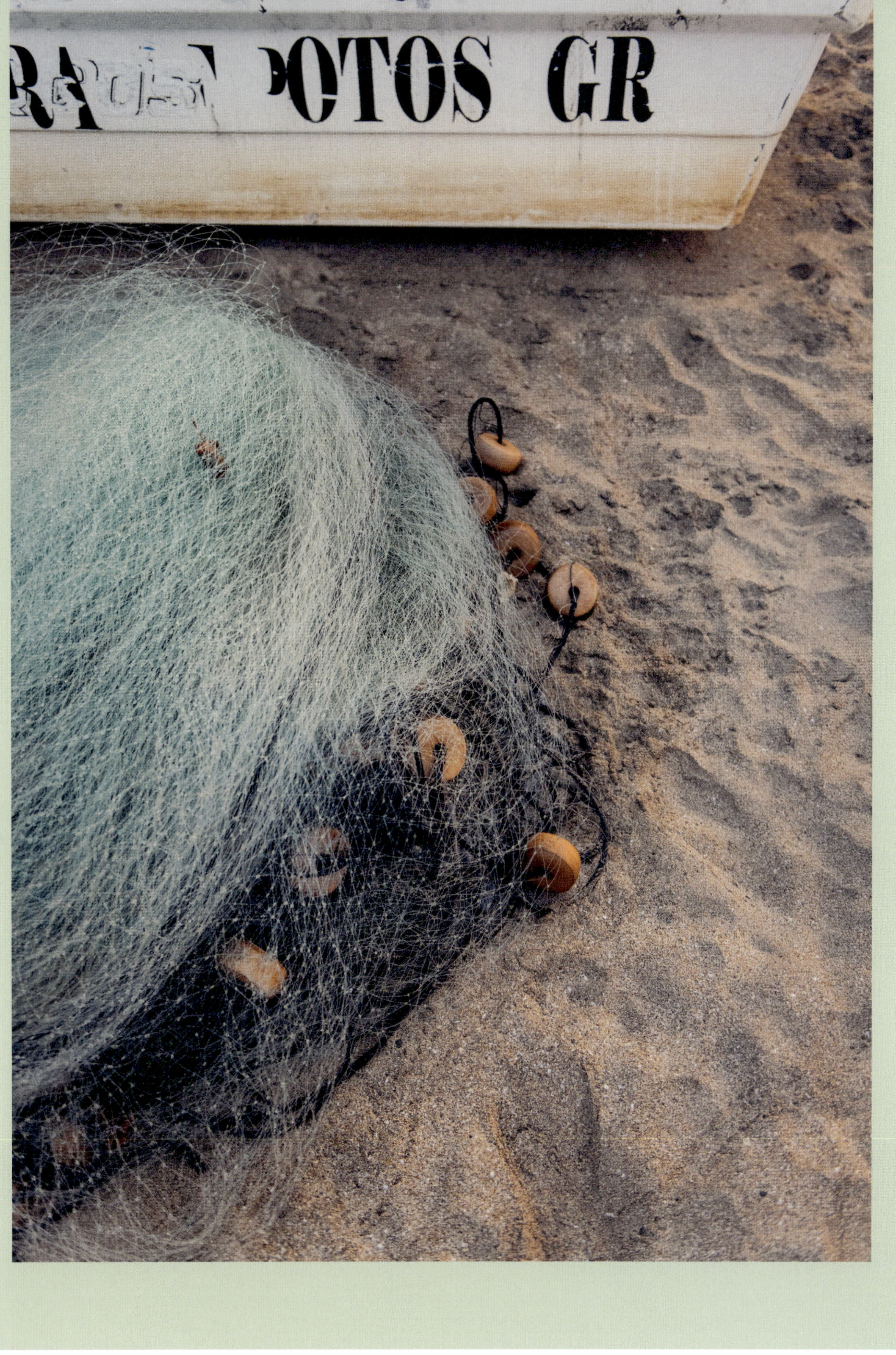
POTOS GR

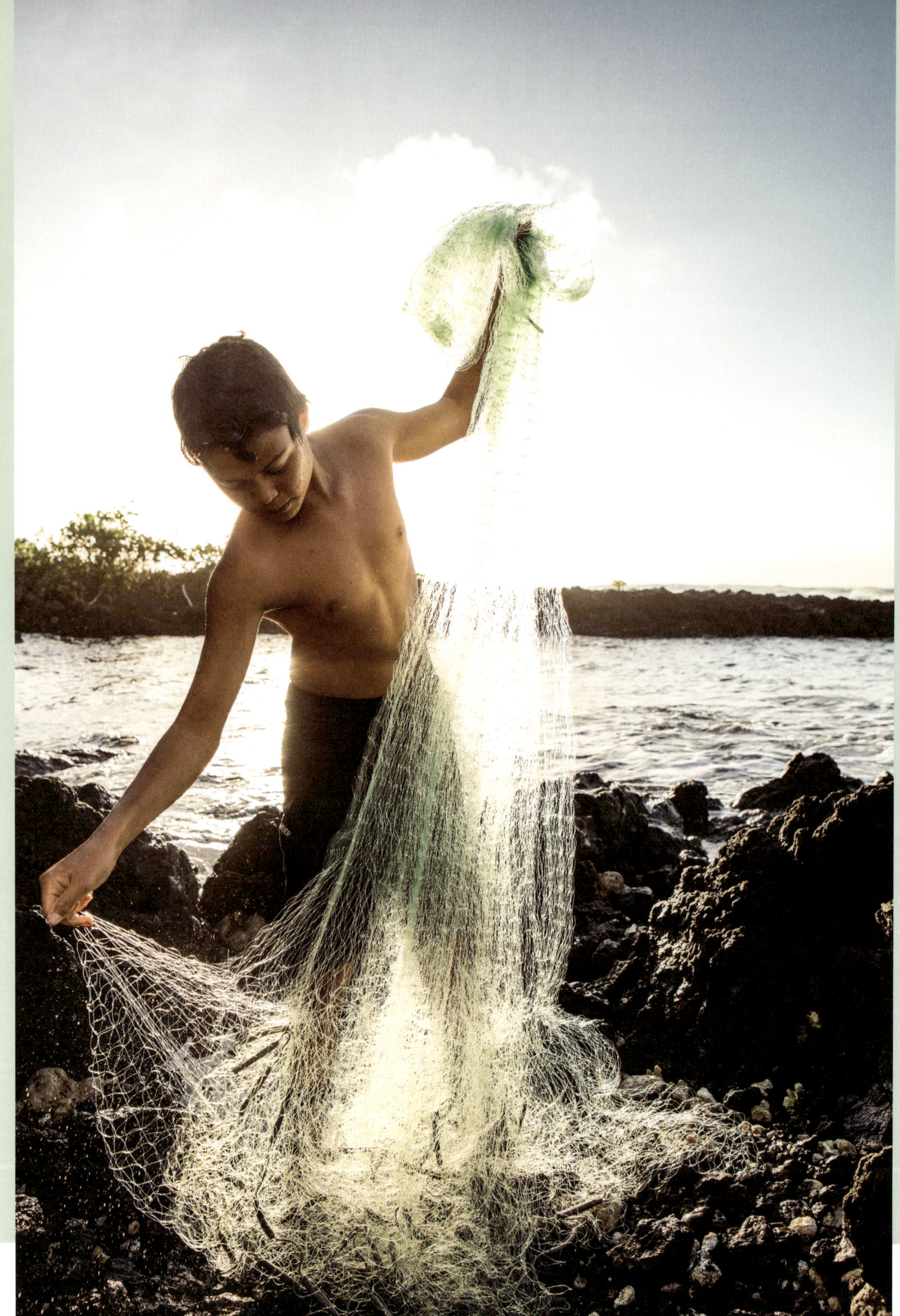

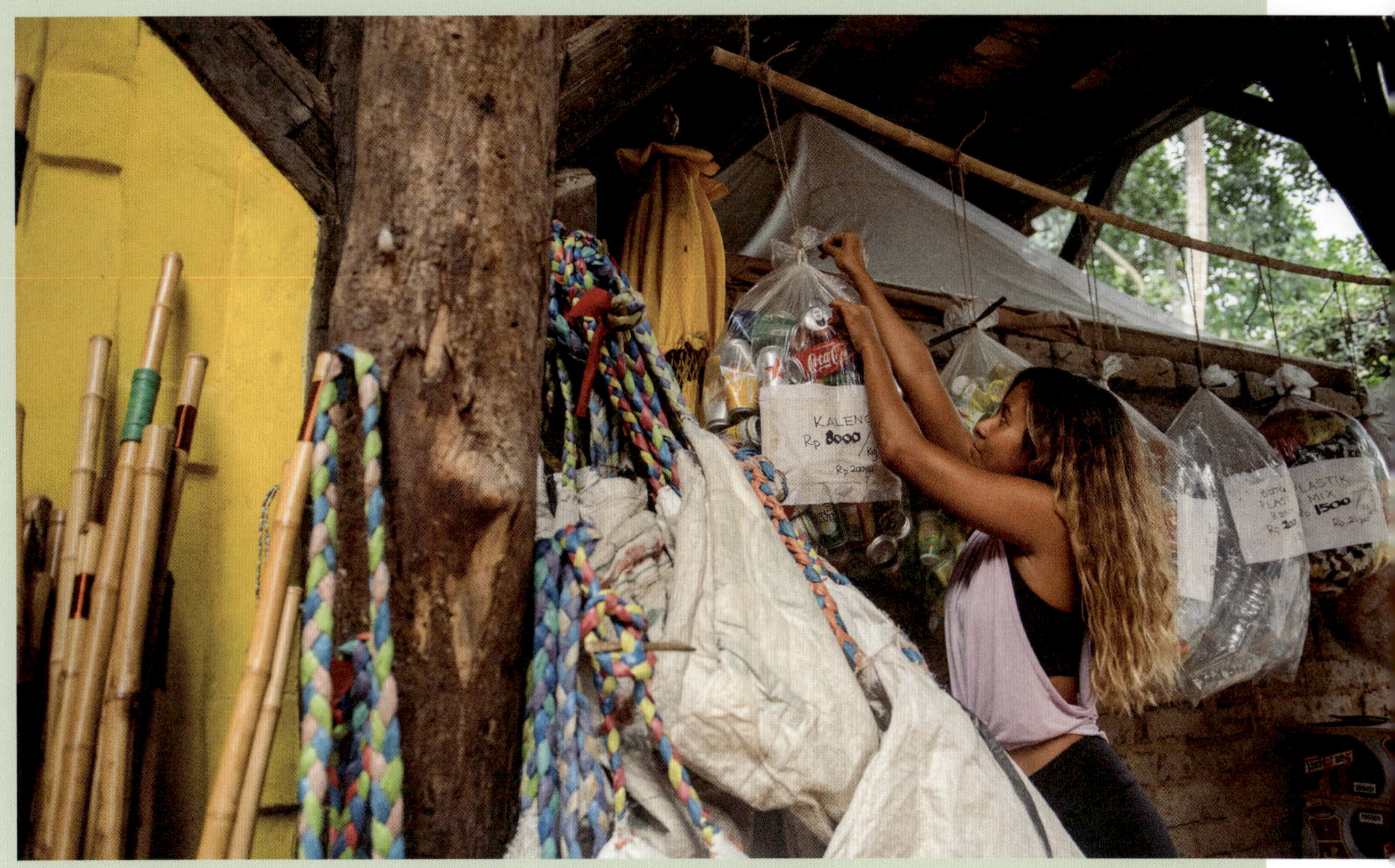

HOW YOU CAN HELP

- Find ways to reduce single-use plastics in your everyday life: bring your own water bottle, use beeswax wrap instead of plastic wrap, and consider refusing all single-use plastic one day a week—inspired by Plastic Free Fridays, a weekly event started by environmentalists Sierra Quitiquit and Meg Haywood Sullivan.

- See if there are any local beach cleanups happening the next time you visit the coast (and if not, consider starting one). In coastal Scotland, a grassroots organization, Plastic@Bay, compiles data to track how much plastic debris winds up on the shore and where it's coming from. Plastic@Bay organizes local beach cleanups and upcycles found plastic, creating tiles, clocks, and more from discarded fishing ropes.

- If you eat fish, get to know your local fishmonger to learn more about where your fish comes from and how it's caught. Make it a priority to support fisheries that use responsible fishing methods.

←
Maui, Hawai'i, United States
Erin Kunkel

↑
Ubud, Bali, Indonesia
Meg Haywood Sullivan

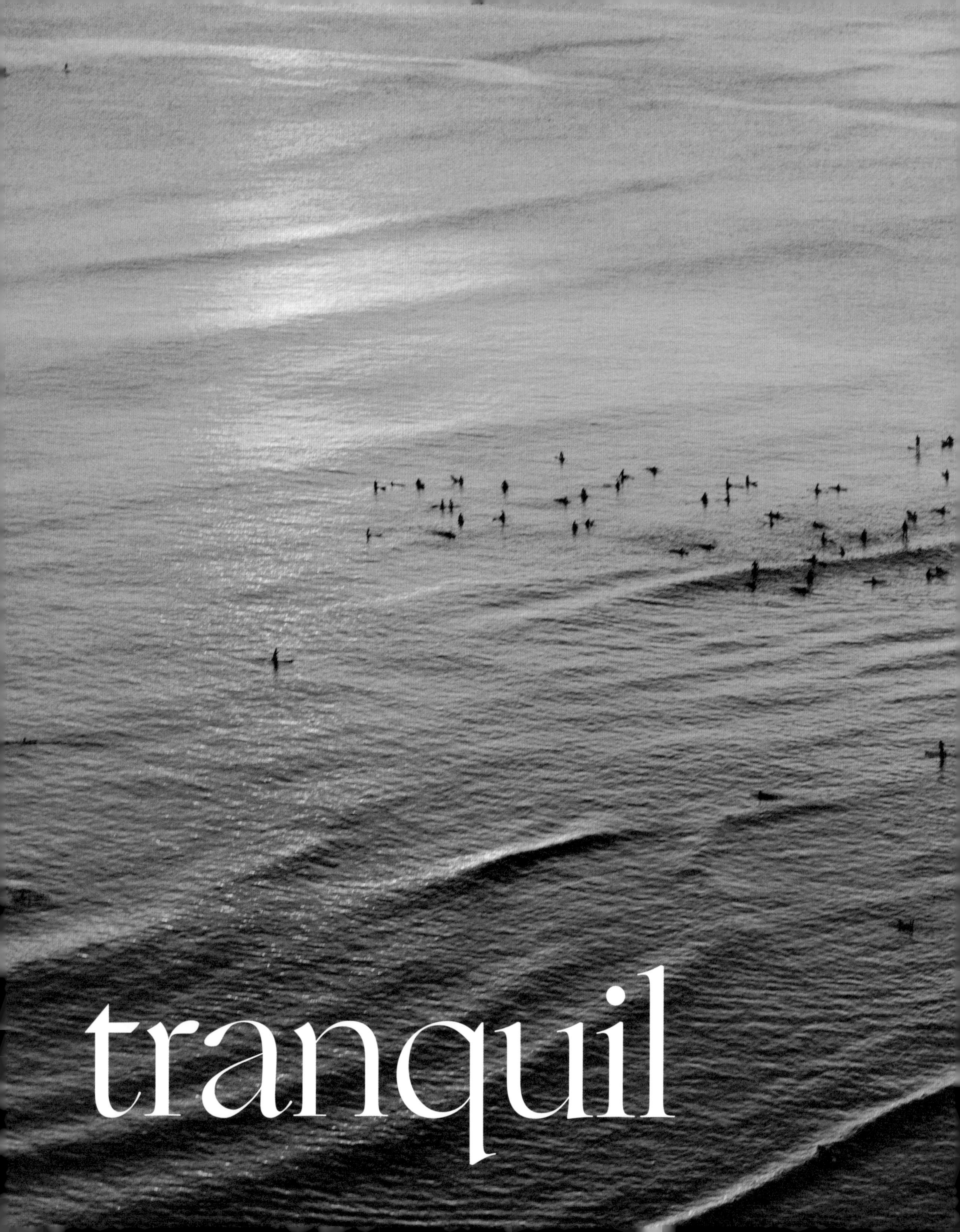

tranquil

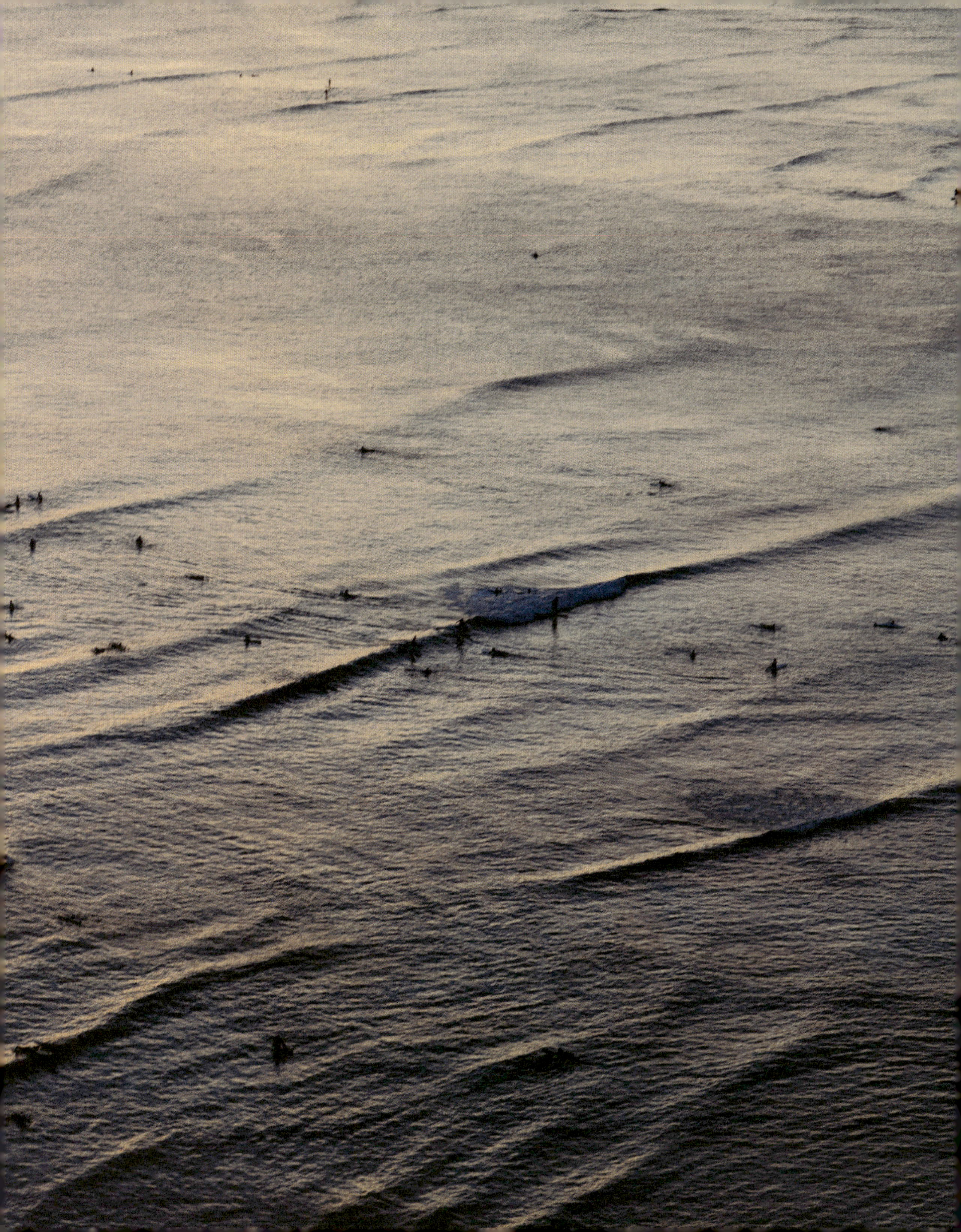

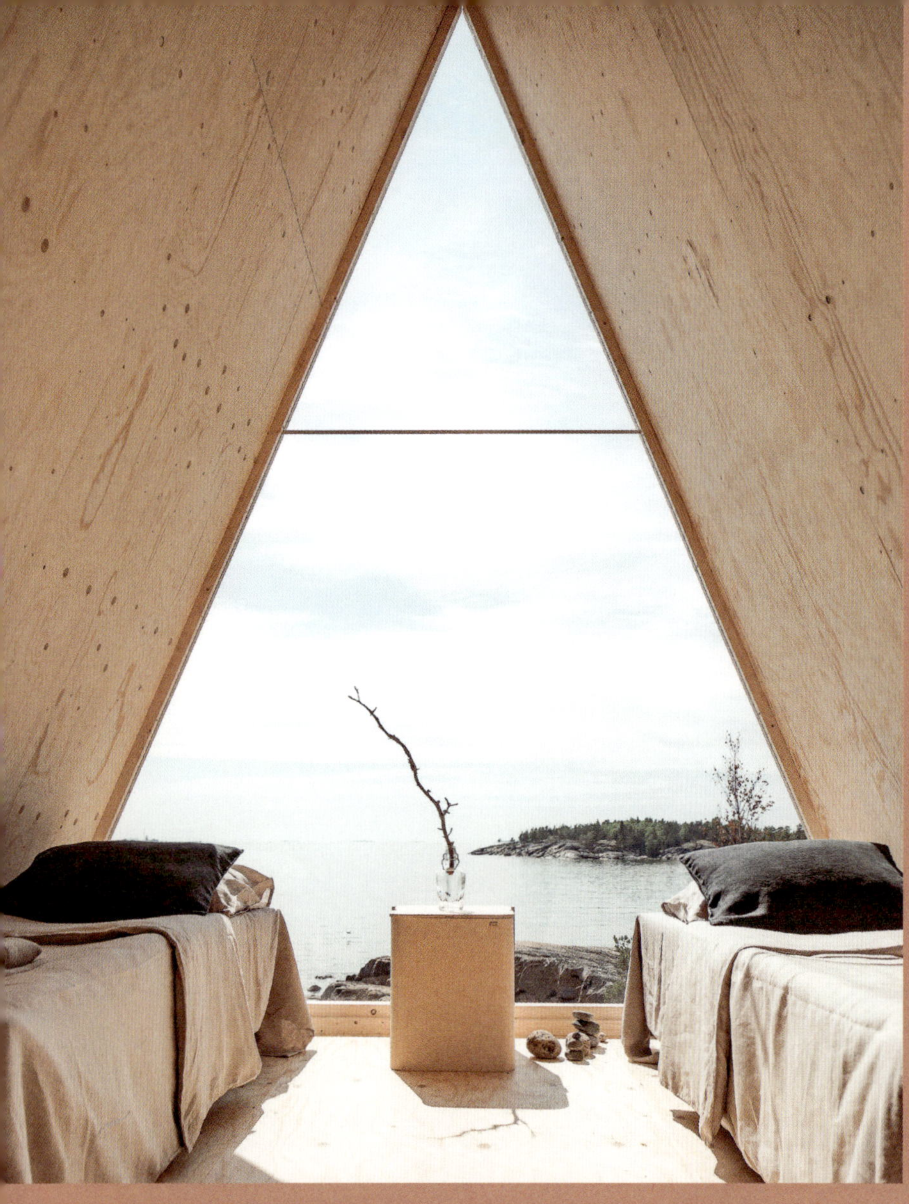

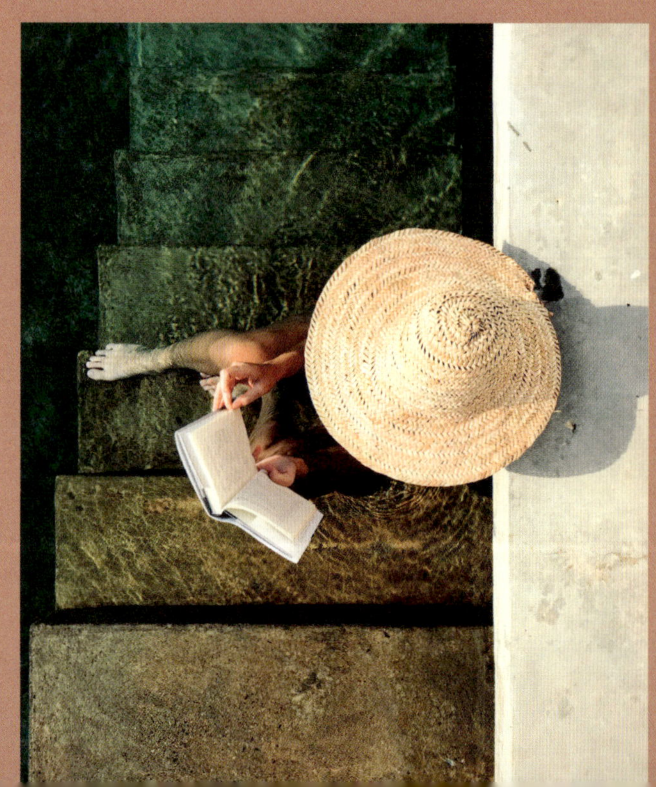

Just a few steps from downtown Honolulu's skyscrapers, locals and tourists alike cherish moments on the water in Waikiki every day.

**Honolulu, O'ahu,
Hawai'i,
United States**
Daeja Fallas

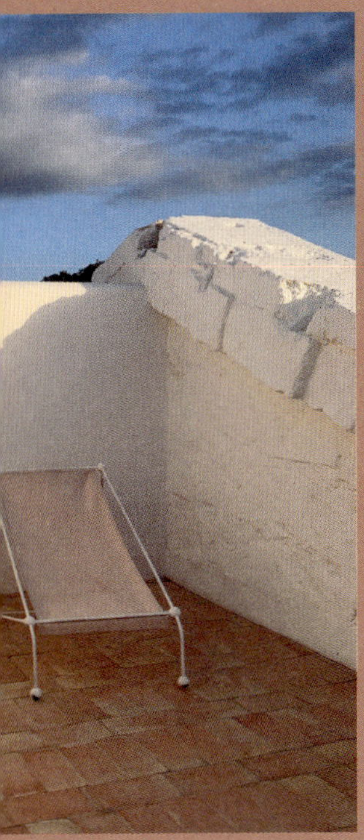

FOR MANY OF US, to arrive at the ocean's shore is to arrive at a feeling of peace. Even when our emotions are in turmoil, the sound of the waves brings a feeling of solace and eternity. We feel a deep sense of serenity while watching a pebble skip across the water's mirrored surface or tracking the gentle crest of a wave as we skim across the sea on a craft. Some divine nature—a force larger than each of us as individuals and more powerful than the magnitude of our problems—relaxes our bodies, eases our minds.

Day-to-day life often moves at a frenetic pace. Life beside, above, within, and beneath the surface of the ocean can sometimes provide an experience of a slower, more serene pace. I recently spent a summer week with my family and some friends on the lagoon at Stinson Beach in Northern California. The lagoon is a marvel, a massive body of water that quietly fills and empties almost completely every day with the tides. During most mornings and sunsets, I would walk the sandy pathways to the dunes where the lagoon alternately spills out into and then later drinks in the Pacific Ocean. I would lay in that spot, captivated by the rhythm of the powerful pelican wings beating and gliding overhead with their webbed feet extending behind them. In the lagoon, seals would whip around the bend in the rushing currents, bobbing their heads up to stare, as curious about me as I was about them.

↑
Menorca, Balearic Islands, Spain

Thayer Allyson Gowdy

↖
Vallisaari Island, Helsinki, Uusimaa, Finland

Robin Falck

←
Playa la Saladita, Guerrero, Mexico

Amy Guittard

↓
**Piha, Auckland,
North Island,
New Zealand**

Ari Westphal

→
**Le Lavandou,
Provence-Alpes-
Côte d'Azur, France**

Arthur Pinault

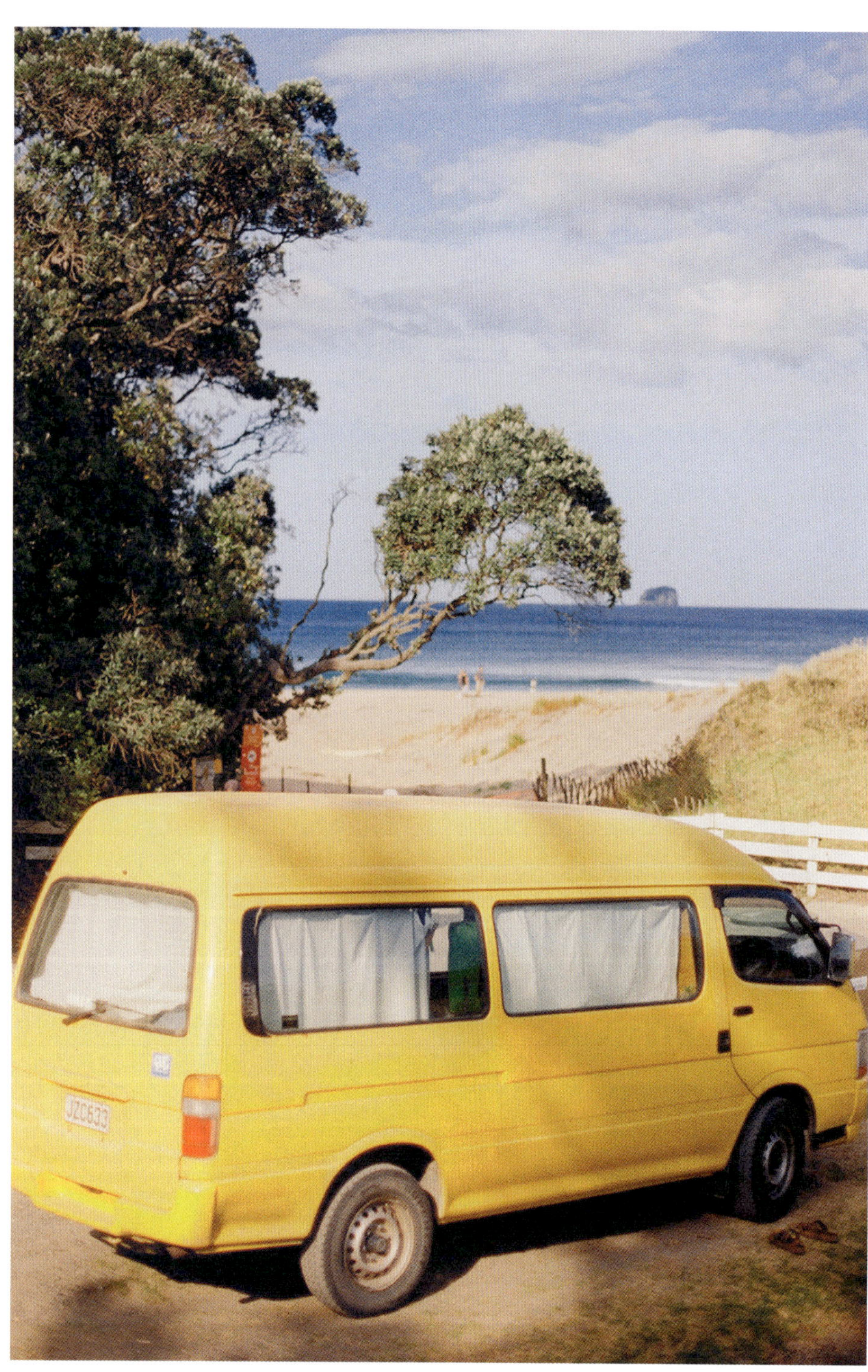

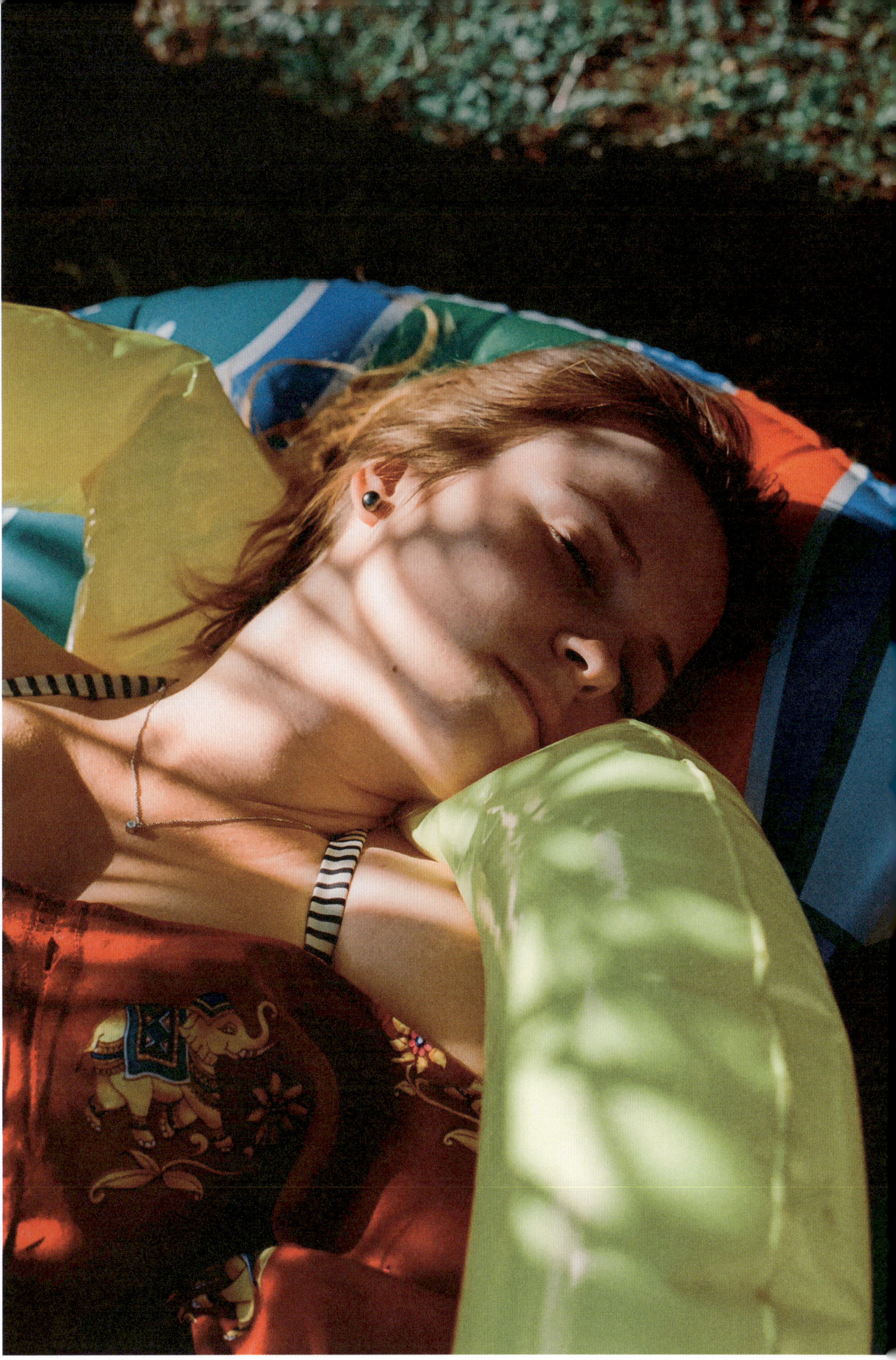

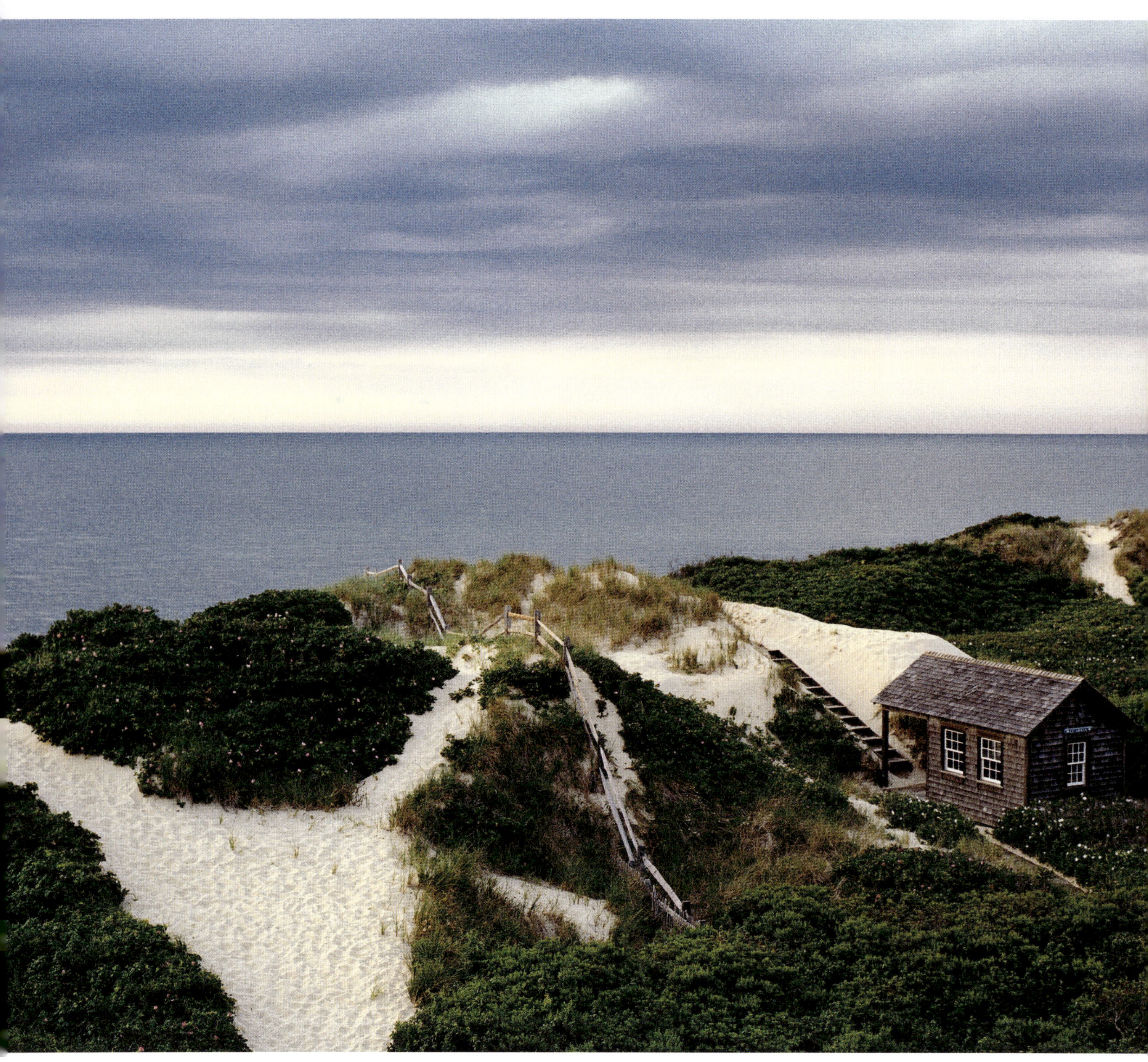

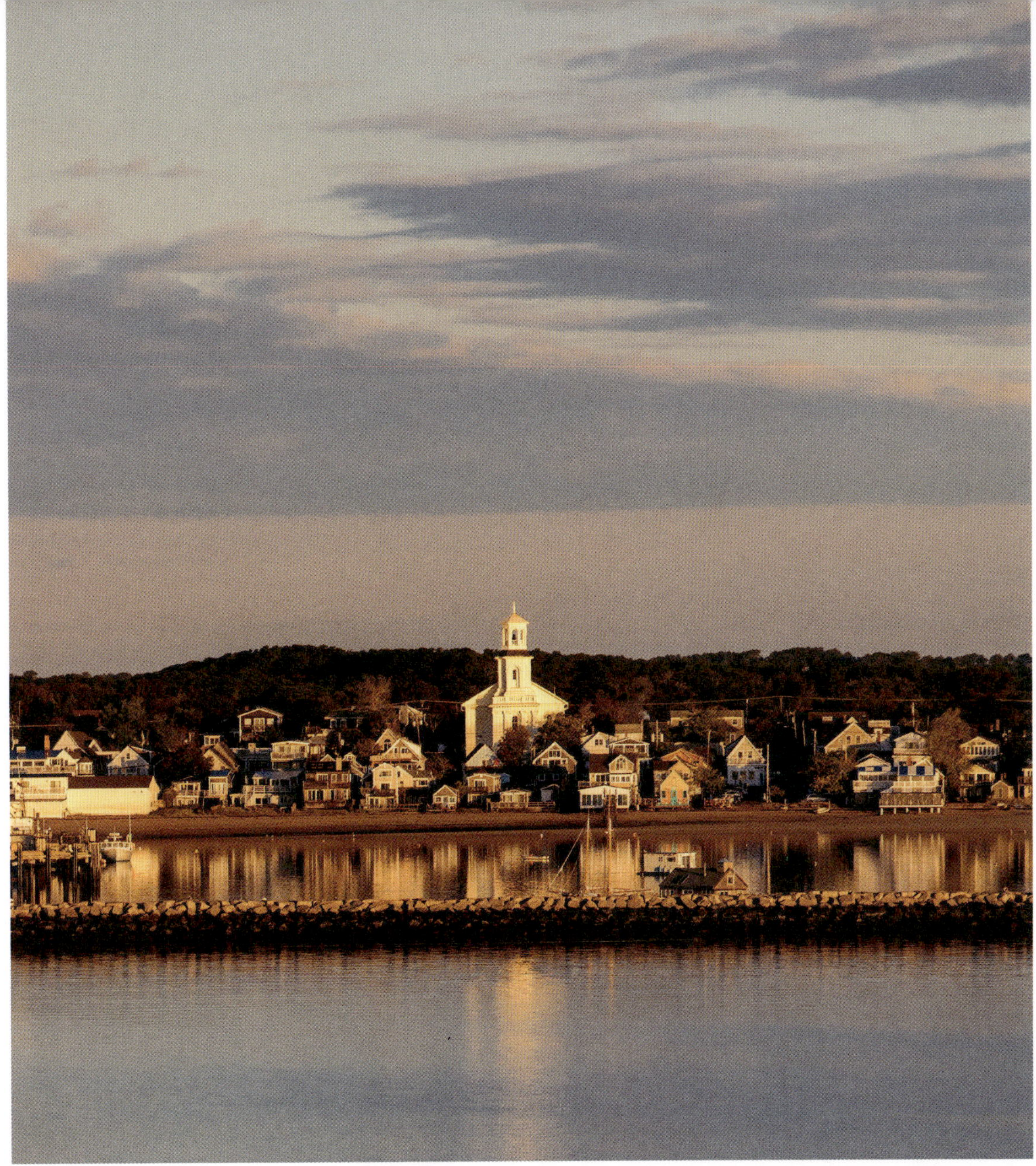

↑

PROVINCETOWN (or P-Town, as it is called locally) is the most popular seaside hamlet on Cape Cod. Located at the very far tip of the curling peninsula, P-Town is known for its art scene and beautiful beaches. While the year-round population is only about three thousand, during the summer months, vacationers and cruise season travelers bring the population as high as sixty thousand. Provincetown is a few hours by car or train from Boston and is also accessible from a variety of ferries and small planes throughout the busier summer months. Provincetown is recognized historically as the first landing spot of the colonial Mayflower and today as a thriving LGBTQ+ community.

**Provincetown,
Massachusetts,
United States**

Marianna Jamadi

↓

TIMBER COVE RESORT is one of the few truly oceanfront hotels in Sonoma County and is surrounded by wild land and trails. Seasonal abalone diving is popular at the tiny harbor in Salt Point State Park just to the north, and from this cliffside perch, you may spot divers headed out in sea kayaks as well as surfers.

**Timber Cove,
California,
United States**

Emily Nathan

→

**Mount Tamalpais
State Park, California,
United States**

Dan Tom

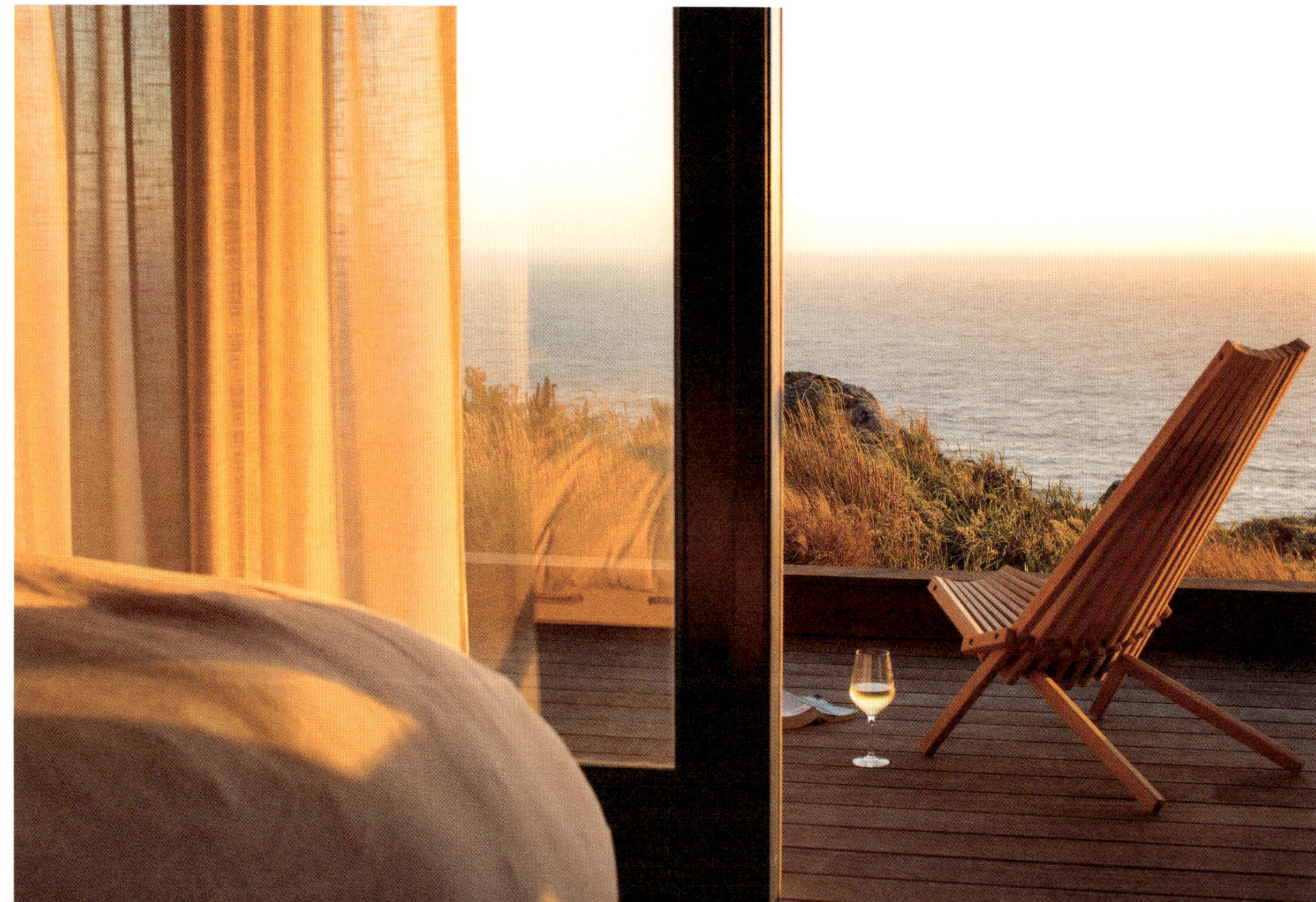

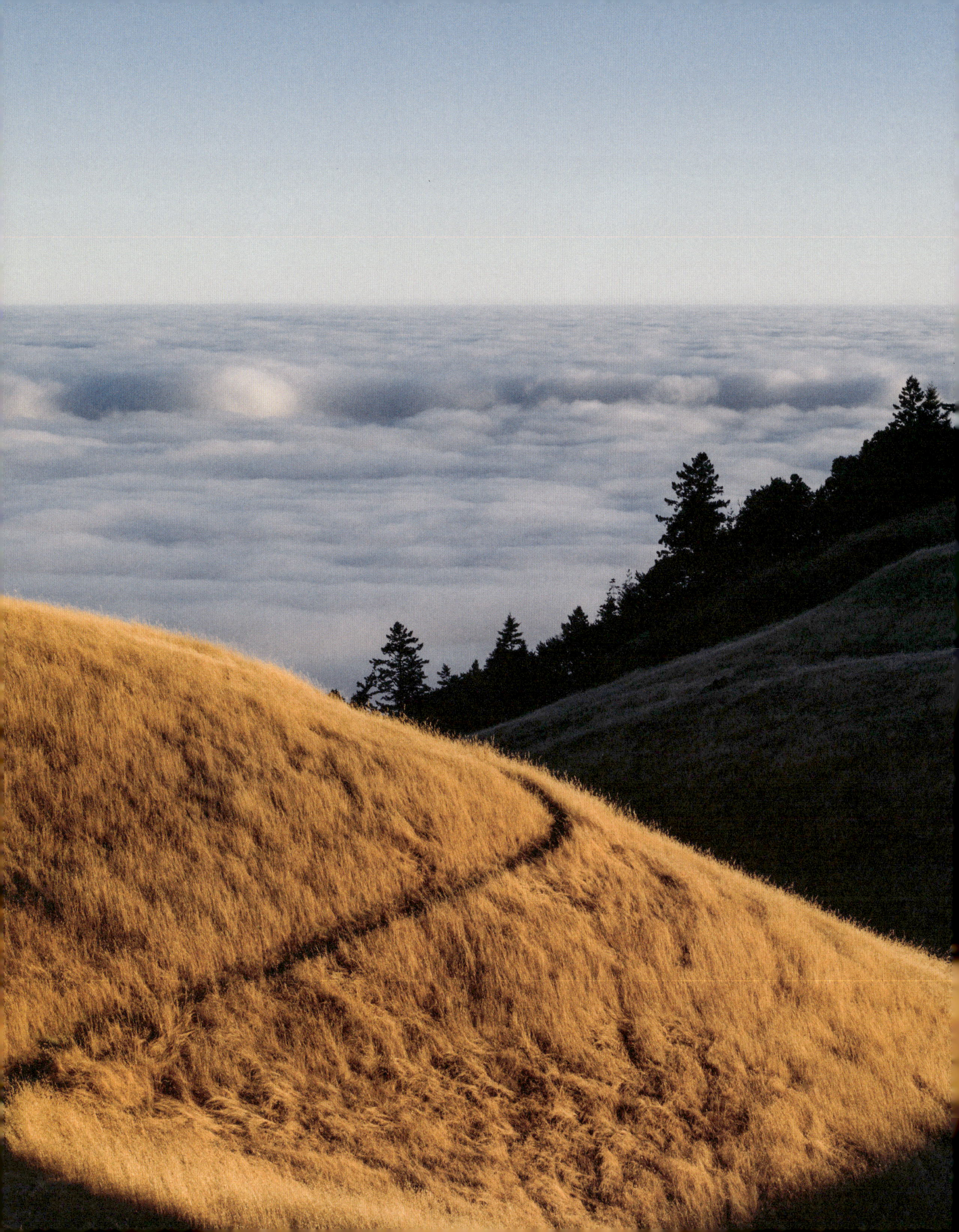

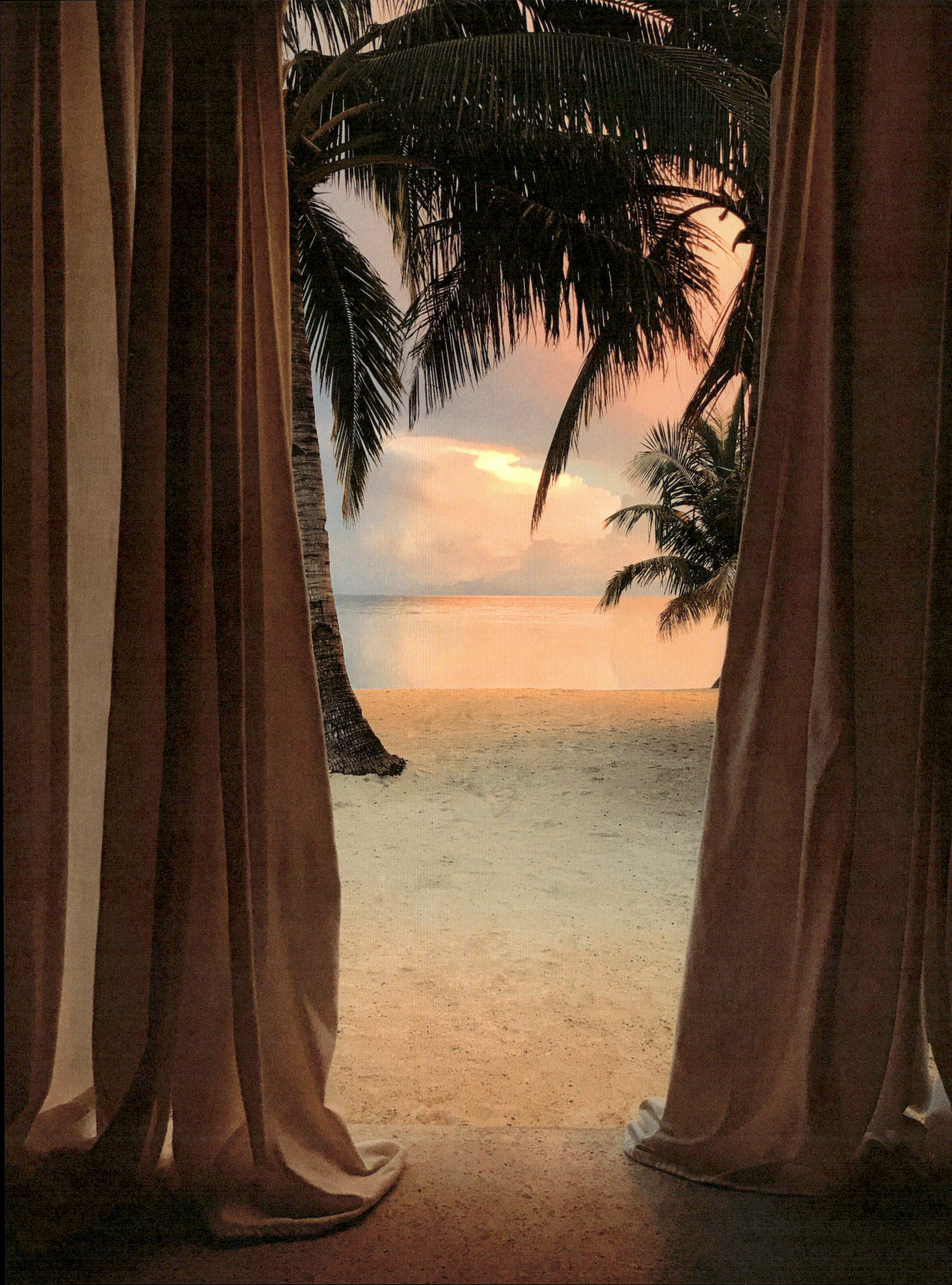

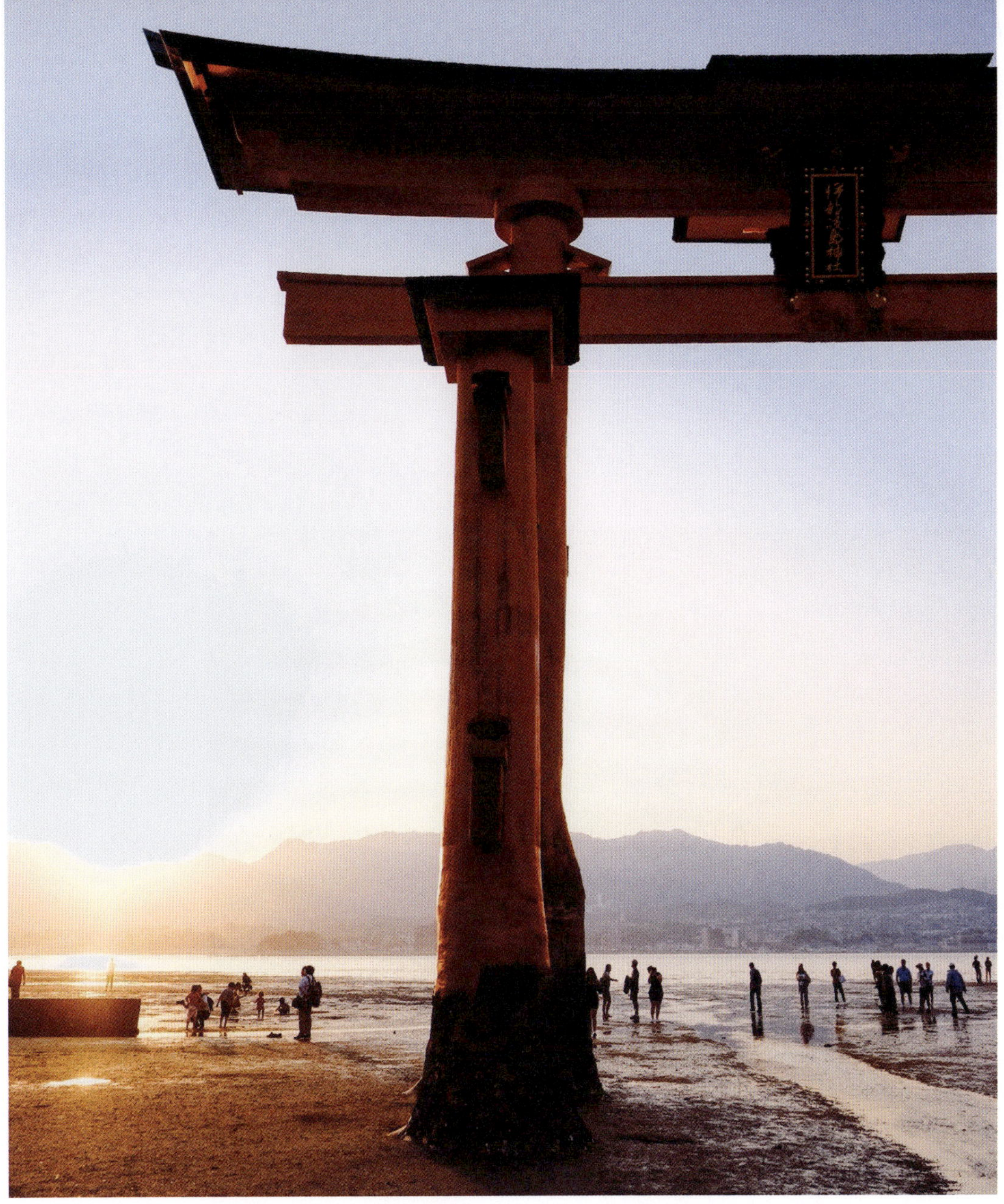

← **Romblon Island, Philippines**

Vianca Soleil Roquero

↑ **ITSUKUSHIMA SHRINE'S TORII** (gateway) on the island of Itsukushima (also called Miyajima) is one of Japan's most popular tourist attractions and a unique construction of a traditional Shinto gate. Parts of the shrine are both a UNESCO World Heritage Site and an official Japanese national treasure. Usually placed on land, this torii, constructed over water, appears to float when the tide is high. The gate is illuminated at night and can be seen from local ryokans (traditional inns) as well as from evening boat tours. Both local and international visitors flock to experience the shrine and gate and photograph its commanding presence in the vast protected landscape. The shrine is dedicated to the sanjoshin (three female deities) that are Shinto goddesses of oceans and storms.

Itsukushima, Hatsukaichi, Hiroshima Prefecture, Japan

Eric John

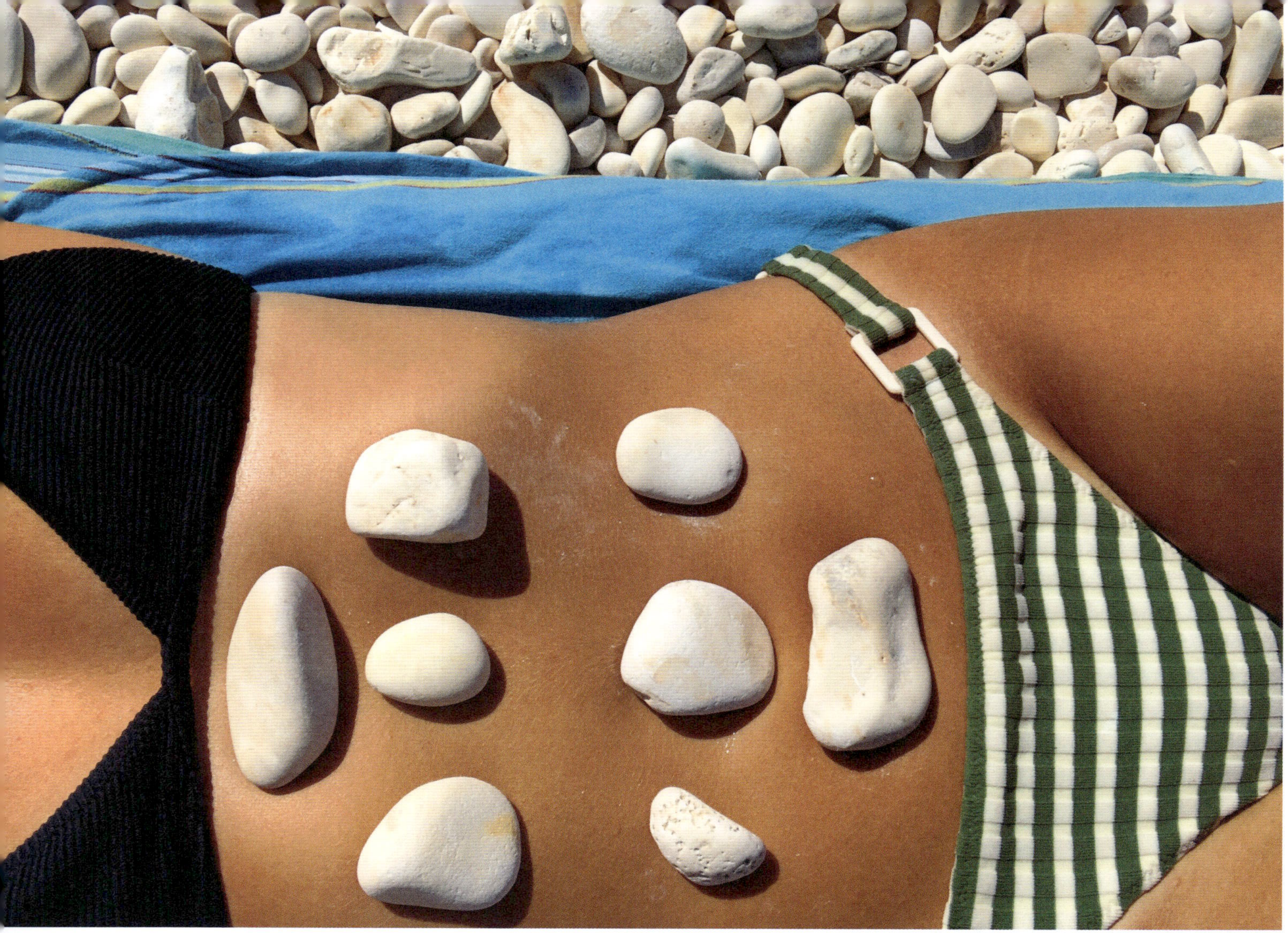

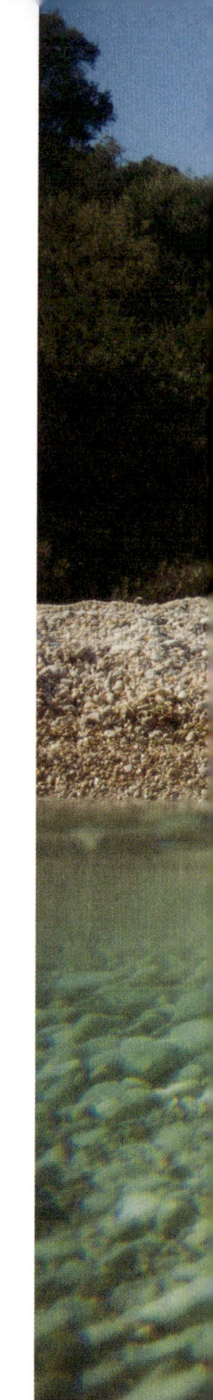

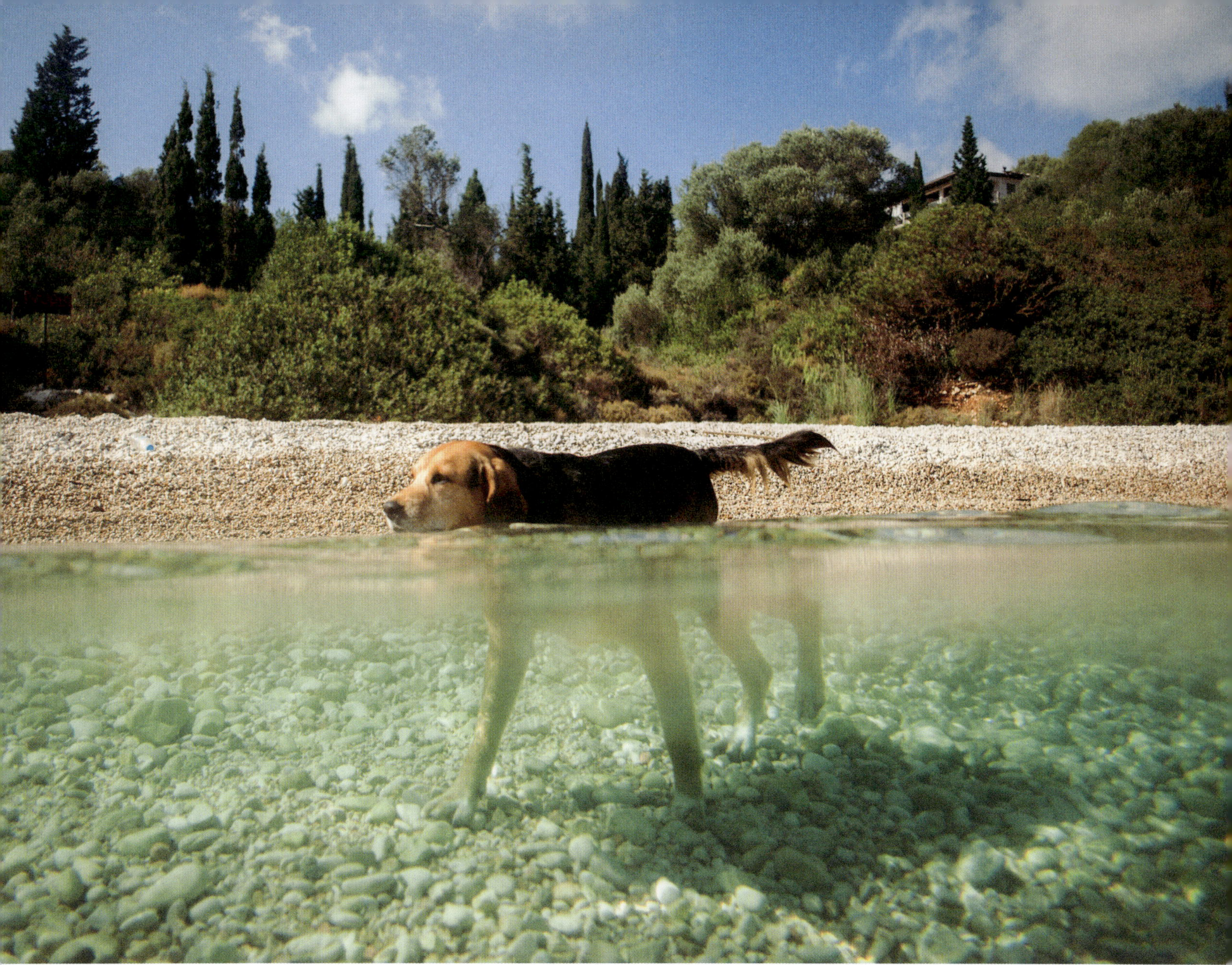

←
**Kefalonia,
Greece**

Ashley Jordan Gordon

↑
**Filiatro, Ithaca,
Greece**

Kerry Murray

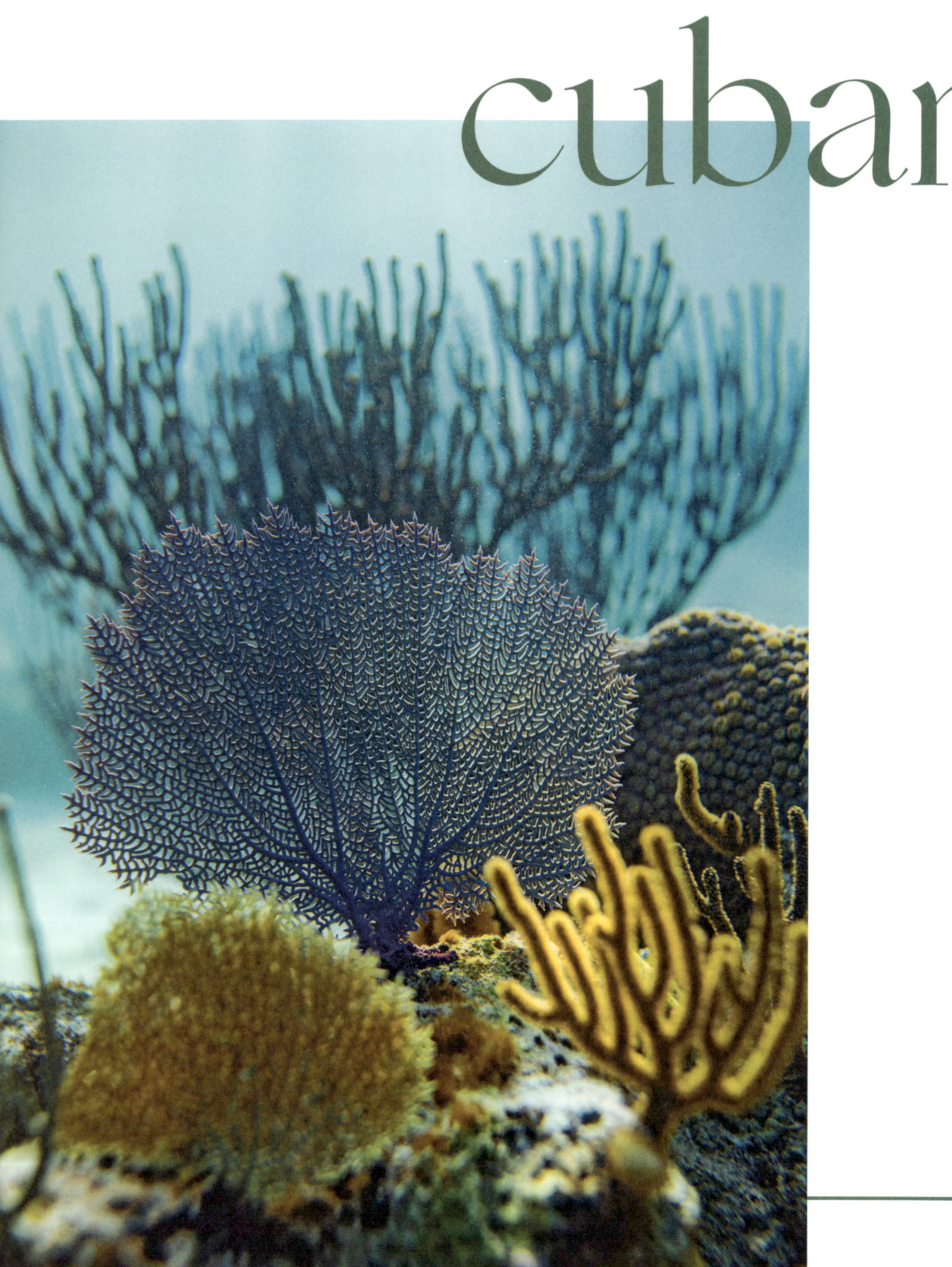
cuban

cayos

CUBA

FEW TRAVELERS HAVE EXPERIENCED the magnificent secluded and pristine beaches, coral reefs, mangroves, and caves within the archipelago of more than four thousand islands that make up the Cuban Keys (called Cayos). The coral reefs in Cuba have fared well, in part because they host a variety of fish, and also because Cuba has limited development and strong environmental protection laws. Cuban farmers tend to use fewer chemicals, so when it rains, cleaner water washes into the ocean. Some describe the Cuban reefs as similar to how other coral reefs looked fifty years ago. About 56 miles southeast of Cuba's coast is the Gardens of the Queen National Park, which is nicknamed "a Crown Jewel of the Caribbean." Here divers will find a half dozen species of sharks, stingrays, and the goliath grouper, which is the size of a small car and raises its young in nearby mangrove swamps. All this makes the waters surrounding the Cuban Cayos a unique destination for snorkelers and divers.

Cuba's Cayos surround the more frequently visited and largest island, Cuba, which shares its name with the national territory. Cuba is just 105 miles southwest, as the bird flies, from Key West in Florida. At the time of Christopher Columbus's arrival, the Tainos were the principal inhabitants of the Caribbean. Tragically, the arrival of Spanish colonizers led to the near decimation of the Taino people, but elements of their culture live on today among indigenous Cubans, particularly through music and food.

Cayo Las Brujas is off the northern coast of the main island of Cuba and connected to the main island by way of a 30-mile pedraplén (causeway). Visitors are surrounded by aqua-blue water as they enter a tropical sanctuary, a solitary respite. The beaches are long stretches of fine white sand that slope gently to shallow and calm water. All Cuban beaches are public and accessible to everyone. Although development restrictions are loosening and some larger properties have been built, travelers will still enjoy the underwater haven of a thriving marine habitat. Cayo Las Brujas is particularly popular for fishing snapper, grouper, and barracuda.

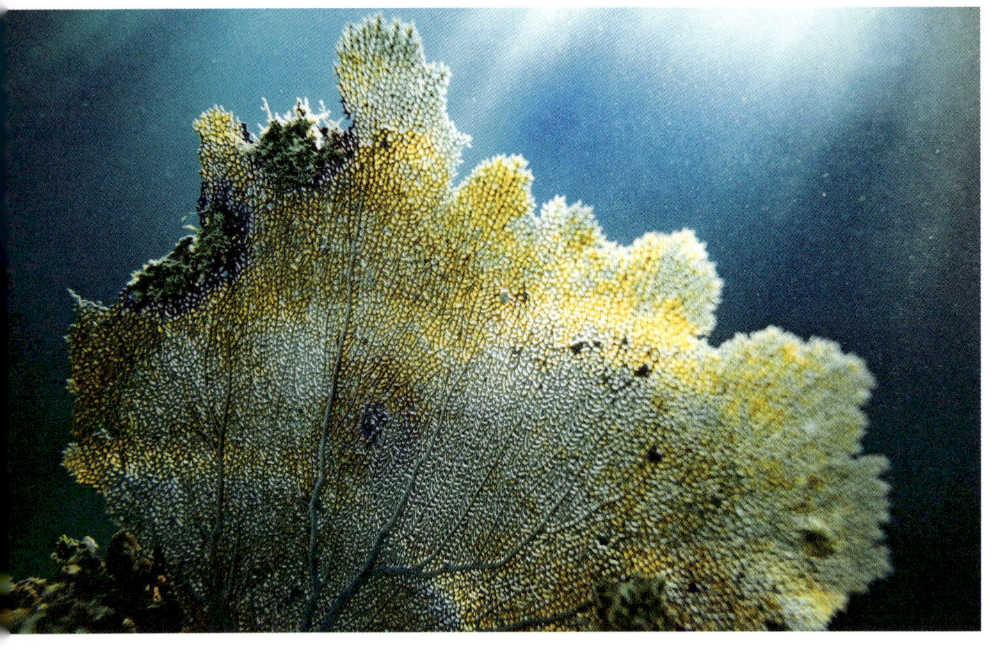

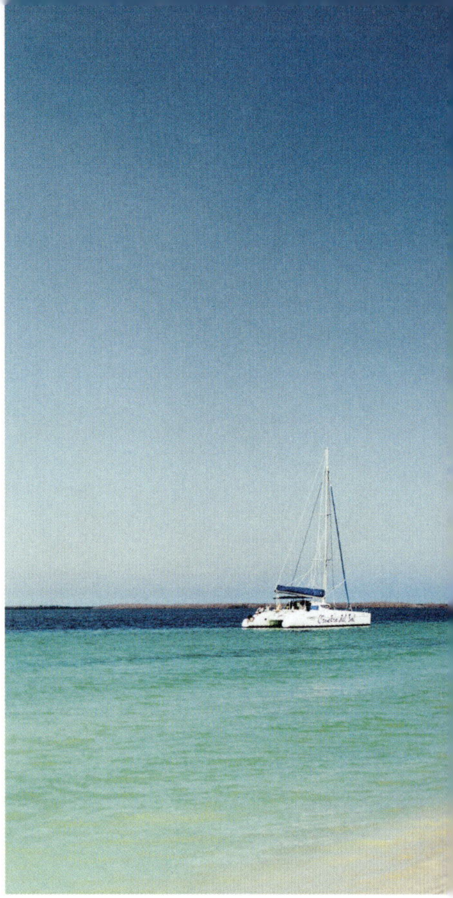

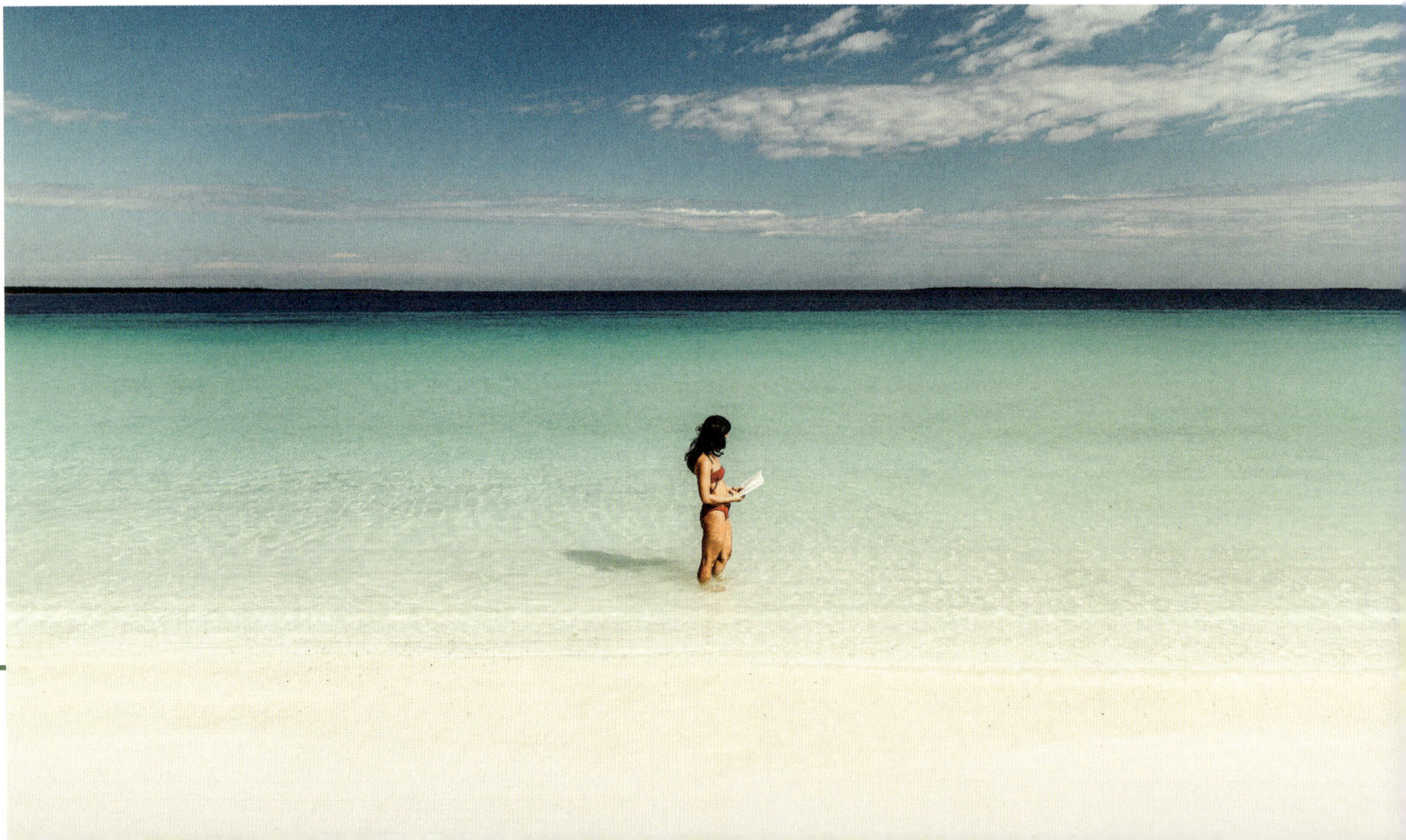

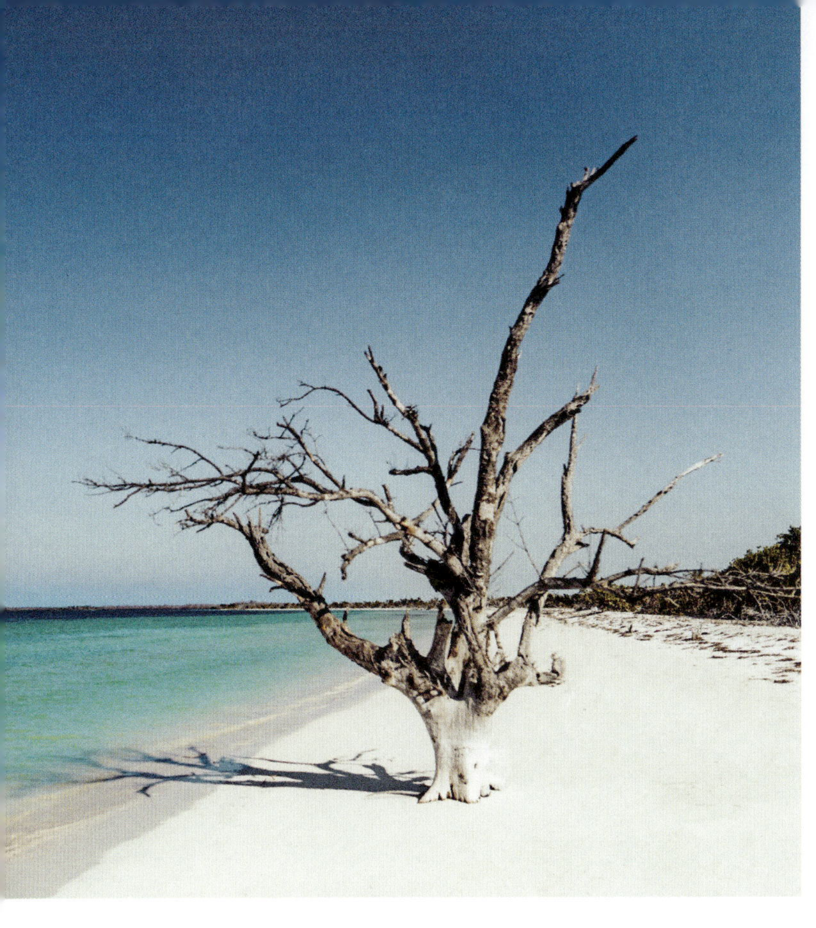

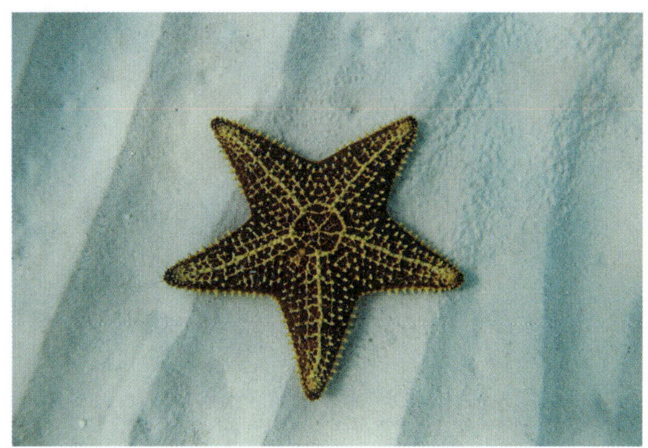

CAYO LAS BRUJAS, CUBA

Photographs by Benjamin Ono

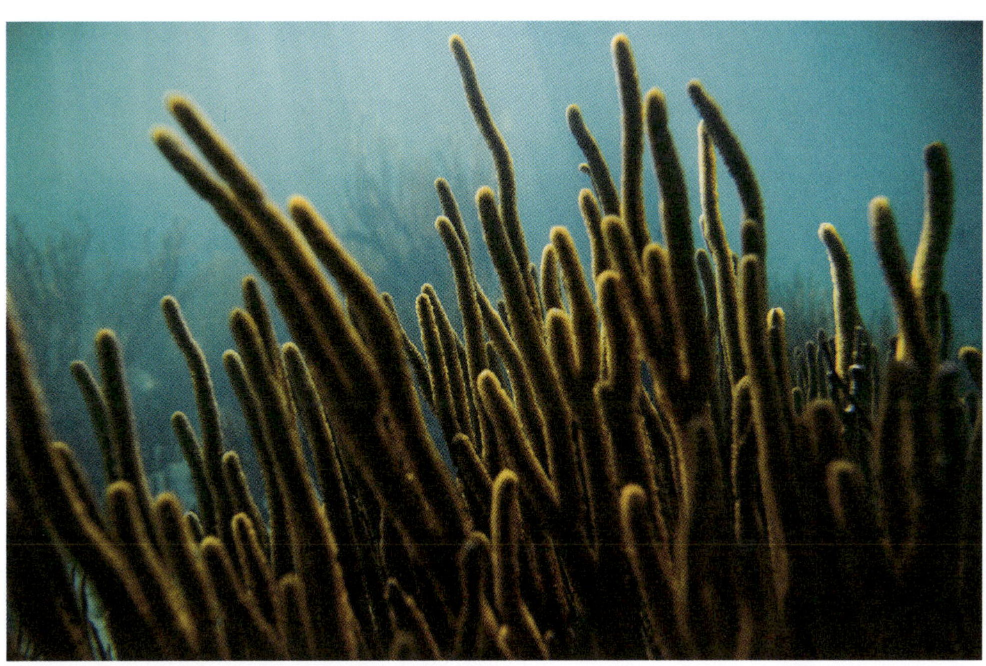

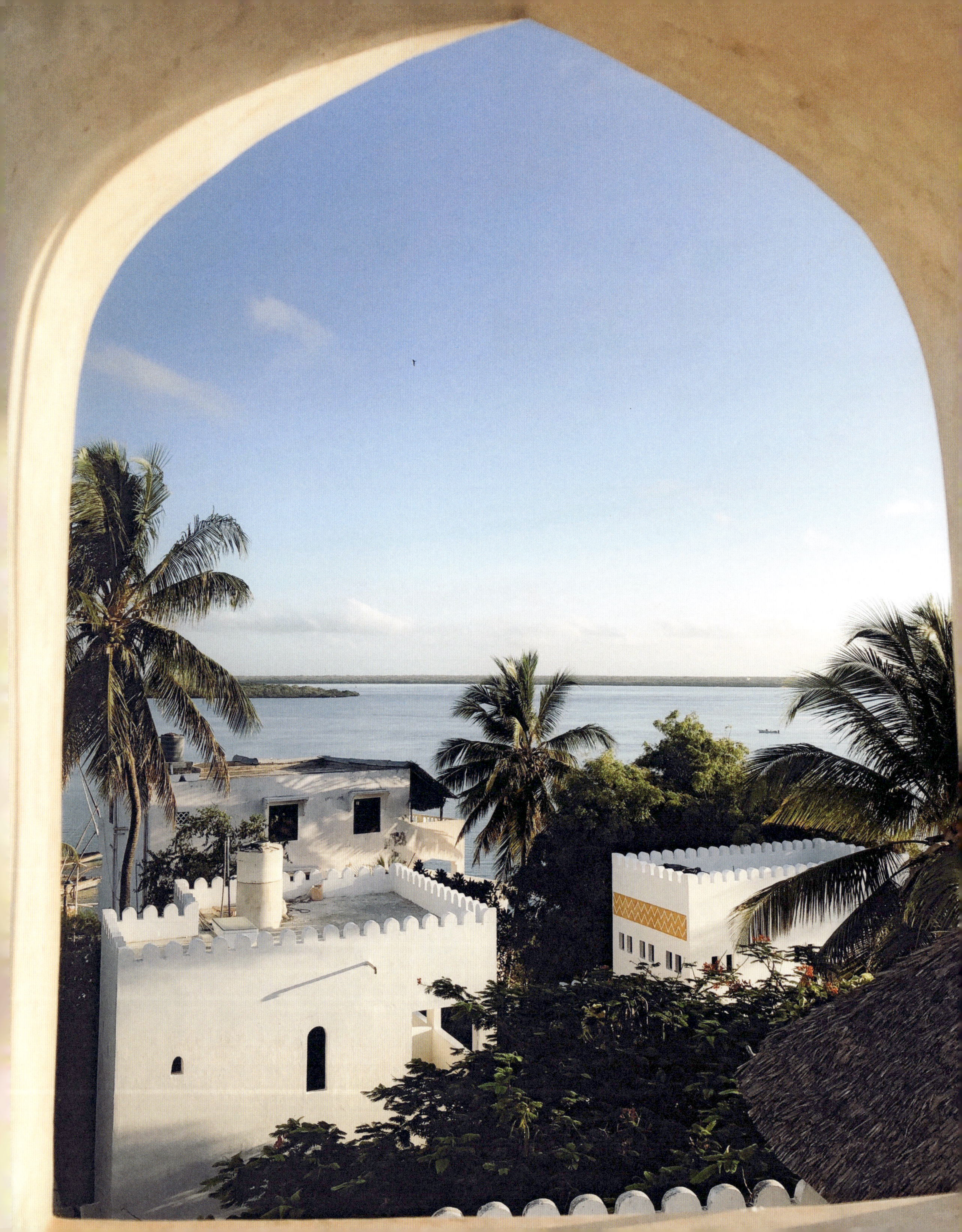

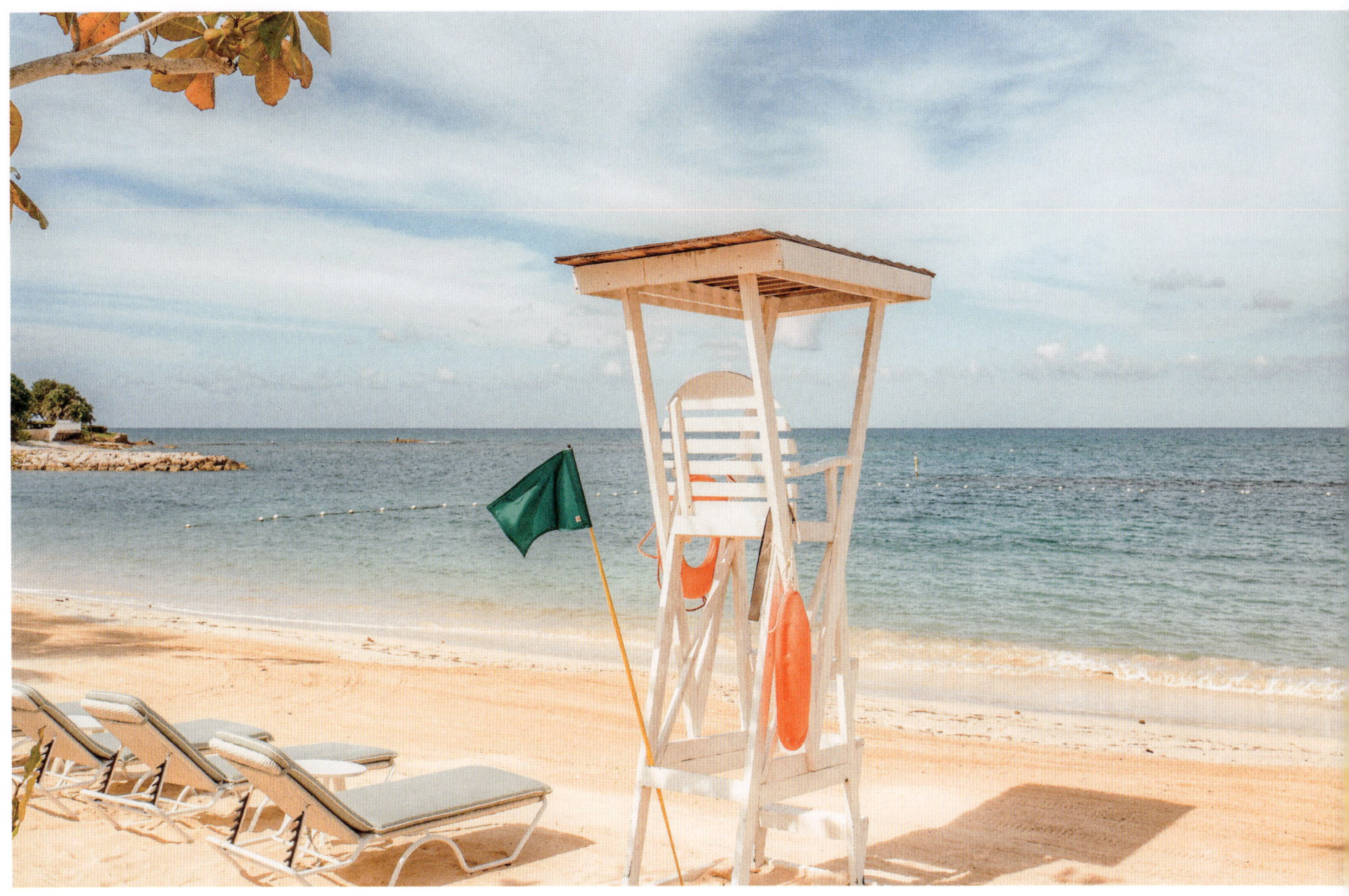

DURING THE MIDDLE AGES, when merchant sailors learned the monsoon weather patterns and increased their travels across the Indian Ocean, the Swahili culture and language and an Indian Ocean trade network emerged. Small East African settlements became wealthy cities as gold, ivory, quartz, and slaves were traded, and Islam took hold.

Lamu, established in 1370 as one of the first Swahili settlements in East Africa, is today the name of the island, city, and port just offshore of Mombasa in Kenya. Shela, pictured here, is one of only four towns on the islands where palm, tamarind, and baobab trees sway over the peaceful Indian Ocean below. The island regained fame in the 1960s and 1970s with the arrival of hippies, rock stars, and European royalty.

There are no cars on the island, so transport is via donkey, on foot, or by traditional hand-built wooden dhows. This image from a local's shower displays the tranquil scene that beguiles travelers to stay and also hints at the prevalent Arabic architecture on the island. In Lamu Town, art galleries and boho boutiques abound. A strong artisan tradition, with a focus on silversmiths and wood carvers, holds to this day. The best season to visit is from October through March.

**Shela Village,
Lamu Island, Kenya**
Sandy Bornman

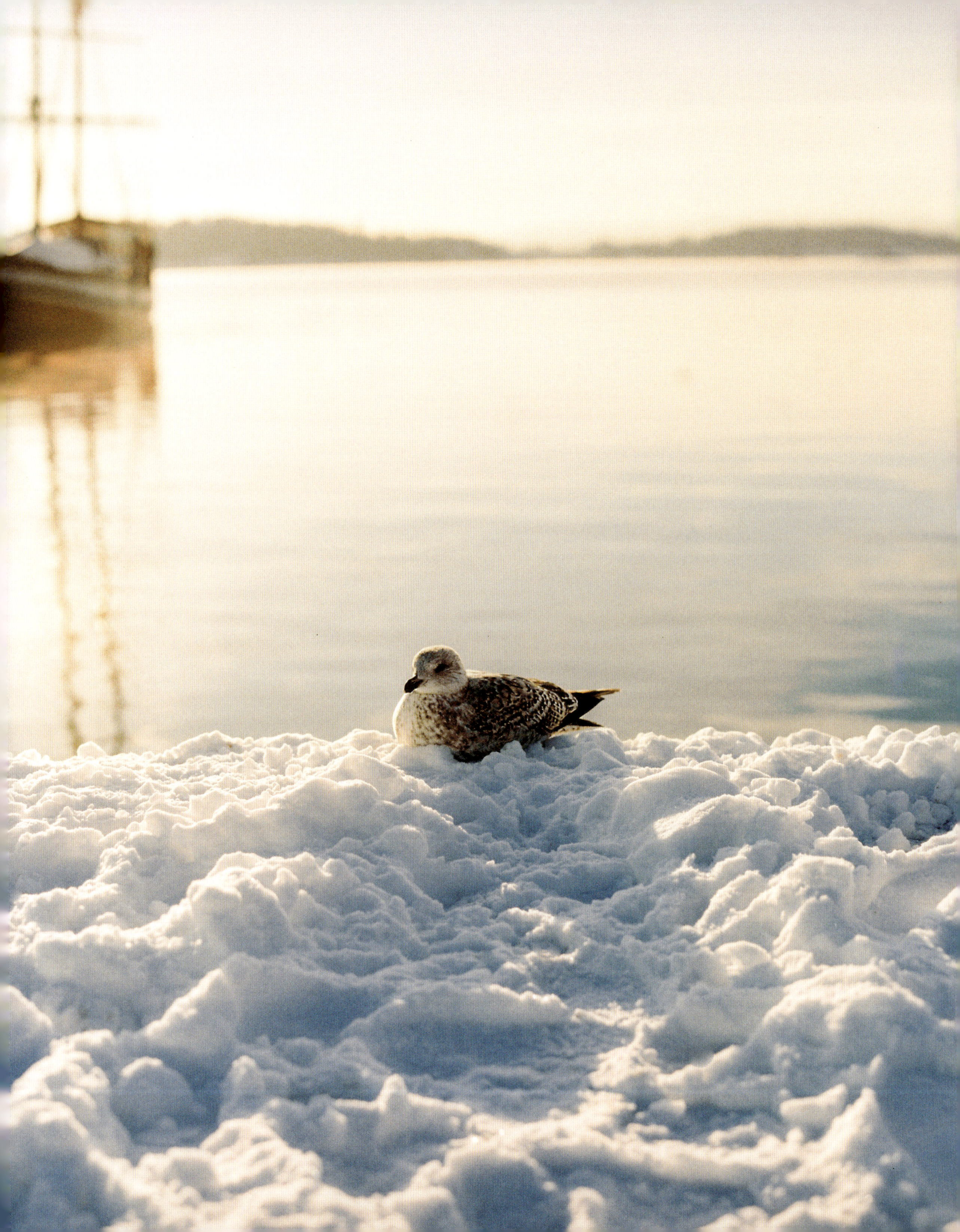

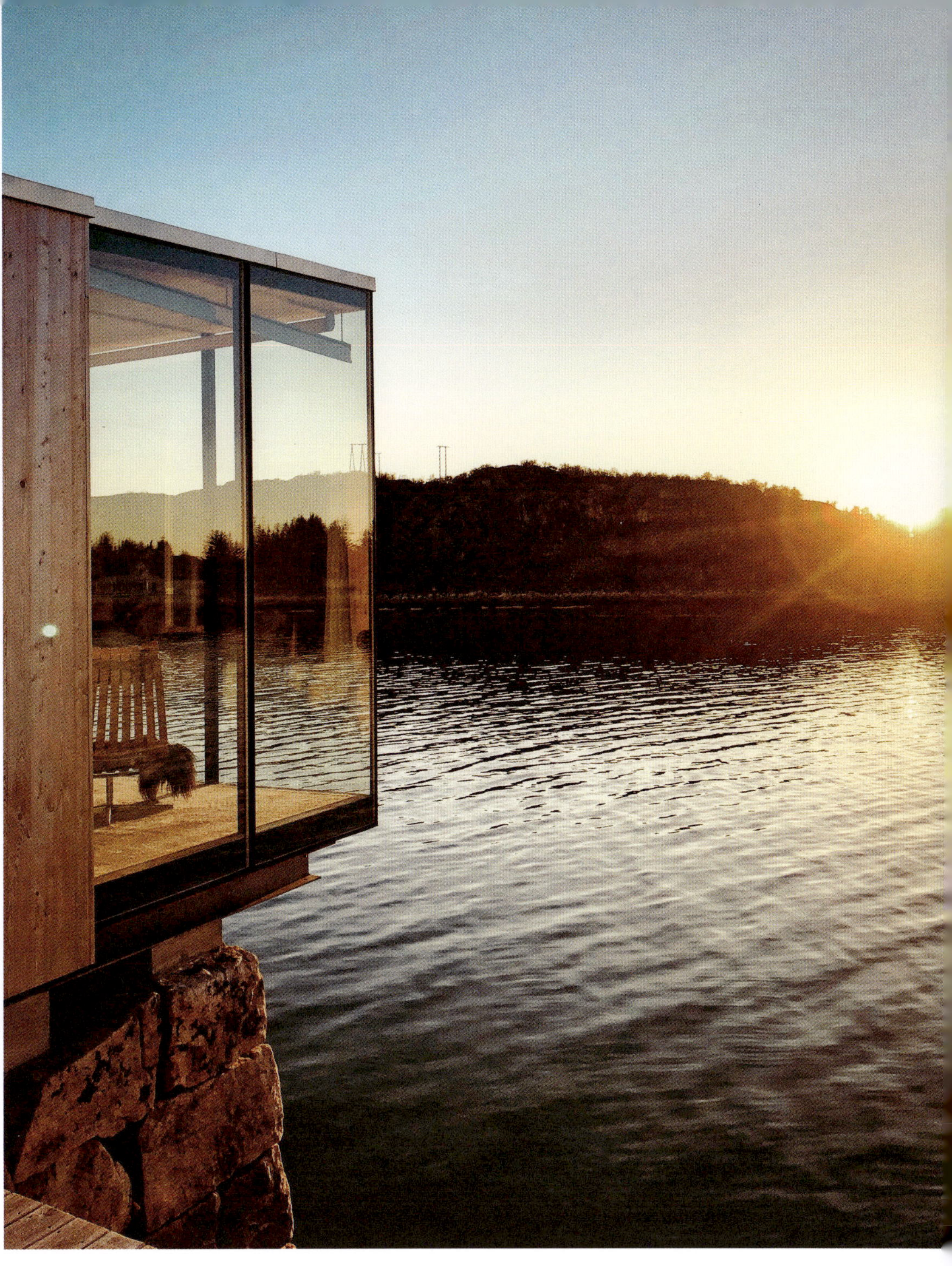

↑
THIS IMAGE SHOWCASES the glow of the midnight sun in Norway on Manshausen, an island south of Lofoten, which is owned by polar explorer, writer, and photographer Børge Ousland. In January of 1997, Ousland became the first person to complete an unsupported solo expedition across the Antarctic (on skis!).

**Manshausen,
Northern Norway**
Alison McCarthy

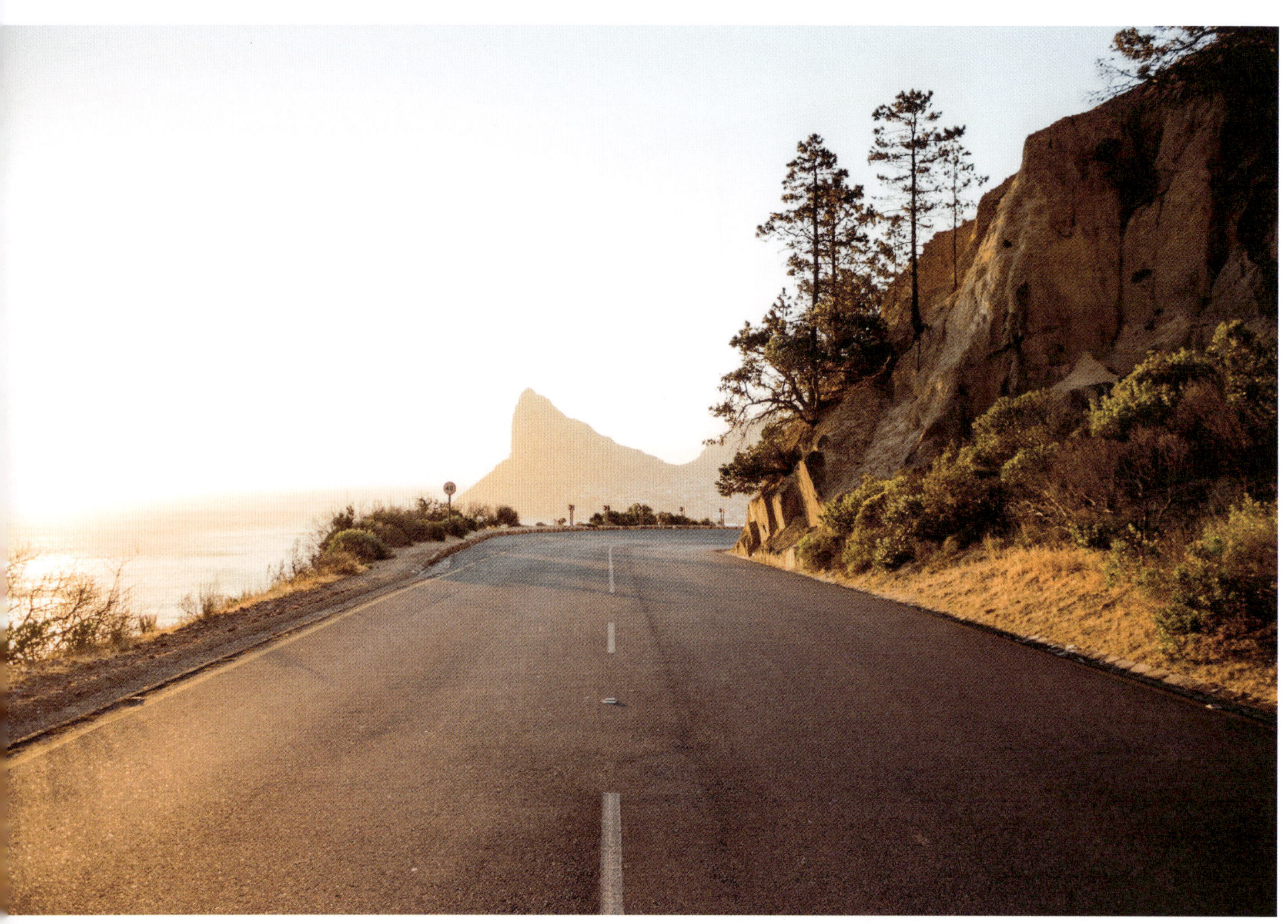

**Cape Town,
South Africa**

Jonny Hayes

**Cap Nègre,
Provence-Alpes-
Côte d'Azur, France**

Arthur Pinault

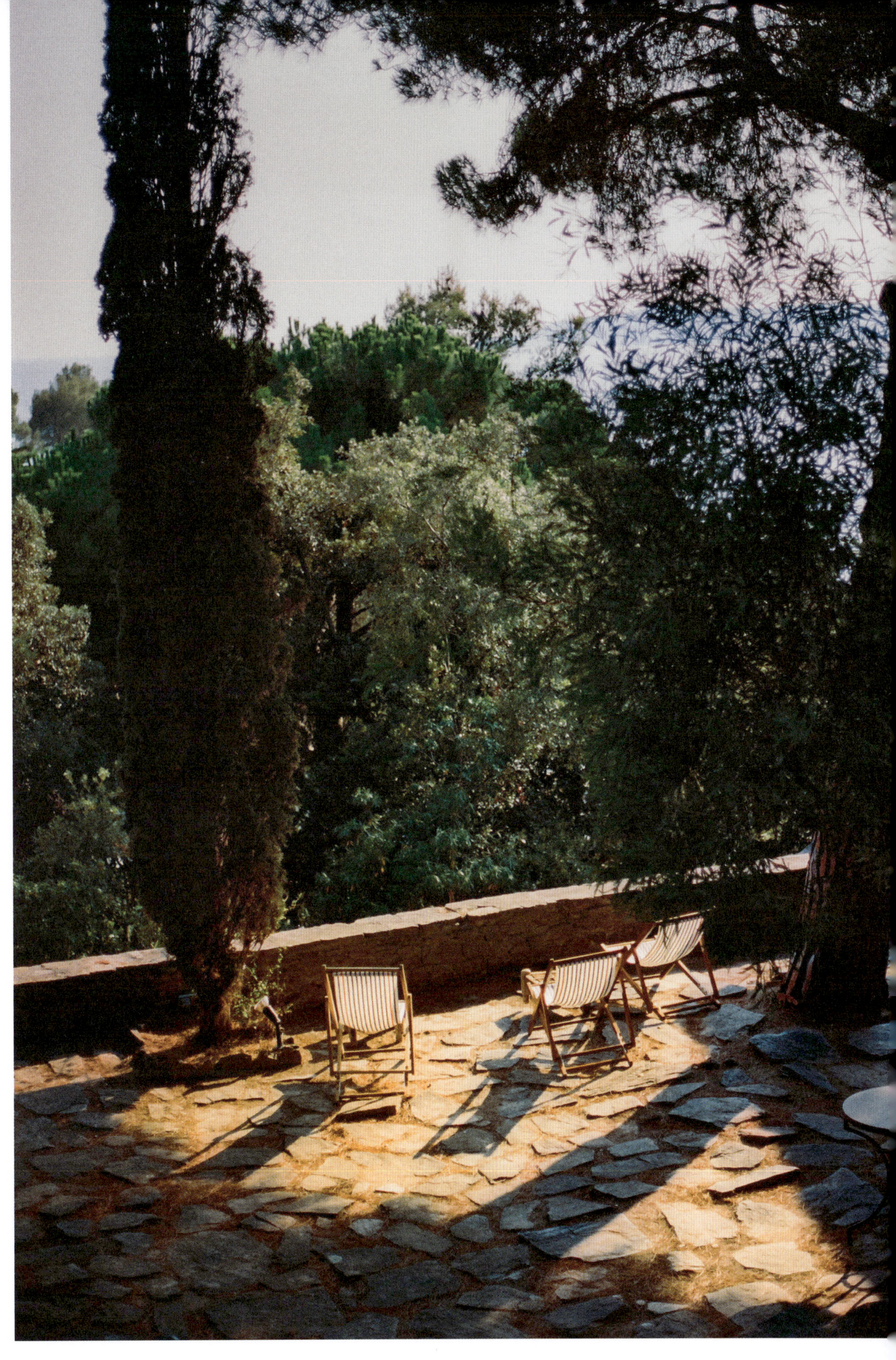

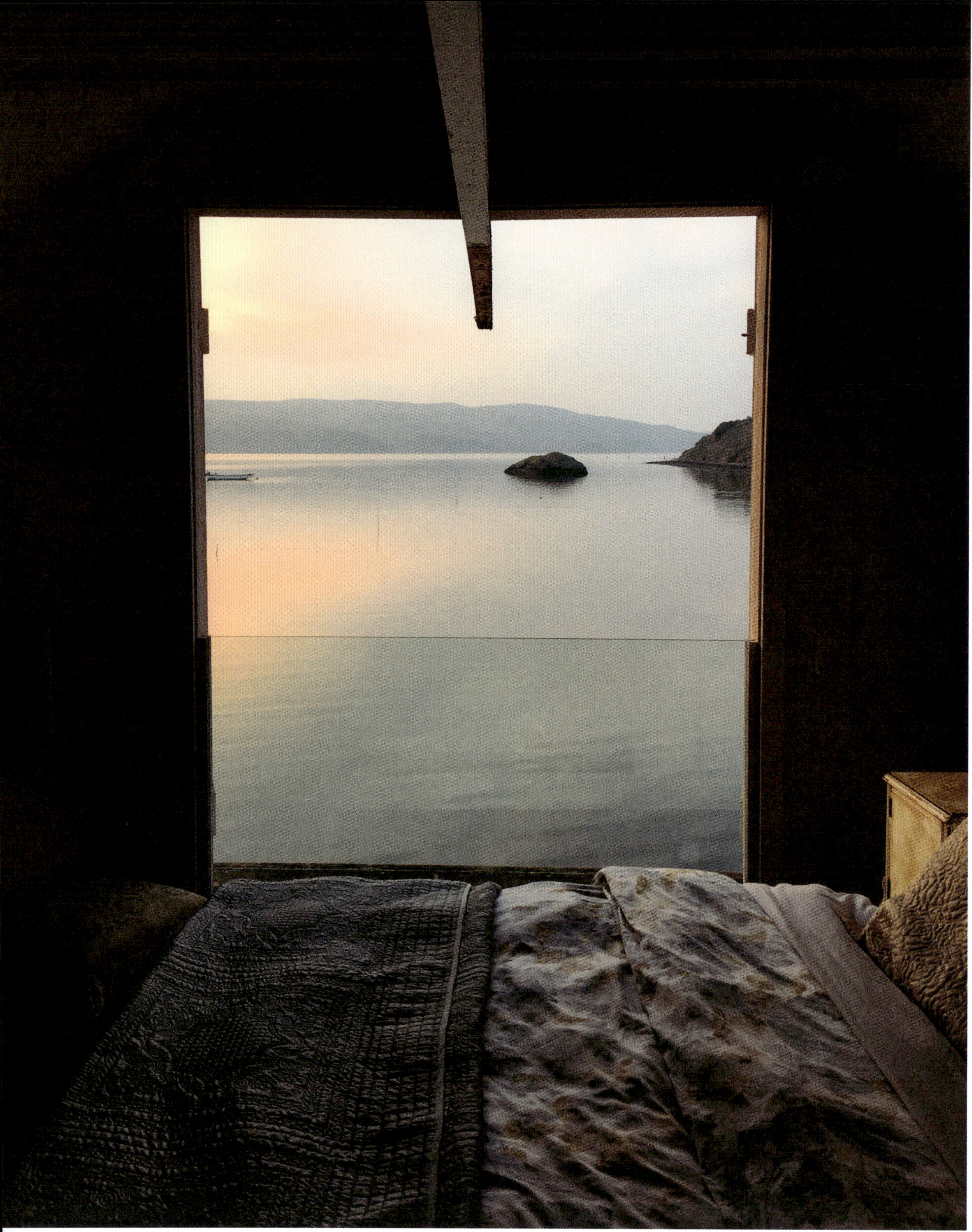

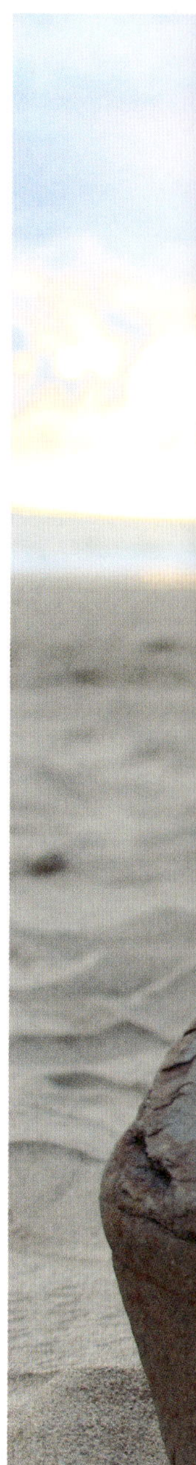

←
**Marshall, California,
United States**

Julia Spiess

↓
**Tomales Bay State
Park, California,
United States**

Jessica Reynaud

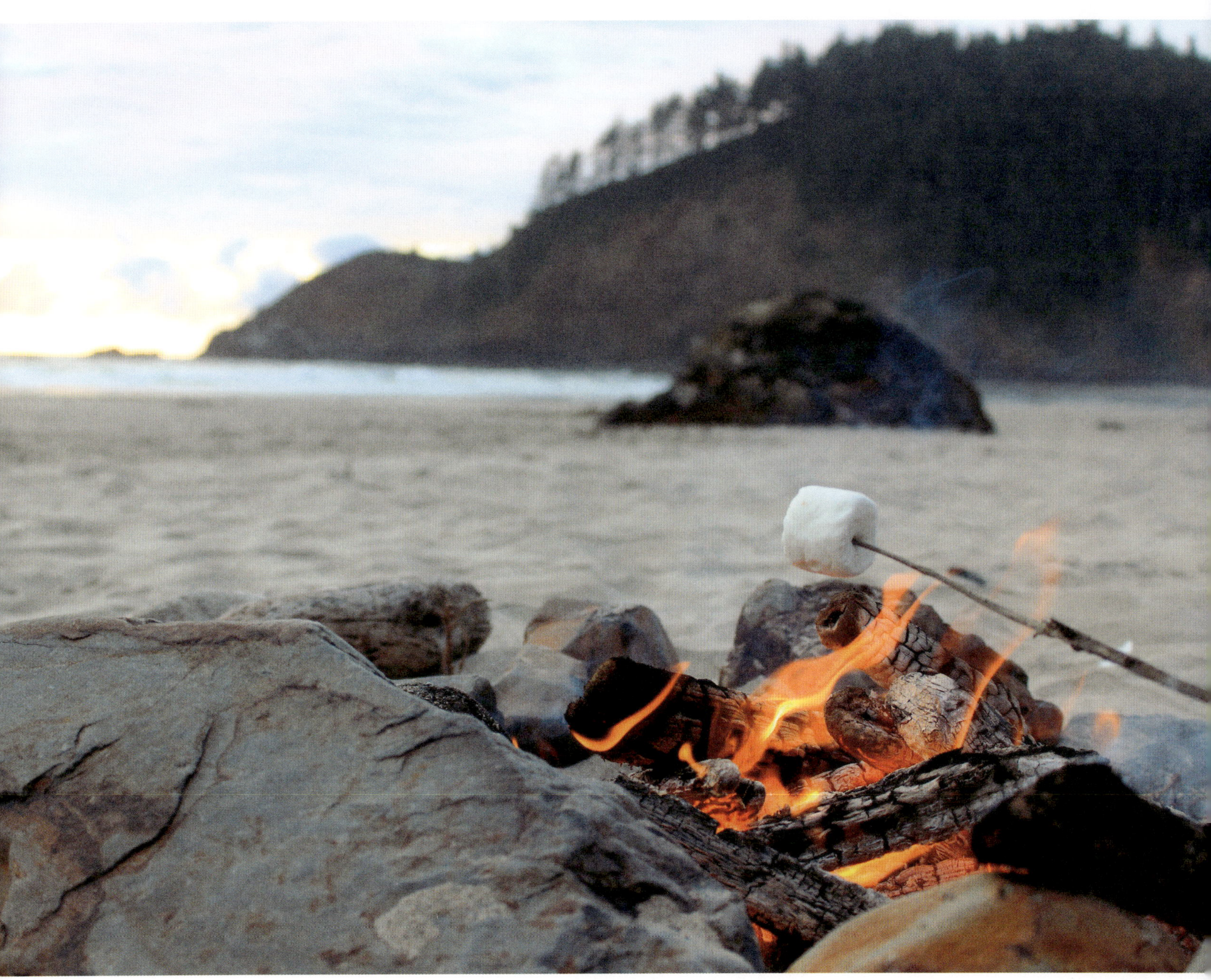

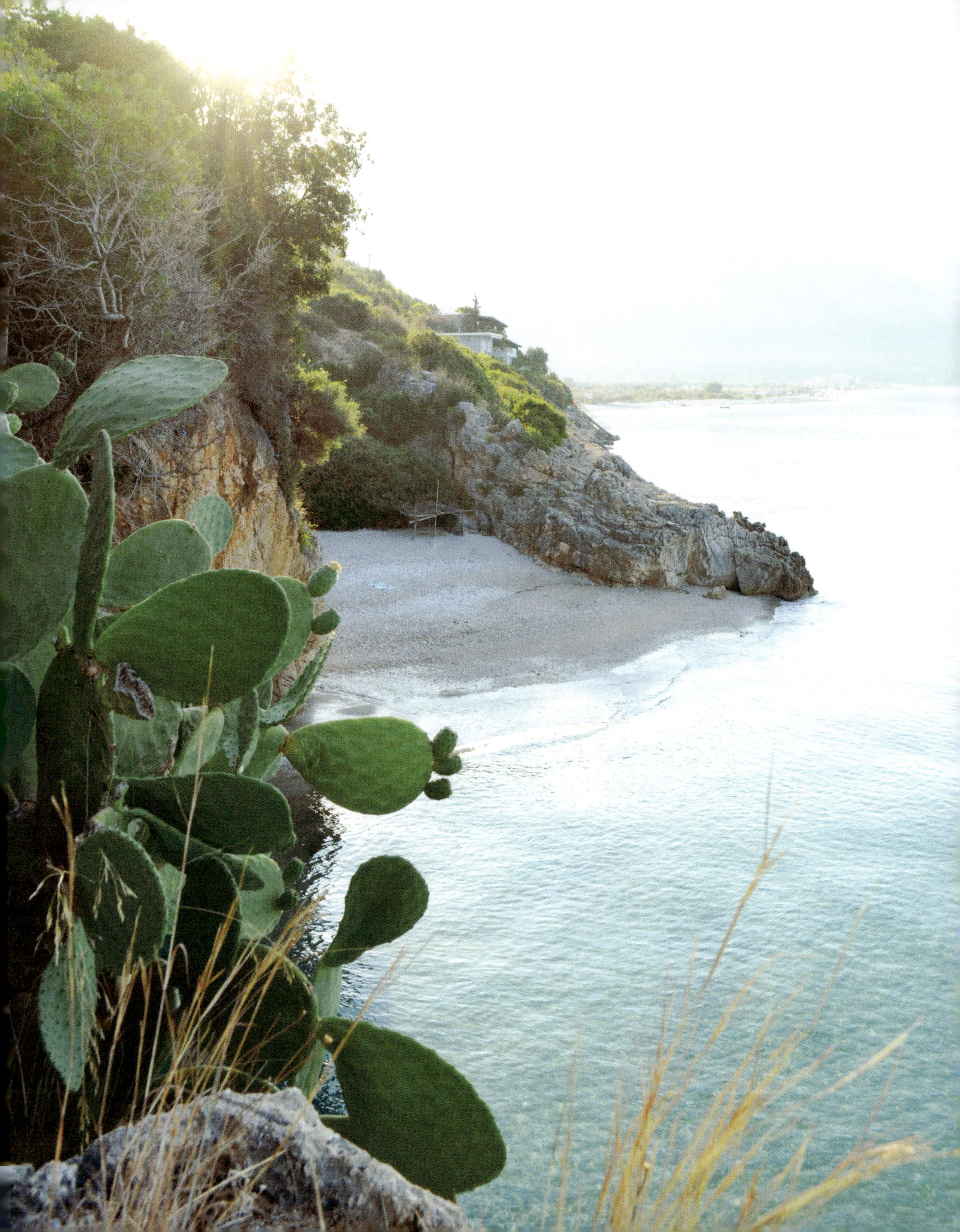

**Qeparo, Vlorë,
Albania**

Fjona Zanaliu

**Tulum,
Mexico**

Anna Pao Cova

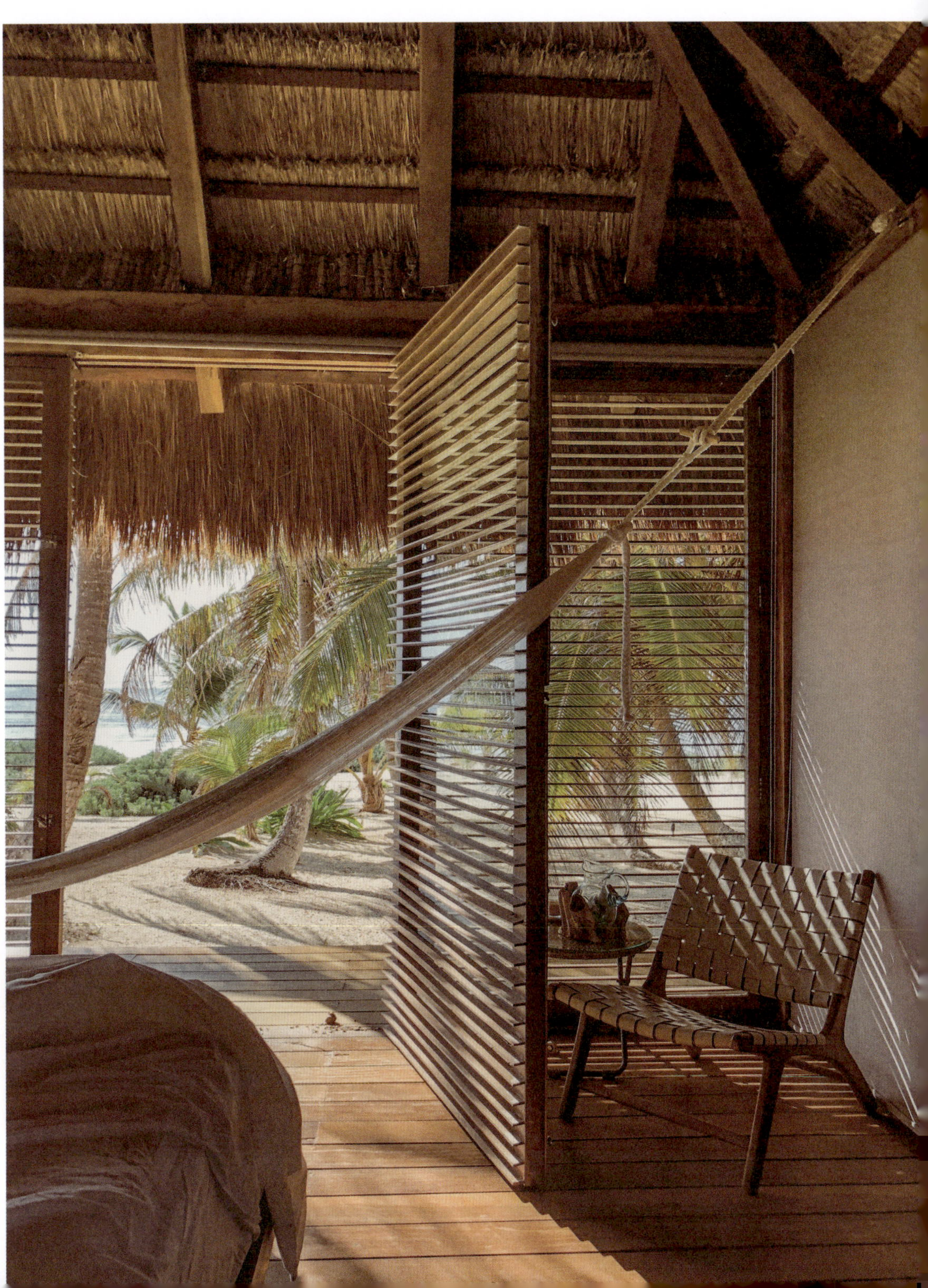

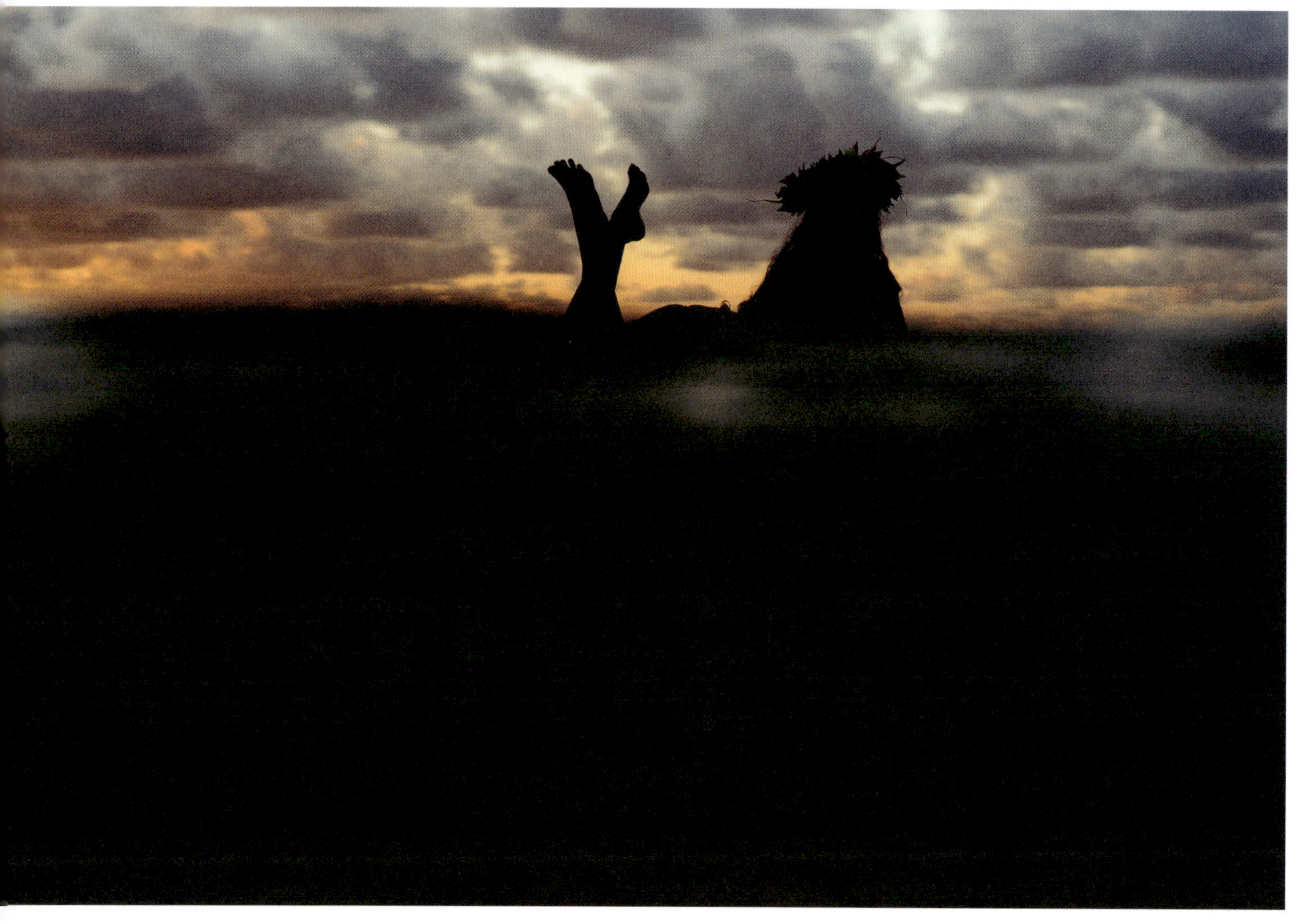

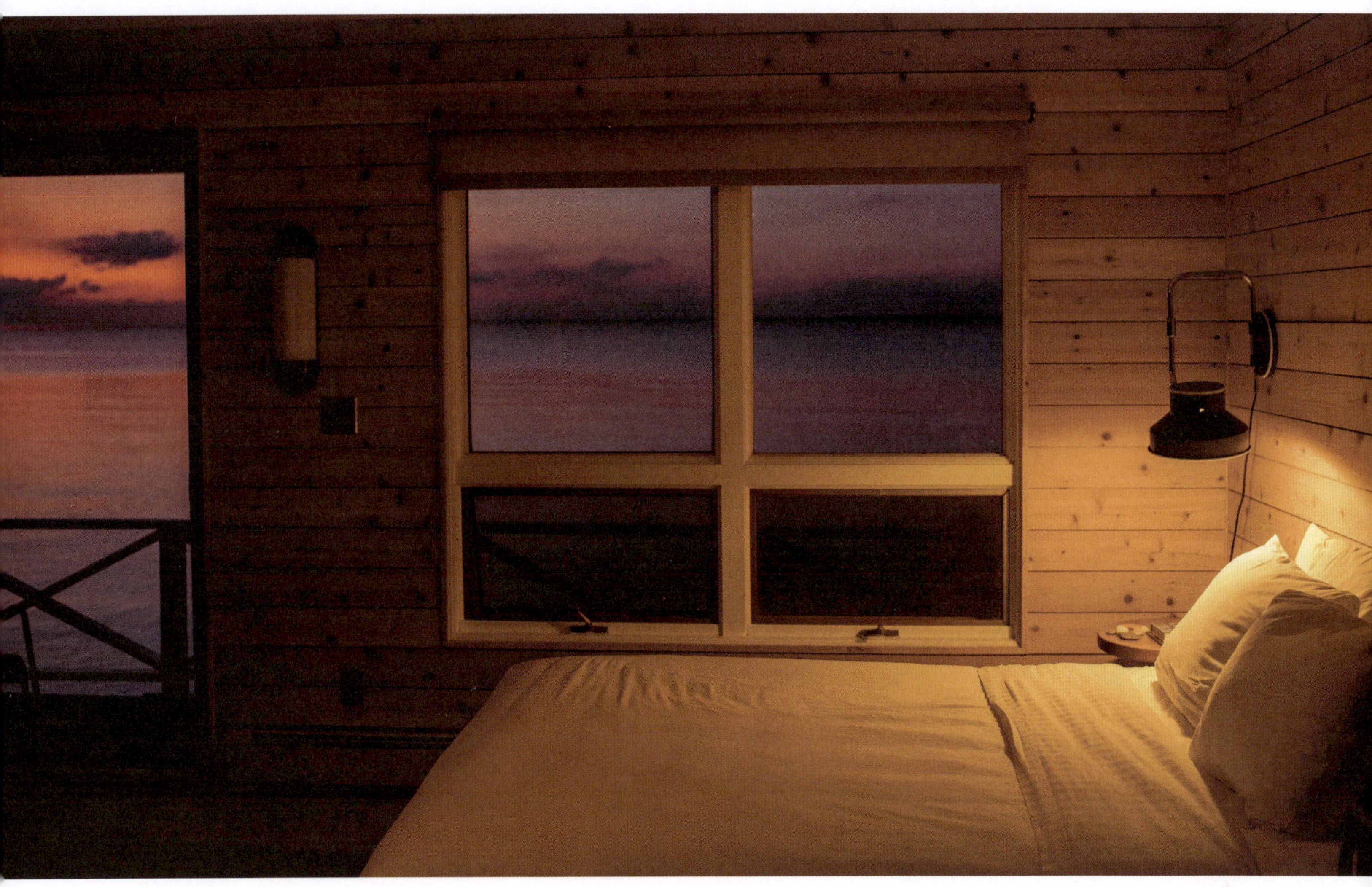

↑
SOUNDVIEW HOTEL, ON the west side of Greenport, offers a commanding view of the serene water of Long Island Sound. Greenport is the second to last town at the tip of Long Island's North Fork (the South Fork ends at the popular surf and beach town of Montauk). In Greenport, the beaches are a mix of smooth granite, agate pebbles, and soft sand. The protected water from the sound is also considerably warmer than the Atlantic coast side of the peninsula. The North Fork of Long Island is accessible easily from New York City via train or car.

**Greenport,
New York,
United States**

Emily Nathan

**Cadaqués,
Girona, Spain**

James Widegren

**Tulum,
Mexico**

Natasha Lee

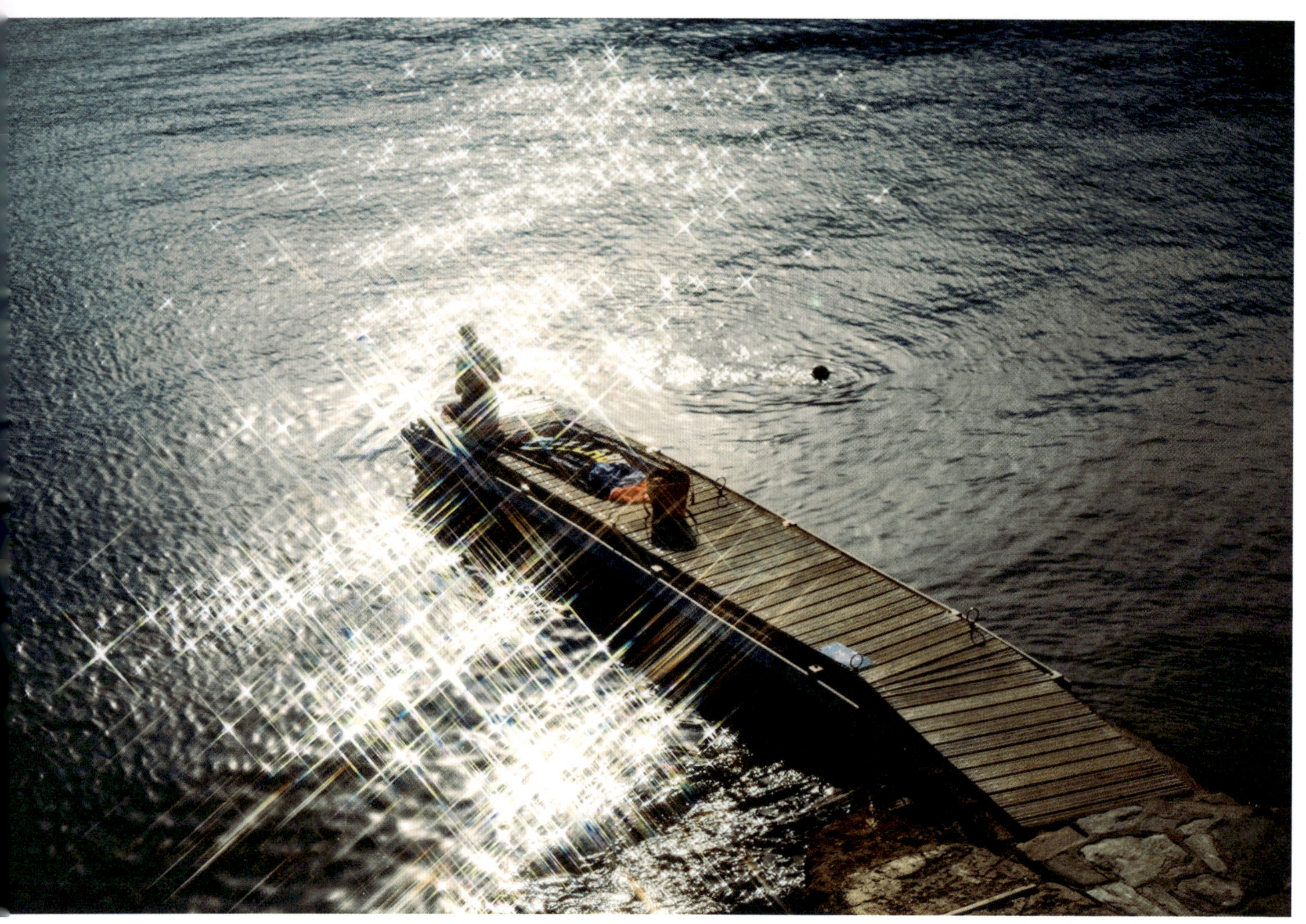

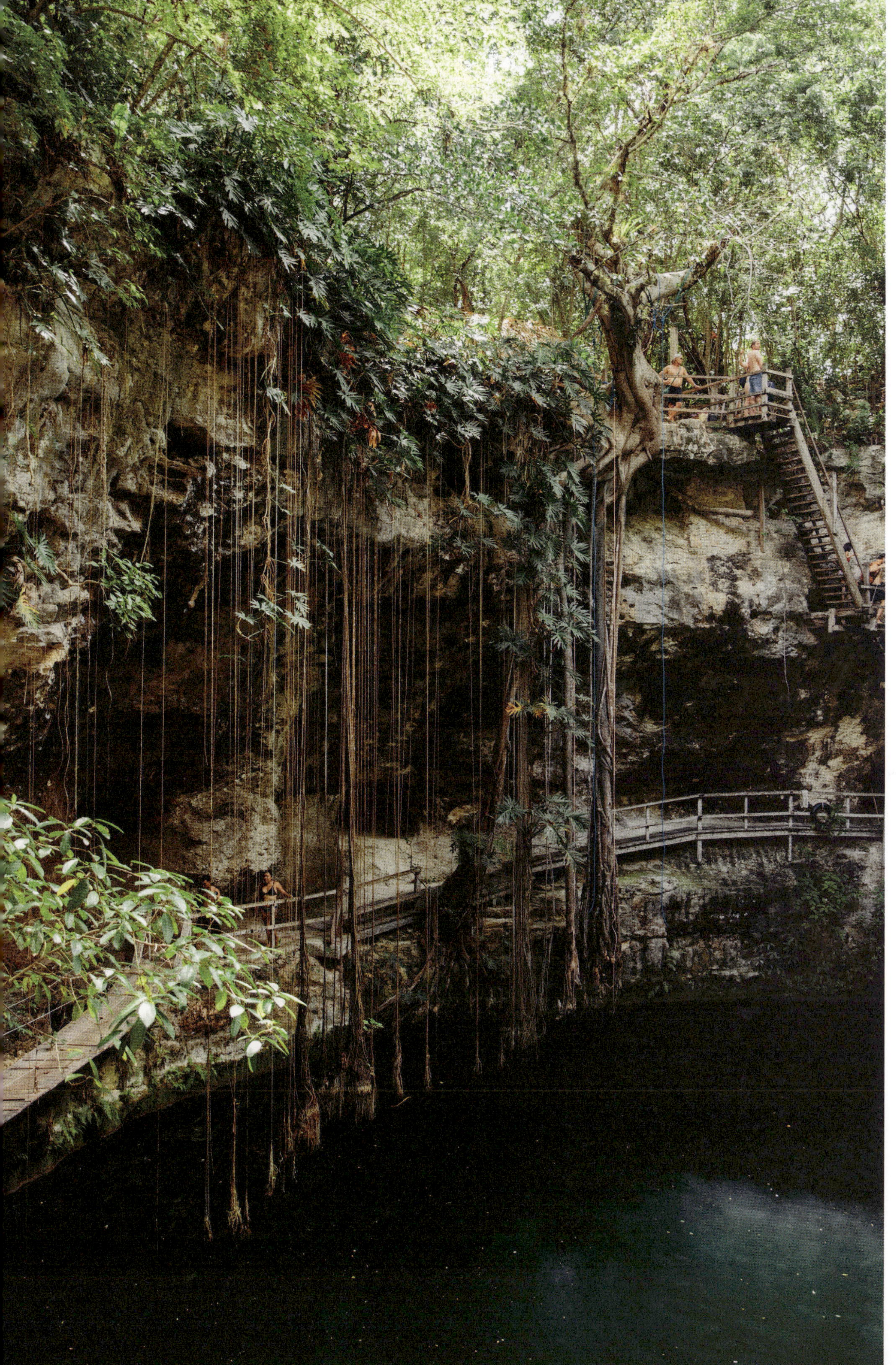

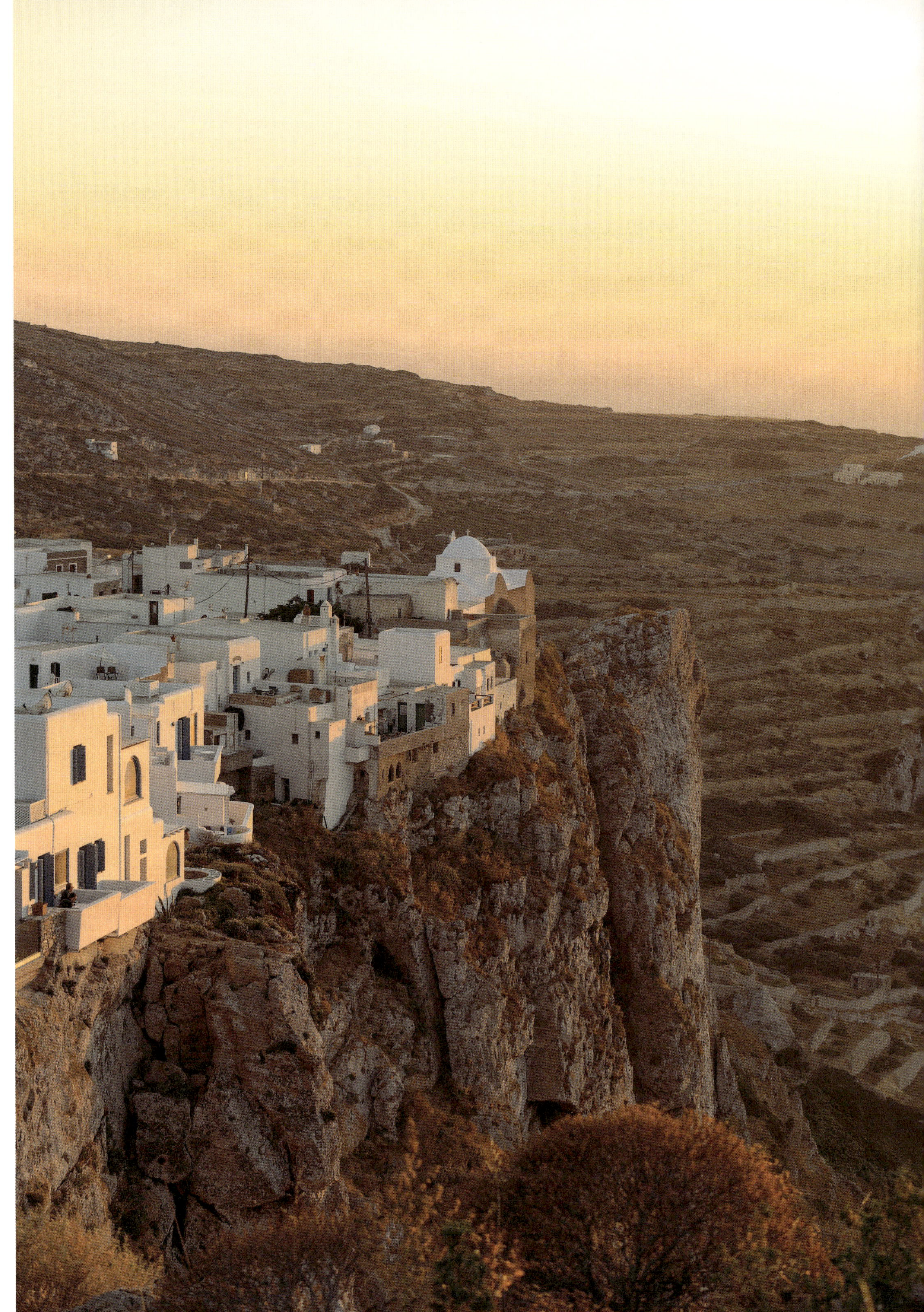

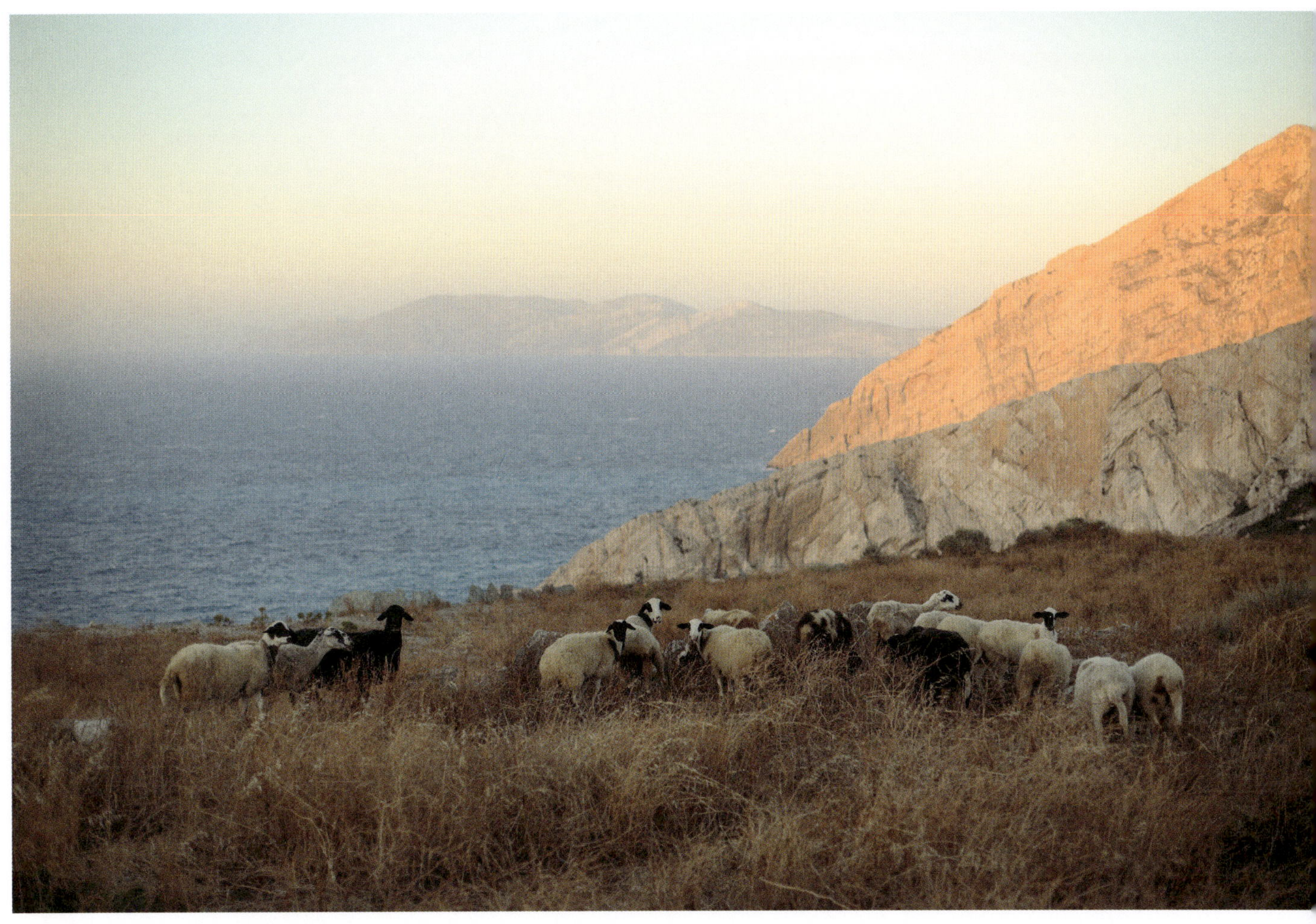

 easy ferry hop for nature enthusiasts visiting the most popular Cycladic island, Milos, on the Aegean Sea just north of Crete. Milos, the southwesternmost island in the chain, is well-known for its stark white limestone cliffs and is a stop on a busy ferry route that hops travelers from popular Santorini to Milos and from Milos to Folegandros. The island is surrounded by a calm, electric-blue sea. It is possible to kayak and camp in near isolation on remarkable and uninhabited beaches. The local cuisine is simple with a focus on tzatziki, fresh octopus, stuffed grape leaves, and massive blocks of feta, all served with local olive oil and honey-drizzled baklava for dessert.

**Hora, Folegandros
Island, Greece**
Jordan Dyck

Like forests underwater, coral reefs are a foundational part of our oceans. Corals are animals, marine invertebrates that live in colonies and secrete calcium carbonate to form a hard skeleton. Coral reefs around the world provide shelter and nourishment to 25 percent of all marine life while occupying only 0.1 percent of the planet's ocean floor. Divers and snorkelers especially celebrate reefs for their beauty and delight in the colorful diversity of fish, mollusks, and other plant and animal species that live among the corals' filigree formations. However, their value extends far beyond their beauty. The health of coral reefs is essential to the well-being of our planet. They provide shelter for fish reproduction, water filtration, shoreline and erosion protection, and the essential oxygen that we breathe while absorbing excess carbon dioxide.

Coral bleaching is the whitening of coral due to the loss or degradation of zooxanthellae, the symbiotic algae that live in the coral. They consume carbon dioxide and the waste of its host while providing oxygen and a steady food source in return. The causes of bleaching are multifaceted and range from an accumulation of high levels of chemicals from sunscreens and personal care products to ocean acidification, increasing temperatures in seawater, and elevated ultraviolet radiation. Dying coral reefs can no longer nourish and support the life of fish and plants that call them home and have devastating effects on local communities, where these ecosystems are intertwined with everyday life. Coral bleaching has become widespread around the world. Healthy reefs with abundant biodiversity are key to sustaining the planet as well as local communities and economies.

**Hāʻena, Kauaʻi,
Hawaiʻi, United States**
Benjamin Ono

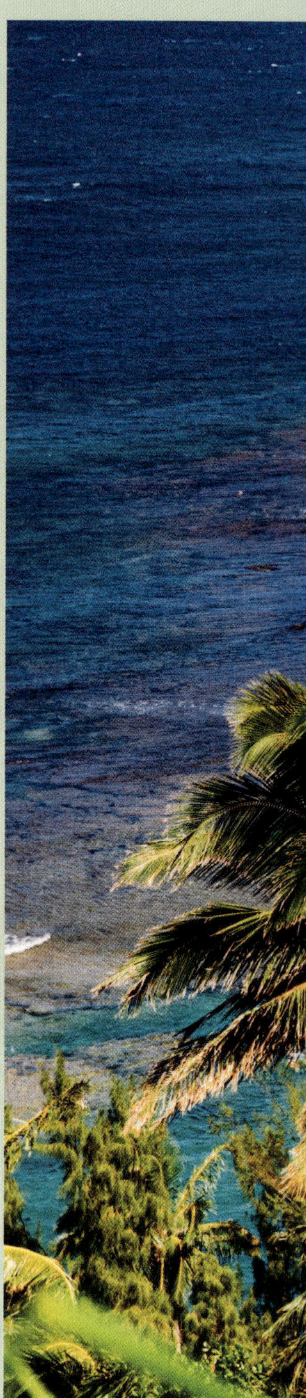

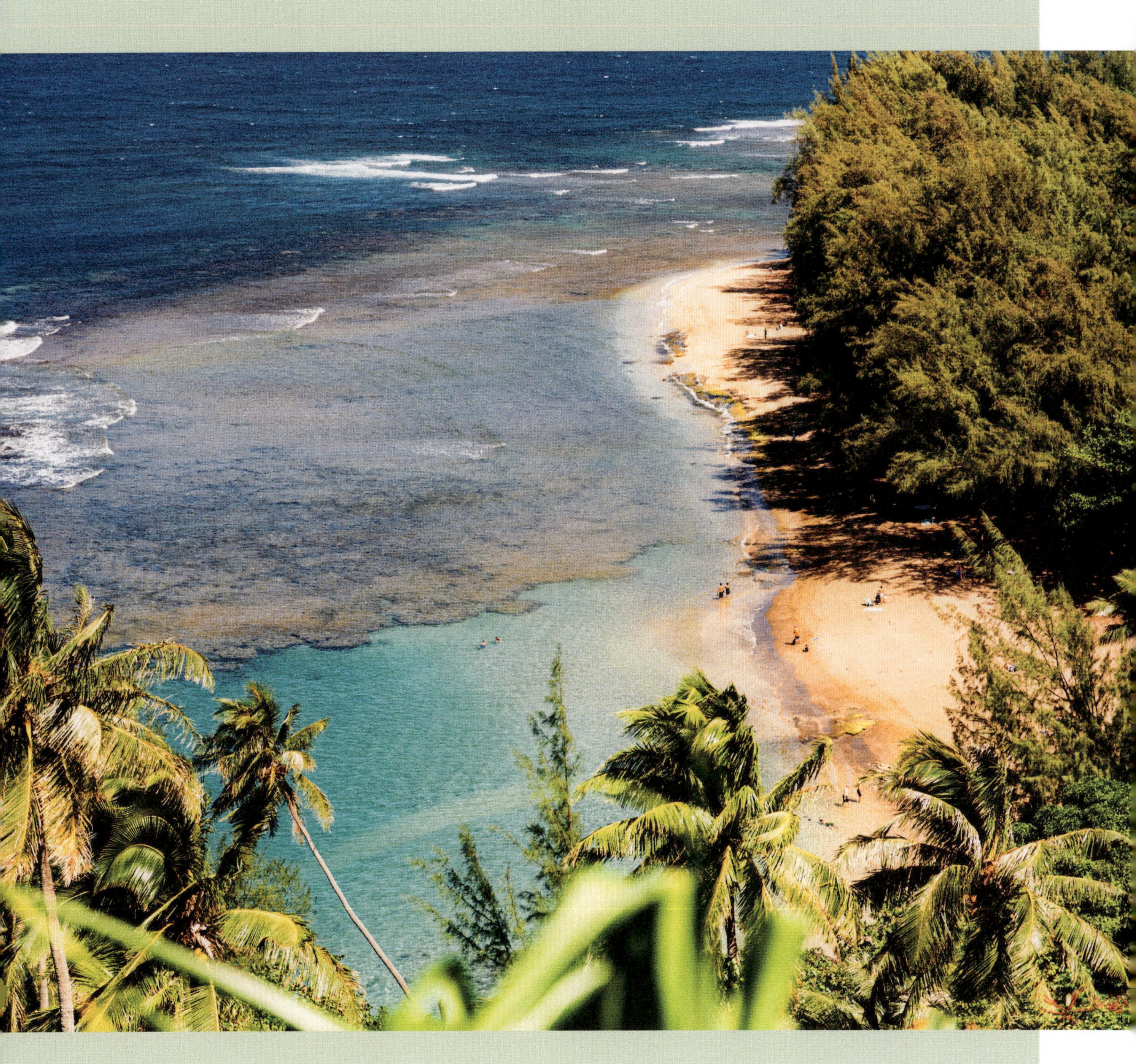

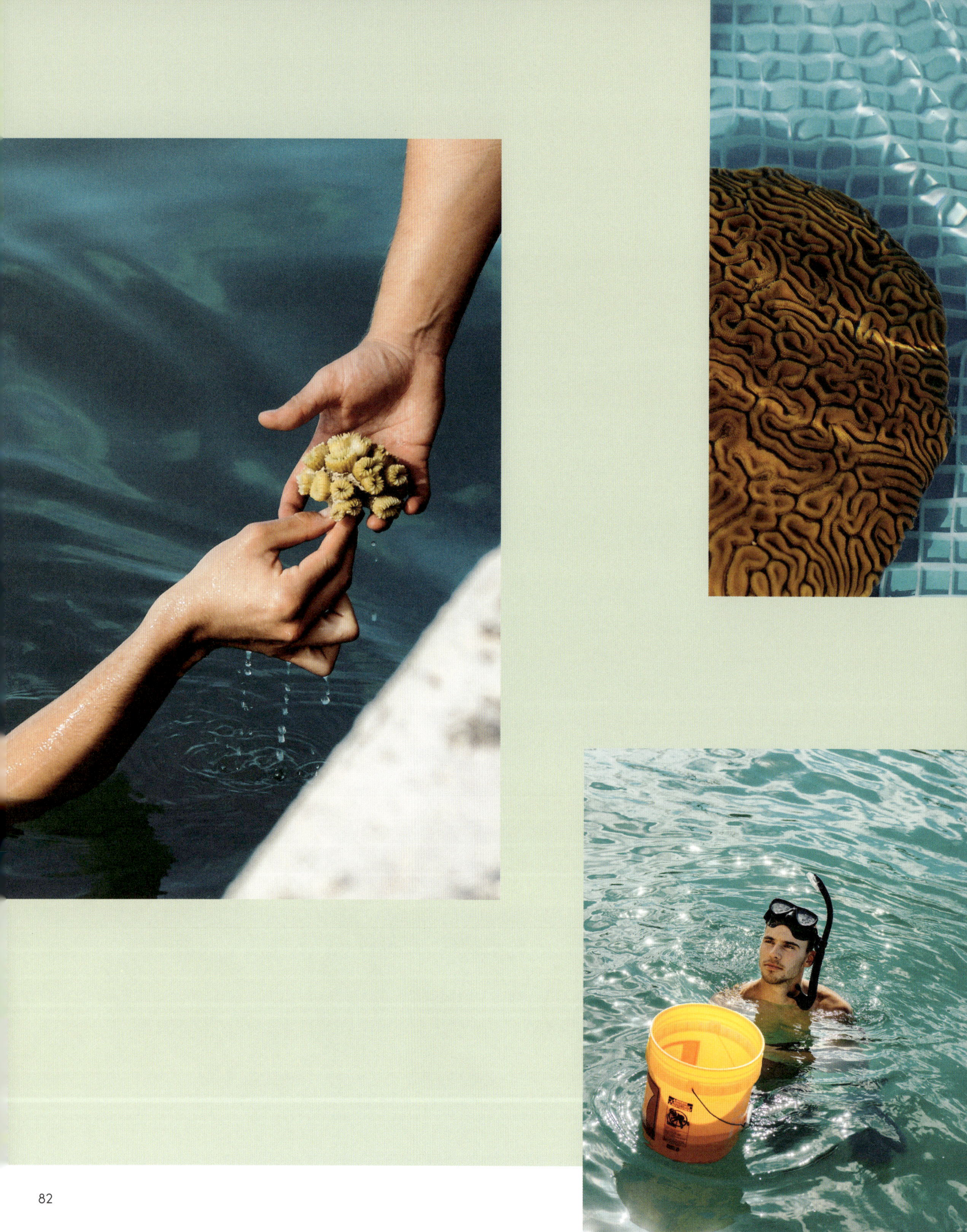

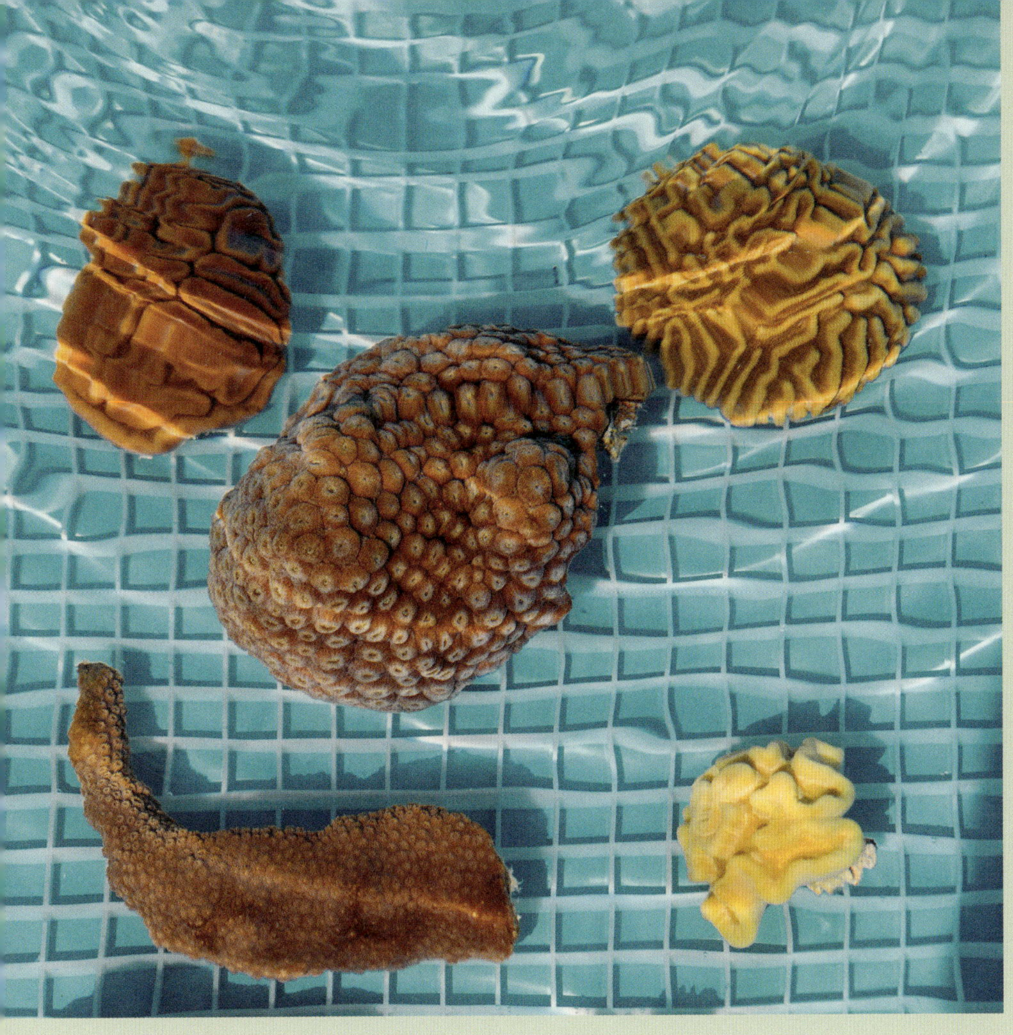

HOW YOU CAN HELP

- Dive and snorkel responsibly near corals—follow local guidelines and never touch the reefs. These photos were taken at a coral revitalization project in the Bahamas, so the coral is being handled safely by professionals.

- Use reef-safe sunscreens whenever possible and consider spending more time in the water in low UV hours when sunscreen is not as necessary. Some sunscreen ingredients, like oxybenzone and octinoxate, can wash off when you swim and damage coral reefs.

- Support nonprofits working on coral revitalization projects; look for local organizations doing reef recovery work when you travel. The Maui Nui Marine Resource Council works to support clean water, healthy coral, and thriving native fish for the islands of Maui County: Maui, Moloka'i, Lanai, and Kaho'olawe.

**Freeport,
Bahamas**
Katelyn Perry

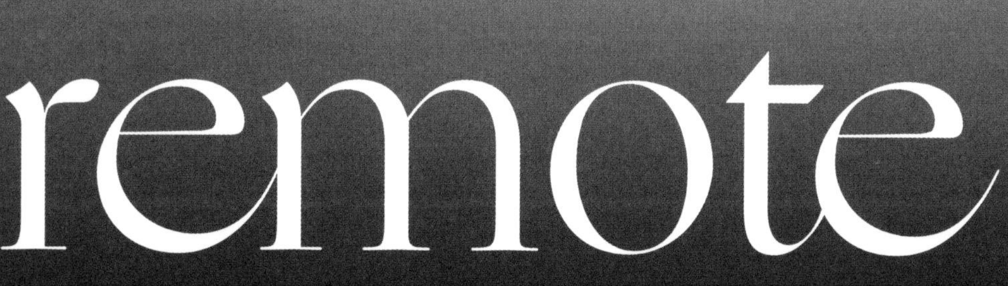

remote

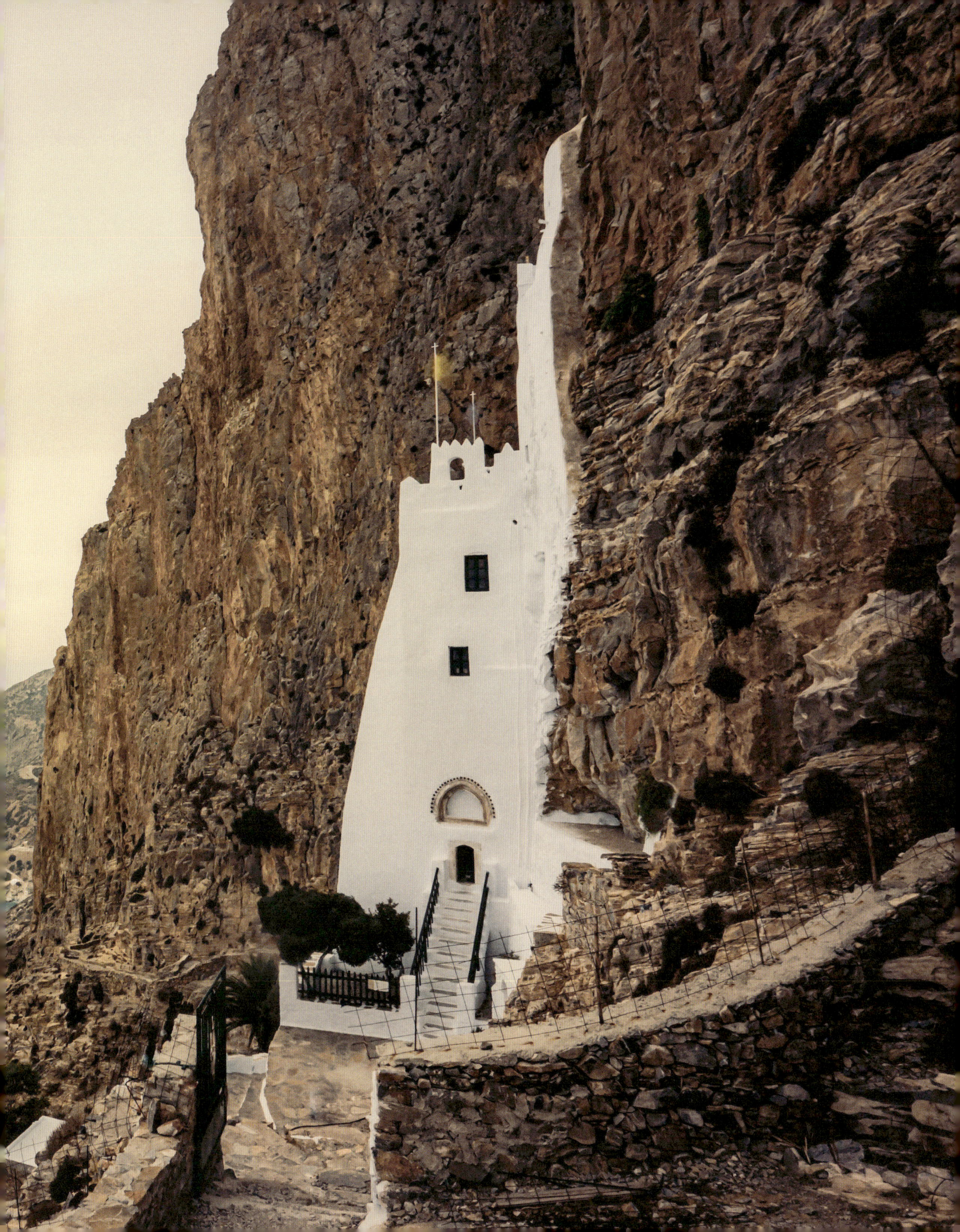

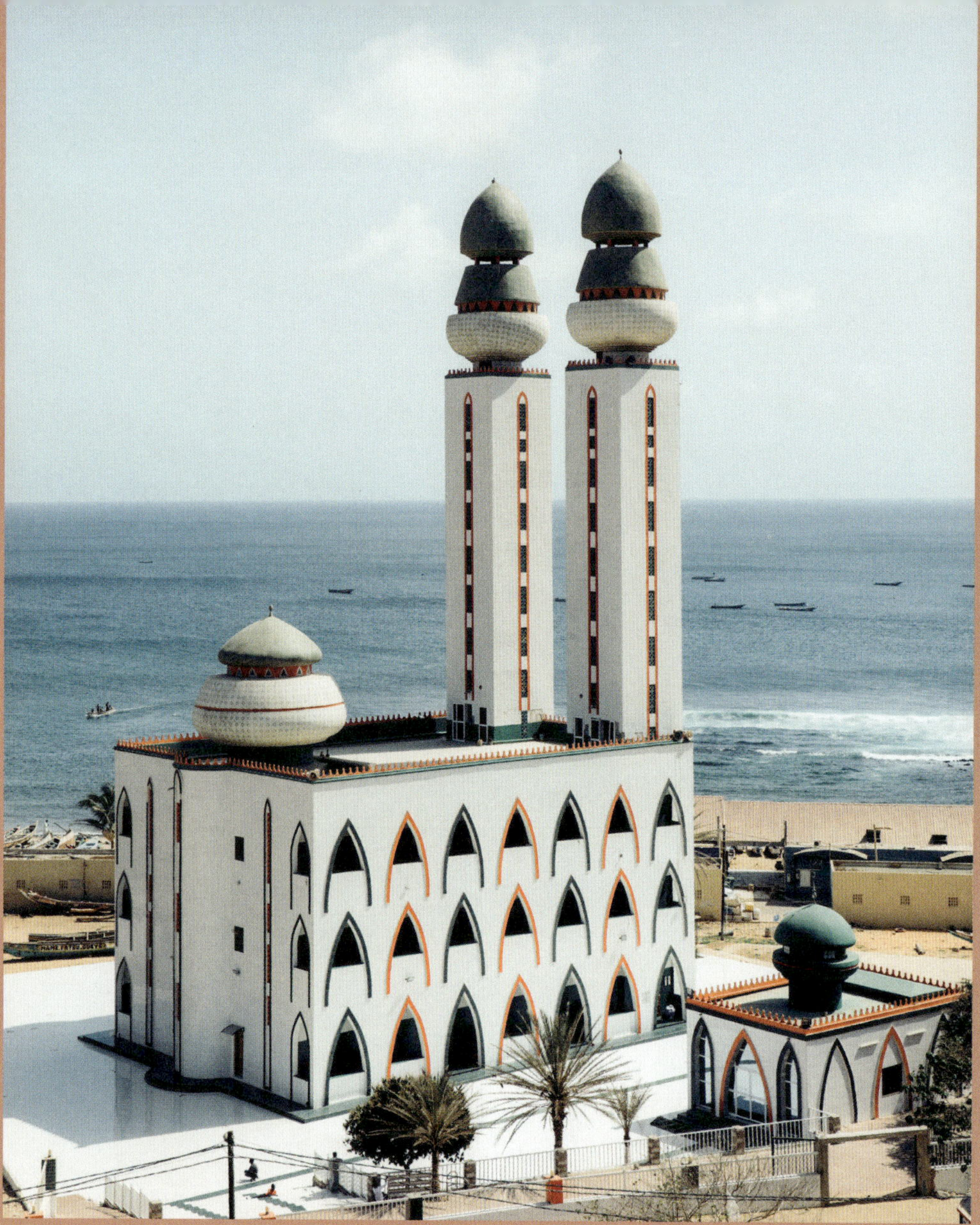

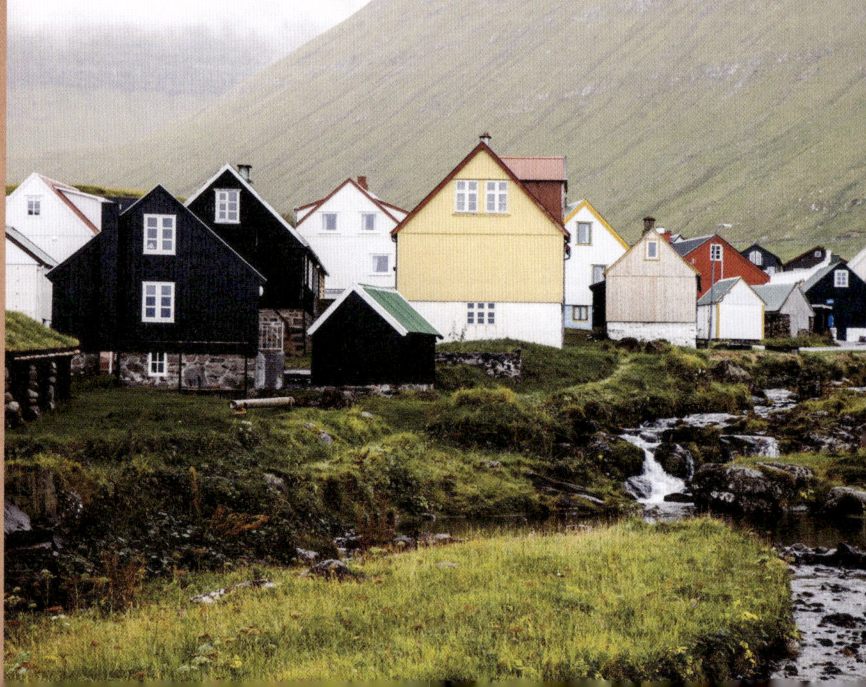

Wear long pants or skirts and walk three
hundred steps up from the site entrance
when visiting the monastery of Hozoviotissa,
the second oldest in Greece, built in 1017,
in the heart of Amorgos Island.

Amorgos, Greece
Denis Dowling

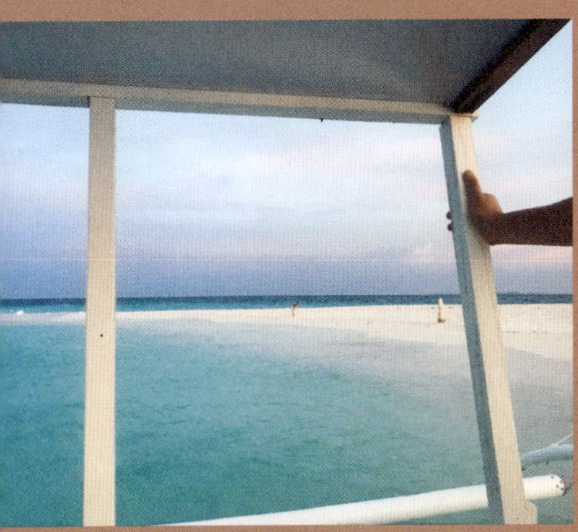

EVEN FOR PEOPLE who appreciate roaming about close to home, there is something special about a hard-won, hard-to-get-to, long-way-from-home adventure. And while travel to remote destinations lights the imaginations of many, only a certain type of person will actually commit to the hassle of a truly remote trip. Remote travelers know how to be okay with delays in schedules, hours spent in airports, and the myriad forms of transportation it might take to get somewhere because they know that the rewards of such journeys are worth it.

Traveling over water to arrive at remote places, as a first or final step, is both a physical and visual reset for our internal clocks. It is an acknowledgment, through seeing and feeling the distance in space and time, of a release. When we transition from experiencing a static landscape to the constantly changing scenes on the water, we feel a certain distance between our known lives and the current moment. There's no rushing required when arriving at the Ranguana Caye in Belize. In Lamu, Kenya, a favorite local saying is "polepole," Swahili for "take it slow." In Costa Rica, a common greeting is "pura vida" ("life is pure"). These expressions are really just other ways of saying "Be here now." In remote locations, people and places are distinctly and deeply interconnected, and the land is often considered to be an integral part of the family by locals (making climate-change displacement particularly devastating). A stand-alone shop in a far-removed port will often also serve as a community hub where gossip and landlines are as important as the coffee, tea, and fuel.

When I traveled through Chile in college with a small group of friends, one friend suggested a visit to the just-opened coastal Parque Pumalín in Northern Patagonia. The journey's numerous legs to get to the park combined with the limitations of a student's budget created an adventure that stays with me to this day. First, I took a taxi to meet my friends at the central bus station in Santiago for the overnight bus trip to Puerto Montt. From Puerto Montt, we boarded an overnight ferry to Chaitén, where I slept on the roof of the ferry, which offered an unobstructed view of docking at that small port at sunrise. After arriving in Chaitén, a minivan took us to the park where we boarded a small speedboat to travel up the fjord. In the fjord, seals swam beside the boat, and sea lions and sea birds crowded the rocks of the surrounding cliffs. Fjords are tidal waterways, and since the tide was low at the time, a tractor truck provided a lift the last bit of the way. I will always remember the journey to that truly remote place that felt a million miles from the suburban existence I knew from home.

Siargao, Philippines
Raquel Guiu Grigelmo

Dakar, Senegal
Sophy Roberts

Gjógv, Eysturoy, Faroe Islands
Jessica Sample

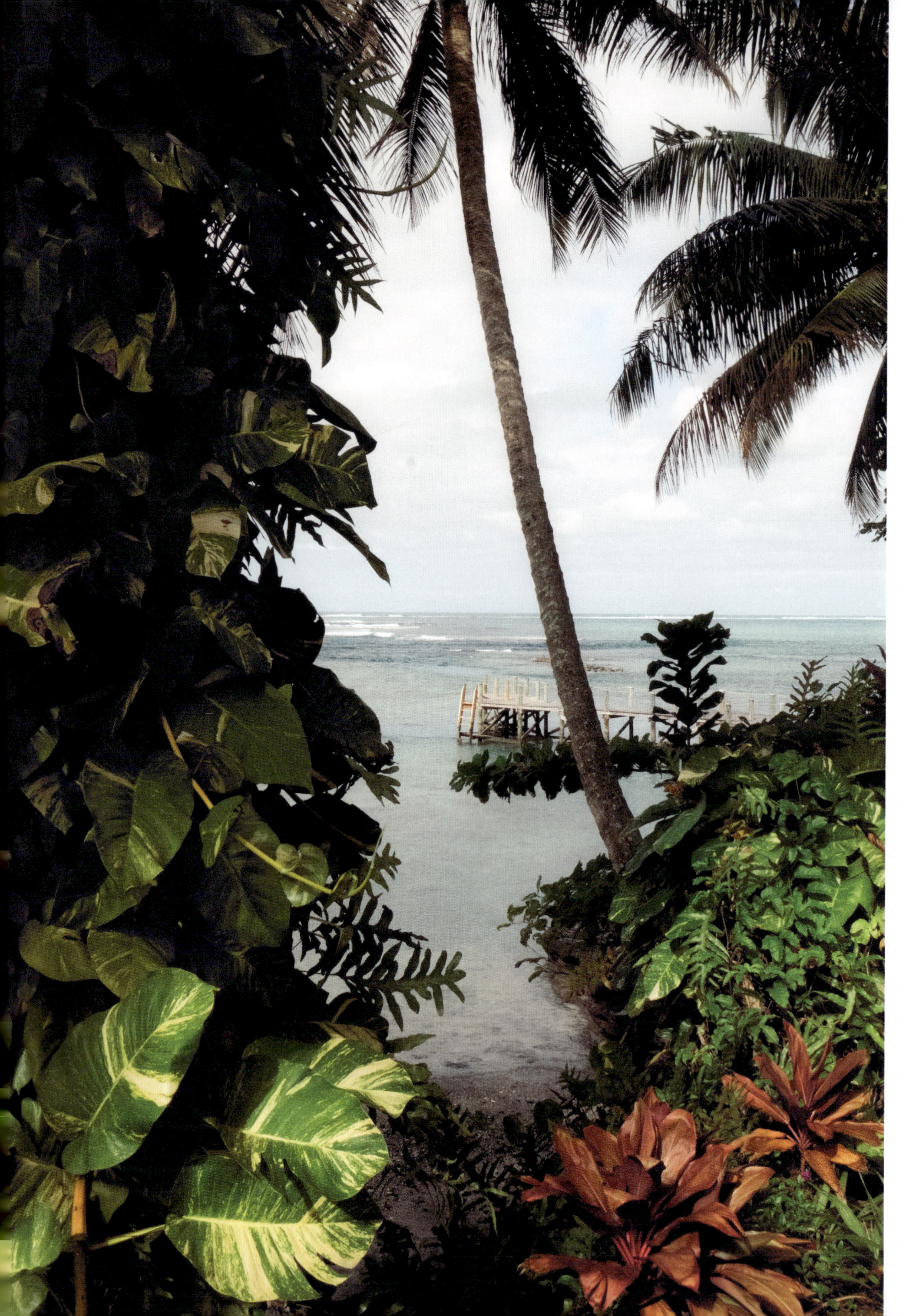

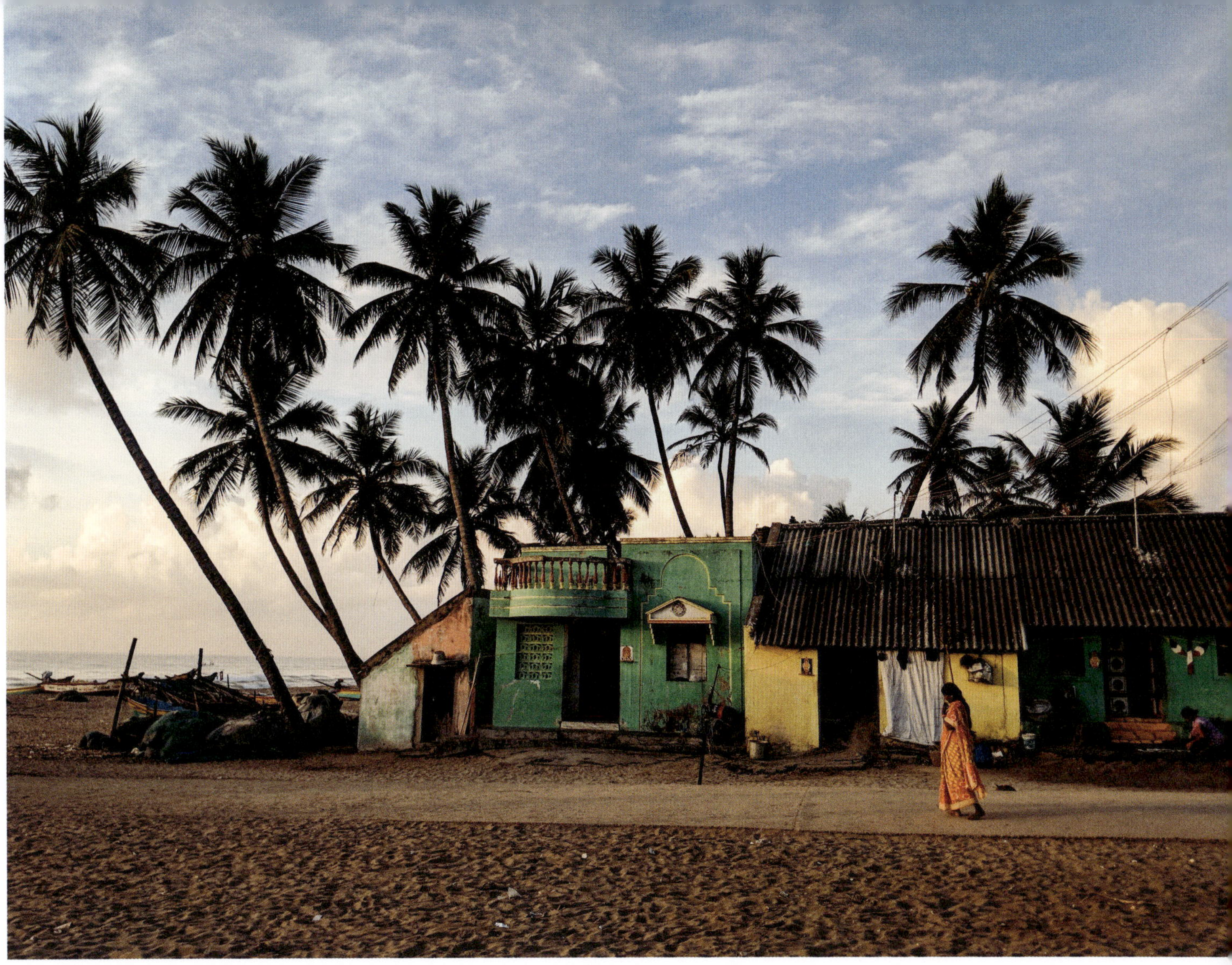

IN AUGUST ON the remote Polynesian island of Upolu, days are spent tasting fresh papaya from family-run fruit stalls, swimming at the empty clear beaches, and basking under the stars at night. Upolu is the smaller of Samoa's two main islands and home to the Samoan capital, Apia. It is famous to travelers for the To-Sua Ocean Trench, a dramatic sinkhole with a long set of wooden steps that take you down to a wooden platform where you can jump in. The island can be reached via walk-on and car ferry from its larger sister island of Sava'i.

**Si'umu, Upolu,
Samoa**

Anna Pihan

THE WORKDAY BEGINS early in the small fishing villages outside of the formerly French colonial town of Pudicherry, with fisherman heading out onto the Indian Ocean in hand-painted boats as the sun rises.

**Nallavadu,
Tamil Nadu, India**

Emily Nathan

THE LOST COAST is a 100-mile stretch of undeveloped coastline in Northern California. There are virtually no roads to the beaches here—if you want to see this pristine stretch of untouched coast, you must hike in, surfboards and all.

**Lost Coast,
California,
United States**
Alex Farnum

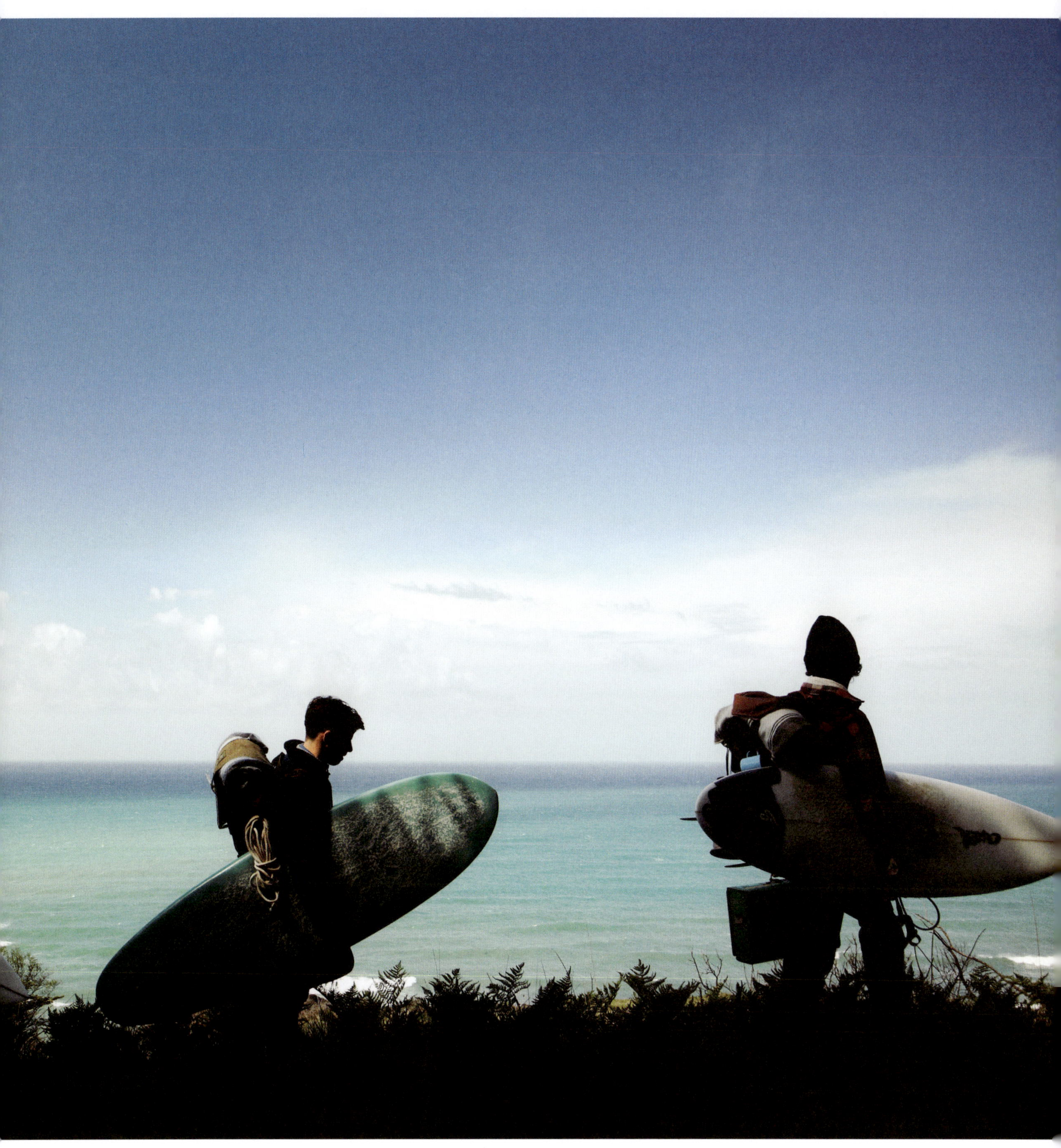

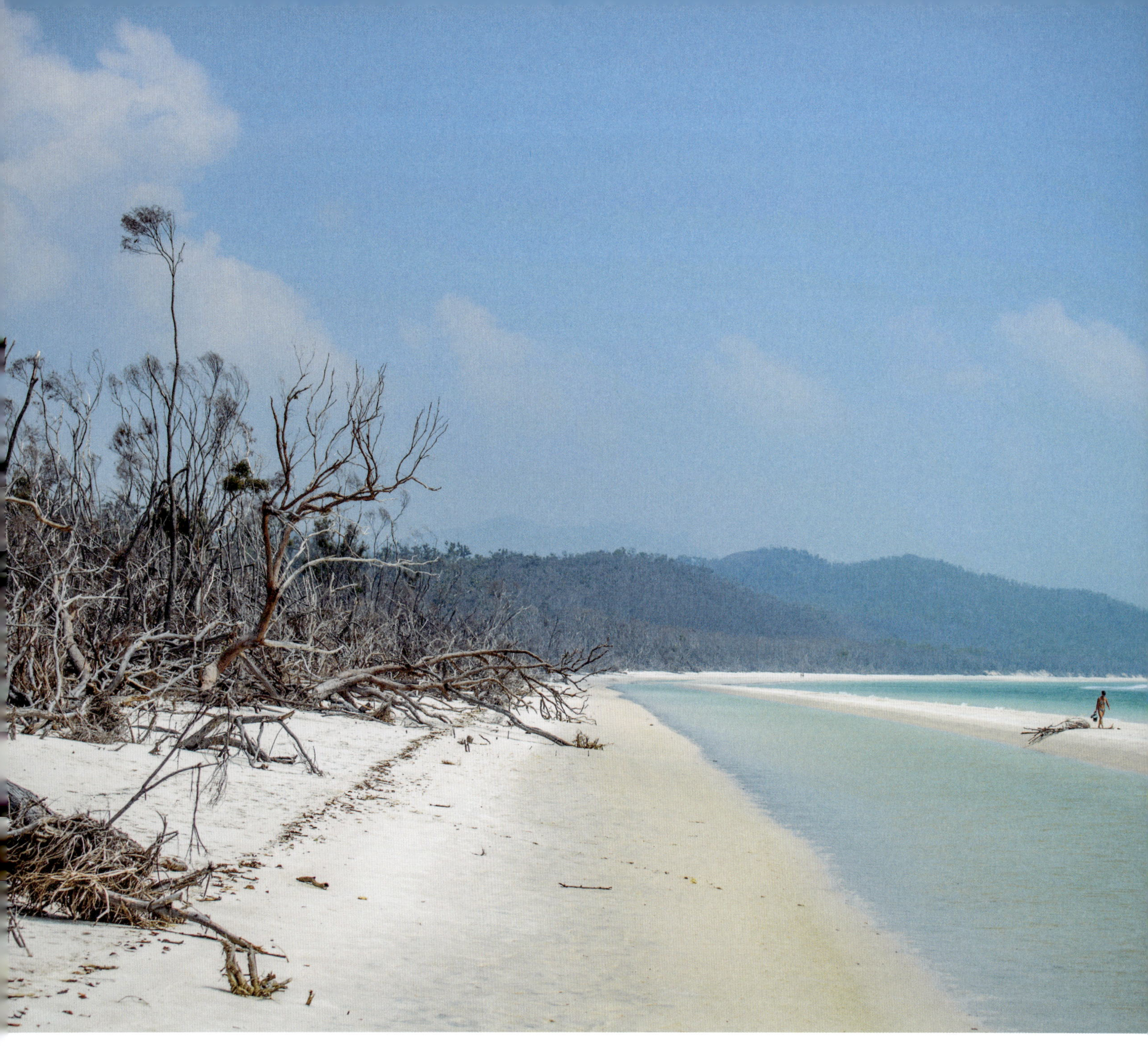

**Whitsunday Island,
Queensland,
Australia**

Alexandra Kryaneva

**Yakushima Island,
Kagoshima
Prefecture, Japan**

Crista Priscilla

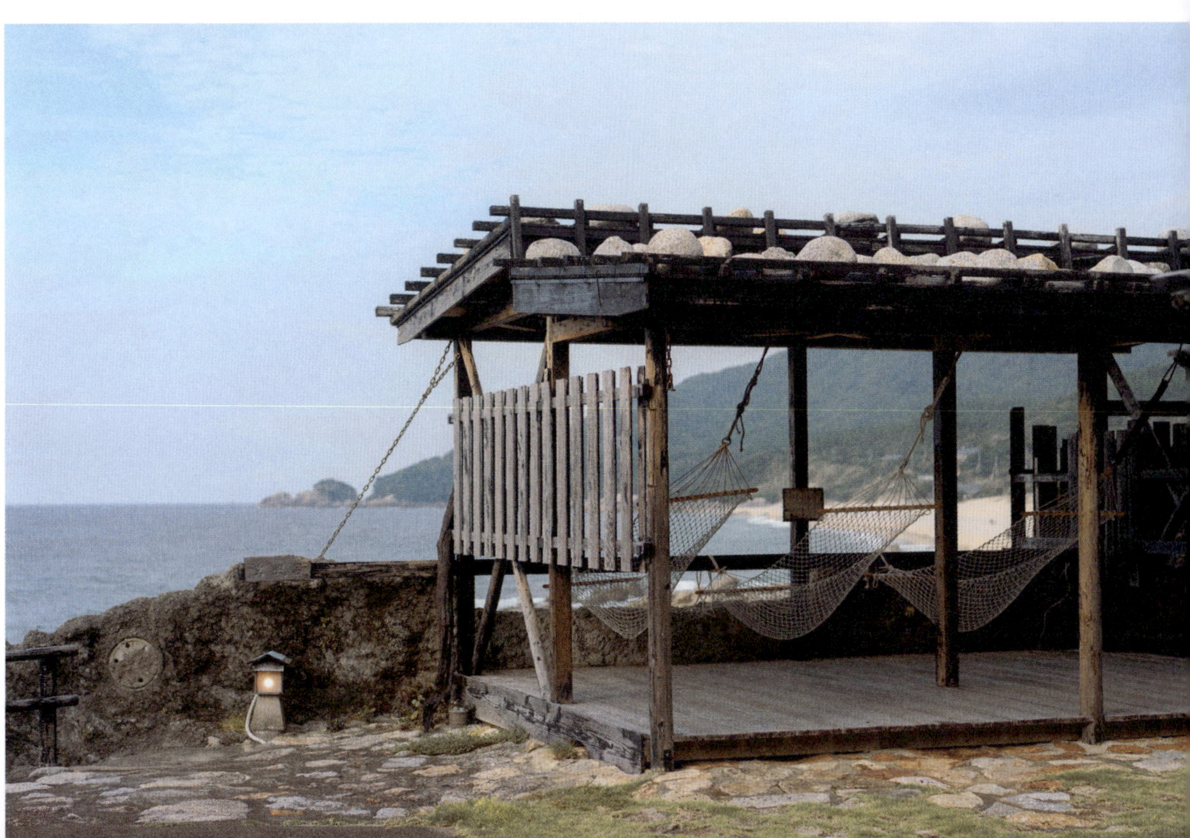

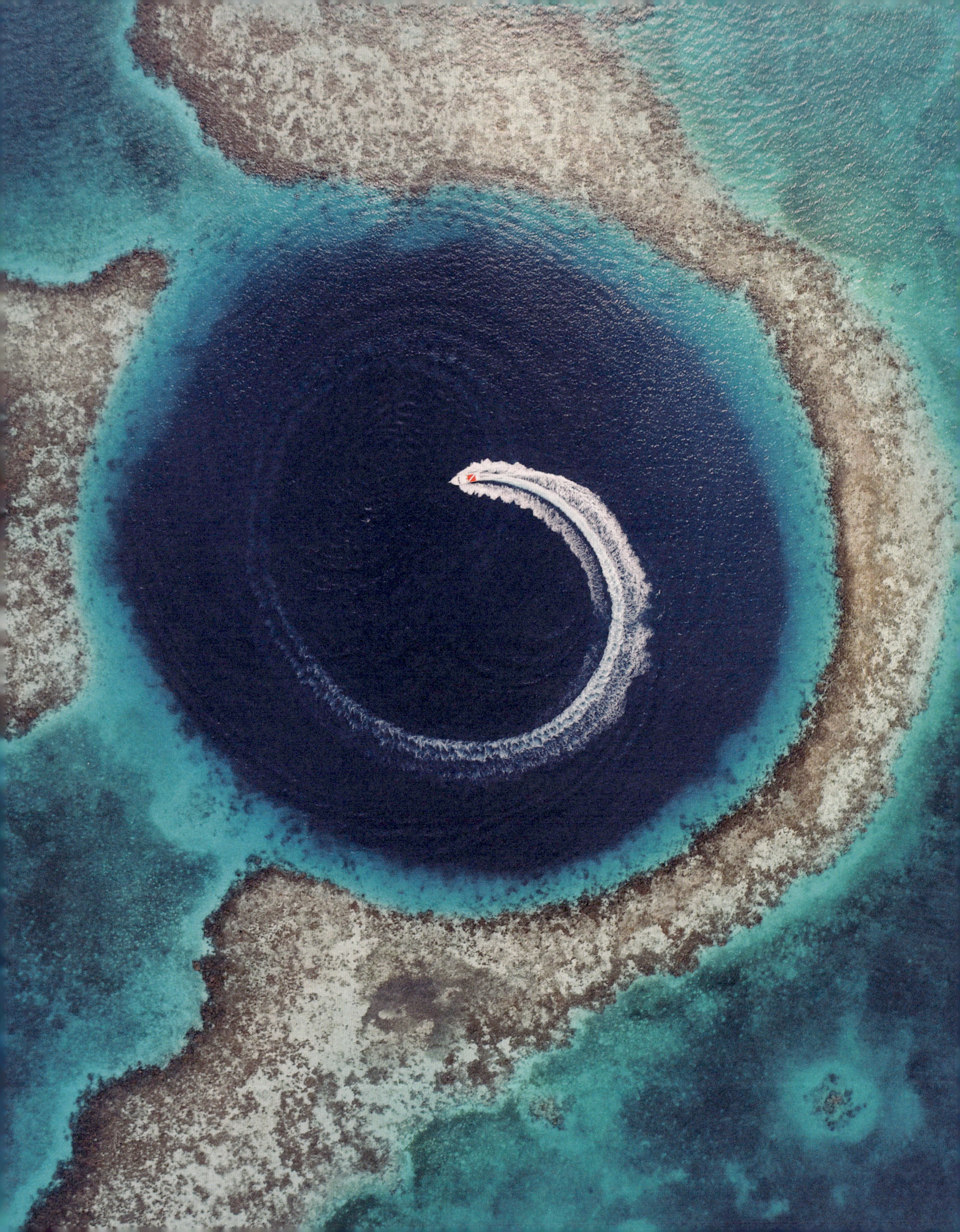

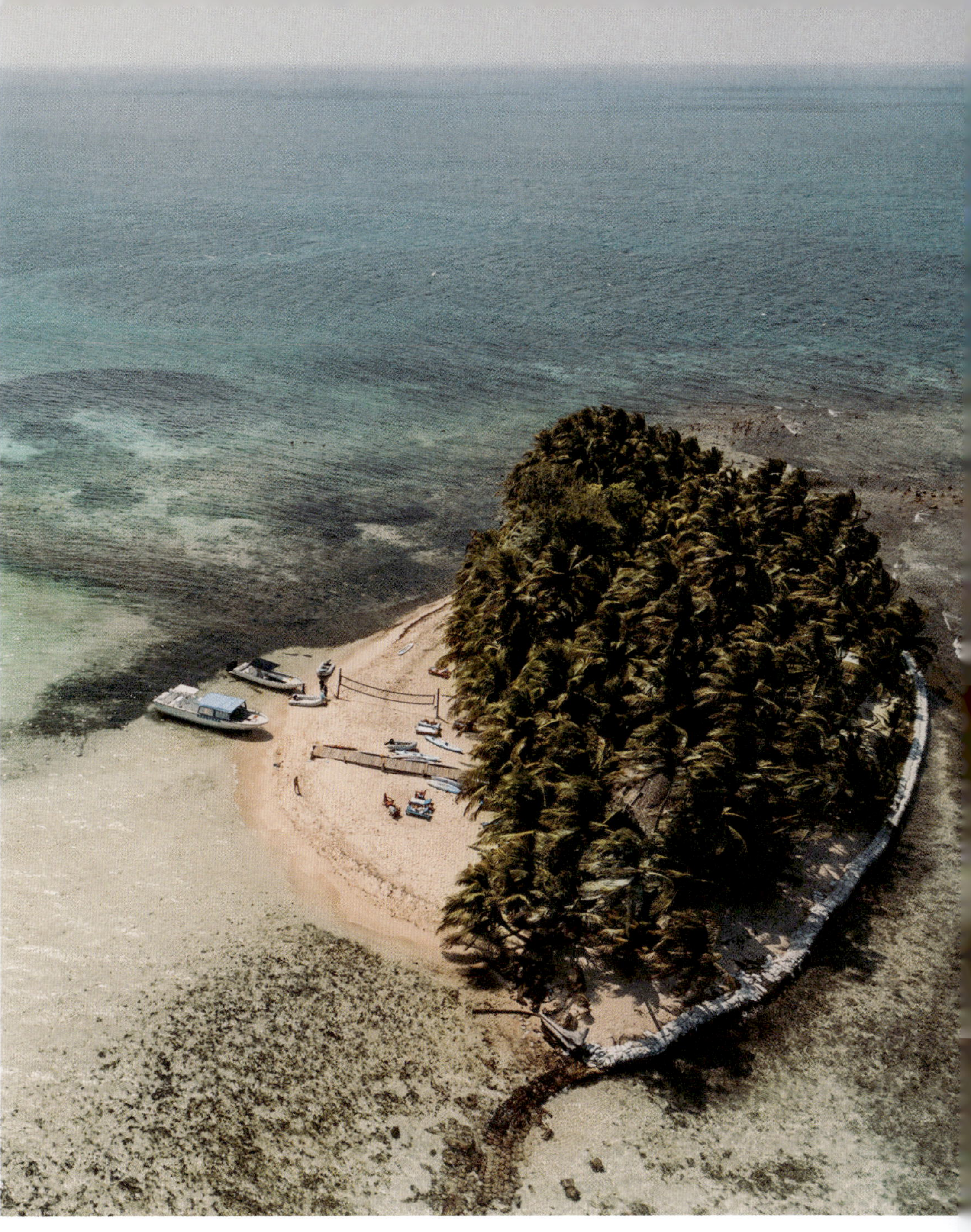

↑
THE PLACENCIA PENINSULA on the Caribbean coast of Belize is perfect for divers and snorkelers. From Belize City you can take a boat (beware of the choppy seas) out to small private islands, such as Ranguana Caye, adjacent to the Belize Barrier Reef, and spend the day exploring the area's crystal clear waters.

**Ranguana Caye,
Toledo, Belize**

Michelle Halpern

**↓
Tofino,
British Columbia,
Canada**

Emily Nathan

**→
Nelson Island,
British Columbia,
Canada**

Grant Harder

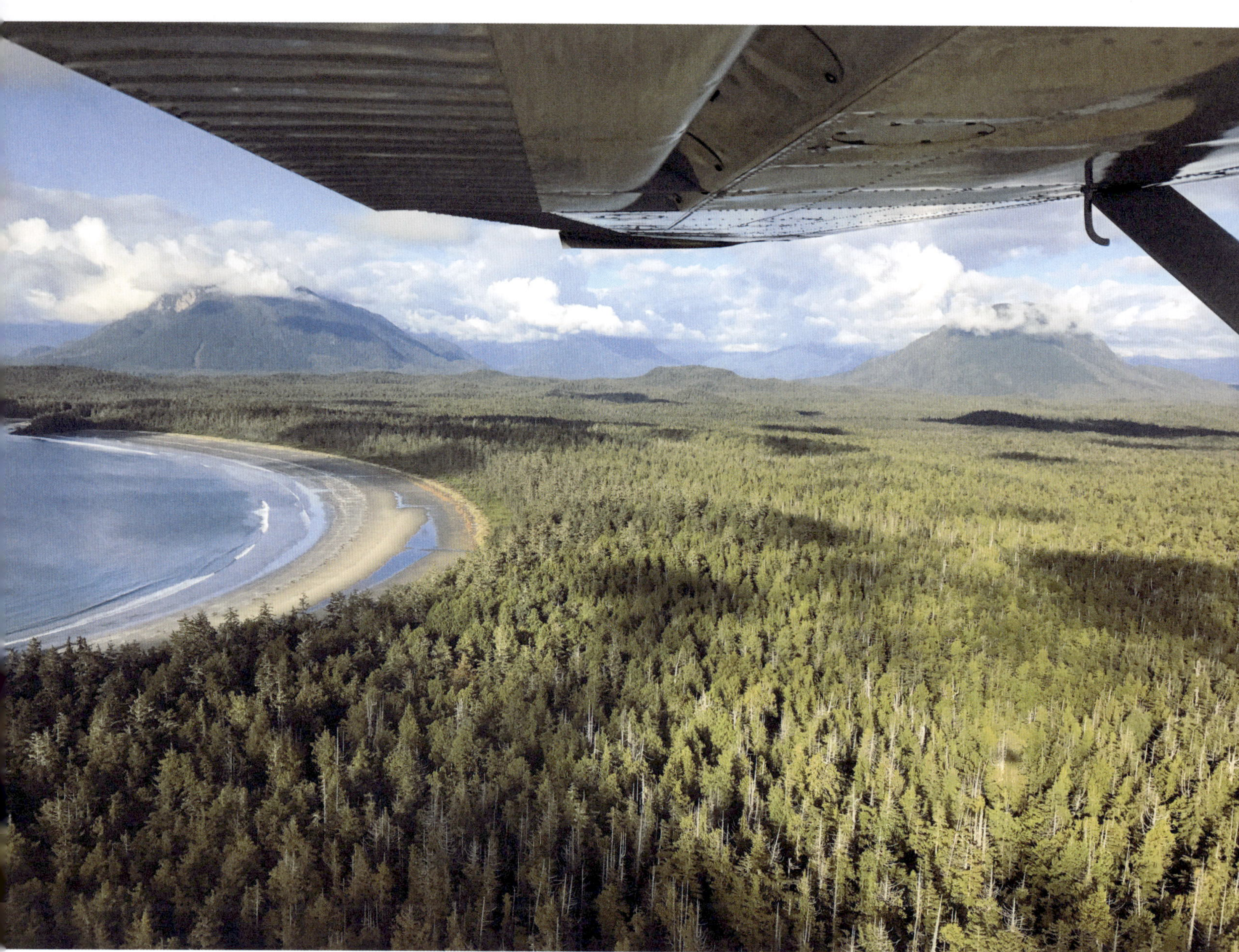

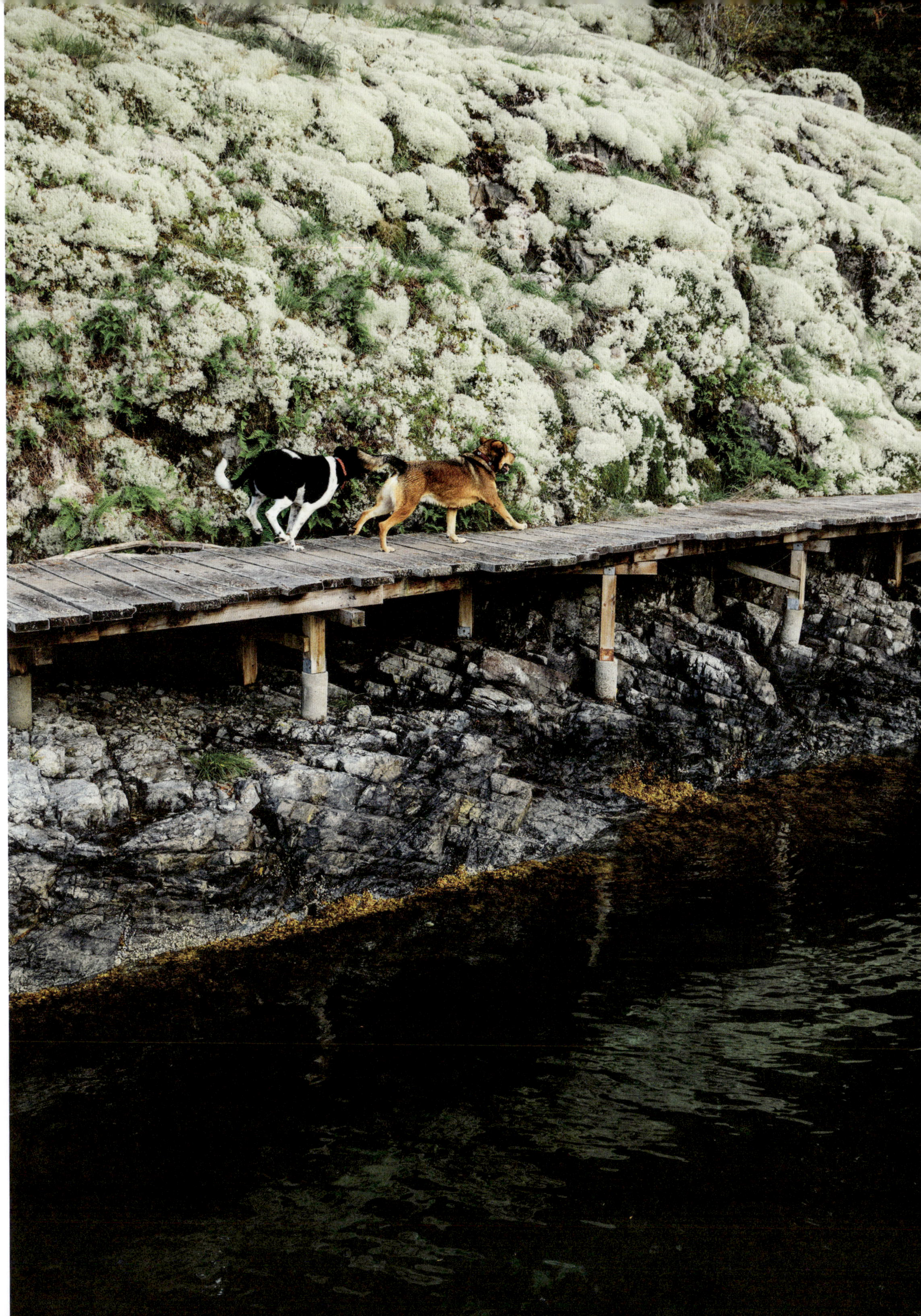

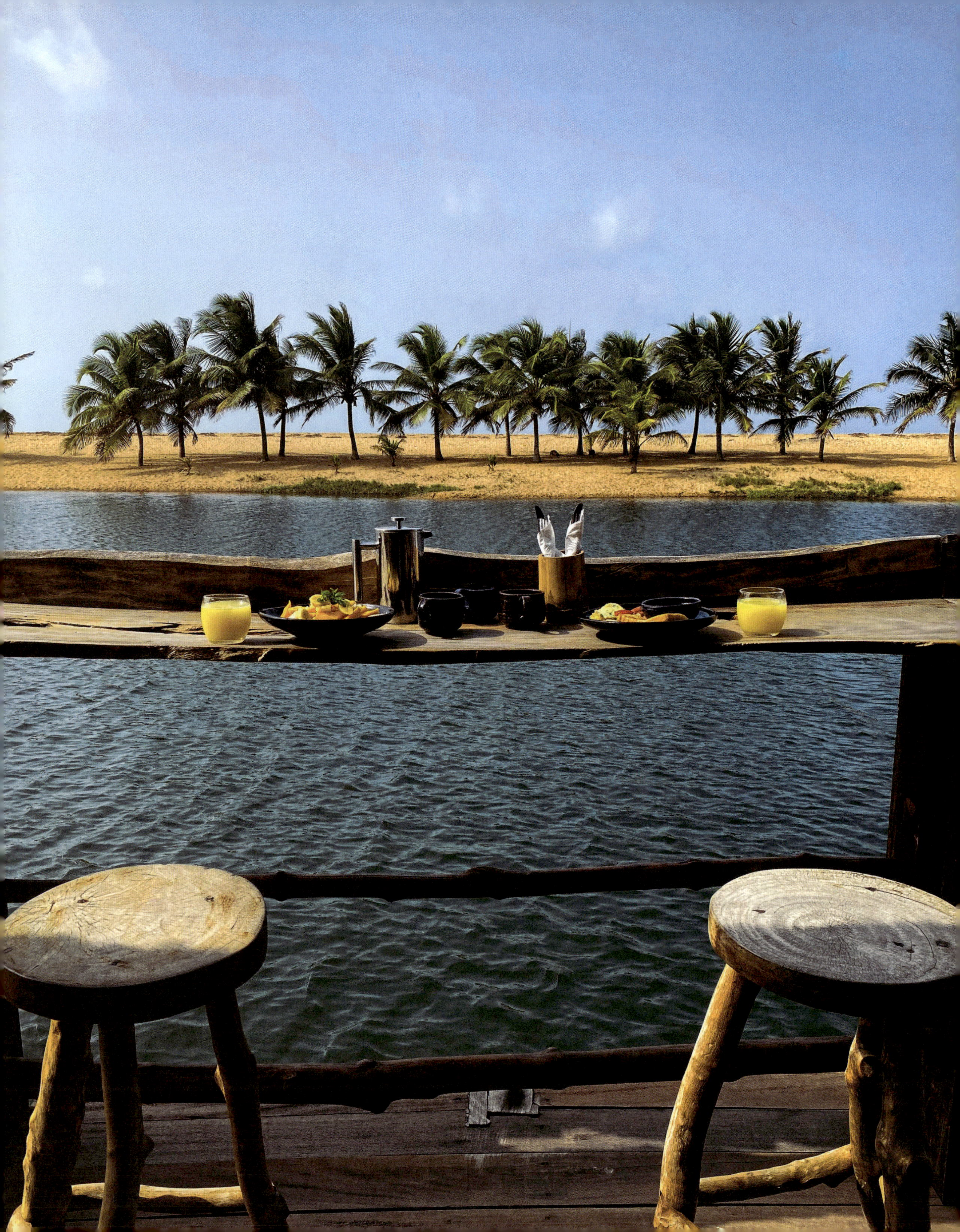

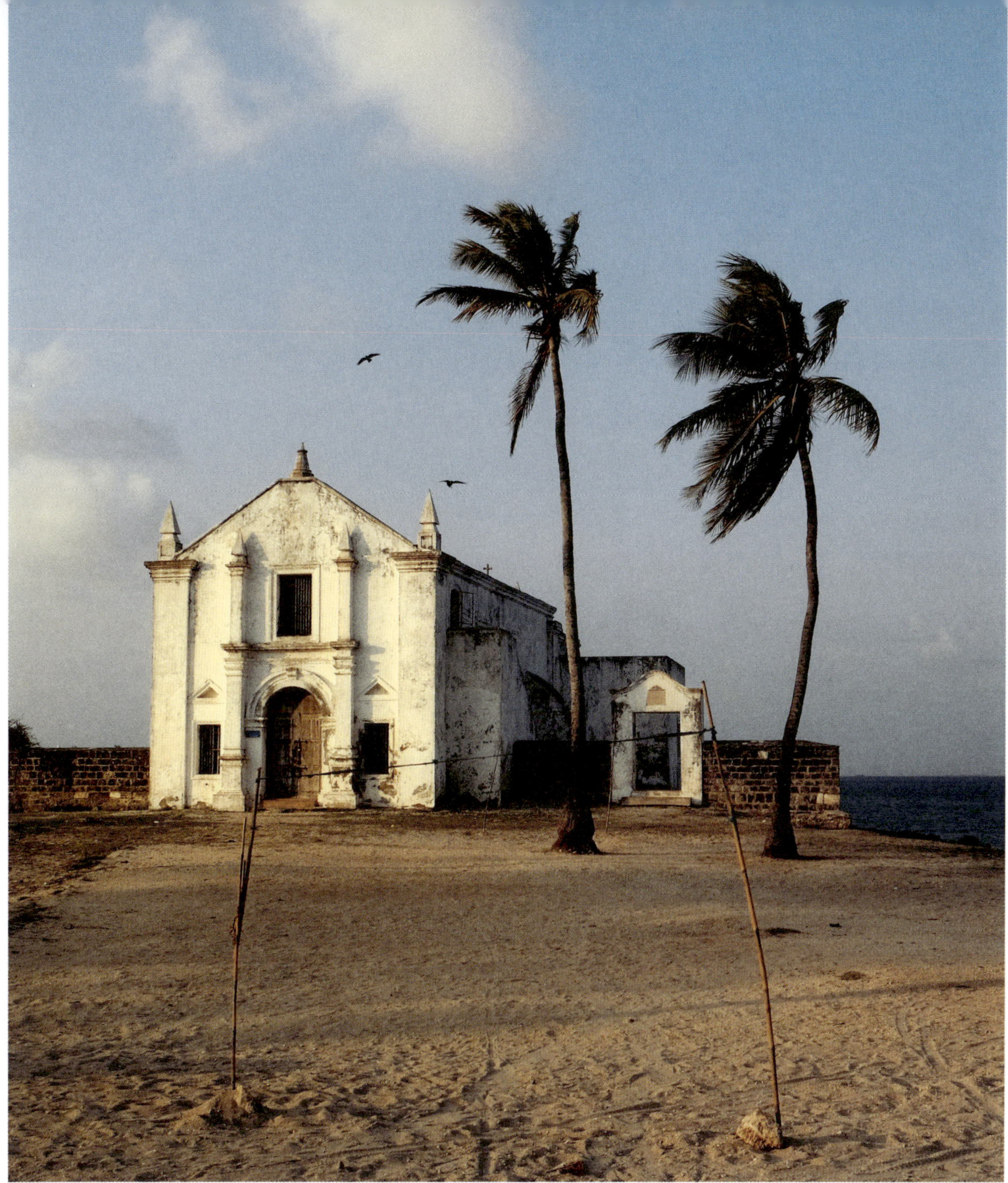

←
**Volta Region,
Ghana**

Douglas Croudace

↑
**Nampula Province,
Mozambique**

Raquel Guiu Grigelmo

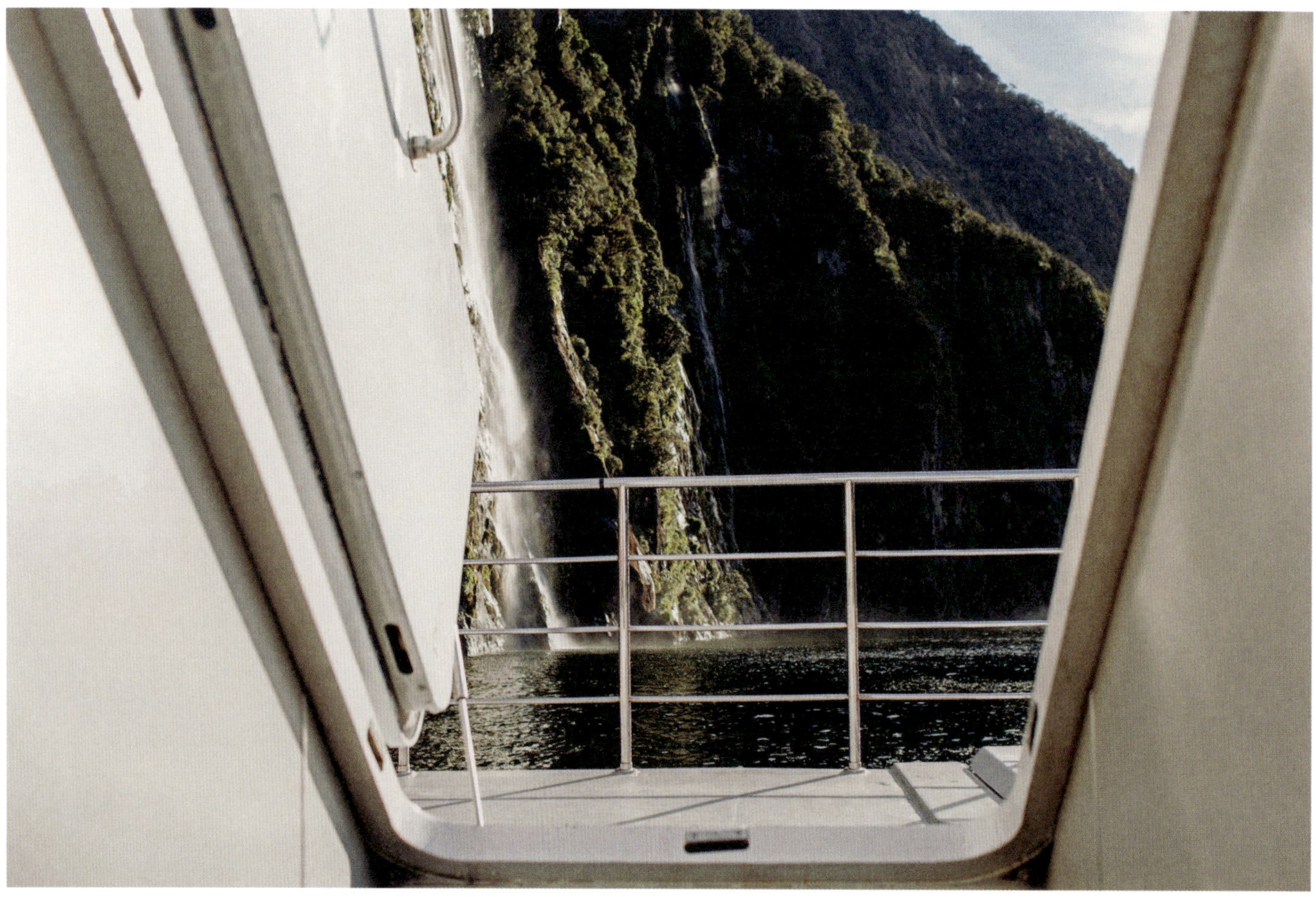

↑

NEW ZEALAND'S MILFORD Sound is about a four-hour drive
from Queenstown or a two-hour trip from the regional hub
of Te Anau. The towering, cathedral-like cliffs surrounding
the sound are green in the summer (December to February)
and covered in snow in the winter, when the region is far
less crowded. The *Fiordland Jewel*, a small cruising vessel
that sleeps twenty, is the only boat that can take visitors on
an overnight trip to experience the magic sound up close.
On these trips, guests can explore the sound from kayaks
and even a submersible craft.

**Milford Sound,
Fiordland, South Island,
New Zealand**

Emily Nathan

→

ACROSS FROM COSTA RICA'S well-known Osa Peninsula
is Golfo Dulce ("Sweet Gulf"), the only tropical fjord in the
Americas. Some of the wildlife that call this beach home are
tiny colorful crabs, Jesus Christ lizards (so named because
they can run across water), and all manner of birds. Be
prepared for dense tropical rainforest (and the bugs that
go with it), as well as hot and humid conditions. To access
the area, visitors fly into (or drive from) the nation's capitol
of San Jose and then take a small plane to Puerto Jiménez
and finally, a breezy boat ride across the bay.

**Golfo Dulce, Puntarenas,
Costa Rica**

Daniel Schwartz

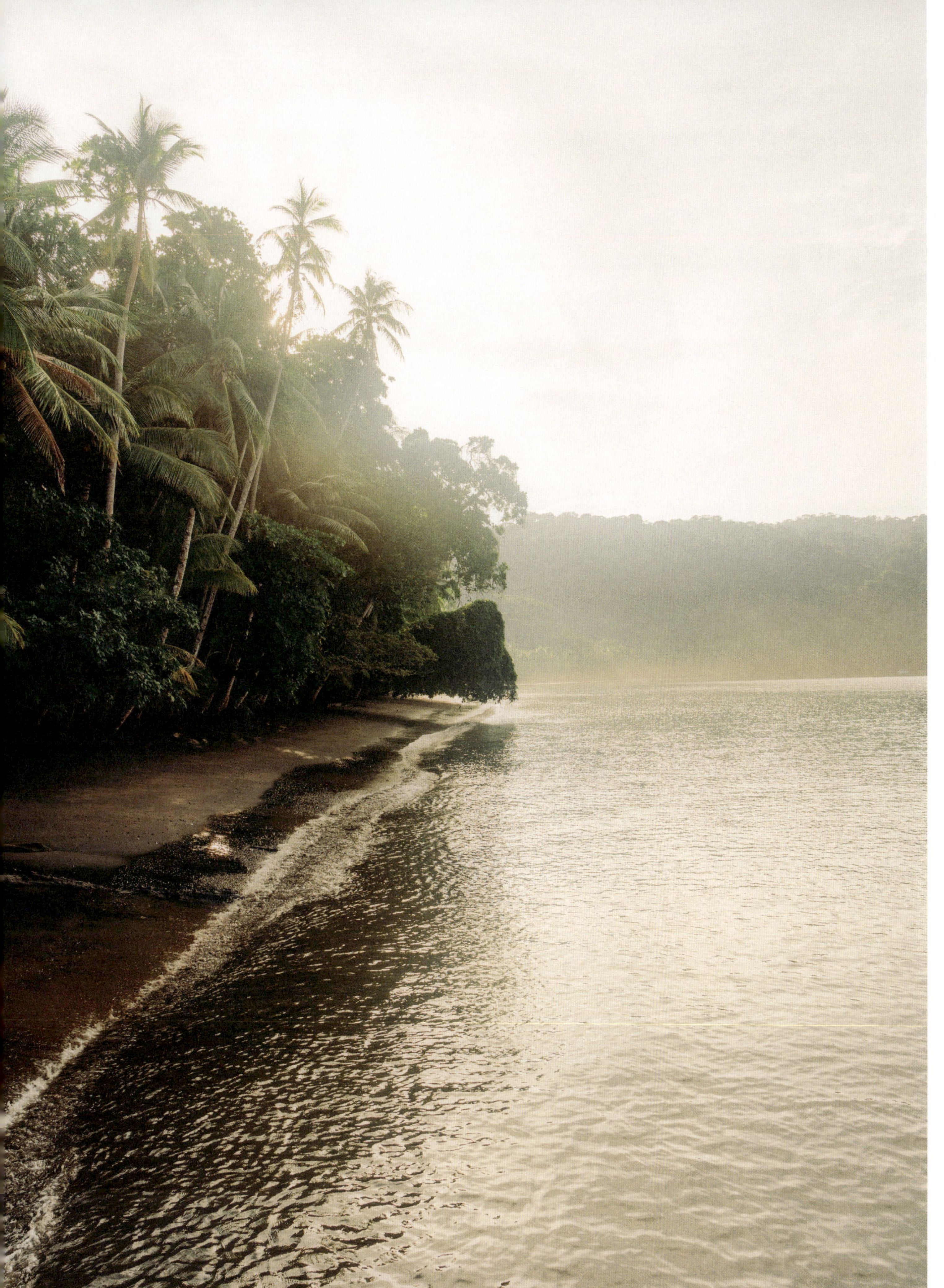

uum

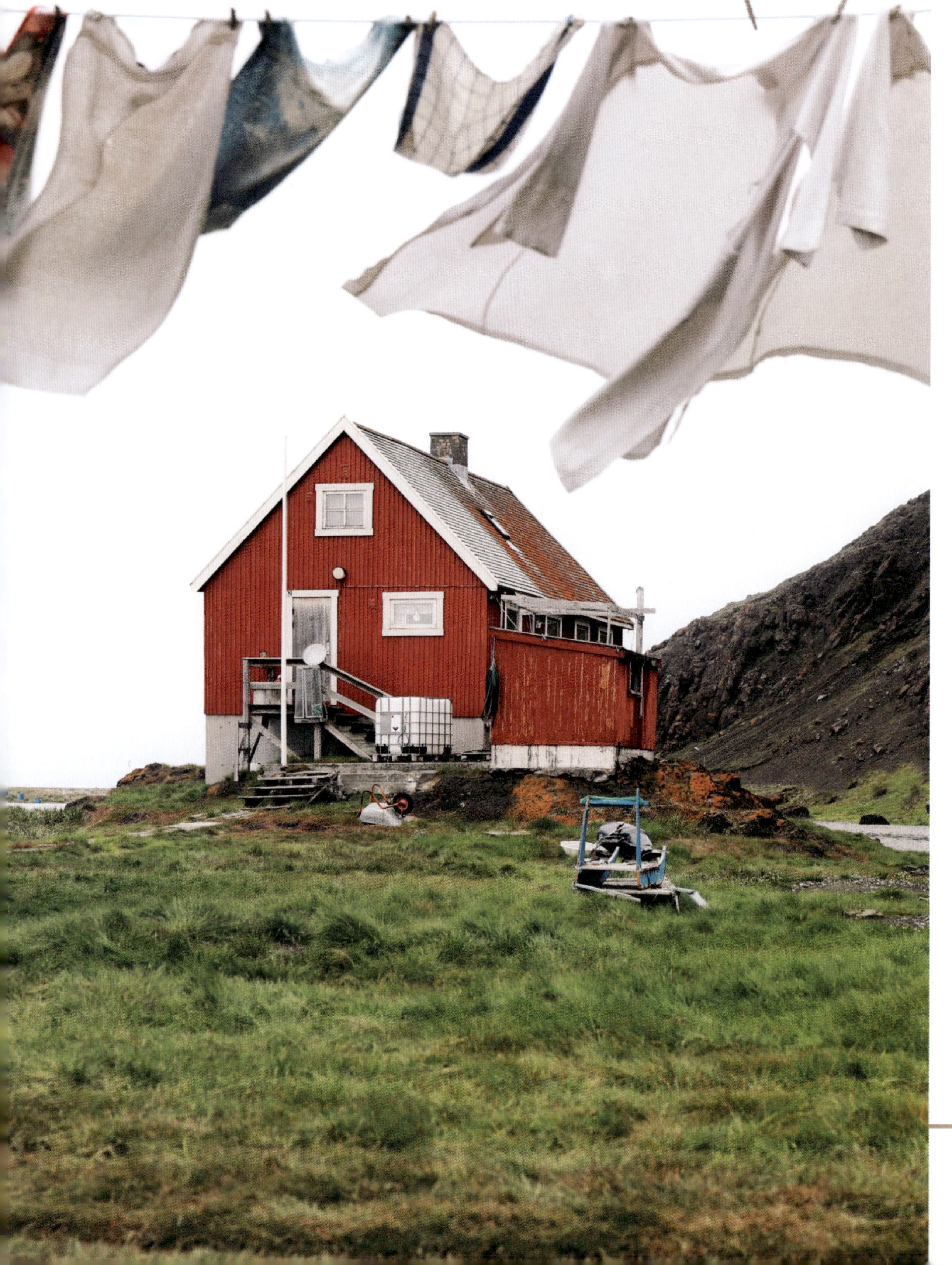

mannaq

GREENLAND

EVERYTHING ABOUT GREENLAND feels remote. The largest island in the world, it is surrounded by the Arctic and Atlantic oceans as well as the Greenland and Lincoln Seas, with three-quarters of the island covered by a permanent ice sheet—the only one located outside of Antarctica. Most residents are Inuit, descendants of migrant travelers who traversed northern Canada from Alaska. Sled dogs are an integral part of life and culture here, as is hunting seal and walrus as well as fishing Atlantic cod and Greenland halibut. When the sea is frozen, dogsleds and snow scooters can be seen gliding across the ice for both work and play. In the summer, transportation for hunting and fishing is all about boats. Visitors can spot a hunter's home by the fish, animal skins, or bones drying outside.

Uummannaq is an island on Greenland's central west coast. The name also refers to the general area of inlets north of the settlement of Niaqornat along the coast of the Nuussuaq Peninsula. Uummannaq Fjord, the largest fjord system in western Greenland, surrounds the island and empties into Baffin Bay. Nearly 400 miles north of the outermost border of the Arctic Circle, the landscape here is mammoth. From a distance, Uummannaq Mountain appears to rise directly from the coastal waters, its dramatic, nearly vertical cliffs reaching about 3,840 feet. The air is very dry, enabling people to see details in mountains and islands miles away. During the winter there

are months of darkness, and in the summer seventeen hours of sunshine a day. Residents and visitors stay up late to watch the northern lights or hike under the midnight sun.

Niaqornat is the smallest settlement in Greenland with a population of less than sixty. The community is spread along on a spit of land between the Nuussuaq Peninsula and a hill jutting out of the sea. There are no commercial hotels; however, travelers inspired (and determined) to visit can look online to find rooms to rent from locals. During the winter, the settlement is serviced only once a week by helicopter from a local hub in Uummannaq, so it can easily end up taking two or three weeks to get there if a trip is disrupted by storms or mechanical issues. Traveling to this area generally does not attract the casual tourist.

Getting to Uummannaq is an exercise in patience (and even though it is slightly more convenient now than when the first explorers set out, it is still a challenge). For travelers who depart from Newfoundland, as photographer Jessie Brinkman Evans did, it can take two trips across the Atlantic, four days of air travel, two more days lost to weather, five planes, and a helicopter. Booking the flights is an eye-twitching process, but dedicated travelers will just have to laugh at it, because it isn't easy and, for some, that can be half the fun. Overnight visitors to Uummannaq usually stay in a private home, though Uummannaq Seasafaris has recently opened a rental house.

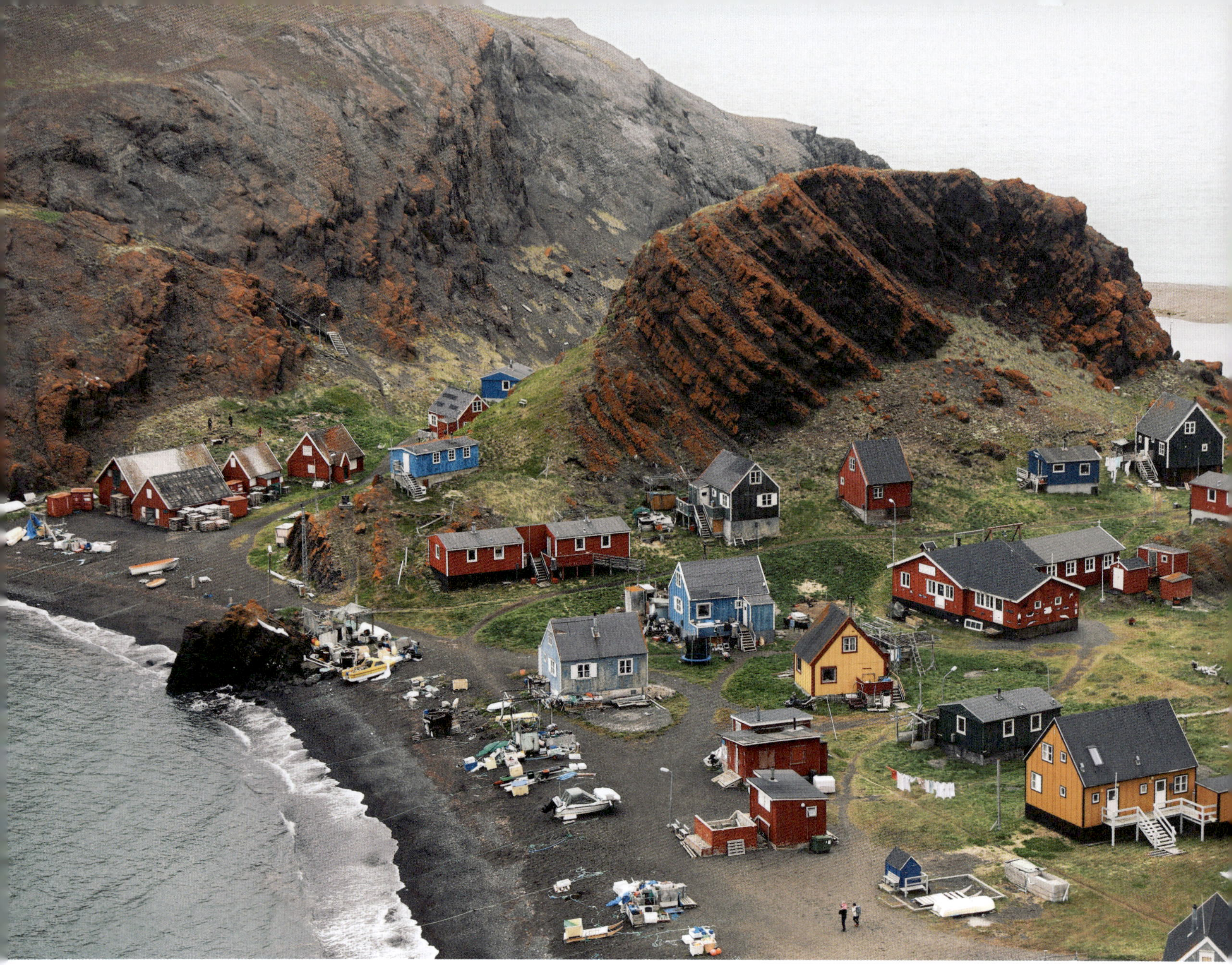

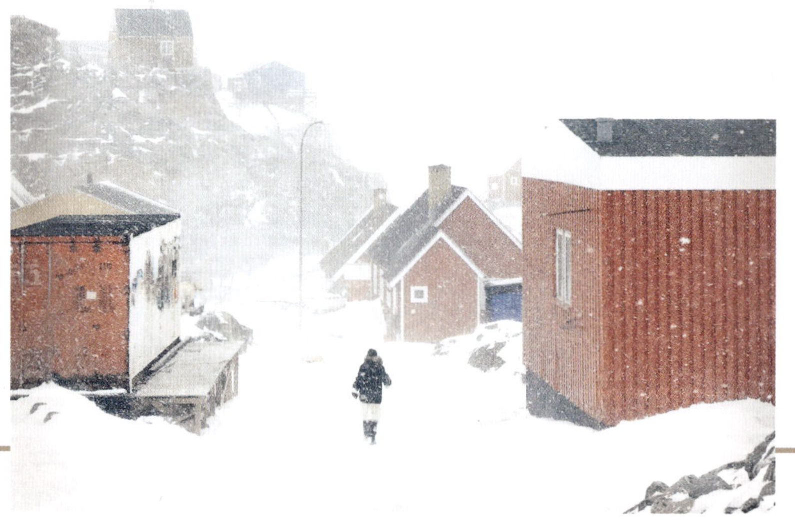

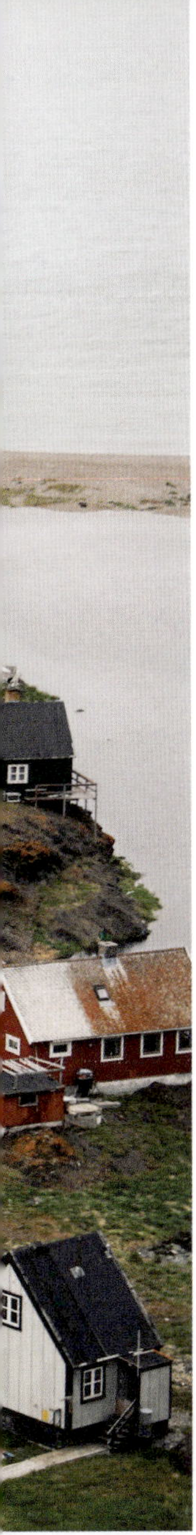

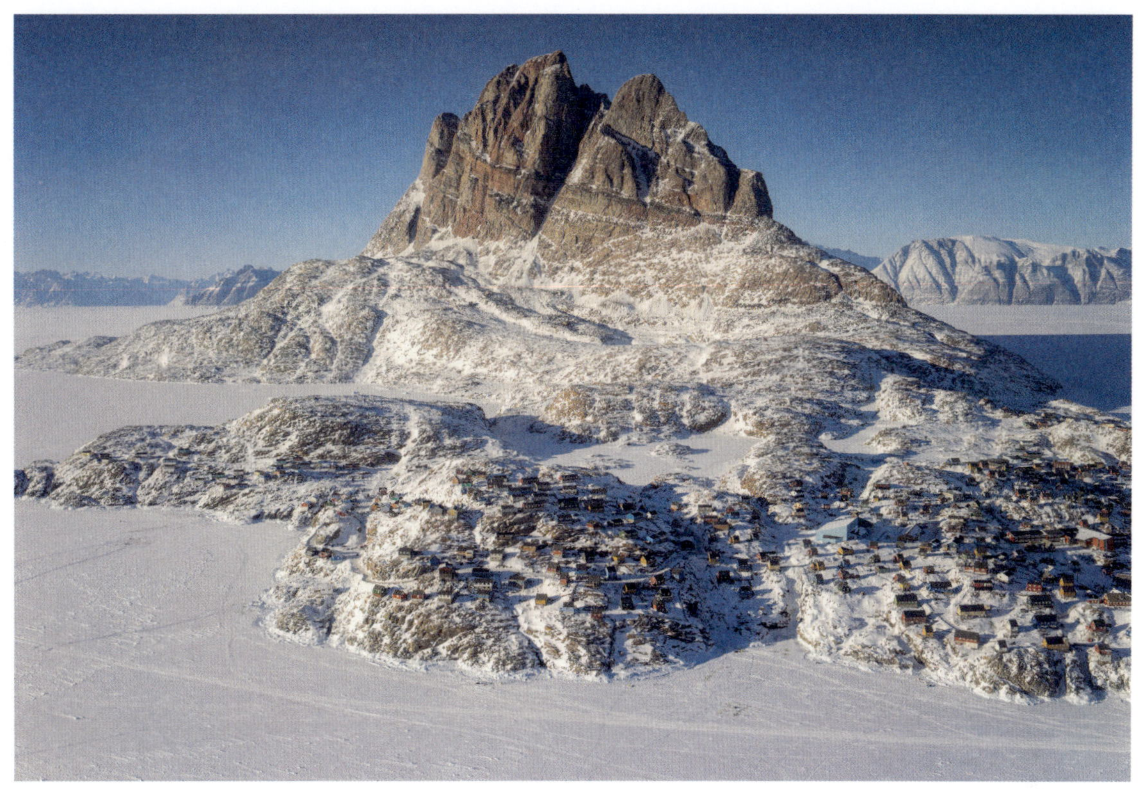

UUMMANNAQ, GREENLAND

Photographs by Jessie Brinkman Evans

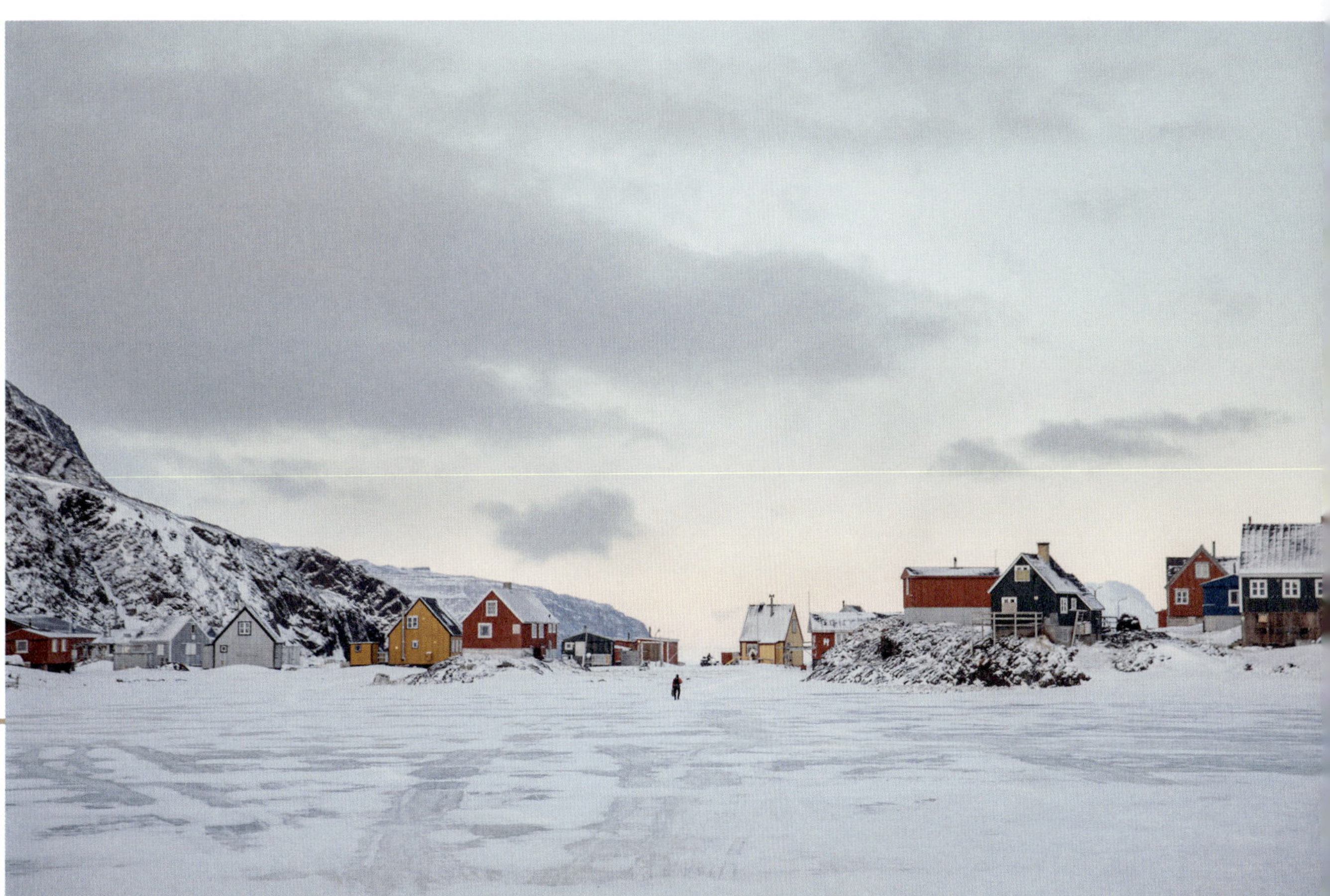

**Dunedin,
South Island,
New Zealand**

Gemma Cagnacci

OVER FIFTEEN HUNDRED islands and cays make up the secluded Raja Ampat Islands of Indonesia. The islands are known for their marine biodiversity, potentially the highest in the world, with thriving coral reefs seeded by both the Indian and Pacific Oceans. They take some time and patience to get to, though—about two days from Europe or North America. Travelers usually fly into to the Indonesian capital of Jakarta, then take a connecting flight to Sorong in West Papua. From Sorong Harbor, catch a two-hour ferry to the administrative island of Waisai, where all the homestays and hotels pick travelers up. From there, it's likely another hour-long boat ride to any final destination.

**Raja Ampat
Islands, West
Papua, Indonesia**

Alexandra Kryaneva

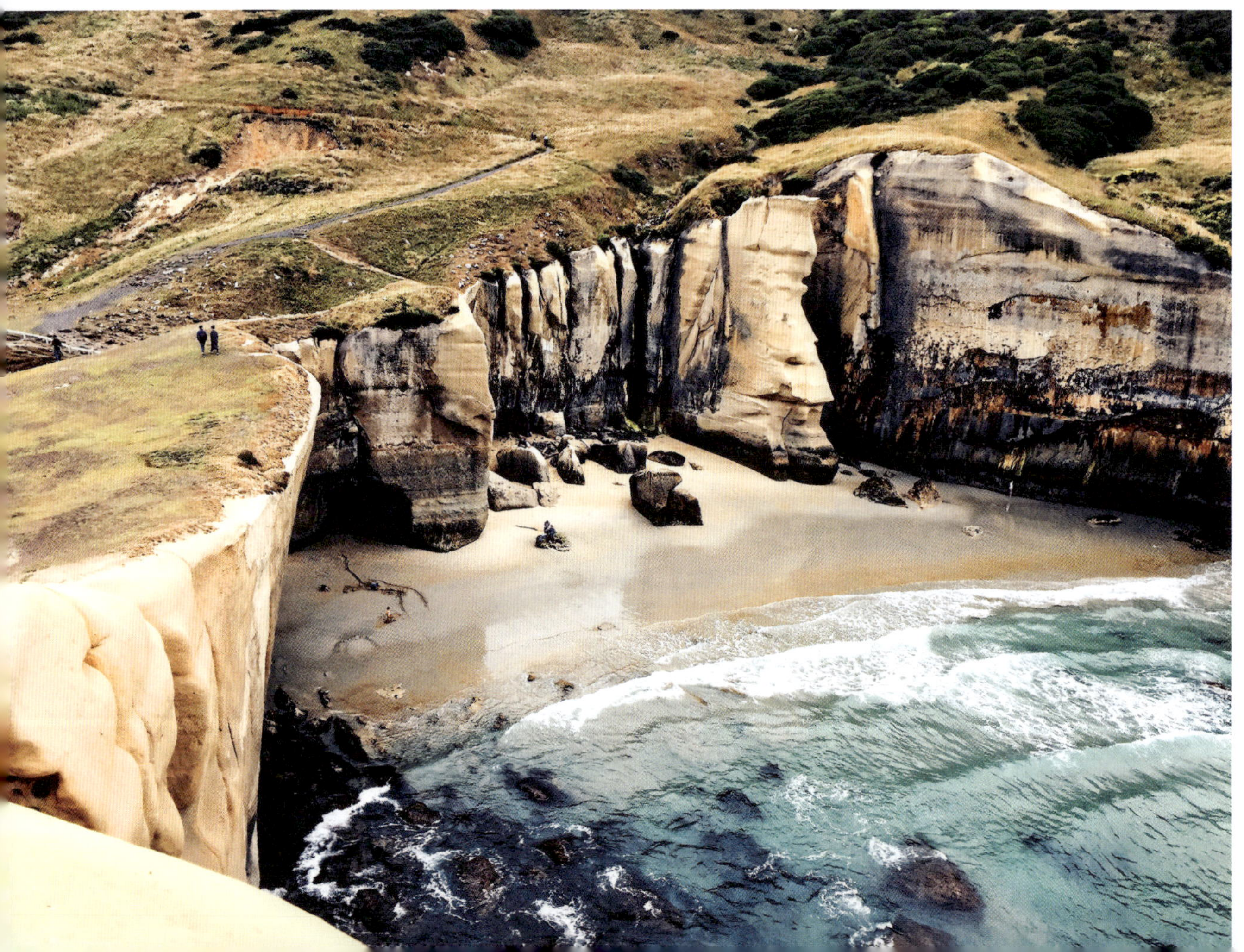

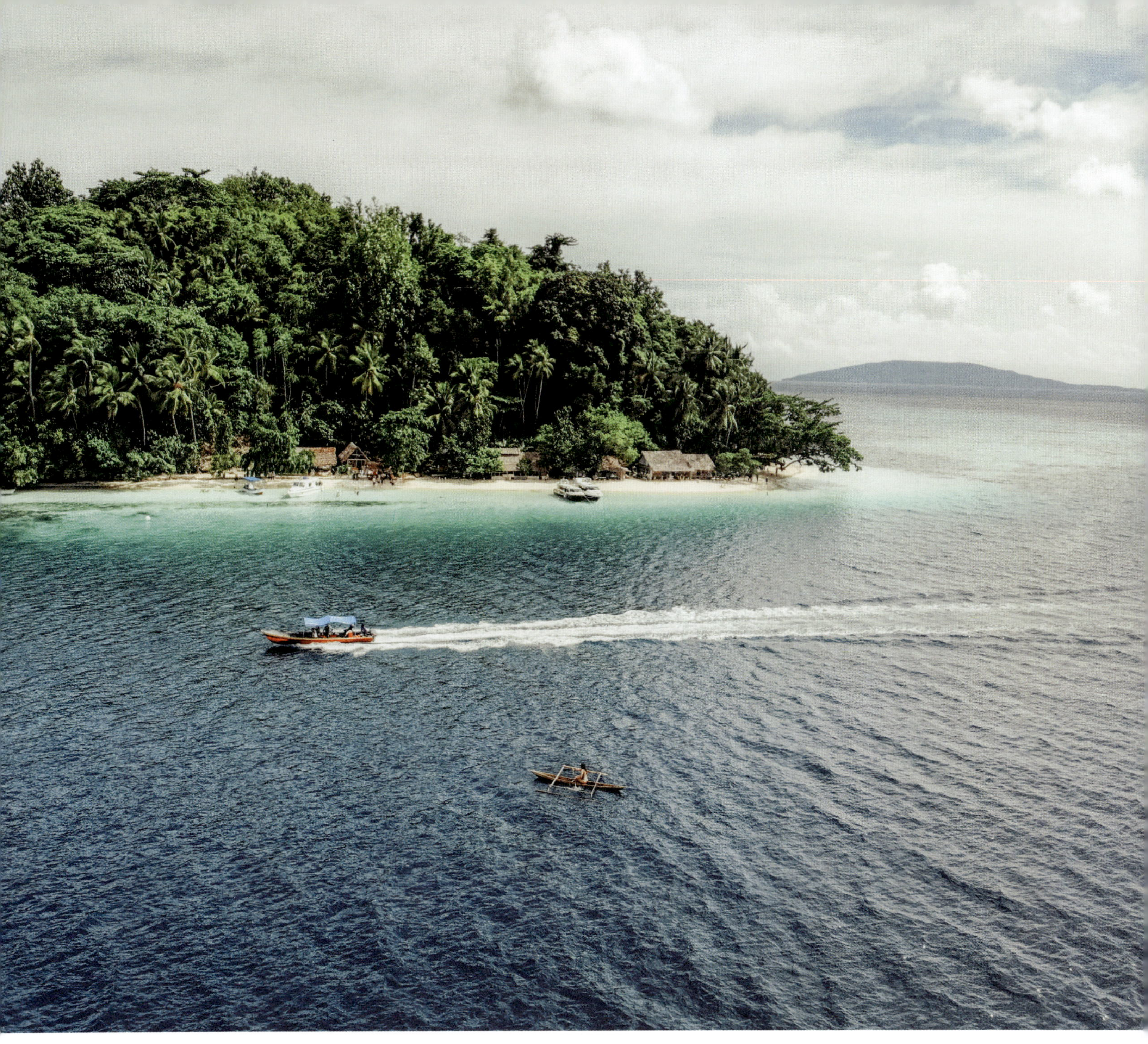

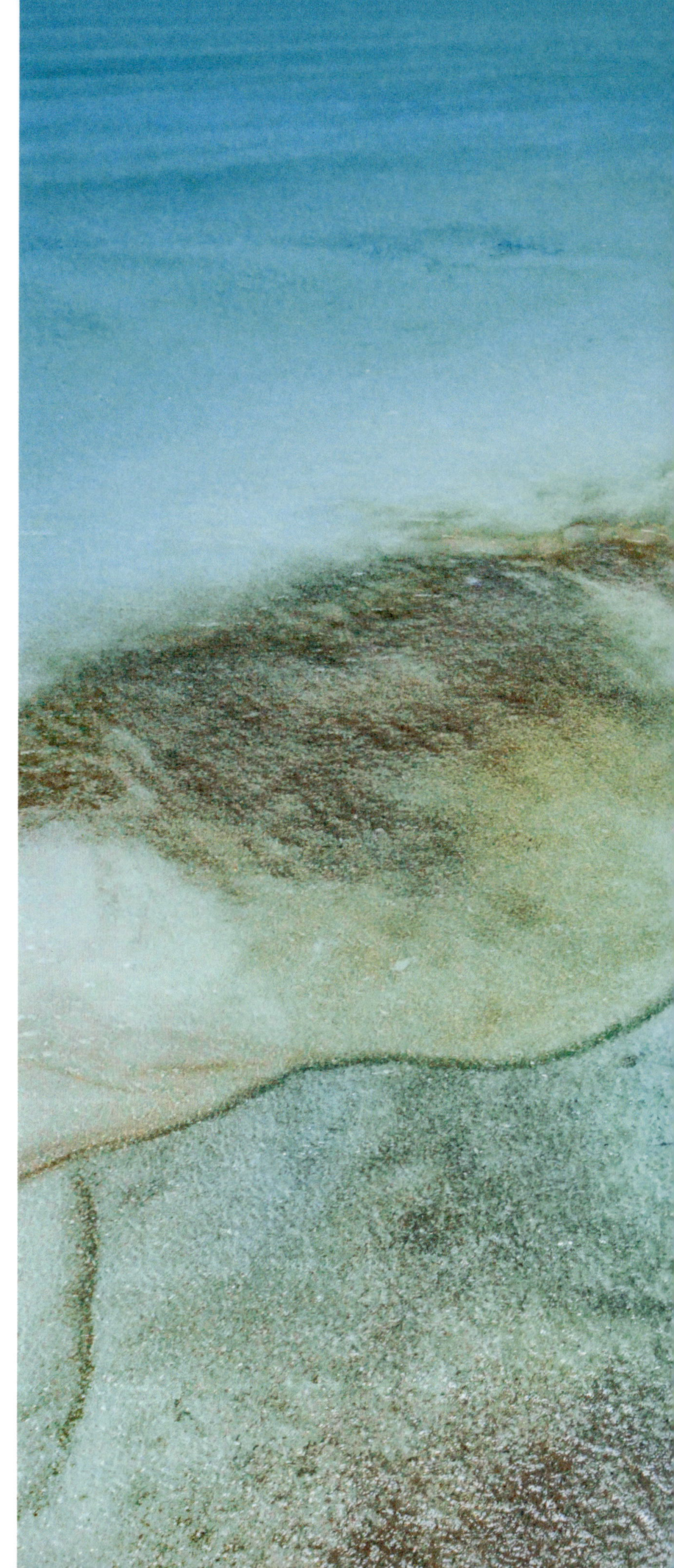

TETI'AROA IS A 2-square-mile slice of white sand and palms that was once a vacation area for Tahitian royalty. The island currently is under a ninety-nine-year lease to the deceased actor Marlon Brando, who visited the island while scouting locations for *Mutiny on the Bounty*, and a luxury hotel, The Brando, is the only accommodation. The lagoon is immaculate for snorkeling and has unbelievable water clarity for photography. From the capital port in Pape'ete, you can reach Teti'aroa atoll via private plane or a catamaran day trip.

**Teti'aroa, Tahiti,
French Polynesia**

Michael Goetze and
Jampal Williamson

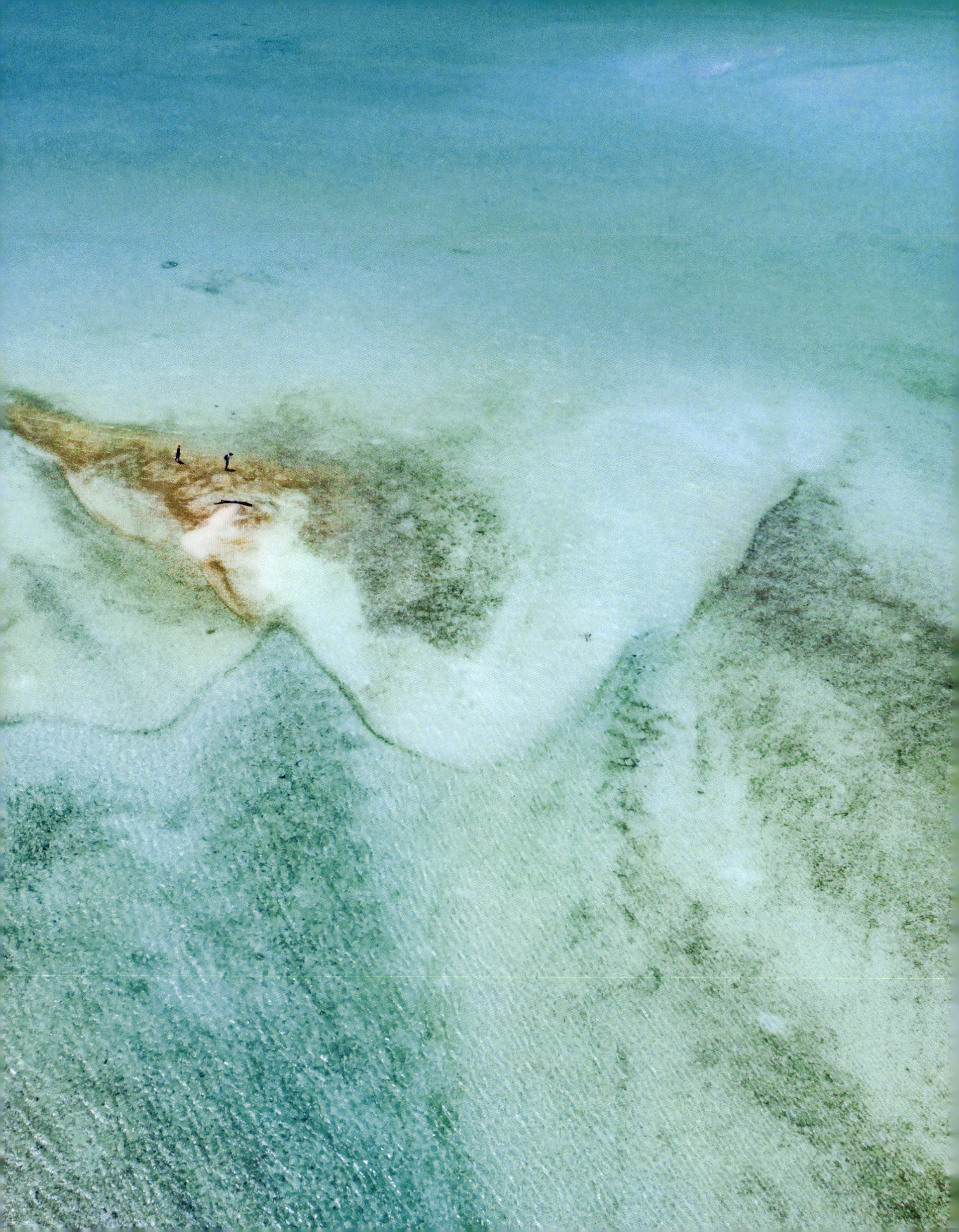

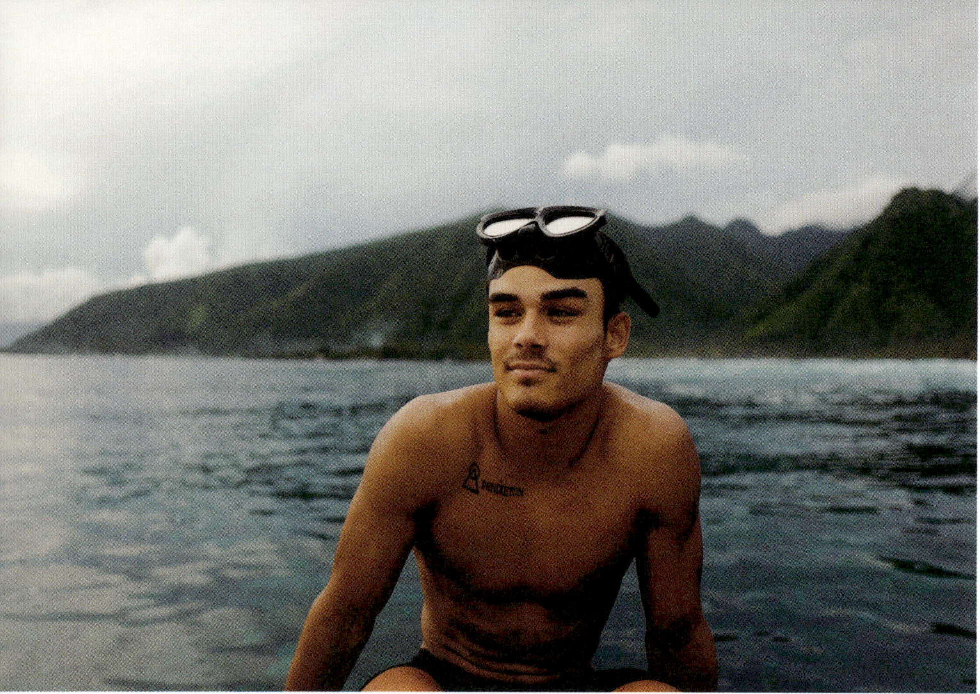

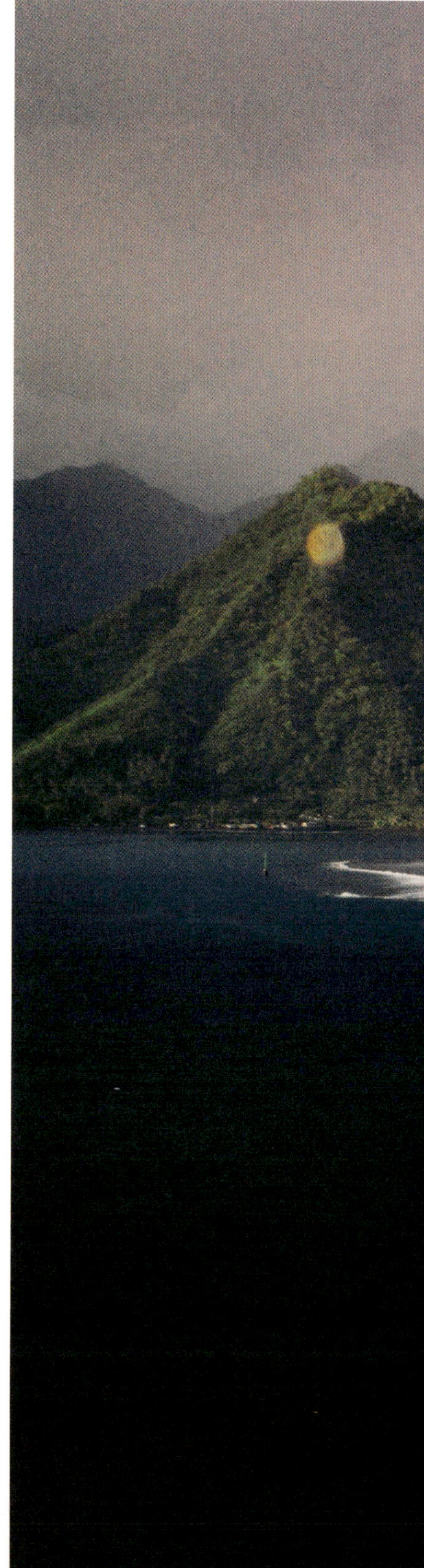

↑
**Teahupo'o, Tahiti,
French Polynesia**

Tyson Wheatley

→
**Teahupo'o, Tahiti,
French Polynesia**

Michael Goetze and
Jampal Williamson

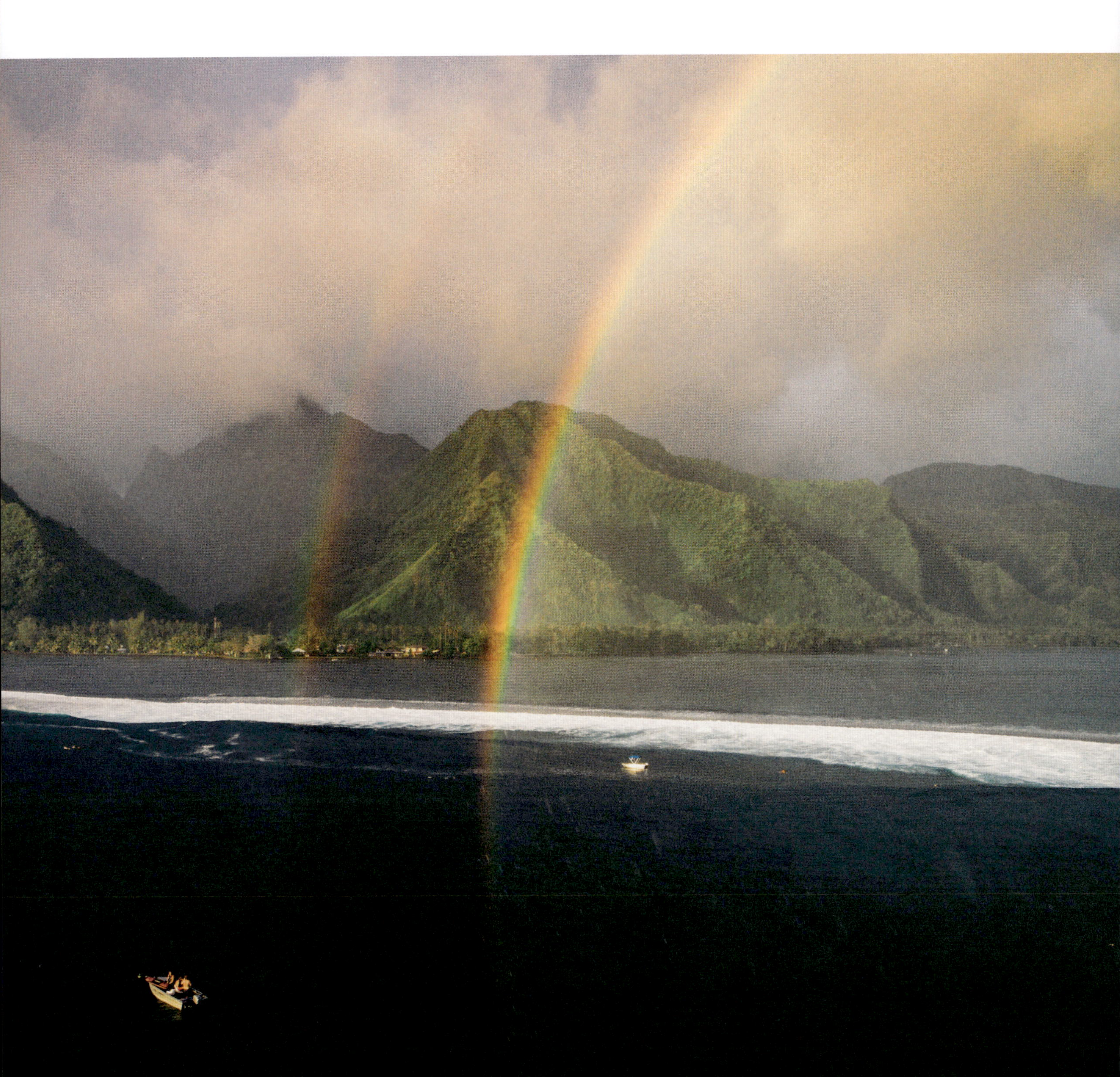

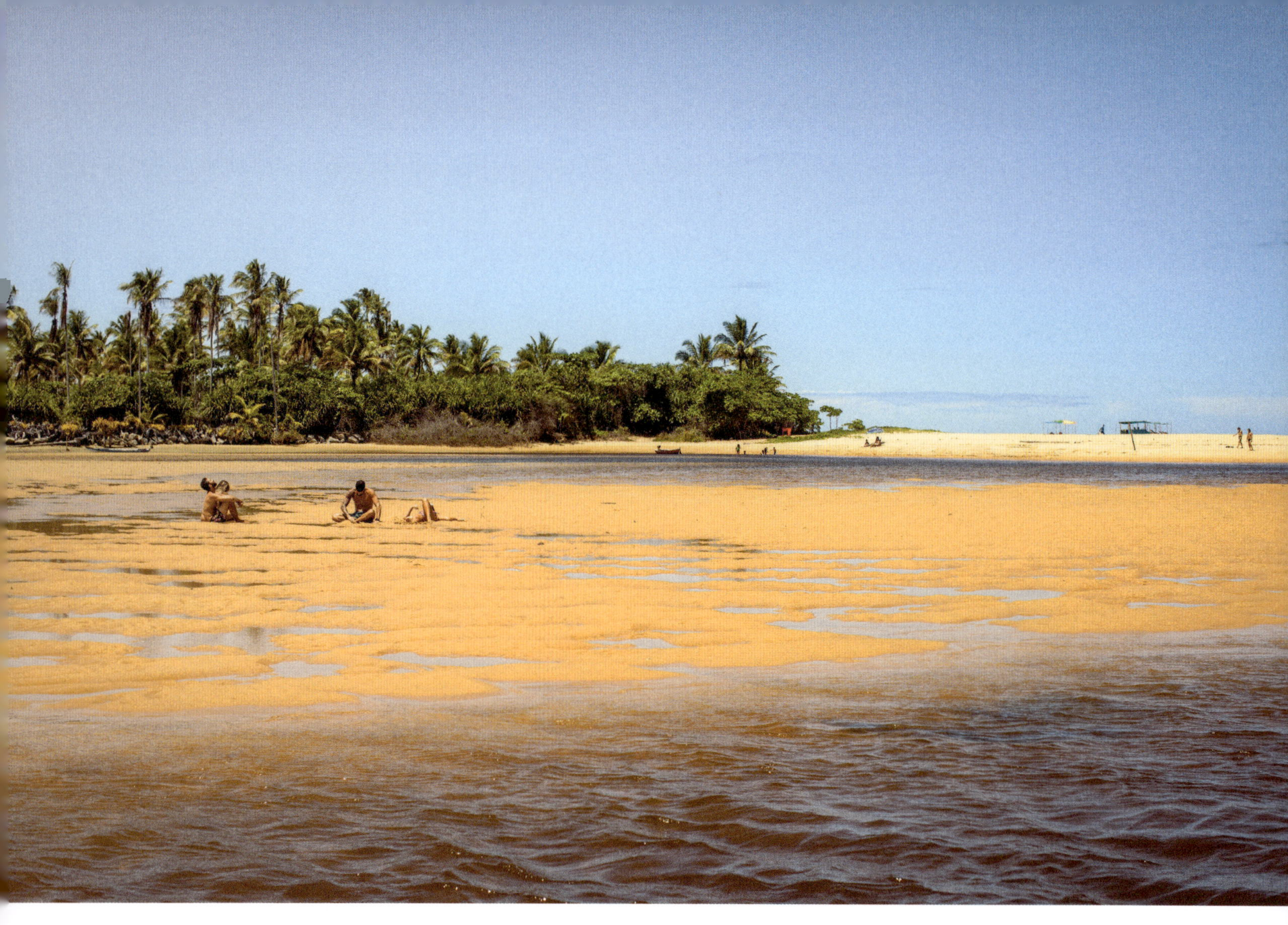

 day trip south from Trancoso that's well worth the hour-plus ride each way (in good weather) along a dirt road that ends at the Caraíva River. Everything and everyone heading into town from the north needs to cross the river in simple wooden boats. In Caraíva, the golden sand streets are lined with little shops and Amazonian tribal vendors selling their crafts, and simple restaurants hug the river. A unique beach scene pops up right where the Caraíva river spills into the warm Atlantic Ocean.

**Caraíva,
Bahia, Brazil**
Emily Nathan

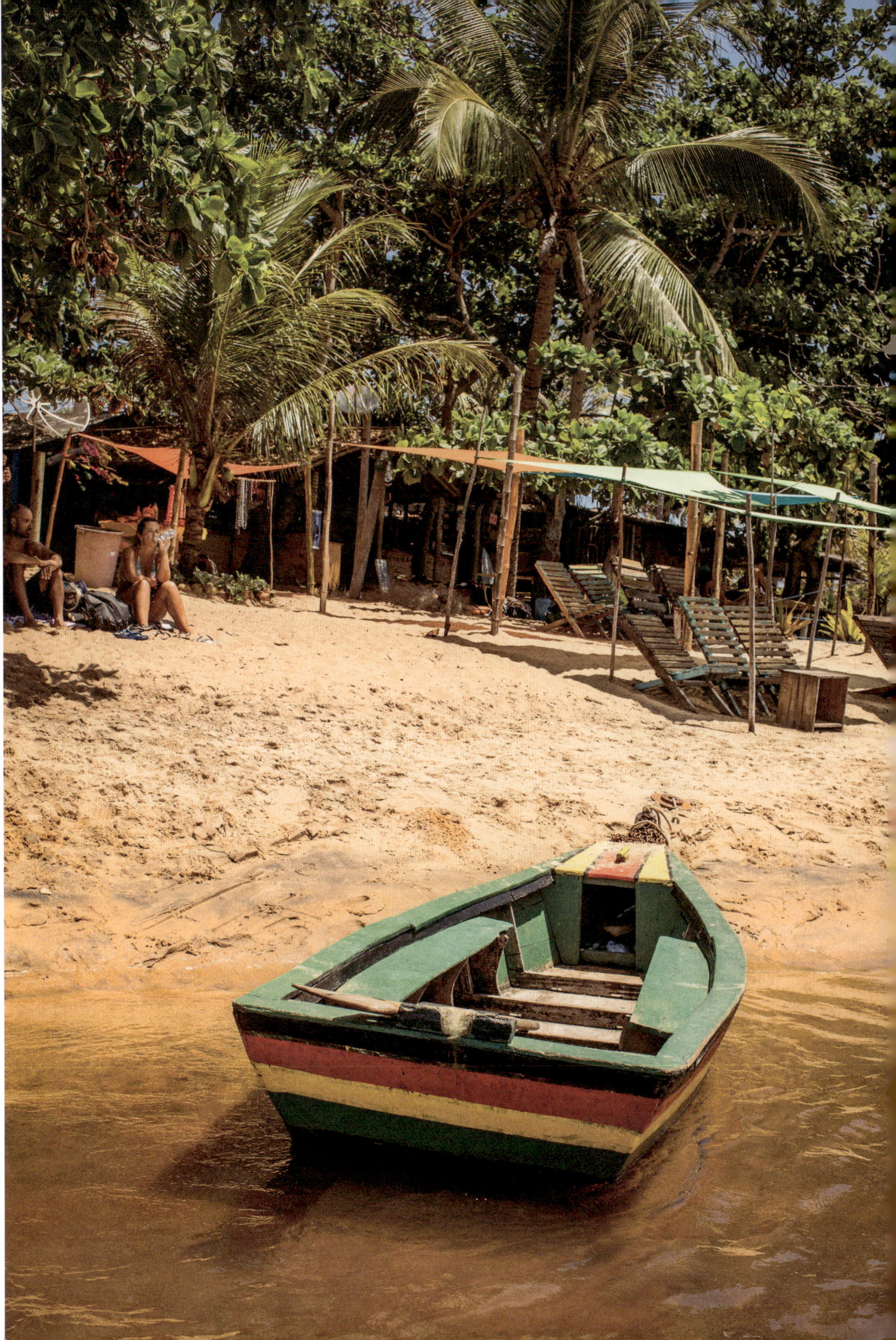

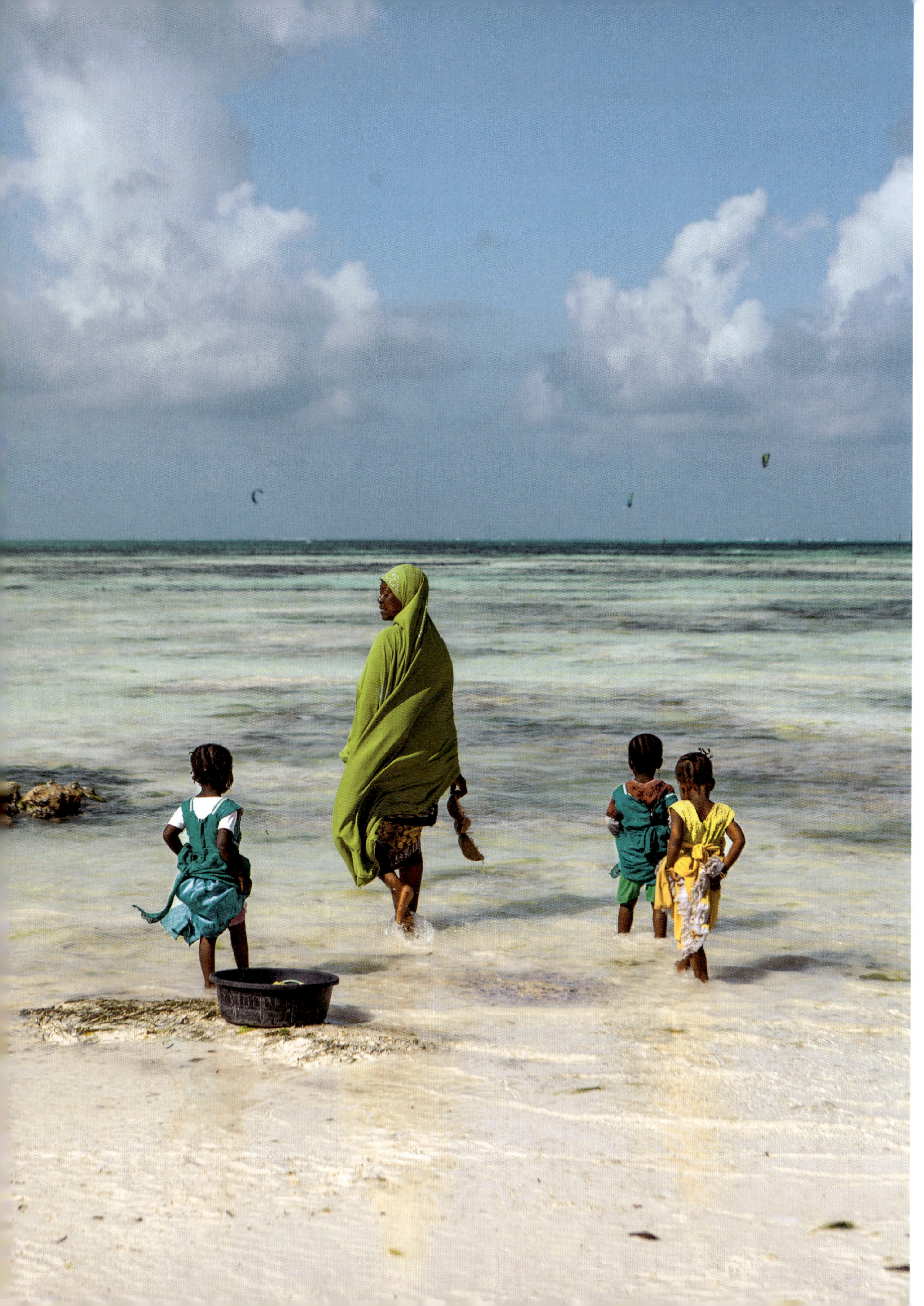

**Jambiani, Zanzibar,
Tanzania**

Wendy Hu

**Inoladoan Island,
Palawan, Philippines**

Raquel Guiu Grigelmo

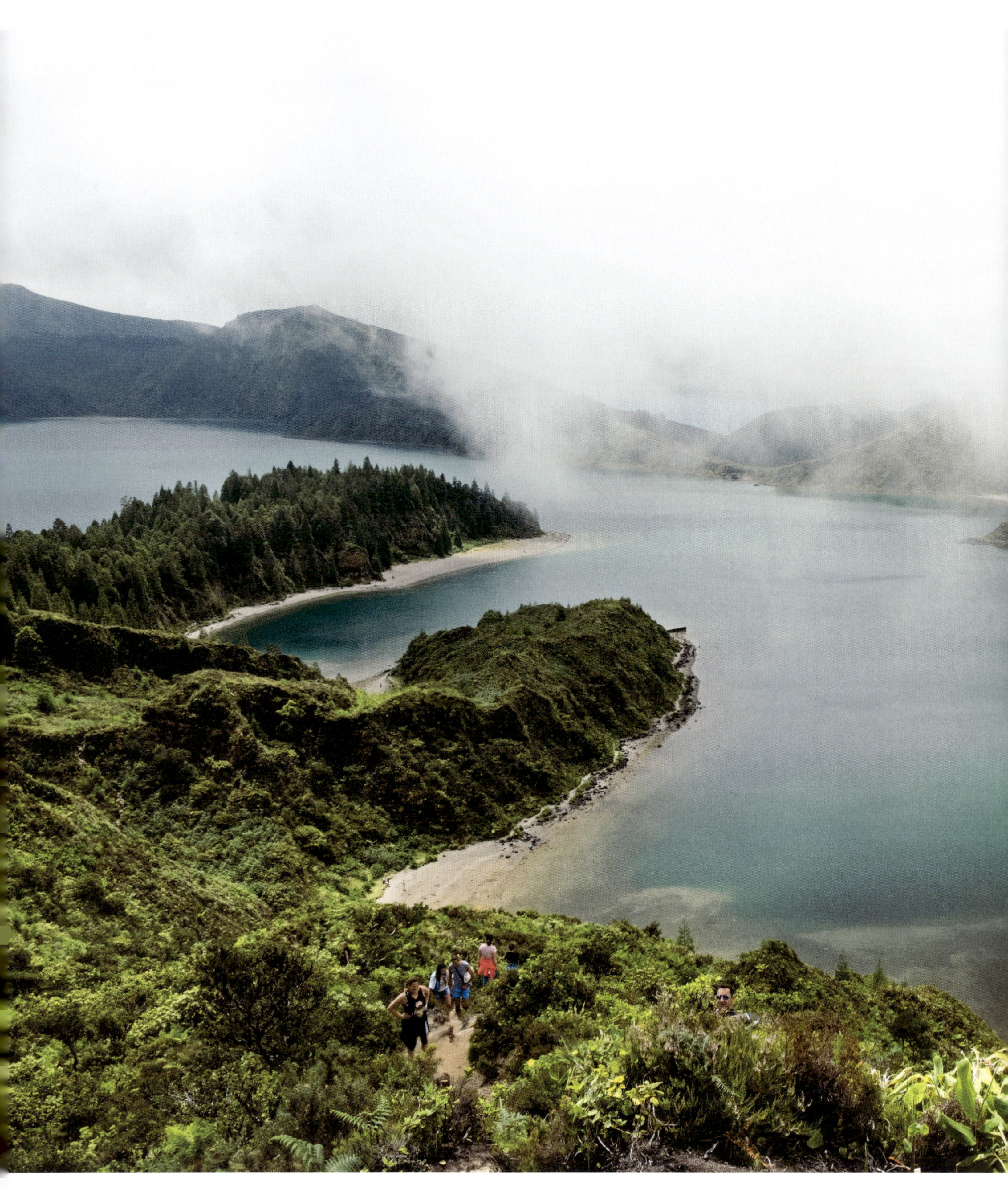

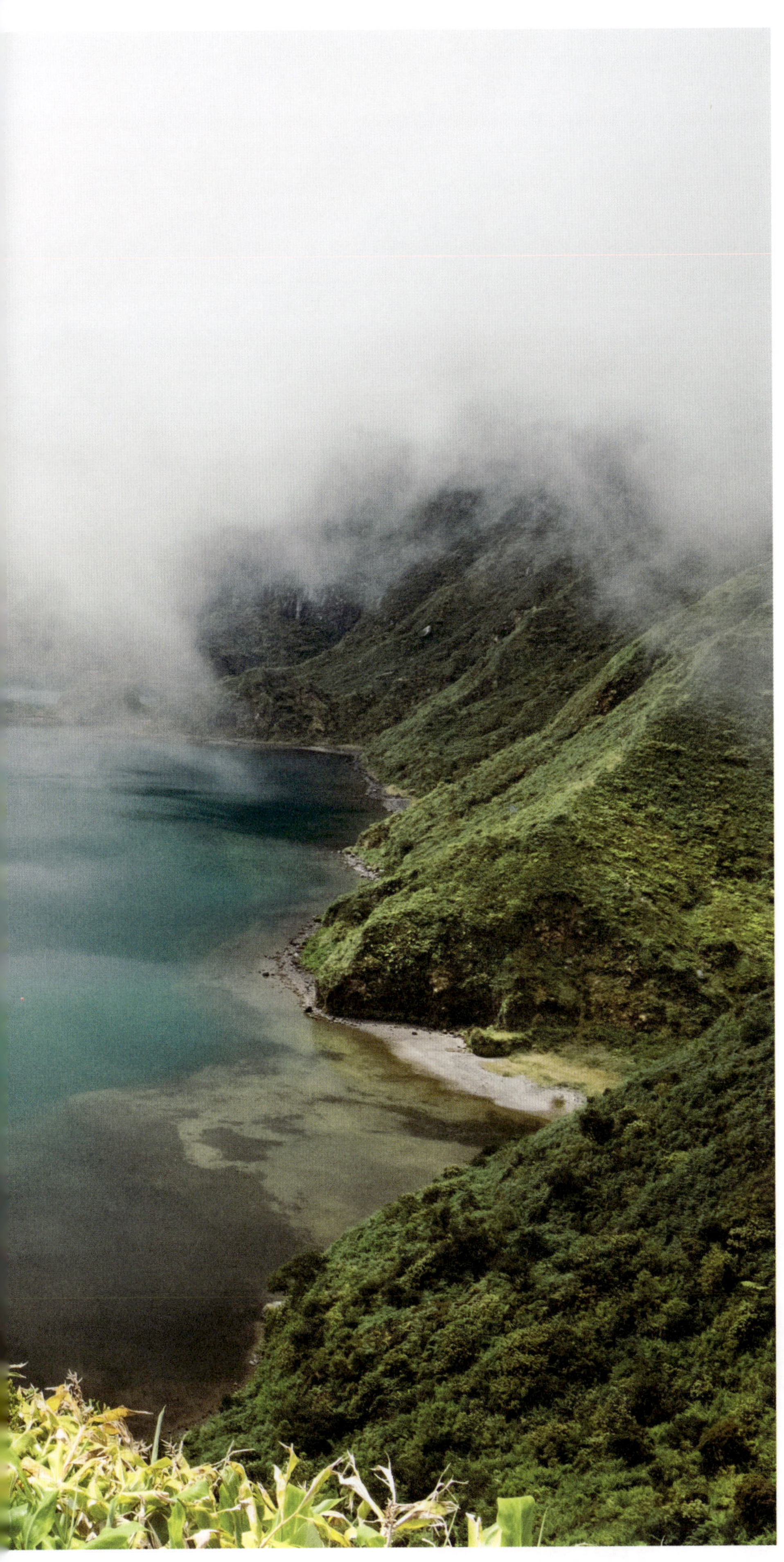

SÃO MIGUEL IS the largest and most populous island in the Azores, an autonomous archipelago of Portugal about 930 miles west of Lisbon in the middle of the Atlantic. Volcanic activity and its aftermath have carved out a wild landscape of verdant craters and lagoons. Sete Cidades ("Seven Cities") is a famous viewpoint and starting spot for a short walk, incredible for either a glowing sunset or a foggy stop.

**São Miguel,
Azores, Portugal**
Jessica Sample

The changing climate knows no borders or boundaries. Antarctica may seem like an icy wasteland, but it's crucial to recognize that it's actually a rich habitat that supports many animals such as penguins, whales, seals, and albatrosses. The animals that live in the Antarctic seabed are sensitive to even small-scale changes, so disruptions to the ecological balance create consequences that resonate across the food chain. Krill, for example, are tiny, shrimplike creatures that are highly dependent on sea ice. For them, sea ice is not only a shelter but also a major source of food; they eat the tiny organisms and algae that live on the ice itself. In recent years, ice in Antarctica has been melting at a rate six times higher than it was in the 1980s. This loss of sea ice has innumerable effects across the continent, including devastating the numbers of krill. They may be tiny, but krill are a keystone species and foundational to the ecosystem. They're an essential food source for many species such as migrating whales and resident seals, and their decline has ripple effects for wildlife across Antarctica.

Ice melt affects more than just local communities, as melting glaciers contribute to a rise in the global sea level. Take Kiribati—a tiny, tropical nation in the middle of the Pacific Ocean that's home to just over 100,000 people. While Kiribati is one of the most isolated places on the planet and produces only 0.6 percent of the world's emissions, it's deeply affected by climate change. Most of Kiribati's population lives on the shallow island of South Tarawa, which sits less than 3 meters above sea level. With climate change accelerating ice melt, Kiribati is losing its landmass, including populated areas, to rising seas. For many of us, places like Antarctica or Kiribati may feel remote and distant, but it's critical to recognize that what we do has implications for even the most remote places.

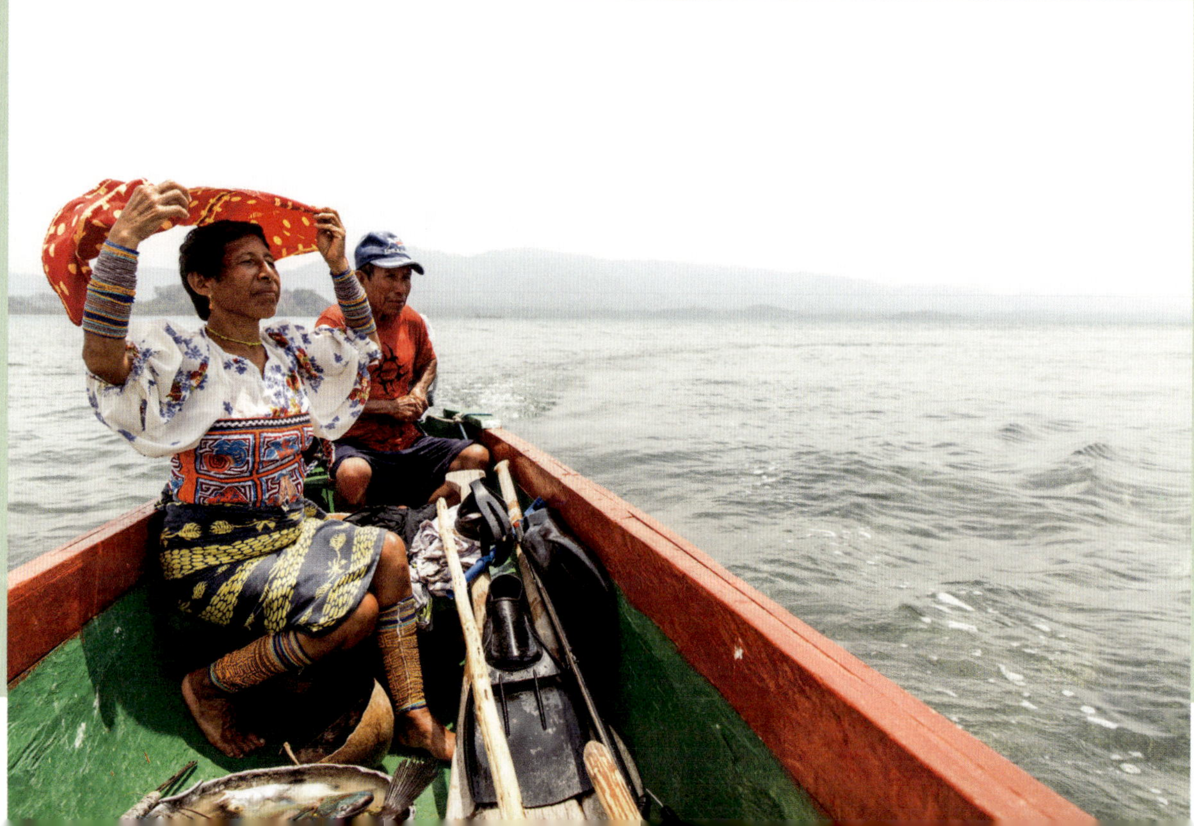

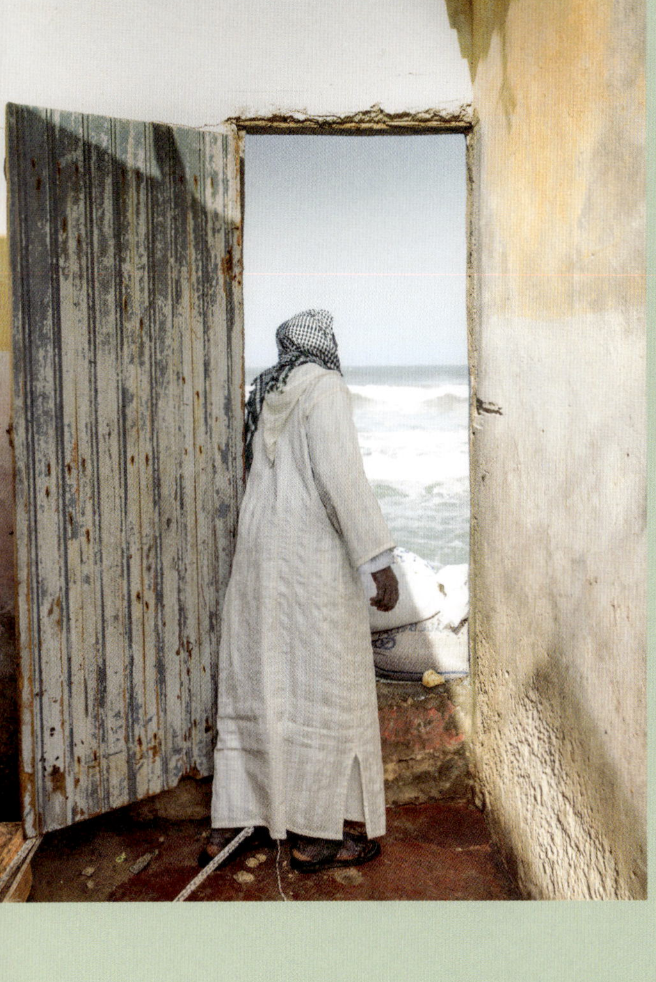

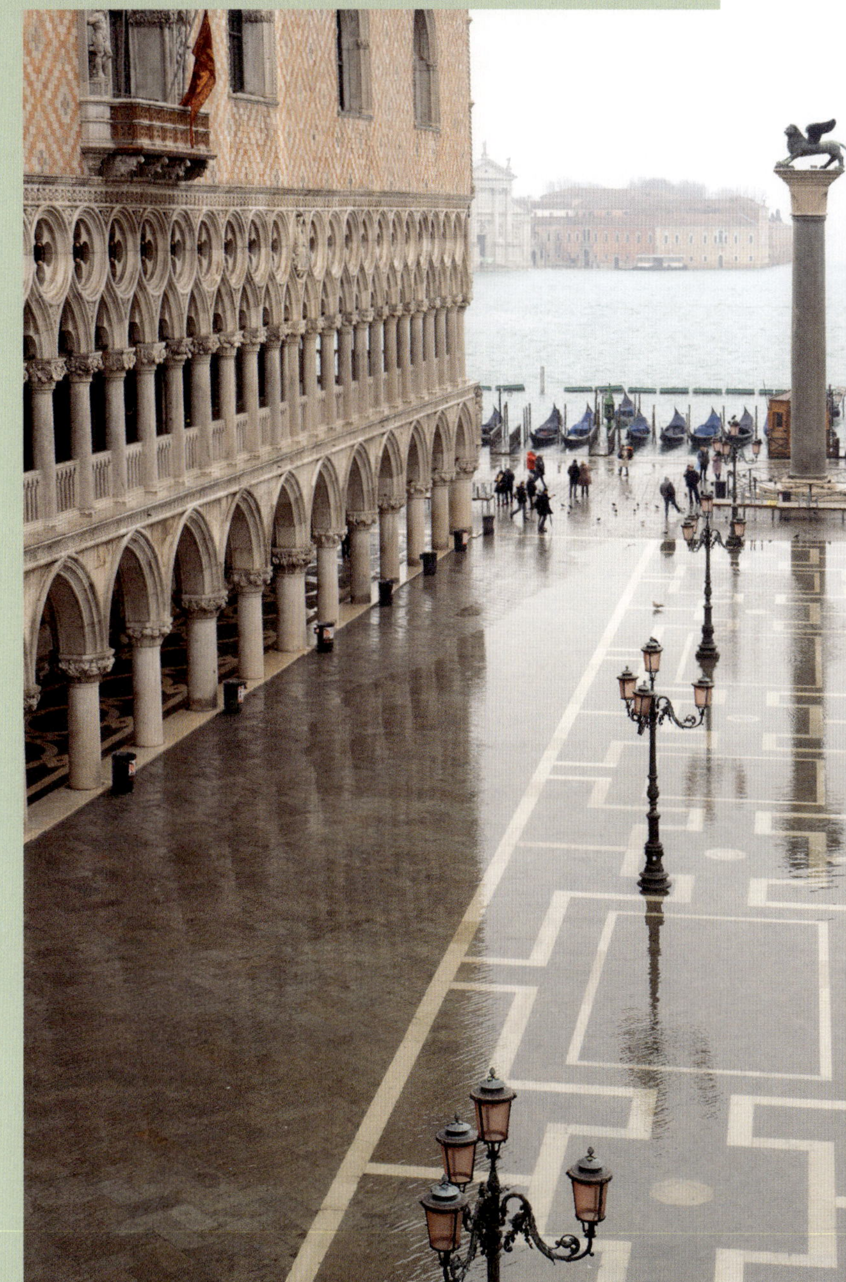

↑
**Guet Ndar,
Saint-Louis
Region, Senegal**
Greta Rybus

→
Venice, Italy
Cécile Herlet Molinié

←
**Guna Yala,
Panama**
Greta Rybus

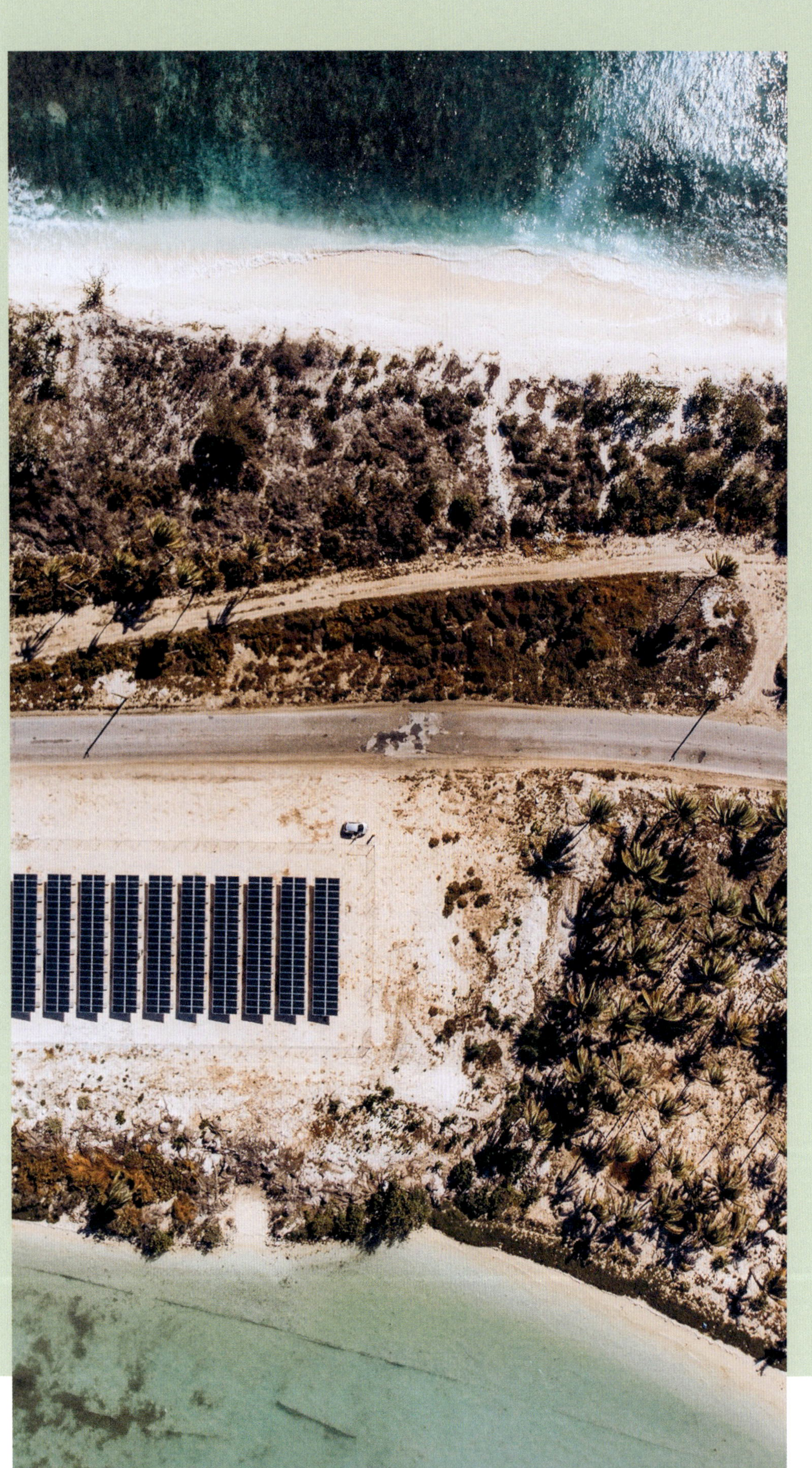

←
**Kiritimati Island,
Kiribati**
Natasha Holland

↑
**Betio Causeway,
South Tarawa, Kiribati**
Natasha Holland

↗
**Gardi Sugdub,
Panama**
Greta Rybus

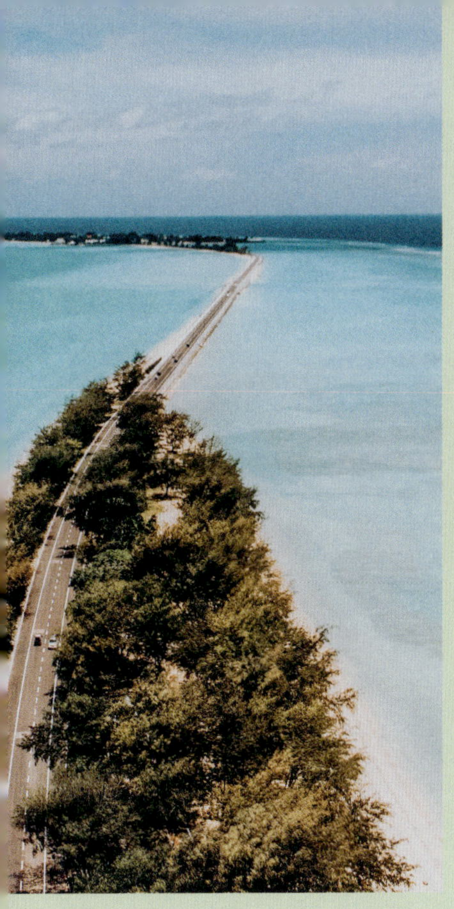

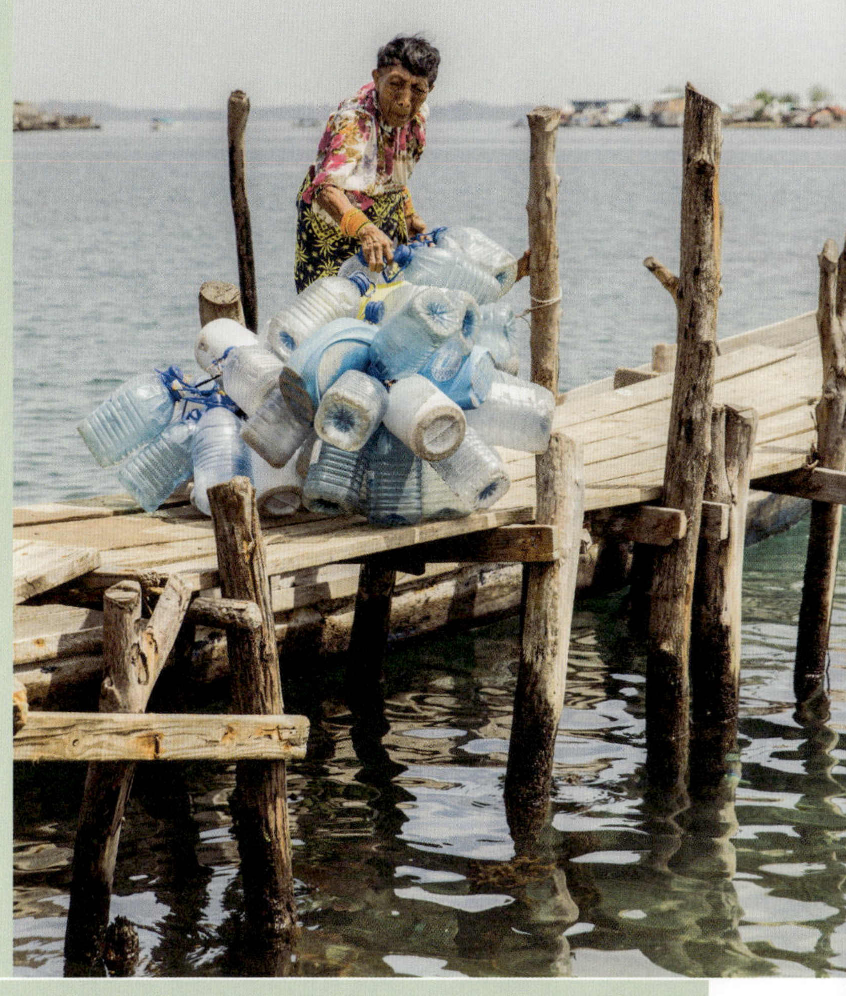

HOW YOU CAN HELP

- Buy used or recycled items whenever possible; start composting your kitchen scraps to reduce waste, or implement strategies to make your home more energy efficient. Small reductions in carbon production help slow the chain of events contributing to rising seas. (For additional ways you can reduce your carbon footprint, see "How You Can Help" on page 167.)

- Write to your representatives in local, state, and federal offices to support legislative initiatives on environmental protections to reduce your community's contribution to carbon emissions.

- Displaced residents from natural disasters are climate refugees, and unfortunately, there is currently no international law to recognize or protect these people. You can support organizations working to raise awareness and relocate people displaced by natural disasters. The Borgen Project currently has online resources on how to connect with these organizations.

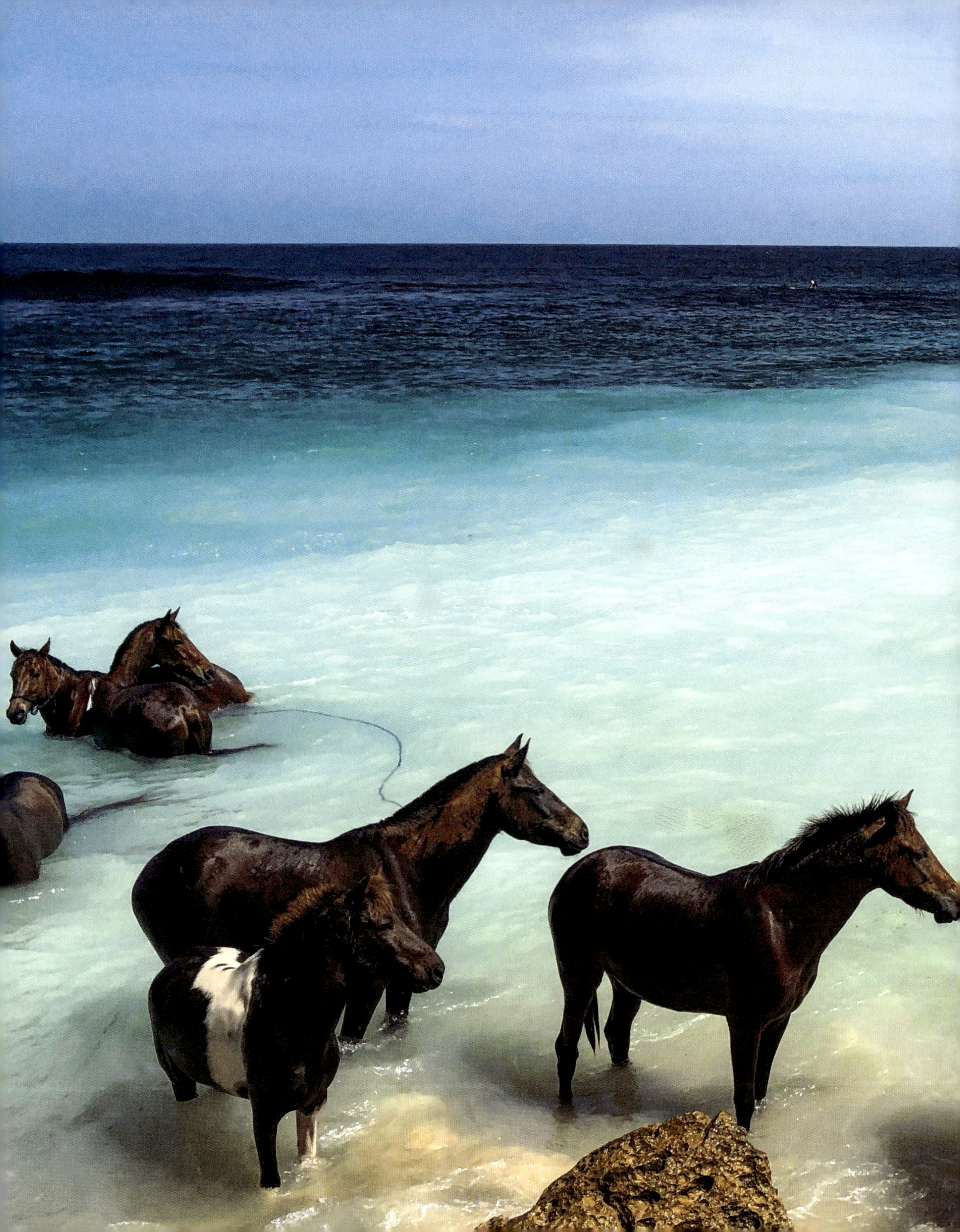

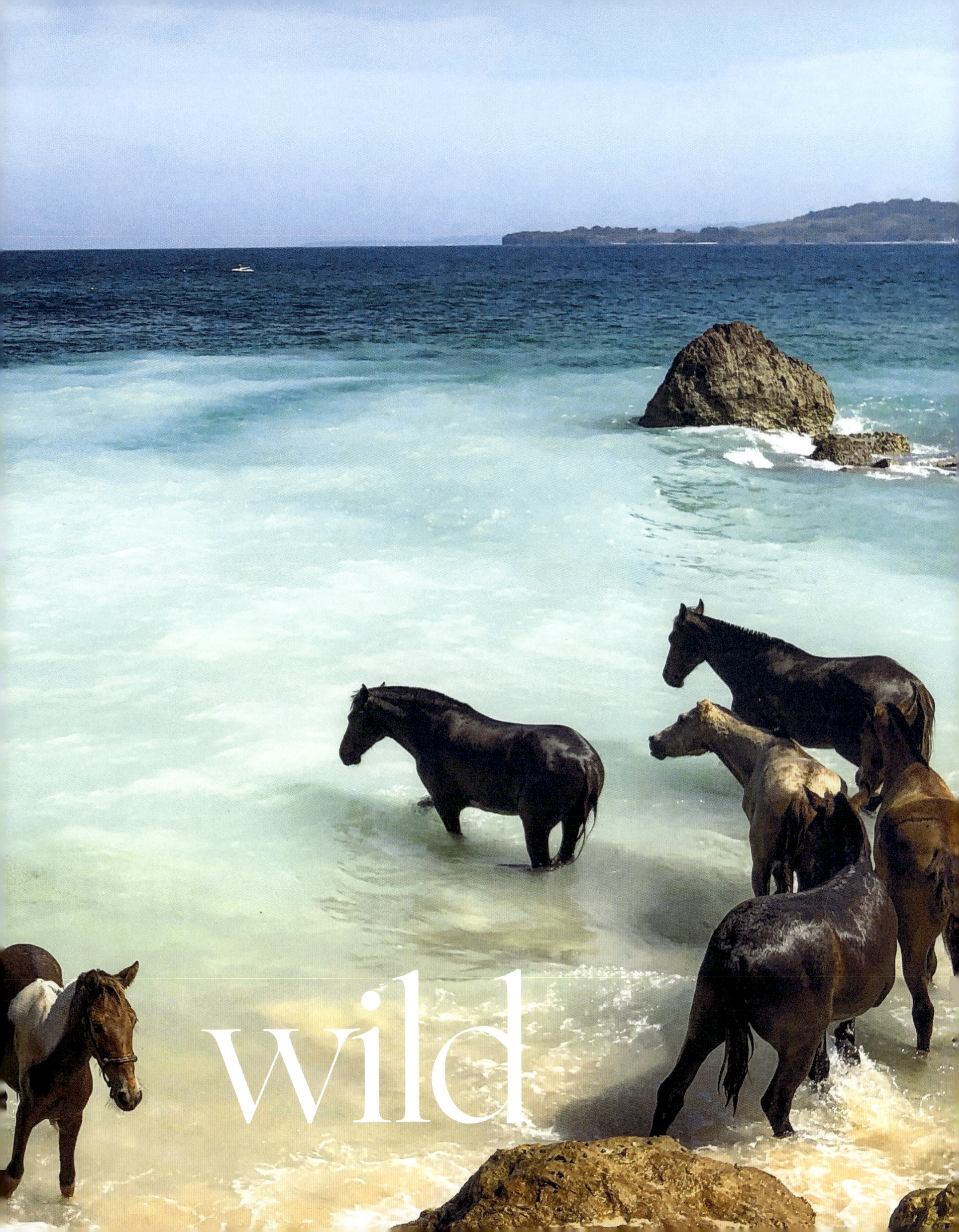
wild

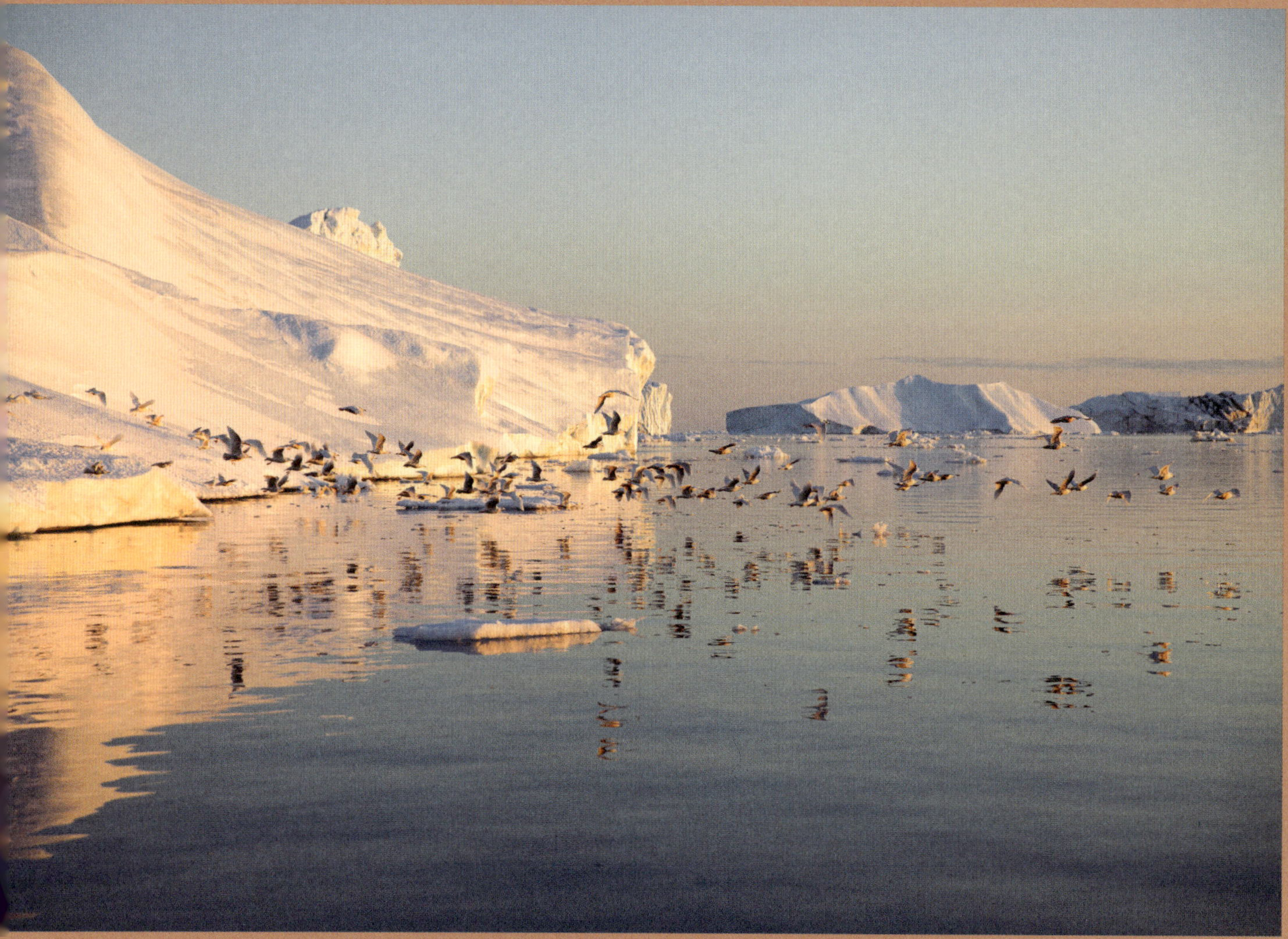

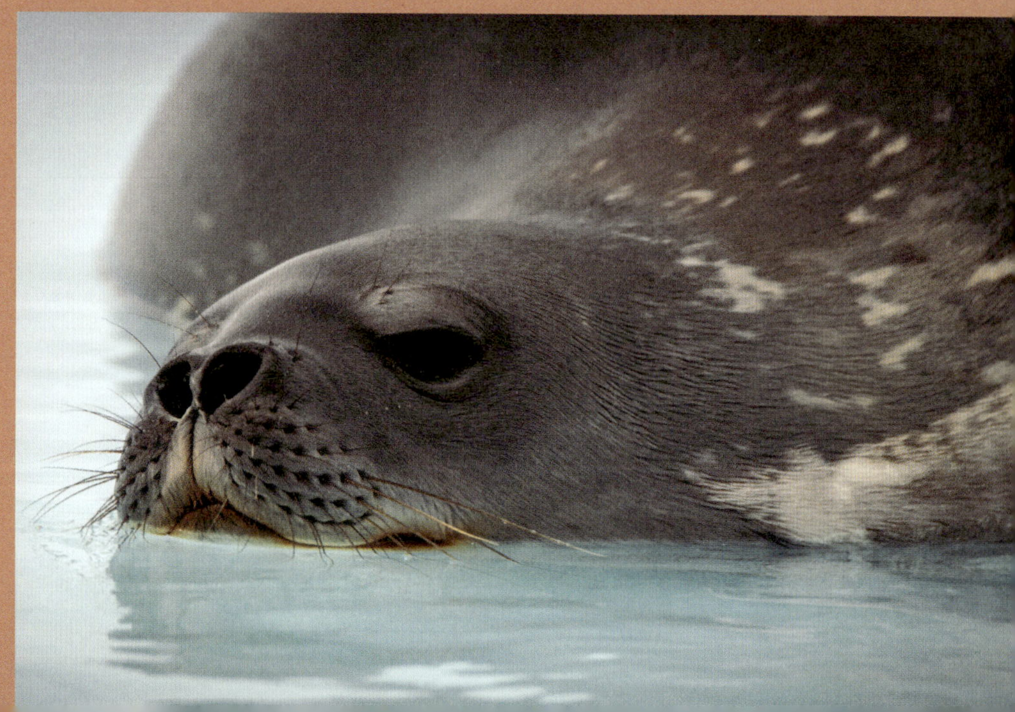

← One hour's flight from Bali, native Sandalwood horses arrive each morning for a swim in this shockingly blue water out front at NIHI Sumba, a sustainable hotel in Indonesia legendary with surfers.

Sumba Island, East Nusa Tenggara, Indonesia
Julien Laracine

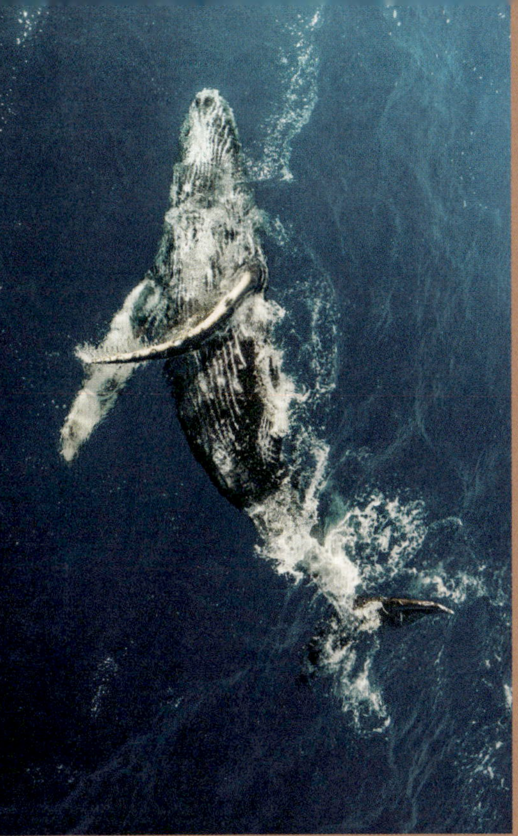

ON THE OCEAN, we are surrounded by life: the birds above, the marine mammals meeting our gaze at the surface, and all the fish and invertebrates below. And yet, even while humans share this planet with countless living species, we tend to focus our attention on ourselves. Our lives, our personal struggles and successes, dominate our thoughts. However, our experiences within wild landscapes and with the creatures that make their homes there can relieve us from our fixation on ourselves and replace it with feelings of joy and childlike wonder.

Kim Goodwin, a wildlife photographer, is devoted to practicing the delicate balance of photographing wildlife while respecting their habitat. In her experience, the best images most often come after waiting quietly for long stretches of time in the same spot and capturing an authentic or unexpected moment for which it's not possible to create a plan. What we see in the images throughout this chapter reflects our desire as humans to immerse ourselves within an environmental landscape where the absence of human development is celebrated, even while we feel the bittersweet irony of our presence there.

On the Pacific Coast of Mexico, I once had the opportunity to watch as newly hatched baby Golfina turtles made their way to the sea. It was sunrise, and the turtles left miniature flipper tracks across the smooth, warm sand, imprinting their geological location for a lifetime as they crossed the beach that one time. I felt uncontained joy, a broad smile on my face, as I witnessed these tiny creatures in their first adventure of many in their lifetime. I knew some might not make it while others could live a hundred years or more, gliding through many thousands of miles of ocean, and returning back to this exact shore during their mating years. Setting off without technology or baggage, these fellow planet travelers were a marvel to me as I spent those few moments with them before they reached the ocean. I sent them off with best wishes and watched in astonishment as they carried their tiny, shelled backs over the white foam, were knocked upside down, and then righted up again by their flippers. They were hardly more perceptible than leaves as they floated off on that wild and incredible sea.

↑
**Maui, Hawai'i,
United States**
Stefan Elmer

↖
**Ilulissat, Avannaata,
Greenland**
Jessie Brinkman Evans

←
**Cuverville Island,
Antarctica**
Kim Goodwin

LA TORTUGA VIVA ("The Living Turtle") is
a sea turtle sanctuary right next to Playa
Viva, a small sustainable hotel property
south of Mexico's west coast beach town
of Zihuatanejo. The sanctuary is part of a
movement in Mexico to restore the numbers
of endangered sea turtles who use the soft
coastal sands to make their nests. Local
volunteers from the neighboring town of
Juluchuca search the beach each night
for the buried nests of green (Golfina) and
leatherback turtles. Once the nests are found
and unearthed, the volunteers relocate the
eggs to a pen safe from local predators
whose populations have gone unchecked.
When the turtle eggs hatch, the volunteers
(and lucky guests at nearby Playa Viva)
carefully bring the babies back to the sand
their mothers buried them in and release
them. The tiny turtles take their first flipper
steps out to the rushing surf and imprint
the beach's location as they go, using what
scientists think is a magnetic field super sense.
The females will return to these same coasts
to make their own nests seven to ten years
later and continue to return throughout their
breeding years.

**Zihuatanejo,
Guerrero, Mexico**
Emily Nathan

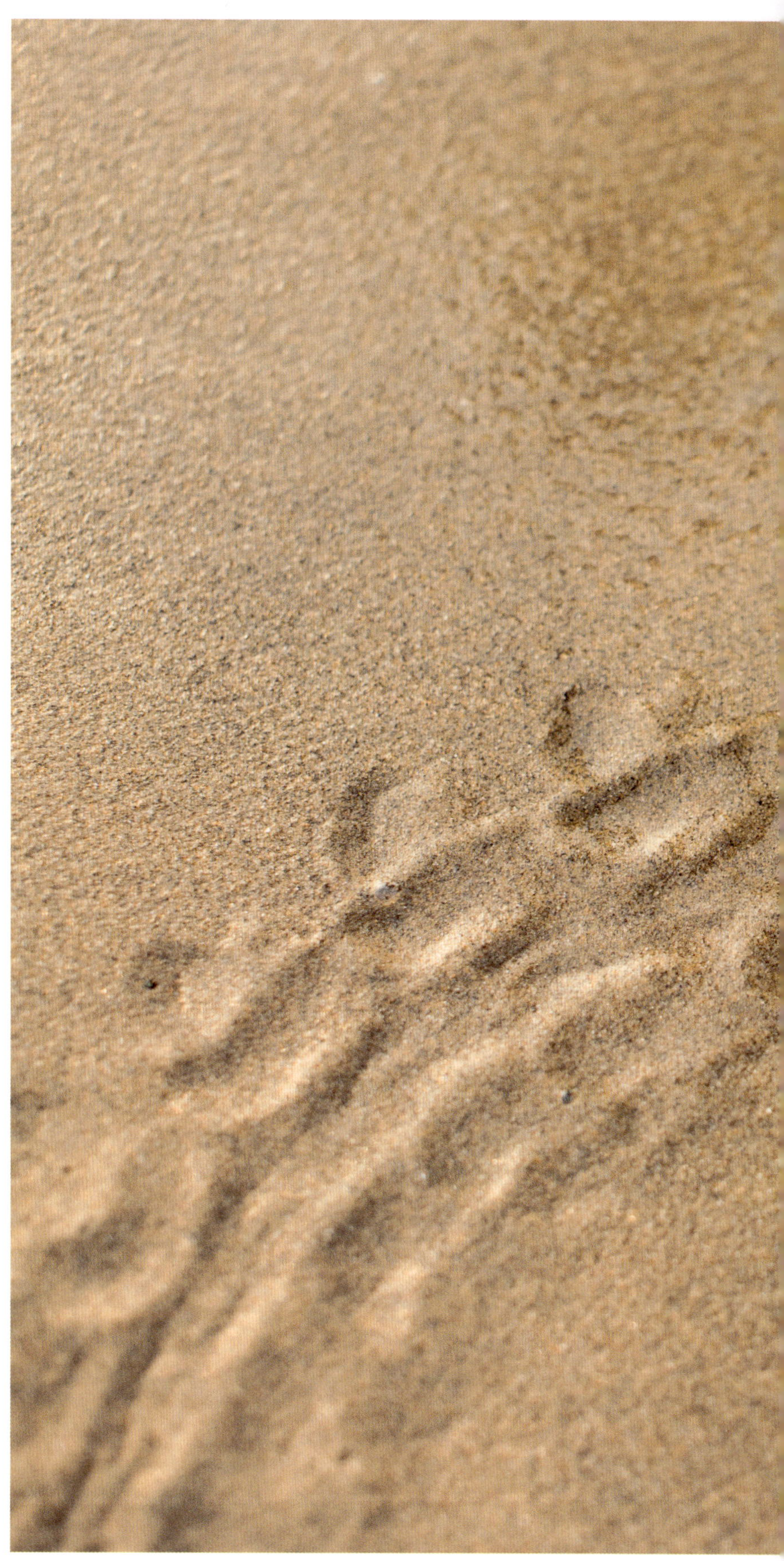

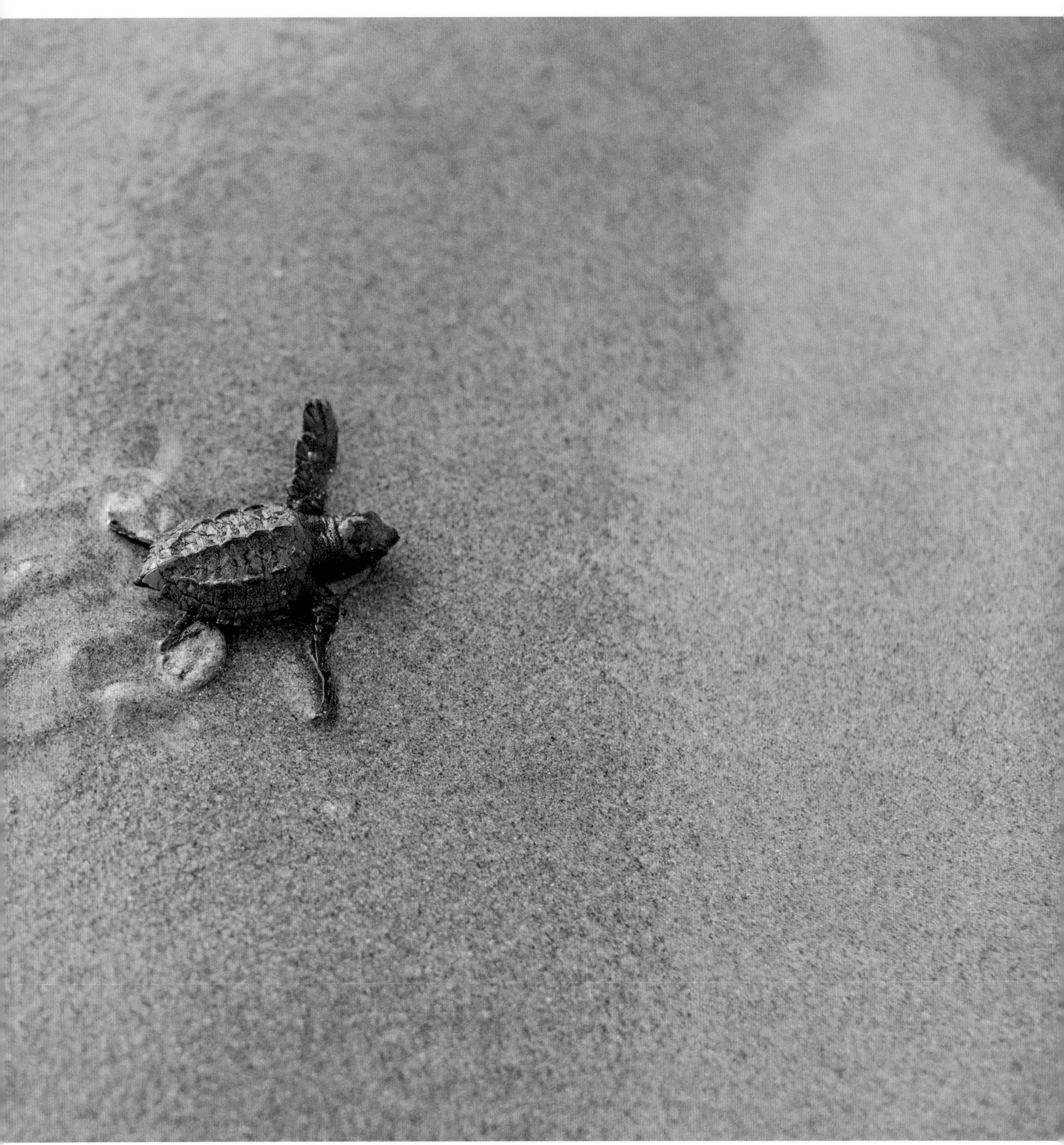

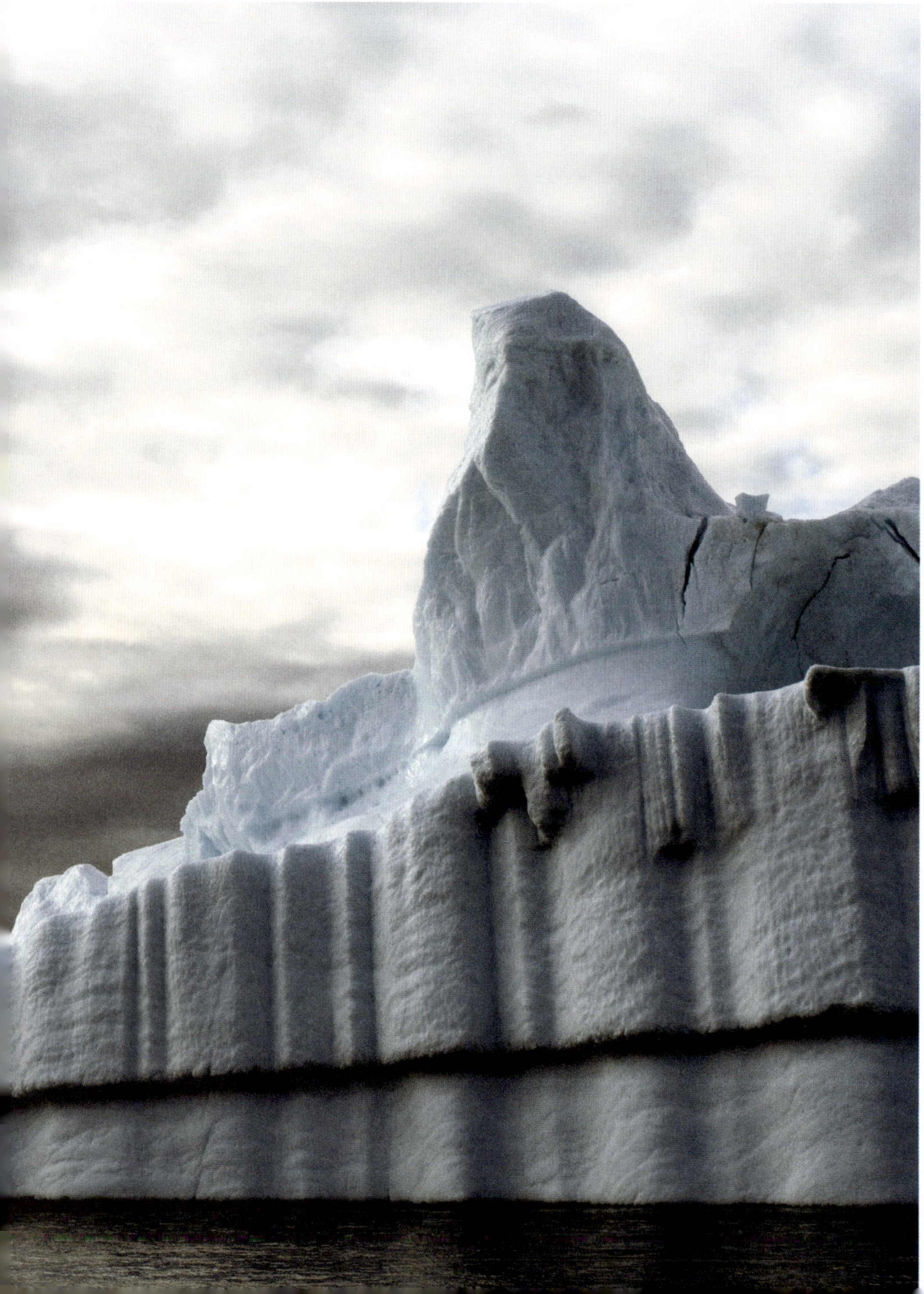

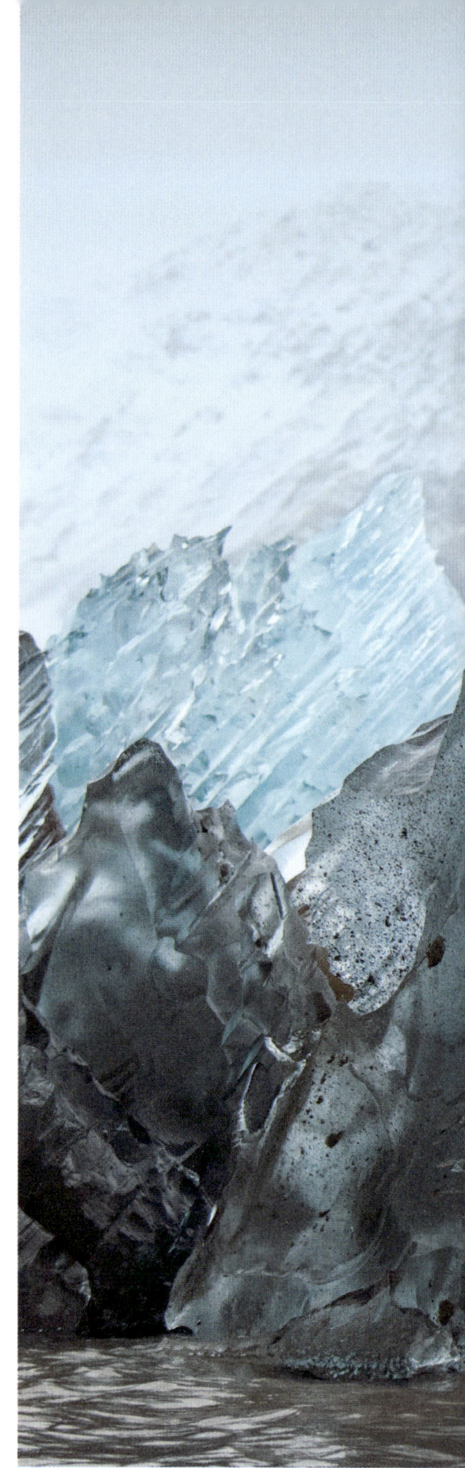

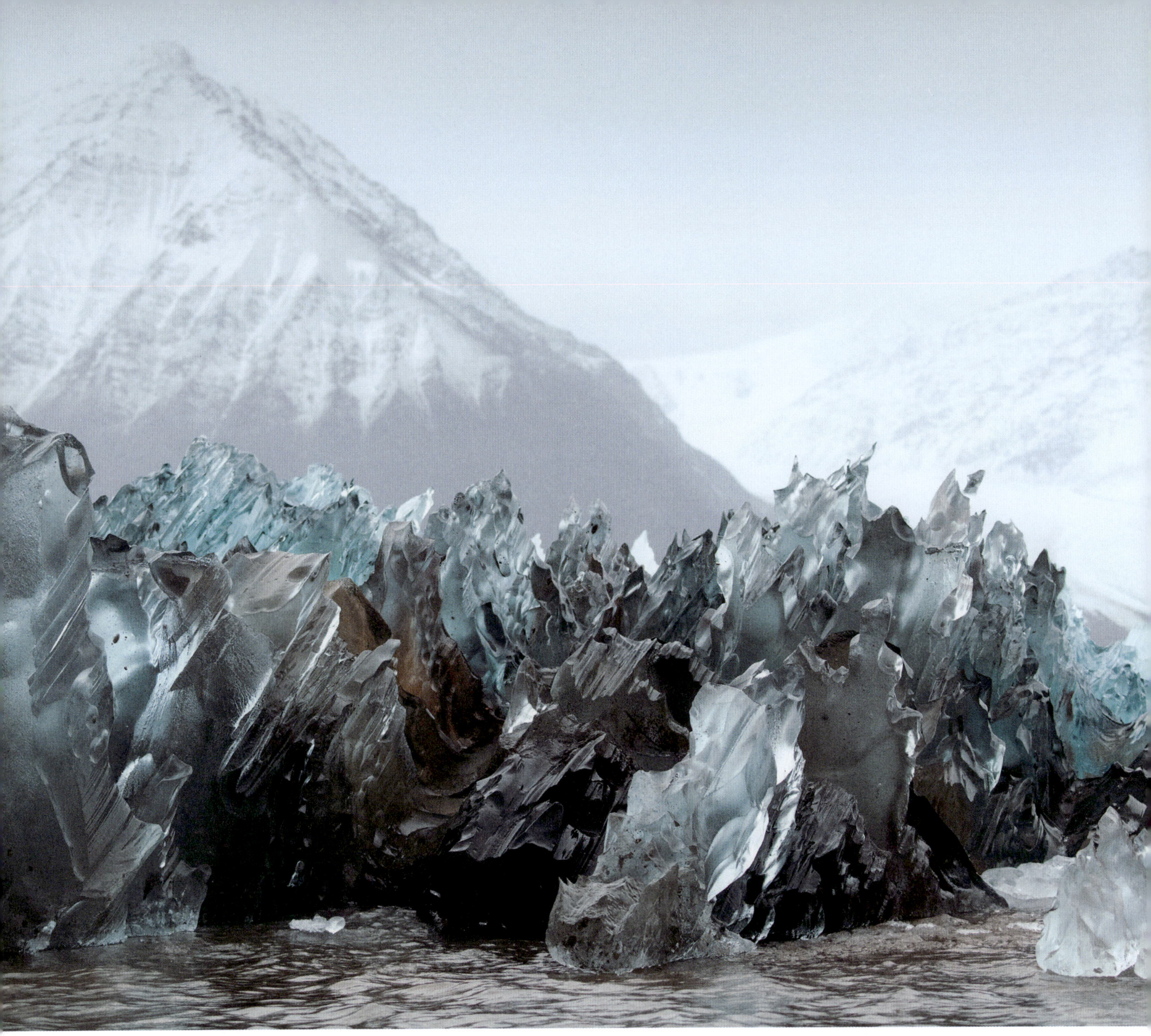

←

**Kulusuk, Sermersooq,
Greenland**

Natalia Horinkova

↑

**Kongsfjorden,
Spitsbergen, Arctic
Ocean, Norway**

Kim Goodwin

↓
**Spitsbergen,
Arctic Ocean, Norway**

Kim Goodwin

→
**Mo'orea,
French Polynesia**

Stefan Elmer

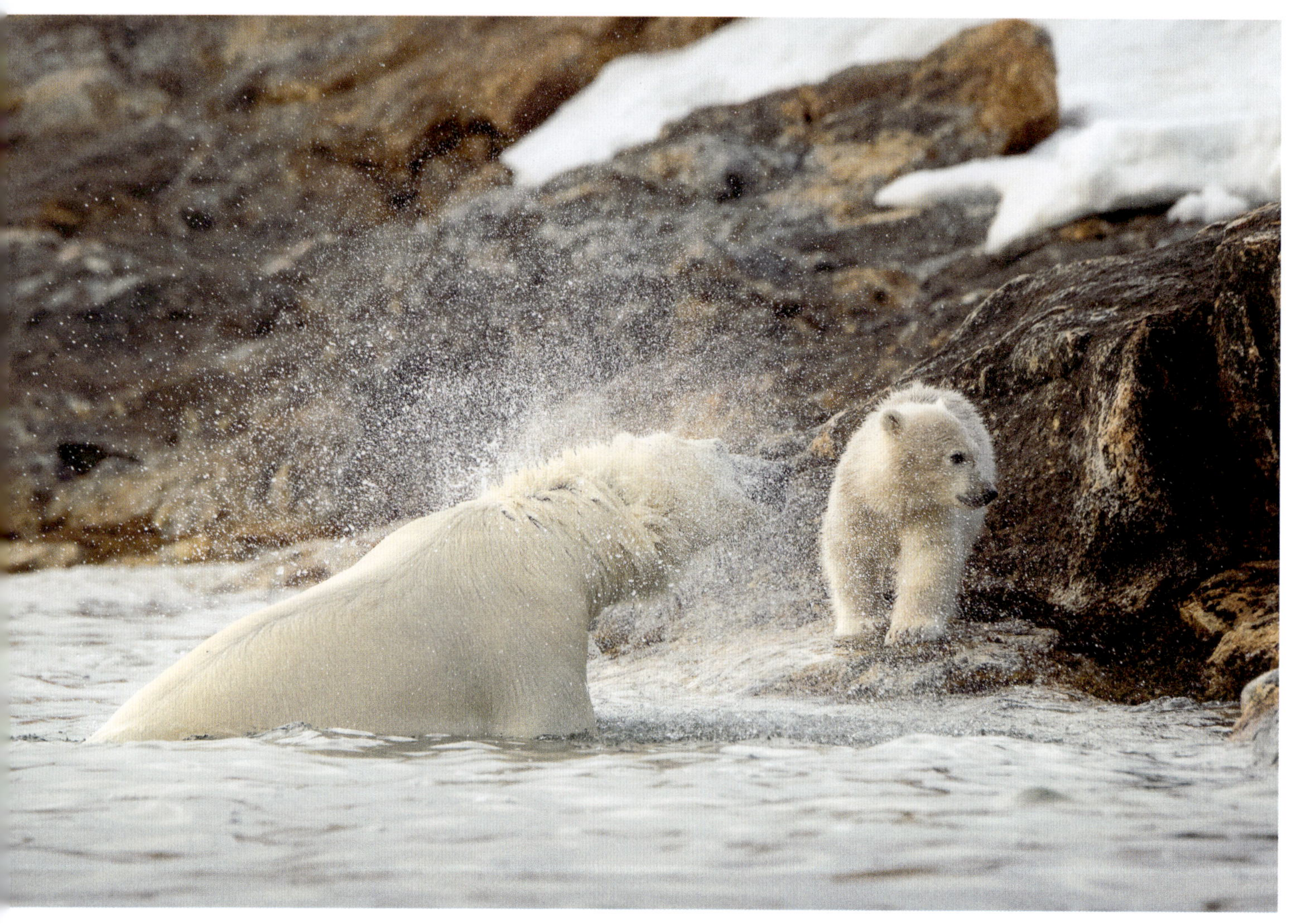

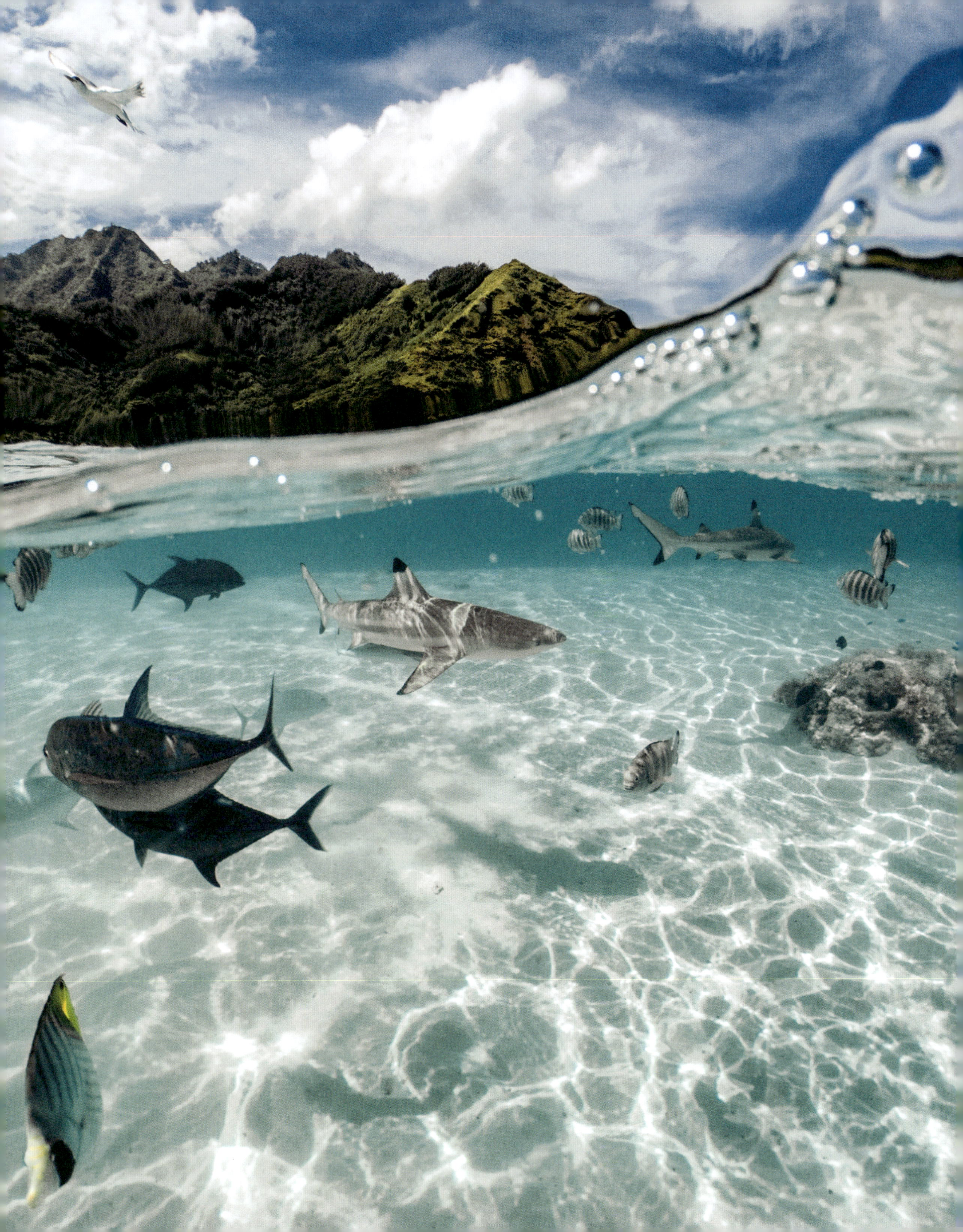

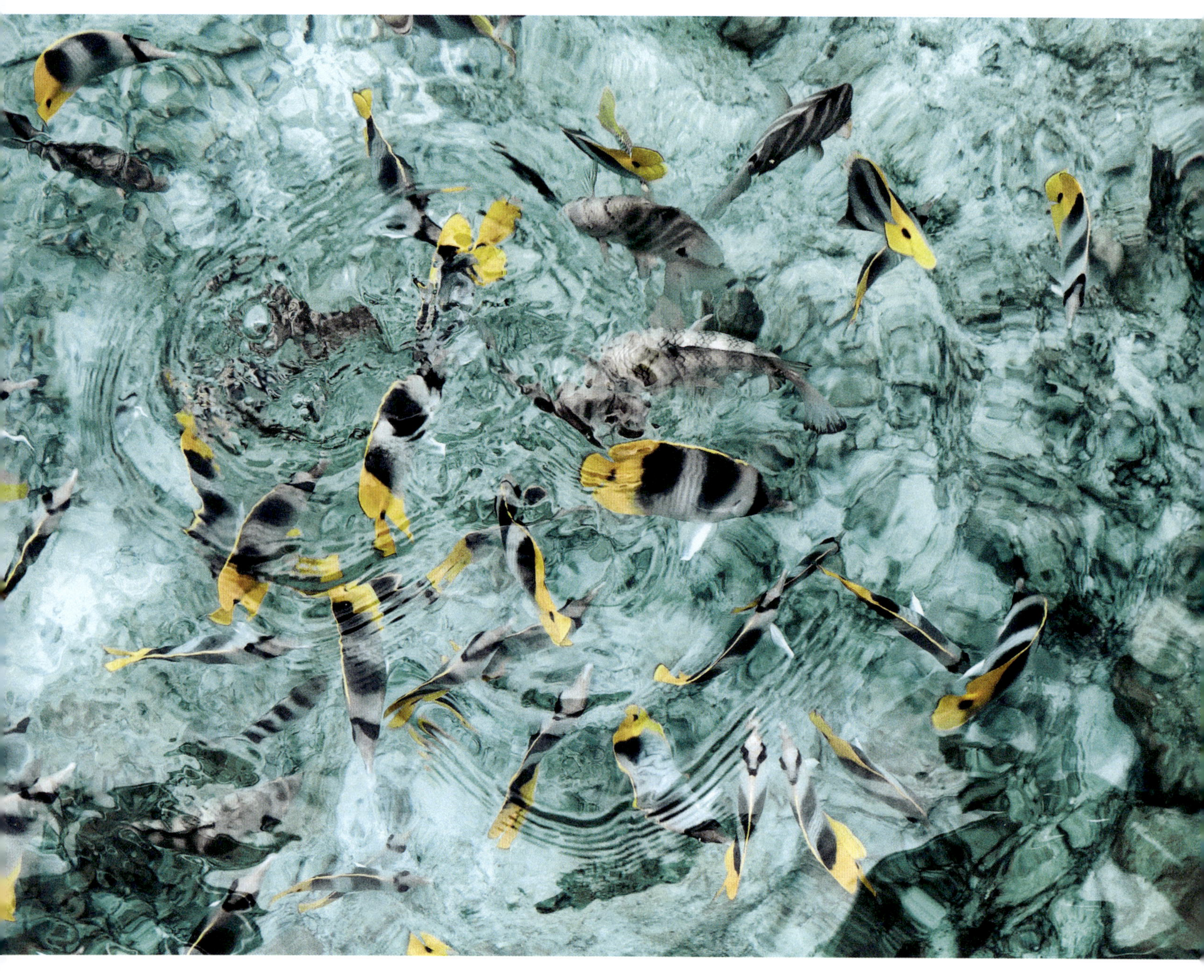

← **Bora Bora,
French Polynesia**
Zeynep Artuk

↓ **Prince William
Sound, Alaska,
United States**
Nels Evangelista

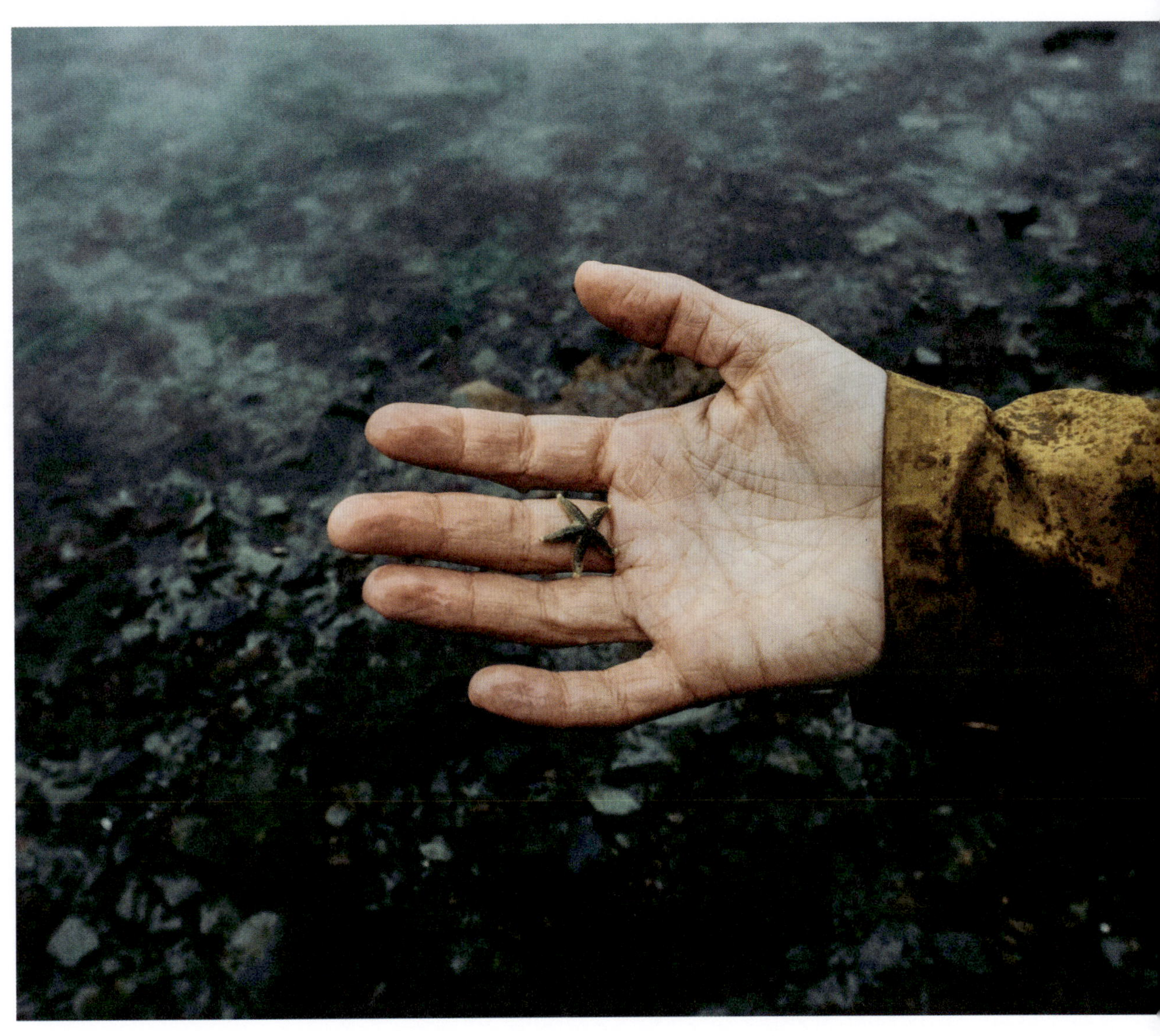

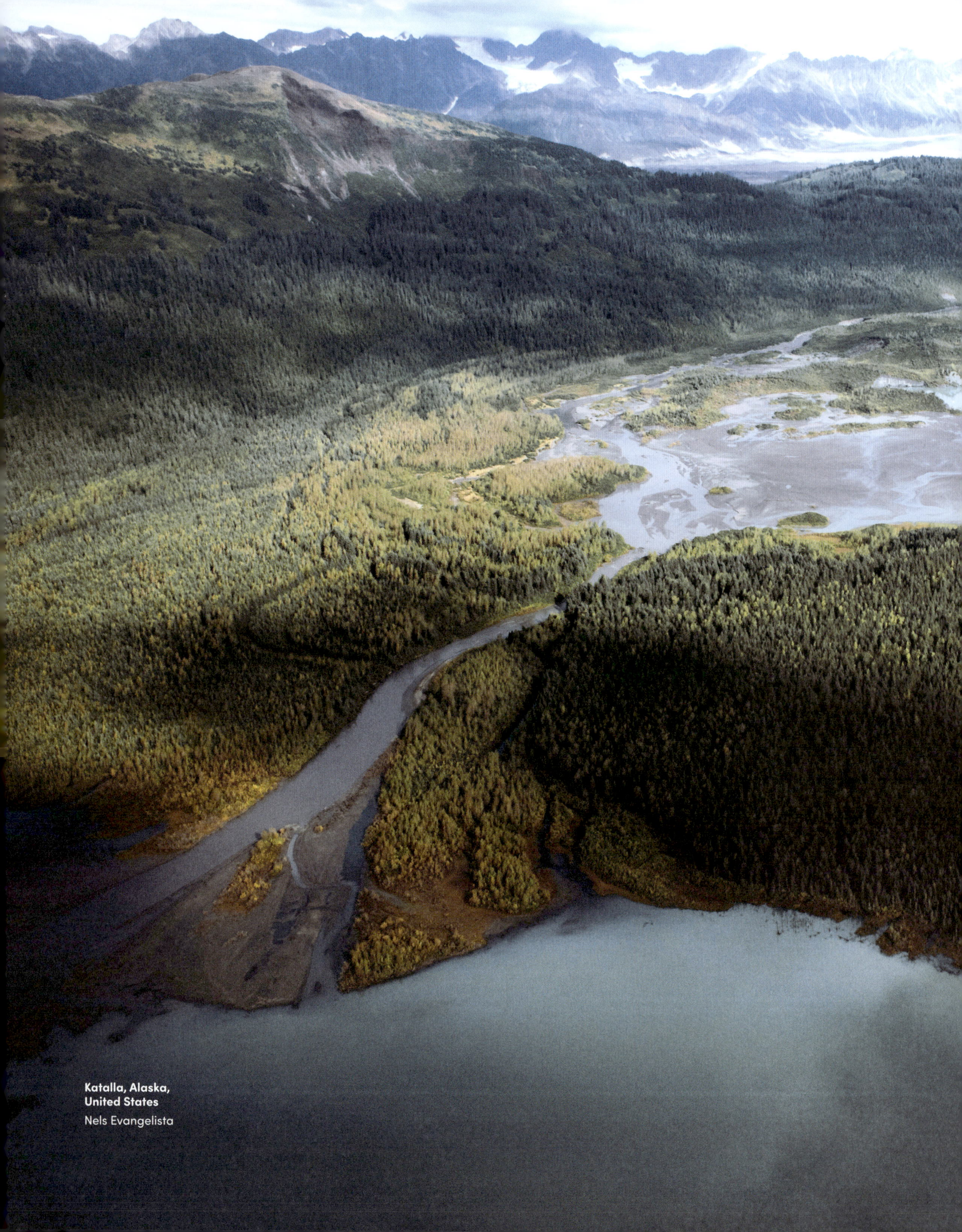

Katalla, Alaska,
United States
Nels Evangelista

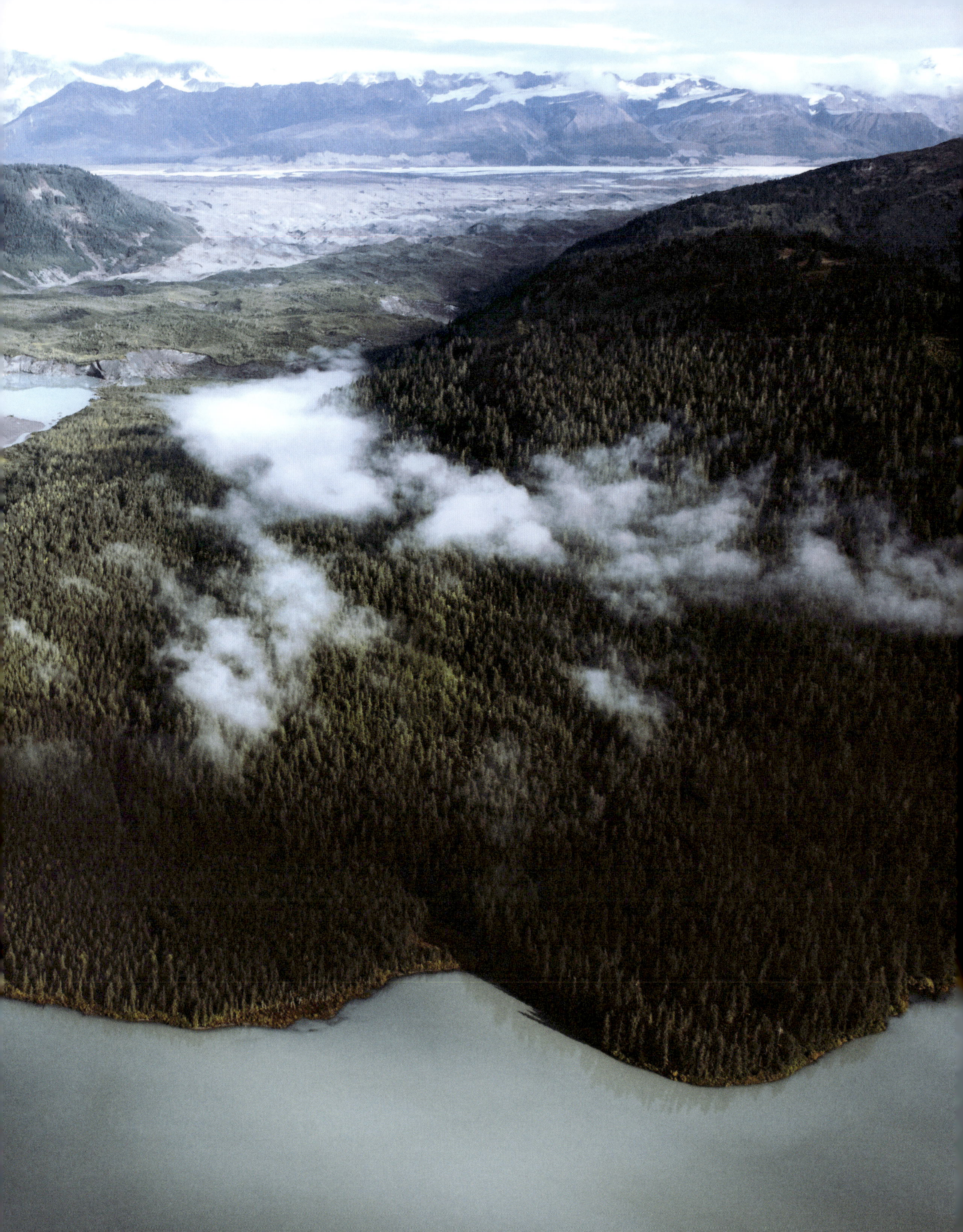

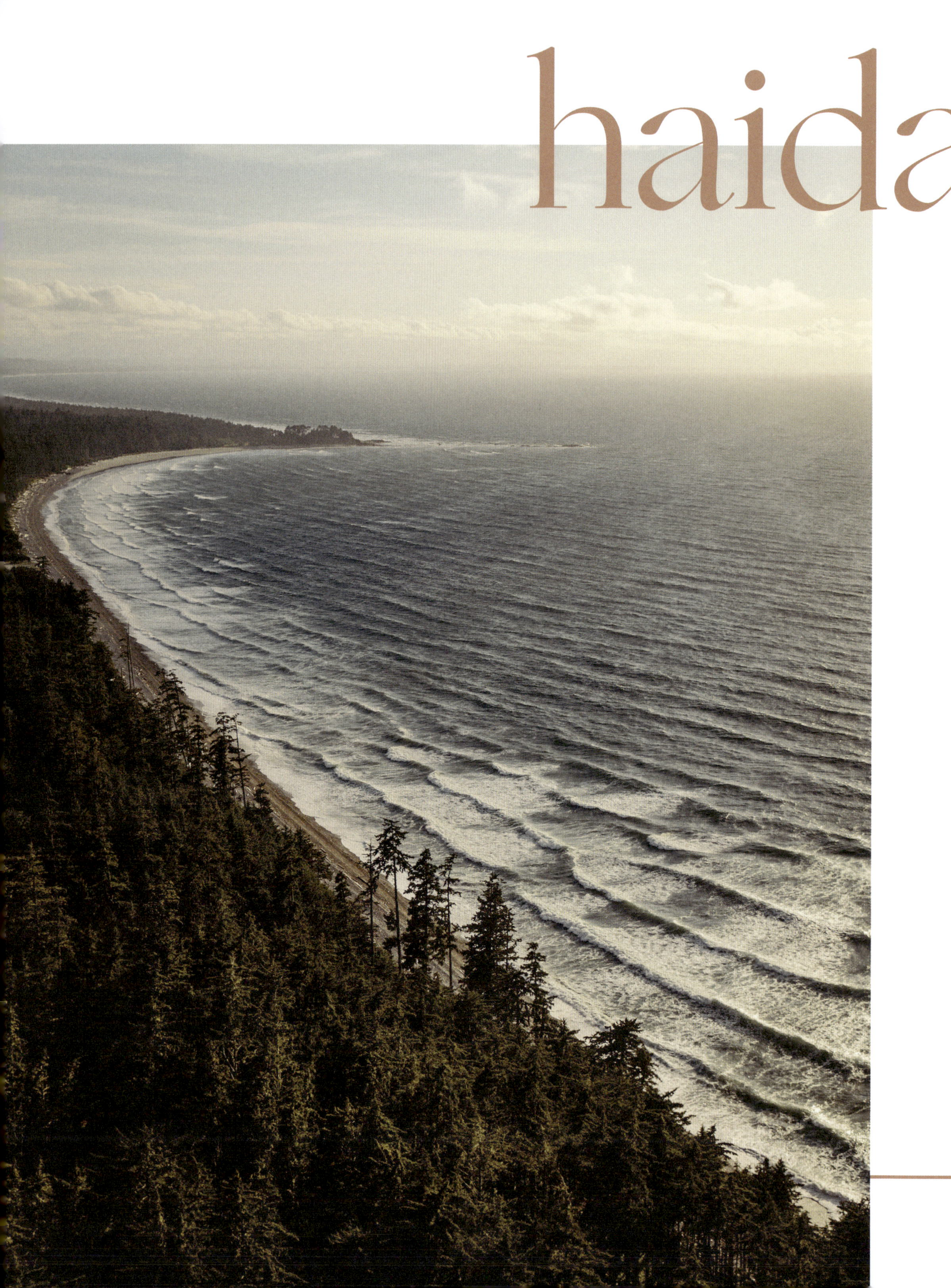

haida

gwaii
BRITISH COLUMBIA

THE HAIDA GWAII ARCHIPELAGO is stormy, rocky, and raw. From Vancouver, it is a straight shot two and a half hours by plane to Masset, which is one of the larger communities on the largest island, Graham Island. Nearby wetlands, sand dunes, rain forests, and beaches and a sparse population provide endless opportunities to immerse in nature. This subtropical rainforest is a habitat for sea lions, puffins, massive box crabs, eagles, grizzly bears, and caribou. It is also home to a host of cultural historic sites for the First Nations, who have lived in the region for thousands of years.

Wilderness lodges, camping, and luxury fishing lodges are all available on the islands. All the Beach You Can Eat provides off-grid cabins in Naikoon Provincial Park right on North Beach in Masset. If you are able, visit Rose Spit, which is at the end of a very narrow part of the island and offers a unique point of view from which you can see open ocean to your right and left.

PHOTOGRAPHS BY GRANT HARDER

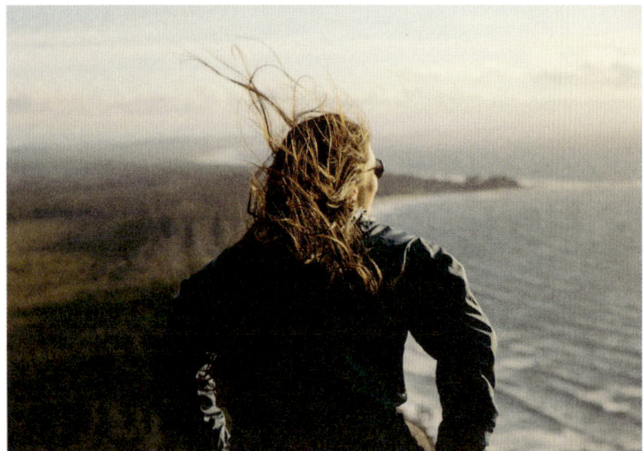

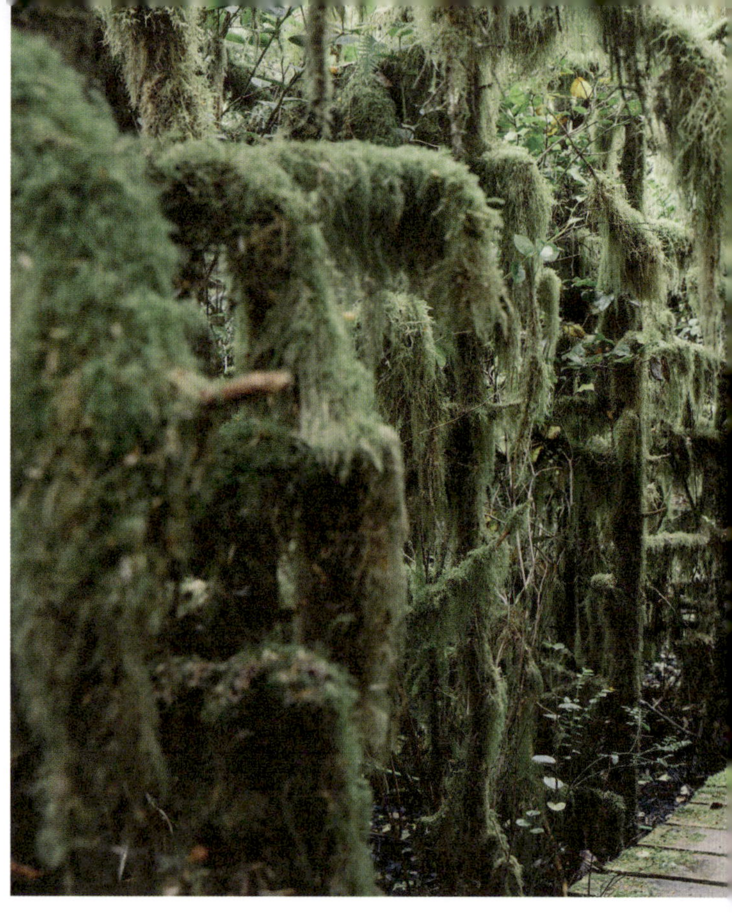

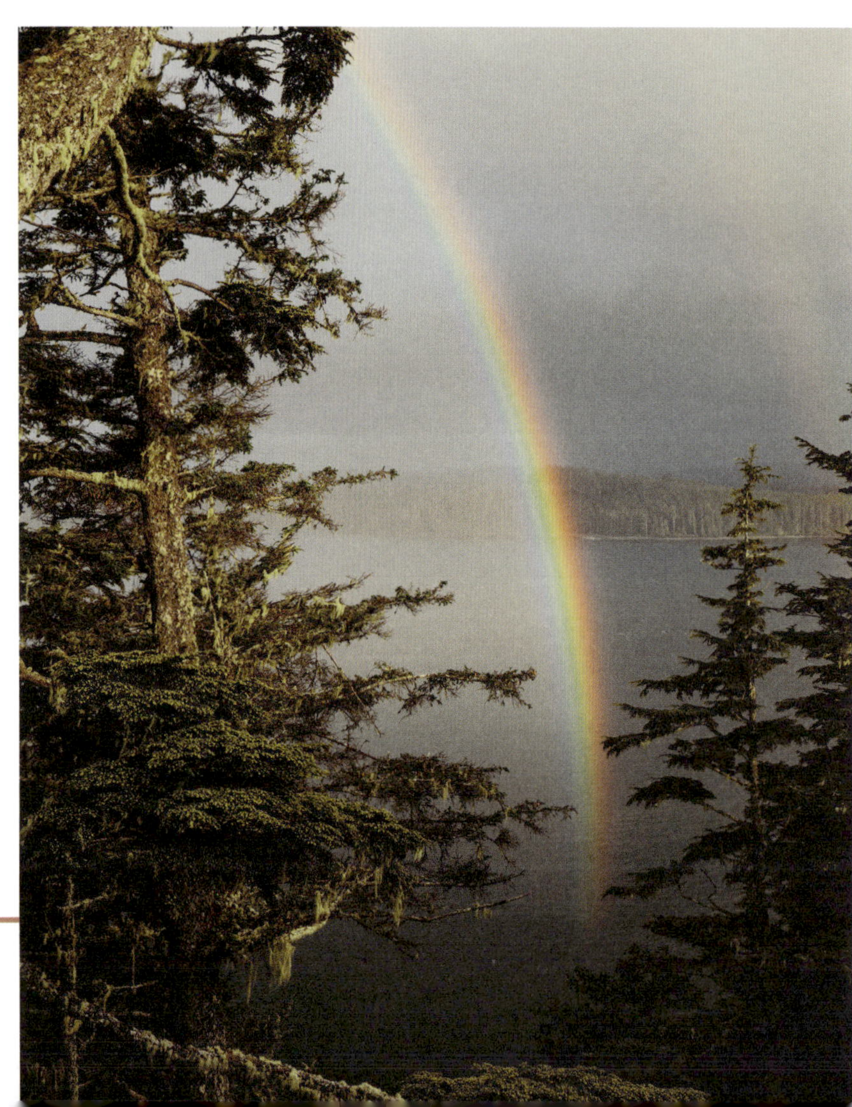

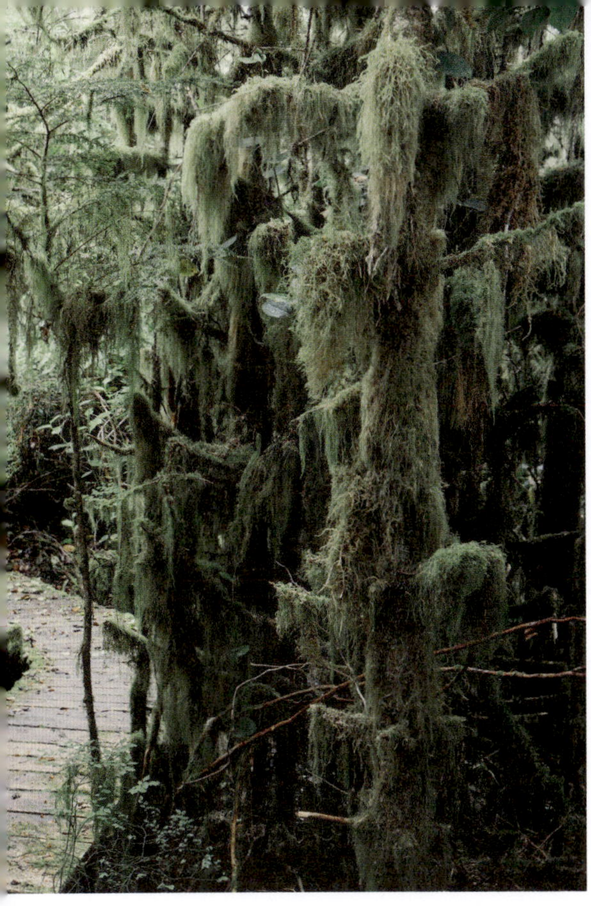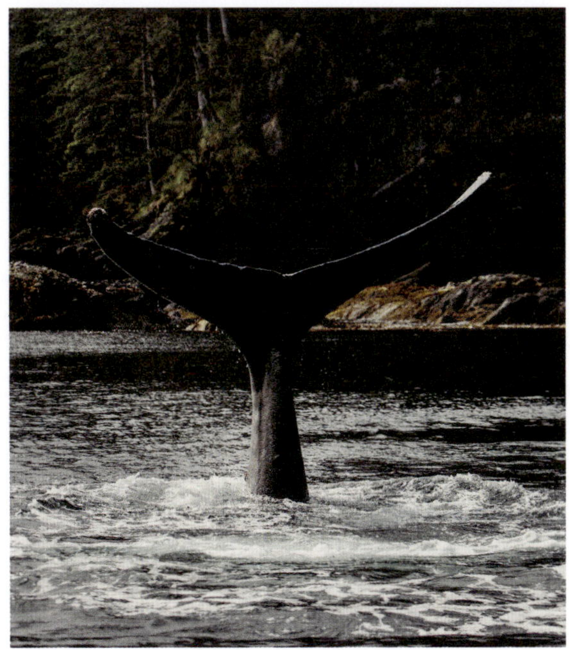

HAIDA GWAII, BRITISH COLUMBIA

Photographs by Grant Harder

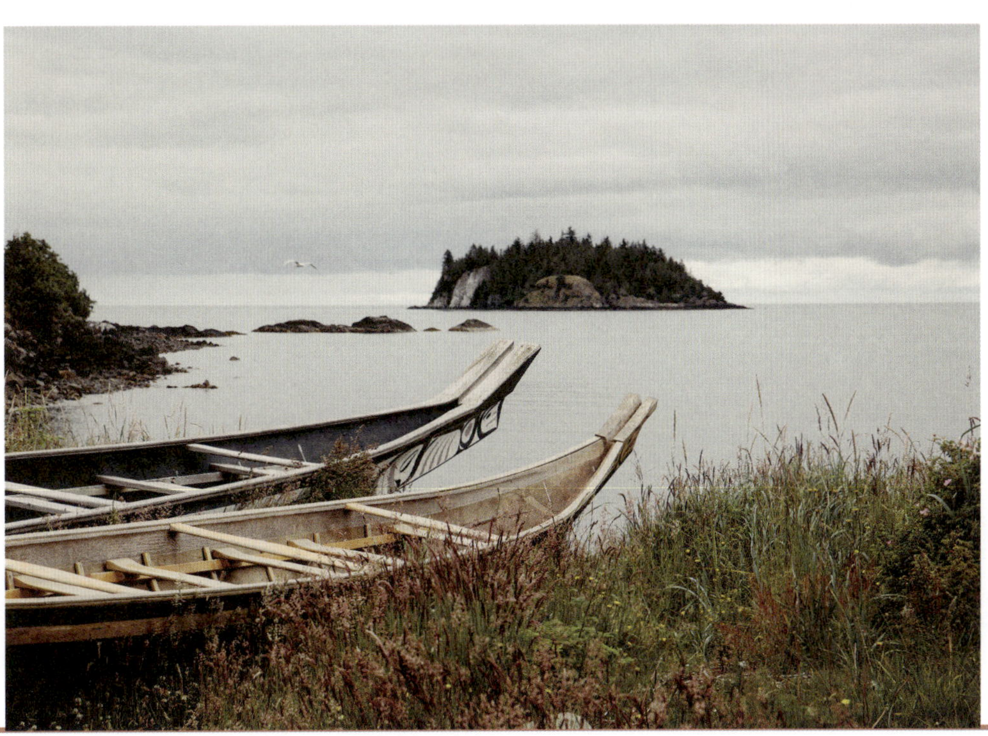

↓
**Johan Petersen
Fjord, Sermersooq,
Greenland**

Natalia Horinkova

→
**Gerlache Strait,
Antarctic Peninsula,
Antarctica**

Reuben Hernandez

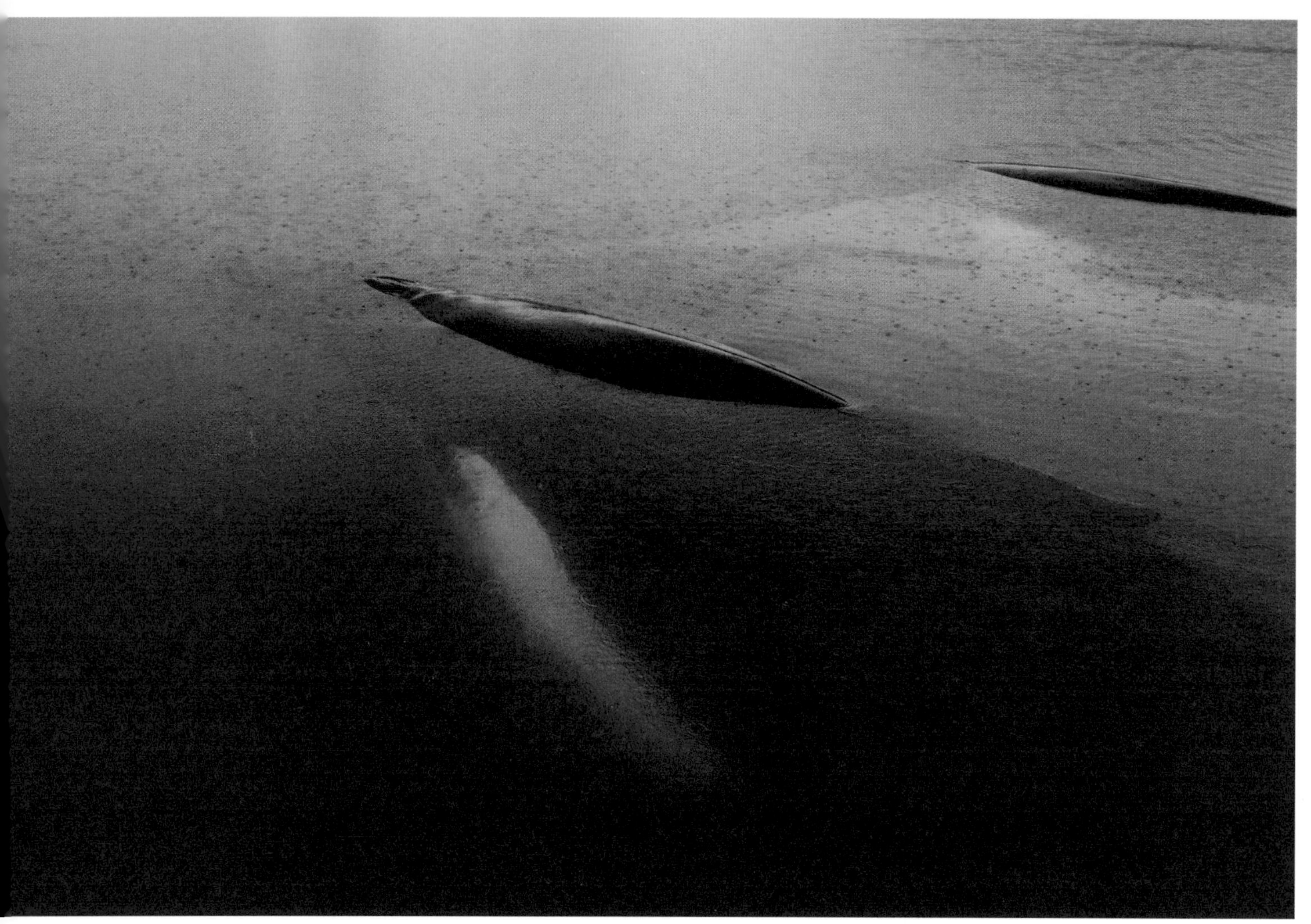

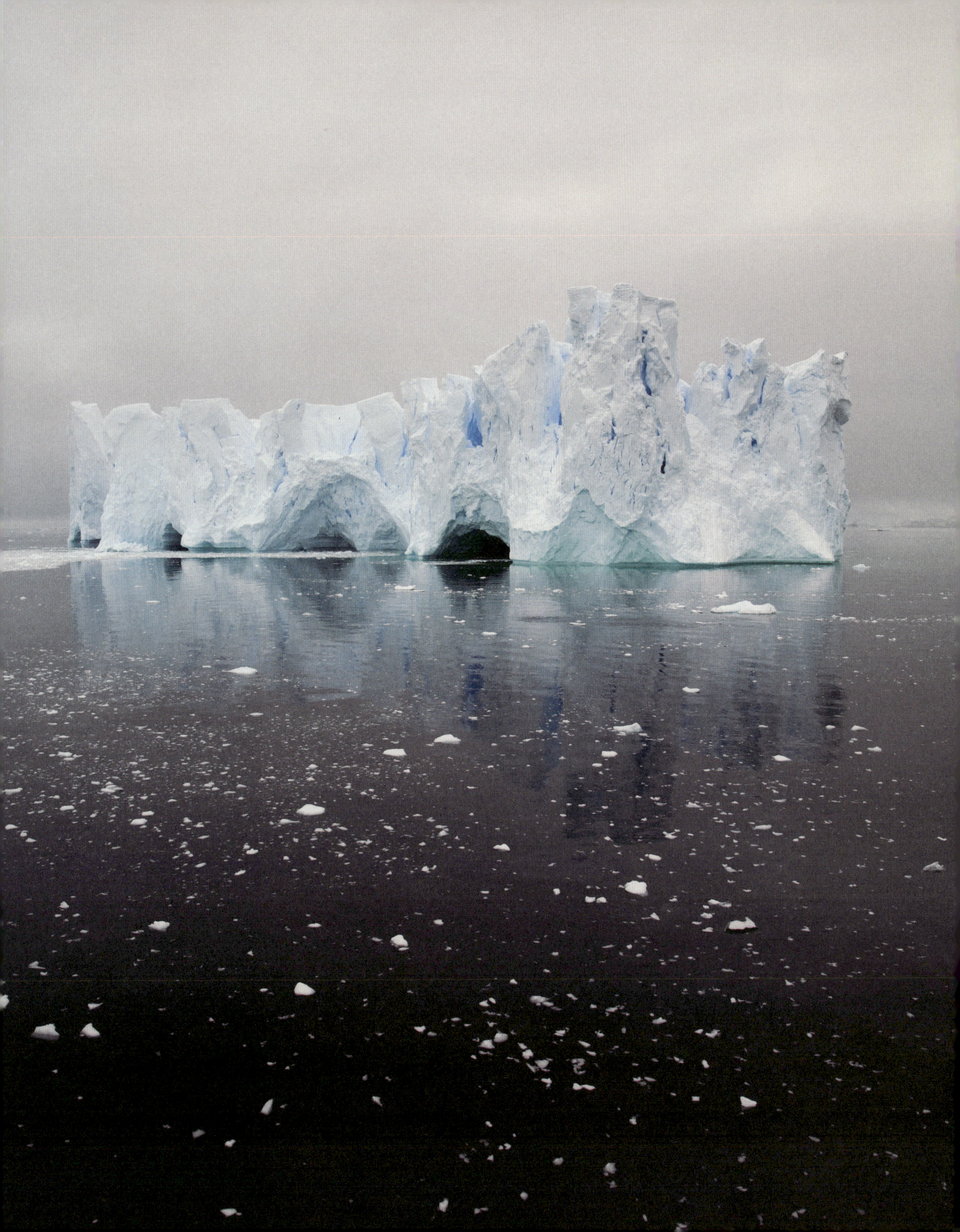

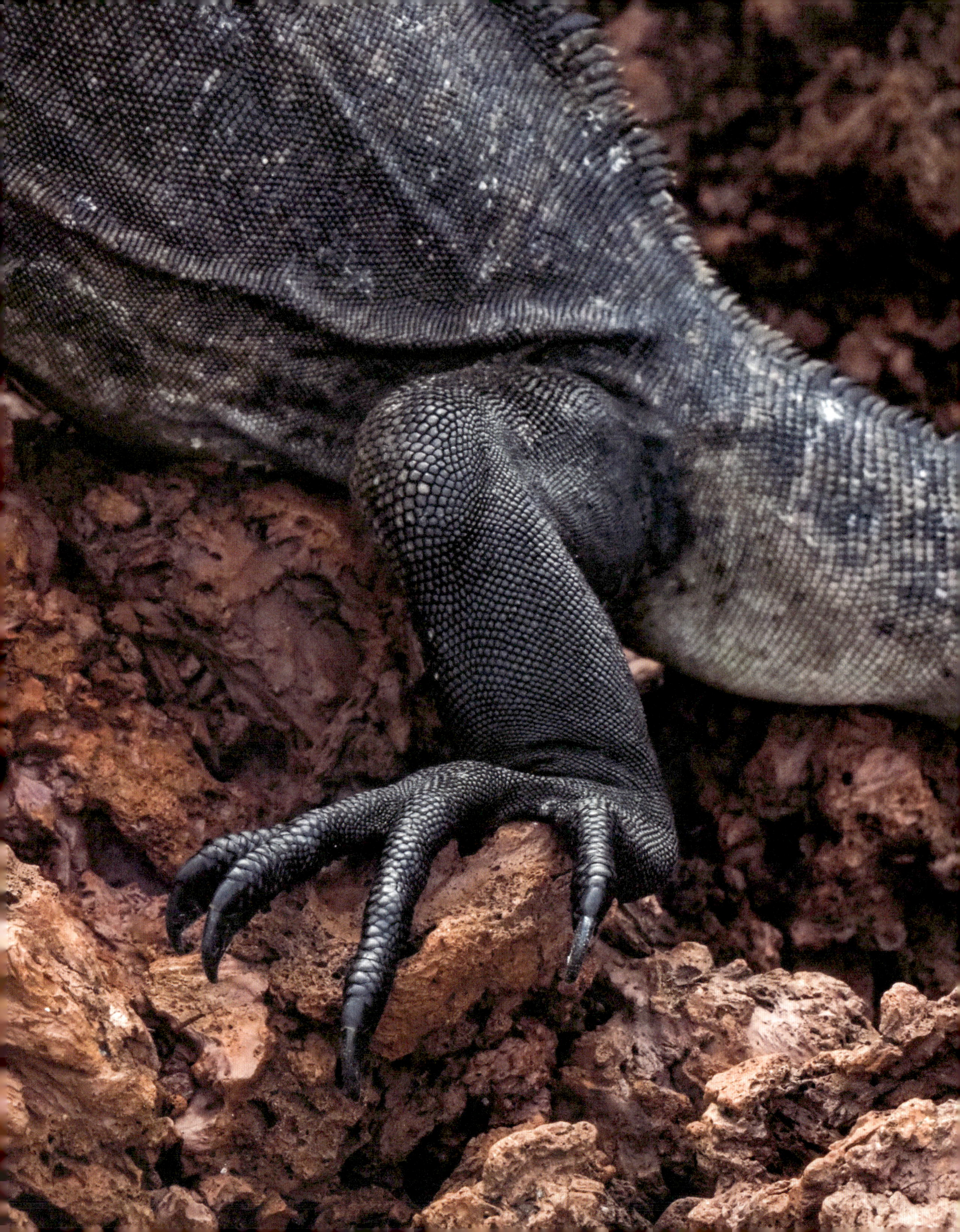

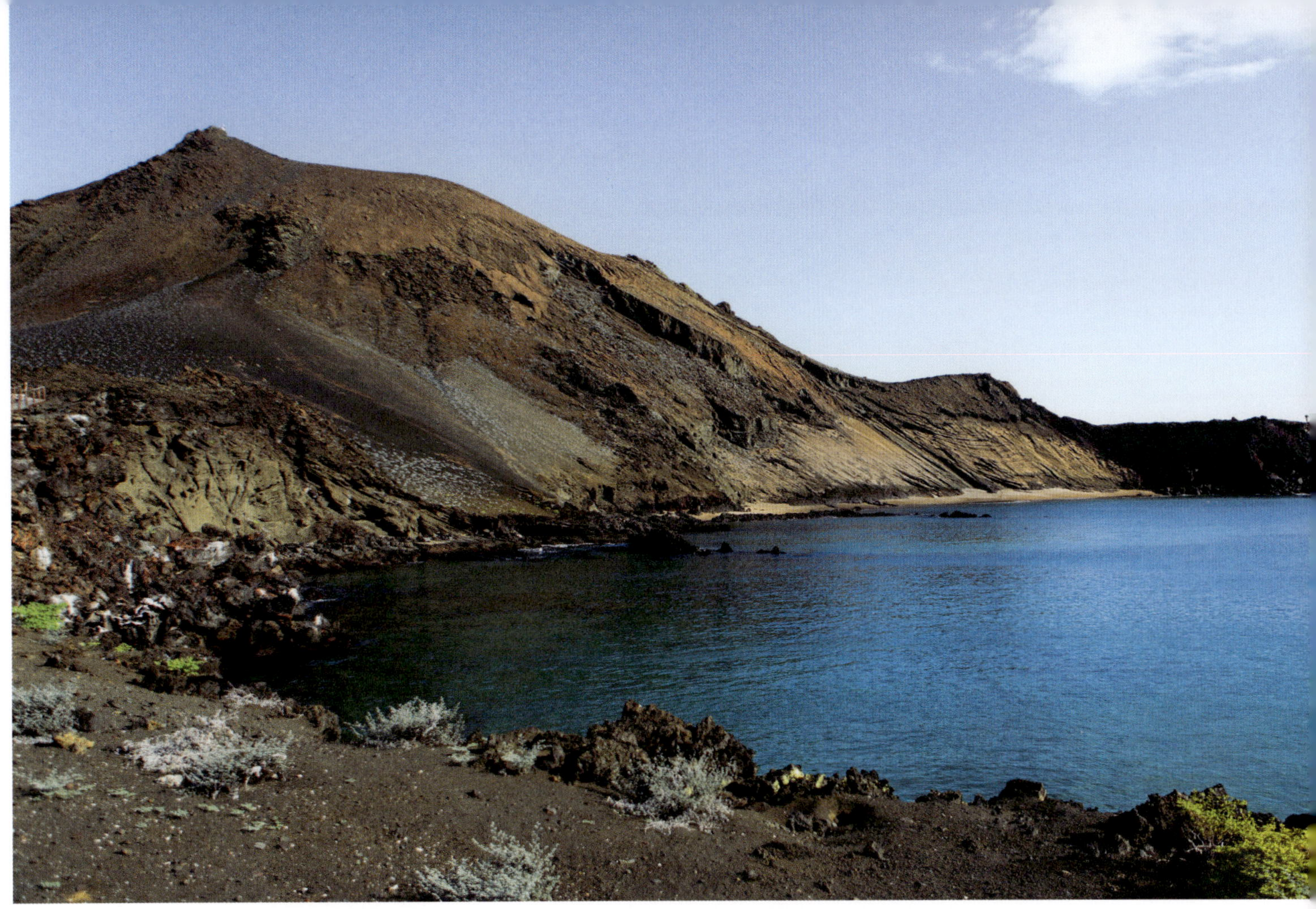

↑
BARTOLOMÉ ISLAND IS a volcanic islet set off the east coast of
Santiago Island in the Galápagos Island chain, an isolated set
of volcanic islands positioned around 600 miles west of mainland
Ecuador. Most travelers arrive in the Galápagos Islands by flying
from either Guayaquil or Quito, opting for a land-based adventure
of the island in an eco lodge or a water-based exploration on a live-
aboard boat. Bartolomé Island is a favorite for hikers, particularly
because of its mountainous terrain. Hiking along the ridge path
rewards you with a vantage point over a number of islands.

**Bartolomé Island,
Galápagos, Ecuador**
Michaela Trimble

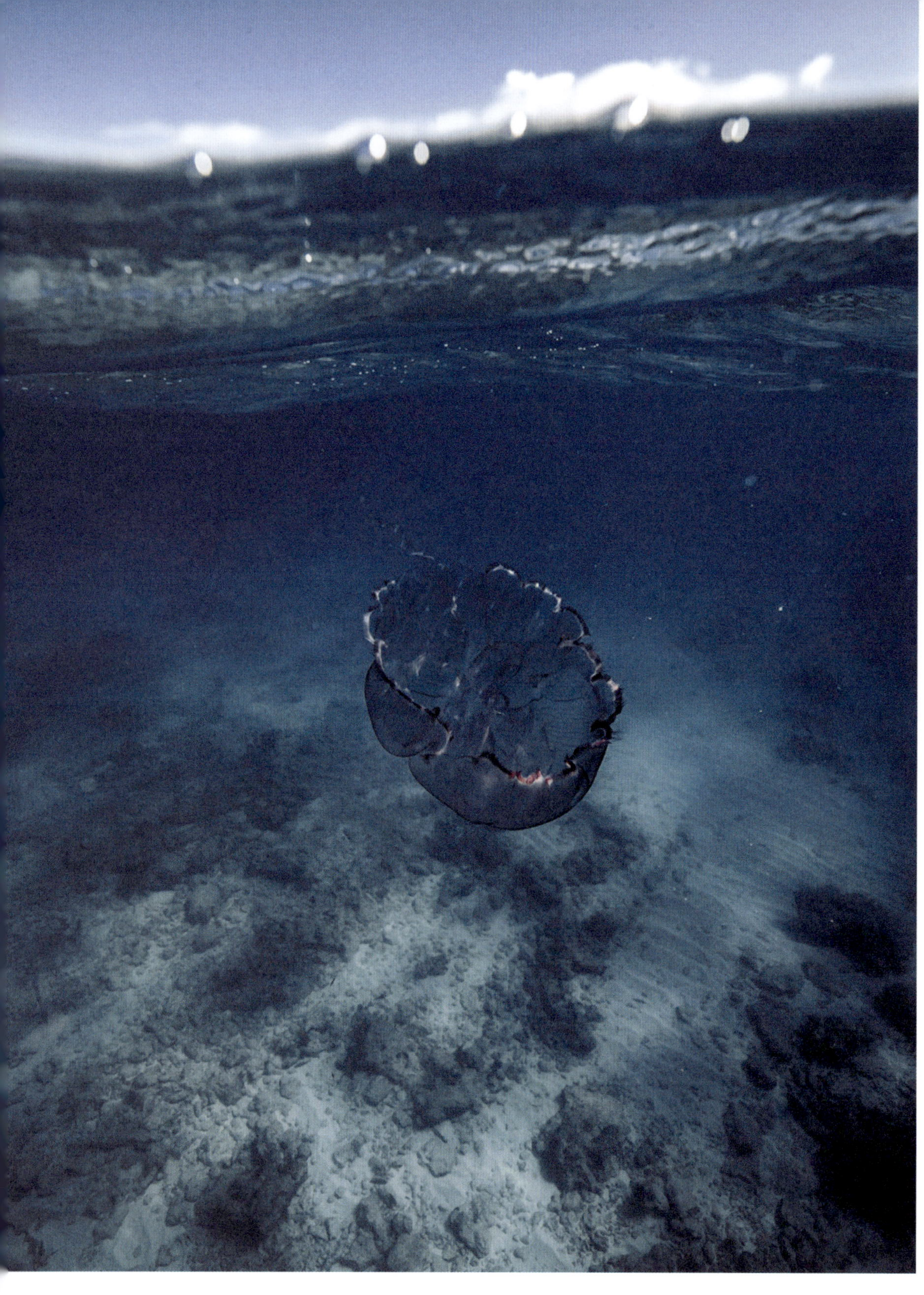

**Islamorada, Florida,
United States**

Austin Aronsson

**Canarreos Archipelago,
Caribbean Sea, Cuba**

Michaela Trimble

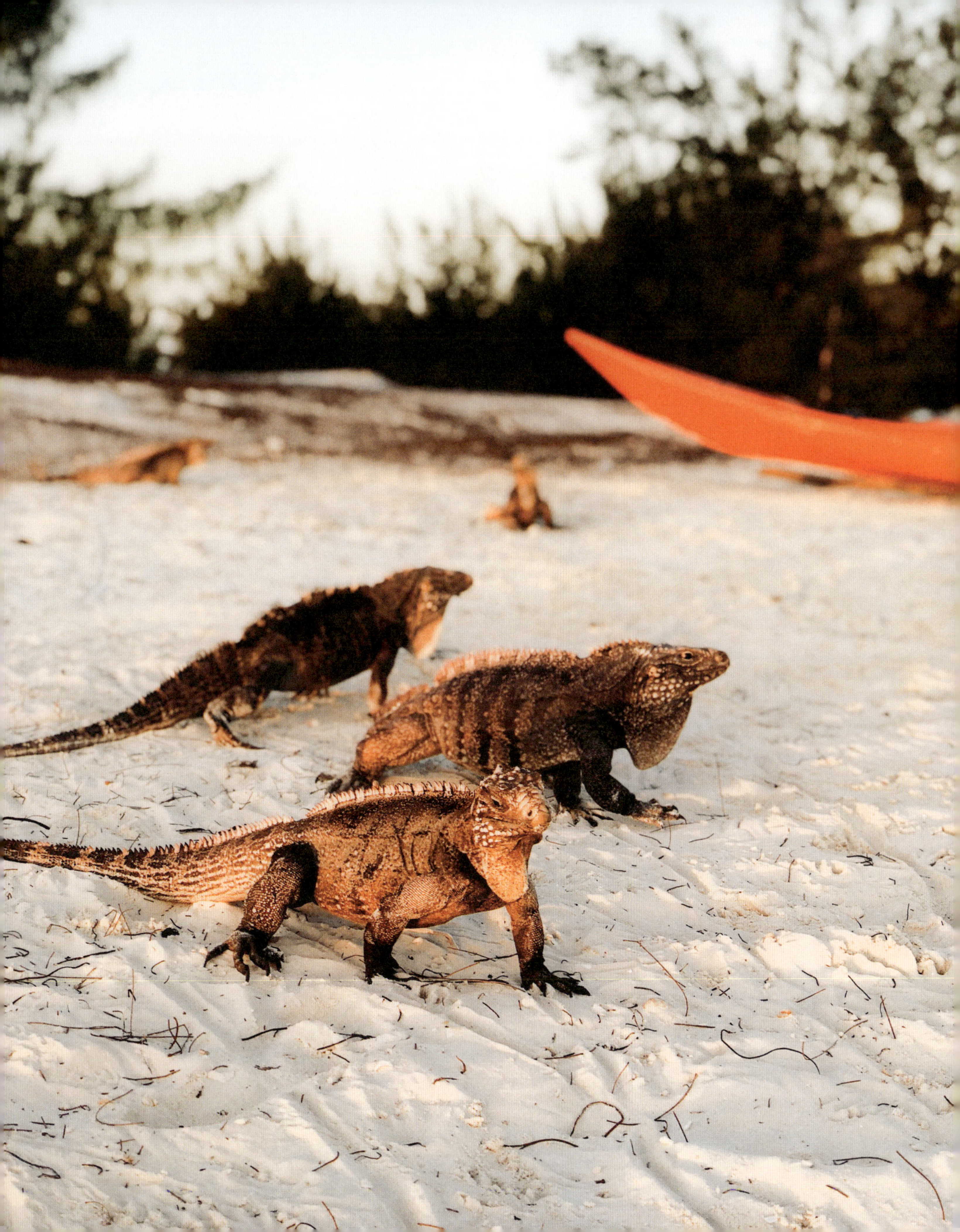

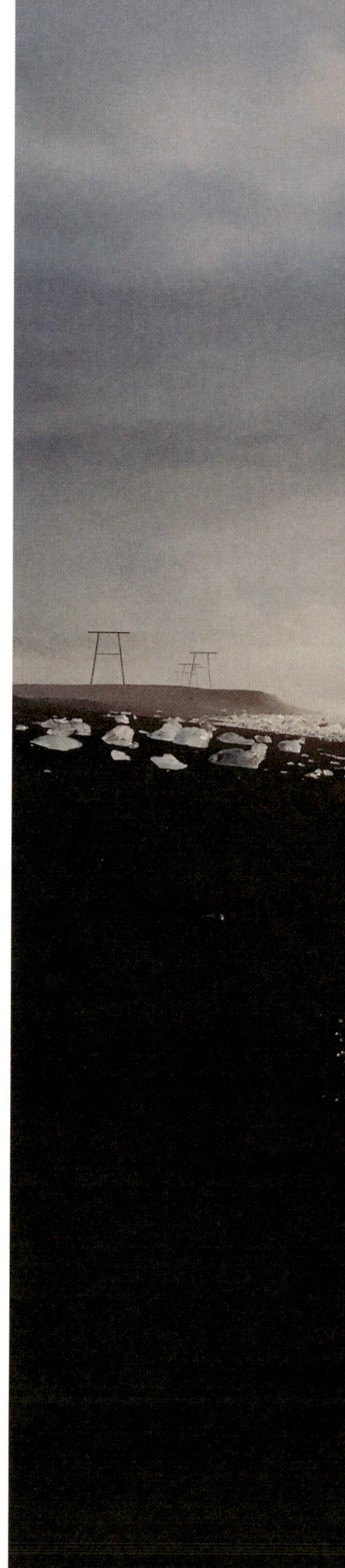

A FIVE-PLUS-HOUR DRIVE southeast from the Icelandic capital of Reykjavík, Diamond Beach is part of the greater Breioamerkursandur glacial plain and close to the Jökulsárlón glacier lagoon. The black sand beach is often deserted and well-known for its seemingly endless shore ice. The broken, glistening pieces of ice reflect surprising colors, and the unusual sight is amplified by the sound of cracking ice and bird calls overhead. Like the sights here, the weather is often dramatic and volatile.

**Diamond Beach,
Iceland**

James Benn

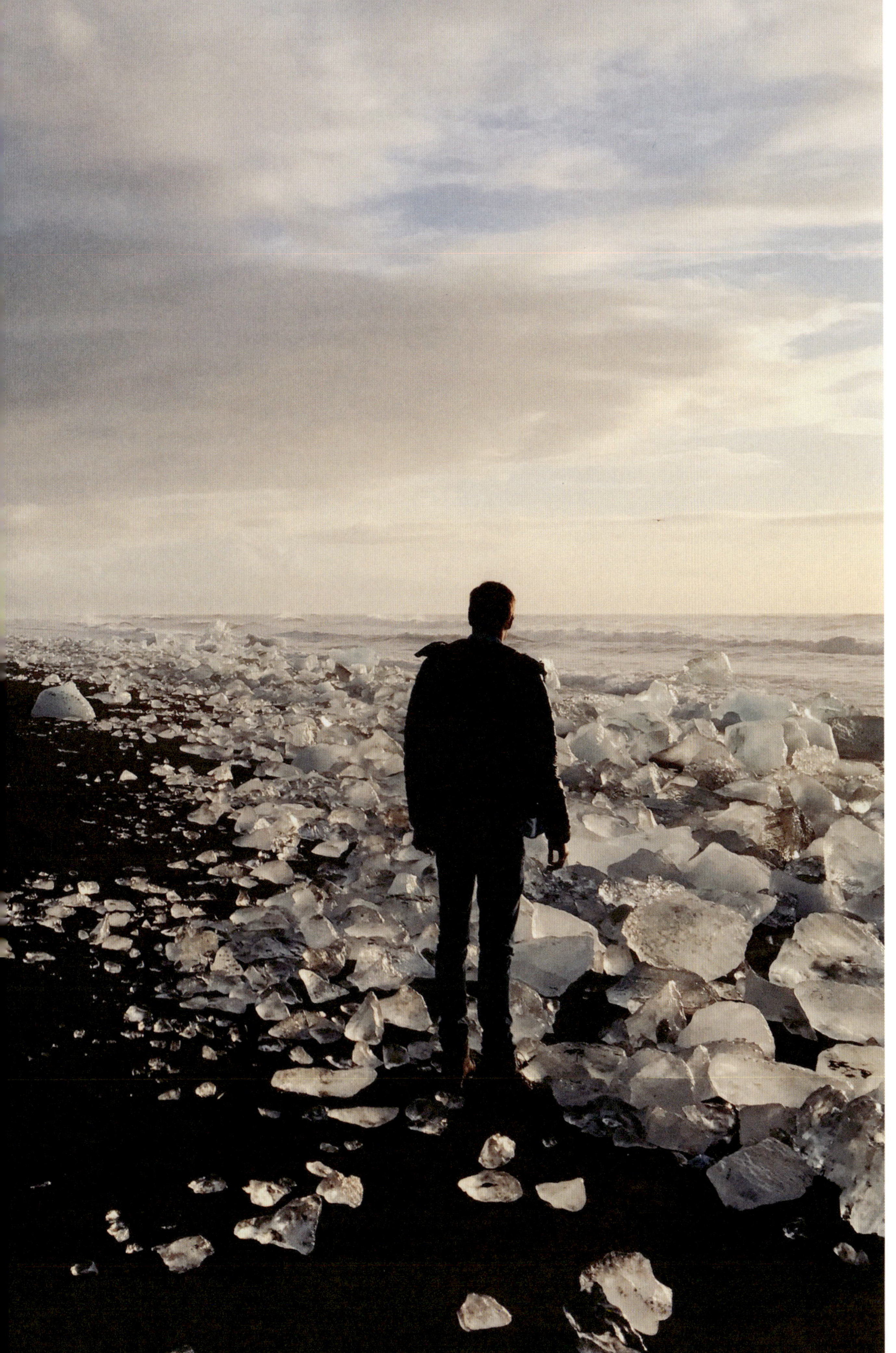

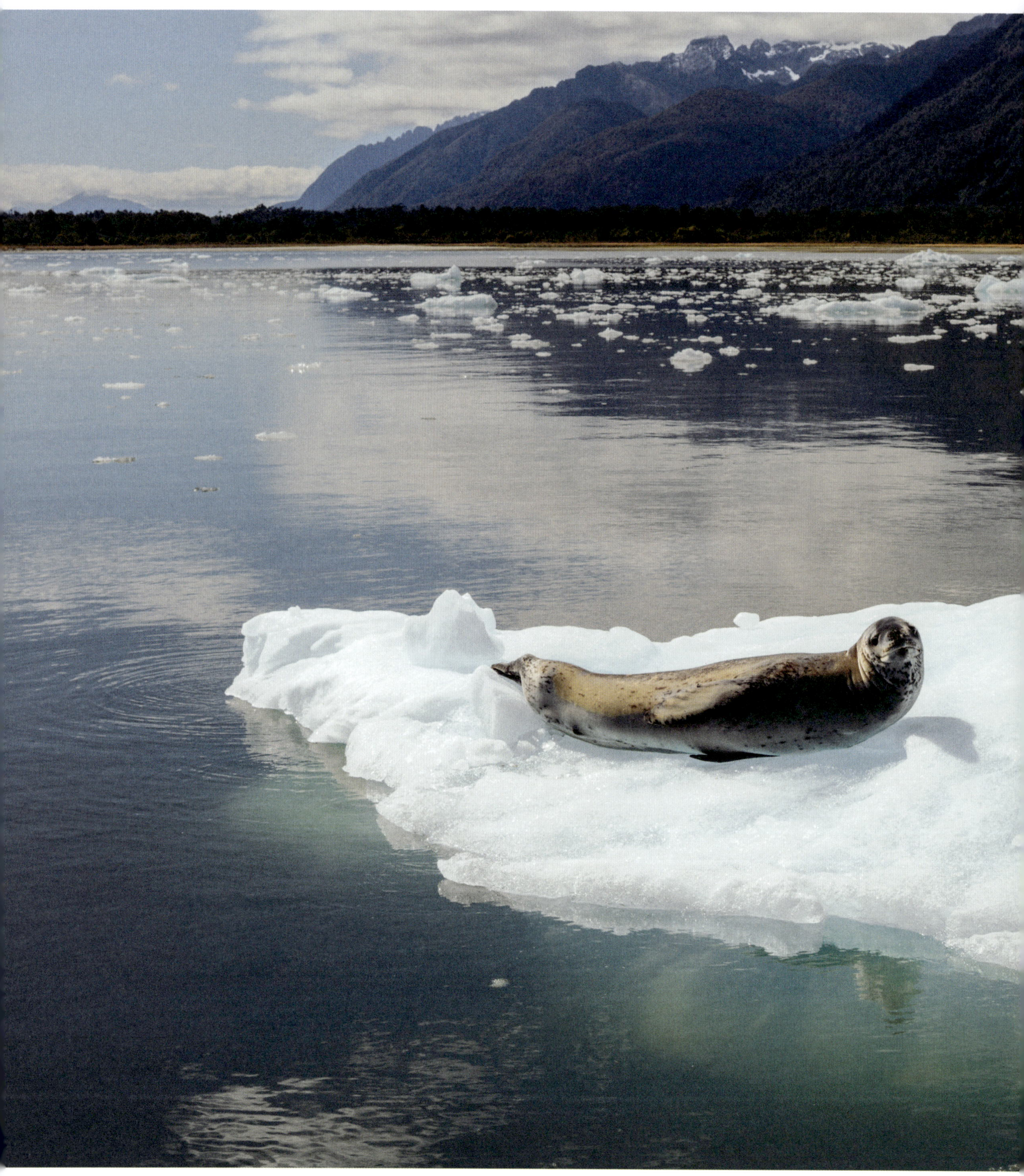

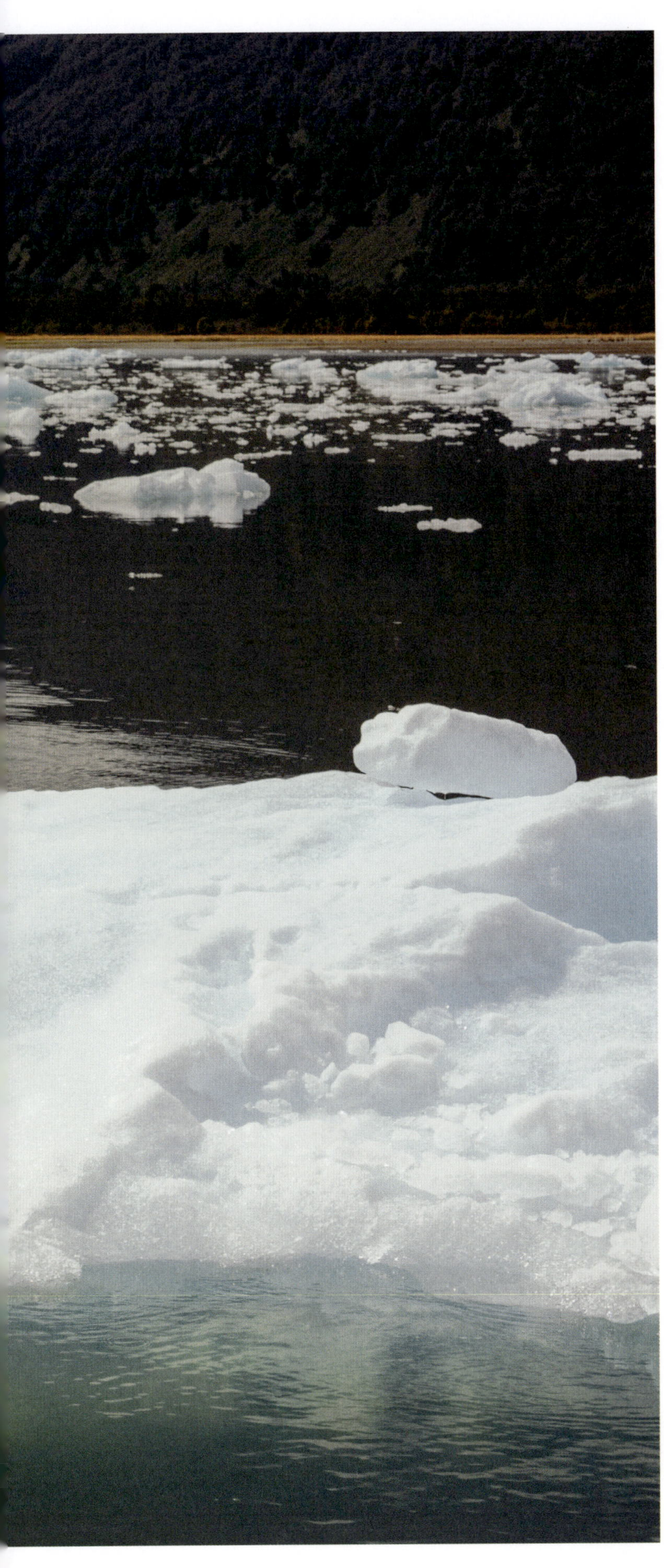

MORE THAN 100 miles south of the adventure travel town of Coyhaique, along the famous dirt highway the Carretera Austral, and west of the Exploradores Valley is the Laguna San Rafael National Park, designated a World Biosphere Reserve by UNESCO in 1979. The lagoon is a coastal Pacific lake formed from meltwater of the San Rafael Glacier, the major attraction in the area. Along with leopard seals, the park waters are home to a unique Chilean dolphin species, elephant seals, ocean and river otters, and many more endemic species. The glacier calves with massive booms as huge pieces of ice crash hundreds of feet down into the lake. To experience the lagoon, travelers will first need to fly (almost always through the nation's capital of Santiago), then hike or drive into Aysén, the region in Northern Patagonia. Take a day trip to Puerto Tranquilo or if visiting for a longer time, hike across parts of the glacier on ice treks as well as climb in nearby Monte San Valentín, the highest Andean peak in Patagonia. Farther south, there is access to the newly open Parque Patagonia that spans from Chile to Argentina.

**Laguna San Rafael
National Park,
Aysén, Chile**
Chiara Zonca

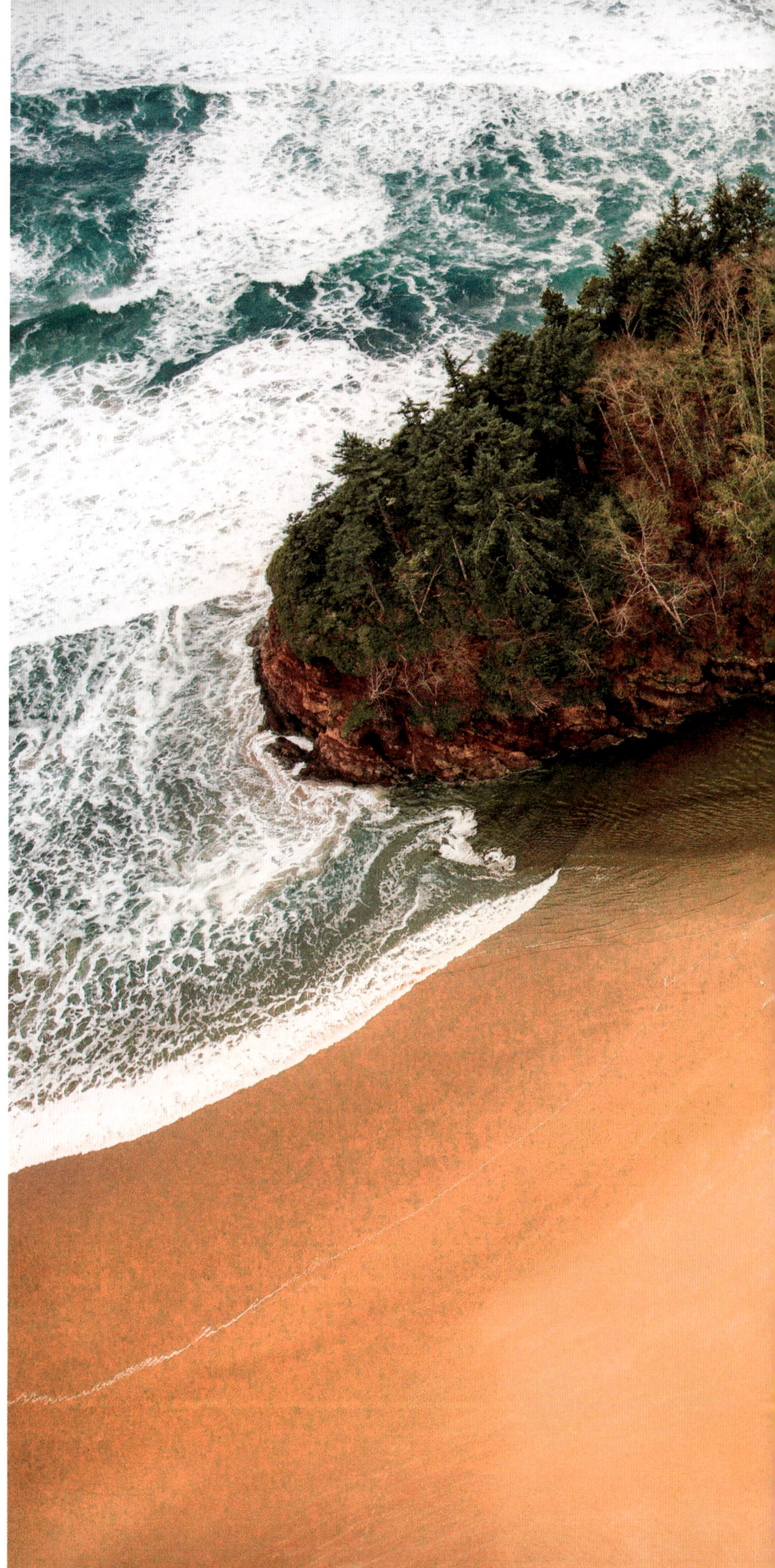

**Neskowin, Oregon,
United States**

Dirk Dallas

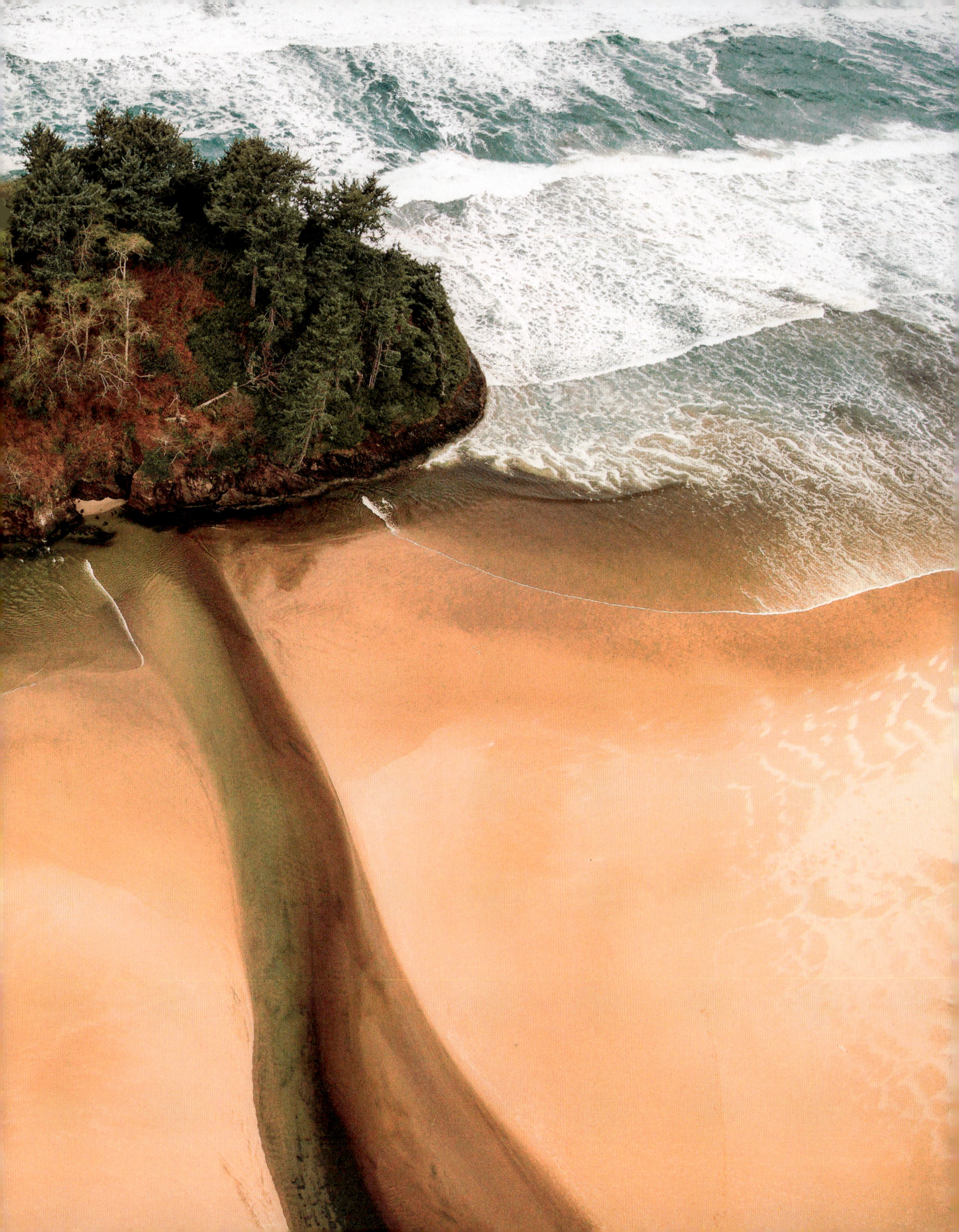

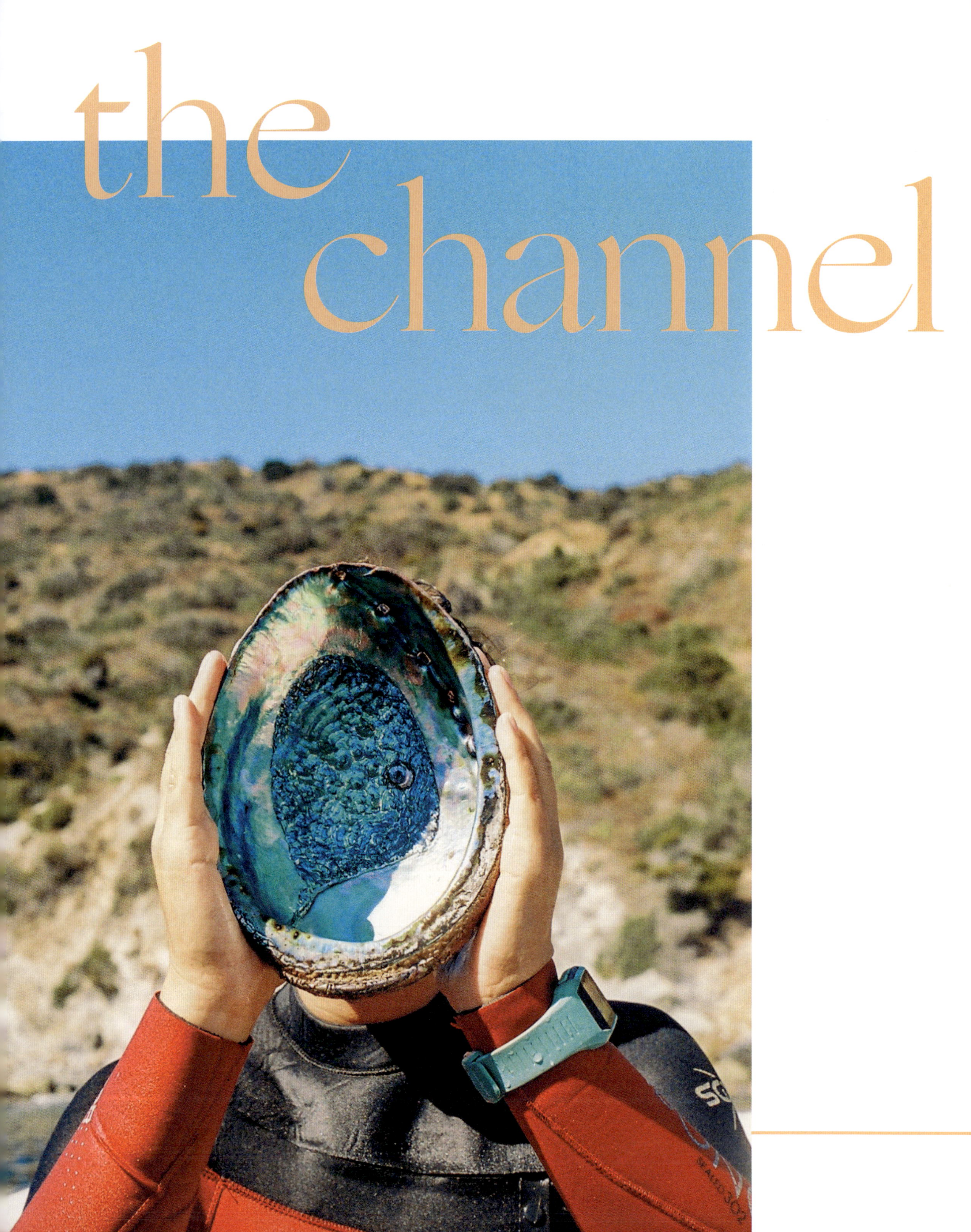
the
channel

islands

UNITED STATES

SOUTHERN CALIFORNIA LOCALS may know of Catalina Island, a getaway destination off the coast of Los Angeles. Yet most will have heard very little about the rest of the seven Channel Islands—an archipelago of volcanic, windswept islands as close as 12 miles from the mainland. Rarely visited yet extraordinarily beautiful, the islands are home to hundreds of species found nowhere else on the planet: island foxes, spotted skunks, island scrub jays, and a subspecies of Torrey pines. The waters surrounding the islands are a designated marine sanctuary, full of dense kelp forests that protect more than a thousand aquatic species.

Visiting the Channel Islands feels like going back in time in California—this is a rare place that has largely escaped development. A stark contrast to its neighboring mainland city of Los Angeles, with layers of highways and sprawling concrete, the Channel Islands are abundantly natural. This is not by luck: the Channel Islands are protected through private ownership, the National Park Service, and the Nature Conservancy. In fact, the islands are one of the greatest conservation success stories on the West Coast. Just thirty years ago, the endemic island fox was at the brink of extinction, with fewer than a hundred left on the islands. The Nature Conservancy began an extensive conservation program that involved relocating eagles, addressing the feral pig overpopulation, and monitoring each island fox individually. Now, the foxes number in the thousands and the program continues to ensure their survival.

Travelers looking to visit the Channel Islands have to take a boat across the choppy Santa Barbara or San Pedro Channel, or charter a small plane. Visitors can stay in the comfort of hotels on Catalina Island or, if preferred, camp on one of the more remote Channel Islands. Out of awareness of this fragile and rare ecosystem, travelers are encouraged to consult the National Parks Service for recommendations on current conditions.

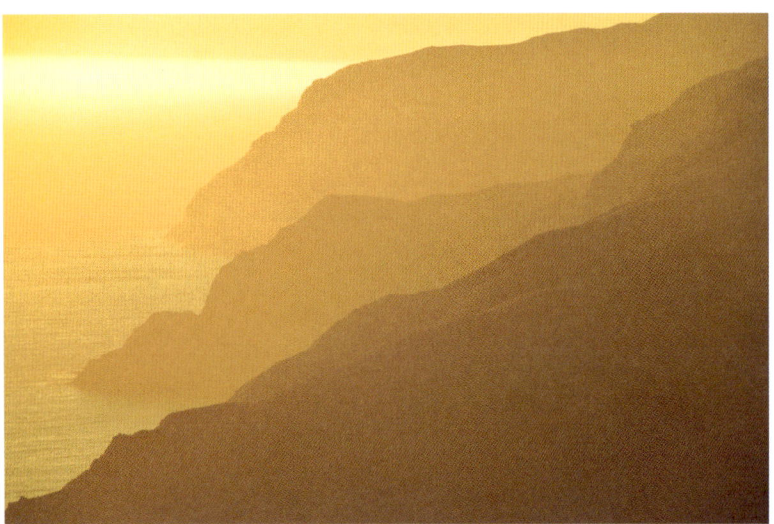

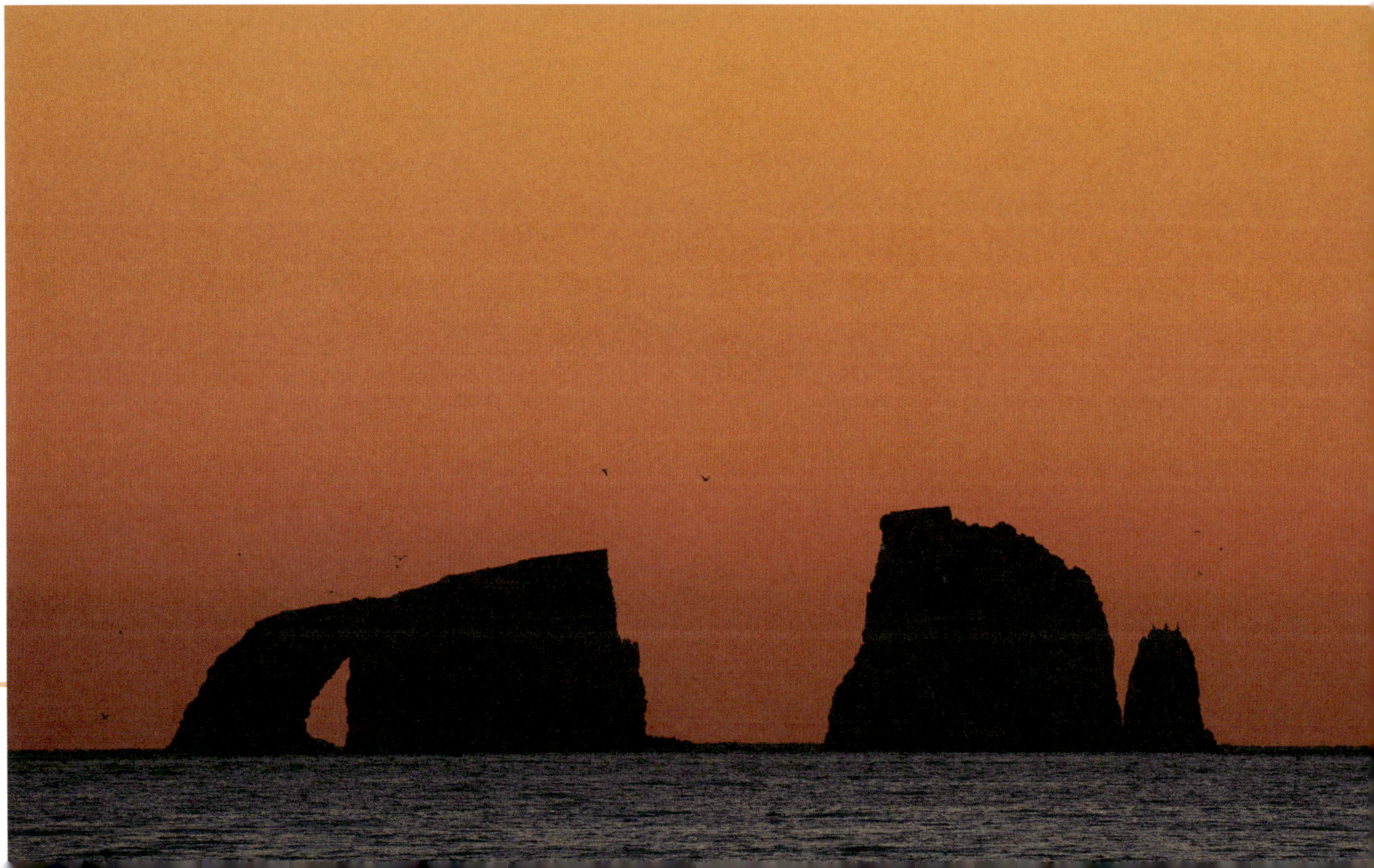

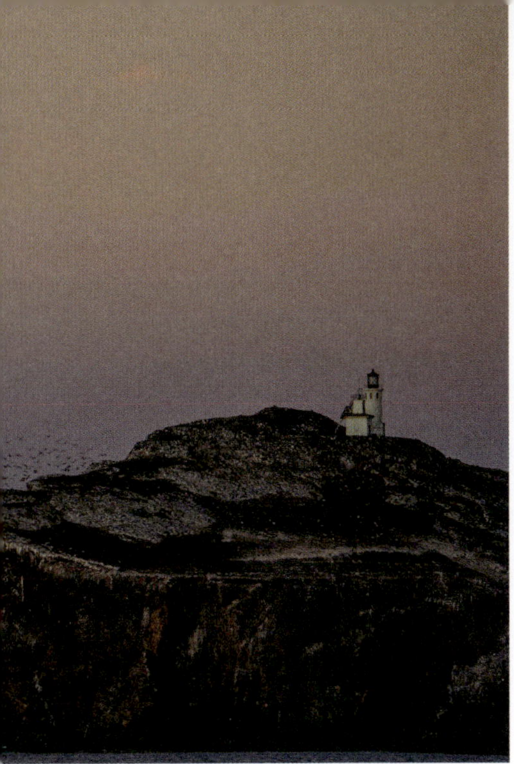

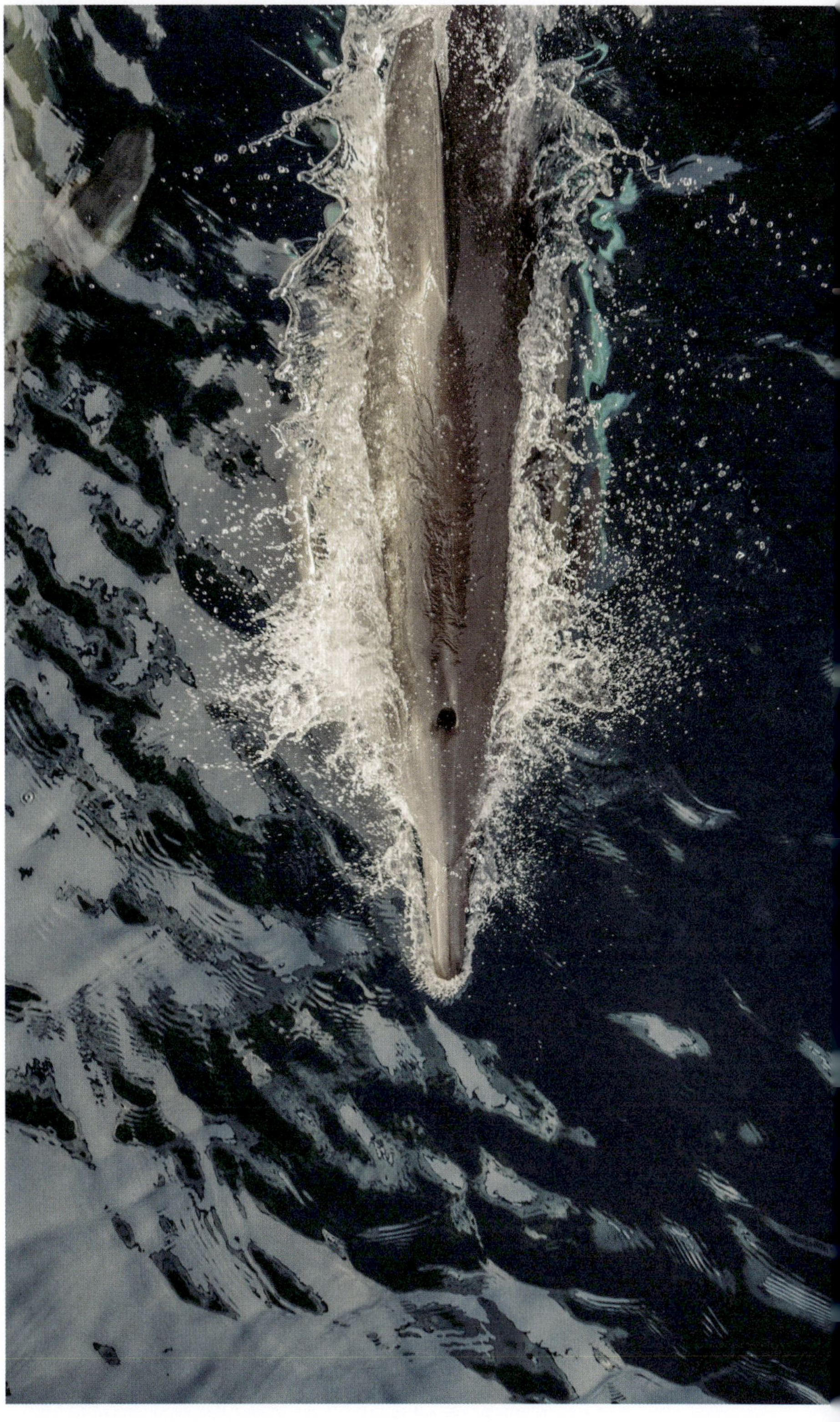

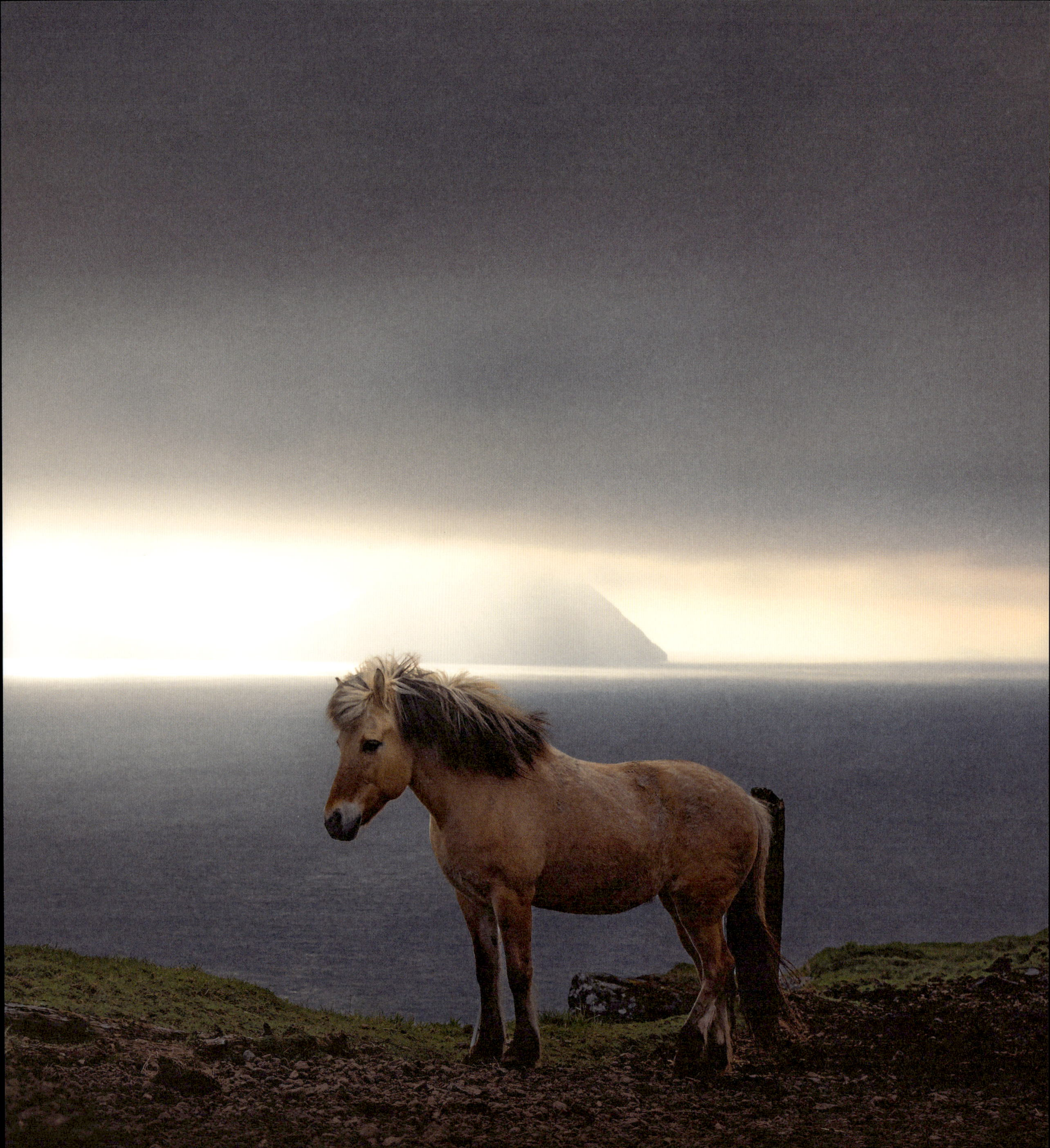

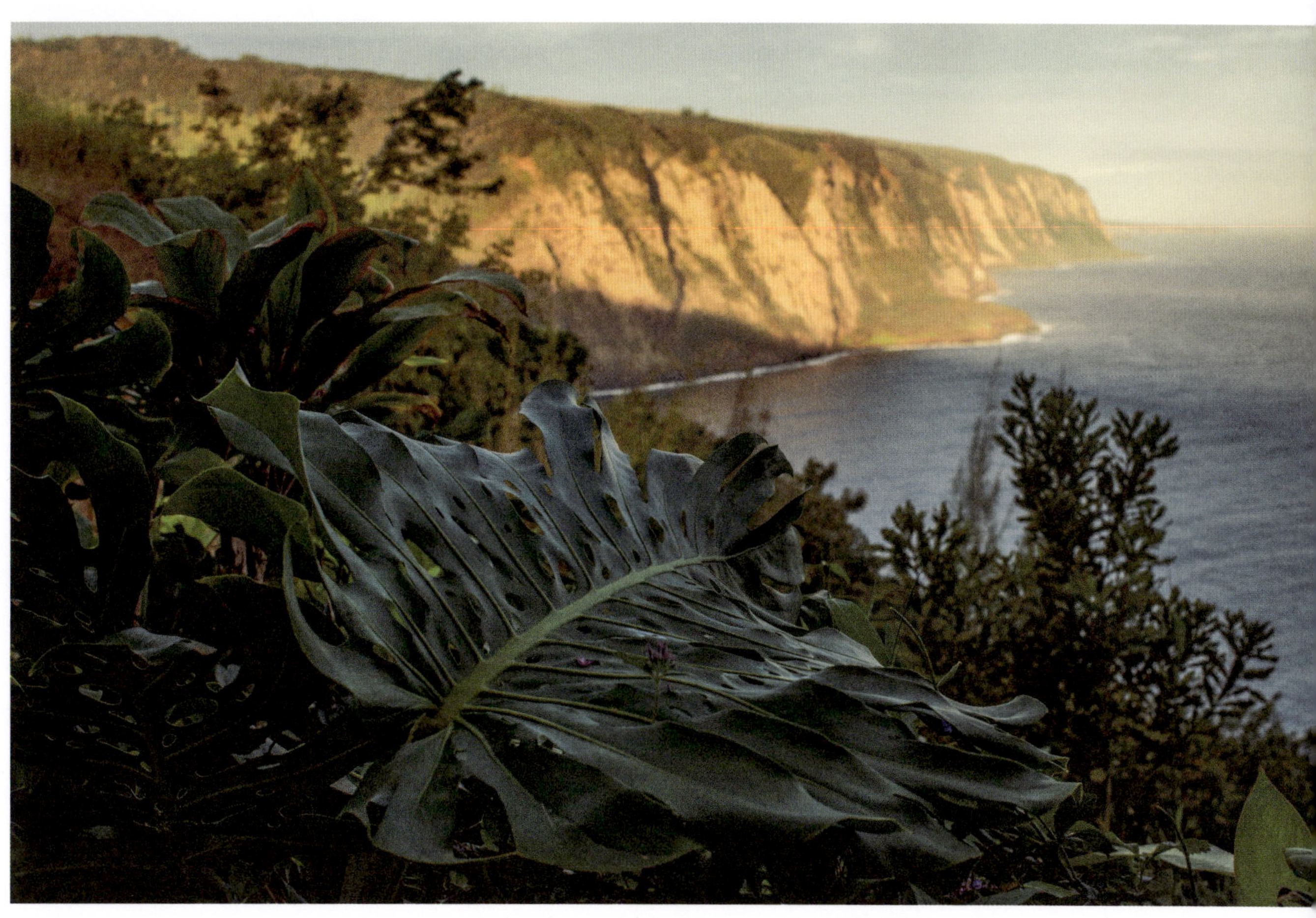

↑

LESS WELL-KNOWN THAN the famous Nā Pali cliffs on Kaua'i, the dramatic cliffs and valleys on the northwest of the Big Island of Hawai'i are just as stunning. The cliffs of Pu'u O Umi Natural Area Reserve are accessed from the north at the Pololū Valley Lookout and from the south, just past the residential hamlet of Kukuihaele (after turning off the road from Honoka'a, at the Waipi'o Valley Lookout). Ancient Hawaiian mythology, still revered across the islands by many Hawaiians today, brings much of the natural landscape of the islands to life with epic tales of the gods who are embodied throughout all the islands. Pele, the goddess of fire and volcanoes, is said to have created the islands of Hawai'i, is believed to reside inside Kīlaeua, an active volcano nearby. The local store in Kukuihaele is a launch spot for day trips that take travelers on open-air jeep rides or hikes into the lush valley below and also sells locally made jewelry, art, and hand-carved hardwood crafts made from local sustainable woods.

**Kukuihaele,
Island of Hawai'i,
Hawai'i, United States**

Emily Nathan

DESOLATION SOUND IS the largest marine park in British Columbia and is accessible only by boat. The topography of the area varies from low rolling hills to steep mountain cliffs with plenty of safe anchorages for the boaters who flock to the area in the summer to swim, scuba dive, fish, and camp. To get to the sound by air, visitors fly from Vancouver to Powell River and then take a thirty-minute cab to a dock. Then they're picked up for the final leg of the journey, a short ride aboard a small motorboat. Desolation Sound is laced with tiny islands both inhabited and not and surrounded by towering forest and deep green water.

**Desolation Sound,
British Columbia, Canada**
Grant Harder

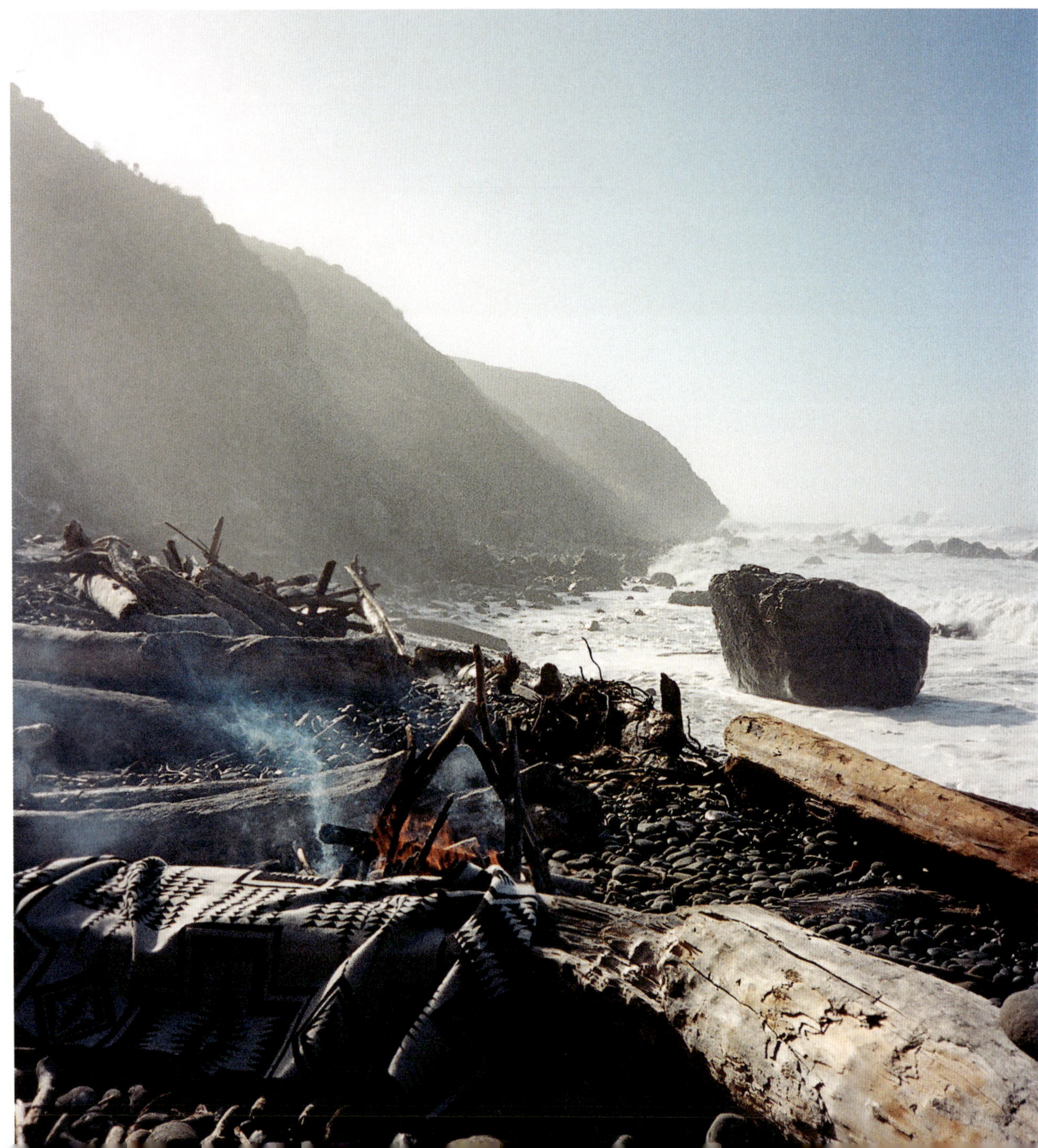

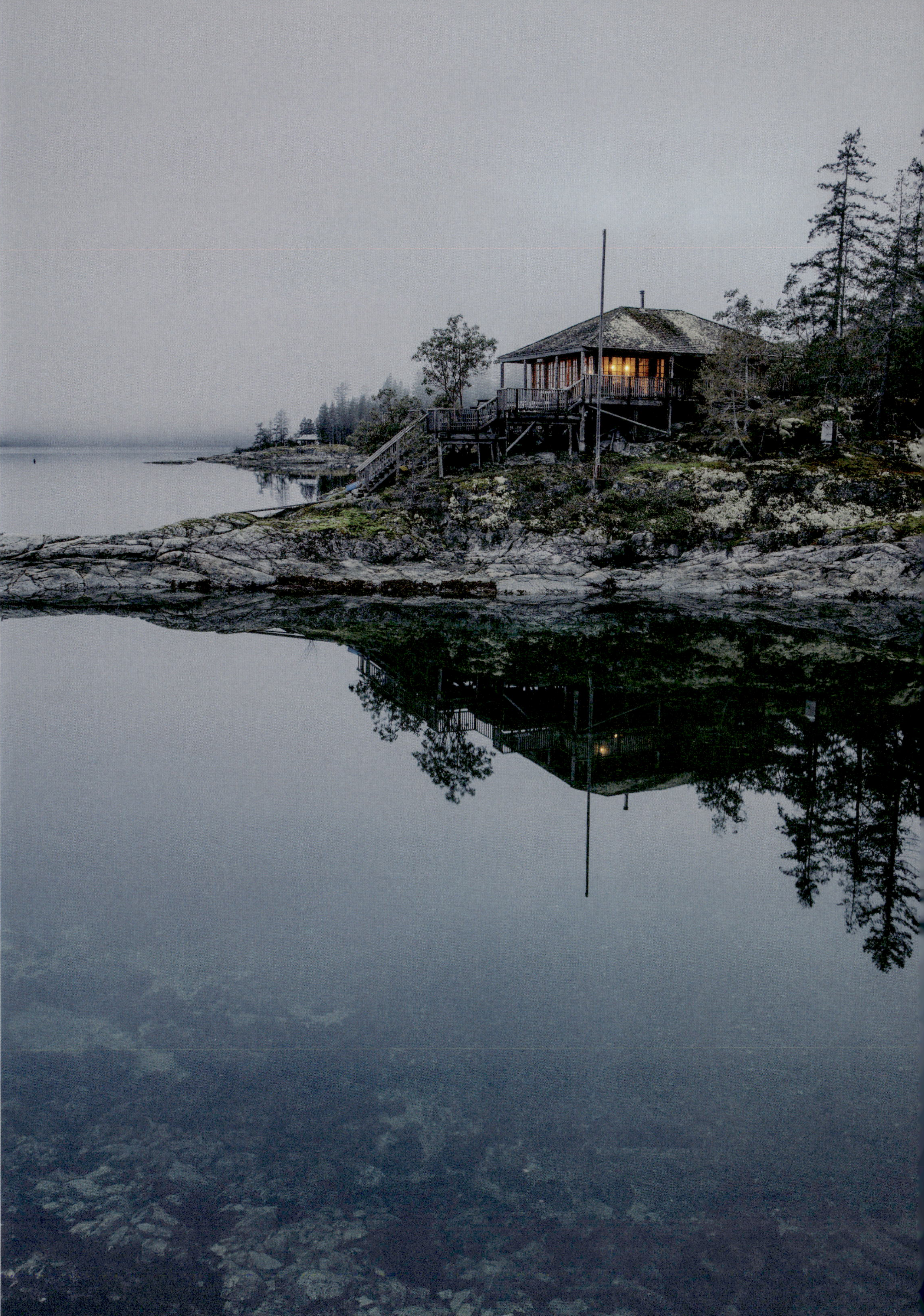

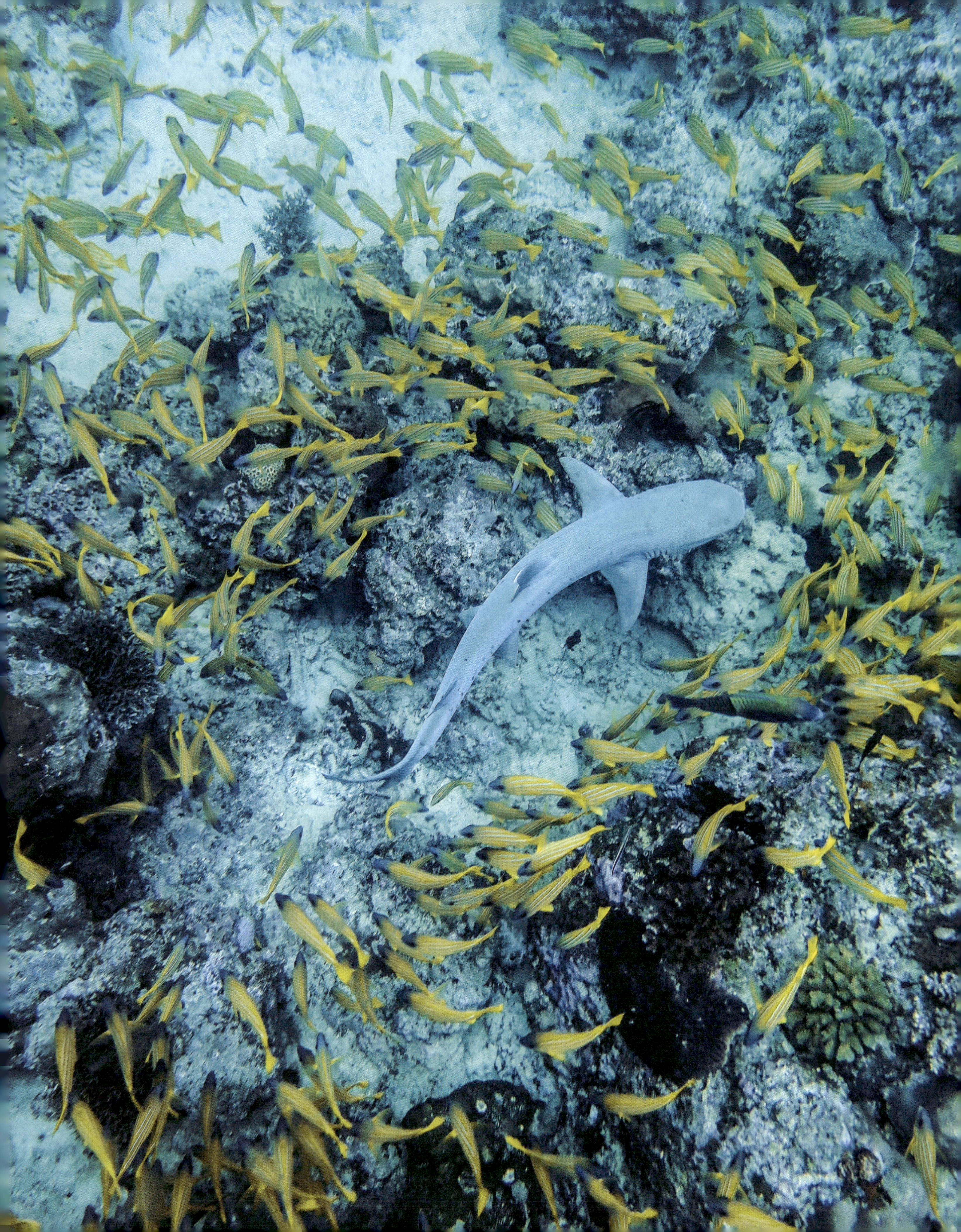

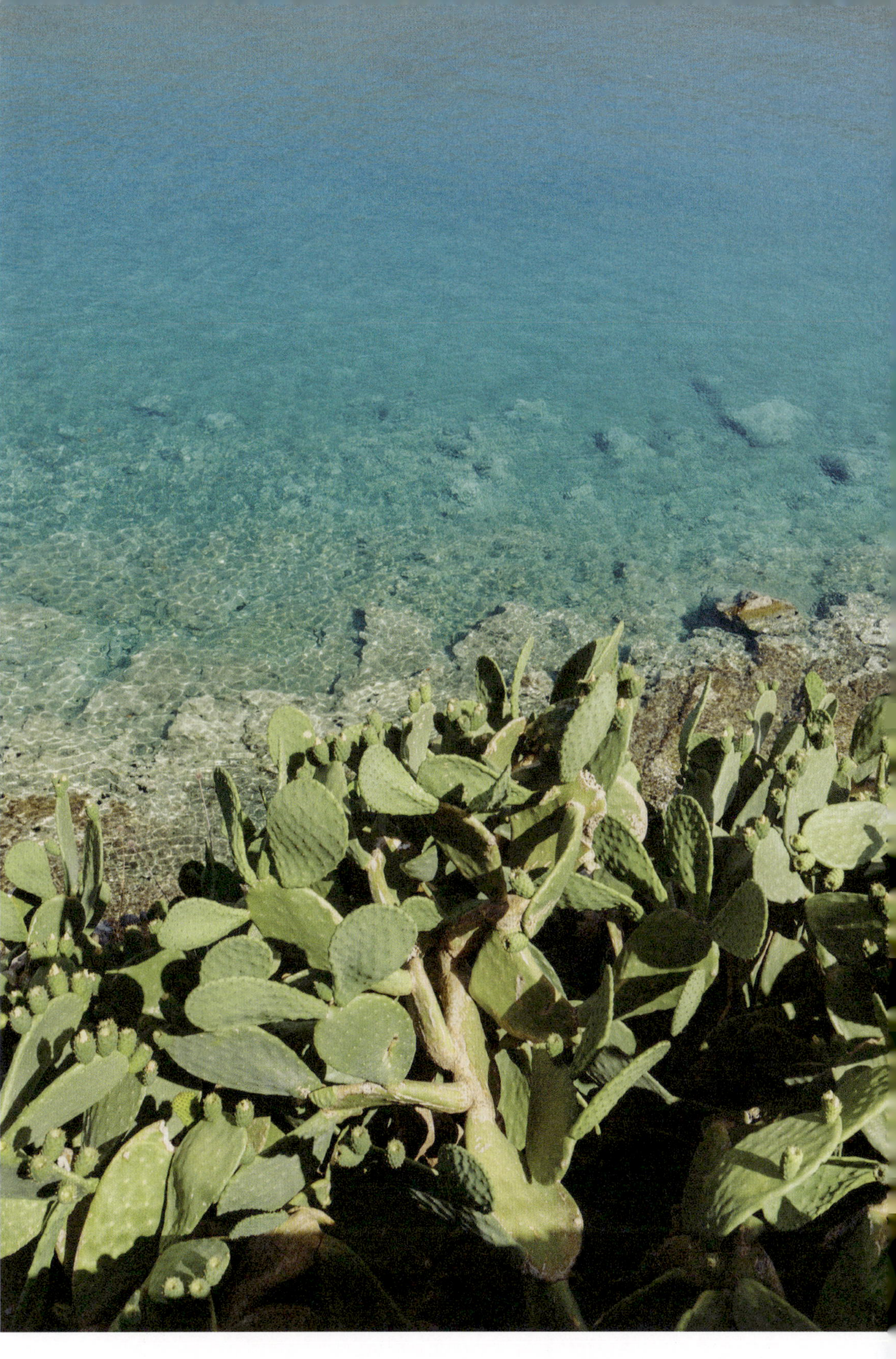

← The Great Barrier
Reef, Coral Sea,
Queensland, Australia

Mateusz Cyrankiewicz

↑ Spinalonga,
Crete, Greece

Louis A. W. Sheridan

↓
**Zihuatanejo,
Guerrero, Mexico**
Gabriel Flores

→
**O'ahu, Hawai'i,
United States**
Meagan Bourne

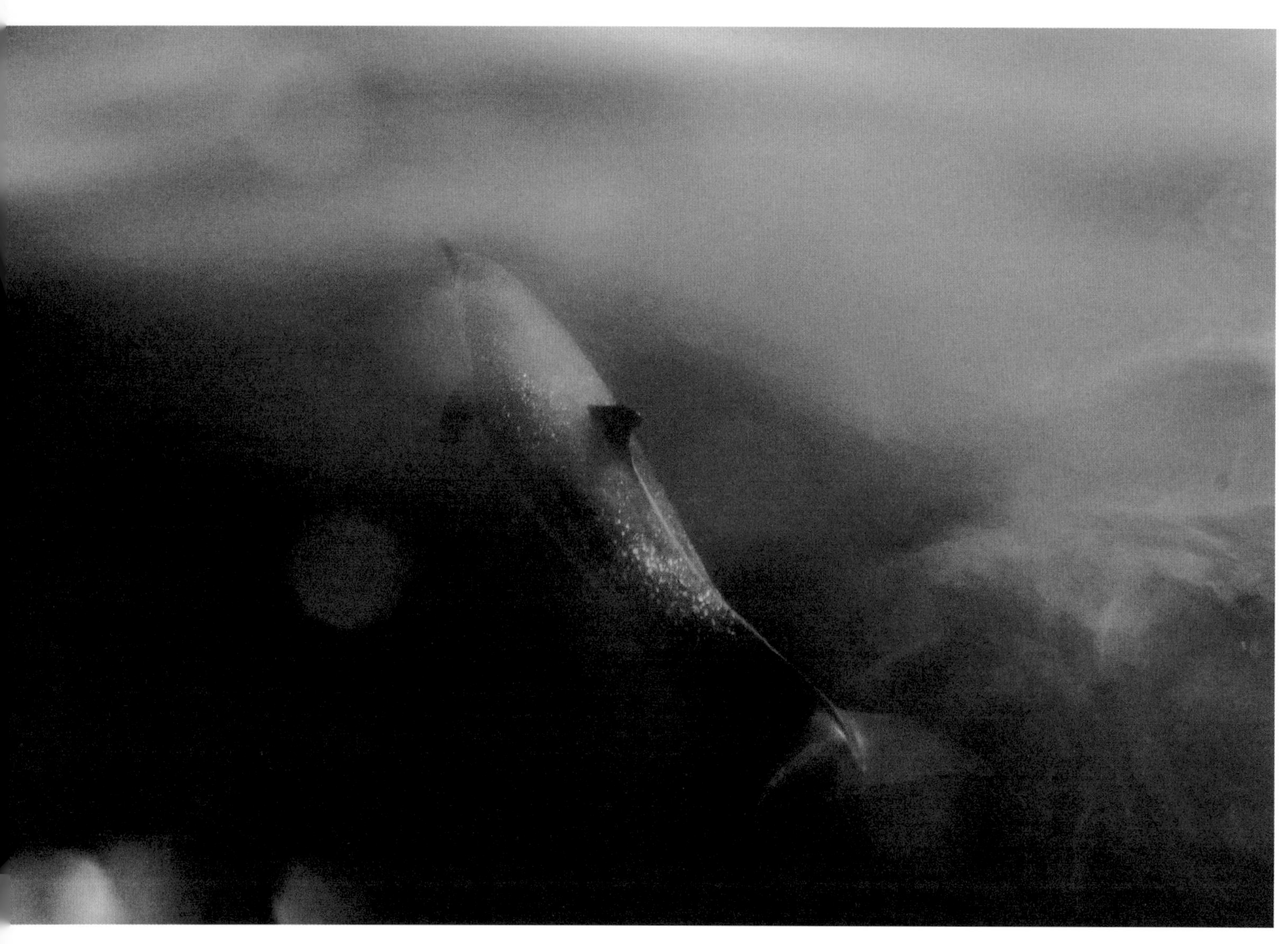

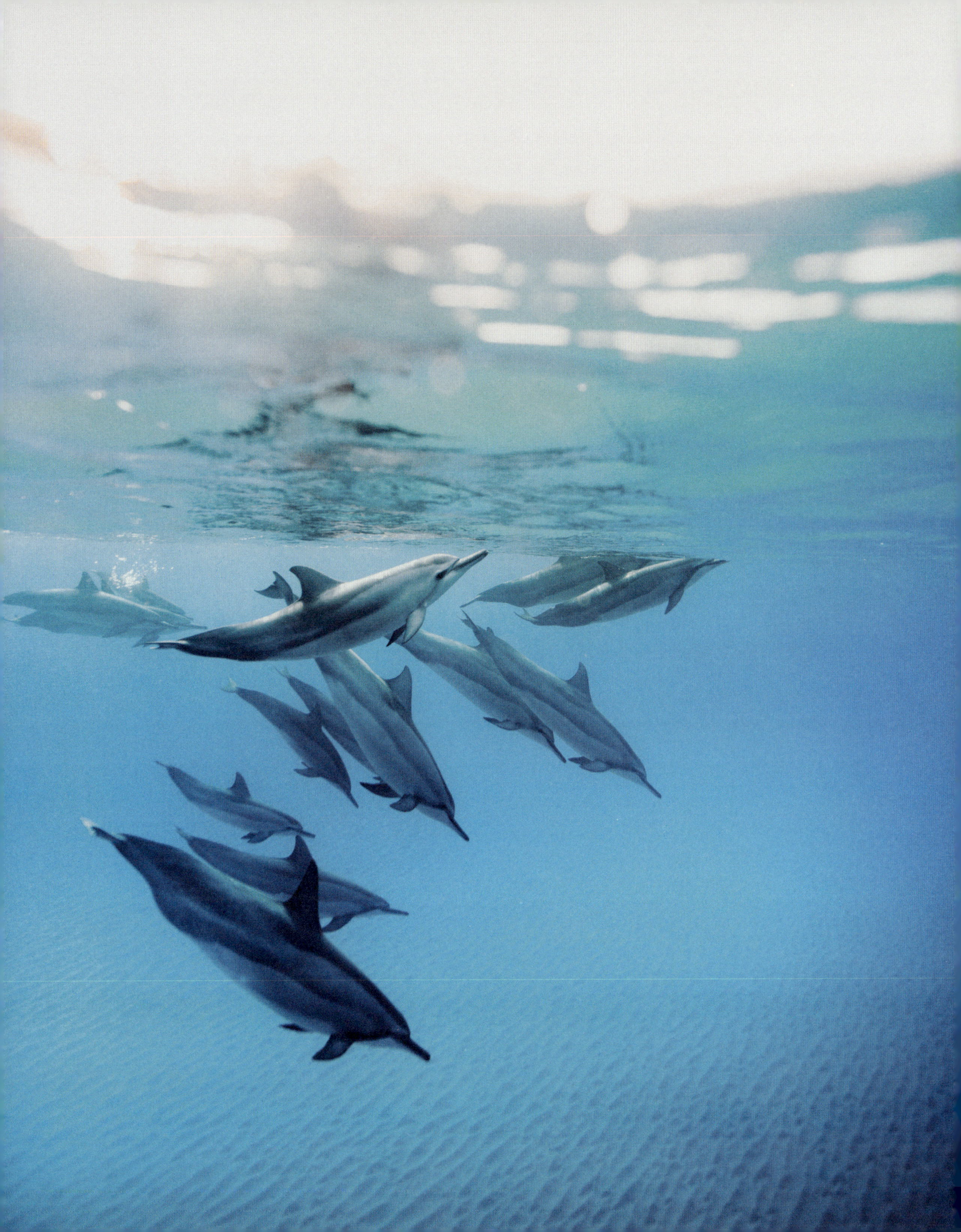

The desert stretches out to the beaches along the shores of the Baja California Sur coastline with fields of chamomile flowers and towering cardon cacti reaching toward the sky. Baja Sur, as it's commonly known, is nearly surrounded by the sea; the Pacific Ocean is to the west, and the Gulf of California is between its eastern shore and the Mexican mainland states of Sinaloa and Sonora. The Gulf of California is full of life: migrating whales, families of sea otters, and countless fish. It is possibly one of the most diverse seas on Earth, and areas of the gulf are classified as UNESCO World Heritage Sites. No matter where you are in Baja Sur, the ocean is never more than an hour's drive away, and many residents in rural communities make their living through fishing or in the service industry at the resorts, restaurants, and shops that depend on the visitors who travel there.

Baja Sur encounters challenges faced by all coastal ecosystems, but one is becoming particularly pernicious: sargassum. This leafy brown algae also appears in astonishingly dense blooms on beaches throughout the Caribbean and on the Caribbean coasts of Mexico and Central America. Scientists believe that increasing sargassum blooms are likely related to warming waters and nutrient pollution, specifically excess nitrogen. There are several contributing causes: runoff from synthetic fertilizers, waste from agricultural animal production, and the burning of fossil fuels, to name a few. Although both warming seas and nitrogen pollution can be attributed to human activity, it's difficult to pinpoint exactly why sargassum blooms are increasing along the coastal waters of Baja Sur. In the Sargasso Sea in the North Atlantic, for example, the floating seaweed is beneficial and provides both shelter and food for marine wildlife. But when it blooms in large quantities along coastlines, sargassum can smother corals and seagrasses and is detrimental to nesting sea turtles and other marine life. It also deters beach visitors, threatening the livelihood of local communities that depend on tourism.

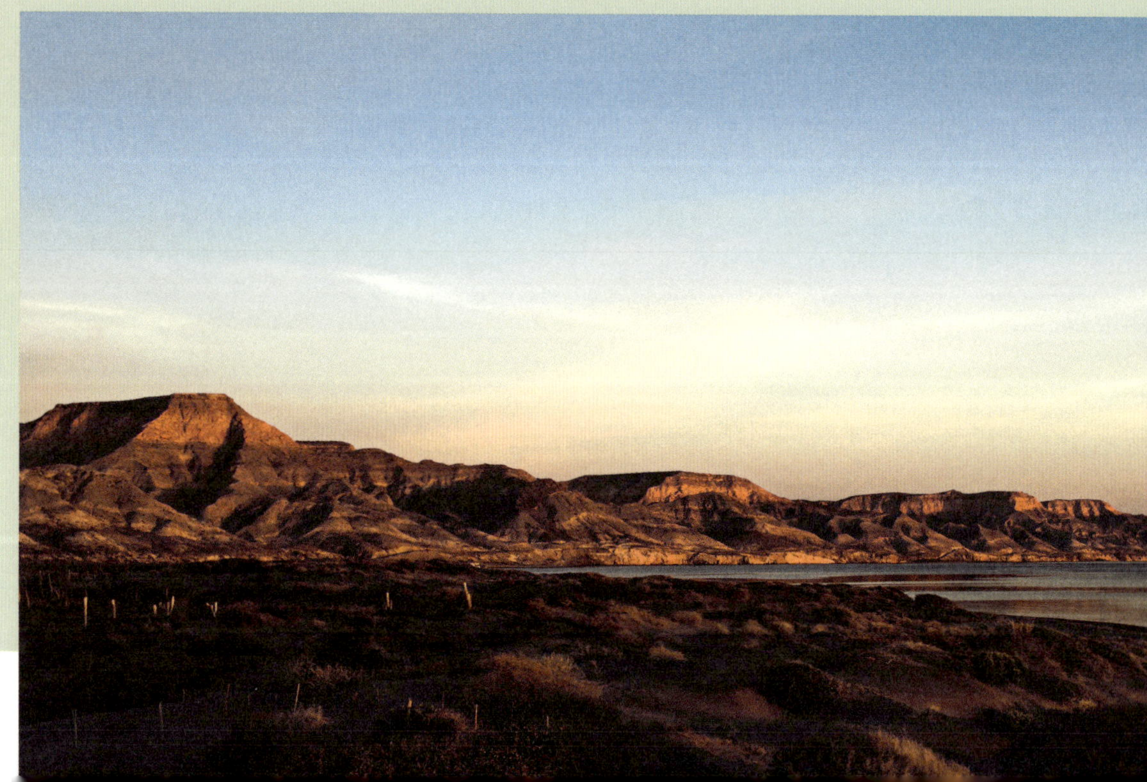

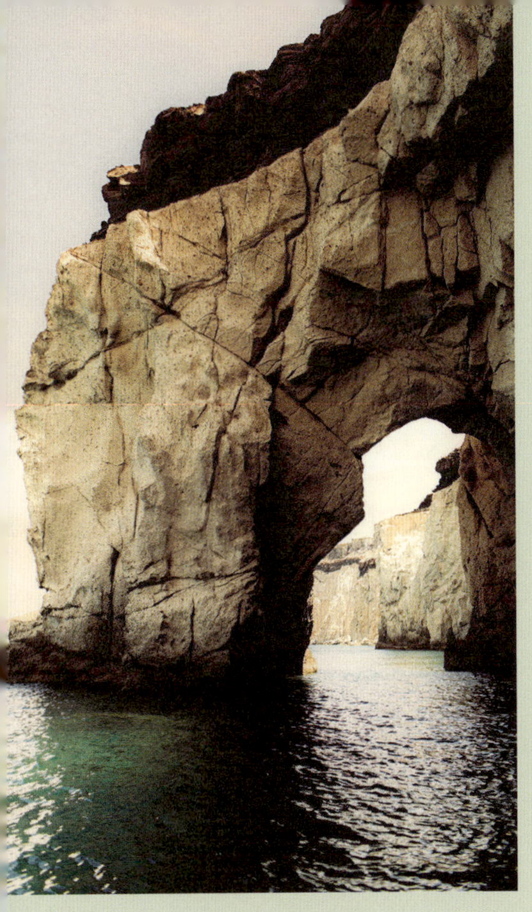

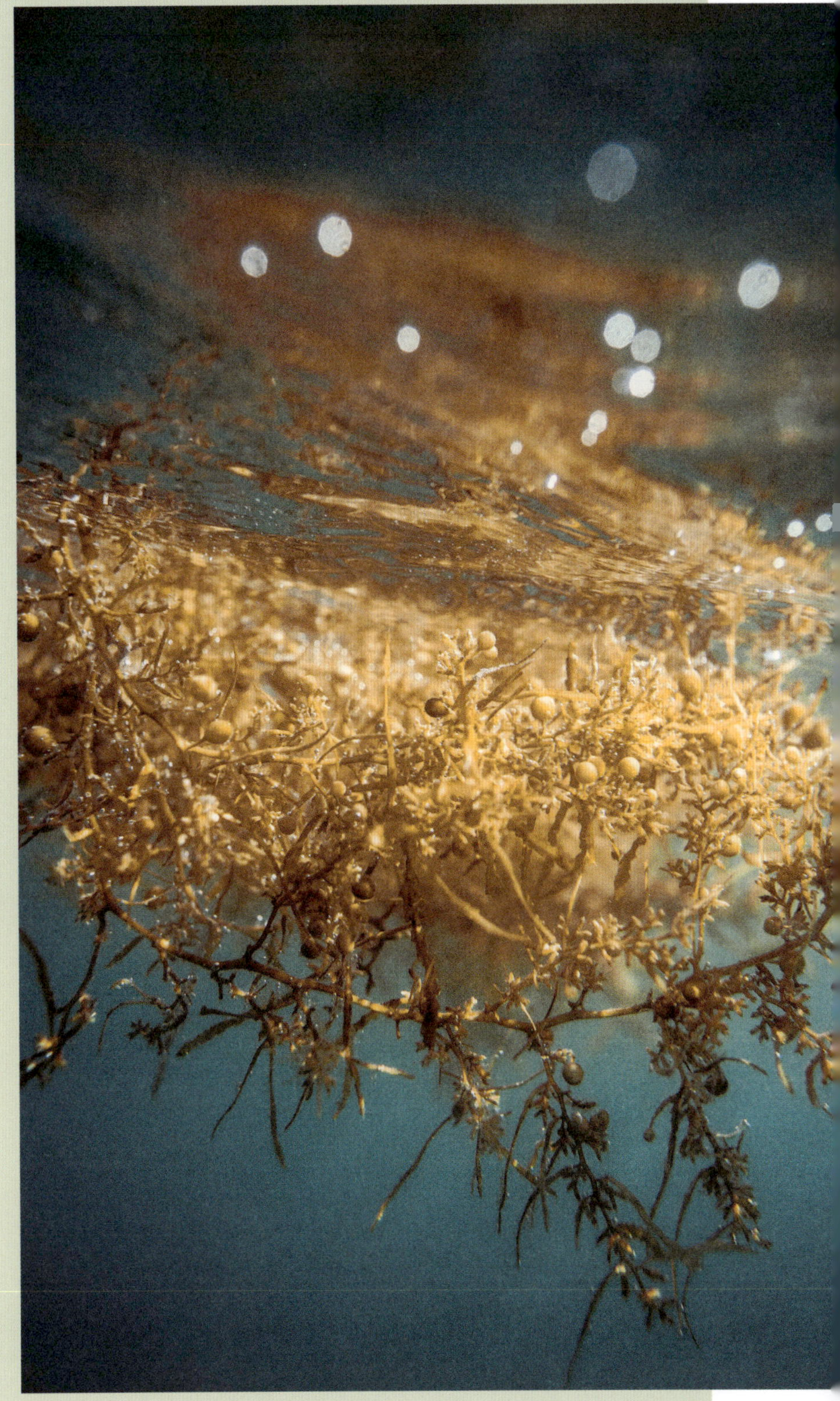

La Paz,
**Baja California
Sur, Mexico**
Gabriel Flores

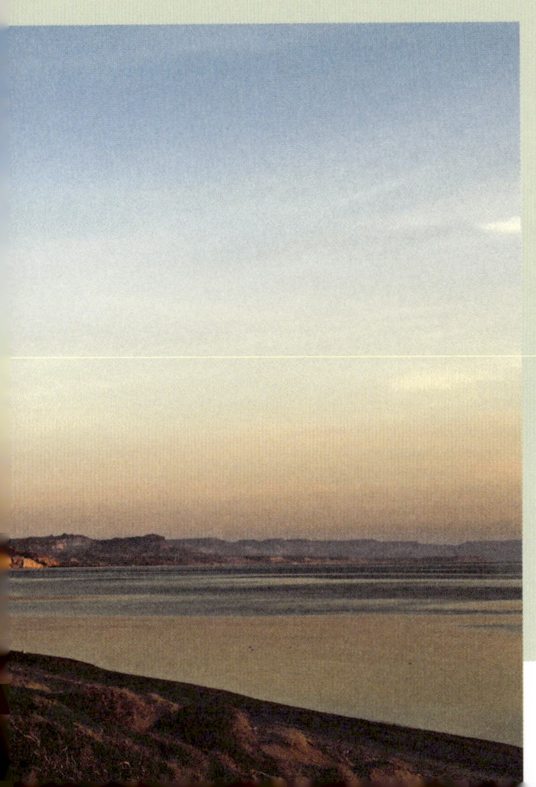

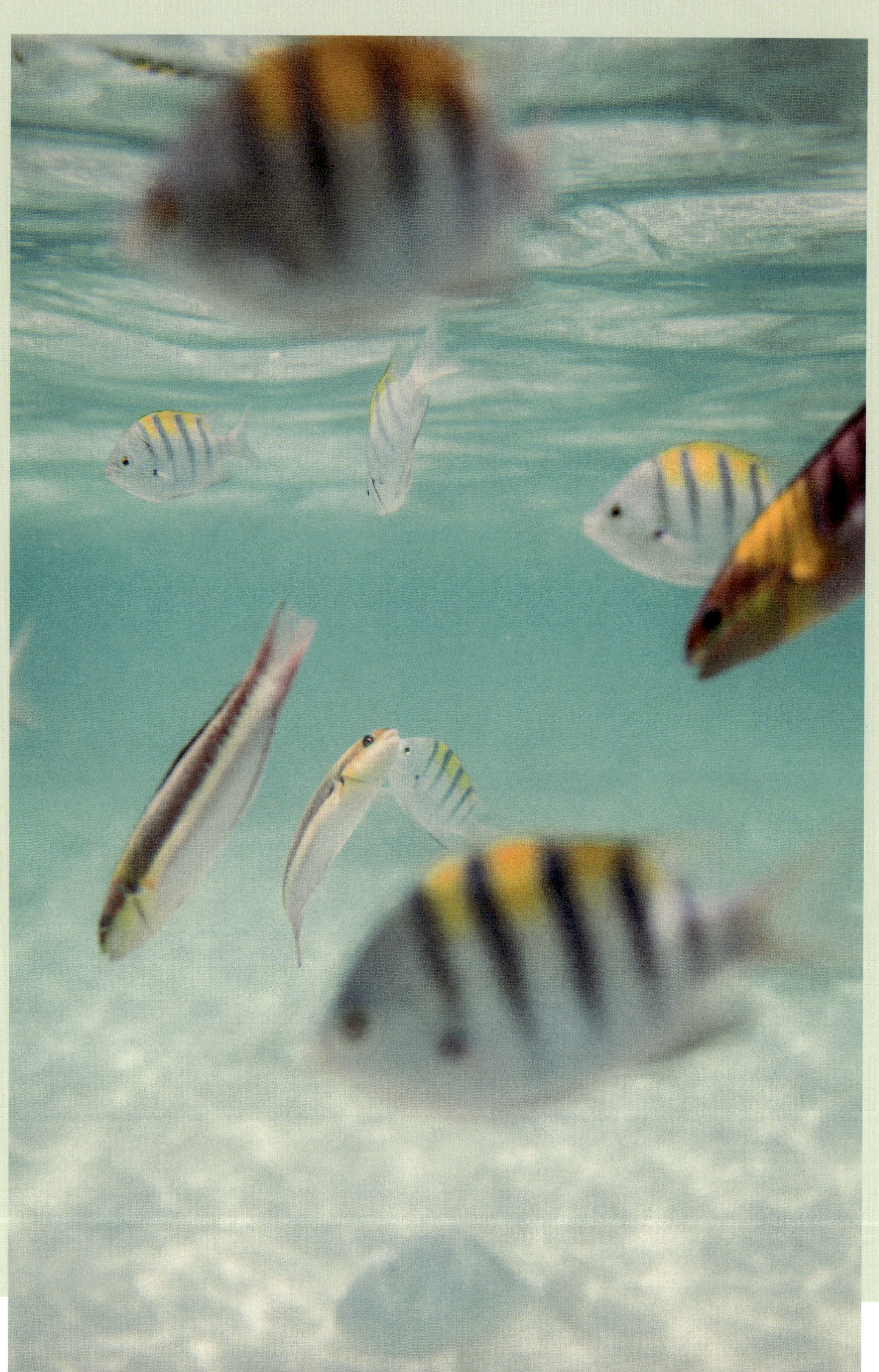

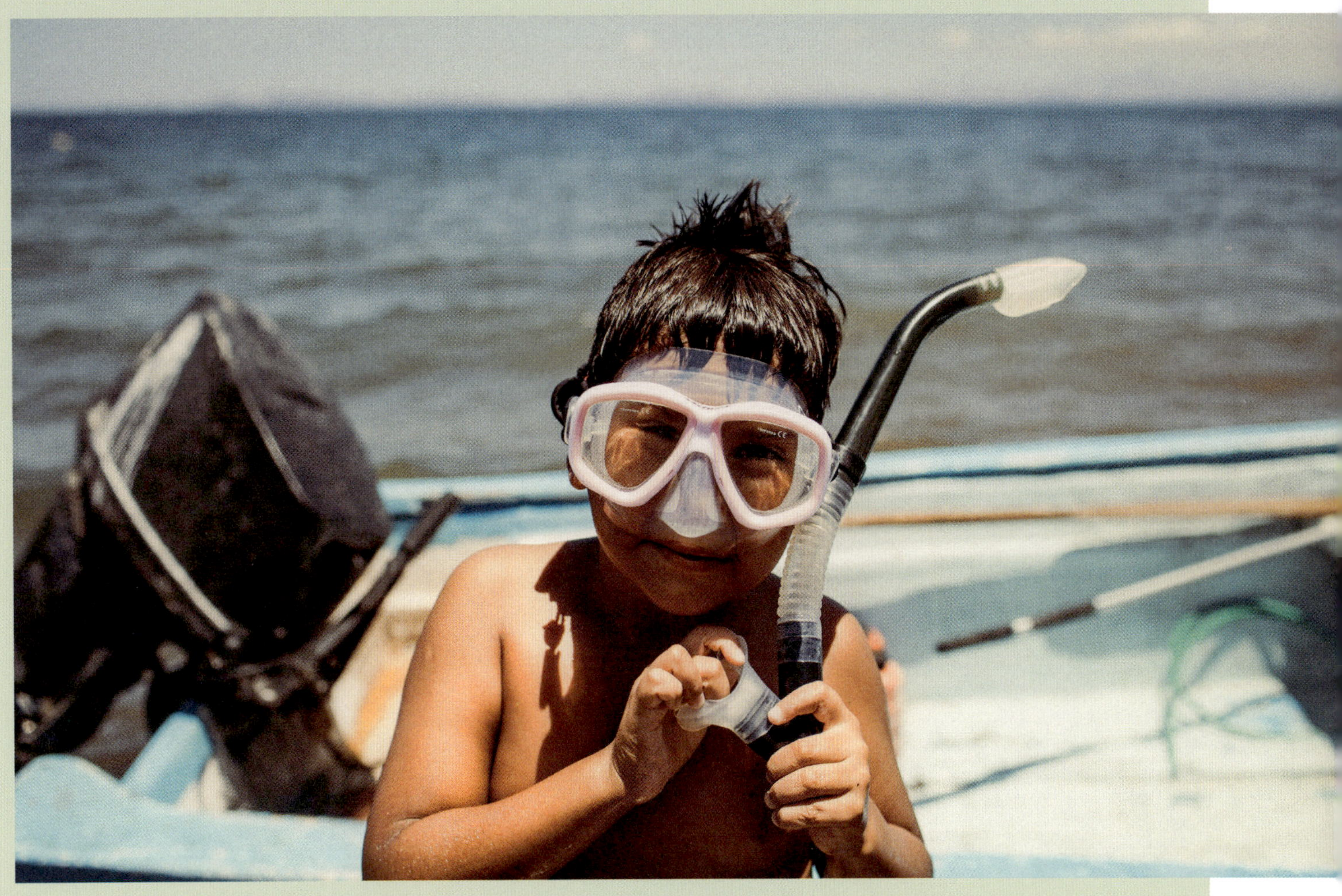

HOW YOU CAN HELP

- Visit Conserva Collective, a conservation nonprofit based out of San José del Cabo. The collective holds educational trips to learn about local environmental issues and harvest sargassum, which they use to make soap or as a building material, in partnership with local artisans.

- Reduce your contribution to nitrogen nutrient pollution. There are many ways to reduce your personal carbon footprint; you can start by eating foods grown locally and from farmers who limit their use of pesticides.

- Use online offsetting tools, such as Co2nsensus, to calculate your carbon footprint for personal and business air travel, donate to an offsetting project, and verify that the projects you donate to are legitimate.

**La Paz, Baja
California Sur, Mexico**
Gabriel Flores

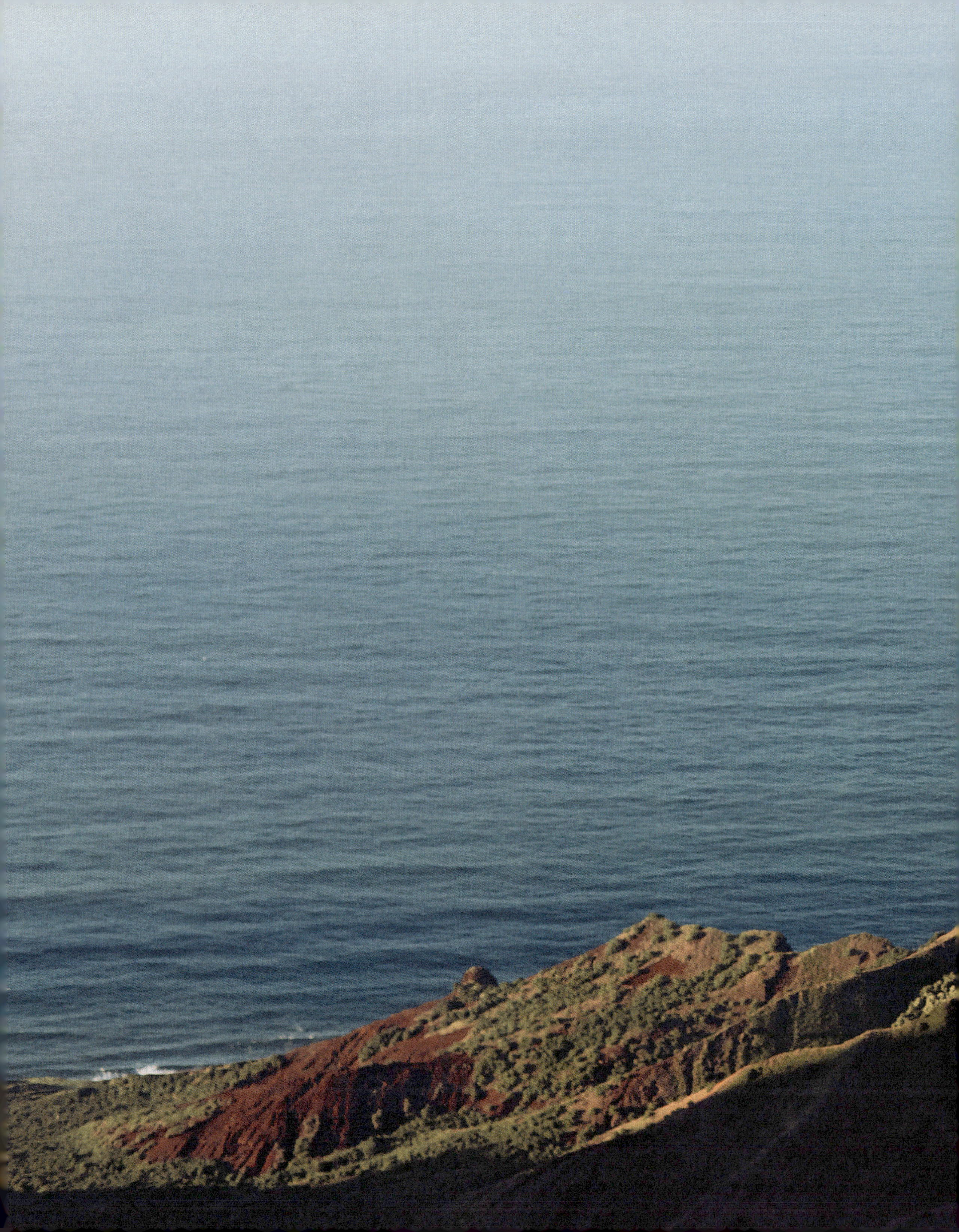

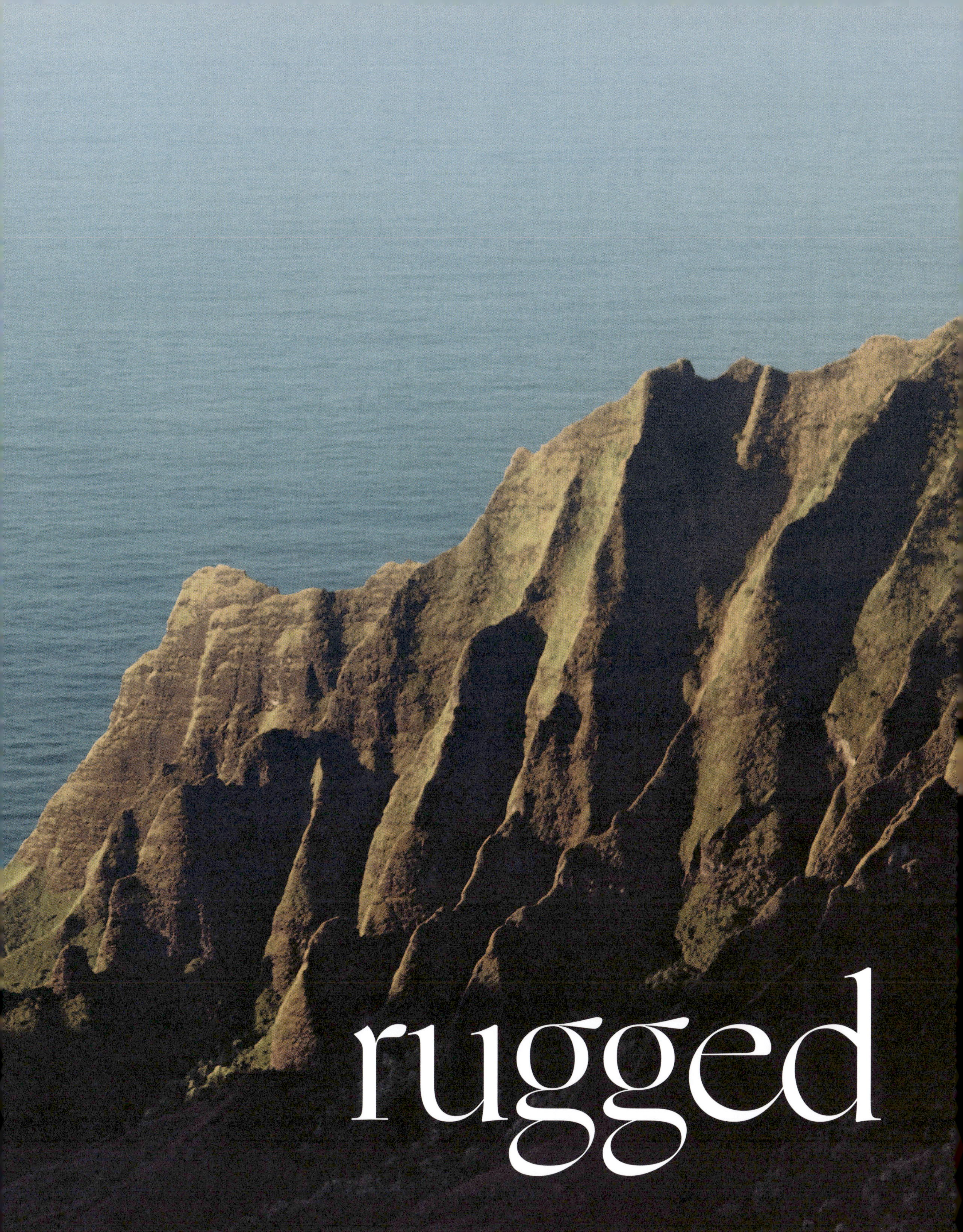
rugged

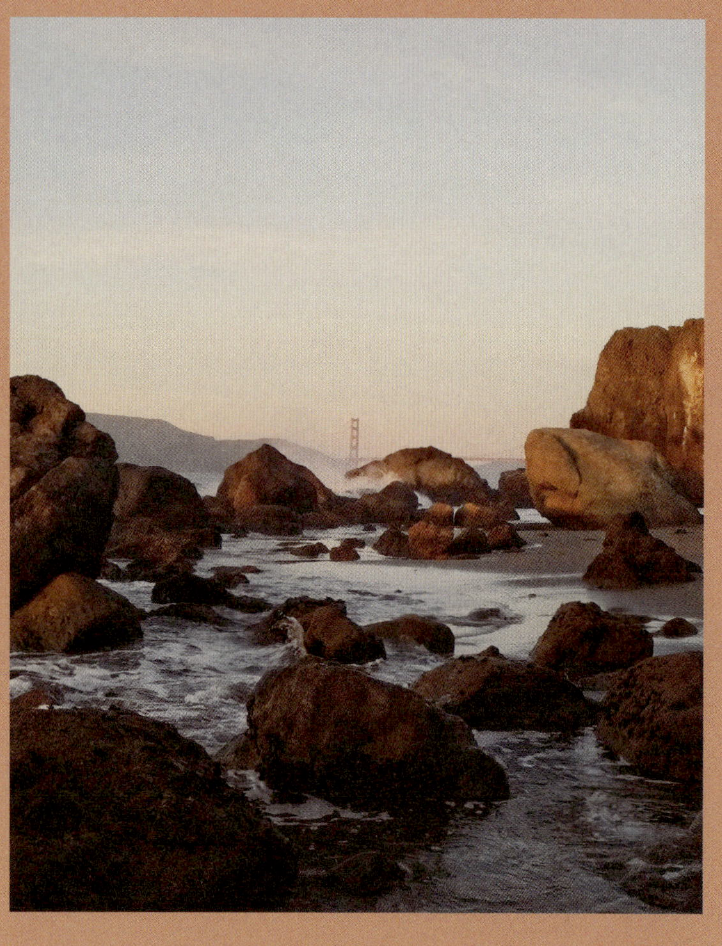

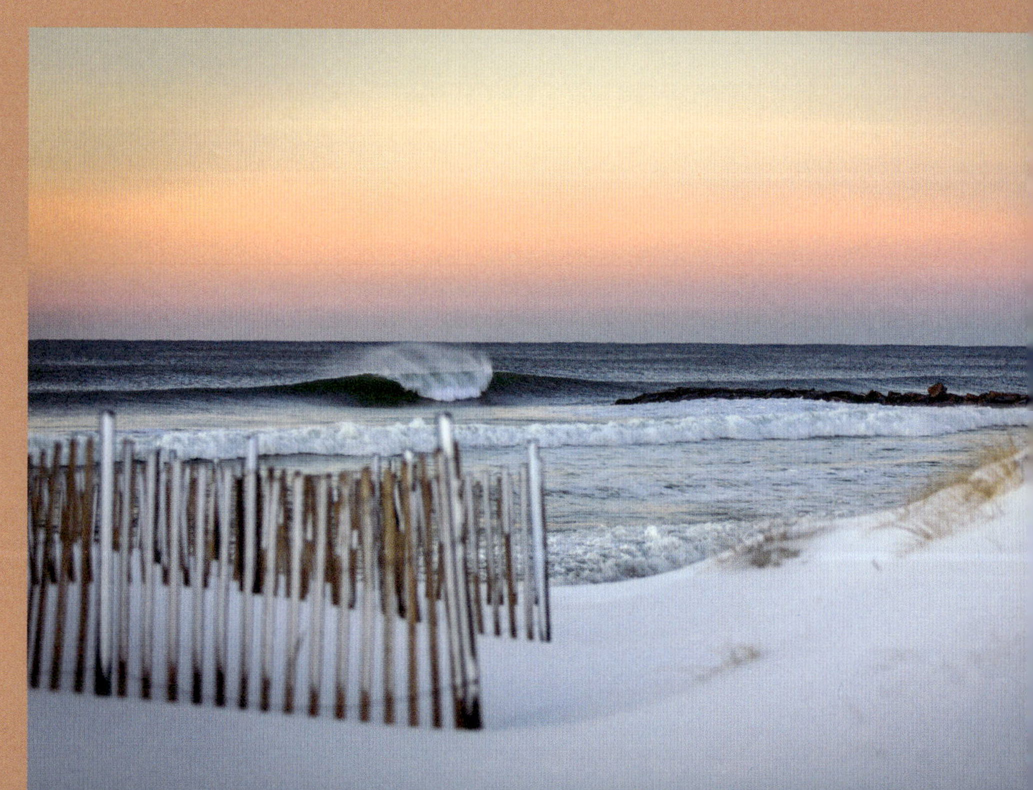

The Nā Pali Coast trail provides year-round access to experience Kaua'i's famous Nā Pali cliffs or for a different perspective you can kayak to take in the inspiring views from the sea.

**Waimea Canyon
State Park, Kaua'i,
Hawai'i, United States**
Emily Nathan

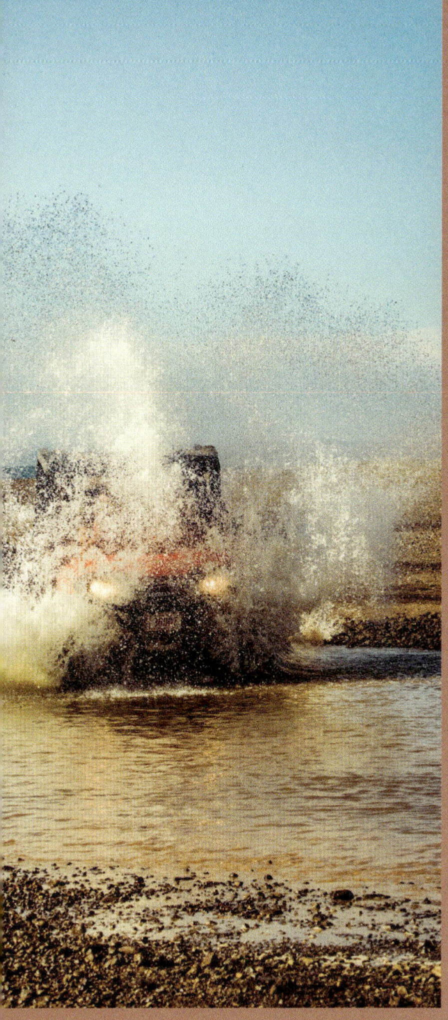

MANY OF OUR FAVORITE stretches of coastline are rugged. Volcanic peaks, steep limestone cliffs, and slick rocky outcroppings call to us. A dramatic coastal landscape can sometimes foreshadow the challenge it takes to get there. The nearest hotel may be a long distance away. When we visit rugged places, we are often not visiting for the amenities, which can be limited. We bring along our own supplies, make contingency plans, and prepare to gear-up for wild weather and unexpected obstacles if needed. Planning for the unexpected is impossible; however, expecting the unexpected is a mindset seasoned travelers often savor. The pleasures found at rugged beaches are often hard-won, but a hot-cooked meal served over a campfire beside the ocean tastes more delicious *because* of the difficulty in reaching the destination.

In Tofino, British Columbia, a few years ago, surrounded by dense forest beside the ocean with the sound of birds and crashing waves, I gathered with my travel group around a massive pot to eat freshly caught local crabs cooked over an outdoor fire. The simple act of eating felt luxurious, despite the rugged conditions. To get there, I'd taken a tiny plane through whiteout conditions from the Vancouver airport to the edge of Vancouver Island, holding my breath most of the flight. After landing, I drove through the rainy darkness to the edge of Pacific Rim National Park. A large cedar-hemlock tree had fallen across the long driveway blocking the entrance to the property at Wya Point. I had no choice but to climb over the trunk, hauling my bags and using a headlamp to find my way to my beachside yurt.

Even in a city like San Francisco, it's possible to experience solitude on the wild dramatic coast at Lands End. Locals love that it's difficult to find some of the smaller, more secluded stretches of shoreline, including Mile Rock Beach. There's no cellular reception along the winding forested trails, so no GPS. Many people simply get lost along the way. The park rangers post markers along the coastal trails that lead there, and there are plenty of maps available, but the combination of captivating dramatic views along the trail, powerful winds, and cold temperatures make for an often secluded beach, even at sunset when the beach is most spectacular. Veterans of the hike and destination know the experience is worth braving the cold winds that rush in from the west; they just pack a warm hat and coat along with their sunset picnic and a flashlight for the dark walk back to the car.

↑
Bahia Herradura, Puntarenas, Costa Rica
Gabriela Herman

↖
San Francisco, California, United States
Dan Tom

←
Westerly, Rhode Island, United States
Read McKendree

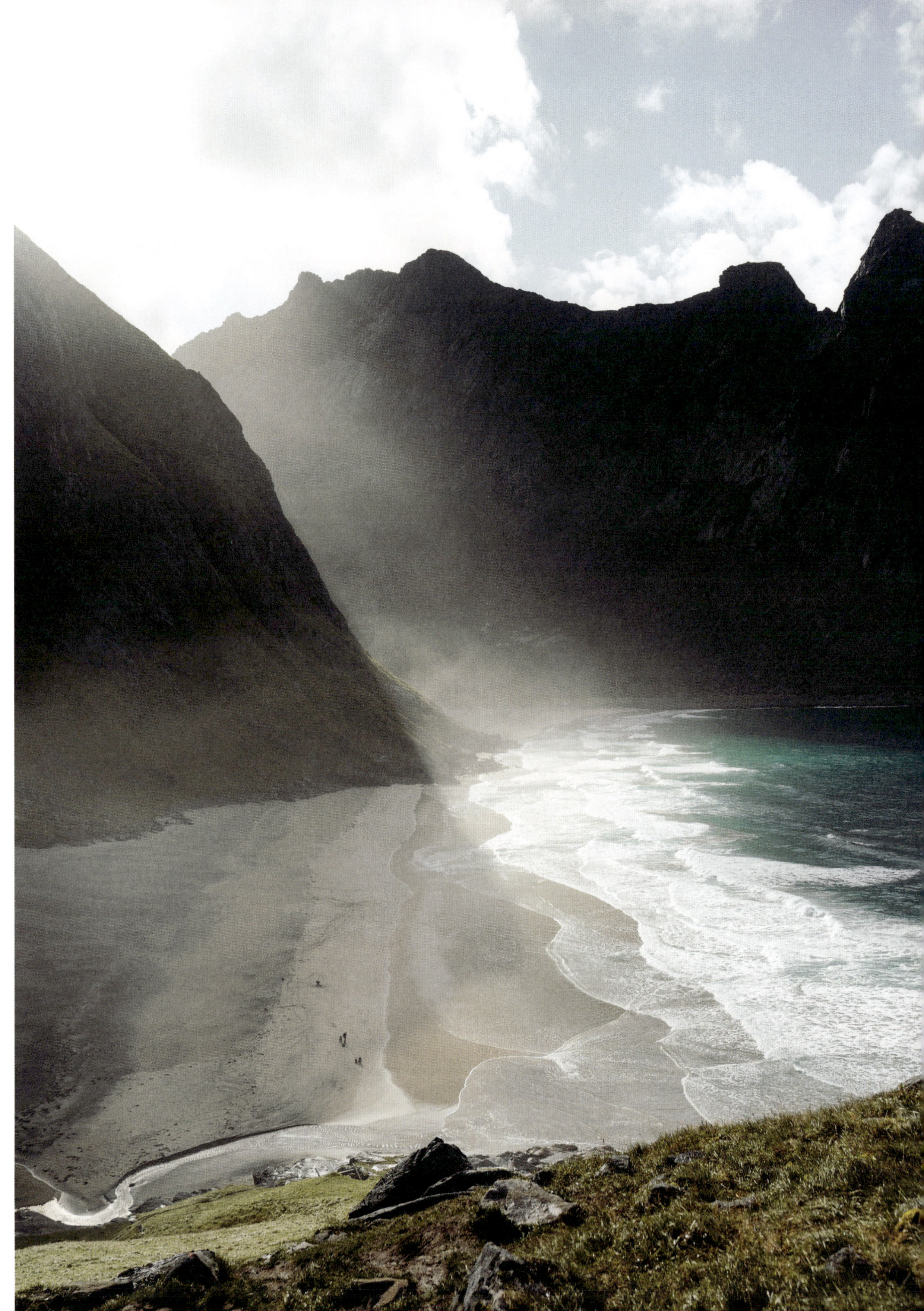

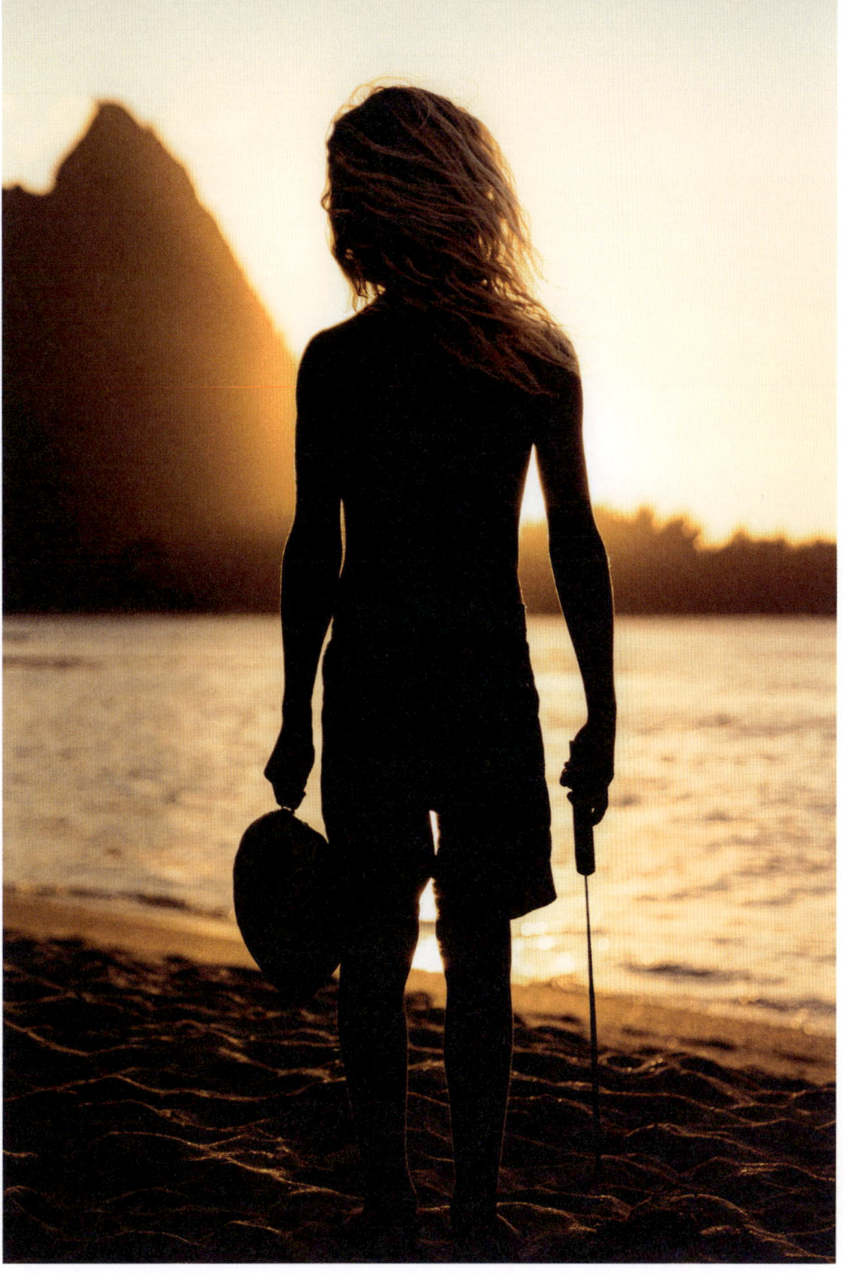

←
A FIVE-AND-A-HALF-MILE, three- to five-hour round-trip hike in the Lofoten Islands is considered moderate. The Ryten hike takes hikers across the peaks to a vista of white sands of Kvalvika Beach. From the vista, there is a choice to either detour down to the beach or continue on up to the peak of Ryten Mountain. The way back takes you across wooden boardwalks and past an elevated lake.

**Kvalvika Beach,
Lofoten, Norway**
Anne-Sophie Rosenvinge

↑
**Hā'ena, Kaua'i,
Hawai'i, United States**
Benjamin Ono

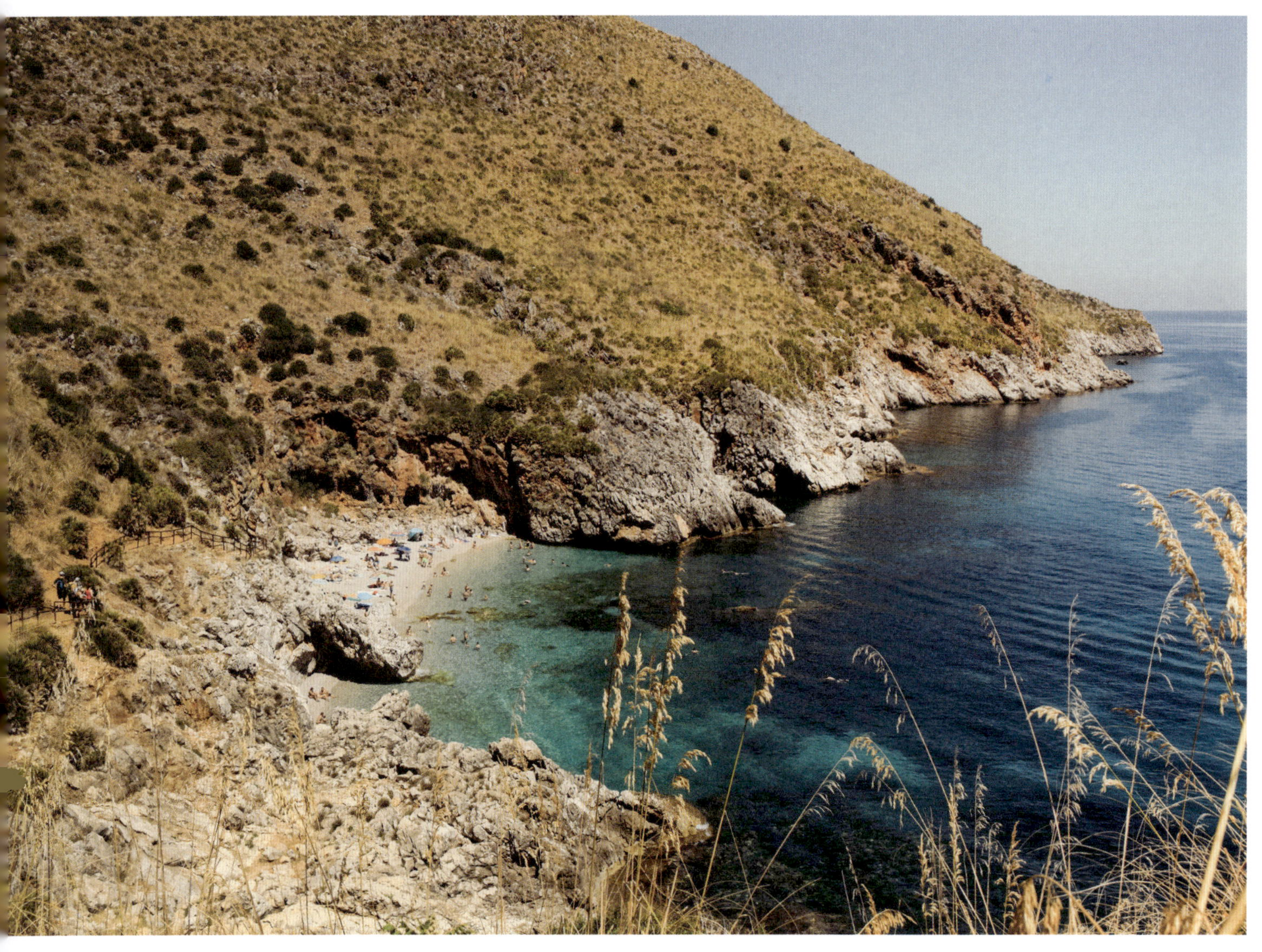

↑
Scopello,
Trapani, Italy

Katie McKnoulty

→
Aigua Xelida,
Girona, Spain

Raquel Guiu Grigelmo

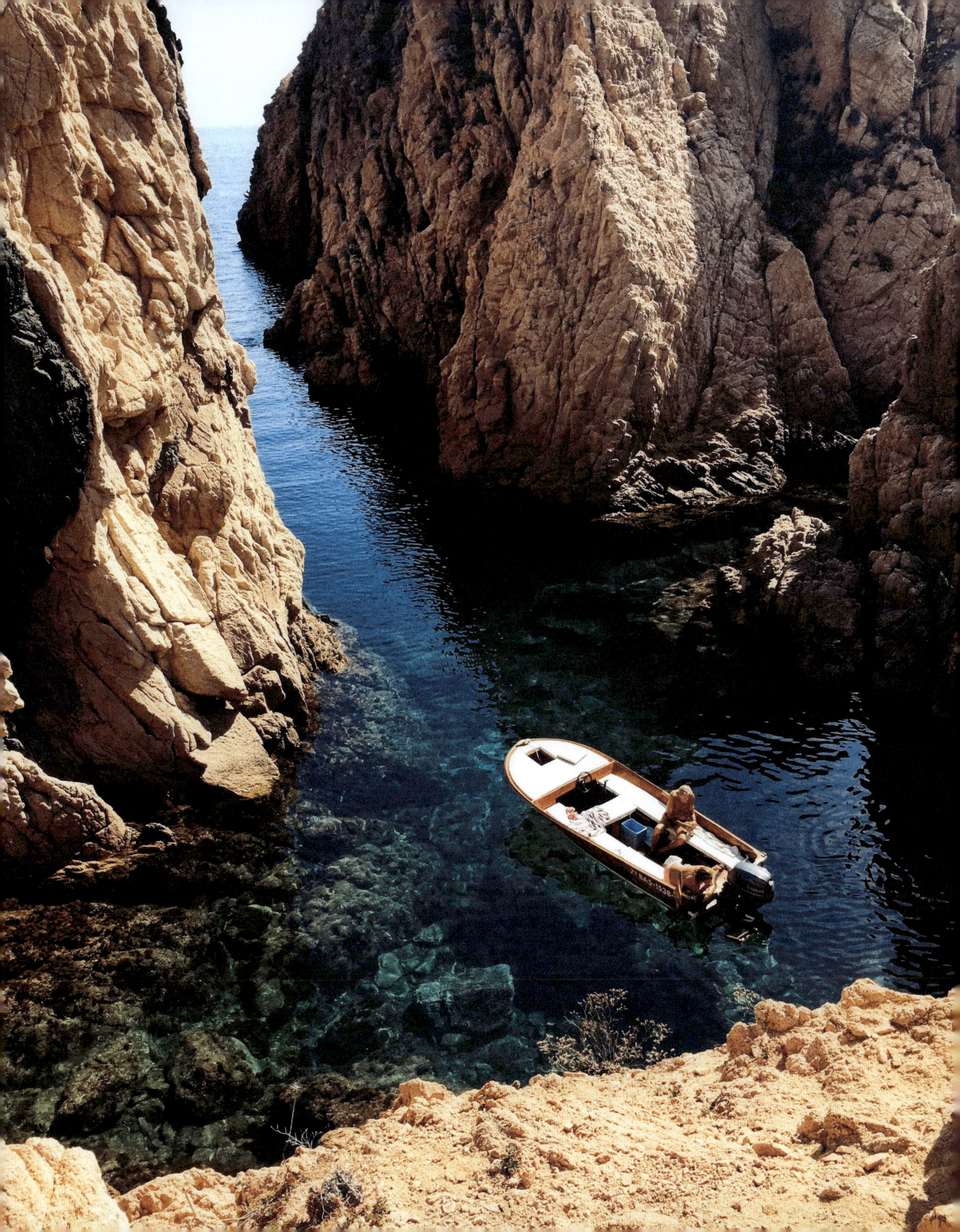

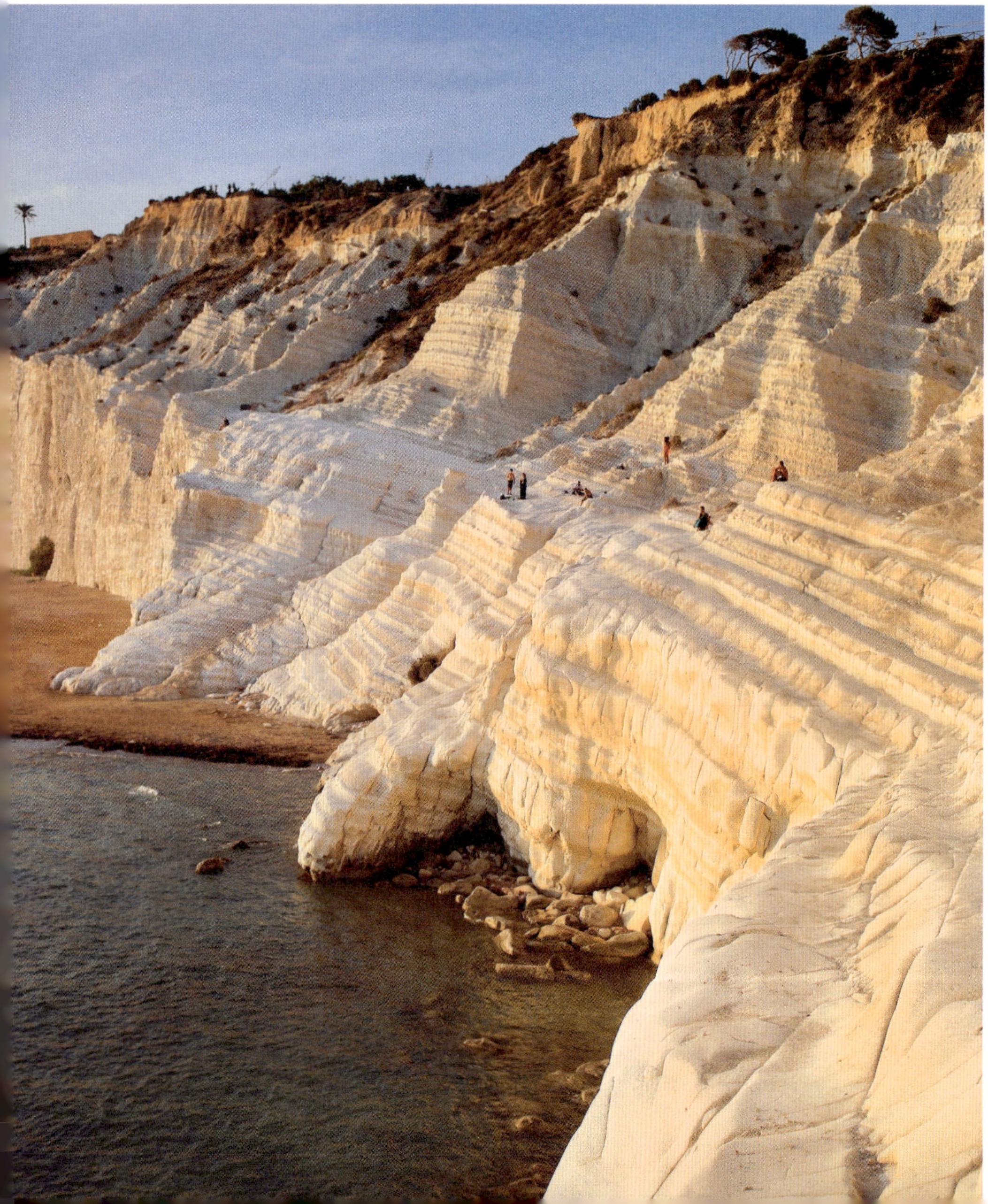

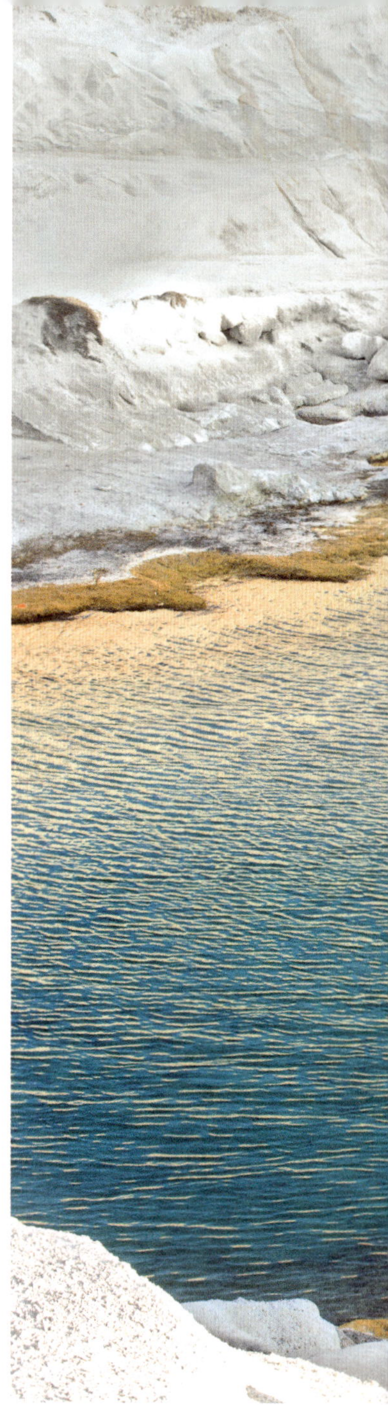

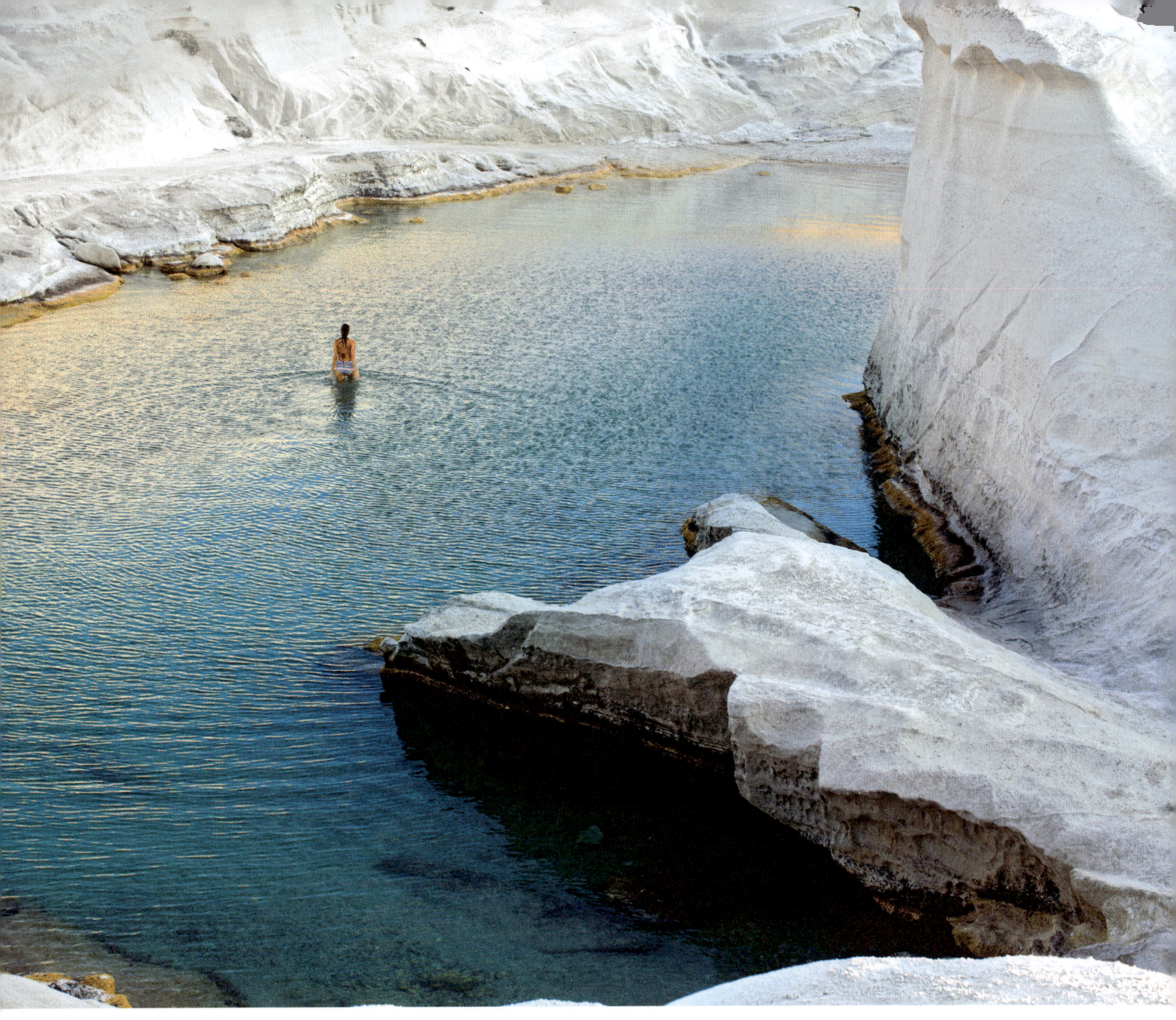

THESE DRAMATIC CLIFFS on the southern coast of
Sicily between Realmonte and Porto Empedocle are
called Scala dei Turchi ("Stair of the Turks"). Although
the location looks as if it were on the moon, there is
regular bus service to the Scala from Porto Empedocle
as well as parking, bathrooms, and dining.

**Porto Empedocle,
Sicily, Italy**

Niki Csányi

THE FAMOUS LUNAR-LOOKING cliffs of Sarakiniko
are centrally located in Milos, just fifteen minutes
away from most of the island. Toward the end
of September, the crowds disperse and you can
have the whole place to yourself.

**Sarakiniko, Milos,
Cyclades, Greece**

Lou Mora

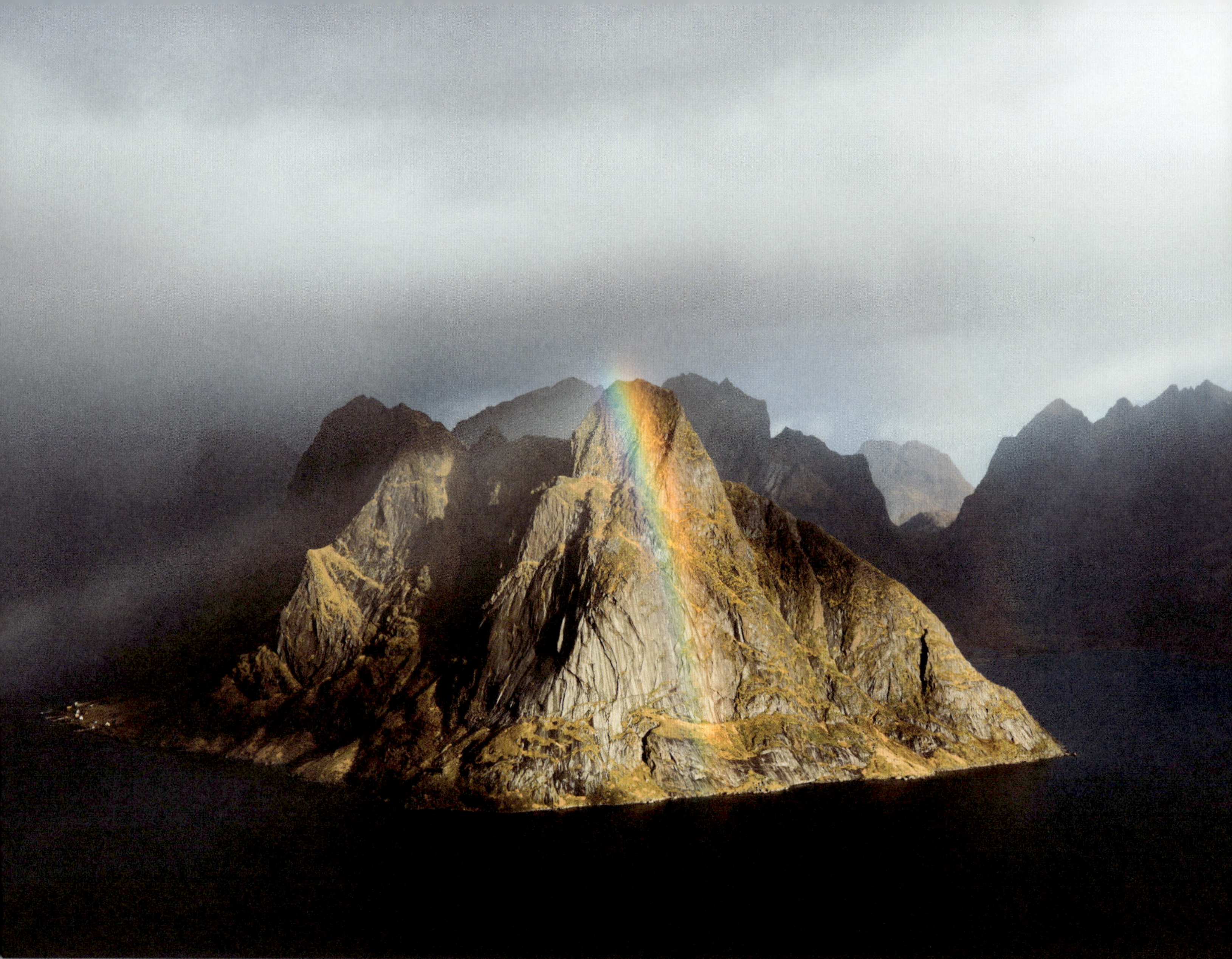

REINEBRINGEN IS A popular short (but hard and steep) hike on Moskenesøya island that overlooks the towns of Reine, Sakrisøy, and Hamnoy in the Lofoten archipelago of Norway. Rain can turn the already steep terrain into an even muddier challenge, but hikers are rewarded with this view from the top (with or without a rainbow). Well above the Arctic Circle in the Norwegian Sea, Lofoten is an hour-long flight from Norway's capital, Oslo. Travelers usually rent a car to explore the area's picturesque fishing villages known for their Viking heritage, midnight sun, and all manner of outdoor adventure opportunities such as cold-water surfing. Lofoten is designated a formal Nordic region Sustainable Destination. As a Sustainable Destination, Lofoten is focused on the preservation of nature and the environment as well as the local culture while actively working to maintain the area as a good place to live for locals.

**Moskenesøya,
Lofoten, Norway**
Joel Hyppönen

→
Lofoten, Norway
Eric Flogny

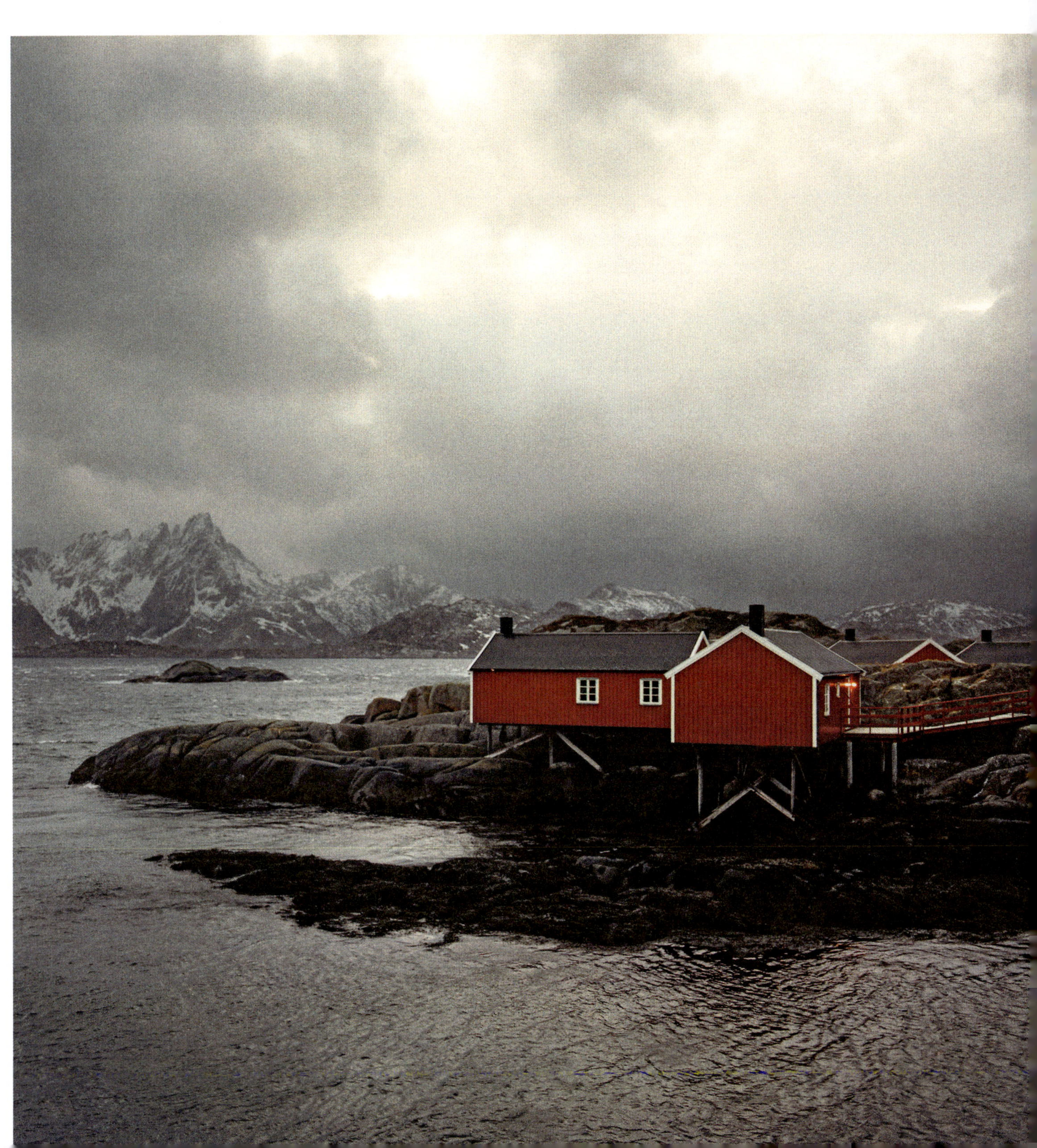

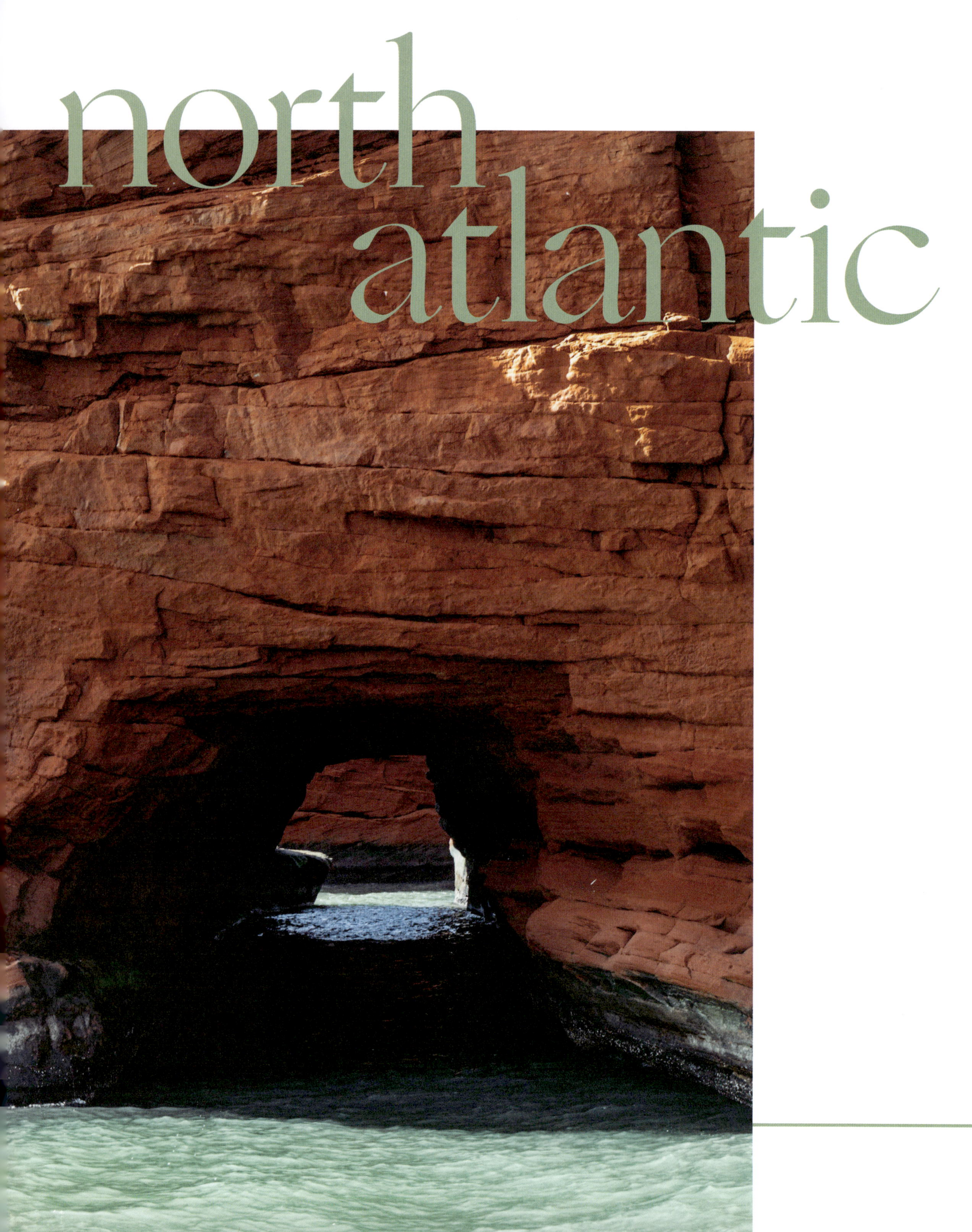
north
atlantic

coast

UNITED STATES AND CANADA

THE NORTH ATLANTIC COAST of Quebec is a rugged natural landscape that doesn't see many tourists. There is little human footprint here, and vast swaths of the land are protected. The landscape along the coast offers a lot of variety, from the brackish water in Saguenay River to sweet towns nestled in deciduous forests along the Saguenay Fjord National Park. Off the coast are the gray and red sandstone Magdalen Islands (Les Îles-de-la-Madeleine), which are closer to Newfoundland than the rest of Quebec. The red cliffs in Cap-aux-Meules have been sculpted by wind and waves and stand as a stark contrast to the gentler surrounding coast.

Nearby, the coast of Maine boasts Acadia National Park, principally located on Mount Desert Island. Acadia was the first American national park to be designated east of the Mississippi River. The vast parklands lure visitors with quiet forests, granite peaks, and a wild coastline. The highest peak in the park is Cadillac Mountain, which is also the highest point on the East Coast. The park entrance is a few miles from the bayside town of Bar Harbor and 177 miles from Portland, Maine, along US Route 1. It is also a short drive southeast of Bangor International Airport and only a few hours south of the Canadian border in New Brunswick.

From various spots in Bar Harbor or inside the park, visitors can hop on a network of free, clean, propane-powered buses, the Island Explorers, that run a 27-mile, three- to four-hour loop and stop at trailheads, island beaches, and towns. The park is a major draw for cruise ships and visitors from outside the region who come to view the fall foliage colors. Remember, though, that even in summer, this is a northern region with unpredictable weather, so travelers should be prepared with weather-resistant clothes and hiking boots. The park is dog friendly and, as in all parks, visitors are reminded to leave no trace.

PHOTOGRAPHS BY MARIANNA JAMADI

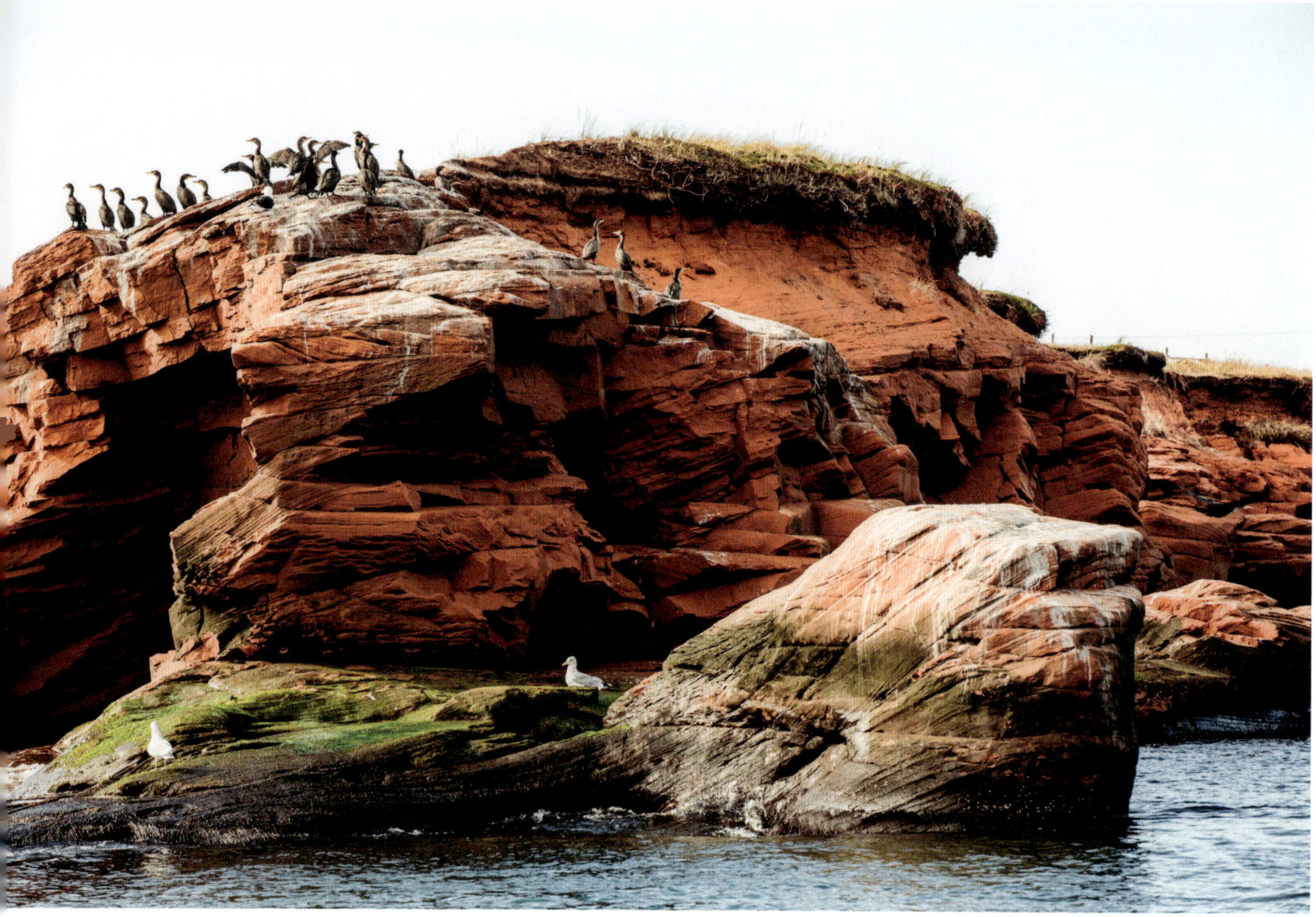

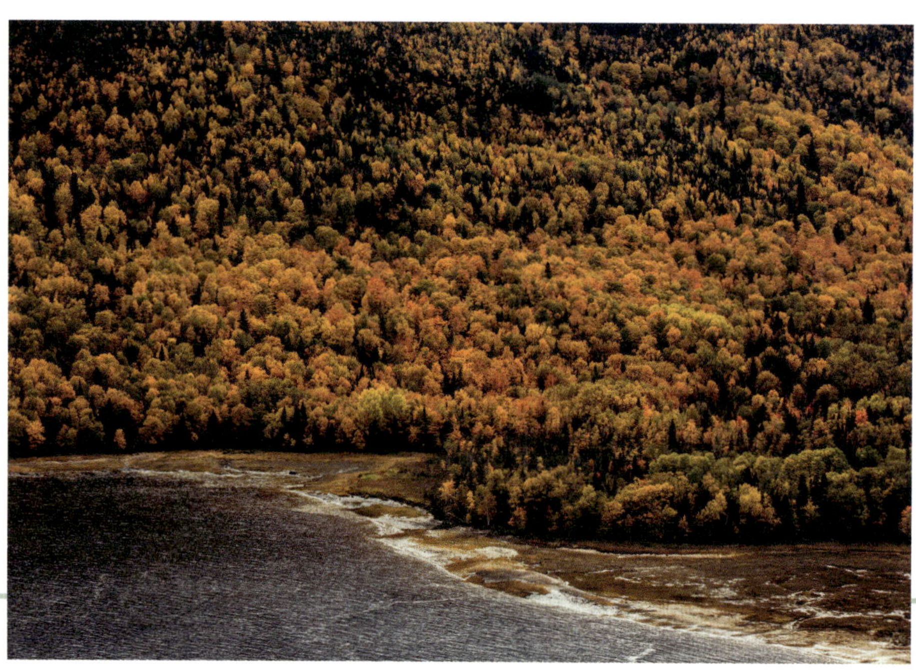

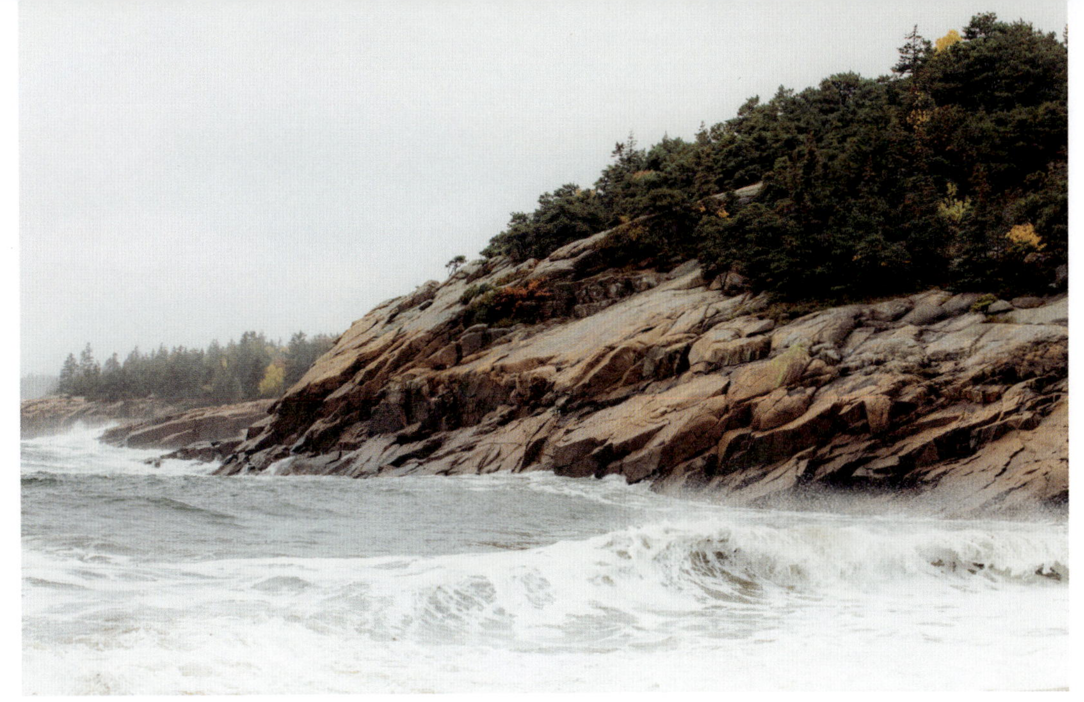

NORTH ATLANTIC COAST

Seabourn Quest, Acadia National Park, Maine and Quebec, Canada

Photographs by Marianna Jamadi

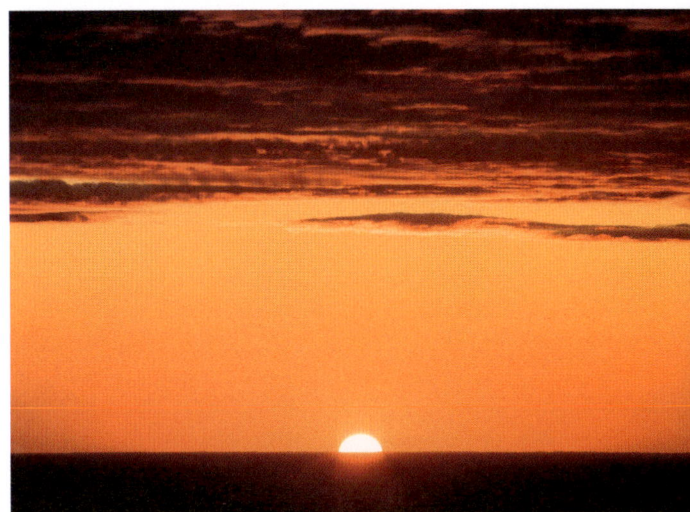

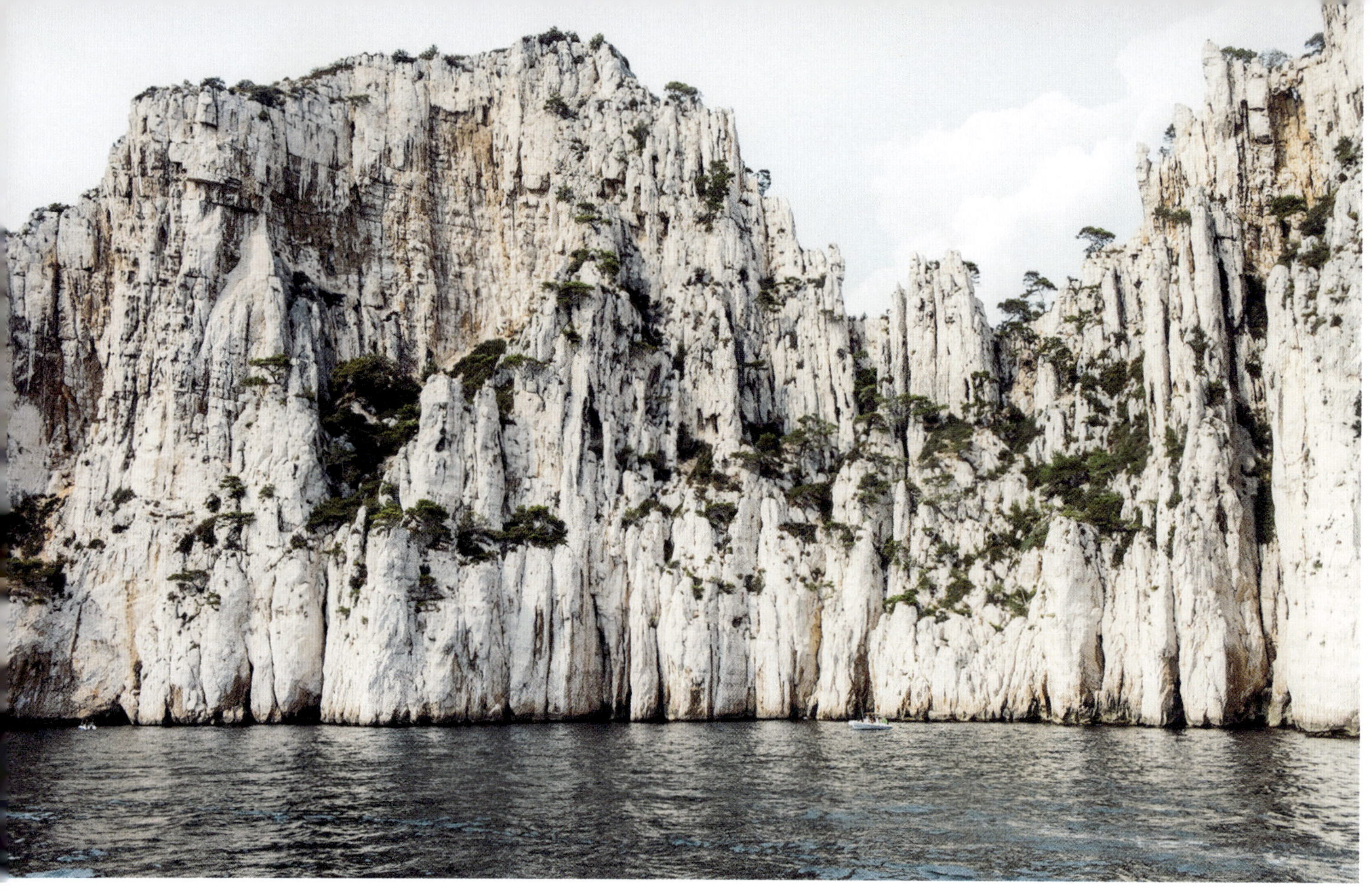

STEEP WHITE CLIFFS characterize the Calanques National Park just outside the popular Mediterranean beach retreat of Cassis in France. Even though summers are hot, travelers hike for hours to swim in the turquoise water of the inlets. For easier access, travelers can charter a speed or sailboat to explore the massive limestone cliffs from another perspective. To get to the Calanques, international travelers typically fly into Paris and take the comfortable high-speed train through the countryside south to Marseille. To explore further, buses or a rental car are needed. In order to protect beaches, cliffs, and coastal flora from erosion caused by increasing tourism, the French government now requires visitors to make free reservations online in advance for certain areas.

**Calanques
National Park,
Bouches-du-
Rhône, France**
Stephanie Eburah

THE SMALL TOWN of Bandon, Oregon, located on the south shore of the mouth of the twisting Coquille River where it empties into the Pacific Ocean, has a variety of accessible state parks and wildlife refuges. Driving south from Portland to the area along Route 1 takes four to five hours, or about two hours from Eugene. Bandon is a popular family and leisure travel spot, though weather can vary dramatically on the northern Pacific coast. All Oregon beaches are public, and places to visit after the beach abound, including local breweries, fish and chips spots, and art galleries, like Washed Ashore, where plastic pollution is turned into educational sculpture.

Locally, camping is available at Bullards Beach State Park, and the Bandon Dunes Golf Course is considered to be the best in the state. It is legal to harvest shellfish and edible marine plants seasonally in Bandon, and fishing licenses can be purchased at local bait shops and hardware stores. As a result, a popular local activity is to rent a crab pot from the Old Town pier and fish for Dungeness crab, feasting for the cost of bait and luck.

**Bandon, Oregon,
United States**
Bénédicte Lassalle

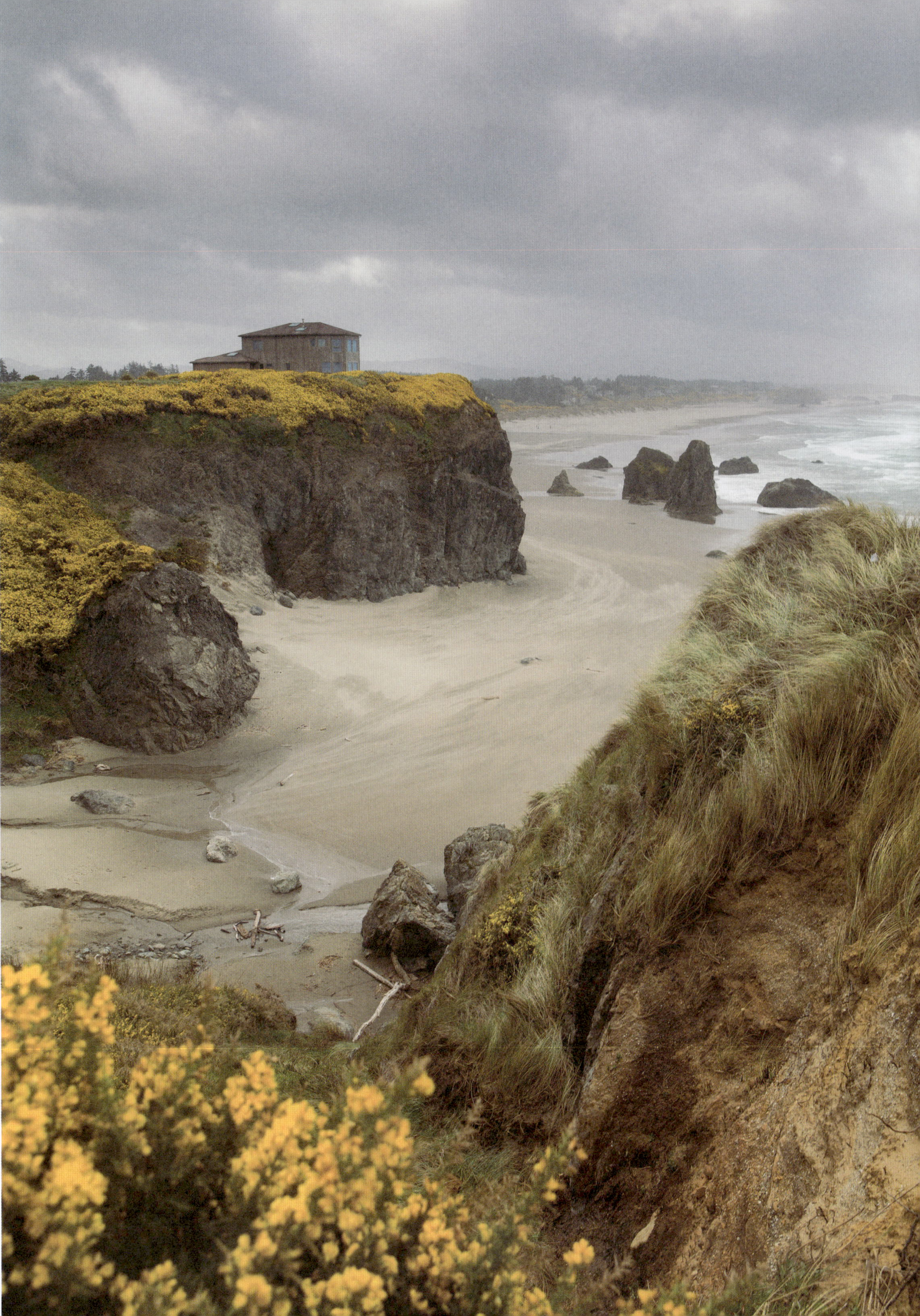

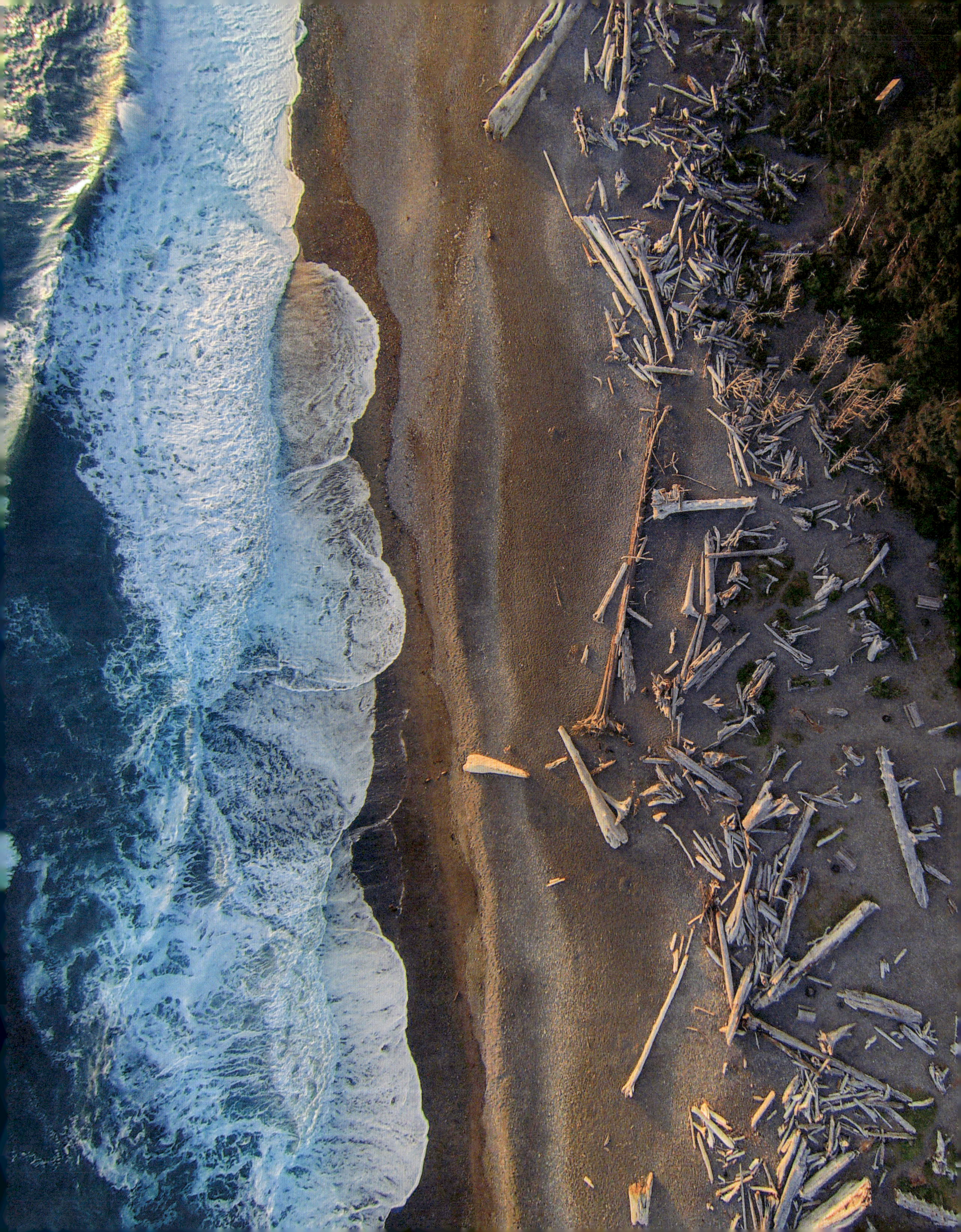

← **Brookings, Oregon,
United States**

Dirk Dallas

↓

THE ISLAND OF Andros is only a two-hour ferry ride from the Athens
port of Rafina, making it an easy weekend escape for Athenians
and international visitors alike who may want to visit the Greek Isles
without having to take additional flights. Chora (or, locally, Xora)
is the main town on the island of Andros. St. Thalassini church is
walkable from Chora, just outside the town border.

**Chora, Andros,
Cyclades, Greece**

Nicole Franzen

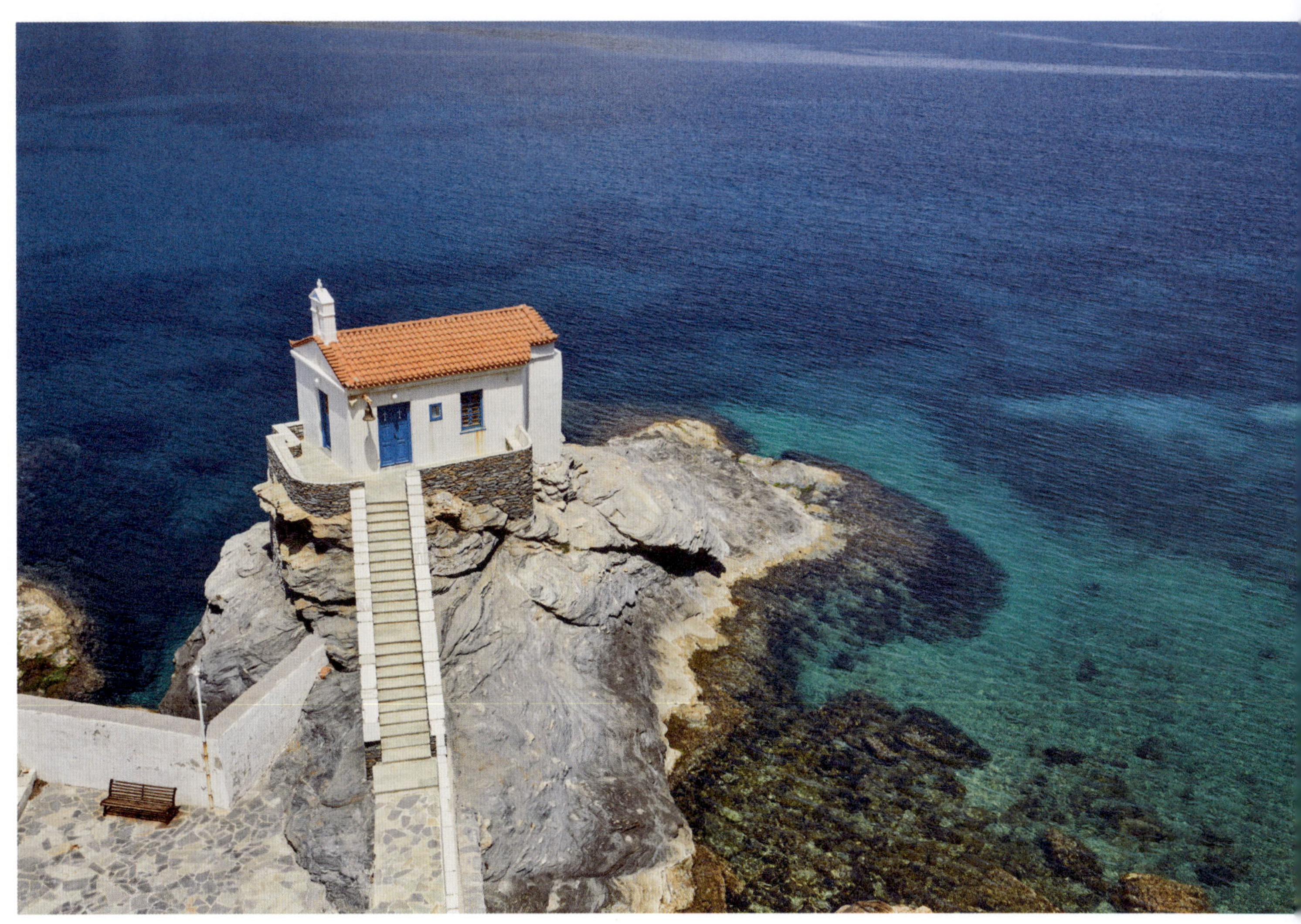

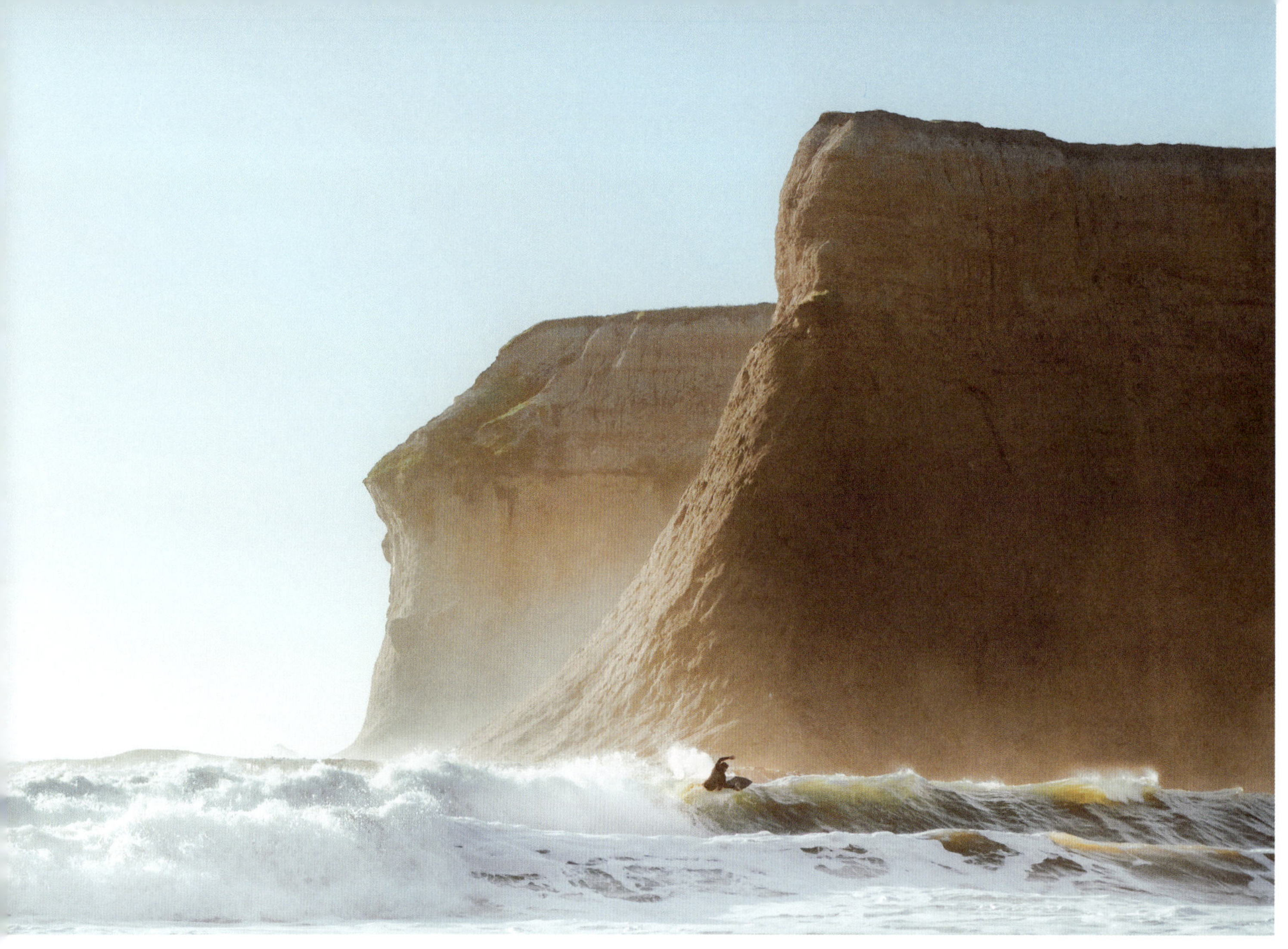

**Half Moon Bay,
California,
United States**

Emilia J. Wroński

BIG SUR, AN unincorporated "town" on California's famous coastal Highway 1, is about a half hour south of the town of Carmel. This stretch of Central California coastline is nestled between redwood forests and the Pacific and is so steep and seasonally wet that it is periodically inaccessible due to landslides. When such road closures occur, locals can get supplies only via boat or routes east through the Santa Lucia Mountains.

The area is notable for its natural beauty but also for the counterculture figures like Henry Miller and Hunter S. Thompson, who spent time living and working in the area in the 1960s. The Henry Miller Library is a treasure in the area and a present-day secret show spot for bands traveling up and down the coast on tour. While the area is sparsely populated, there are all manner of places to stay and dine, with cherished camping spots, inexpensive (and luxurious) cabins, short-term vacation rentals, inns, and a few luxury hotels and cliffside bars.

**Big Sur, California,
United States**

Marianna Jamadi

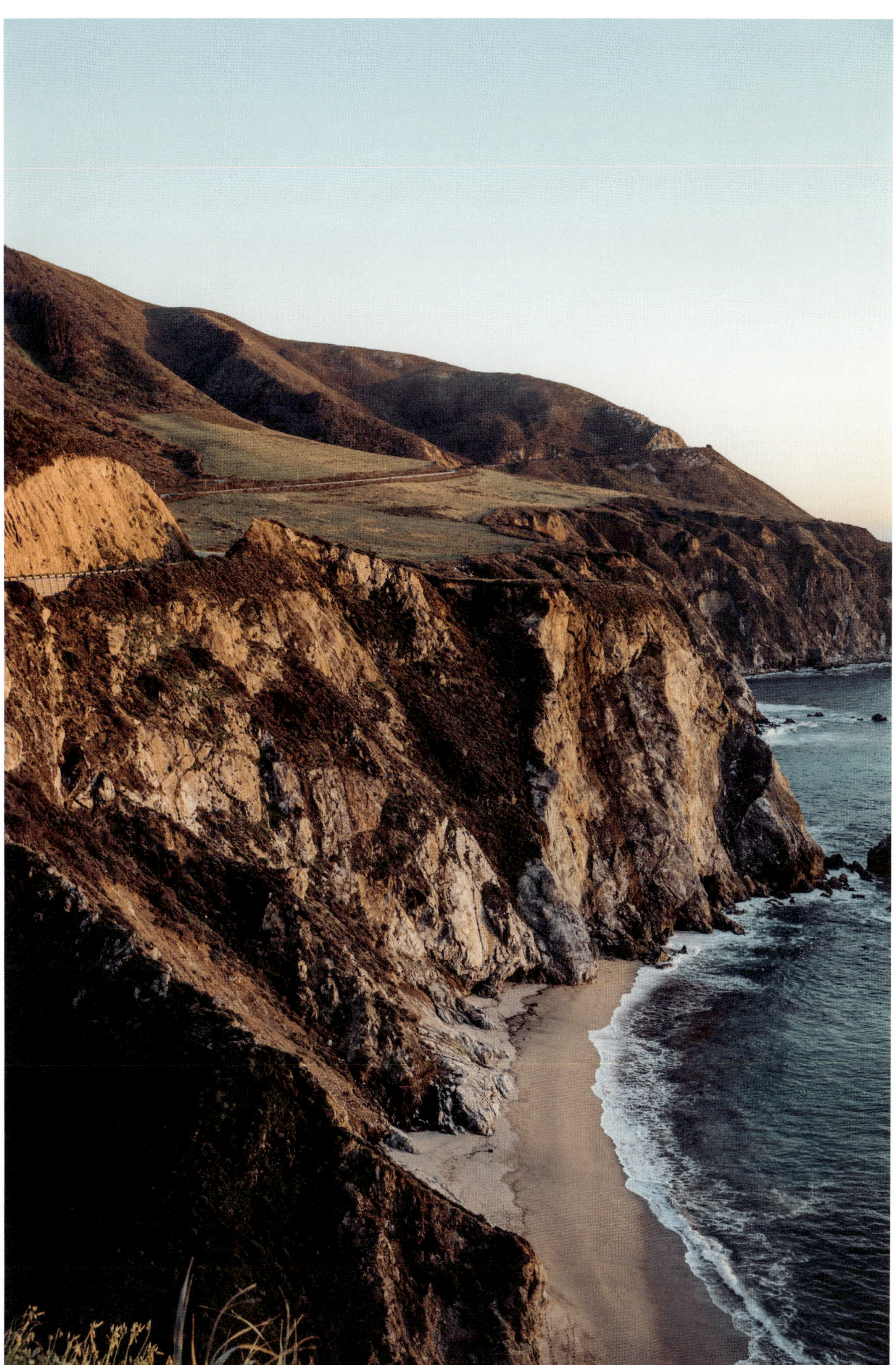

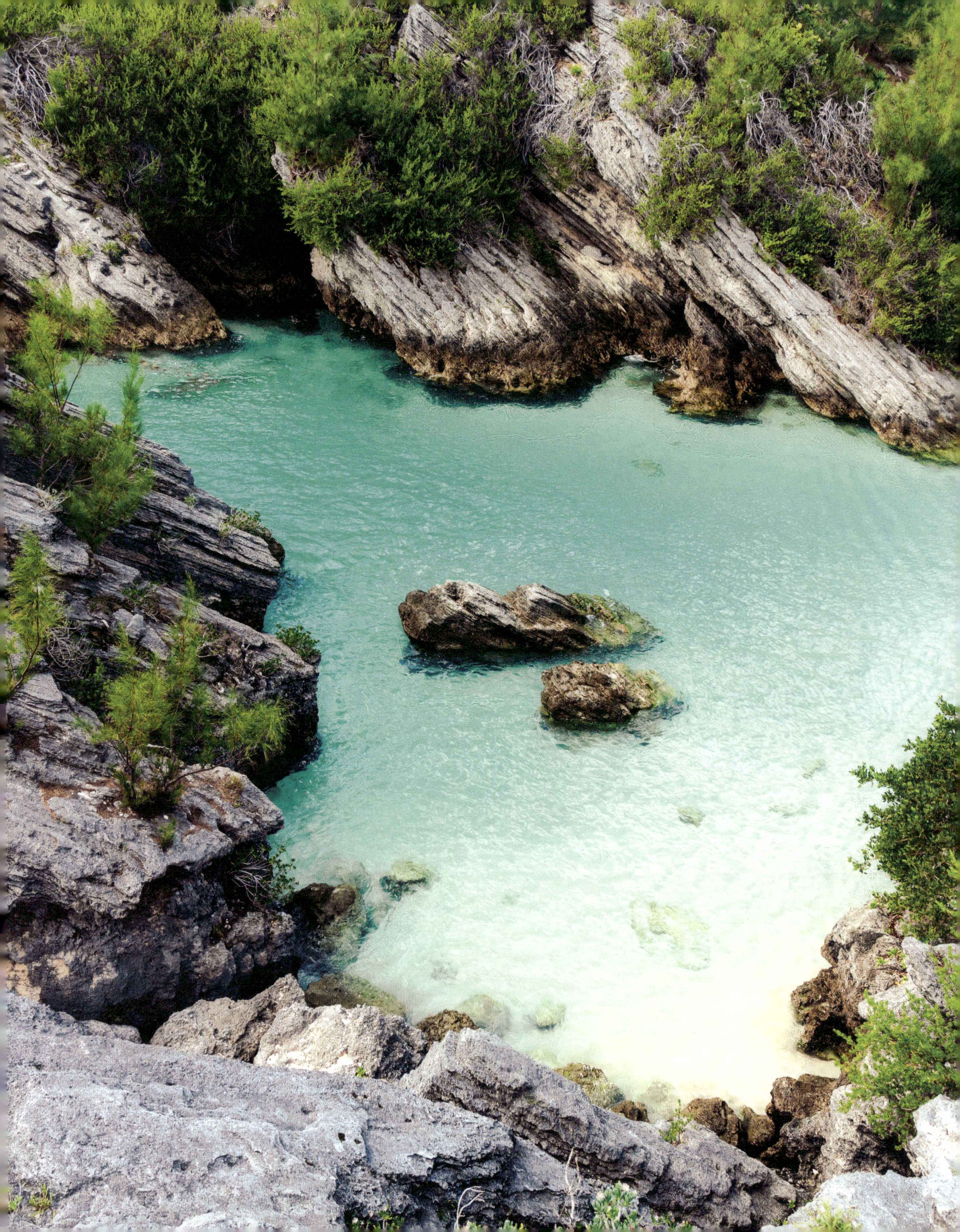

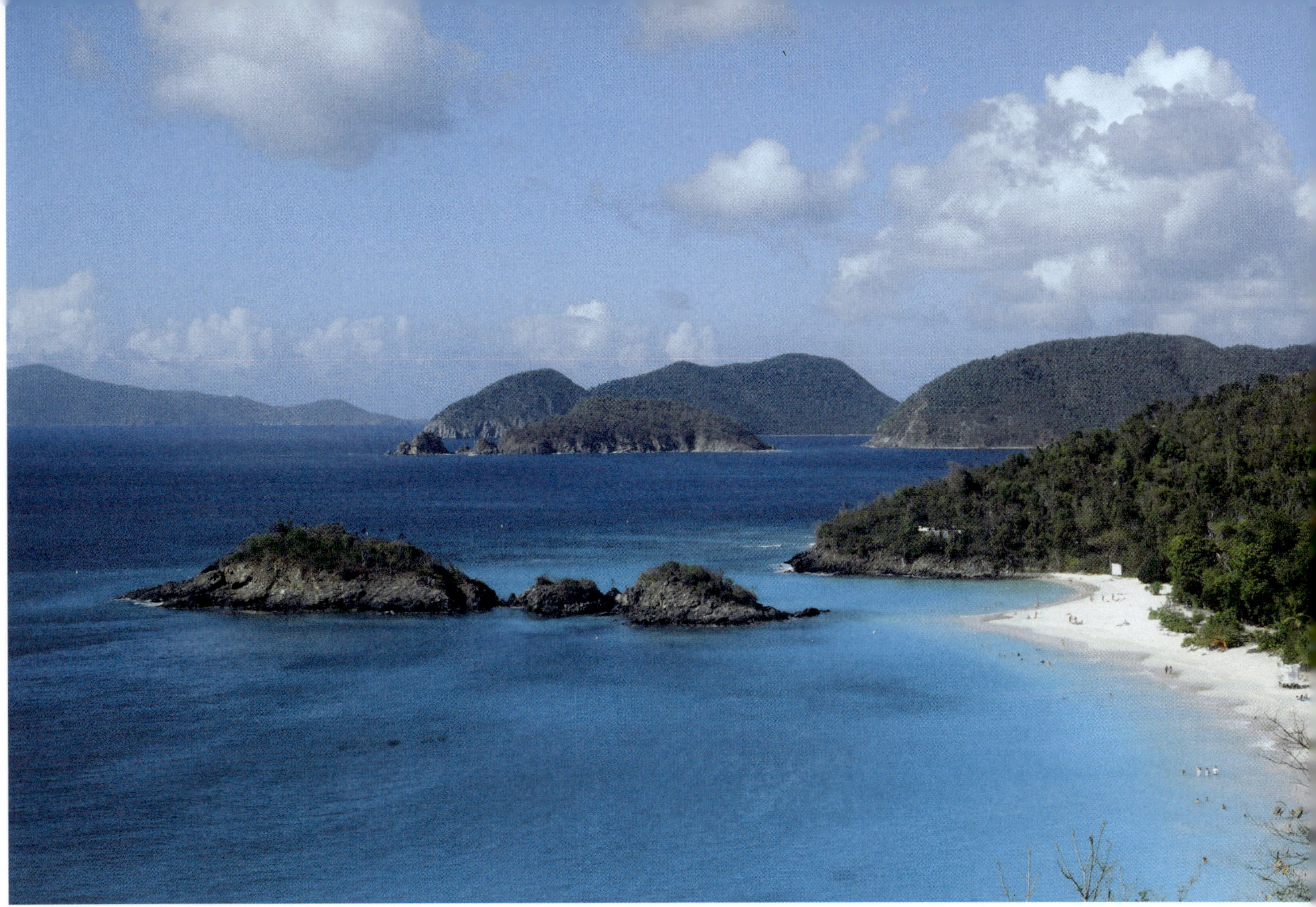

← **IN THE MIDDLE** of the island of Bermuda, along a stretch of more famous beaches, Jobson's Cove is surrounded by limestone rocks that buffer both the breeze and the waves. There are no standard cars on Bermuda, but you can rent a tiny electric vehicle and park at the western edge of Warwick Long Bay and cross the beach on foot or on horseback.

**Jobson's Cove,
Warwick Parish,
Bermuda**

Daniel Schwartz

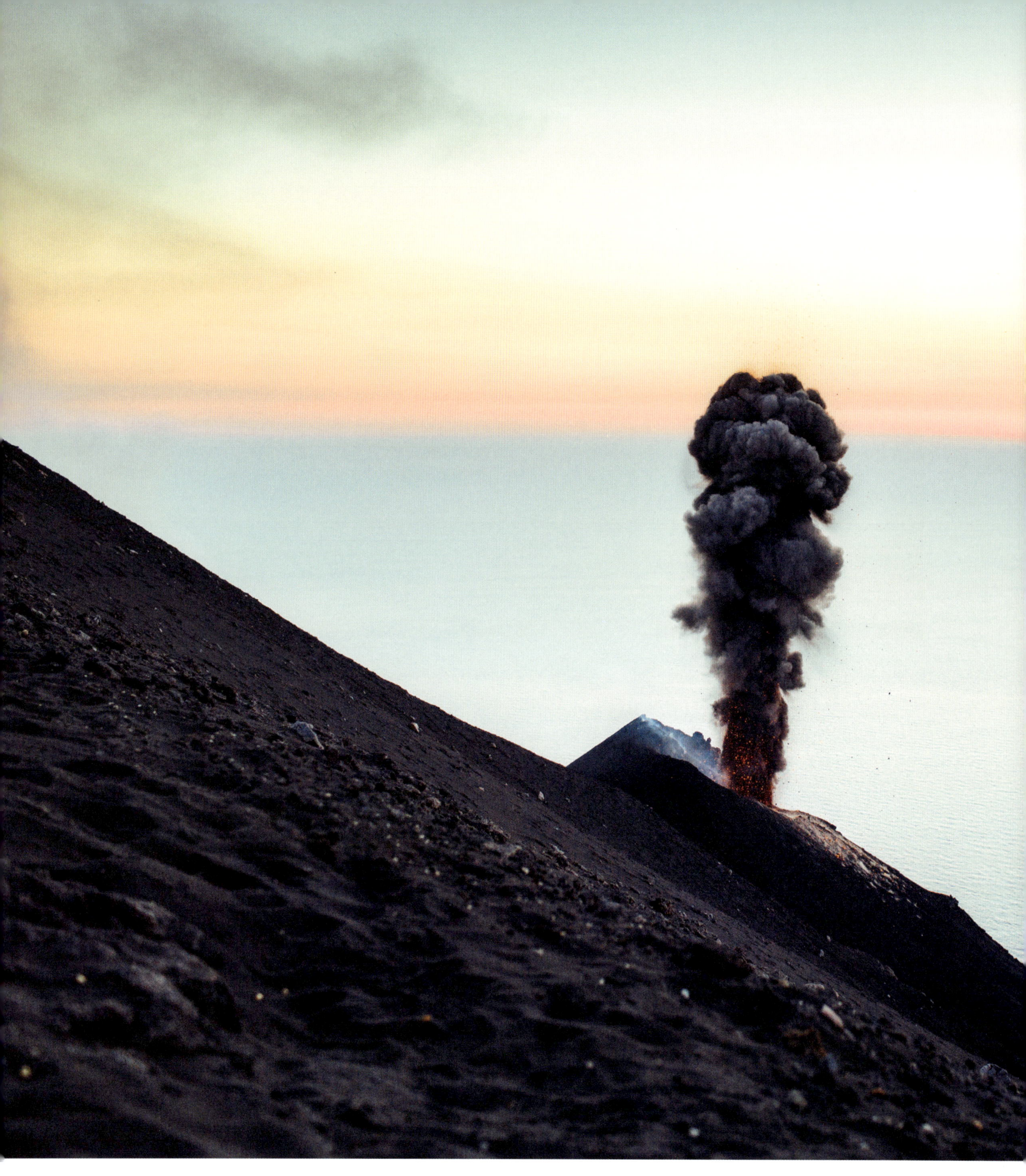

IN THE GLITTERING Tyrrhenian Sea off the west coast of Italy, north of Sicily, the island of Stromboli is named for its active volcano, Mount Stromboli. The peak of Stromboli has three active craters that explode regularly, spewing ash, lava, and stones up to several hundred feet in the air. While the explosions are generally somewhat predictable, as recently as 2019 a massive unexpected eruption surprised visitors on the island and on boats just off the coast. Luckily, no one was harmed since local regulations have kept visitors at a safe distance.

To photograph and experience the volcano, always check with local notices first. Travelers can explore by themselves from a hike, join a group, or hire a private guide on the island. In the busy summer months, travelers should bring lots of water, snacks, and backup clothes to be prepared for blazing heat.

**Stromboli,
Sicily, Italy**
Finn Beales

Along the coastline in southern England lie the vast white cliffs called the Seven Sisters. The stark beauty of these chalky cliffs was created by erosion, from thousands of years of the wind and the sea breaking against the coastline. In recent years, this natural process of erosion has become unnaturally intensified, and now these iconic cliffs are eroding ten times faster than before. This has largely been driven by increasing storm intensity, higher seas, and greater intensity of waves, all caused by climate change. Human management such as gravel extraction has also taken a toll, stripping away protective beaches from some of the cliffs and making them even more vulnerable to erosion from the ever-increasing intensity of storms.

Around the world, coastal erosion like this leads to a loss of land, which negatively impacts wildlife as well as human communities. In places like the Seven Sisters area of England, the erosion rate was 2 to 6 centimeters a year for the past 7,000 years. Over the last 150 years, the erosion rate has made an astonishing increase to 22 to 23 centimeters a year.

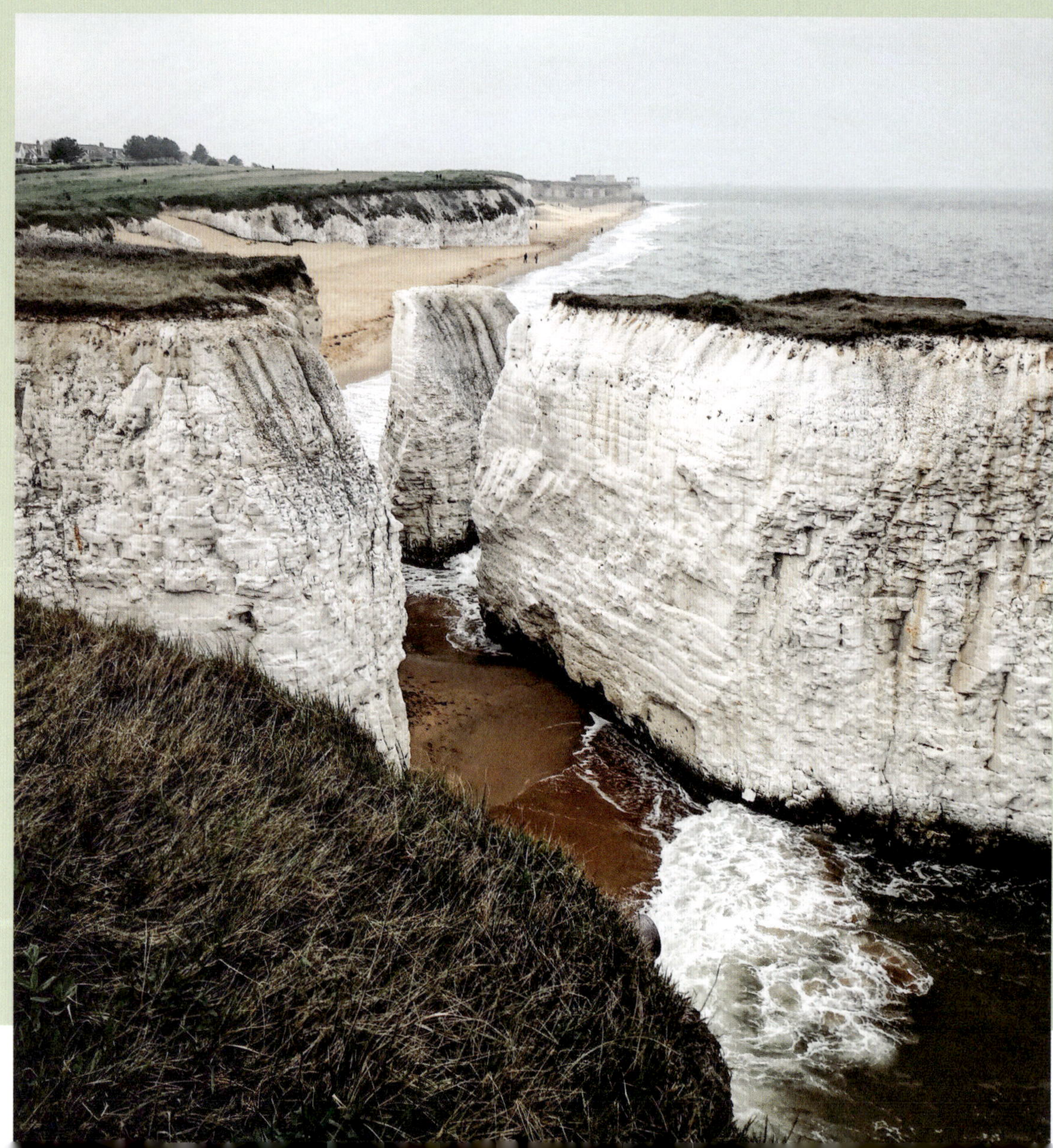

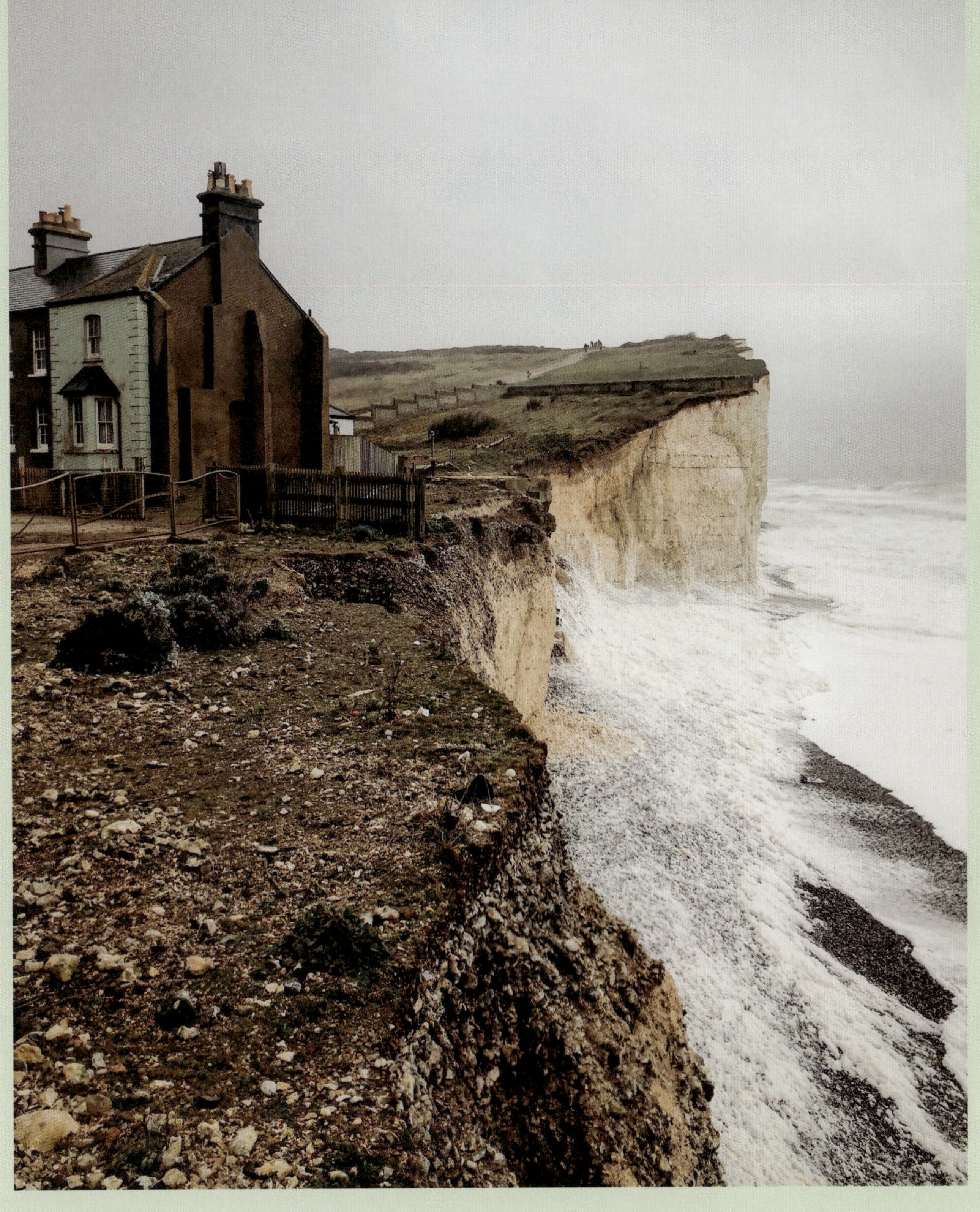

**Seven Sisters,
East Sussex, England**

Joe Pickard

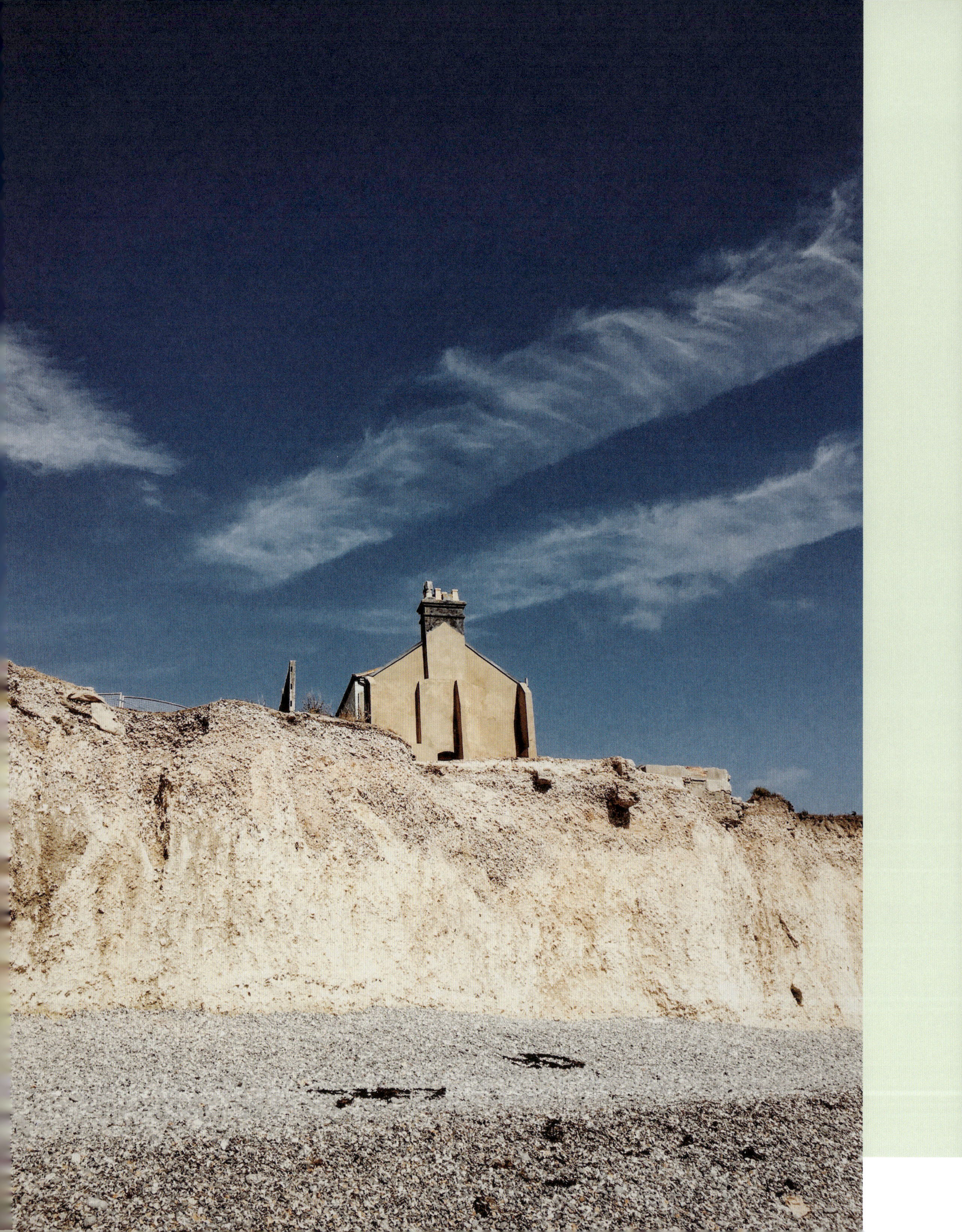

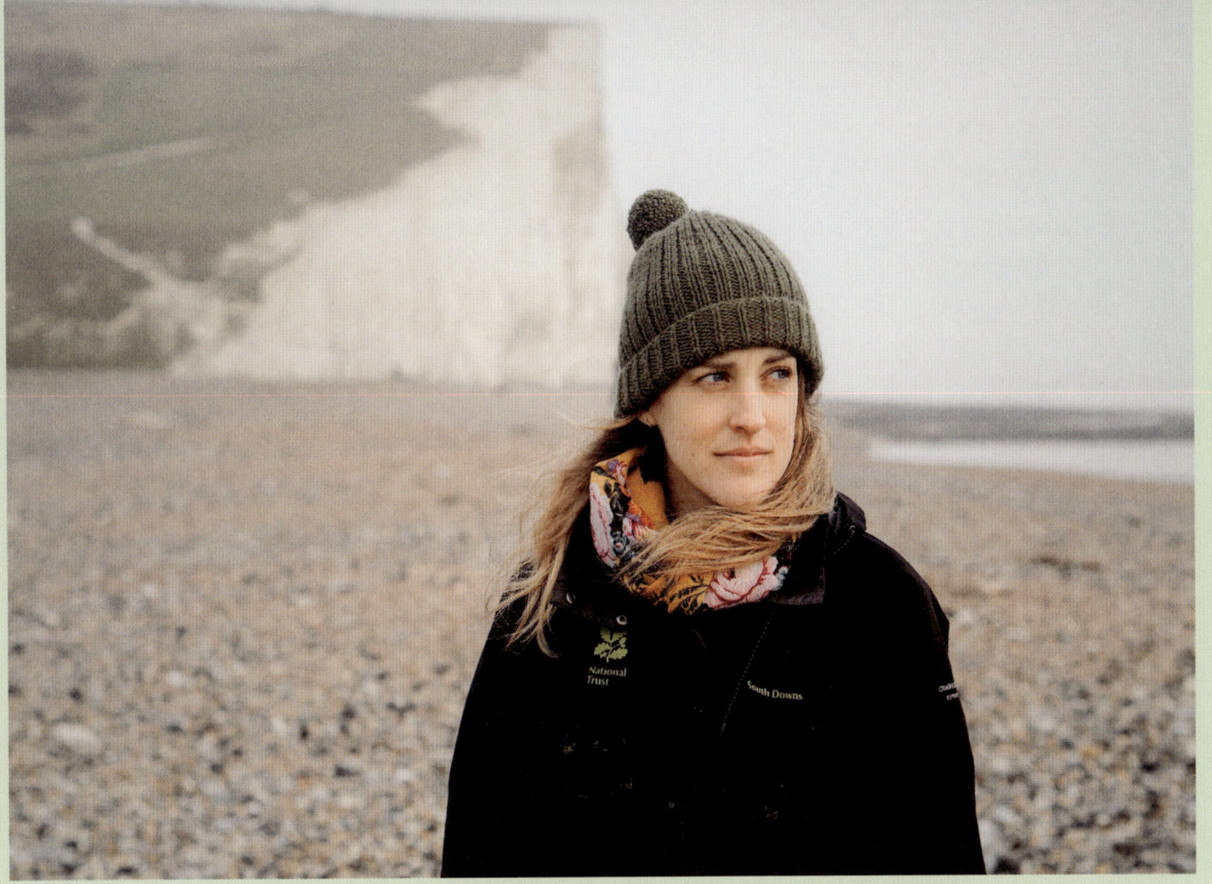

↑
**Cuckmere Haven,
East Sussex, England**
Joe Pickard

HOW YOU CAN HELP

- If you're traveling to a cliffside place, be aware of the risks of cliff erosion. Standing near the edge is dangerous, and a great photo is not worth the risk to yourself or the environment.

- Support organizations like the National Trust in the United Kingdom, which are working on initiatives to help mitigate this impact of climate change.

- Land management options include barriers such as walls and fencing as well as transferring sand and gravel from one beach to shore up a more vulnerable beach. However, these strategies are temporary, and in the case of transferring sand and gravel, you're depriving one beach of its stability in order to support another. Reducing the human activity that leads to global warming and intensifying weather appears to be the strongest and most effective action we can take.

←
**Birling Gap,
East Sussex, England**
Joe Pickard

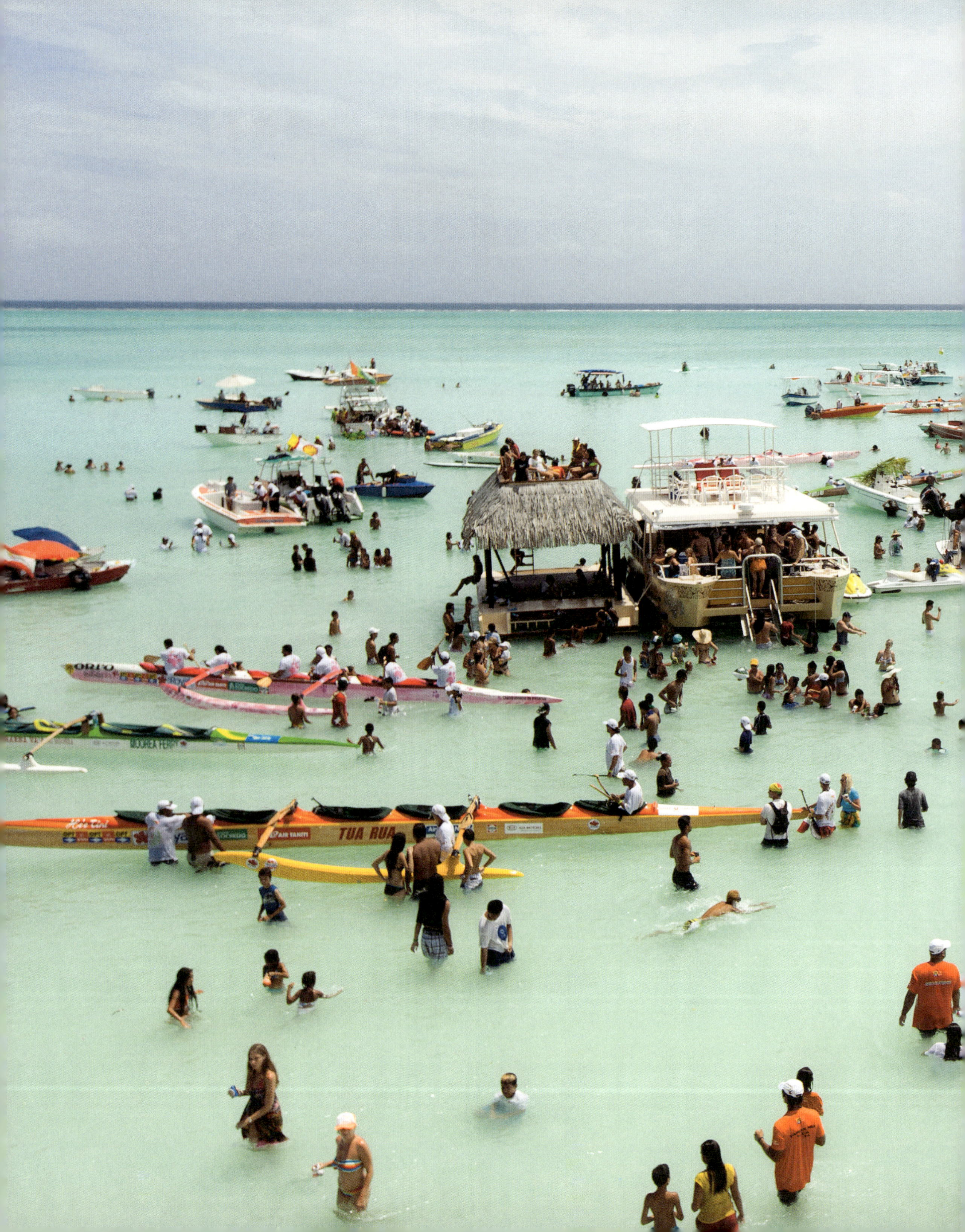

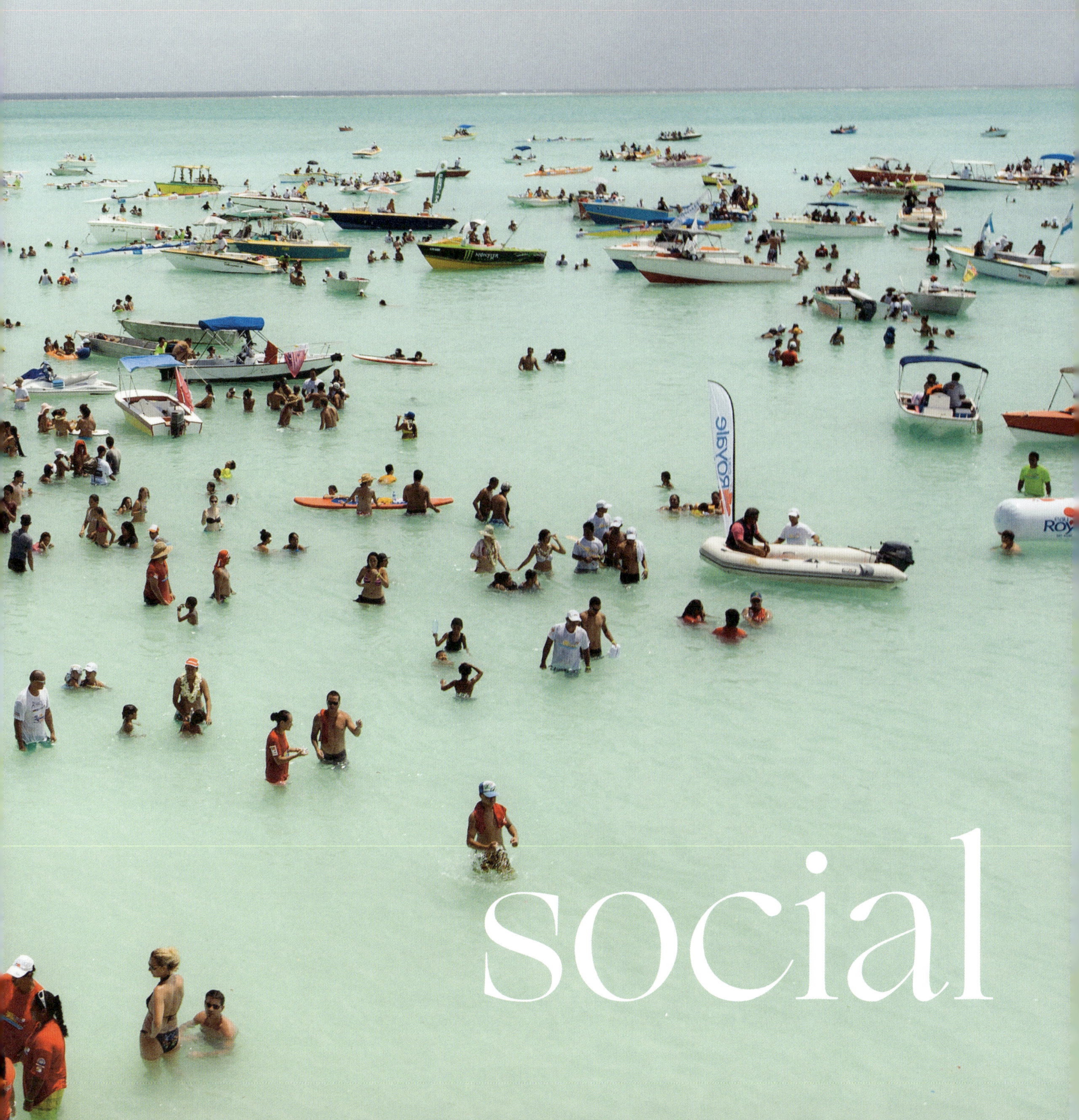
social

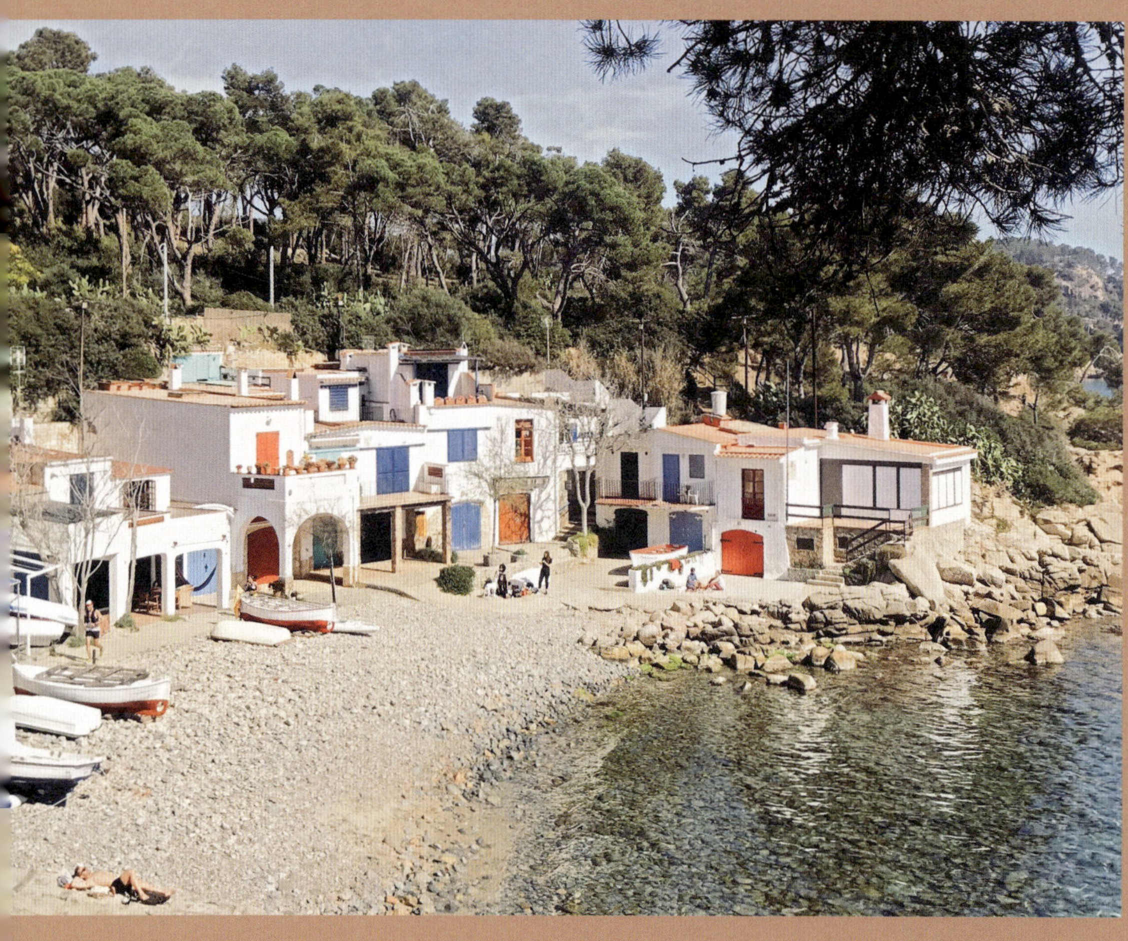

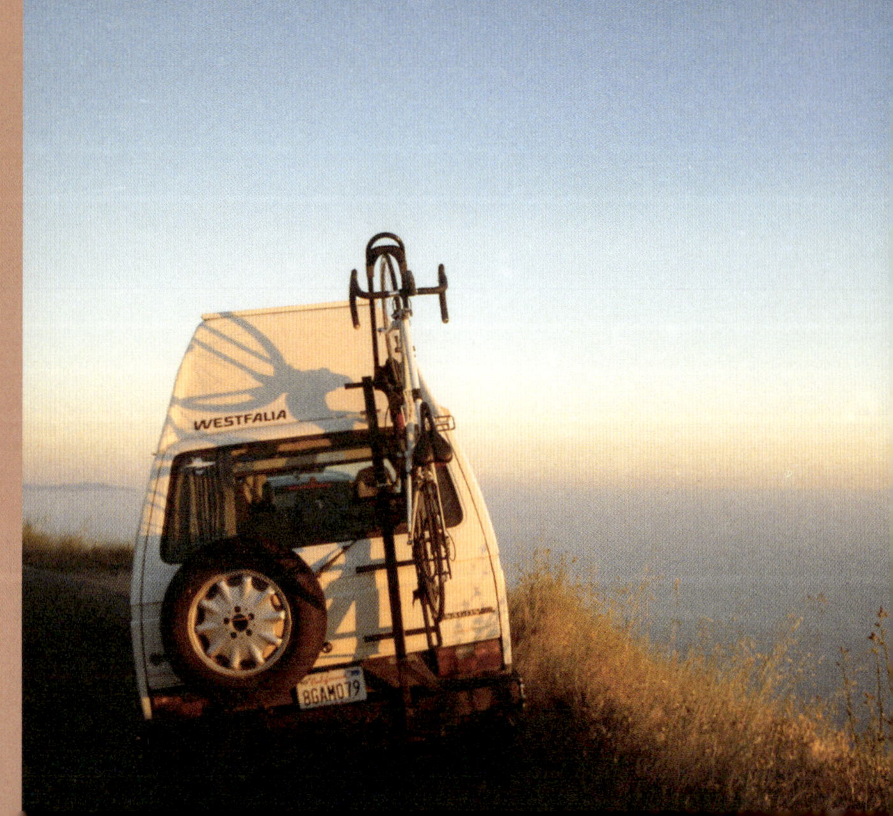

← The atoll of Bora Bora is a dream destination to many, including traditional canoe racers who compete in the annual three-day Hawaiki Nui Va'a outrigger canoe race, which passes through the islands of Huahine, Raiatea, and Taha'a.

**Matira Beach,
Bora Bora,
French Polynesia**
Shelly Strazis

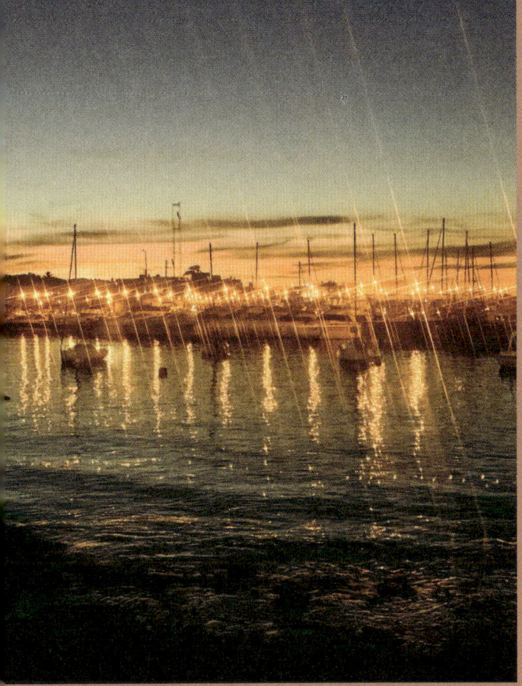

RED-AND-WHITE CANDY-STRIPED umbrellas, long boardwalks, white sand beaches, ports of call, marinas—humanity is drawn to the ocean, a fluid counterweight to our lives on the earth. More than that, we are drawn to being *together* at the shore—to gather and be social, to celebrate and relax with loved ones, to be among people. We come to the coasts for commerce, contemplation, relaxation, awe, recreation, and sport. For travelers, inlanders, and coastal residents alike, planning to share a meal with family and friends at a seaside restaurant or packing a picnic to eat with a group during a day at the beach elevates these simple pleasures and brings excitement to the routine of daily life.

There's an easy familiarity the world over when meeting strangers at the beach. Although you may not know the local customs, the relaxed cadence of the day's schedule breaks down common social barriers. Experienced travelers on extended stays in remote beach towns know that it takes only a day or two before they're recognized by locals and fellow travelers.

For a few summers when my son was little, my family and I would spend a week on Rye Beach with extended family, all piled into one old rental house on the very short New Hampshire coastline (only 18.5 miles long). Quickly, a beach routine separate from our day-to-day life emerged, familiar to all who spend vacation time at the beach. Mornings are quiet, save for the familiar interruptions of sounds of pans clanking, drawers and doors opening and closing, generations of voices intermingling as families make breakfast for kids. A toddler shouts, birds call, and a car horn honks or a siren rings out. Dogs walk with their owners; fishermen come in from the sea and chat beside their trucks. By midday, everyone shows up on the shore to cool off, carrying beach chairs and towels, toys and books. In the afternoon, the grills fire up, and then kids, tired from being knocked over and over by the waves, change into dry clothes and stand in line for ice cream. We bring our lives to the coast, but the coast is also a way of life and we shift our routines to meet it.

↑
**Punta del Este,
Maldonado, Uruguay**
Nina Romani

↖
**Palamós, Costa
Brava, Girona, Spain**
Raquel Guiu Grigelmo

←
**Marin County,
California,
United States**
Skyler Carrico

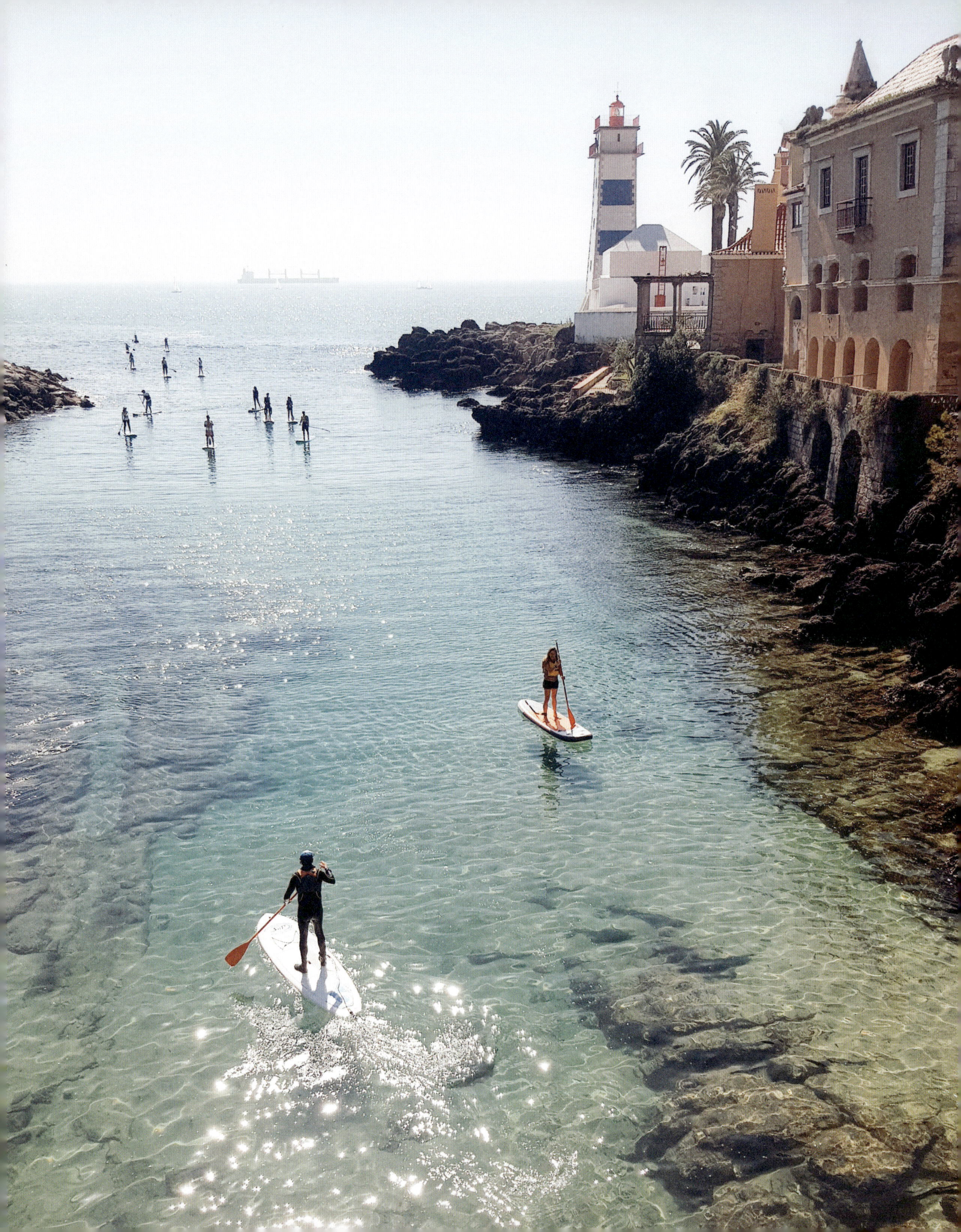

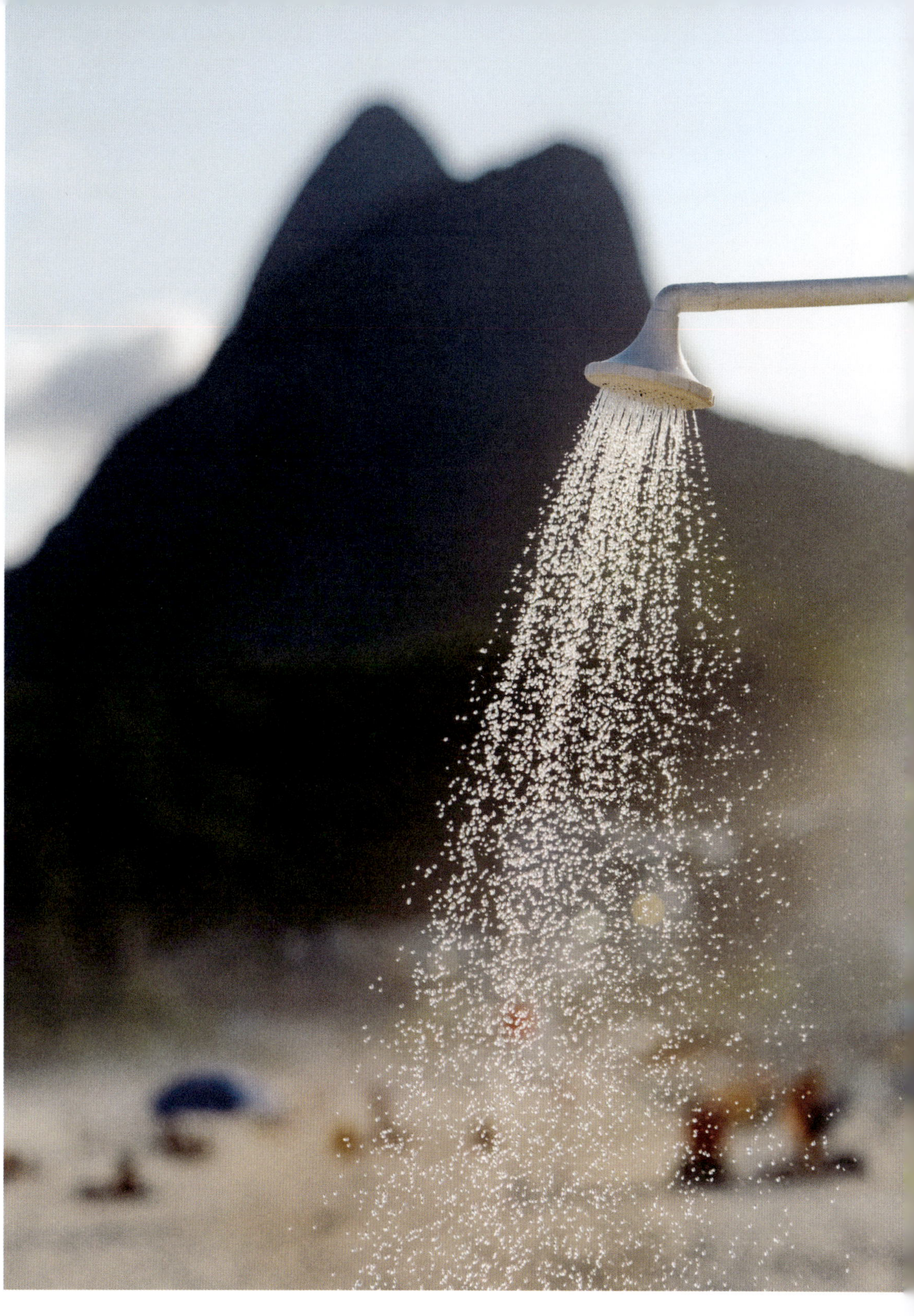

←
**Cascais, Lisbon
District, Portugal**

Natalia Horinkova

↑
**Rio de Janeiro,
Brazil**

Via Tolila by Lauren
and Annael Tolila

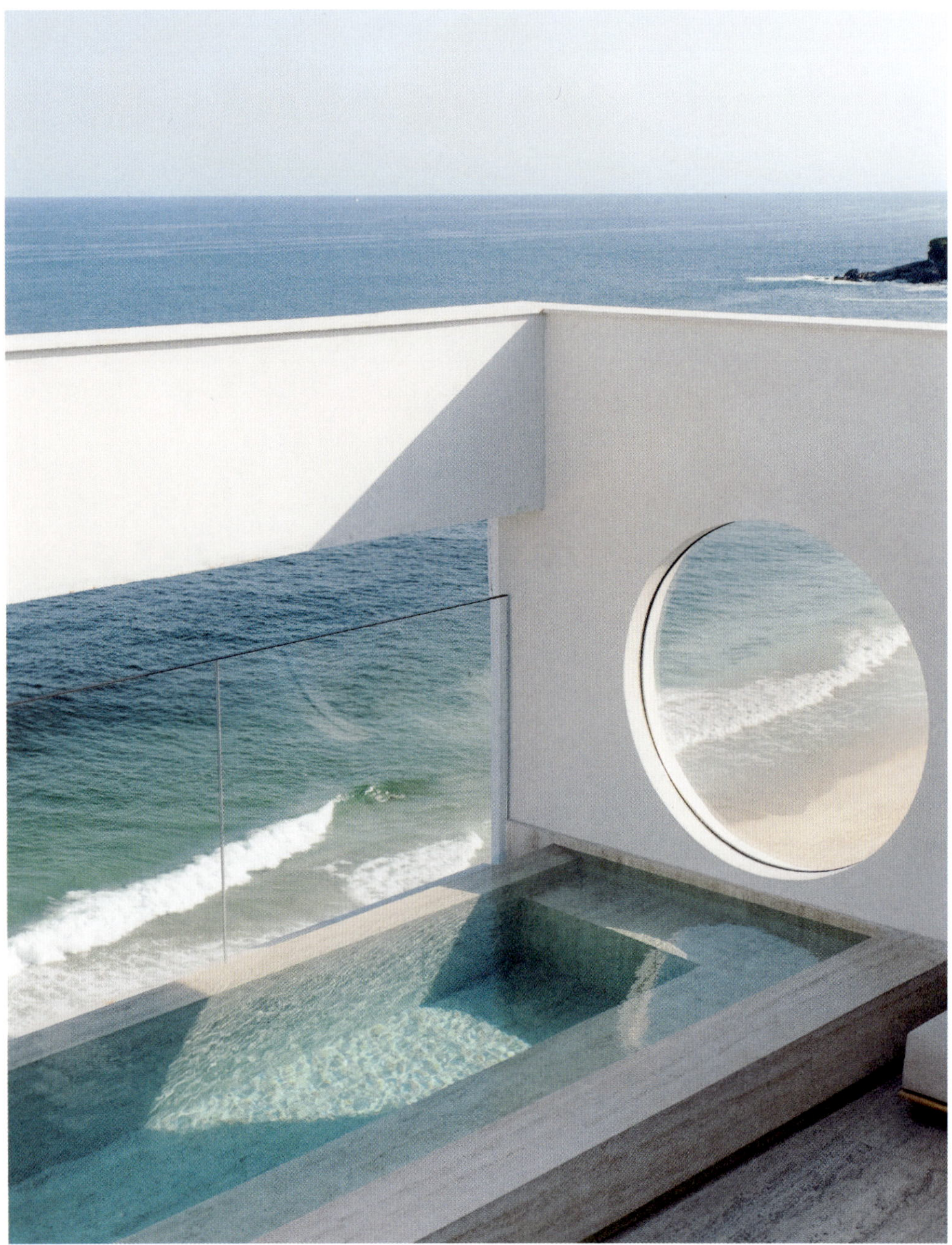

↑
**Rio de Janeiro,
Brazil**

Via Tolila by Lauren
and Annael Tolila

→
**Cabo San Lucas,
Baja California Sur,
Mexico**

Romana Lilic

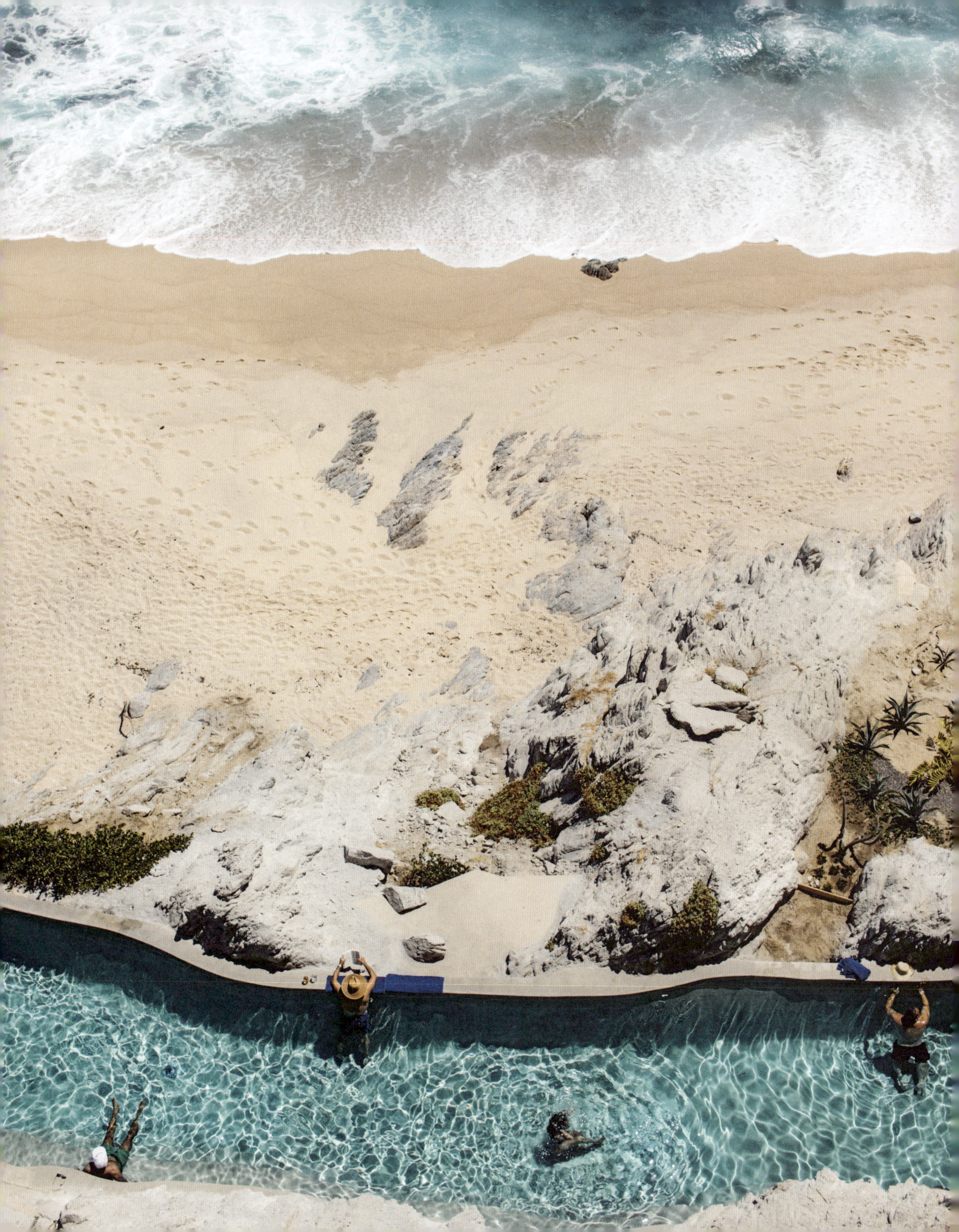

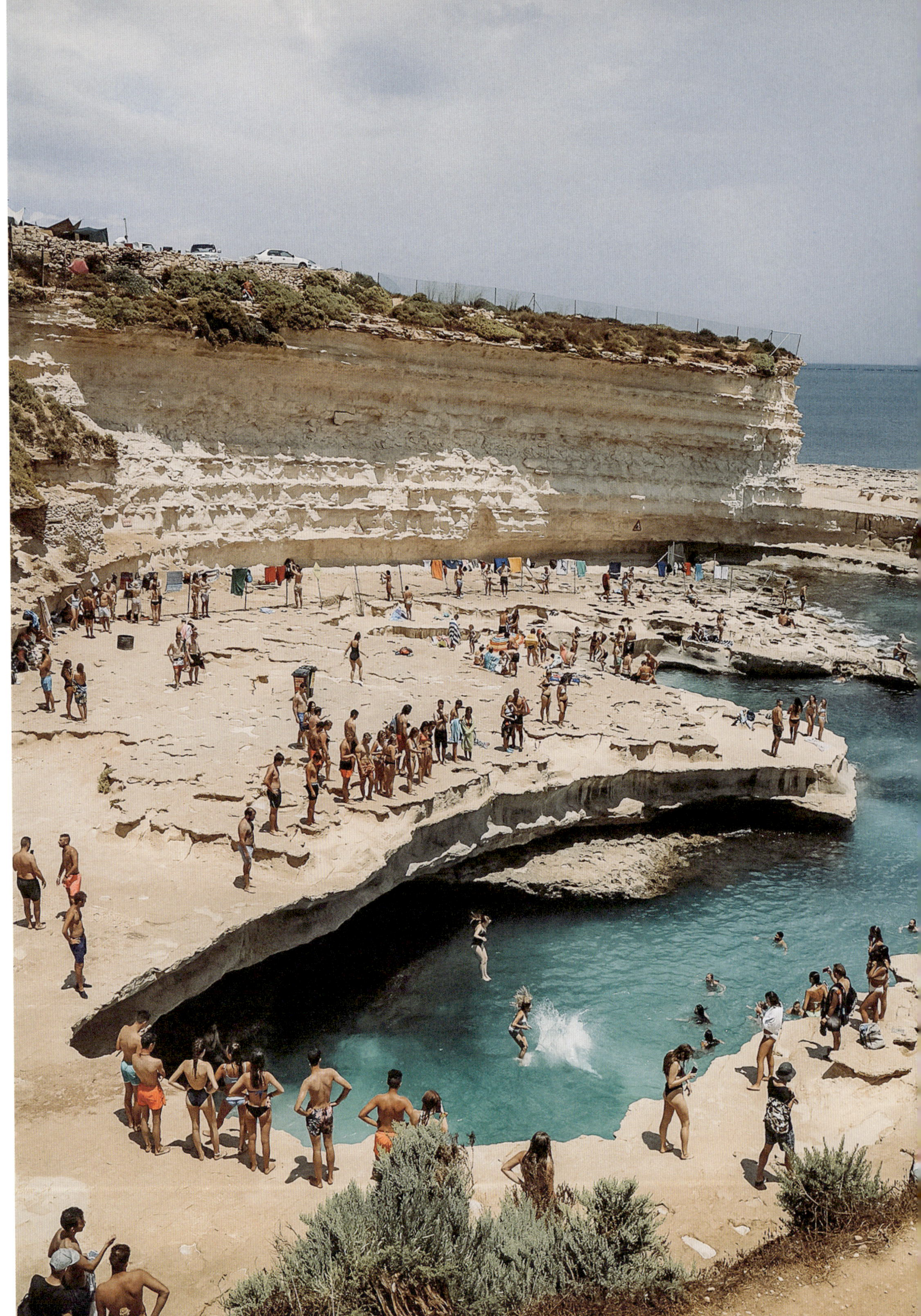

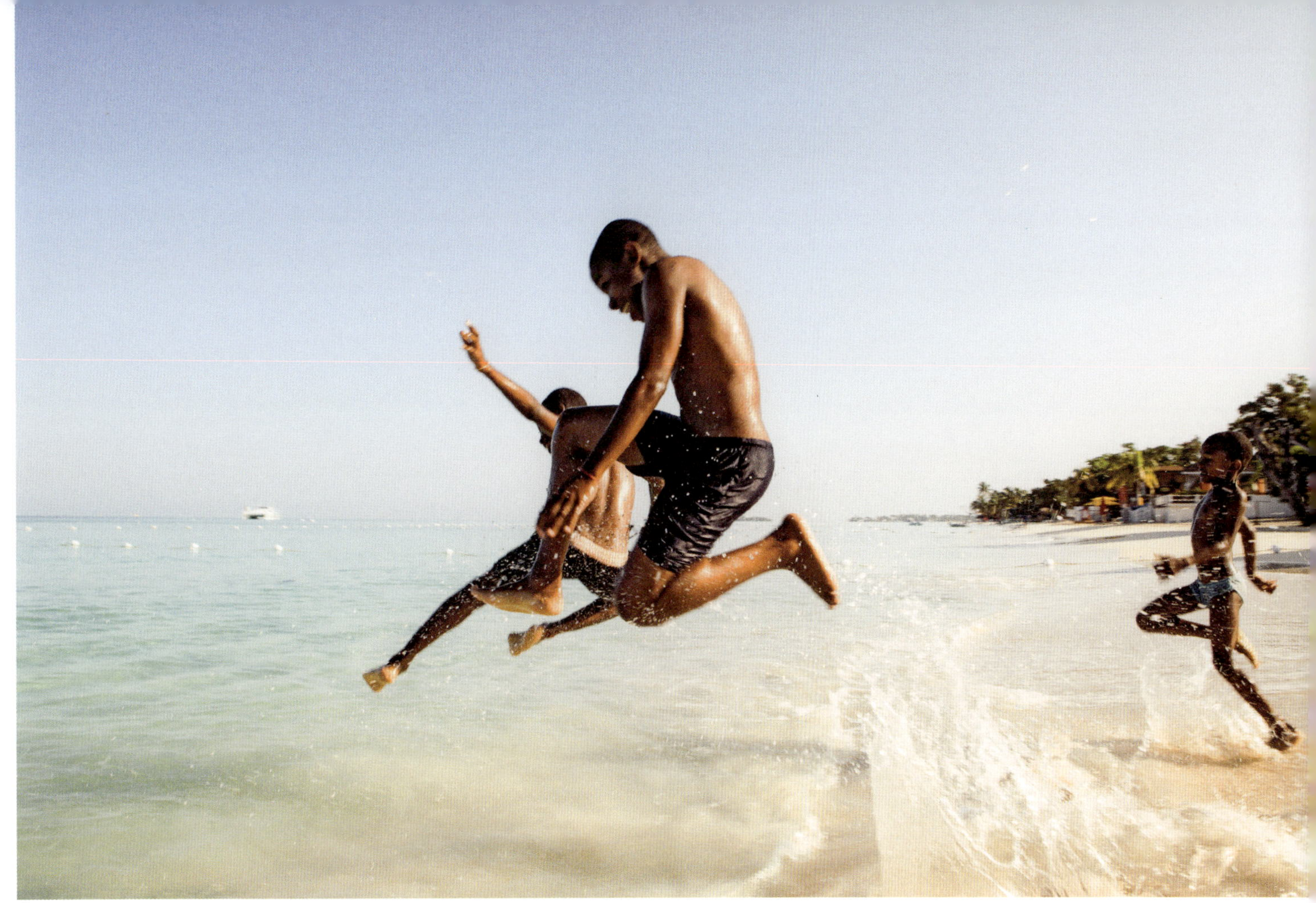

Erin Kunkel

←

ONE OF THE smallest countries in the world, the Republic of Malta is an island nation comprising an archipelago of islands in the central Mediterranean: south of Italy, north of Libya, and east of Tunisia. Twenty minutes from the capital, Valletta, is the fishing village of Marsaxlokk, and east of town on the southeast corner of the island is St. Peter's Pool. Since there is no public transport to either place, visitors can walk or take a private boat or car. The walk to the pool takes around thirty minutes from Marsaxlokk and passes through indistinct fields that ultimately open up to reveal the pool naturally carved out of stone. Descending the hill toward the bay, visitors will find sunbathers on the surrounding flat rocks and see the spectacle of people taking turns to backflip, dive, or simply jump into the brilliantly blue water below. For those who don't want to take the leap, there are ladders, as well as steps carved in the stone.

**Marsaxlokk,
South Eastern
Region, Malta**
Isabel Chai

Stone Town, Zanzibar City, Tanzania

Sam Vox

A MASSIVE CITY at the crossroads of Asia and Europe, Istanbul is the historic, cultural, and population center of Turkey built on the banks of the Bosporus. On both the Black Sea and the Mediterranean Sea, Istanbul has been a strategic position for ruling empires for thousands of years. Today in a city of 15 million with endless opportunities to explore, there is always an alley to wind up and a new vista to discover. Here a rooftop view overlooks Ortaköy Mosque and the Bosporus Bridge below.

Istanbul, Turkey

Rigoberta Jellini

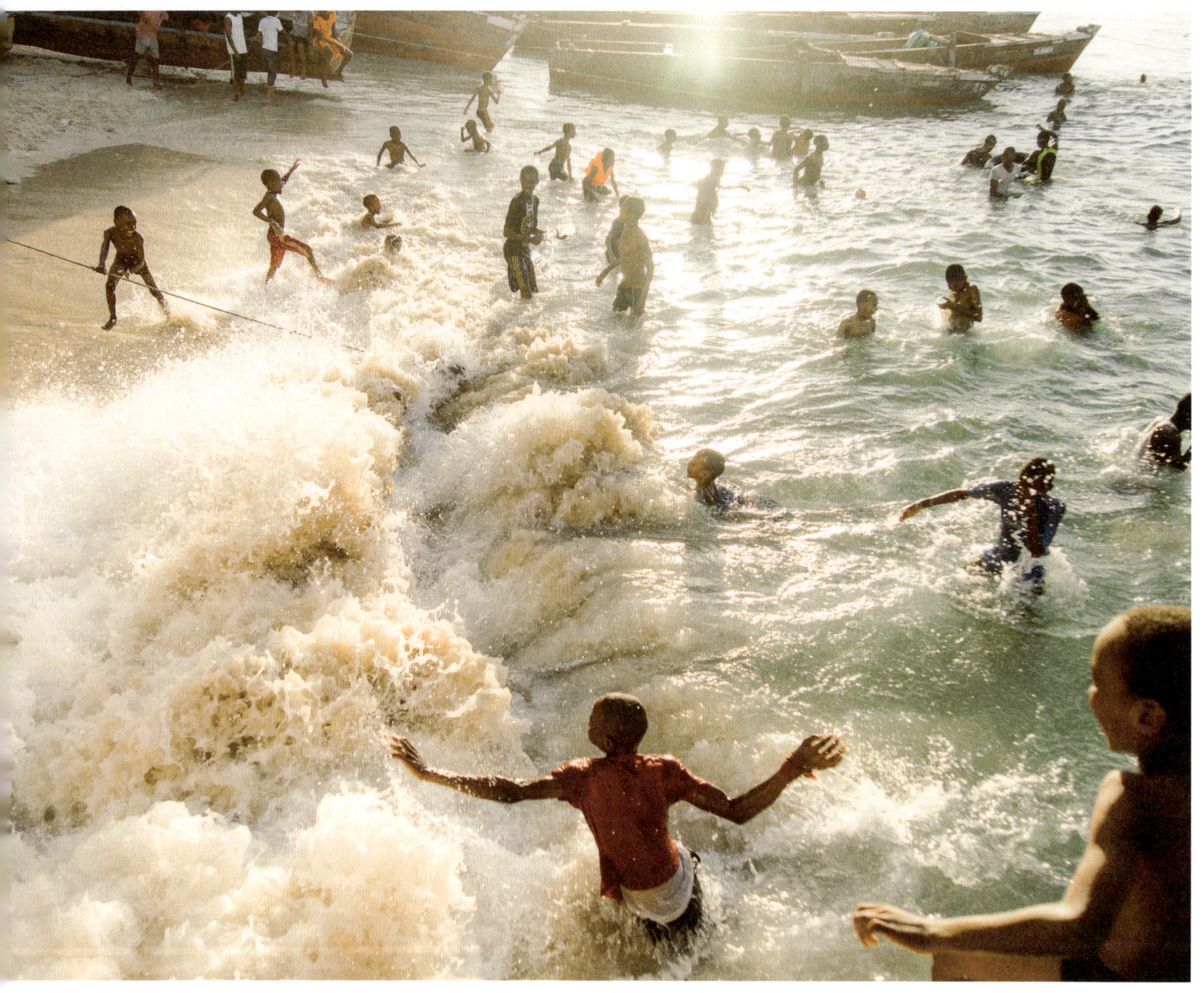

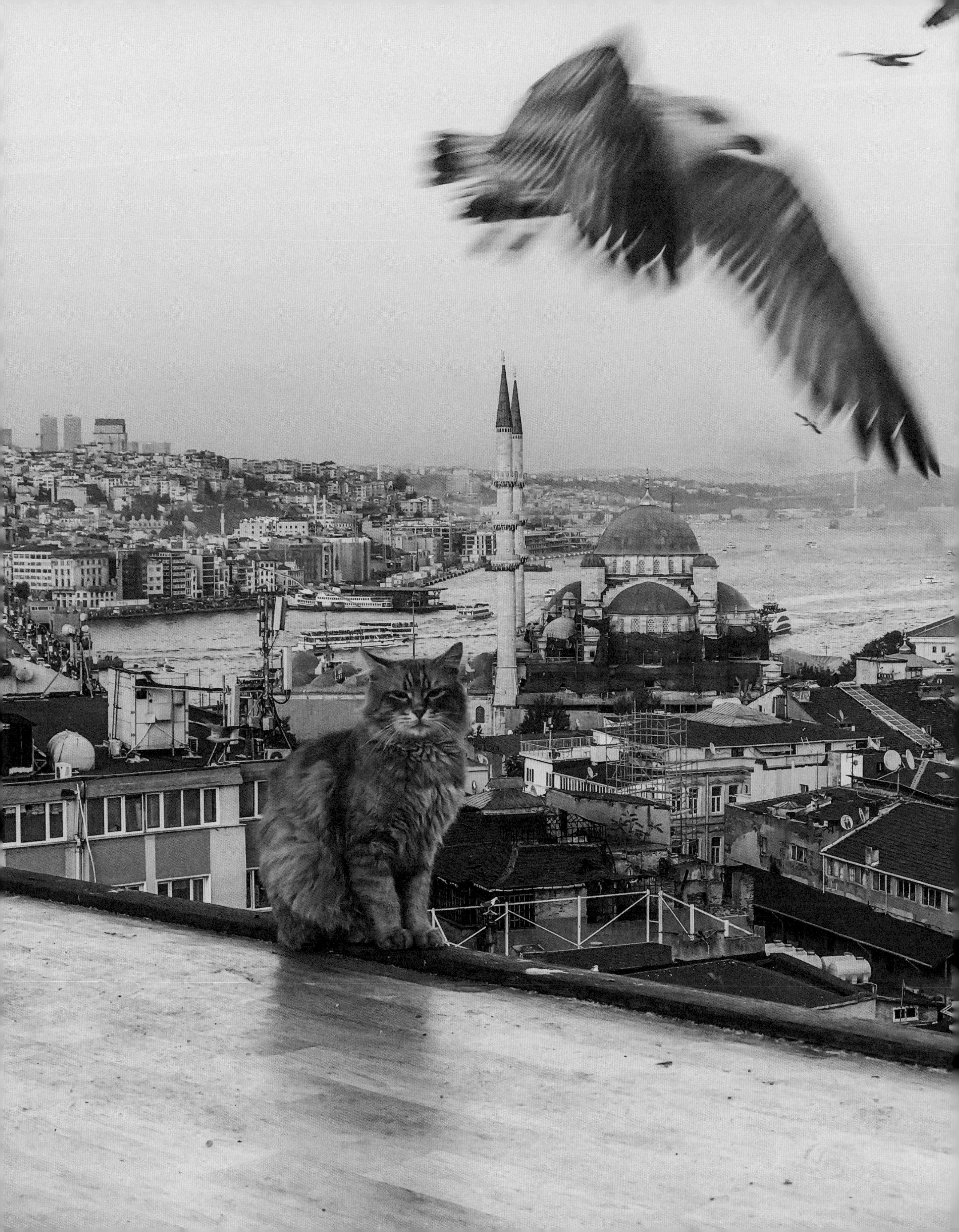

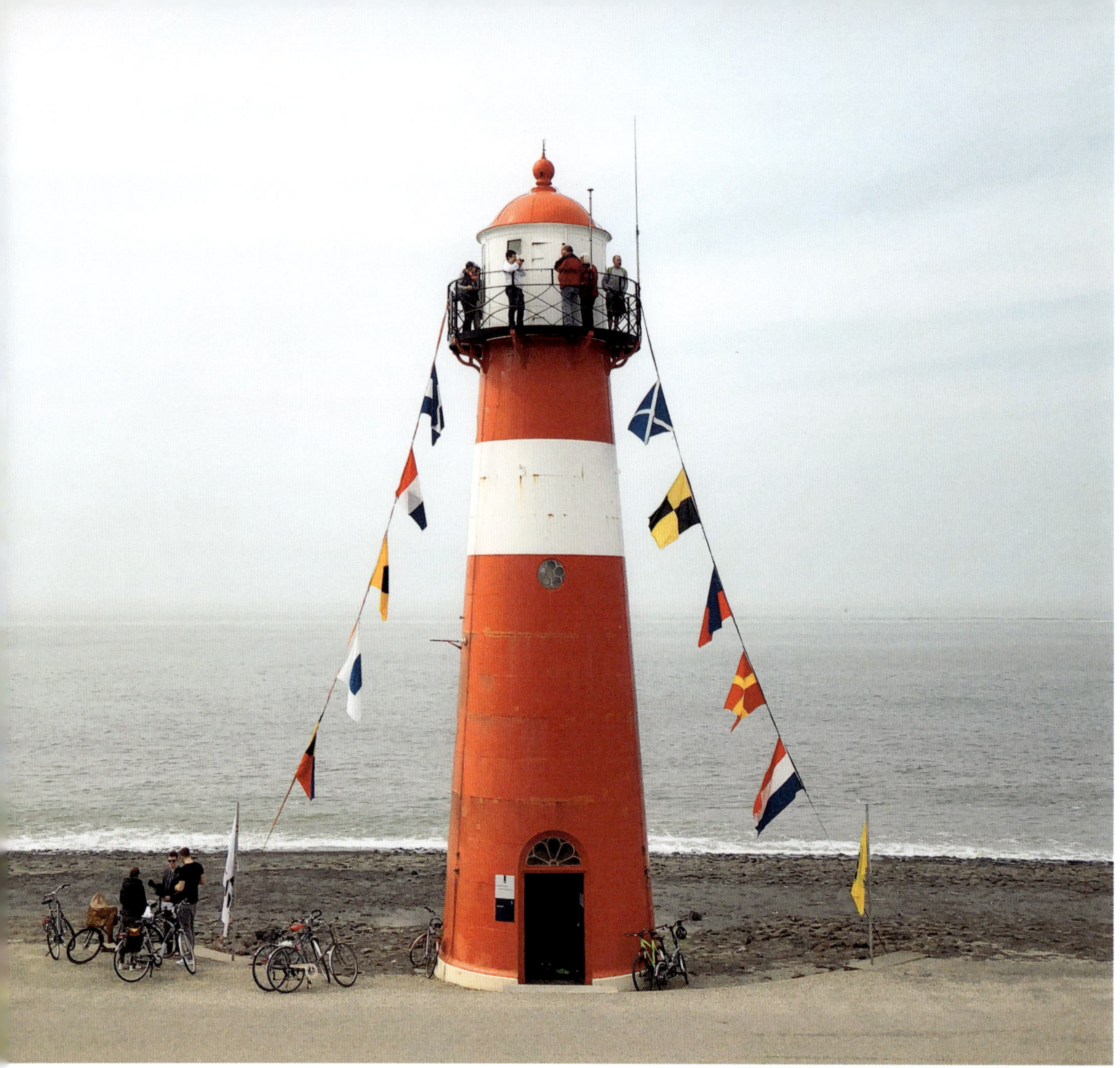

THOUGH OFFICIALLY IN the Netherlands, the Vuurtoren Noorderhoofd, or North Head Lighthouse, on the North Sea is one-half of a pair of lighthouses that guide large ships into the Scheldt estuary and lead them to the Belgian port cities of Flushing, Terneuzen, Ghent, and Antwerp. The lighthouse sits at the edge of a dam that was destroyed during WWII, right off of the coastal highway N287, so a drive-by view and quick picture is possible through a rolled-down car window, but remember to be mindful of the passing cyclists. There is off-street parking available for those who want to go inside the lighthouse or explore the beaches nearby.

**Westkapelle,
Zeeland, Netherlands**

Kate Davison

SURROUNDED BY JUNGLE and situated on a harbor, Paraty is a colonial gold-rush town on the Costa Verde. Once a month, when there is a full moon, the tide rises to its highest point and flows into the streets through specially constructed openings in the seawall.

**Paraty, Rio de Janeiro
State, Brazil**

Gabriela Mateus

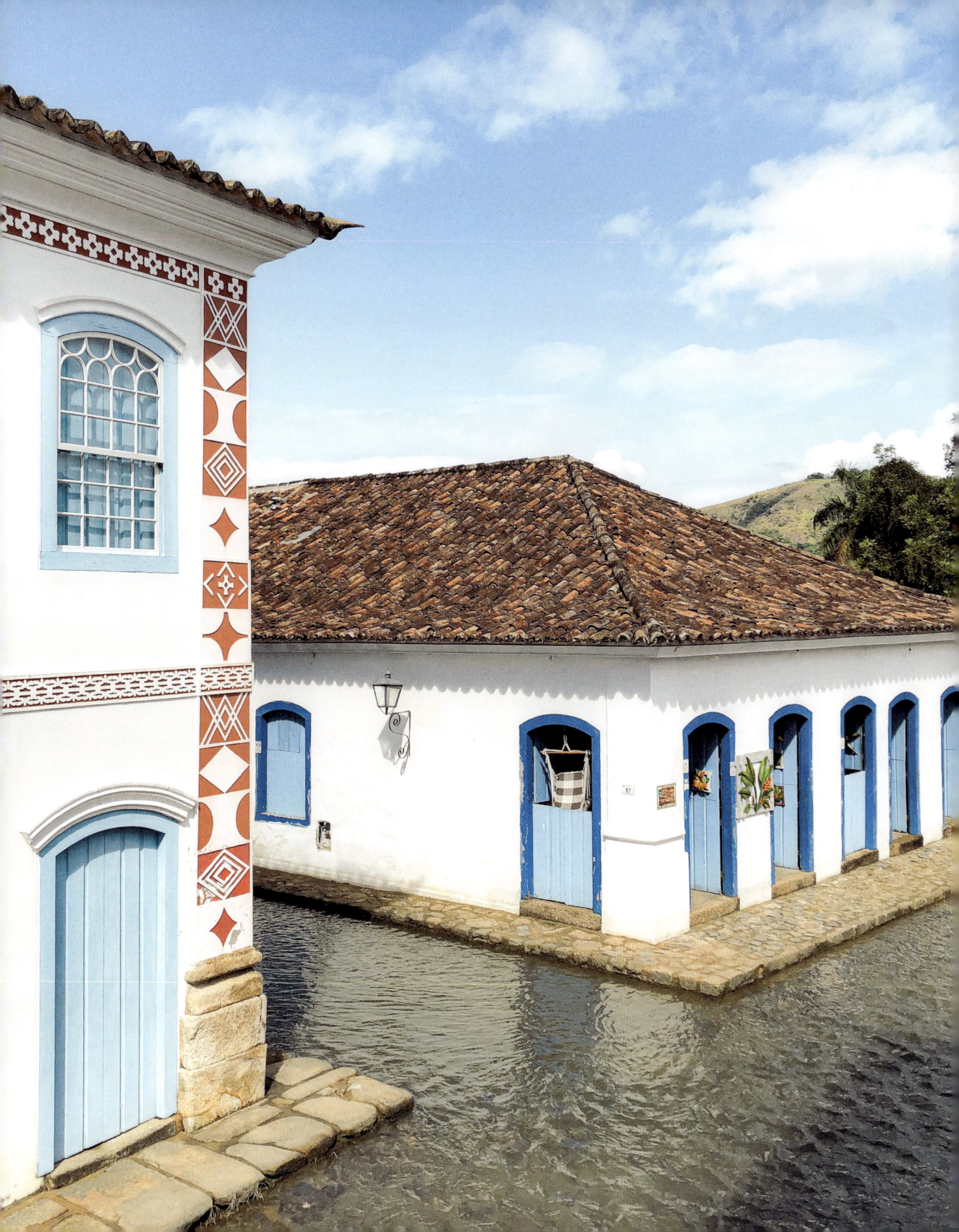

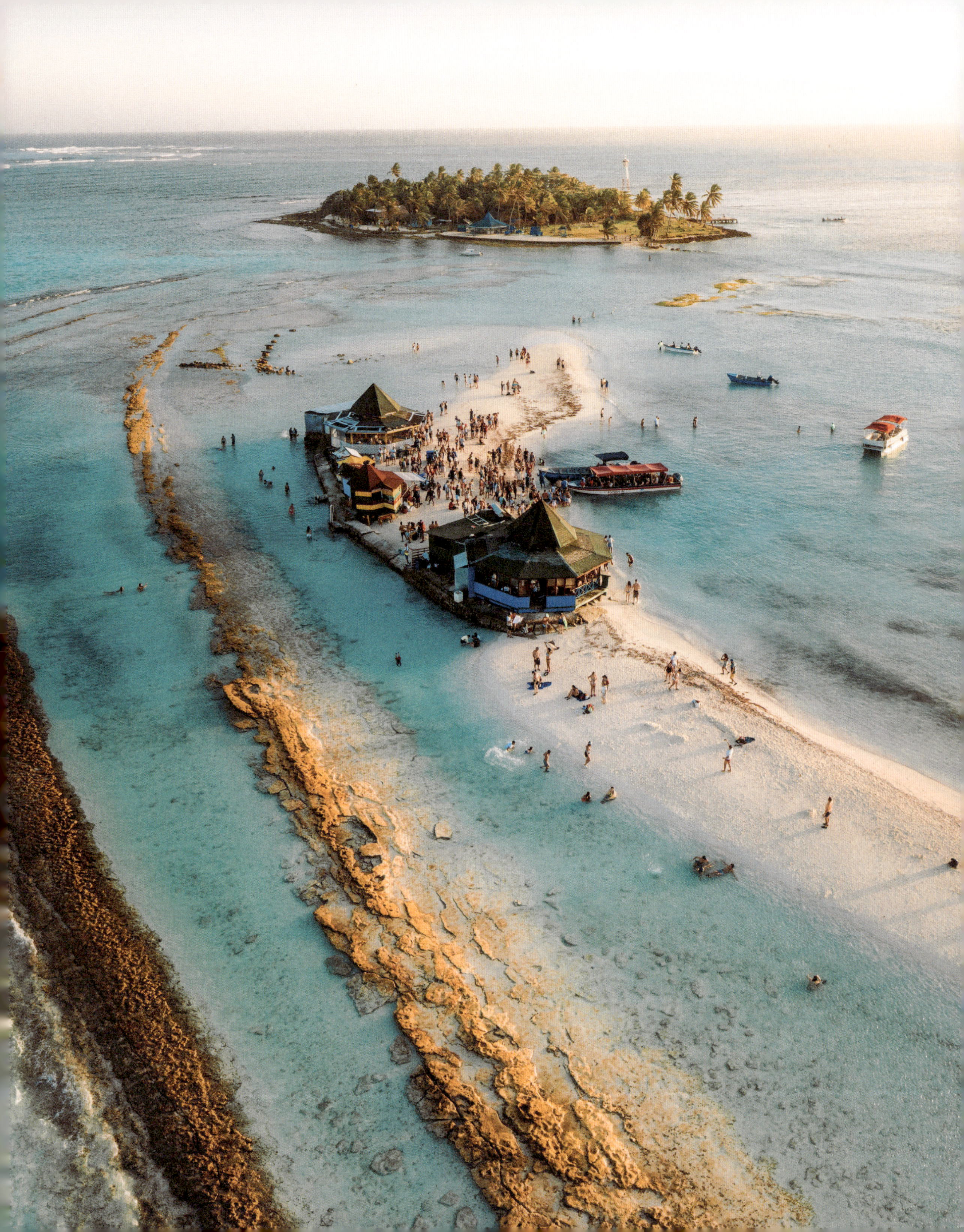

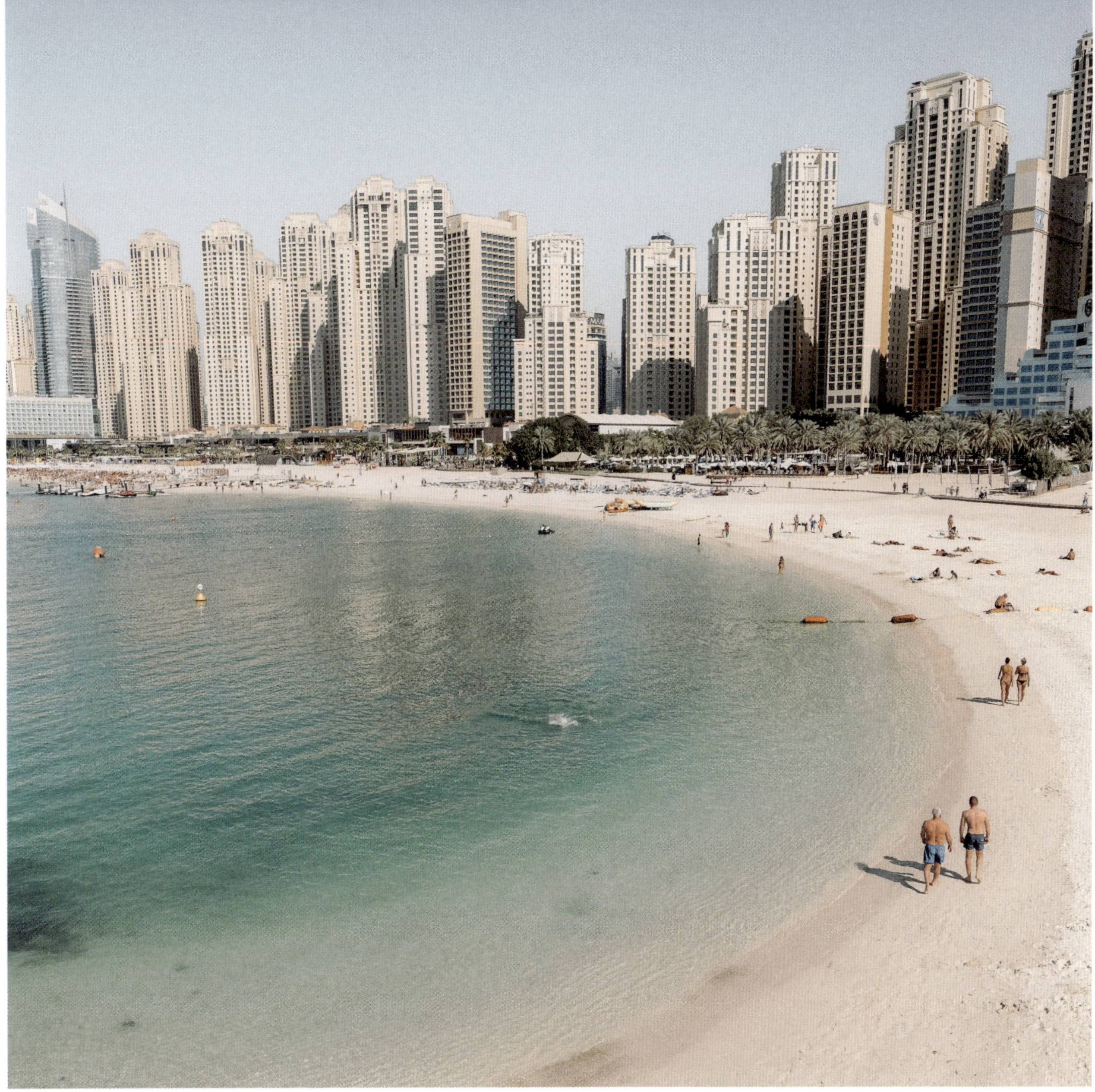

← A UNIQUE CORAL reef, El Acuario has a sandy ocean floor and gorgeous light blue water that has made it a famous snorkel spot. To visit, hire a boat for a day trip from the neighboring Cayo Acuario.

**El Acuario, San Andrés,
Colombia**
Adolfo Muro

↑ JBR BEACH, LINED with restaurants, bars, and shops, is a city beach popular with visitors and locals. The wide expanse of soft white sand lapping warm turquoise water faces the towers of the Dubai Marina to the east and the Arabian Gulf to the west. Such a pristine beach in the middle of an upscale urban center gives the beach a unique refined but casual flavor. An airline gateway to the Middle East, Dubai is also well-known for extreme sports activities. Looking up from this beach, visitors will see a cascade of skydivers landing at the nearby Skydive Dubai landing zone.

**Dubai,
United Arab Emirates**
Özgur Gemici

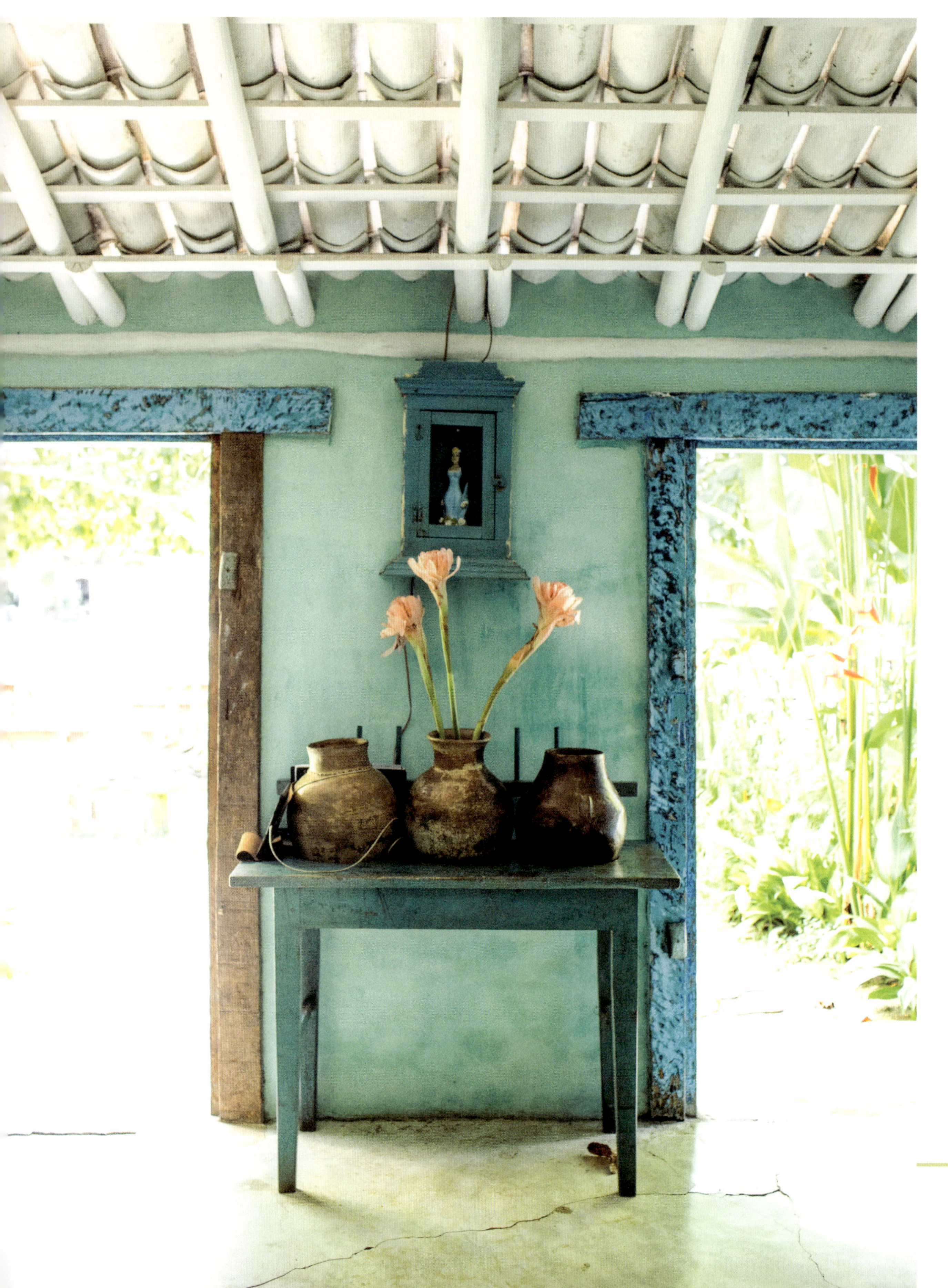

trancoso

BRAZIL

TRANCOSO IS A MAGICAL little beach town on the Atlantic Ocean in Bahia, Brazil. On this "discovery coast" (the first place the Portuguese landed in Brazil in 1500), amber-colored rivers wind to the sea, arriving at sandy beaches after crossing through lush protected jungle, mangroves, palm, and cashew trees. Brazil's federal environmental agency is expanding its national parks and preserves to maintain what's left of the Atlantic rain forest. Trancoso is also the starting point of an environmental protection area, APA Caraíva-Trancoso, where tourist development is limited. Along the coast is the Corumbau Marine Extractive Reserve, 8 nautical miles wide and spanning 40 miles of the Brazilian coastline, including reefs that support the greatest marine biodiversity in the South Atlantic. The region is a breeding ground for humpback whales and loggerhead sea turtles. The reserve was created in part to protect the traditional fishing communities who rely on the fish and shrimp caught there, since predatory industrial fisheries were endangering the stocks.

The centerpiece of town is a UNESCO-protected whitewashed church, the Igreja de São João Batista, founded by Jesuit priests in 1583, and a town square that extends just past it called the Quadrado. Though quadrado means "square," it is in fact a rectangle of several blocks lined with candy-colored UNESCO-protected homes that have been turned into hotels, guesthouses (pousadas), shops, restaurants, and bars. The church is surrounded by tamarind trees and overlooks the electric-blue ocean. During the day, the Quadrado is virtually shuttered as tourists slowly make their way across the square and down a bumpy dirt road (as likely to be taken by a horse as by a car) to the beach below. At the beach, travelers find local vendors selling sunhats and mesh beachwear, artisan cacao, beach cafés, and the beach club of the UXUA Casa Hotel, which features a bar made of an antique wooden boat. Everything closes just before sunset, when the crowds wend their way back up to the Quadrado to dine, drink, and dance to sounds of local forró or axé music.

Trancoso had been a quiet fishing village until the 1970s, when it started to become known for its beaches and began attracting hippies (locally called biribandos) and artists. The town has now become popular with both Brazilian and international celebrities as well as tourists who appreciate its loving spirit and its abundance of macrobiotic foods. To get to Trancoso (if you're not backpacking in from Caraíva, a few miles down the road), take a connecting flight from Rio de Janeiro or São Paulo to the Porto Seguro regional airport; then drive an easy hour and a half to town. There's also a small-aircraft airport just outside of town.

PHOTOGRAPHS BY EMILY NATHAN

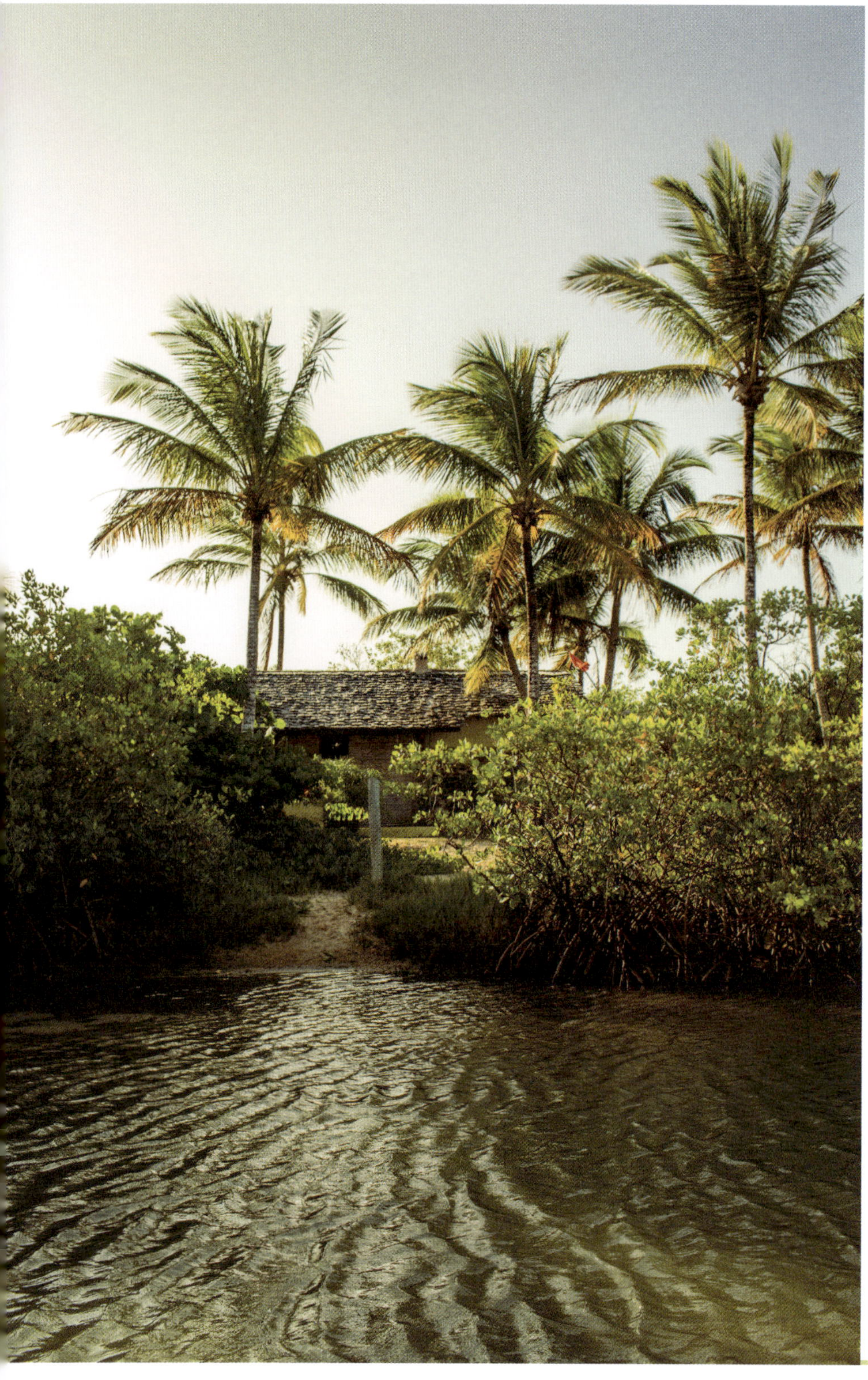

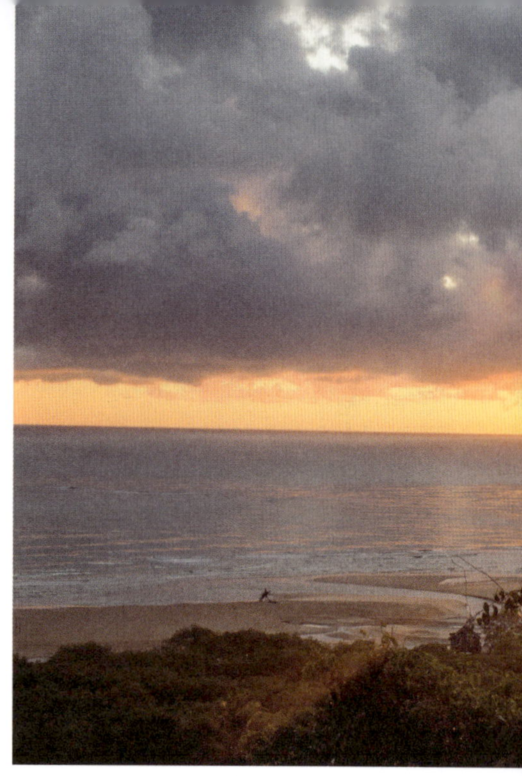

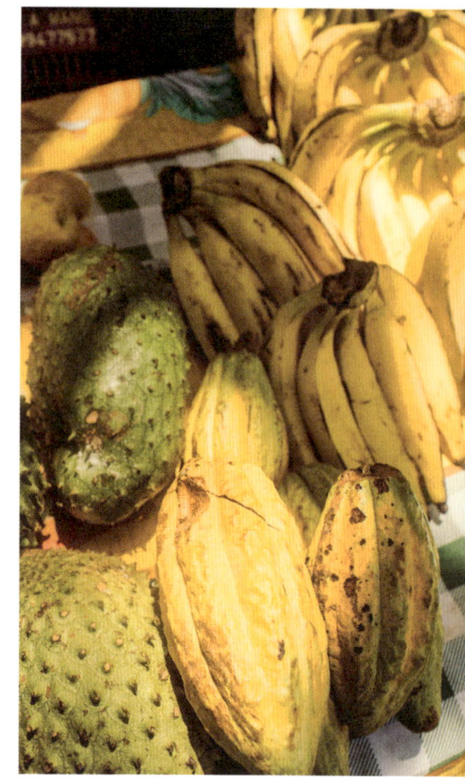

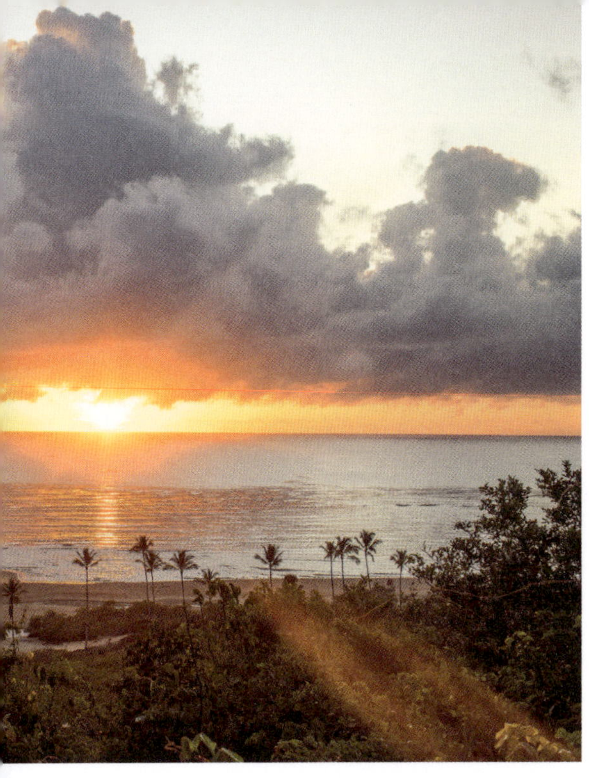

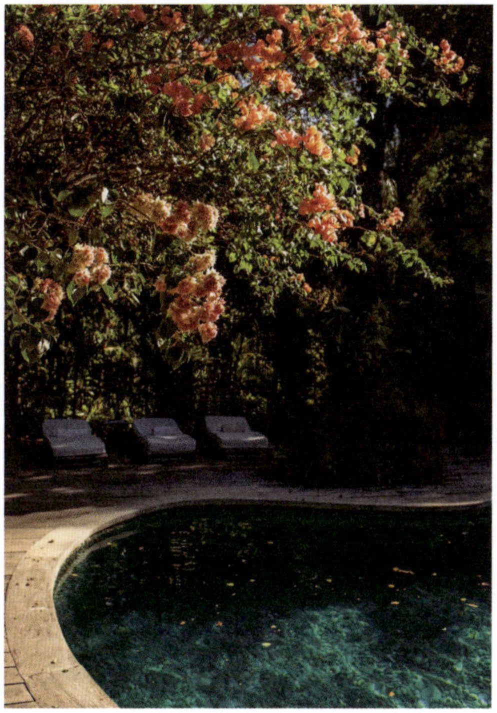

TRANCOSO, BRAZIL

Photographs by Emily Nathan

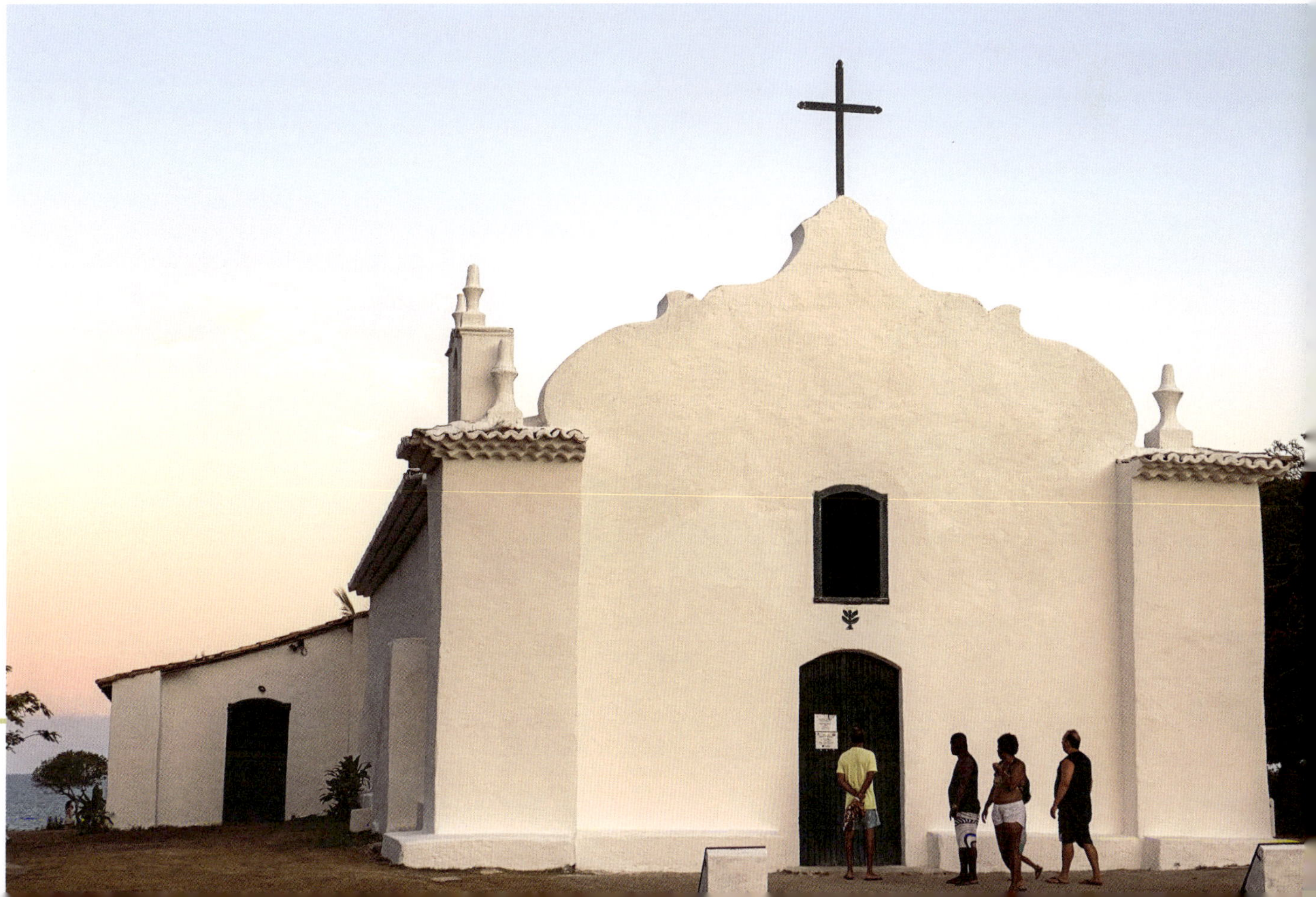

Unguja, Zanzibar,
Tanzania
Sam Vox

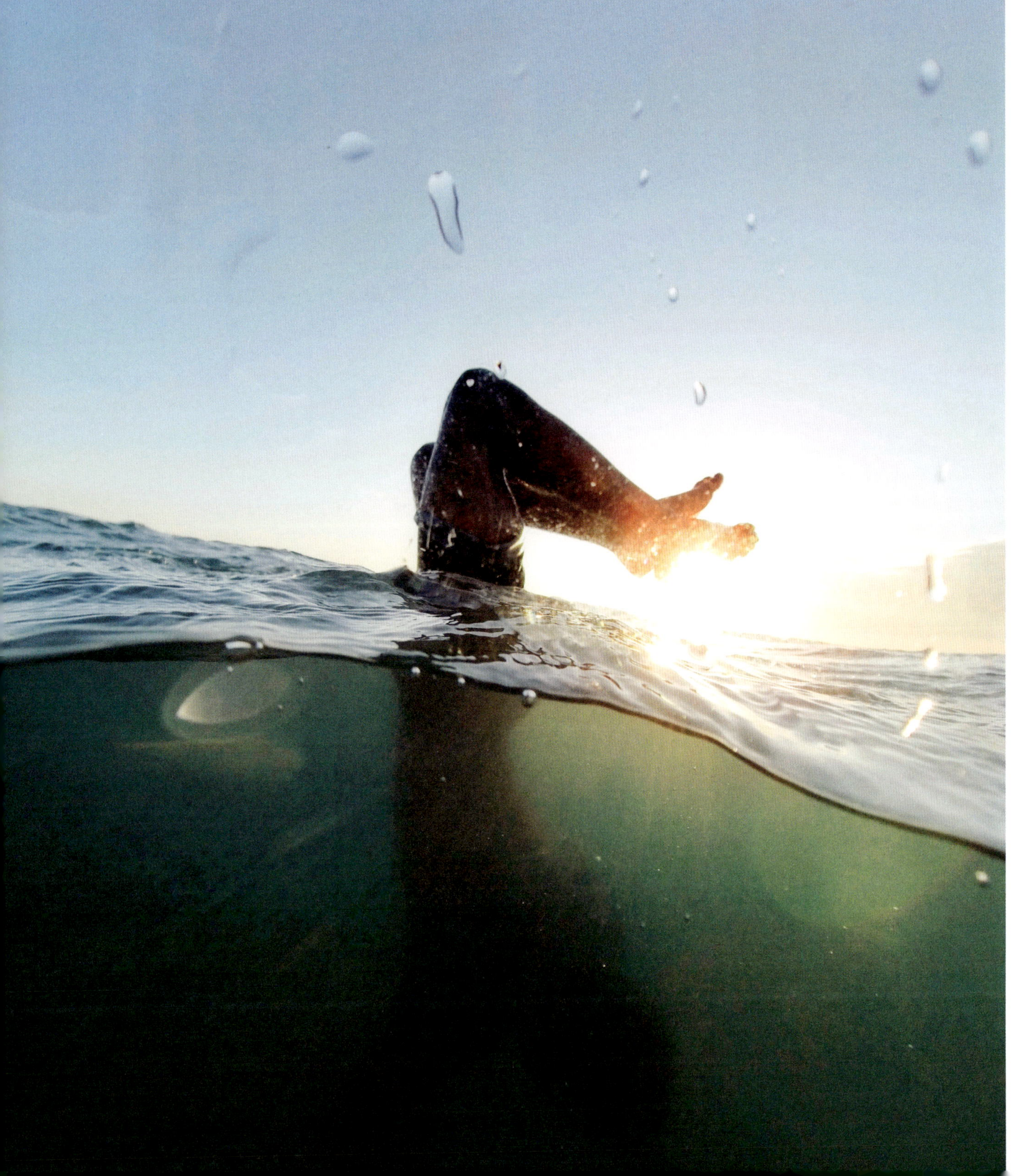

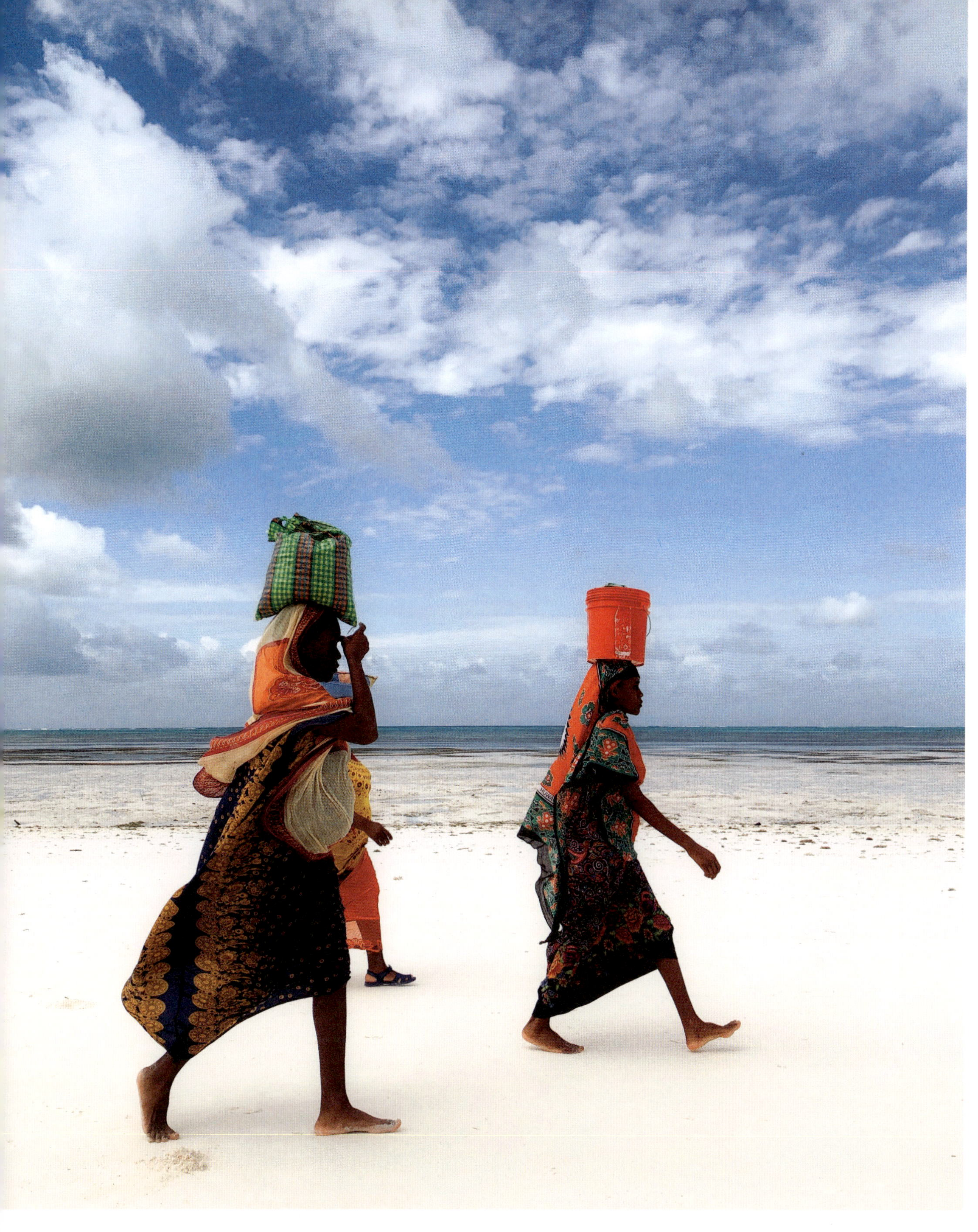

MALTA IS AN easy direct flight from many European cities. A half-hour ferry will take you across to the neighboring Maltese island of Gozo. Gozo is filled with beautiful bays and coves for snorkeling and diving, but divers especially love the limestone sinkhole known as the Blue Hole, with its electric-blue, crystal clear water. The hole is around 50 feet deep and is a marvelous underwater sight for swimmers and divers alike.

**San Lawrenz,
Gozo, Malta**

Holly Farrier

**San Juan,
Puerto Rico**

Gabriela Herman

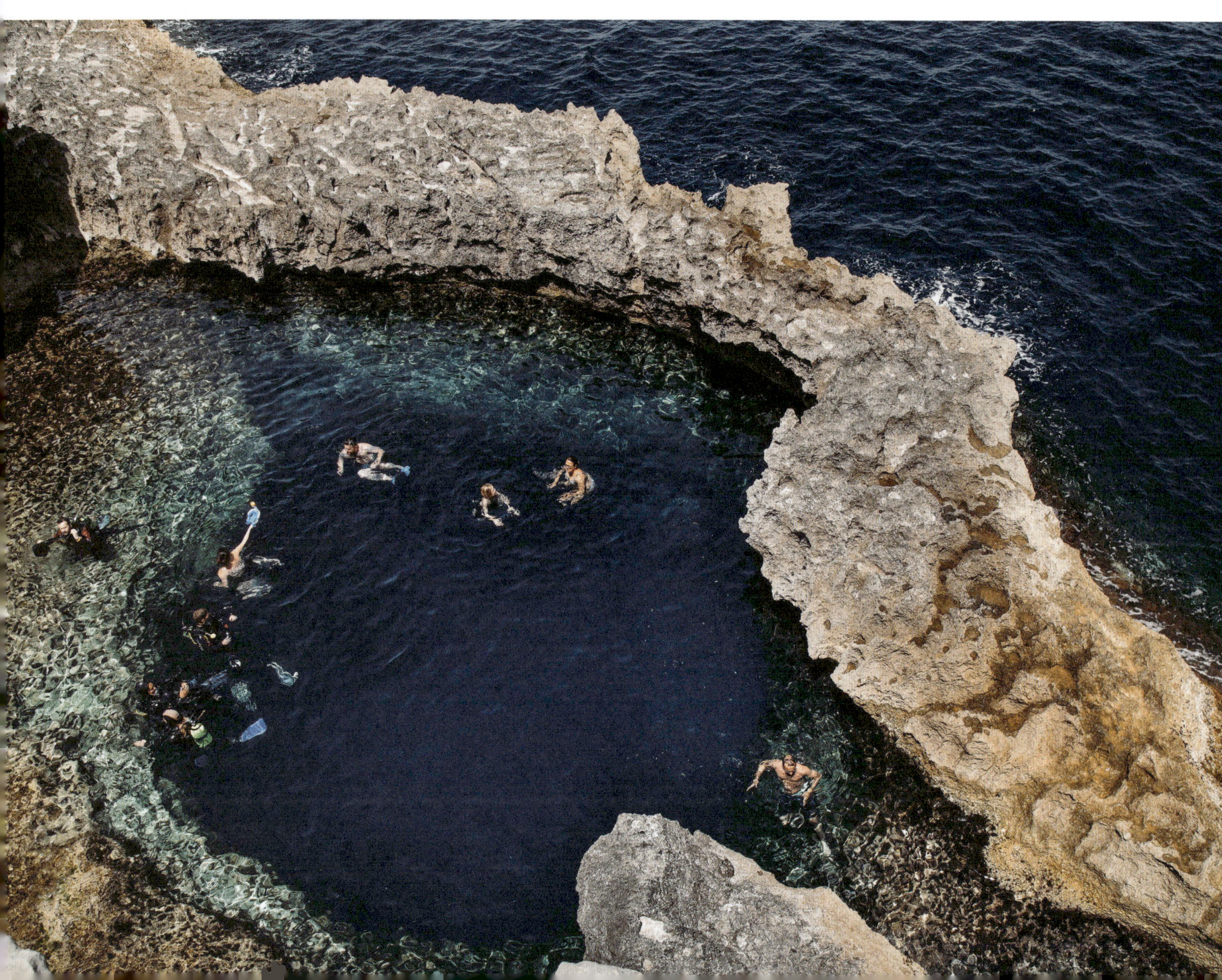

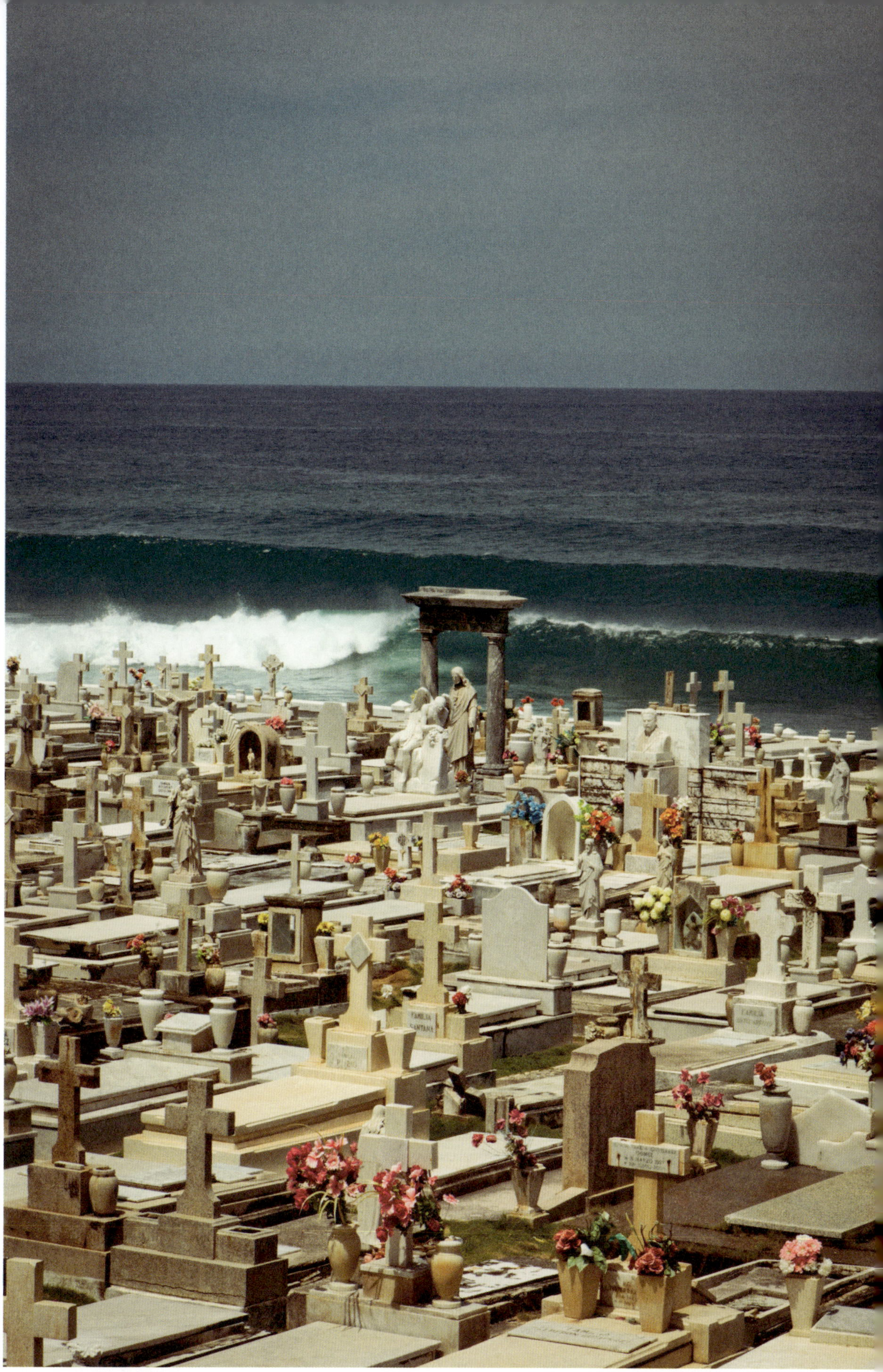

↓
**Hon Ga Choi Island,
Hạ Long Bay, Quảng
Ninh Province, Vietnam**
Courtney Kinnare

→
**Lanikai, Oʻahu,
Hawaiʻi, United States**
Stefan and
Audrey Elmer

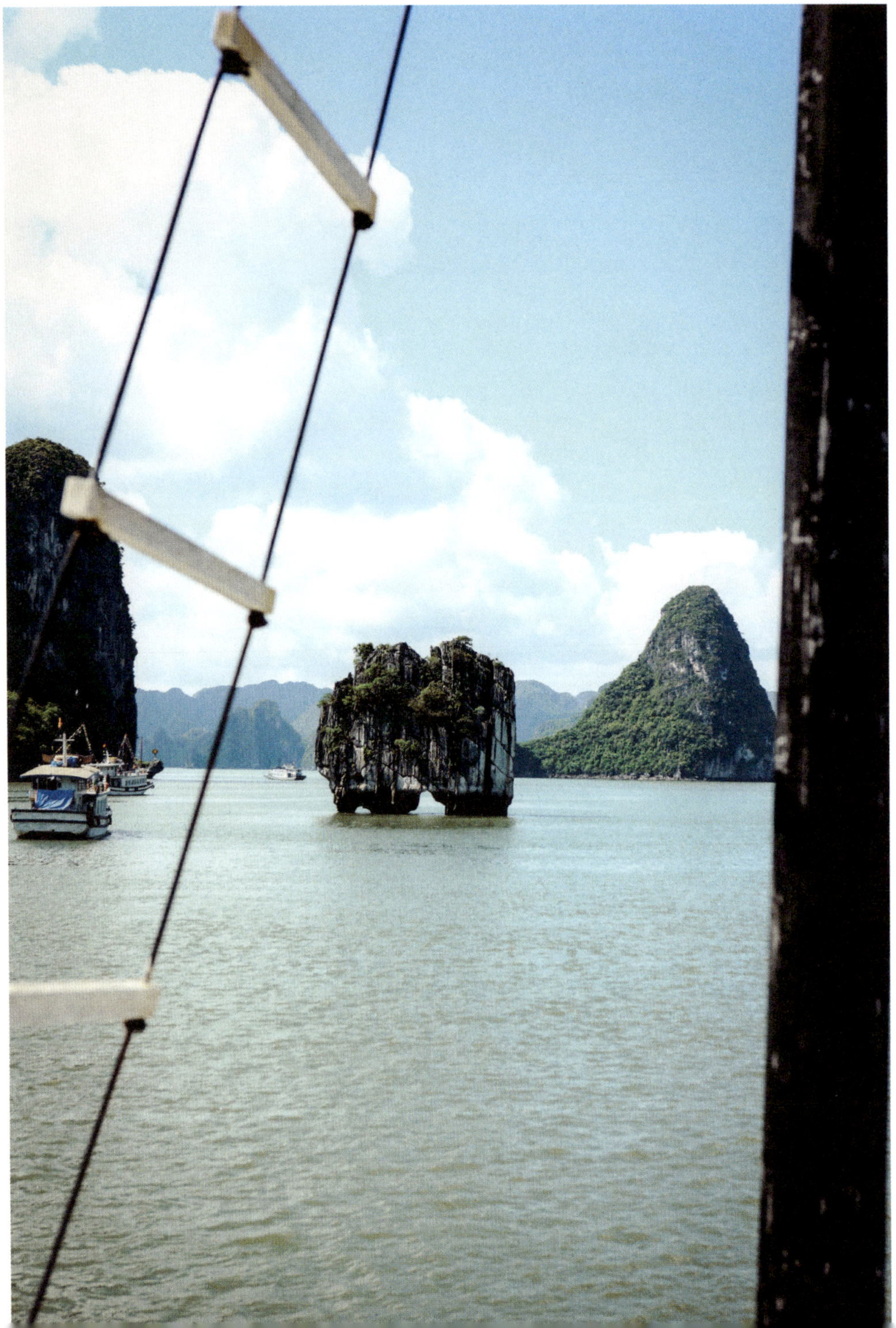

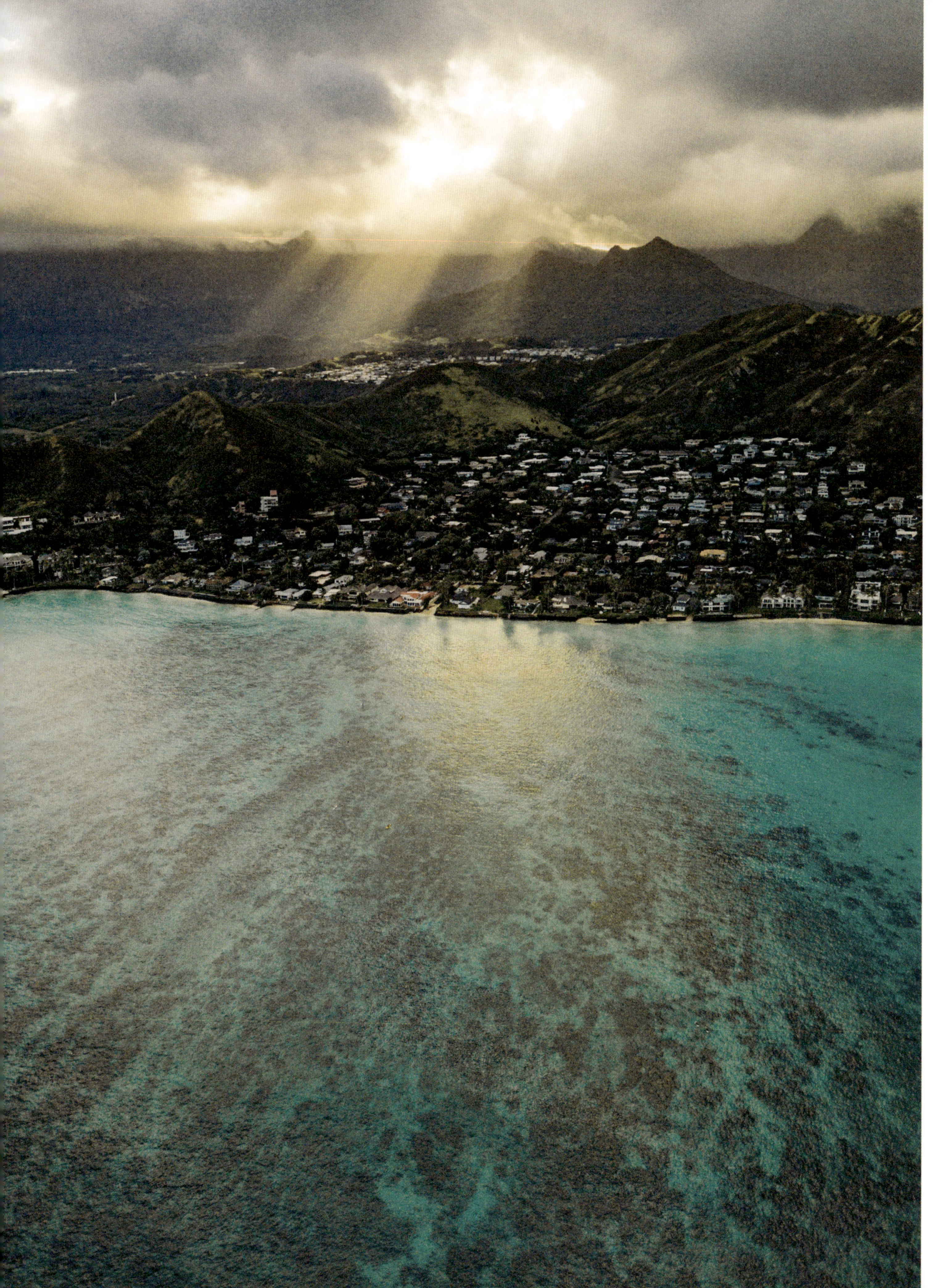

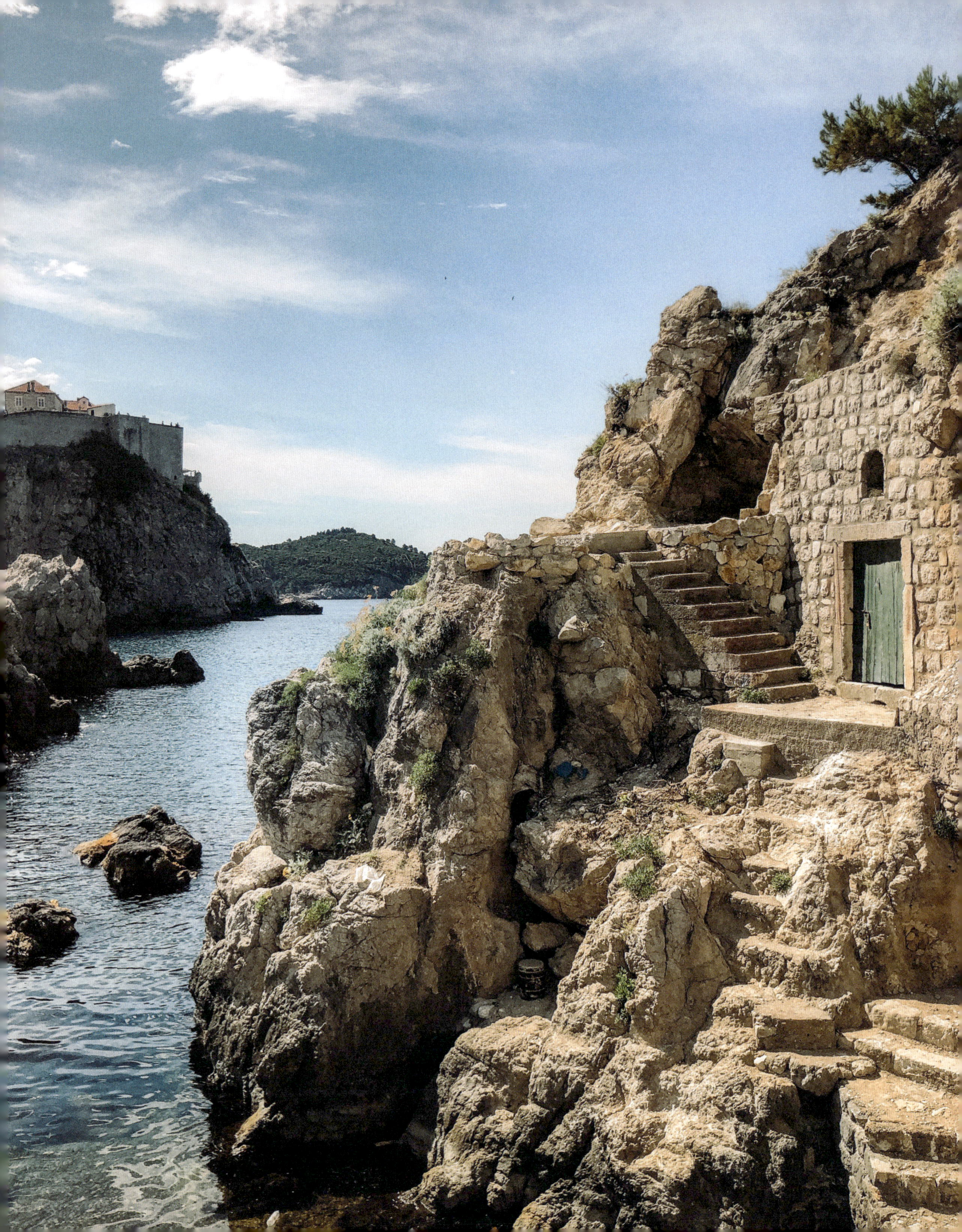

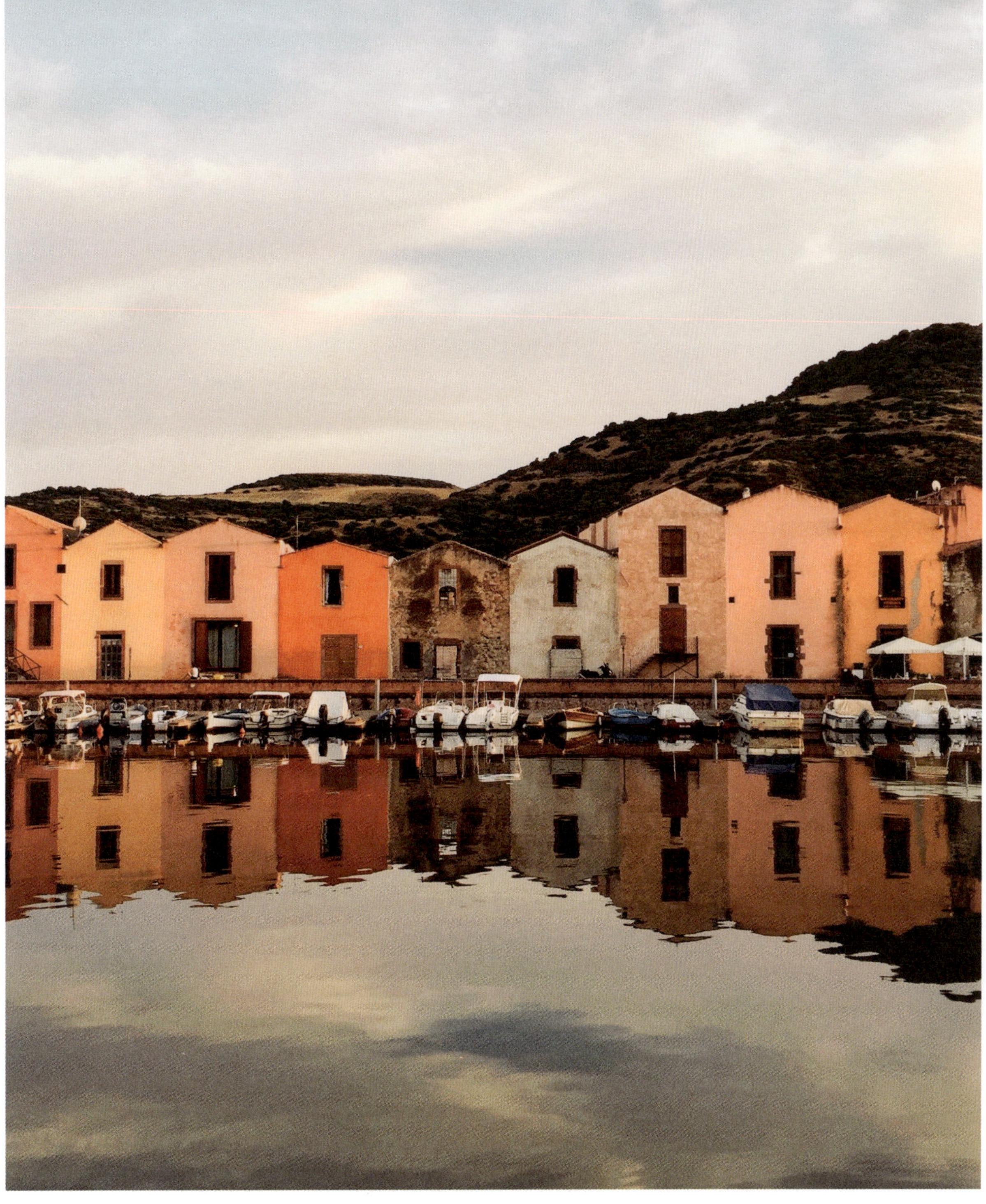

← **Dubrovnik,
Dalmatia,
Croatia**

Amanda Nevarez

↑ **Bosa,
Sardinia,
Italy**

Renata Ravot

↓
**Amalfi,
Salerno,
Italy**

Anne-Sophie
Rosenvinge

→
**Ischia,
Campania,
Italy**

Lucy Laucht

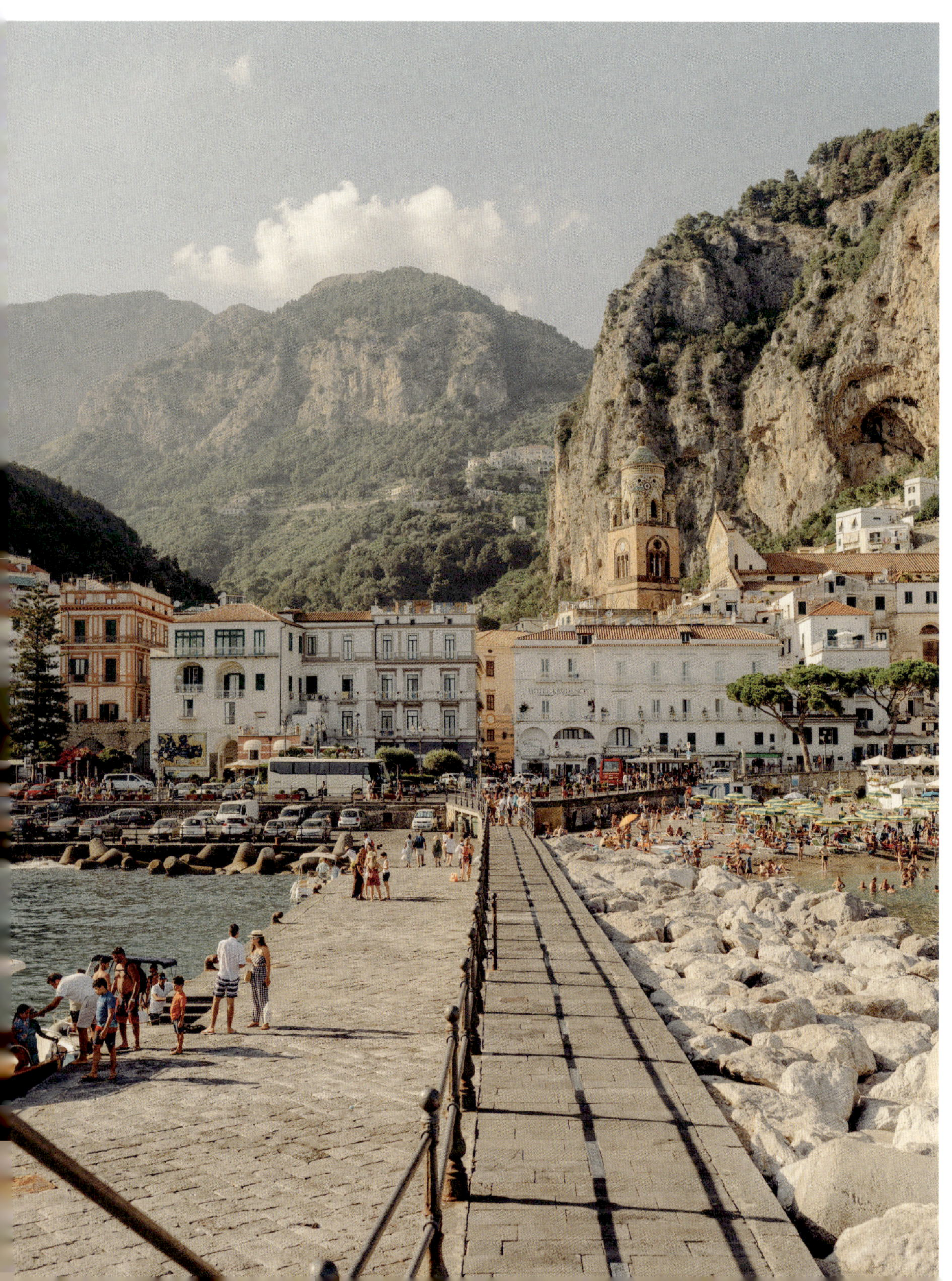

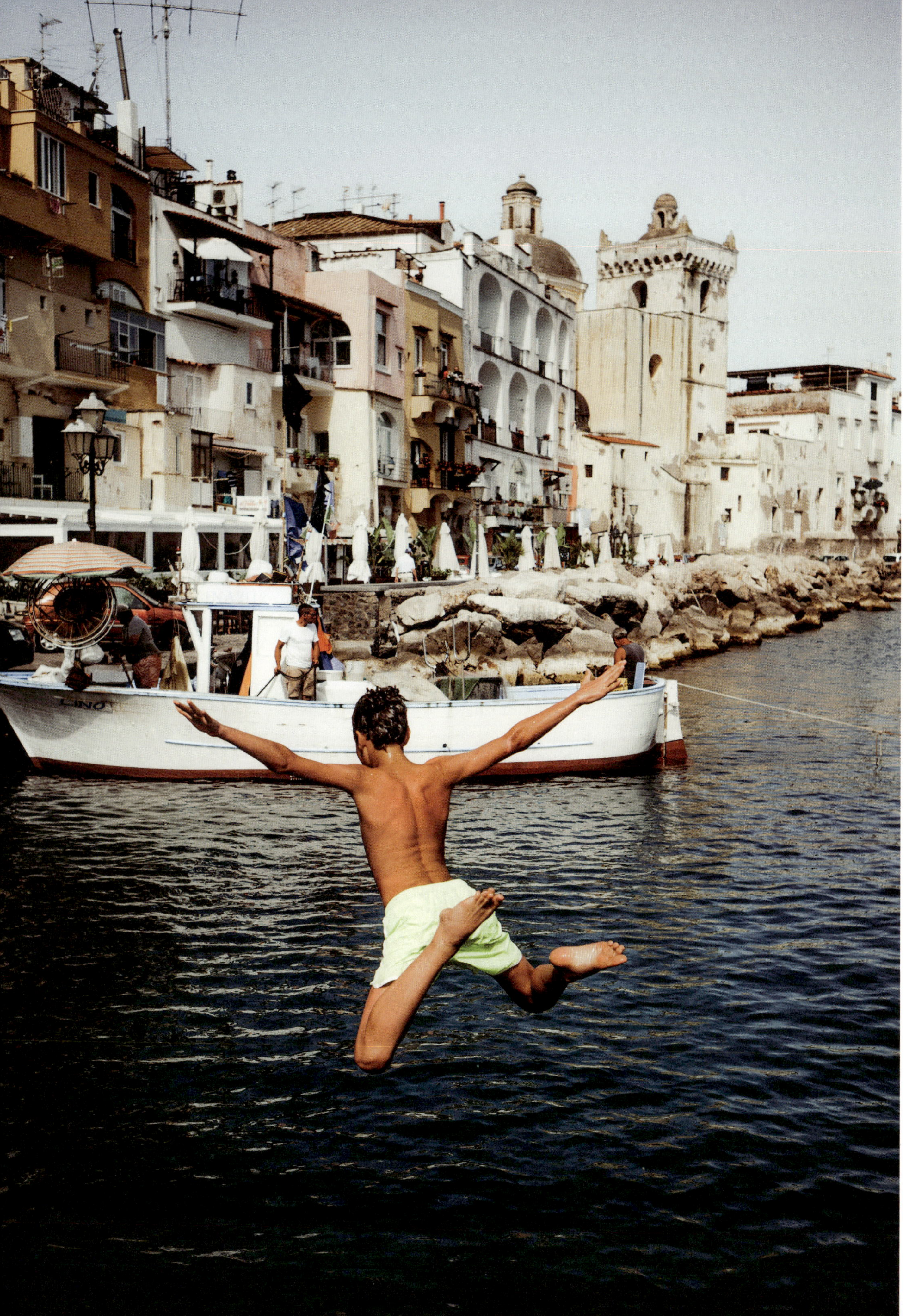

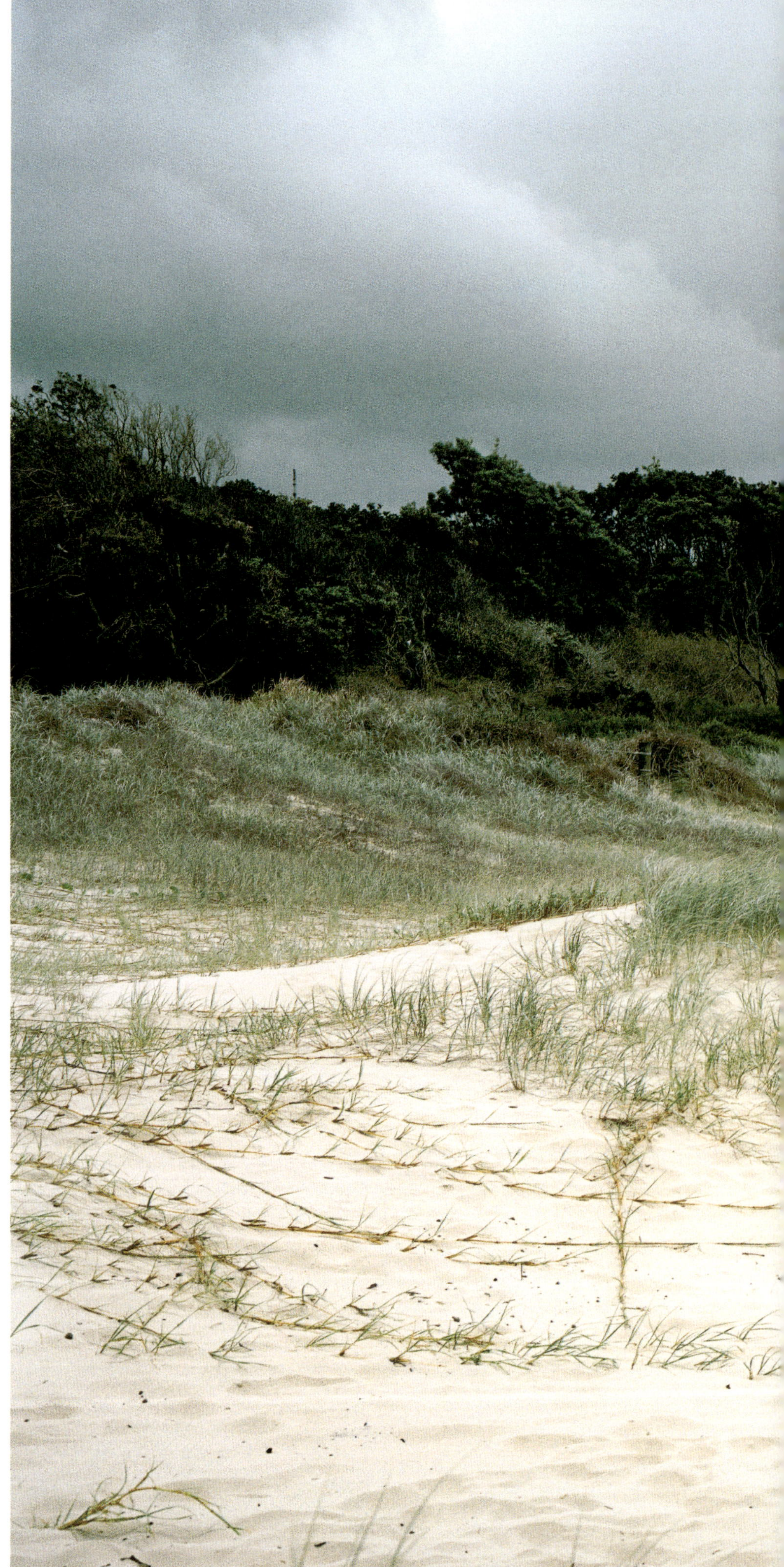

Byron Bay, New South Wales, Australia

Emily Nathan

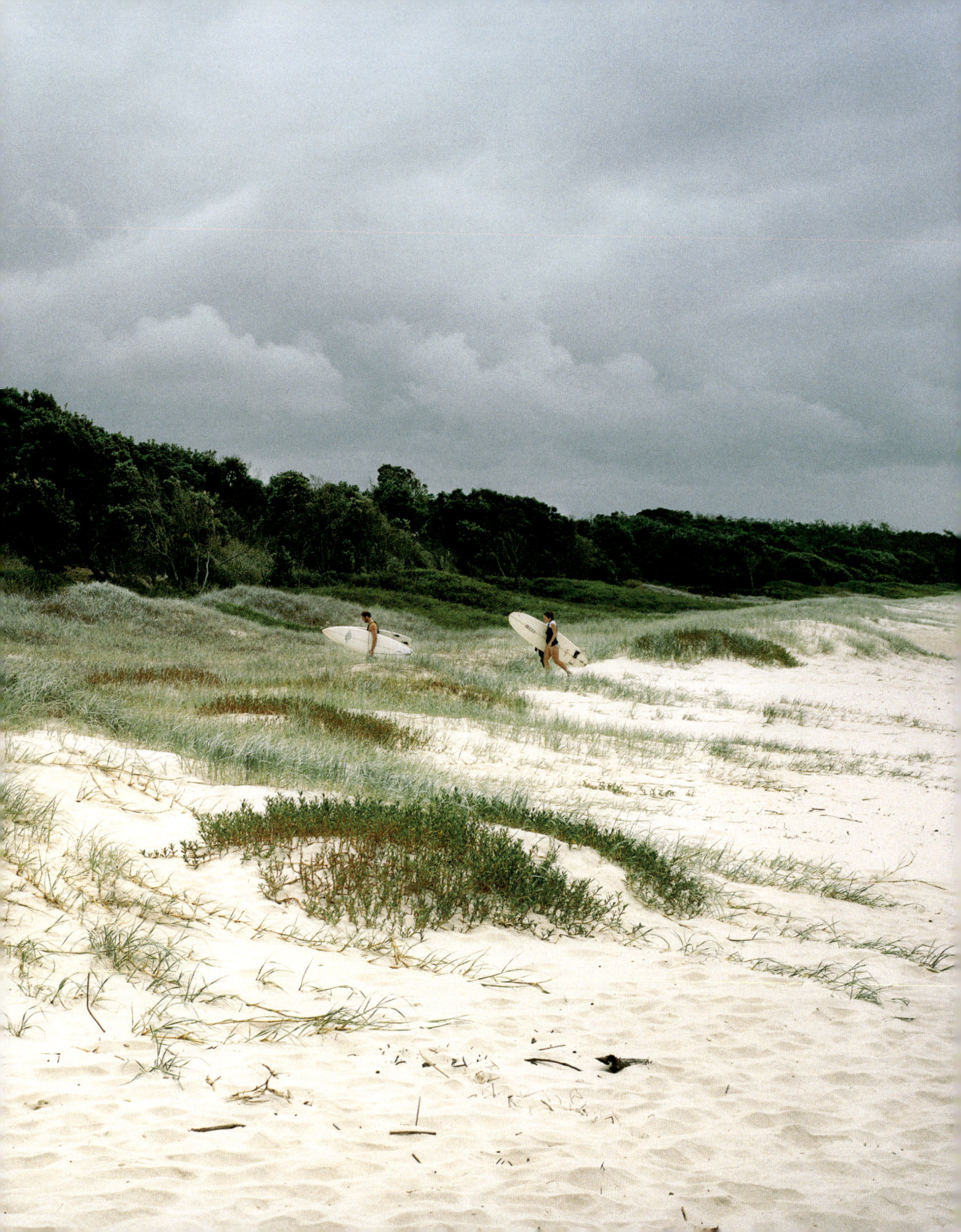

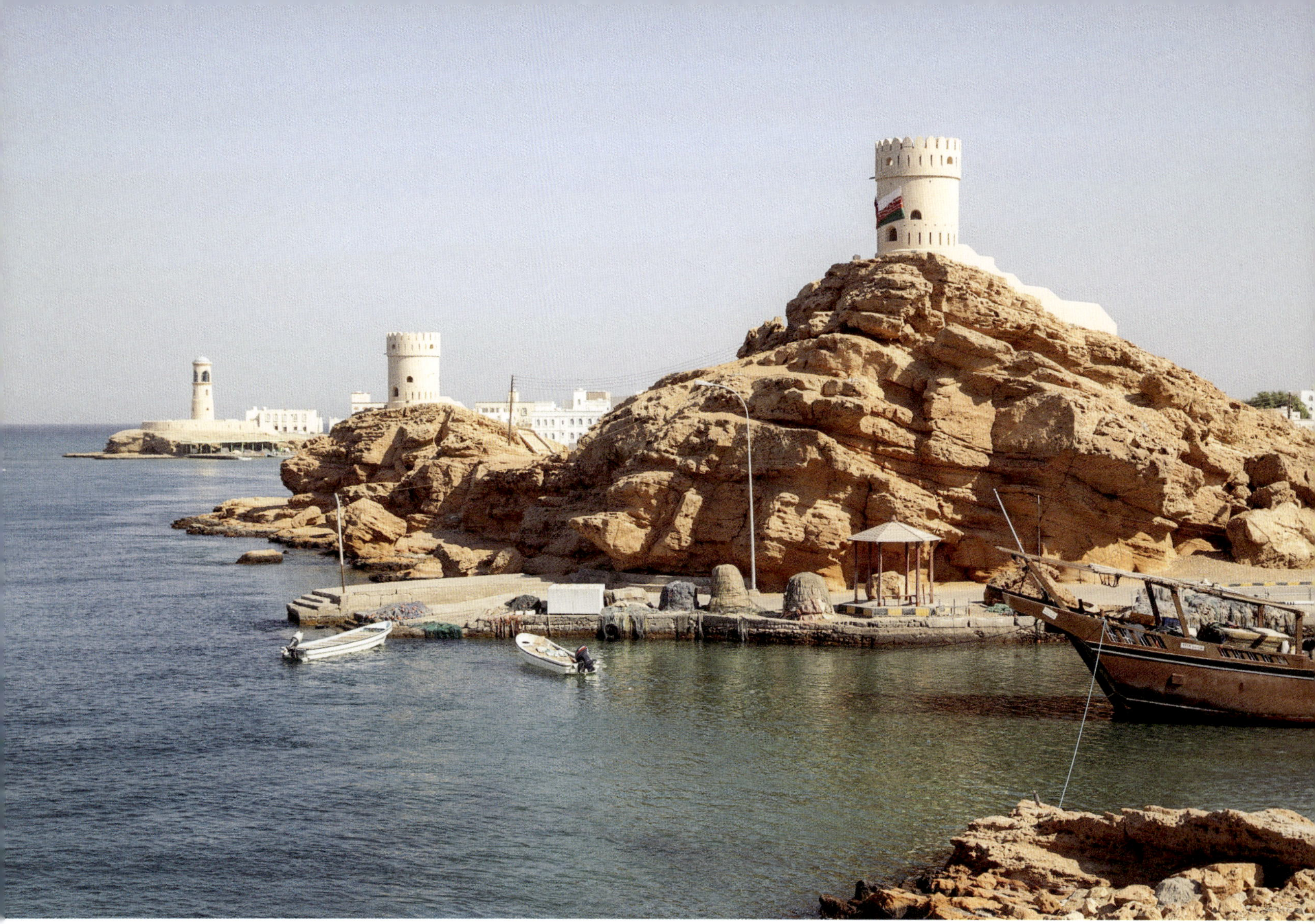

THE TOWN OF Sur is located about a two-hour drive south of
Muscat and is a great pit stop on the way to Ras al Jinz Turtle
Reserve, Wadi Bani Khalid, or Wahiba Sands. You can find a
road-trip snack of shawarma and karak tea at local coffee shops,
and spot the old dhows (traditional fishing boats) if you wander
down to the beach in town. The highway between Muscat and
Sur is scenic, passing rivers and small traditional villages against
a backdrop of desert cliffs. Though public transportation is scarce
in Oman, renting a car and navigating the roads is easy and is
the best way to explore (pick up a copy of the fabulous Explorer
guidebook *Oman Off-Road* before you leave home). It is a very
safe country, and the locals are particularly friendly, so if you're
ever in a fix, just ask an Omani; they will likely be happy to help you
out (and may even offer you some Omani coffee and dates, too).

**Sur, Ash Sharqiyah
Region, Oman**

Jade Spadina

**Nash Island, Maine,
United States**

Greta Rybus

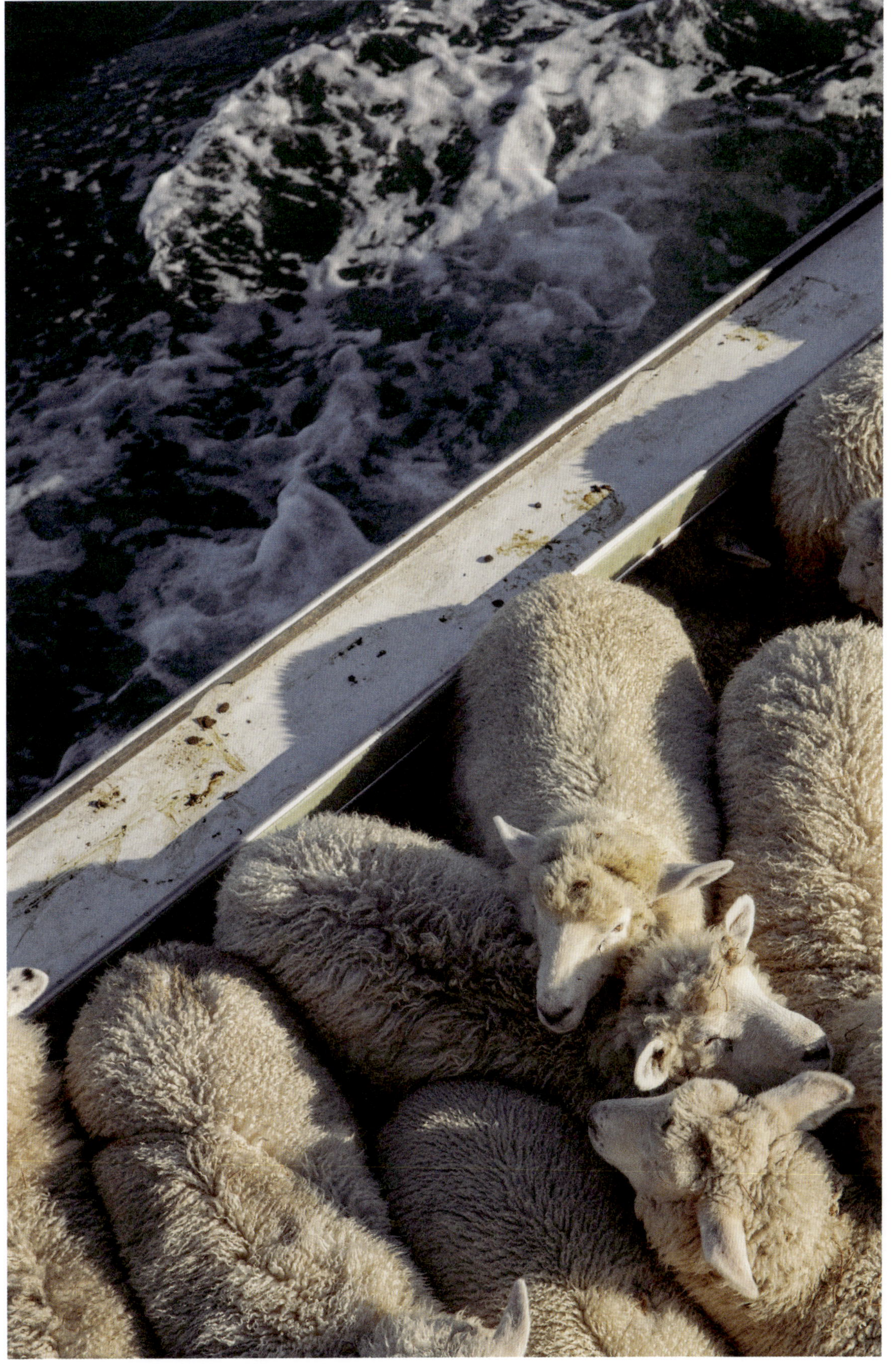

**St. Petersburg,
Russia**

Tatiana Nadyseva

THIS SURF TRADITION to honor the dead, potentially dating back to the 1920s era of the Waikiki Beach Boys and Duke Kahanamoku, has migrated around the world. During a paddle out, participants on surfboards link hands for a moment of silence. After the ceremony, participants throw flowers and leis into the circle and splash water into the air. This image was taken during the protests for racial justice in 2020.

**Honolulu, Oʻahu,
Hawaiʻi, United States**

Matty Leong

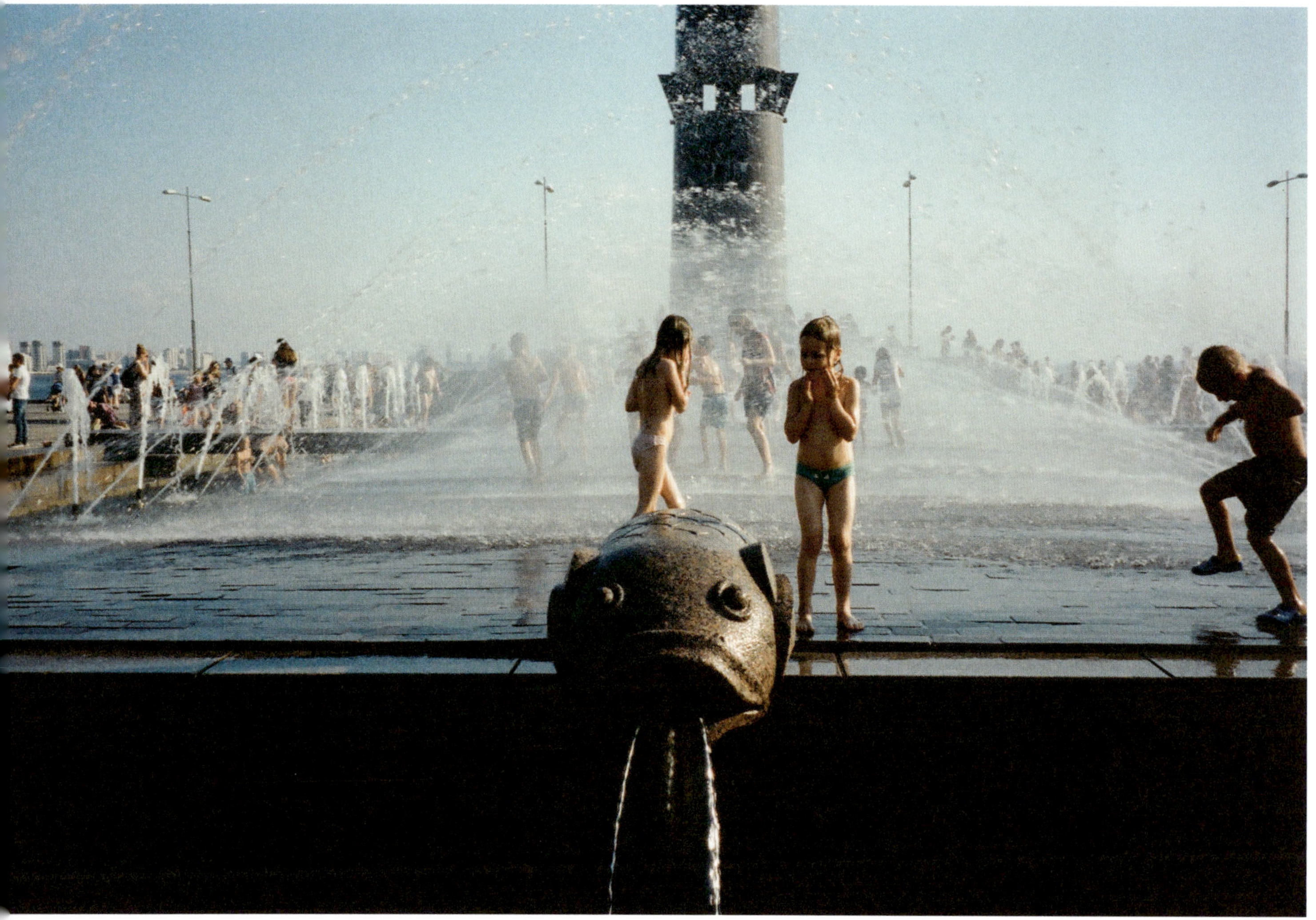

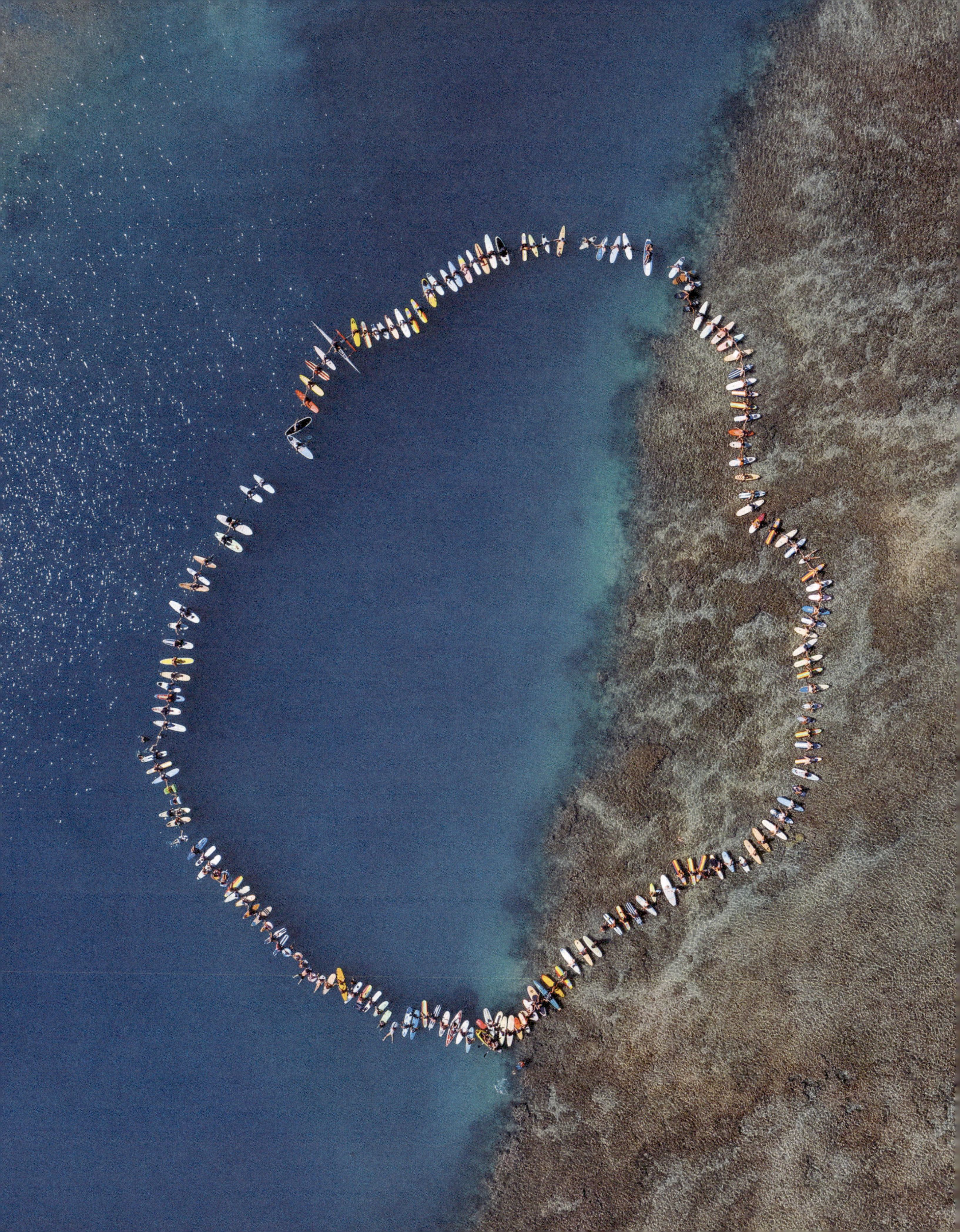

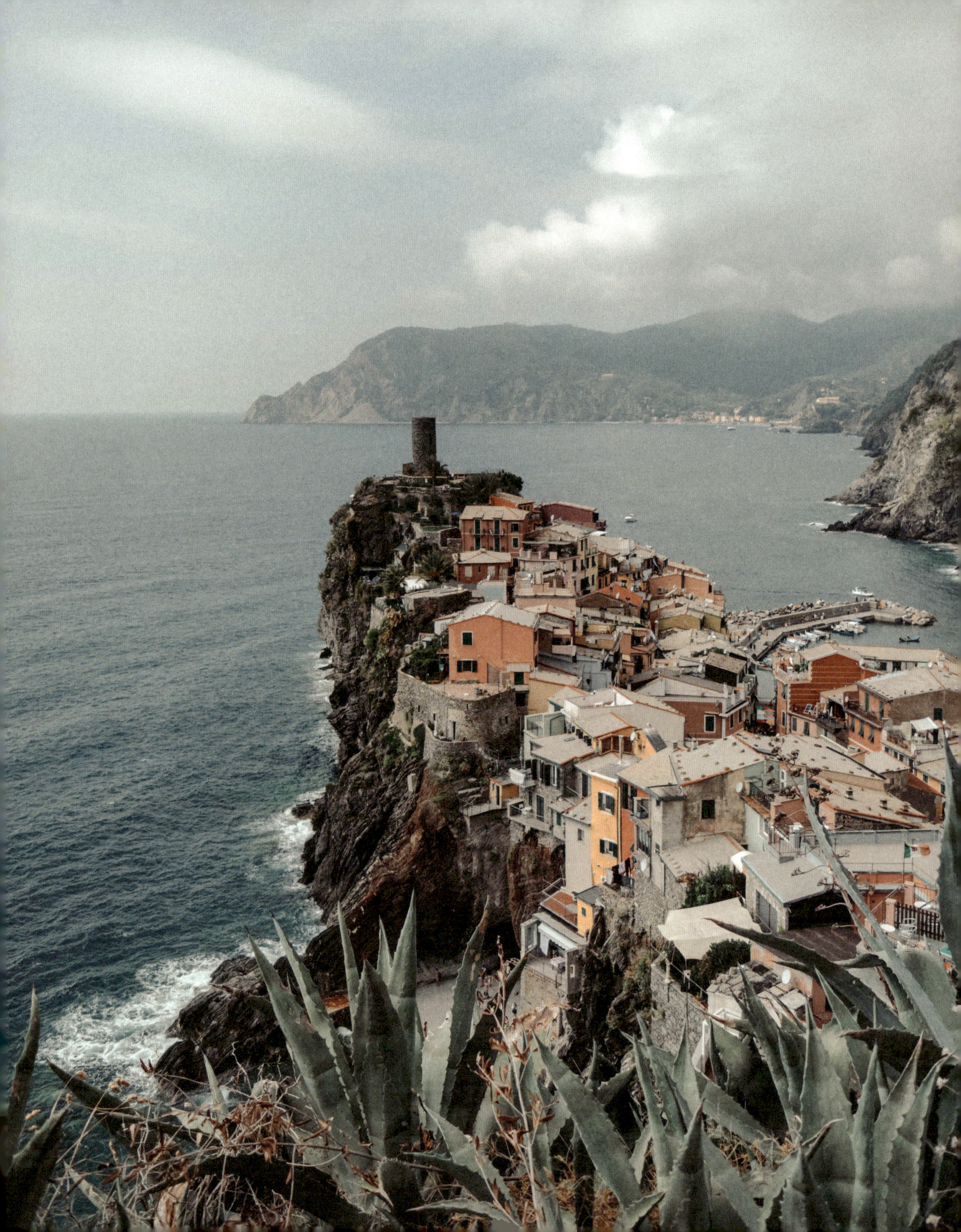

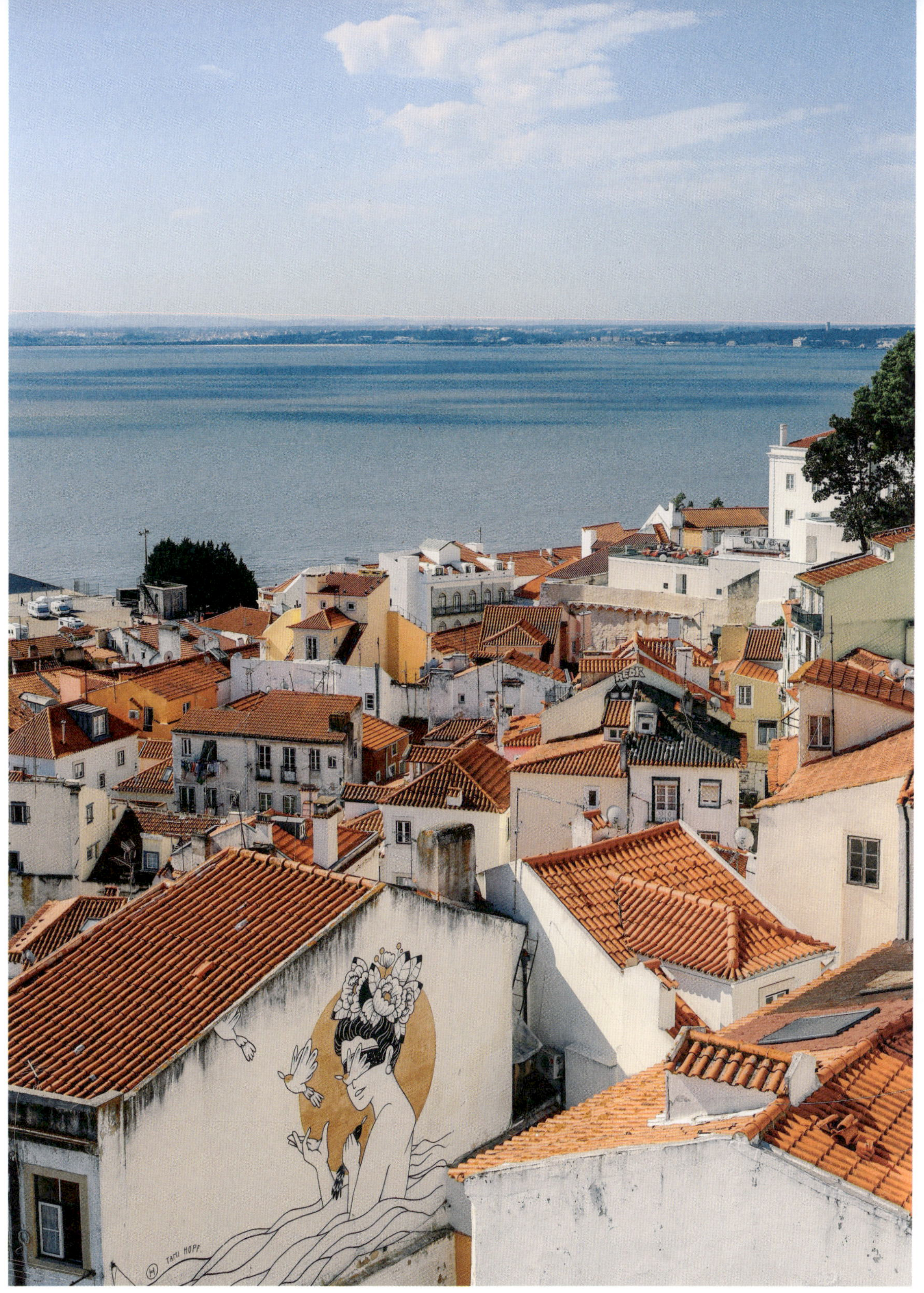

← **Vernazza,
Liguria, Italy**

Jessica Lu

↑ **Lisbon,
Portugal**

Sezgi Olgaç

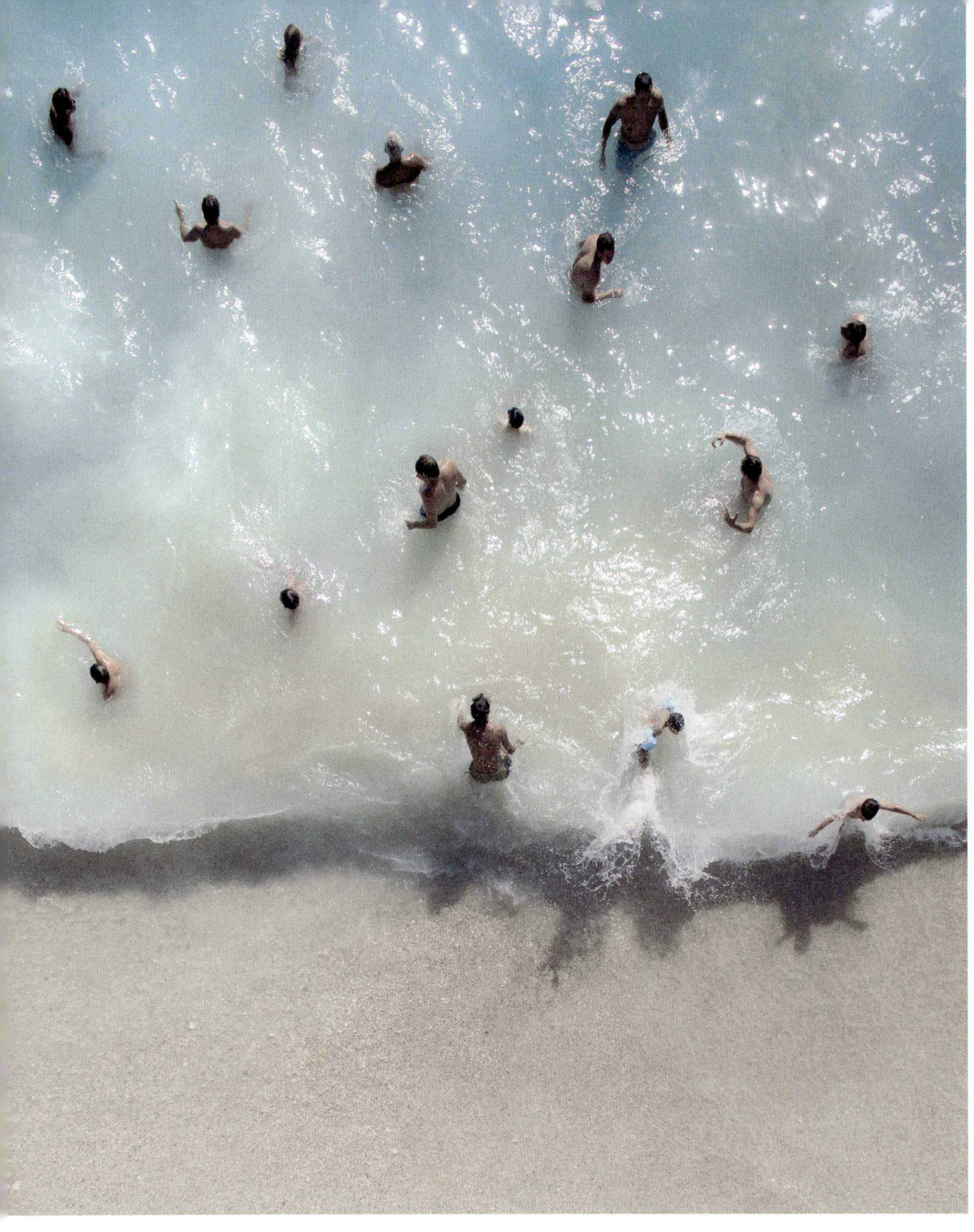

↑
Lefkada Island,
Lefkada Region,
Greece

Costas Spathis

→
Wollongong,
New South Wales,
Australia

Adams Rozmus

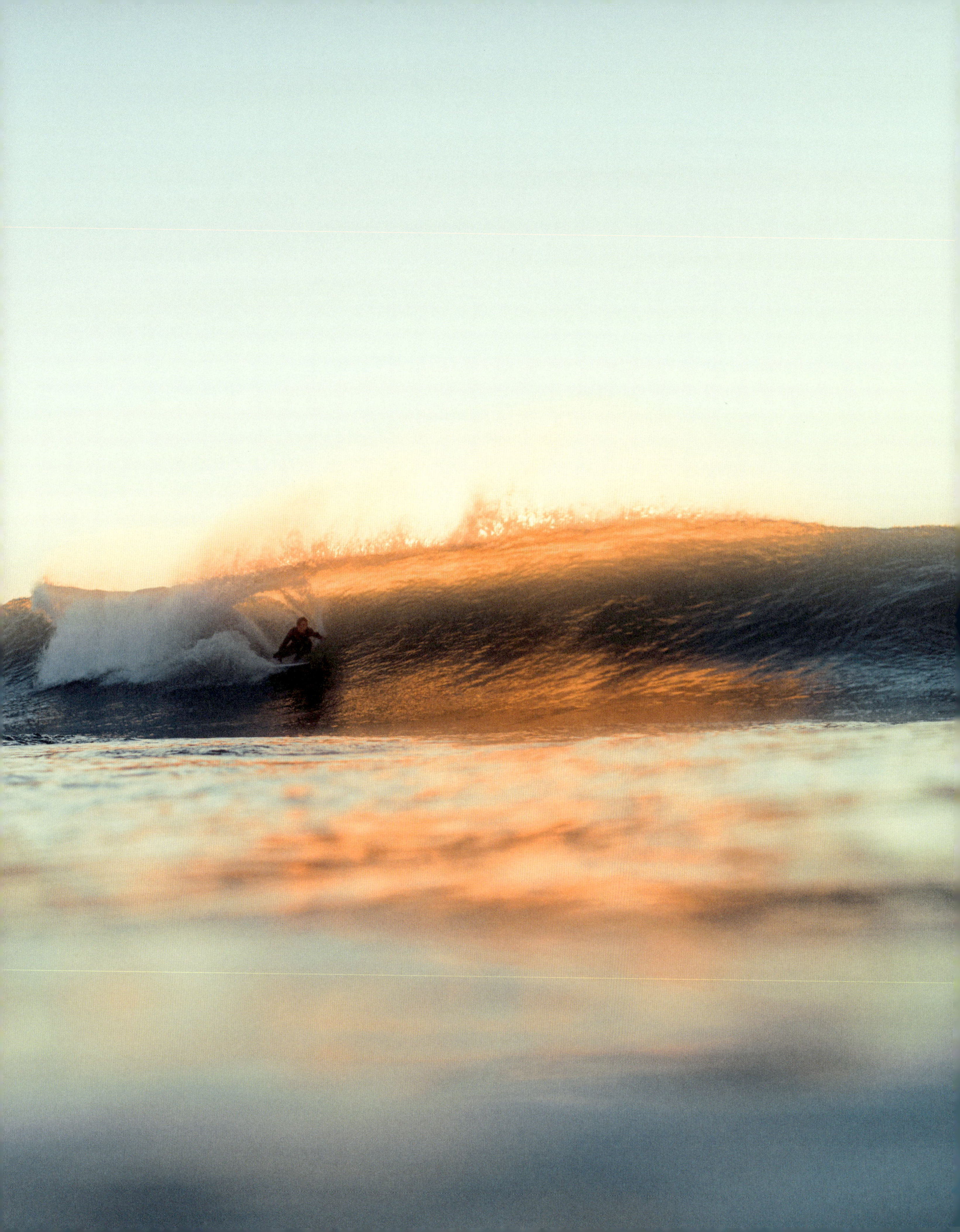

OVERTOURISM

Only about ten thousand people live on the Greek islands of Santorini, but the dramatic cliffside architecture attracts around two million travelers annually. The majority of them visit the tiny, postcard-perfect town of Oia, with its iconic, whitewashed buildings set high within the rock precipice overlooking an idyllic Aegean sea. But this small island community was built for its local population, not for the enormous number of people who visit every day. Besides diminishing the local character of the place and disrupting the lives of locals who live there, overtourism on Santorini has put a strain on infrastructure and waste management. Huge daily numbers of tourists and cruise ships produce a large amount of trash and waste, some of which makes its way into Santorini's waterways and seas every day.

Travel has become more popular and accessible than ever before, and social media (especially geo tagging) has helped drive overtourism to specific locations around the world. To help mitigate the impacts of tourism, some places are working proactively to manage it, bringing in the right amount of travelers to support the local economy while not overtaxing the community and ecosystem. The tiny Brazilian island of Fernando de Noronha is one such place—a model for sustainable travel. The island has a quota for how many tourists can visit and strict measures to protect the local ecology; a tax for visitors based on the length of stay goes toward local conservation efforts, mandatory recycling, and a ban on disposable plastics.

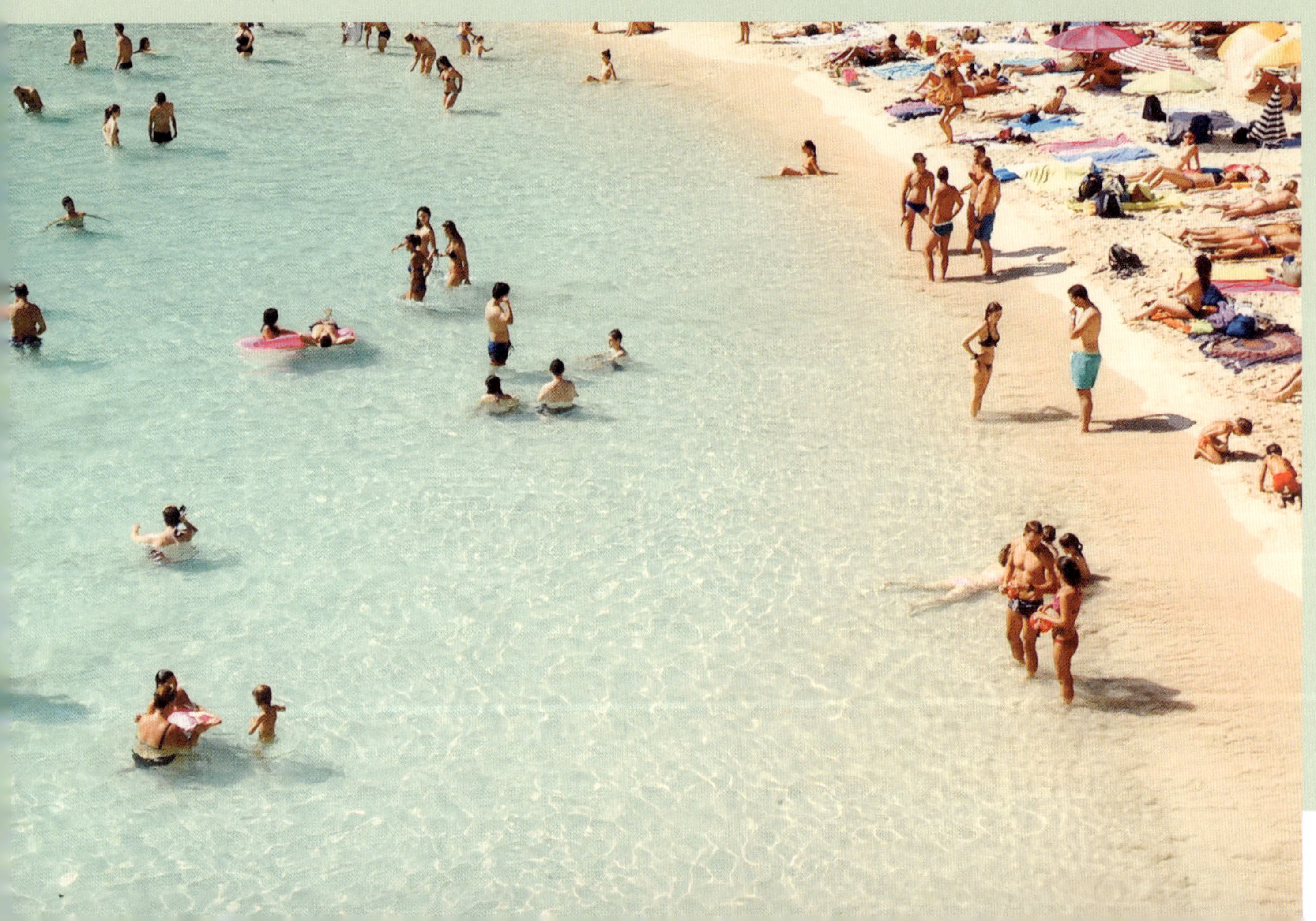

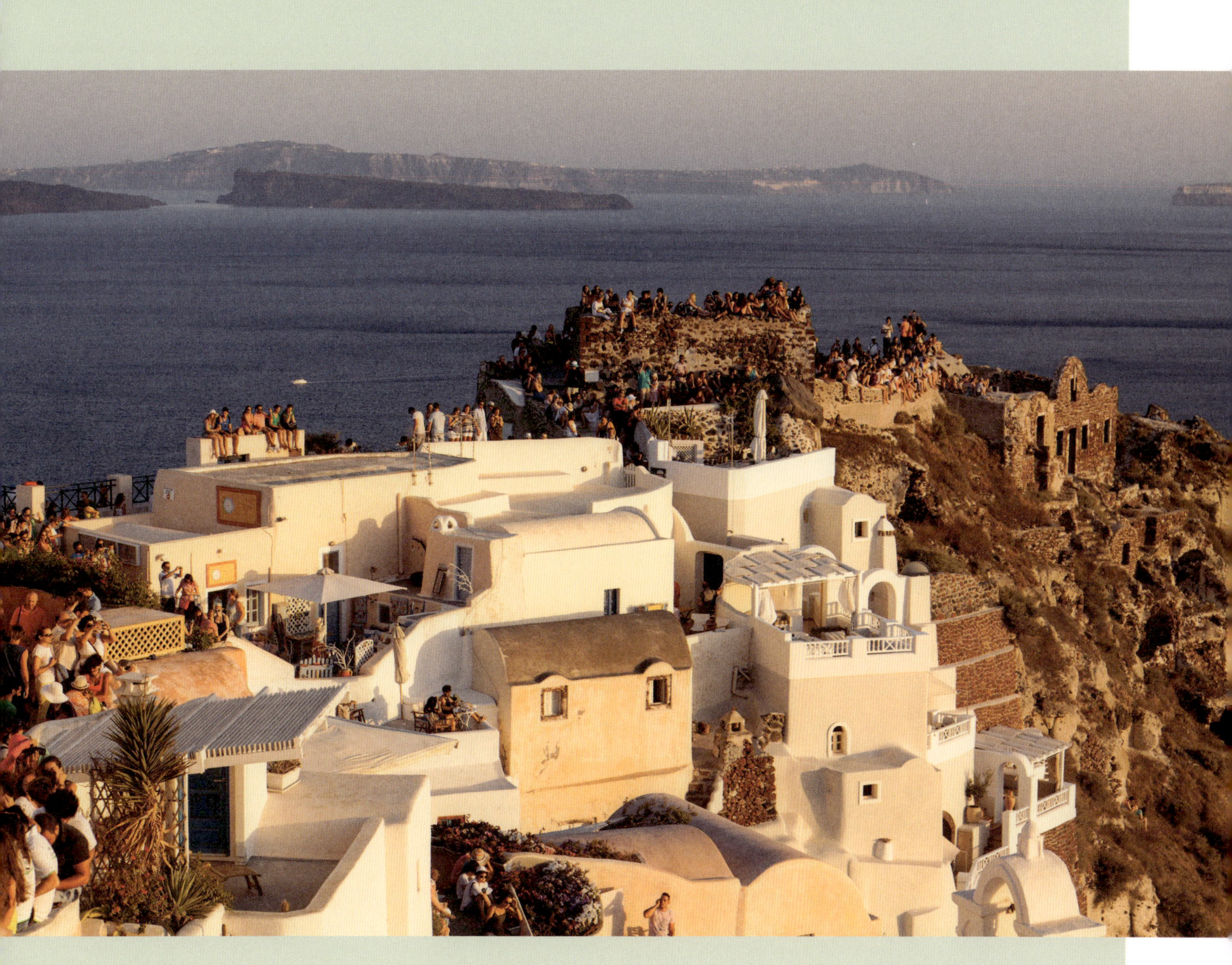

←
Menorca, Balearic
Islands, Spain

Raquel Guiu Grigelmo

↑
Santorini,
Greece

Andrea Bakacs

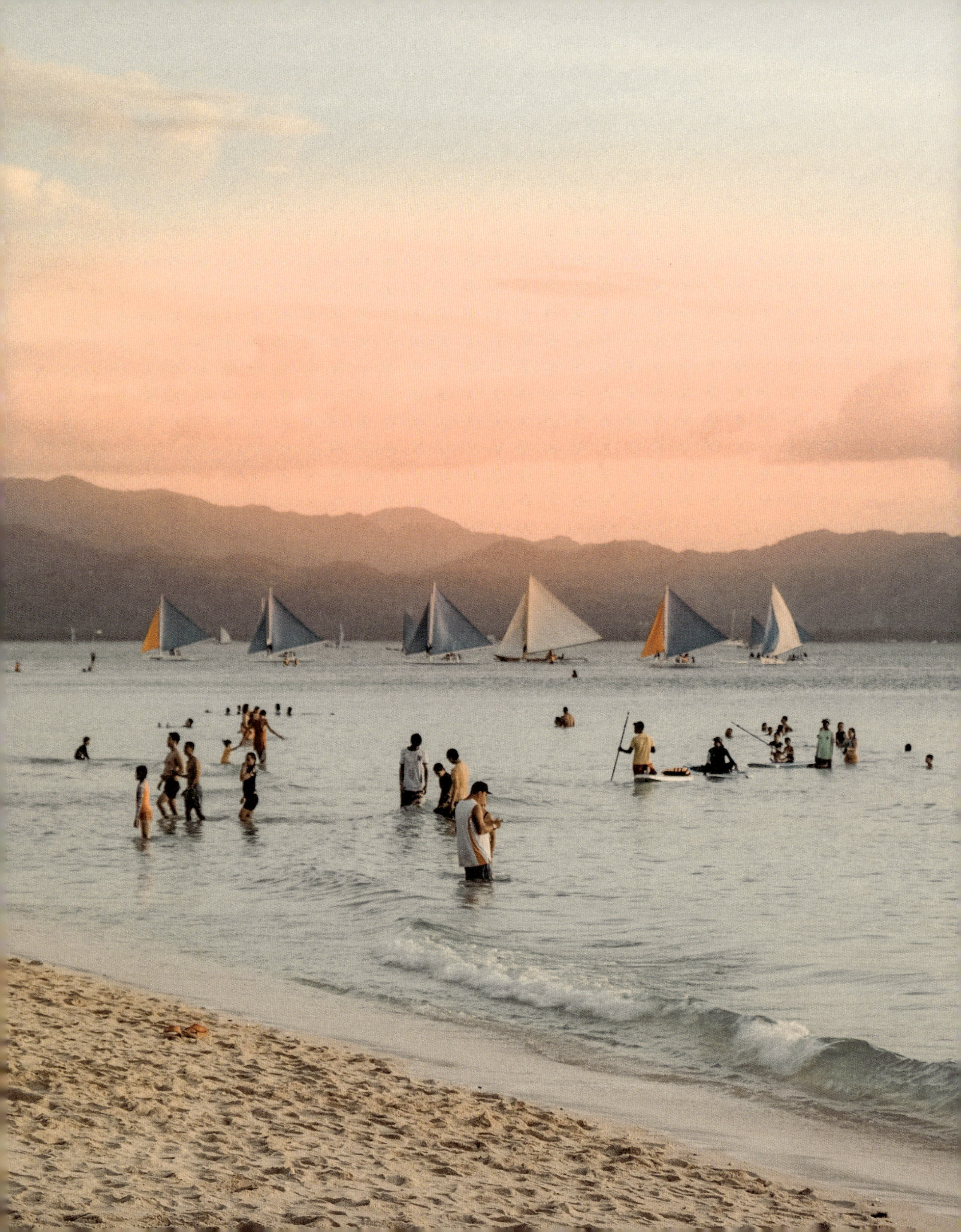

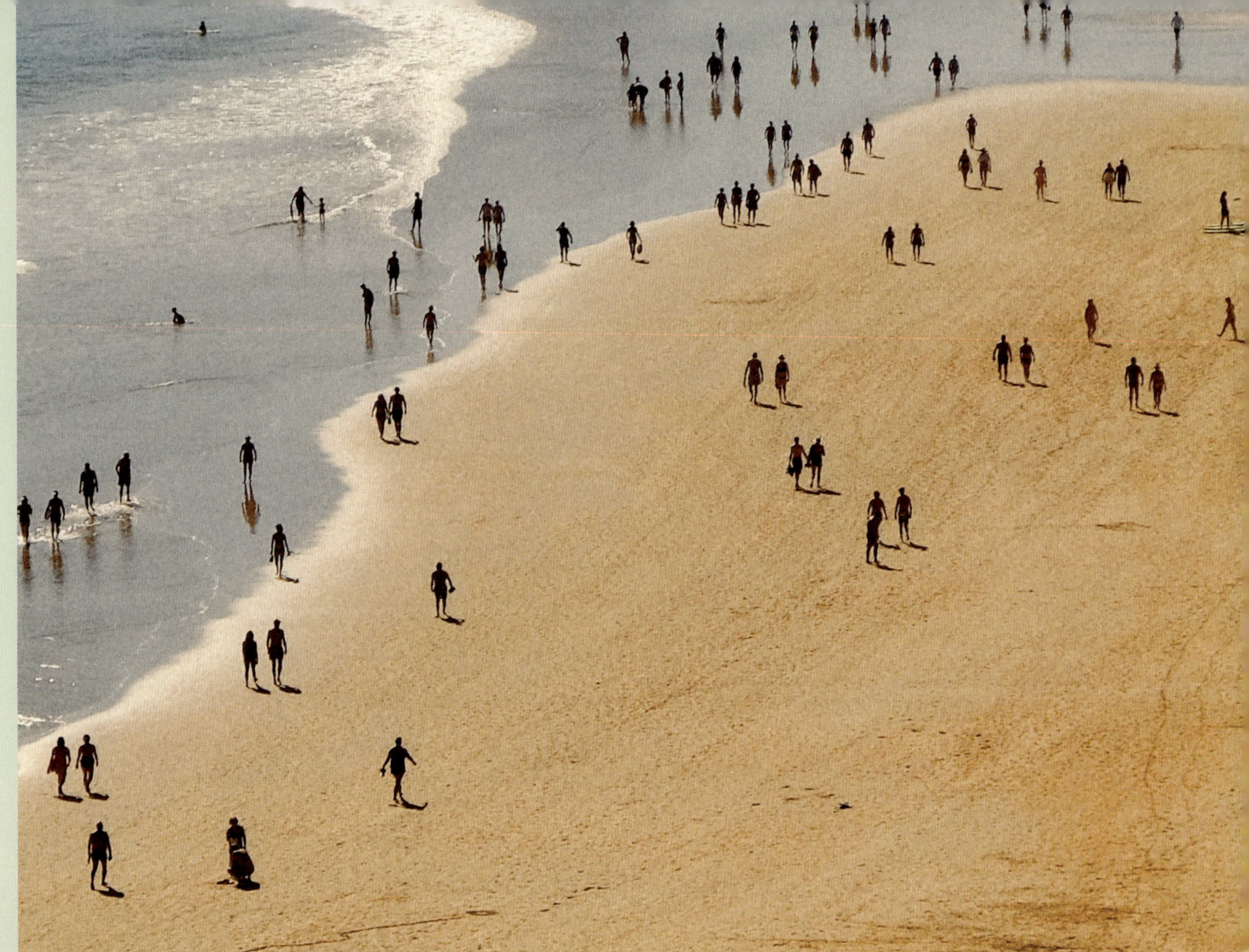

HOW YOU CAN HELP

- Choose your destinations responsibly and thoughtfully. There are so many beautiful, fascinating destinations in this world, so consider a more off-the-beaten-path destination.

- When you do travel, shop and dine at local businesses, and perhaps even consider volunteering. Be respectful of the local customs and character, and acknowledge that you're visiting someone's home.

- Support legislation that helps regulate tourism numbers through caps, taxes, and environmental protections.

←
**Boracay Island,
Aklan Province,
Philippines**

Arjhay De Leon

↑
**Santander,
Cantabria, Spain**

Raquel Guiu Grigelmo

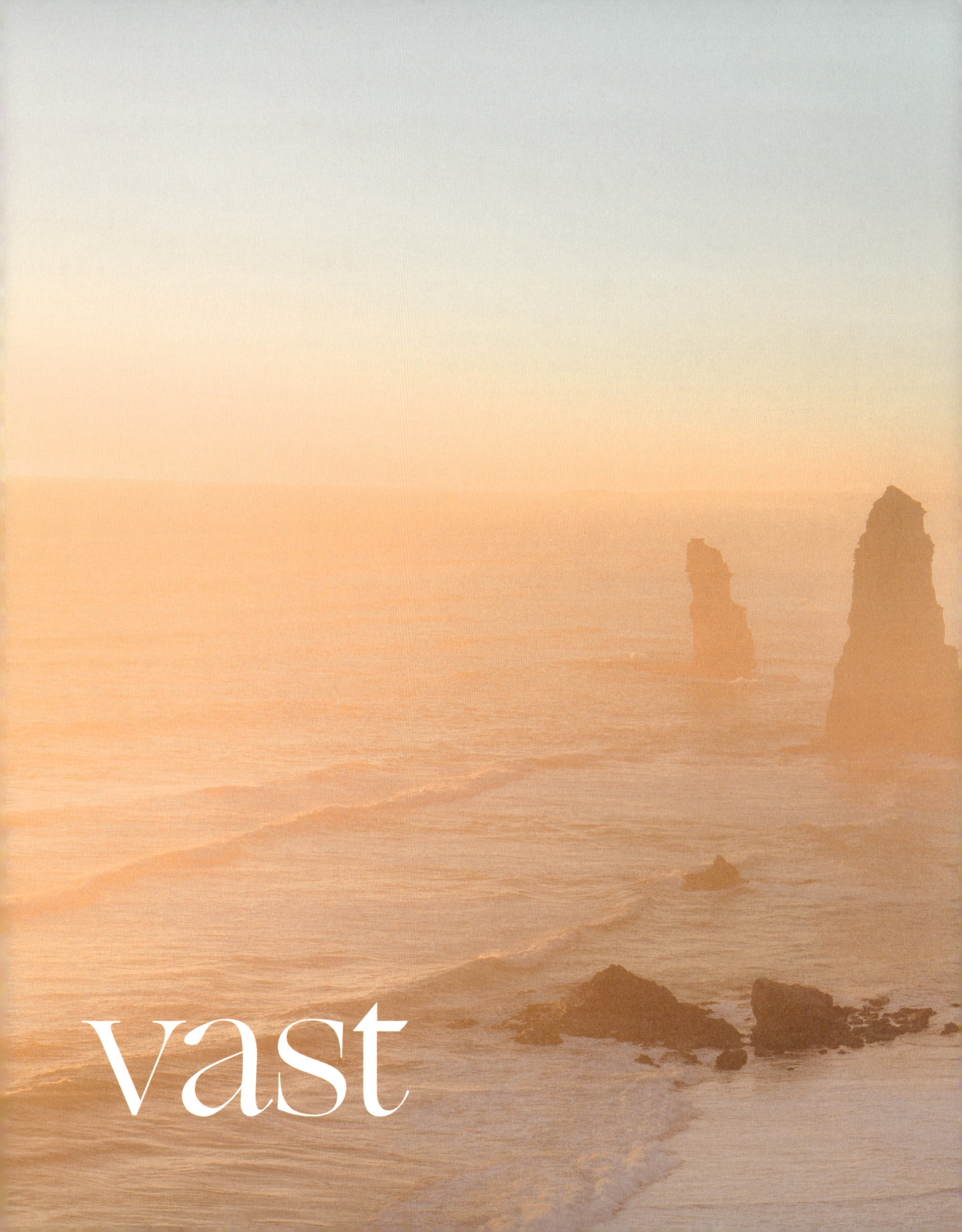
vast

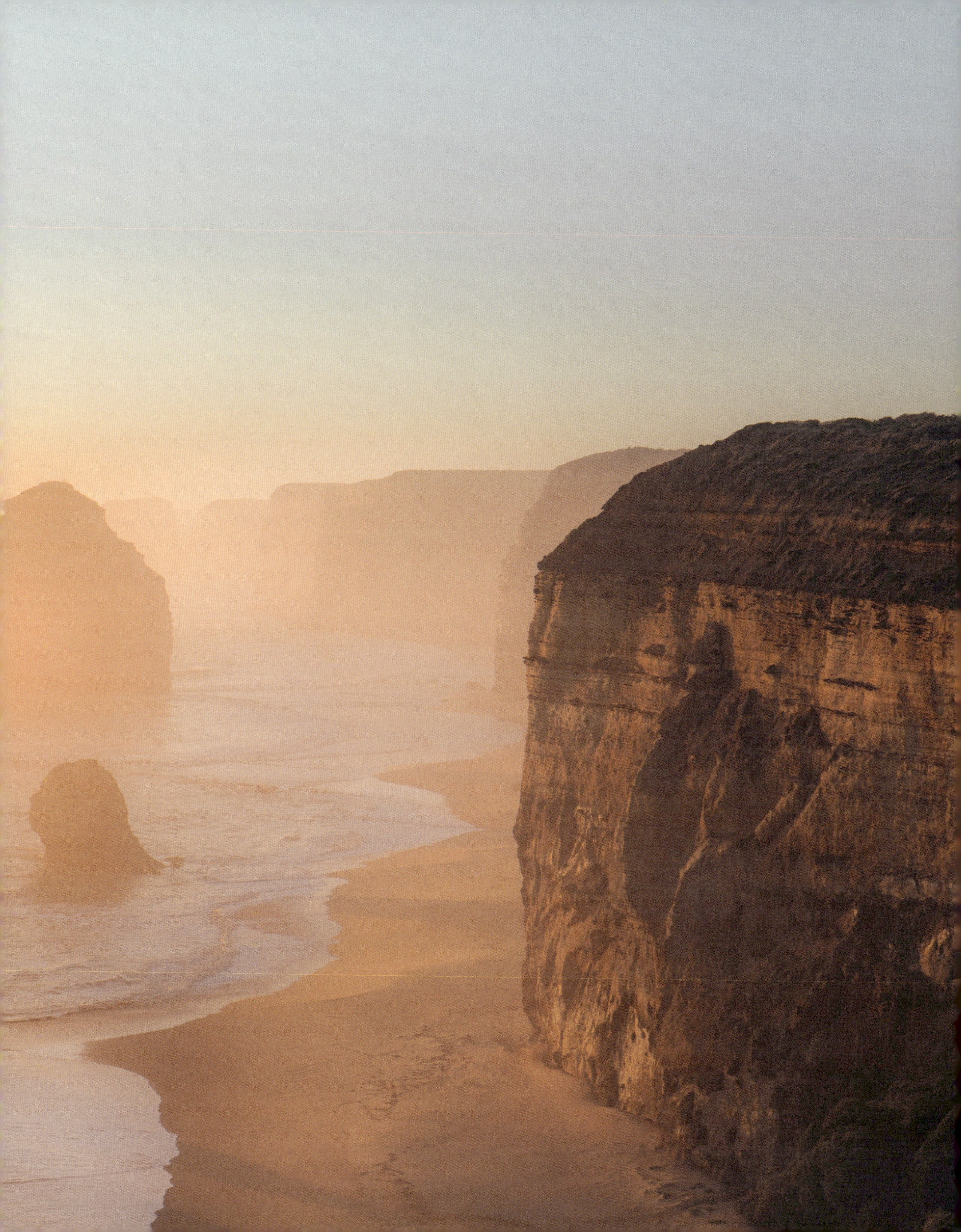

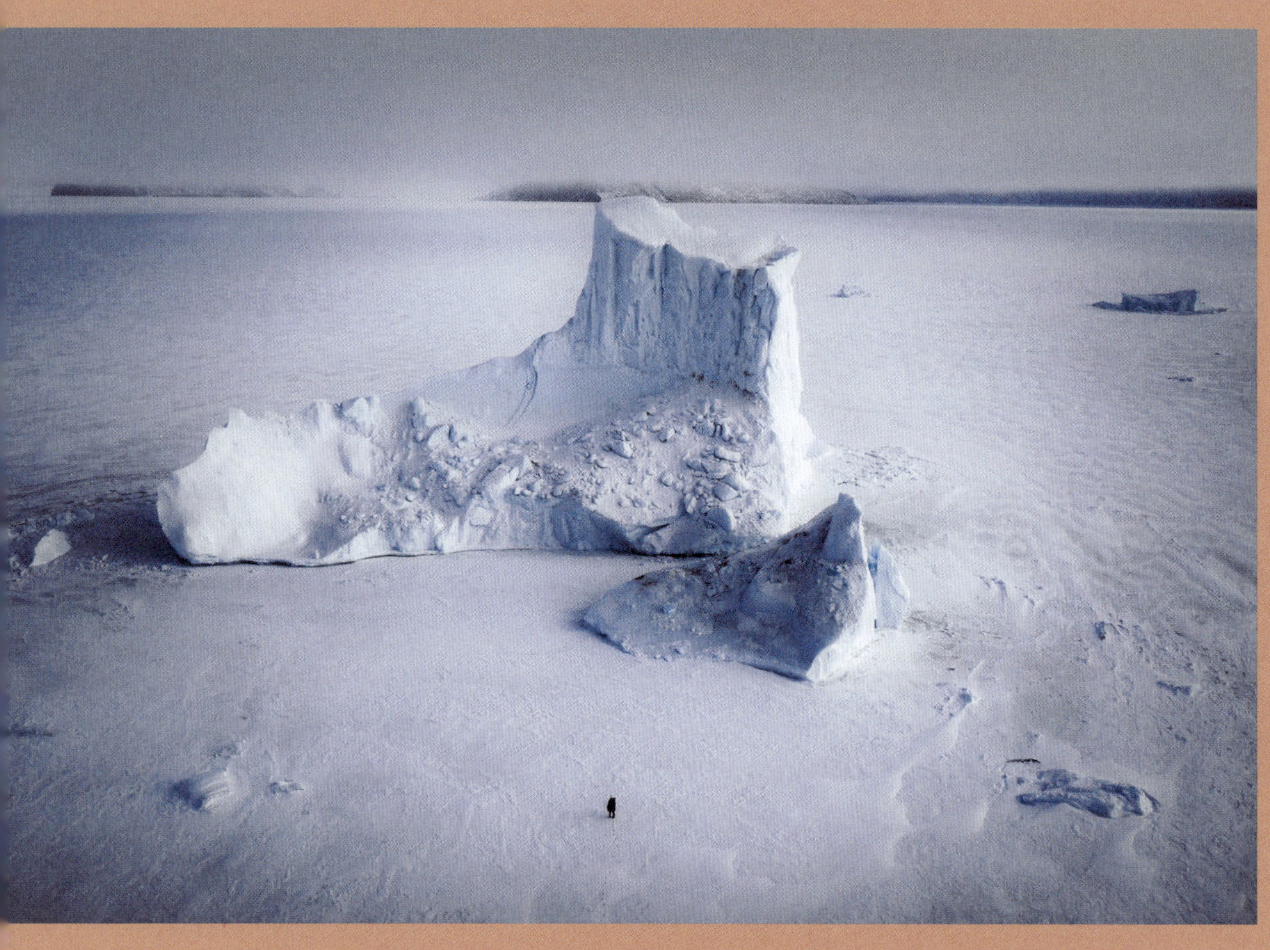

The world-renowned pillars of limestone called the Twelve Apostles, off the mainland of Australia in the Southern Ocean, is a popular day trip from Melbourne.

Port Campbell National Park, Victoria, Australia

Carley Rudd

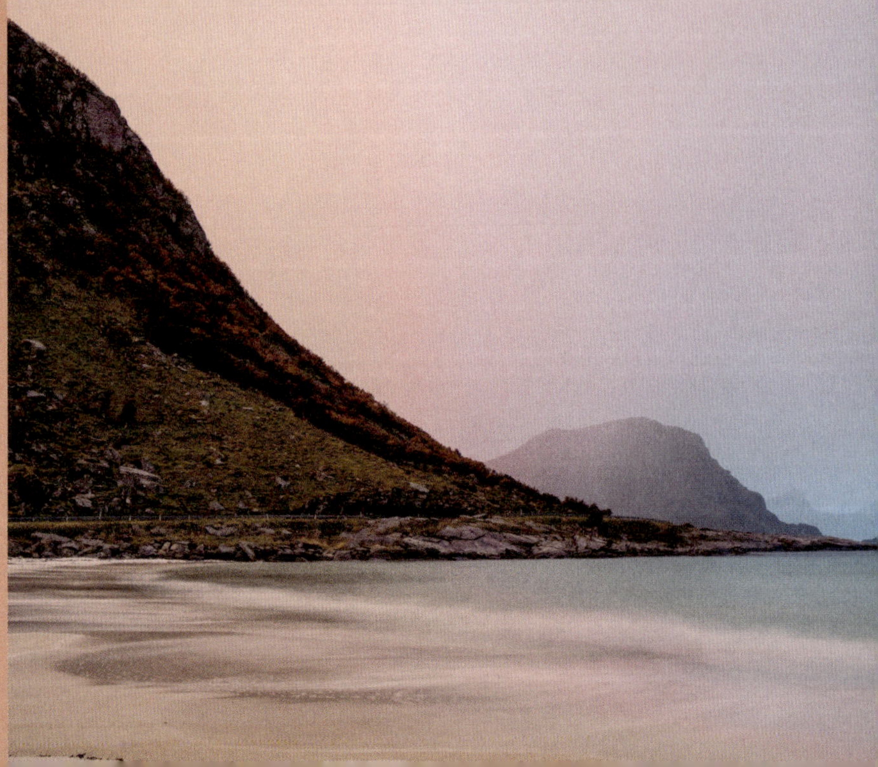

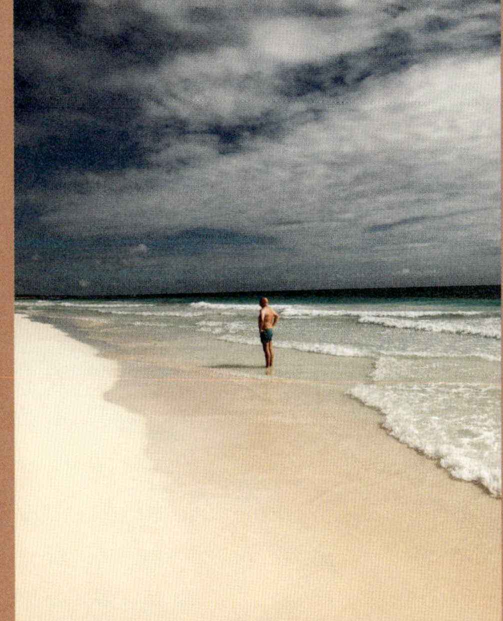

WHEN WE LOOK OUT over the wide-open sea, whether from a boat, a plane, a cliff, or the shore, we can see the enormity of our planet. The curved horizon of our globe is apparent, and the history of centuries, of millennia, can be seen etched onto cliffs, glaciers, and shifting sand. An open mind often comes along with an open landscape.

Vast ocean landscapes are nature's fortune-tellers and historians, the horizon informing us of what weather we have in store and what weather has just passed. When we look up at the unobstructed nighttime sky or watch clouds roll over the ocean, we see not just the landscape, but ourselves more clearly—tiny beings on a large planet in an even larger sea, the universe, undulating with stars.

A few years ago, I went with a group to Playa Viva, an eco-resort on the coast of Mexico just outside Zihuatanejo. The resort is essentially a big open kitchen and a few hand-built wooden cabanas perched just above the soft beach in the jungle. At night, the windows of my room were open to the air and there were no city lights. The sound of the ocean roars through the spaces, and in the evening it feels as though the blackness outside could go on forever.

One night after dinner, a friend in our group started calling everyone to the beach. I ran barefoot into the dark to find my friend. When I found her, I could see what she was shouting about—tiny bioluminescent organisms were making the waves glow. Tears welling in my eyes, I imagined the tiny organisms as a mirror image of the stars above. The stars were infinitely vast above me, and the bioluminescence unfathomably small throughout the dark ocean. My life was a miniature speck between those two matching realities on that beach in the dark, and I felt somehow reassured about my own elemental existence as my feet were lapped by the warm waves.

↑
**Tulum,
Quintana Roo,
Mexico**
Alena Paramita

↖
**Uummannaq
Fjord, Avannaata,
Greenland**
Emilie Ristevski

←
**Bøstad, Lofoten,
Norway**
David Leøng

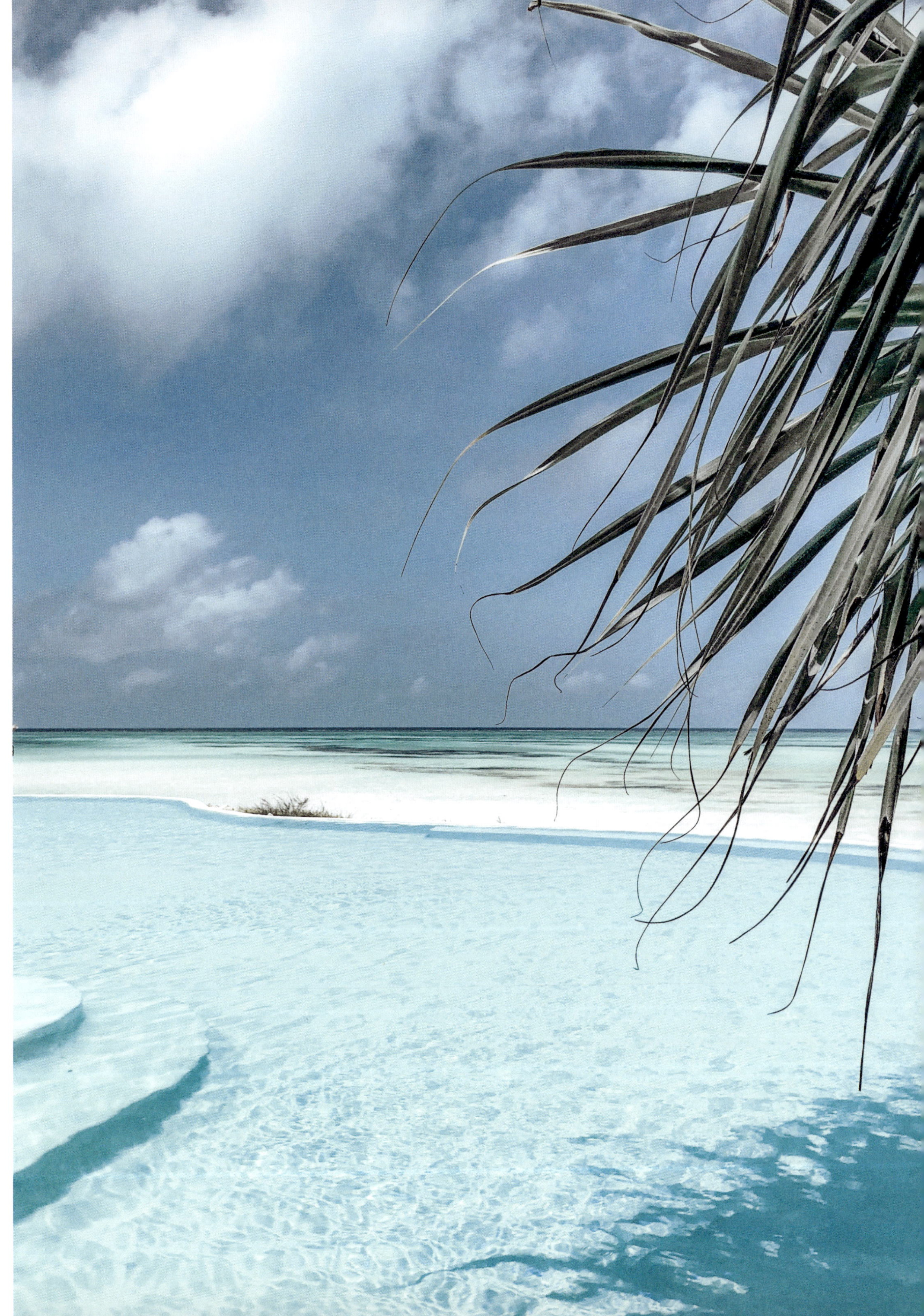

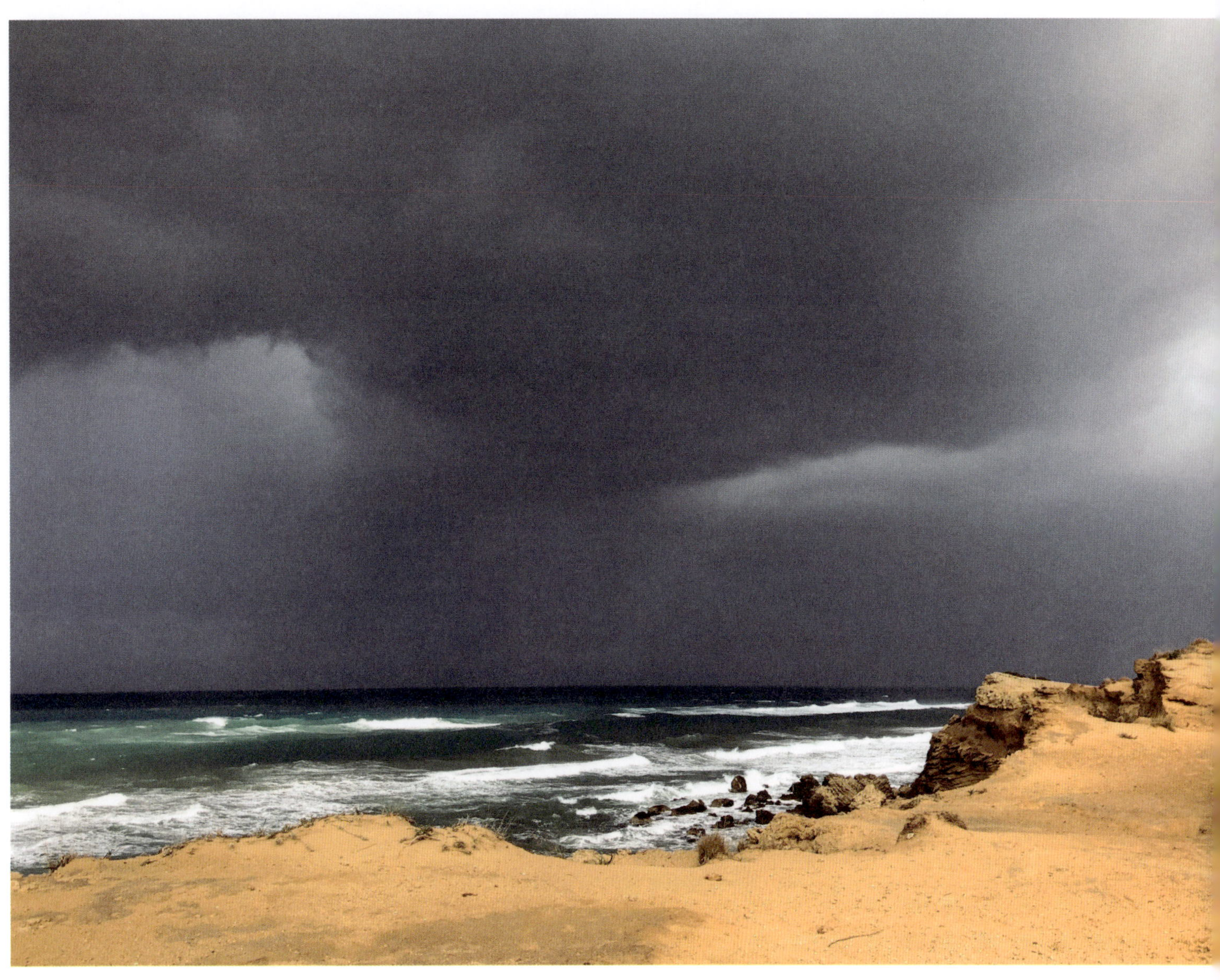

← **Pongwe, Zanzibar, Tanzania**

Amanda Nevarez

↑ **Mikhmoret, Hefer Valley, Israel**

Trine S. Ben Aish

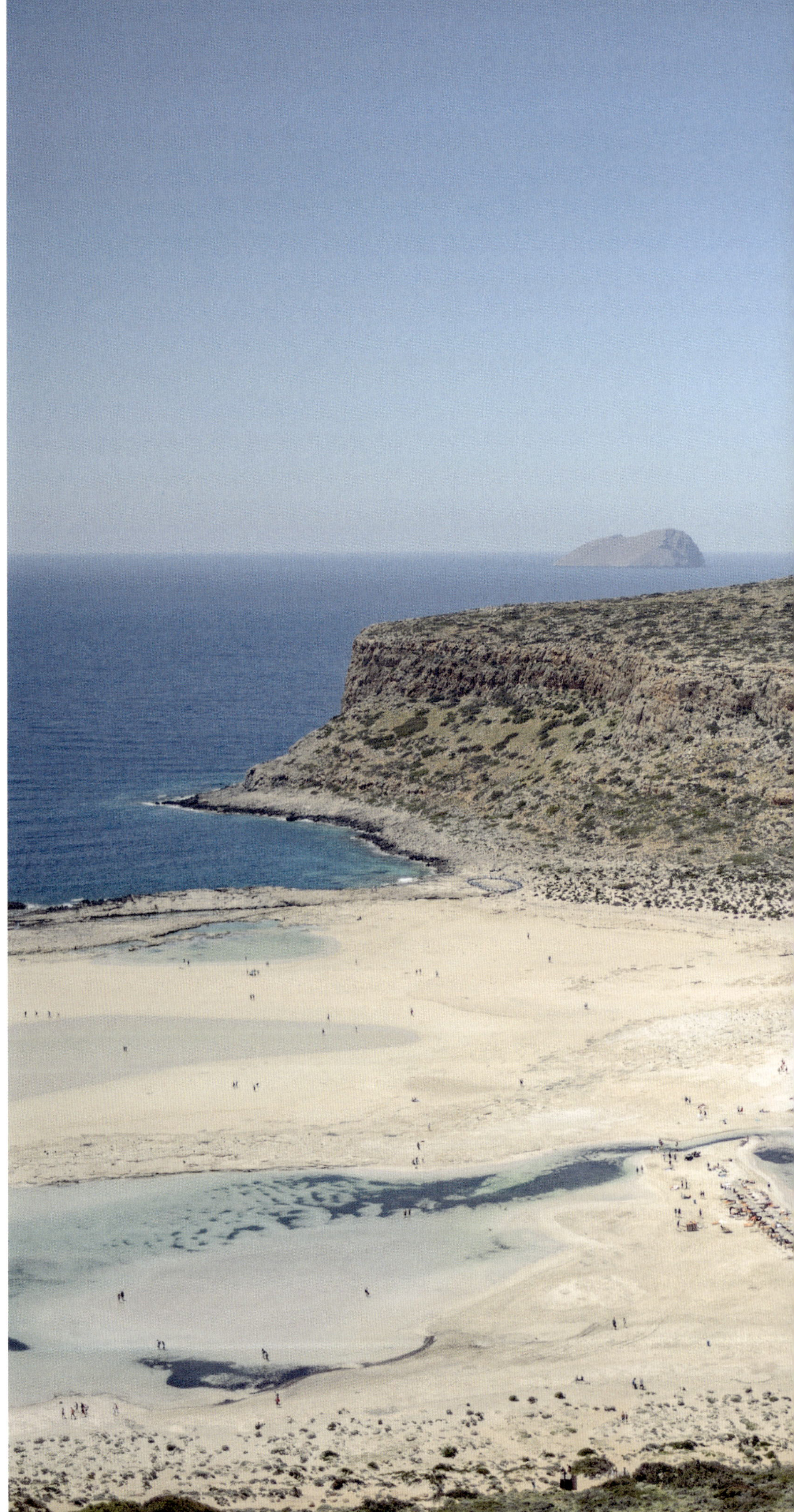

**Balos, Crete,
Greece**
Alexandra Kryaneva

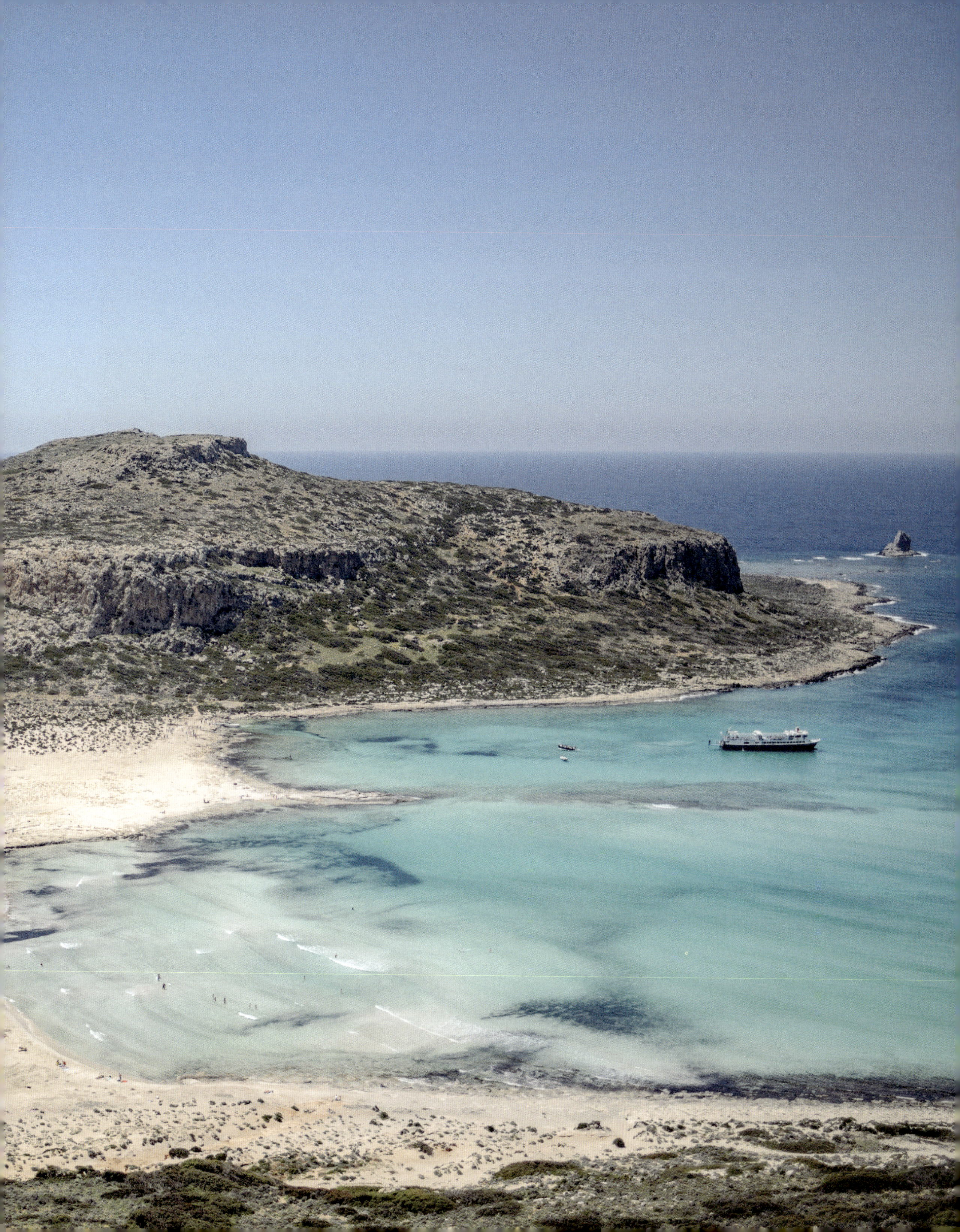

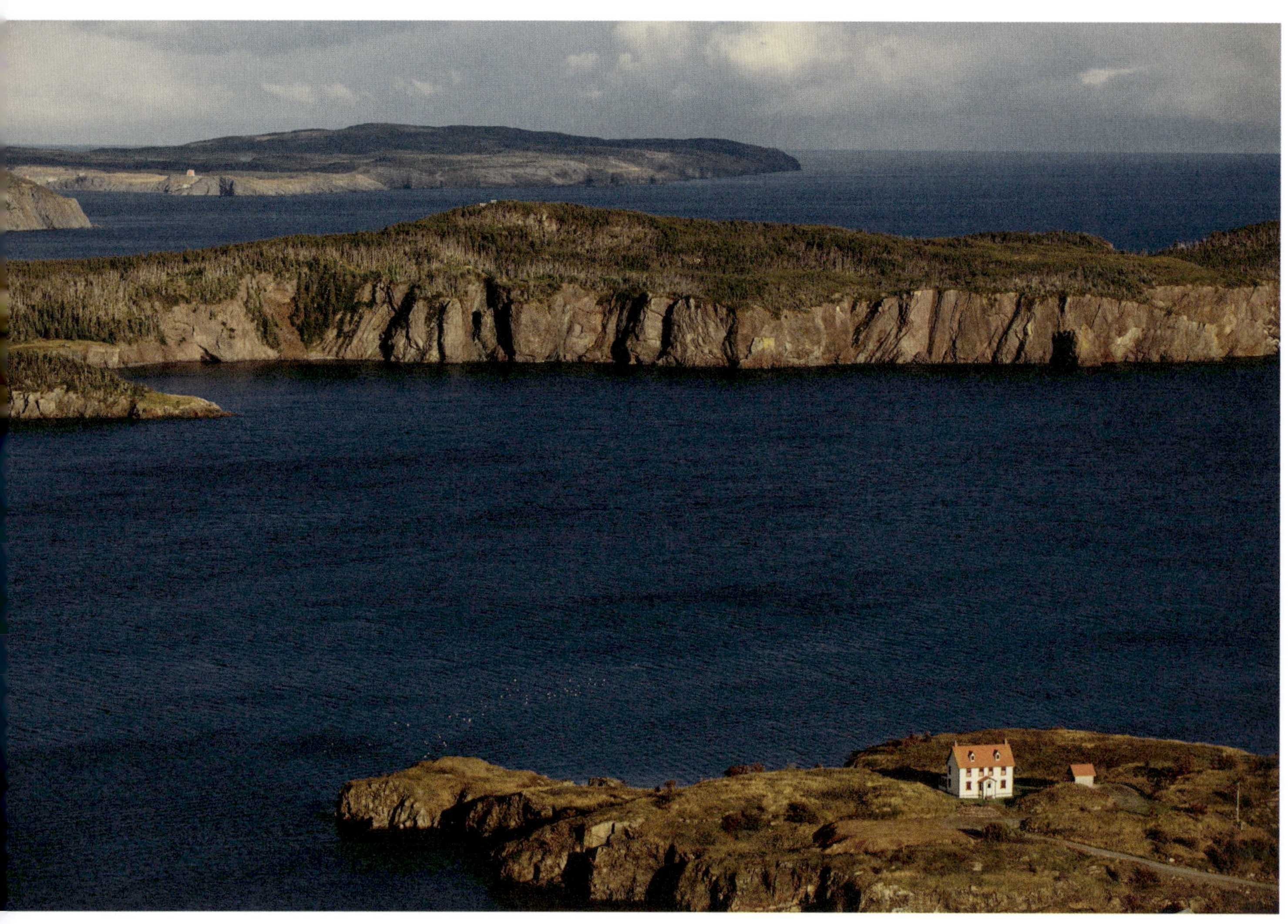

BONAVISTA IS A small town on the western protected side of the northernmost reaches of the island of Newfoundland, almost due south from Greenland across the Sea of Labrador. Just off the coast of the Bonavista Peninsula, the island of Elliston is known for its accessible and thriving Atlantic puffin colony. Built on a wide-open plain, the historic colonial town of Bonavista had a population that peaked around 1900, when close to twenty-thousand people filled the town to fish the waters rich with fish and seal. Today the population is just about three thousand.

**Bonavista,
Newfoundland,
Canada**
Grant Harder

HẠ LONG BAY is a UNESCO World Heritage Site (and popular backpacker bucket-list spot) with more than a thousand forested karst islands. Popularity has led to an increase in plastic pollution and diminished water cleanliness, so travelers are reminded (as always) to make sure to treat the area with respect. Hundreds of boats depart from the city of Hạ Long daily for day trips as well as overnight stays. Visitors can kayak, rock climb, sail, snorkel, and dive in less-traveled sections of the bay as well as hidden lagoons and floating villages.

Hiking Bai Tho Mountain (Poem Mountain) in town is not officially sanctioned, but many travelers still make their way through narrow alleys and through a paid private entrance in order to capture this view. If you do go on the forty-five-minute hike, bring water, snacks, and mosquito repellent, and wear shoes suitable for a tropical hike.

Travelers usually opt to arrive at Hạ Long Bay via taxi or minibus transfer (rather than the cheaper but slower local trains and buses), finding tickets online or easily from the many travel agencies in the tourist-heavy Old Quarter of Hanoi.

Hạ Long Bay, Quảng
Ninh Province, Vietnam
Courtney Kinnare

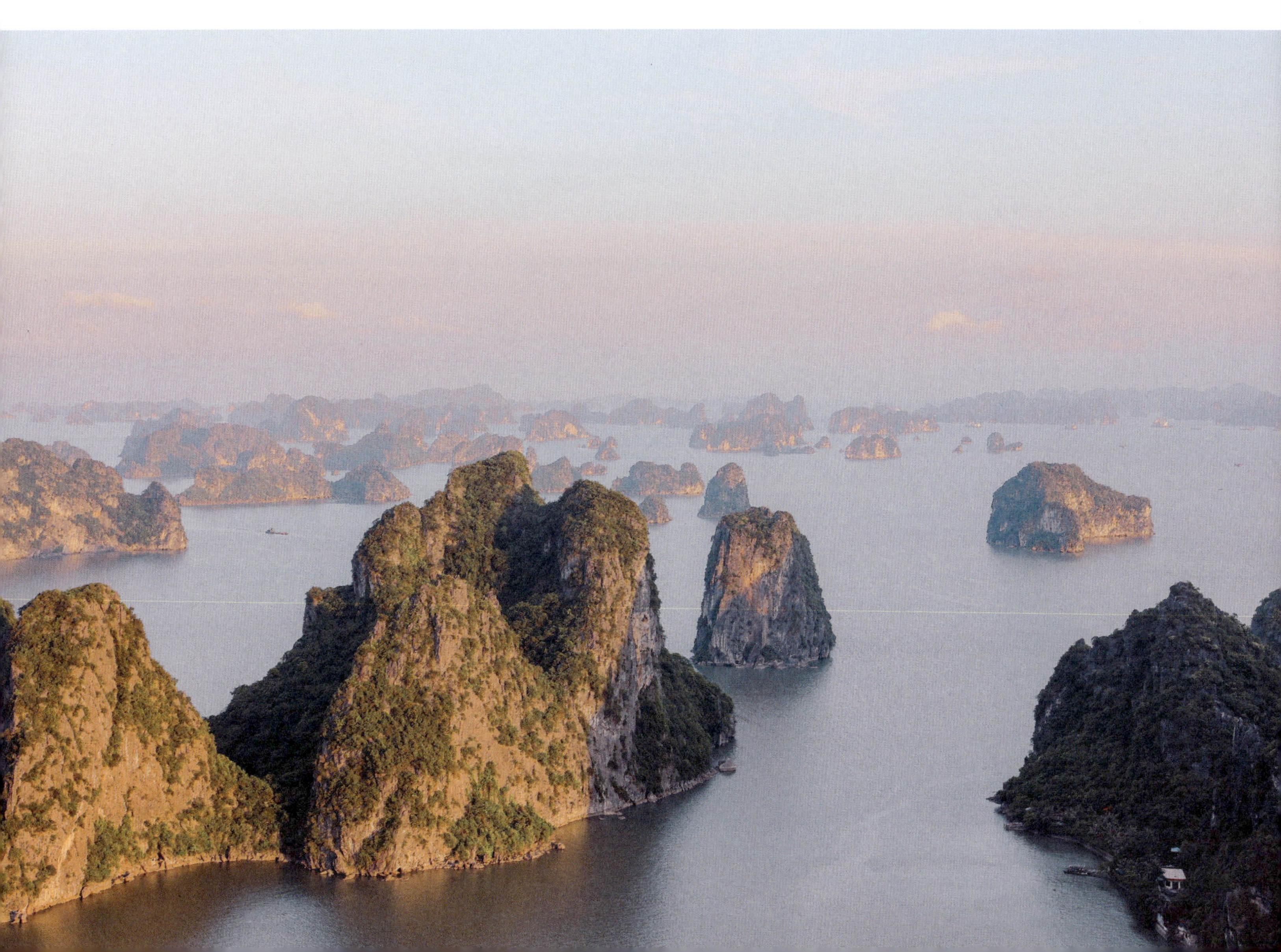

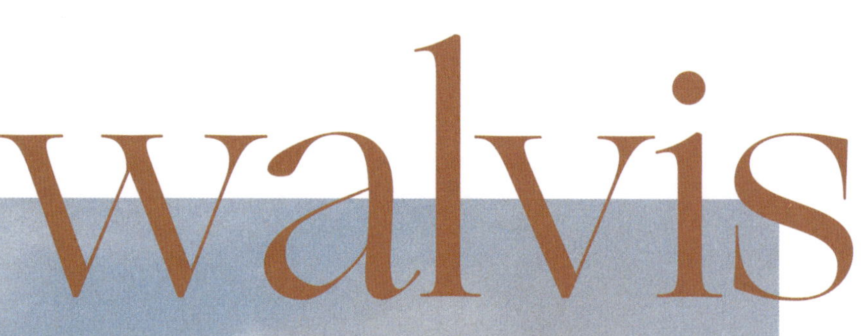
walvis

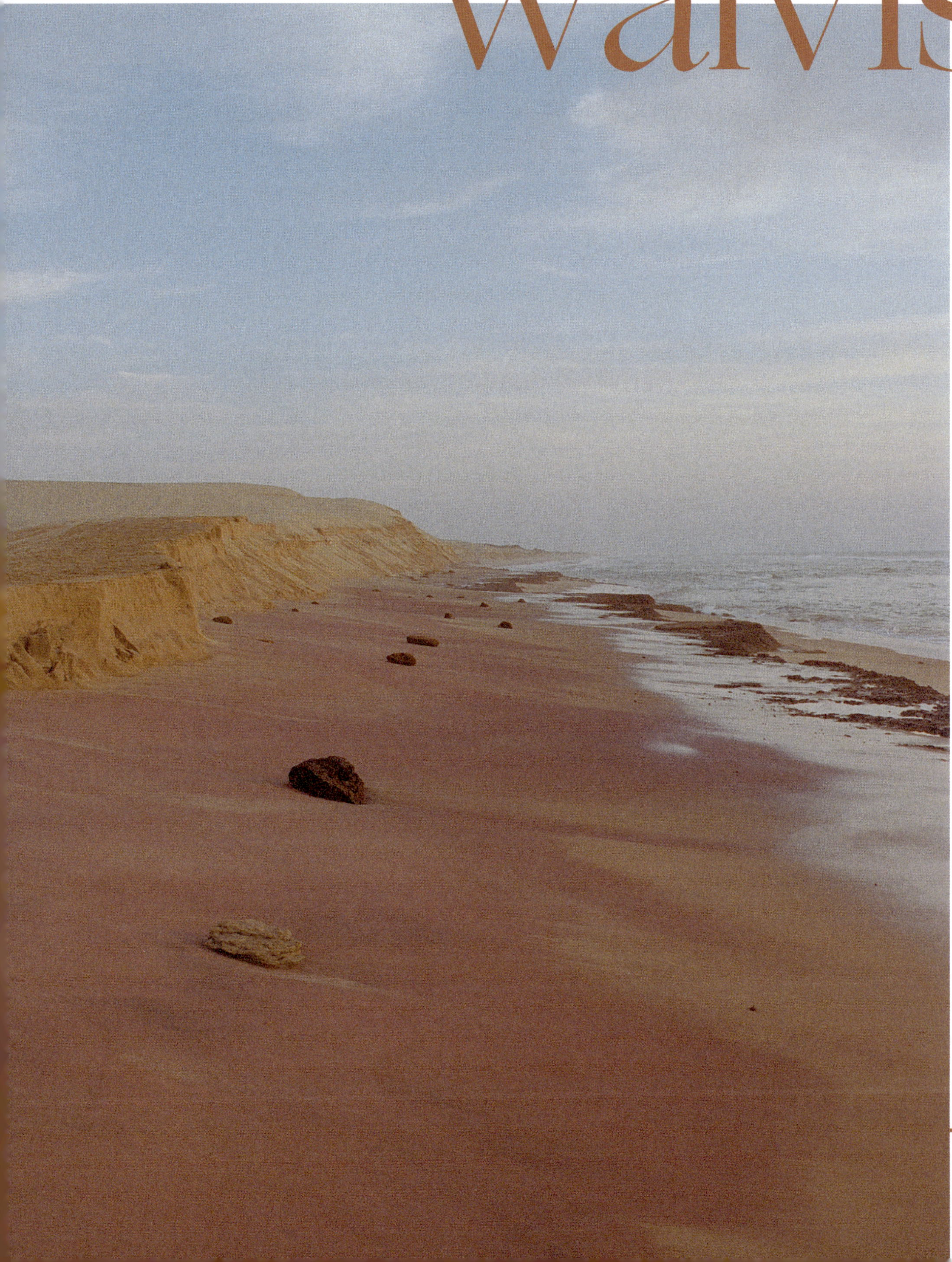

bay

NAMIBIA

NAMIBIA, LOCATED ON THE southwestern coast of Africa, is full of wide-open spaces. There are very few trees or buildings to limit the views of the Atlantic coastline, the deserts, or the savannahs that make up this country's primarily dry landscapes. The city of Walvis Bay, which in Afrikaans means "Bay of Whales" and speaks to the area's historical connection to colonialists, is a city on a bay of the same name along the central coastline of Namibia. The majority of its residents are native Bantu people. The Herero people, a local Bantu ethnic group, call it Ezorongondo. The bay is a natural deepwater harbor, and the coastal waters are rich in marine life, including oysters, rock lobster, seals, pelicans, and dolphins, as well as humpback and other whales in July and August. The Walvis Bay area is best explored more deeply on a bike with fat tires.

Across the bay from town, Walvis Peninsula is nearly surrounded by water, with Walvis Bay on the eastern shore and the Atlantic Ocean on the west. The only way to reach the peninsula and its isolated beaches is with a 4x4 truck or by boat. Because the cold Atlantic waters and the warmer desert temperatures meet here, the peninsula and Walvis Bay are often wrapped in thick fog, especially in the morning. The lighthouse and the Pelican Point Lodge are the only buildings on this remote, sandy stretch of the coast. On the long drive to reach the hotel, the feeling of isolation is absolute, with golden sand stretching as far as the eye can see. Travelers who venture here will experience seemingly endless unobstructed views of waves and sand, the highest dunes in the world meeting the ocean in a dreamlike scene, and perhaps a cormorant or flamingo feeding in the lagoon. It feels blissfully solitary.

To get to Walvis Bay, connect through the capital city, Windhoek, and then drive roughly five hours west (or take a short hopper flight). The nearby regional capital of Swakopmund, which has more accommodation and leisure options such as Sandwich Harbour tours, is a short thirty- to forty-minute drive from Walvis Bay. Sandwich Harbour is famous for its towering sand dunes. Before becoming a destination for travelers, the harbor was an abandoned commercial port that once serviced the whaling industry. Be sure to check the tides before heading out; daily rising tides sweep over the single path to the harbor.

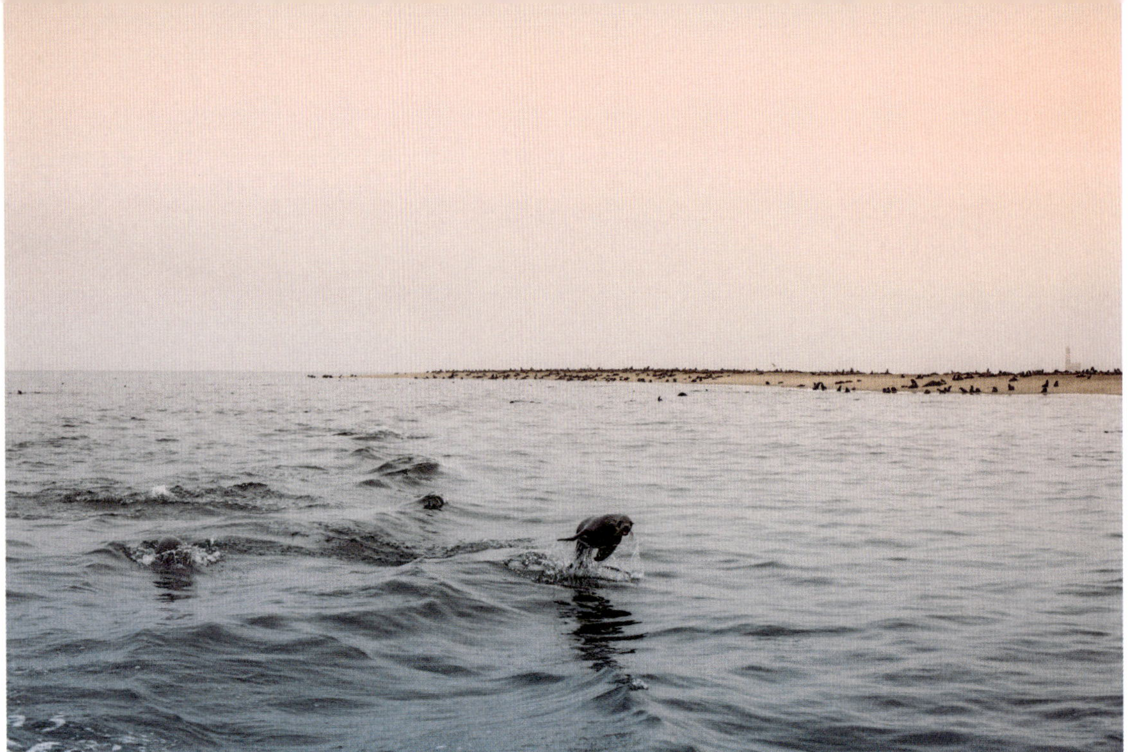

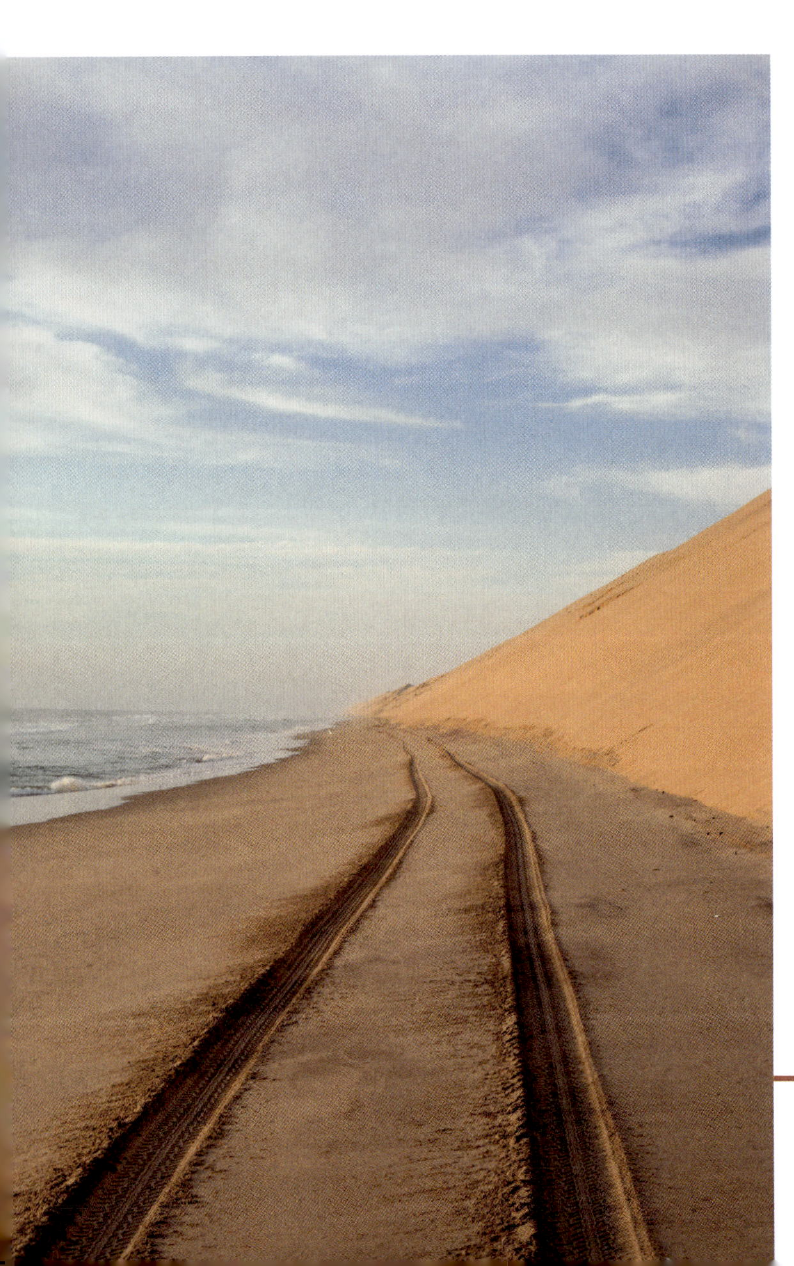

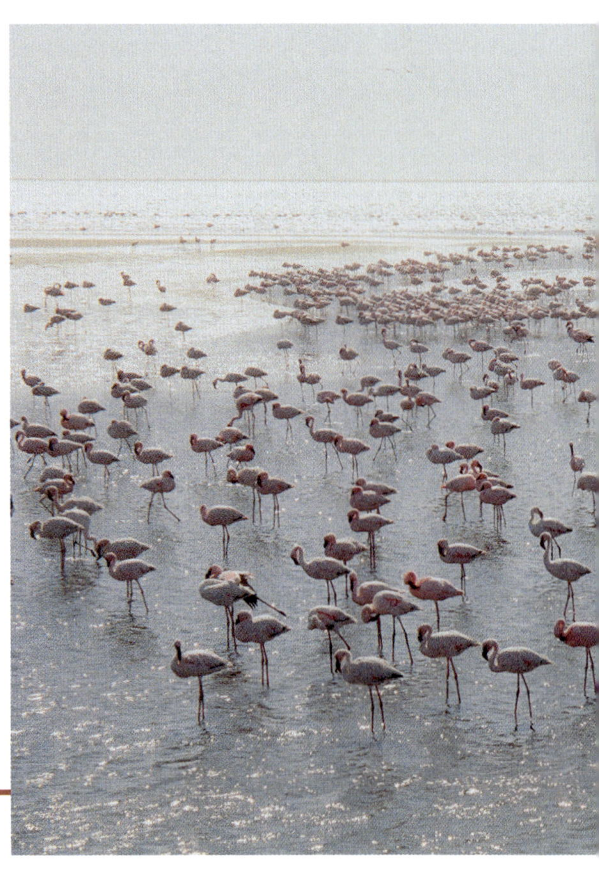

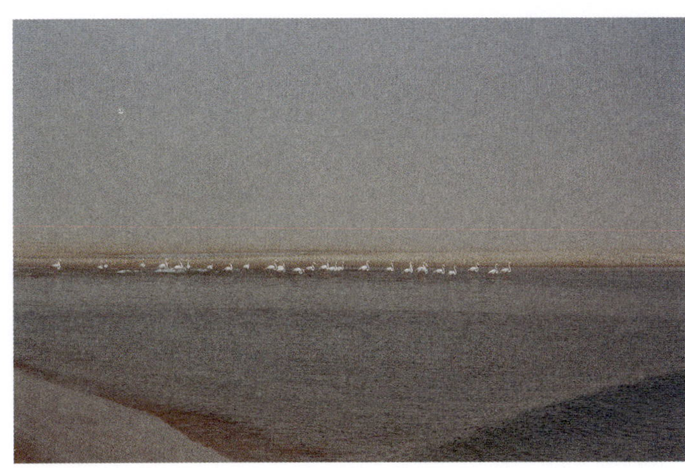

WALVIS BAY, NAMIBIA

Photographs by Chiara Zonca

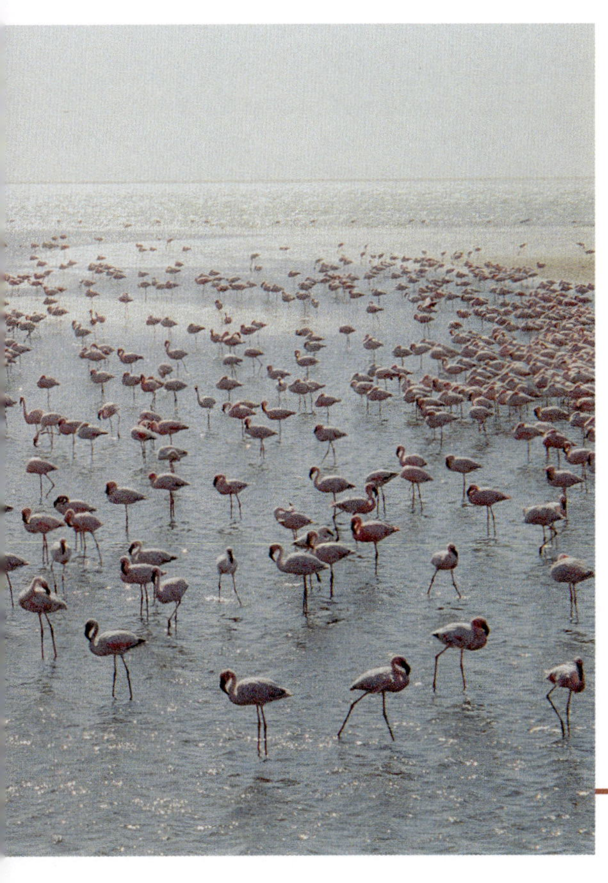

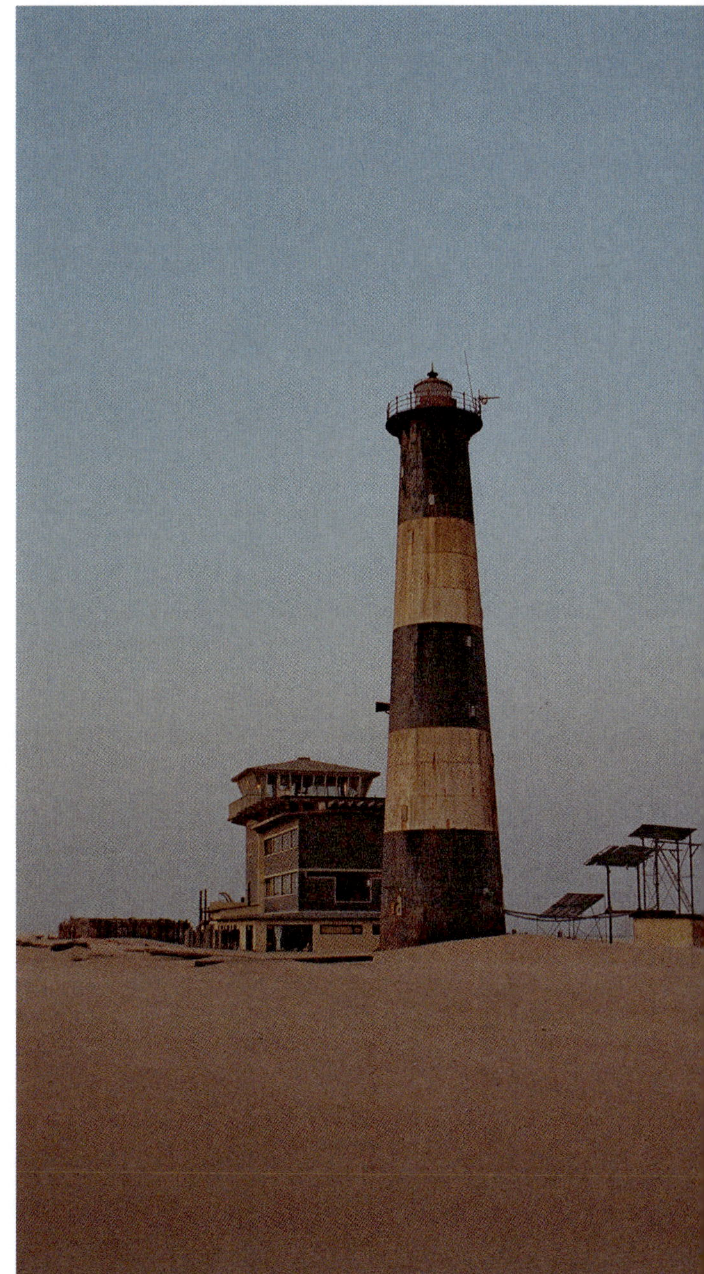

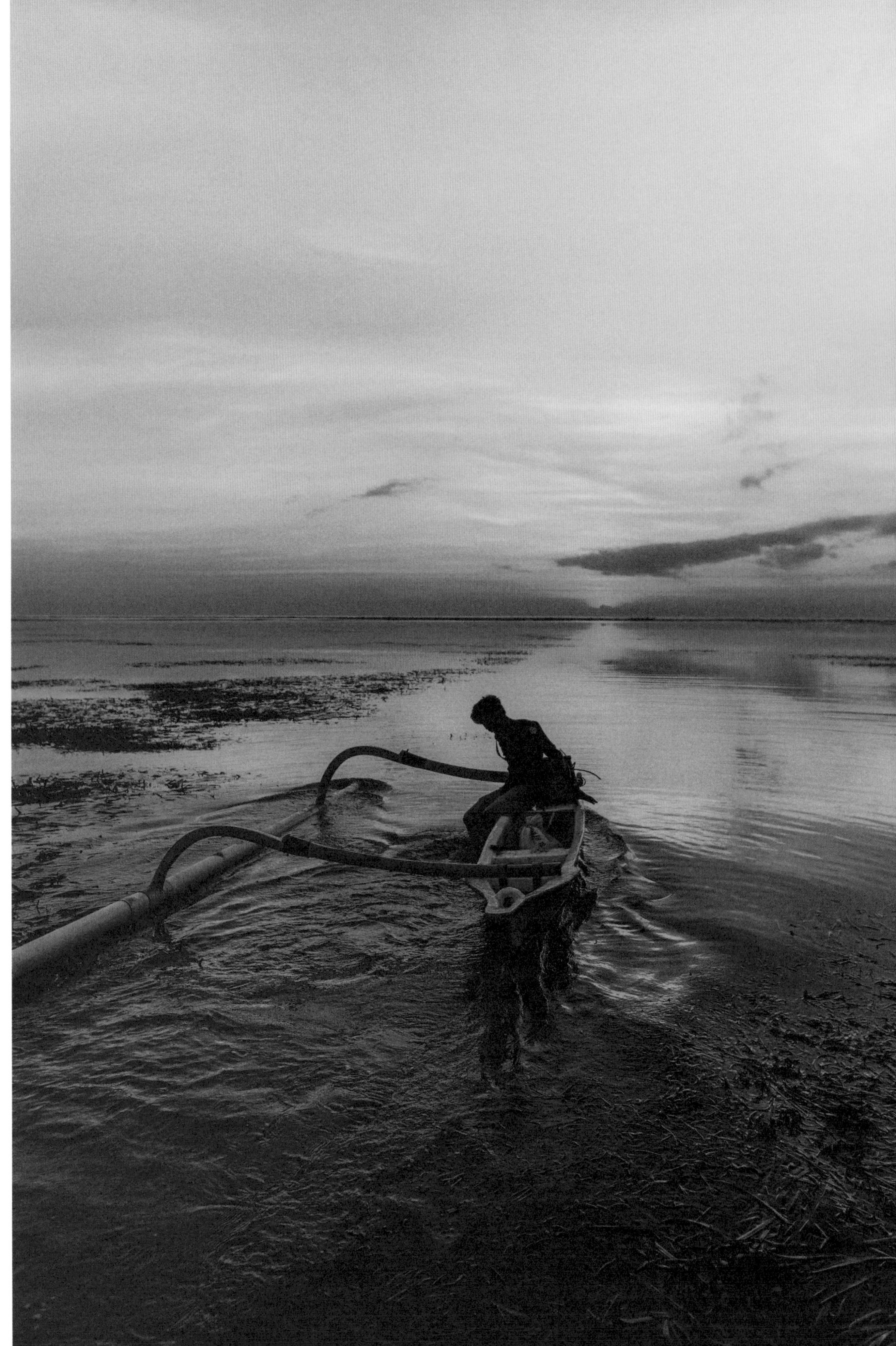

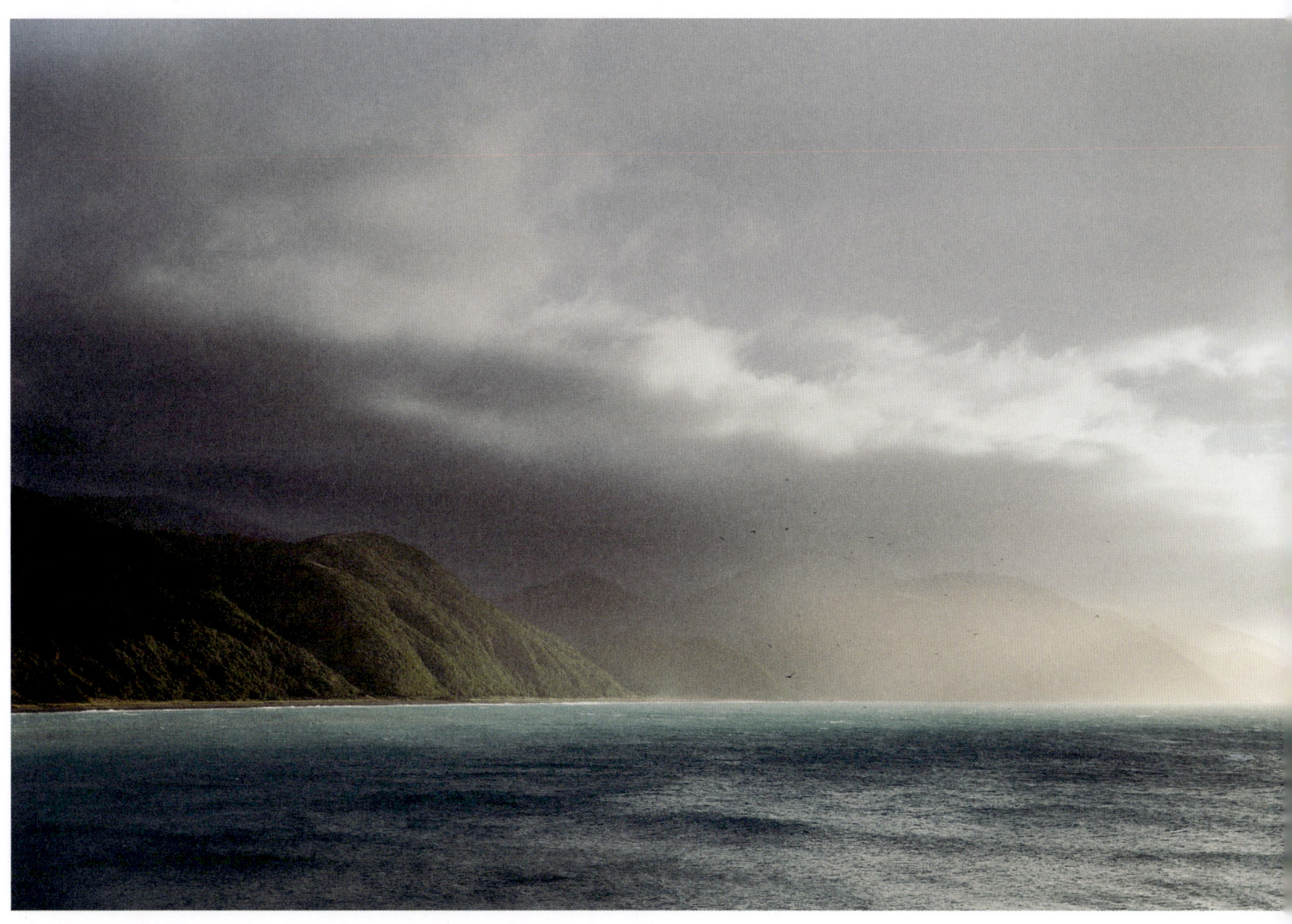

←
**Sanur, Bali,
Indonesia**
Tino Renato

↑
**Kaikoura, Canterbury,
South Island,
New Zealand**
Bénédicte Lassalle

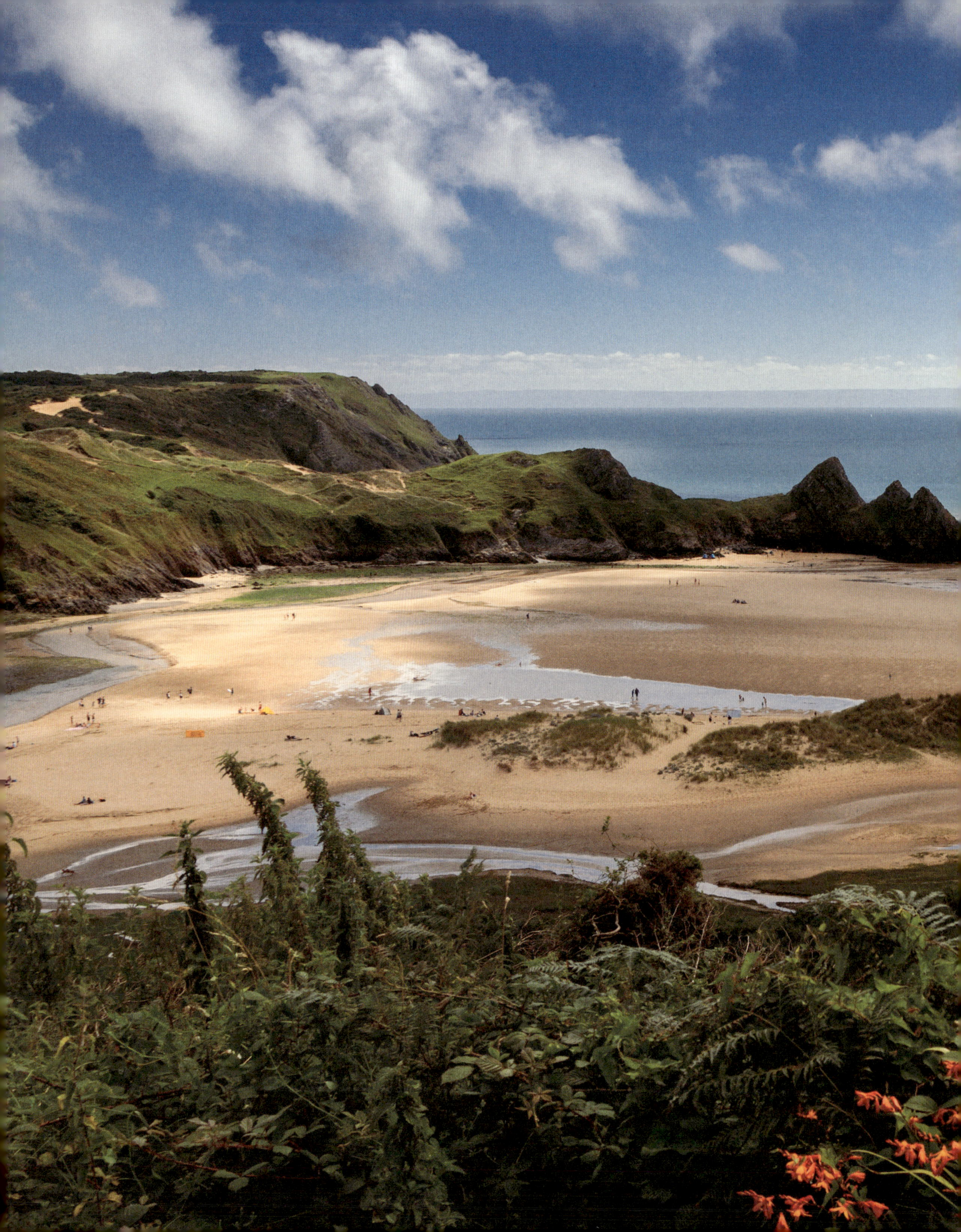

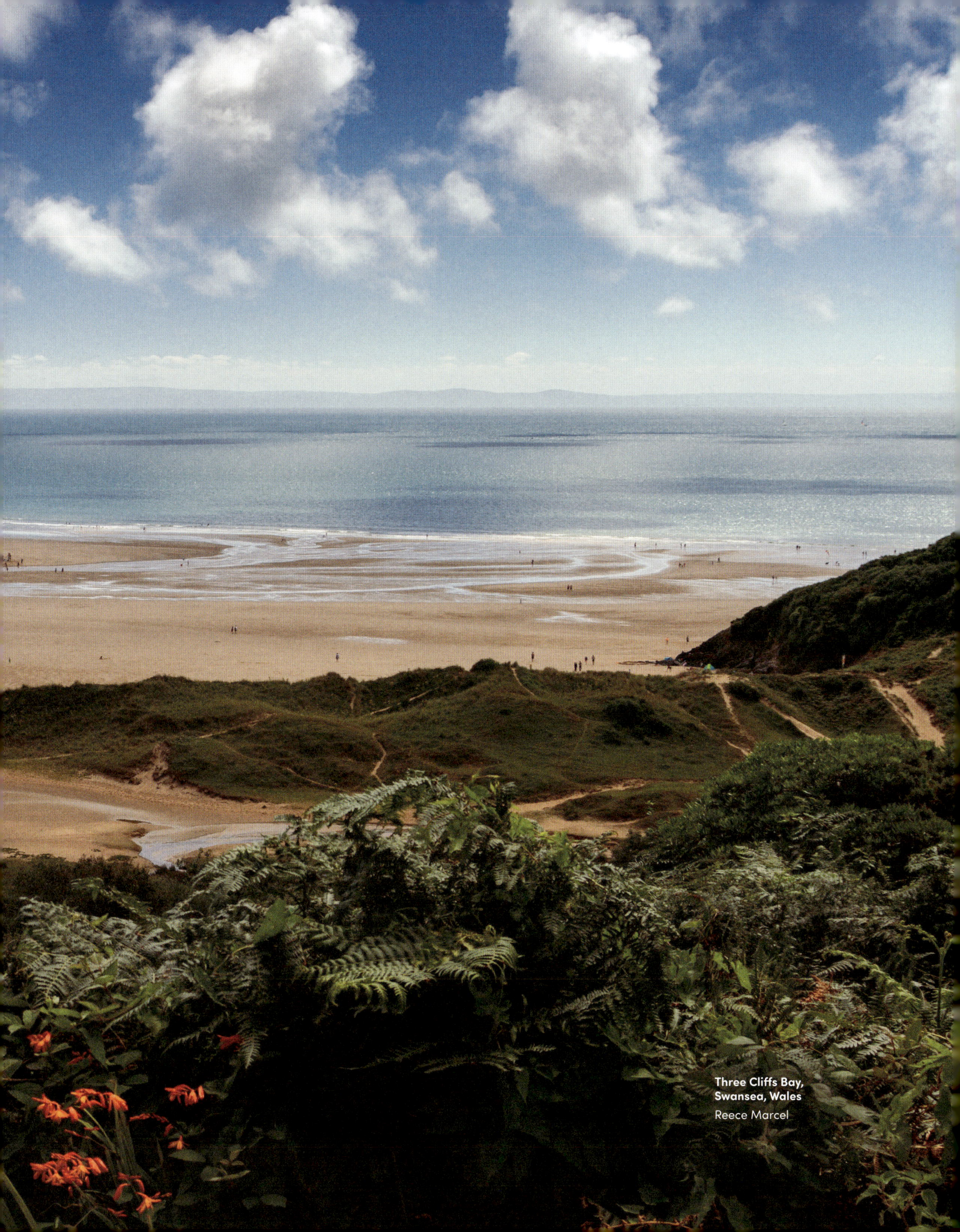

Three Cliffs Bay, Swansea, Wales
Reece Marcel

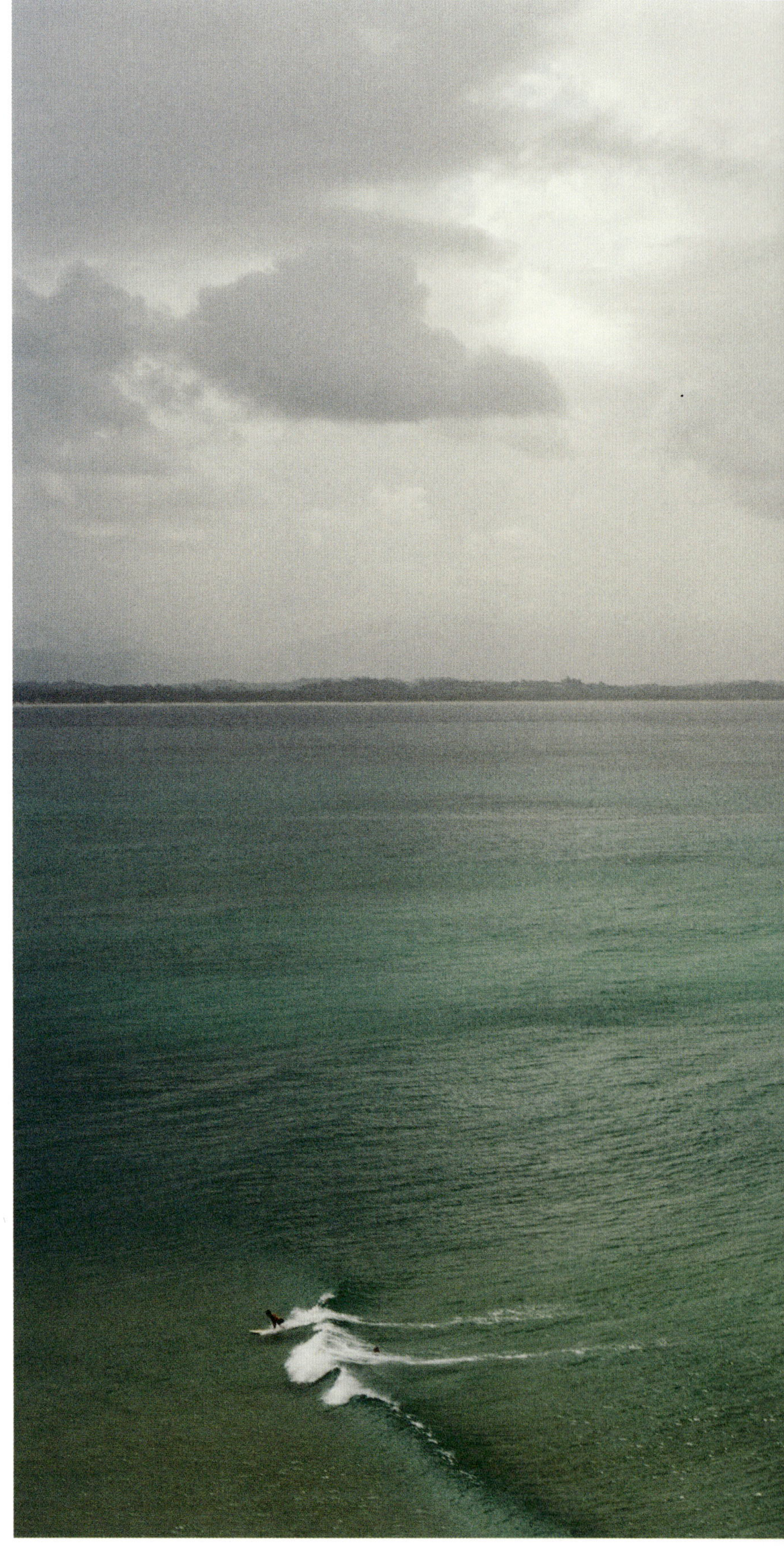

BYRON BAY (or Byron as locals call it) is a surf hamlet on the Australian east coast. Byron is in the province of New South Wales (the same as Sydney to the south), but it is closer to Queensland's capital, Brisbane, which is about two hours north on a major highway. The countryside outside Byron, known as Byron Shire, is peppered with small towns filled with farmers' markets, surf shops, and farm-to-table-restaurants, as well as shops with upscale furniture, linens, and crystals.

The lighthouse at the top of Cape Byron State Conservation Area overlooks Wategos Beach at the point of the eponymous bay below and is also a perfect perch for whale watching.

**Byron Bay,
New South Wales,
Australia**

Emily Nathan

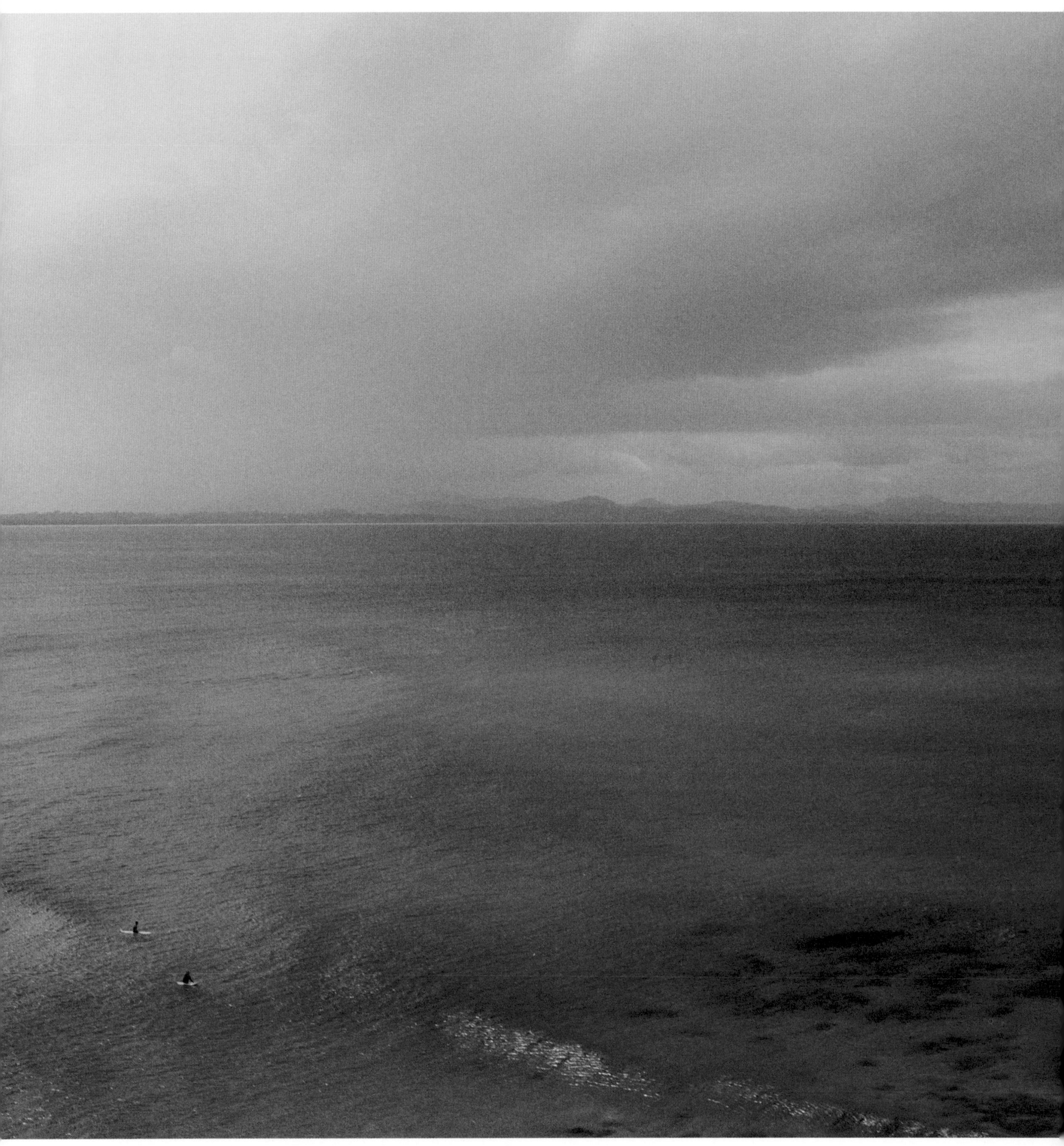

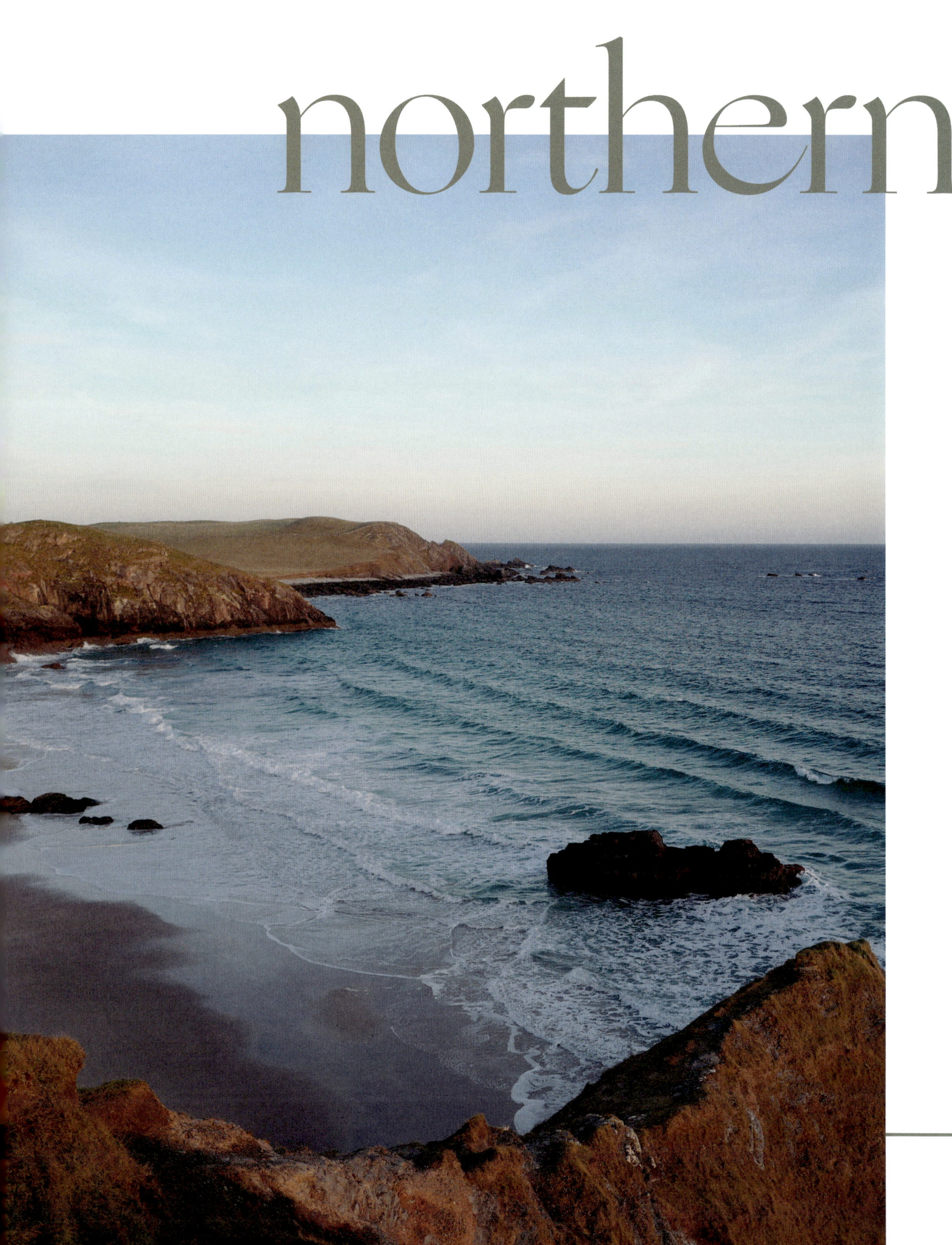

northern

scotland

UNITED KINGDOM

MACKAY COUNTRY, or northern Sutherland as this area in northern Scotland is generally known, is not just rural—it's wild, rugged, and surprisingly vast. Watching the clouds move across the enormous expanse of sky is a spectacle in its own right. Here the Atlantic Ocean meets the far north Scottish Highlands at a dramatic coastline that's sparsely populated, save for an abundance of wildlife. The history of the land includes wars for independence and clan conflicts; however, these days, this is a place with more sheep than people, and if a traveler encounters someone, it's likely to be a shepherd or a scallop diver by the sea. The entire region's population is near 2,600 people, which is less than one person per square kilometer. Most local families have lived here in the territory of the Clan Mackay for generations, in isolated crofts or small villages. The area is so sparse that a village name on the map in this region could turn out to be a single building that was abandoned a long time ago.

The people living here know each other well. Even though the community is diffused across the land, people are connected through communal gathering places, like a town shop, where the latest local gossip is exchanged. The little seaside town of Durness has a shop that is also a post office, a twenty-four-hour gas station, the village hall, a pub, and a bed and breakfast. It's a little hub of civilization, as is the nearby Balnakeil Craft Village, which has studios, galleries, a chocolate shop, and a golf course with sheep grazing around its holes.

The light, like the weather, is ever changing. When the skies are filled with stars during the winter months, the northern lights can sometimes be seen above the sea. The people who live by the sea in the far north, be they locals or transplants, have chosen its unspoiled natural beauty over the comforts of city life, and a love of the ocean is the core of the community.

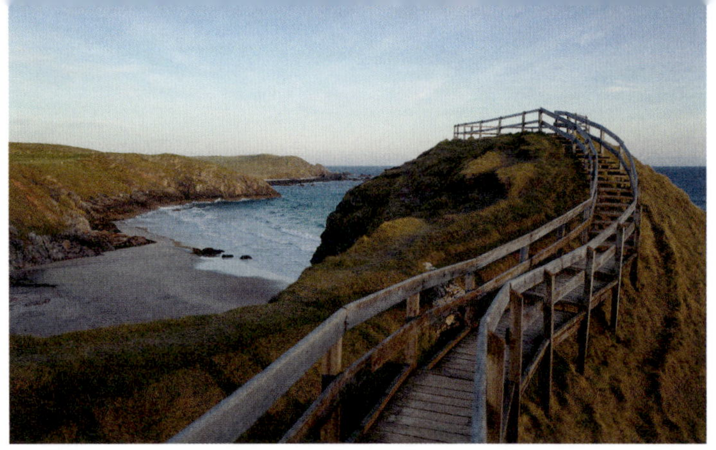

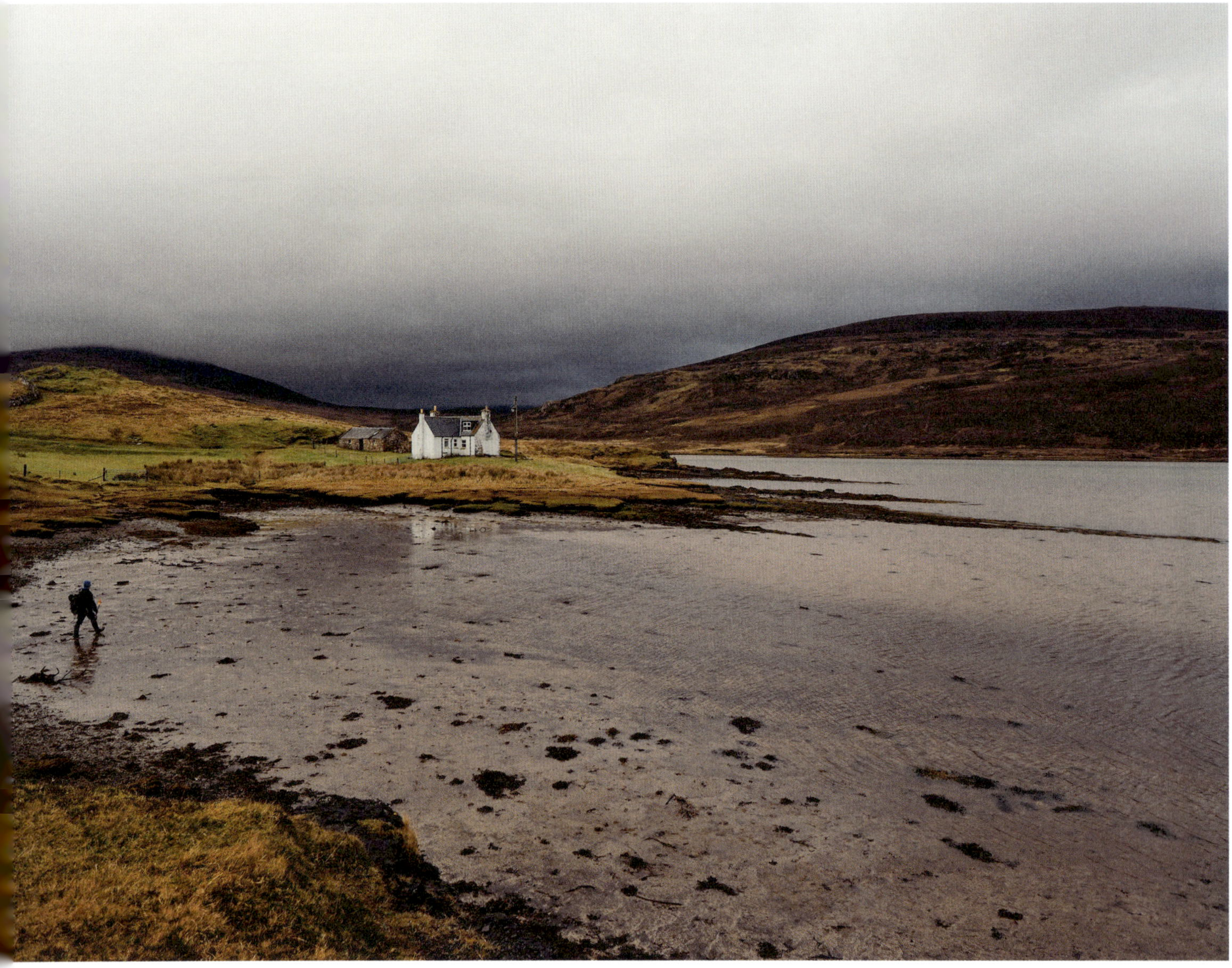

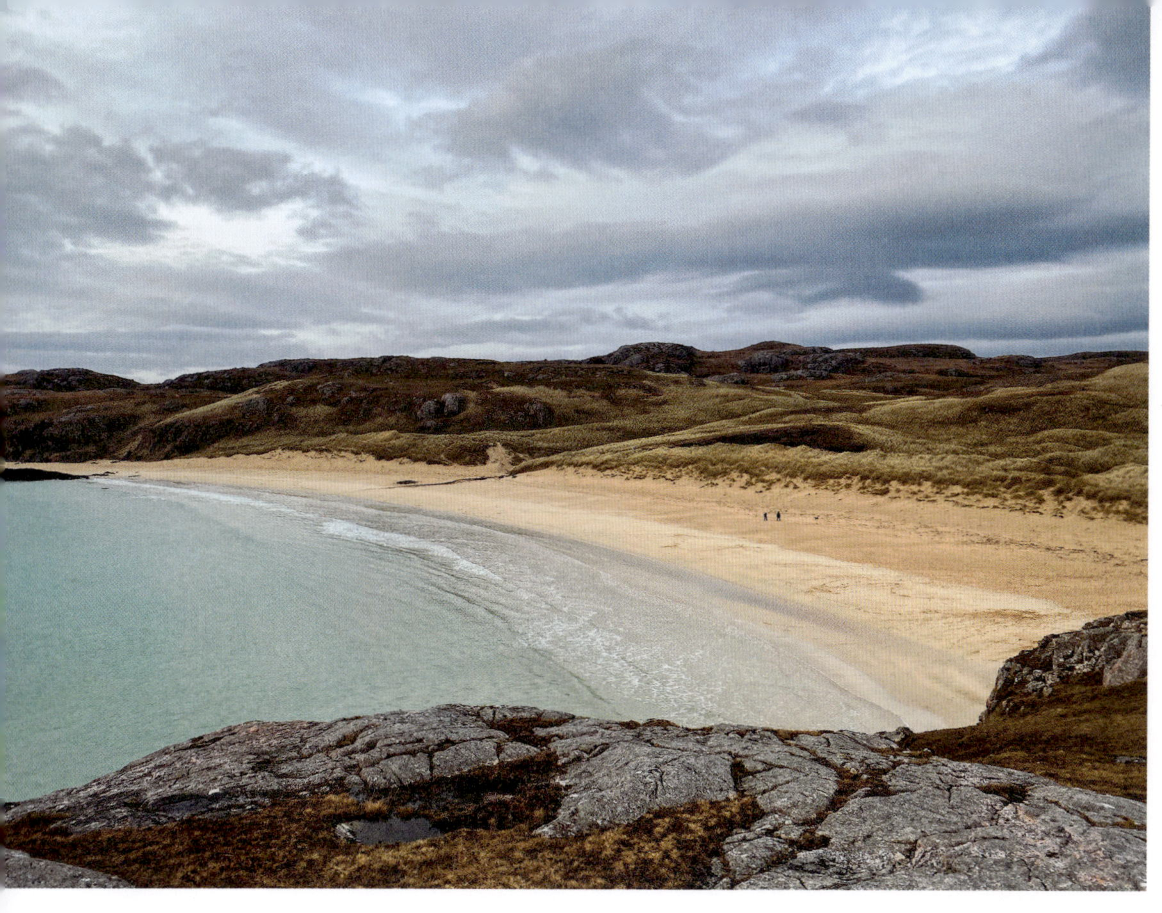

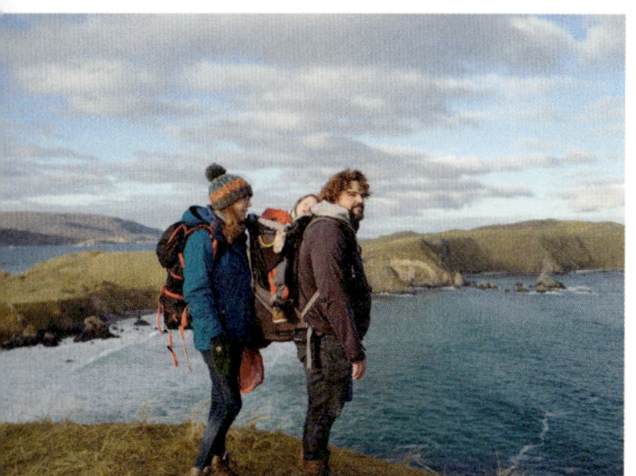

NORTHERN SCOTLAND, UNITED KINGDOM

Photographs by Elke Frotscher

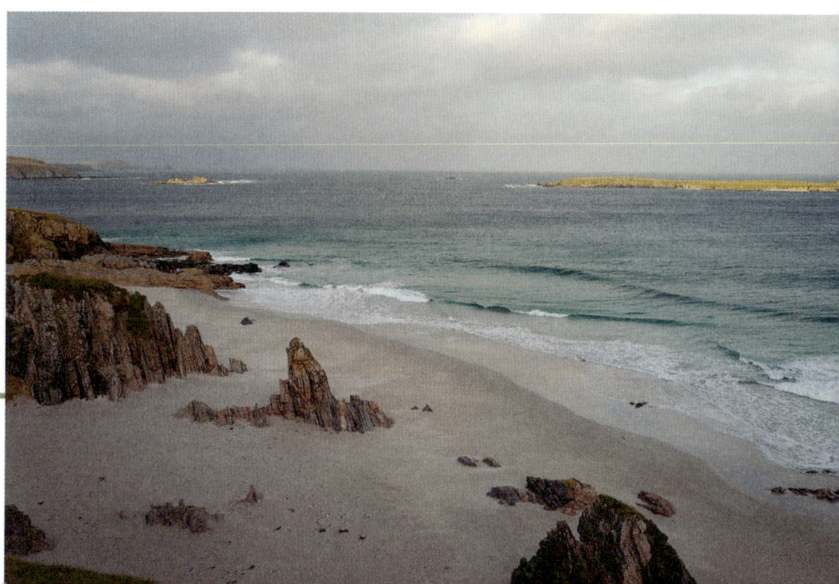

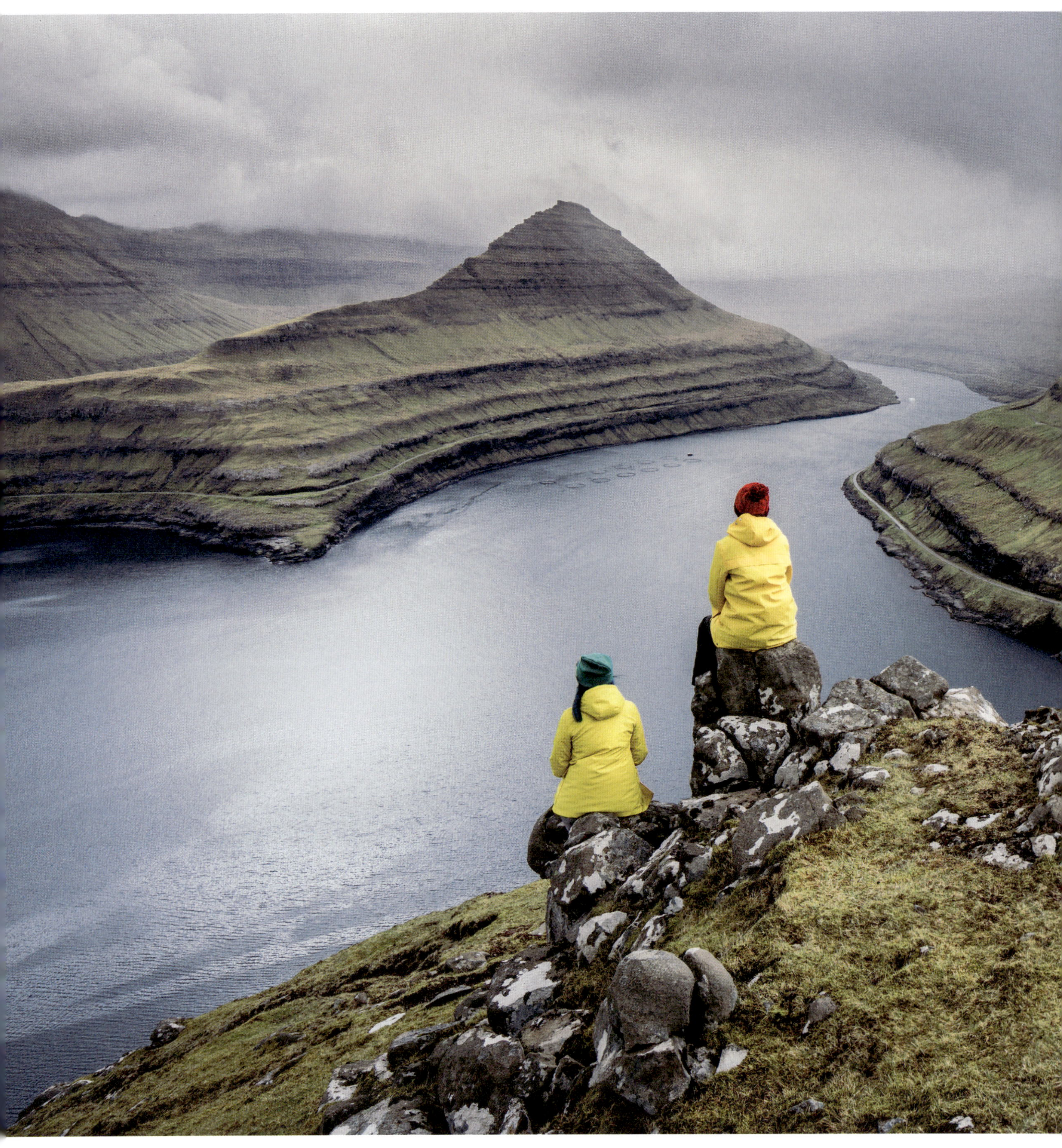

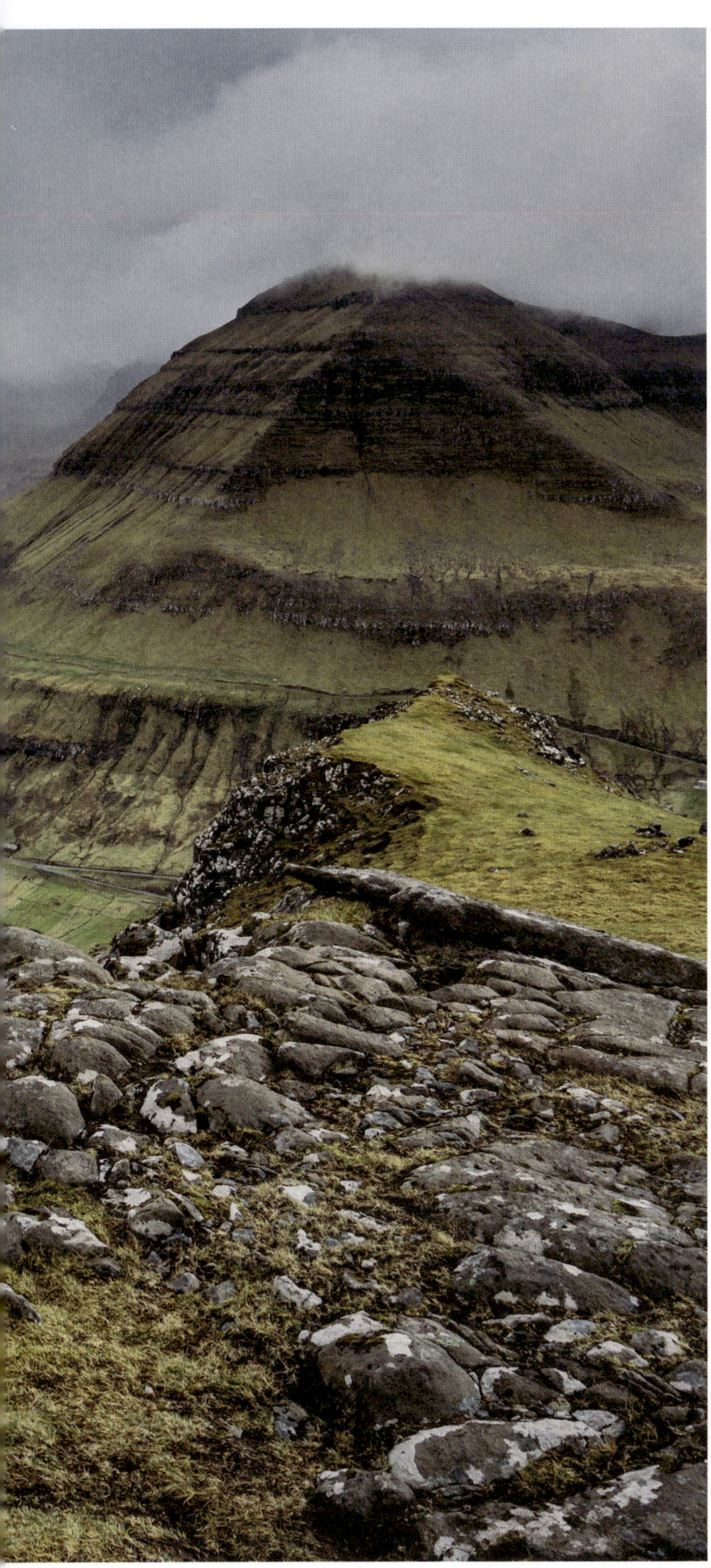

THE EIGHTEEN SMALL islands that comprise the Faroe Islands are relatively easy to access via nonstop flights from Iceland, Denmark, and Scotland. Officially part of the Danish Kingdom, the islands are an autonomous archipelago halfway between Norway and Iceland in the North Atlantic. The islands are a little world unto themselves with unique landscapes and culture. The usually wet, windy, and cool weather has shaped the steep cliffs and deep fjords into a visual marvel.

To get to this lookout above Funningur, it's a short steep hike from the high point on the road between Gjógv and Funningur, which takes about thirty minutes. Funningur is on the island of Eysturoy, the second largest in the chain in both size and population. Many photographers seek out the Faroe Islands as a place for landscape photography or workshops. This location is a perfect example of how to add subjects into a landscape image while at the same time isolating the subjects against the background below.

**Funningur, Eysturoy,
Faroe Islands**
Jeff Bartlett

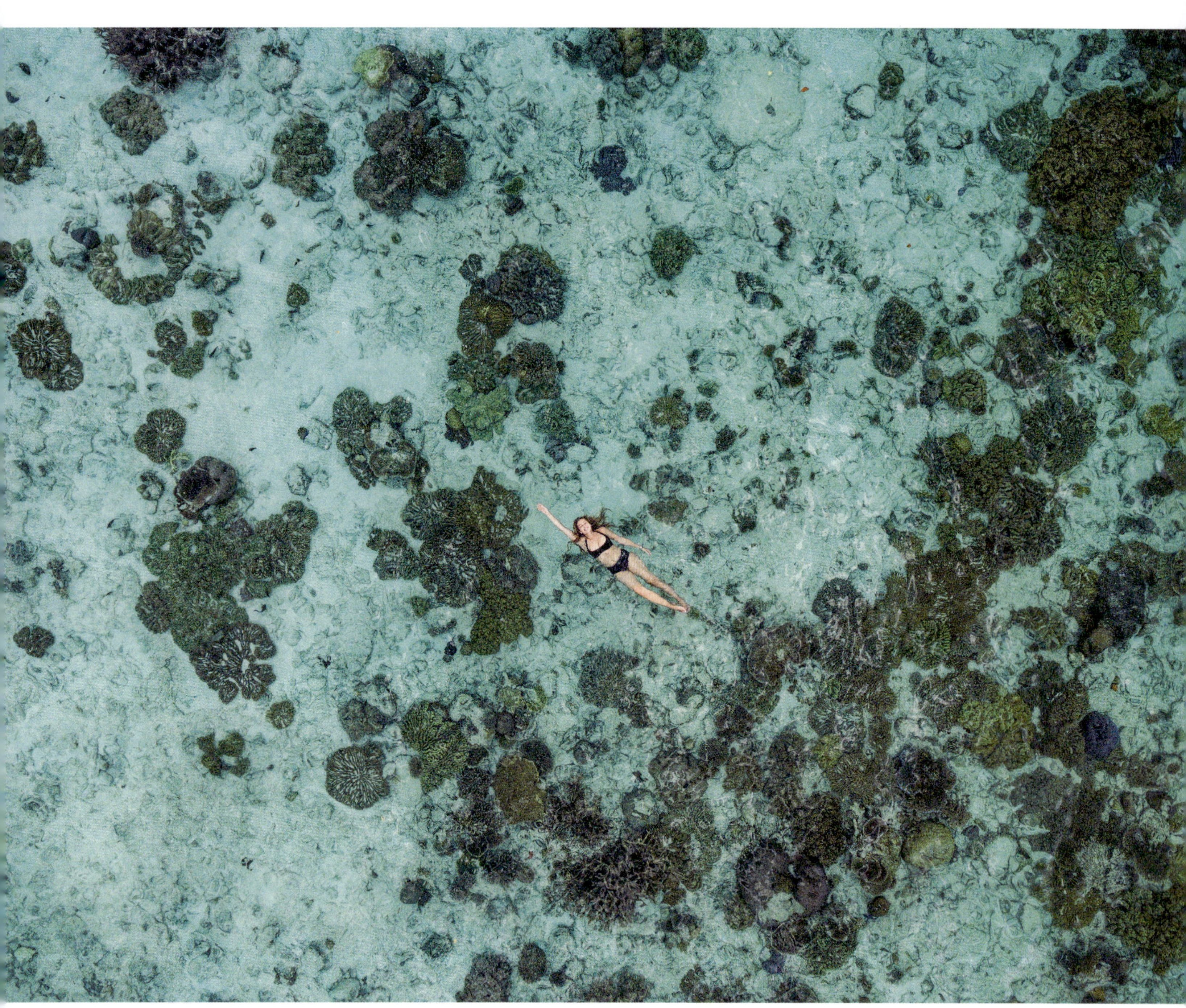

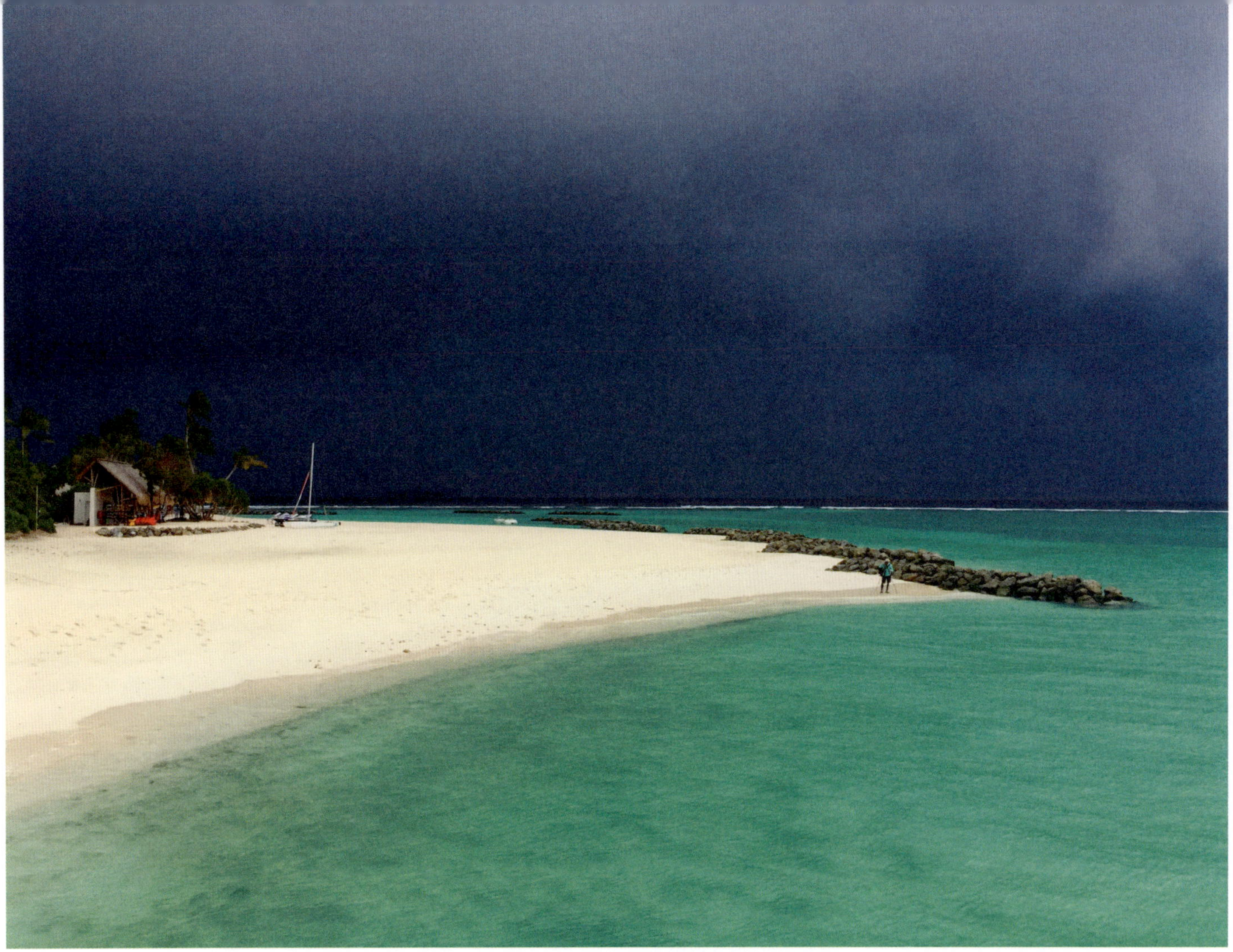

← **Raja Ampat Islands, West Papua, Indonesia**

Alexandra Kryaneva

↑ **THE MALDIVES IS** an equatorial nation of more than a thousand islands in the Indian Ocean southwest of India. The islands are commonly grouped into two chains of twenty-six atolls that stretch north-south over 500 miles of ocean, but with a land area that covers only around 200 square miles. Travelers and scientists come for the clear, warm waters and biodiversity. Visitors typically arrive at the main airport in Malé and then take hopper flights or boats on to a variety of luxury resorts, but it is also possible to backpack and work or volunteer.

Fasmendhoo Island, Raa Atoll, Maldives

Jeralyn Gerba

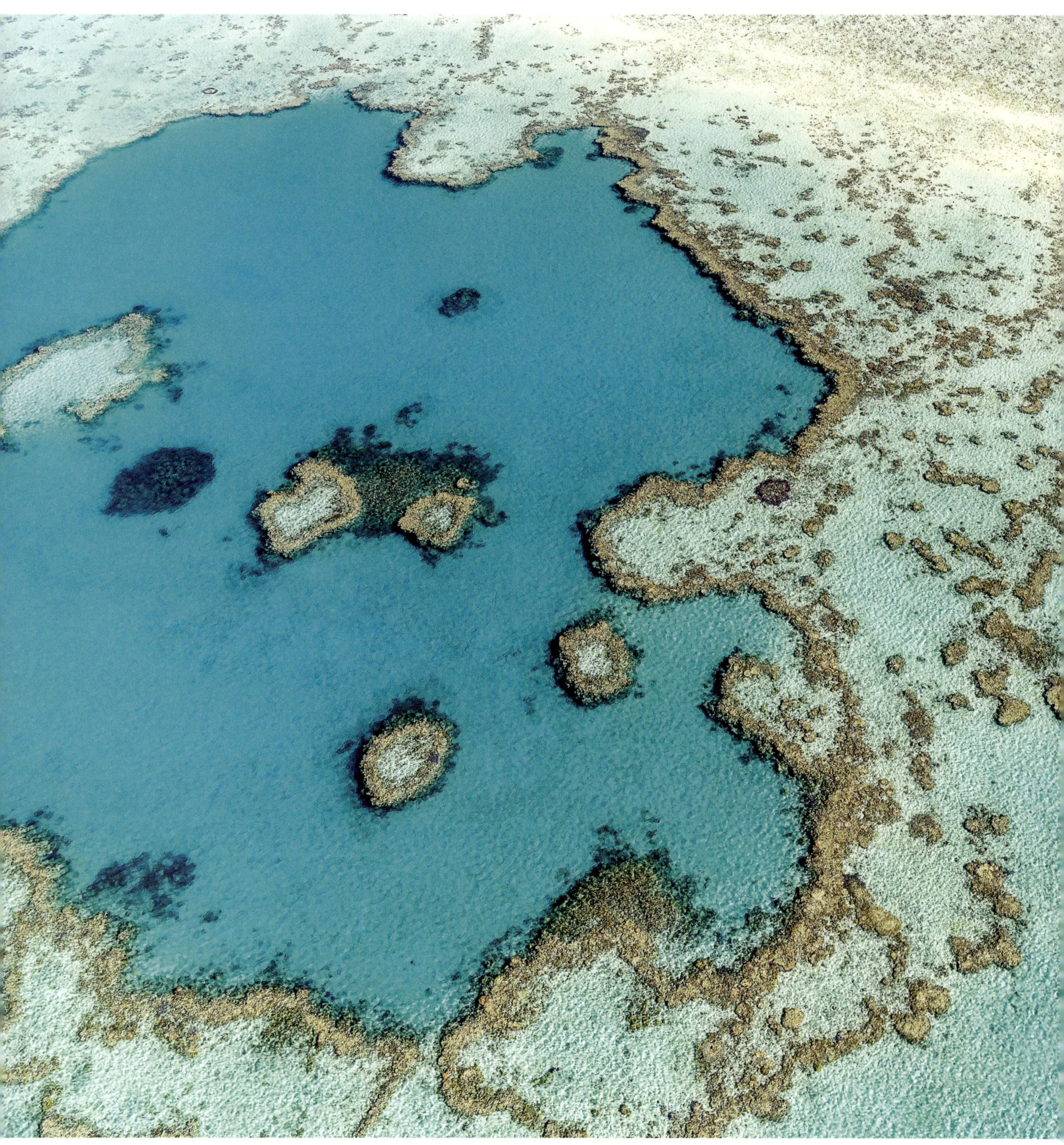

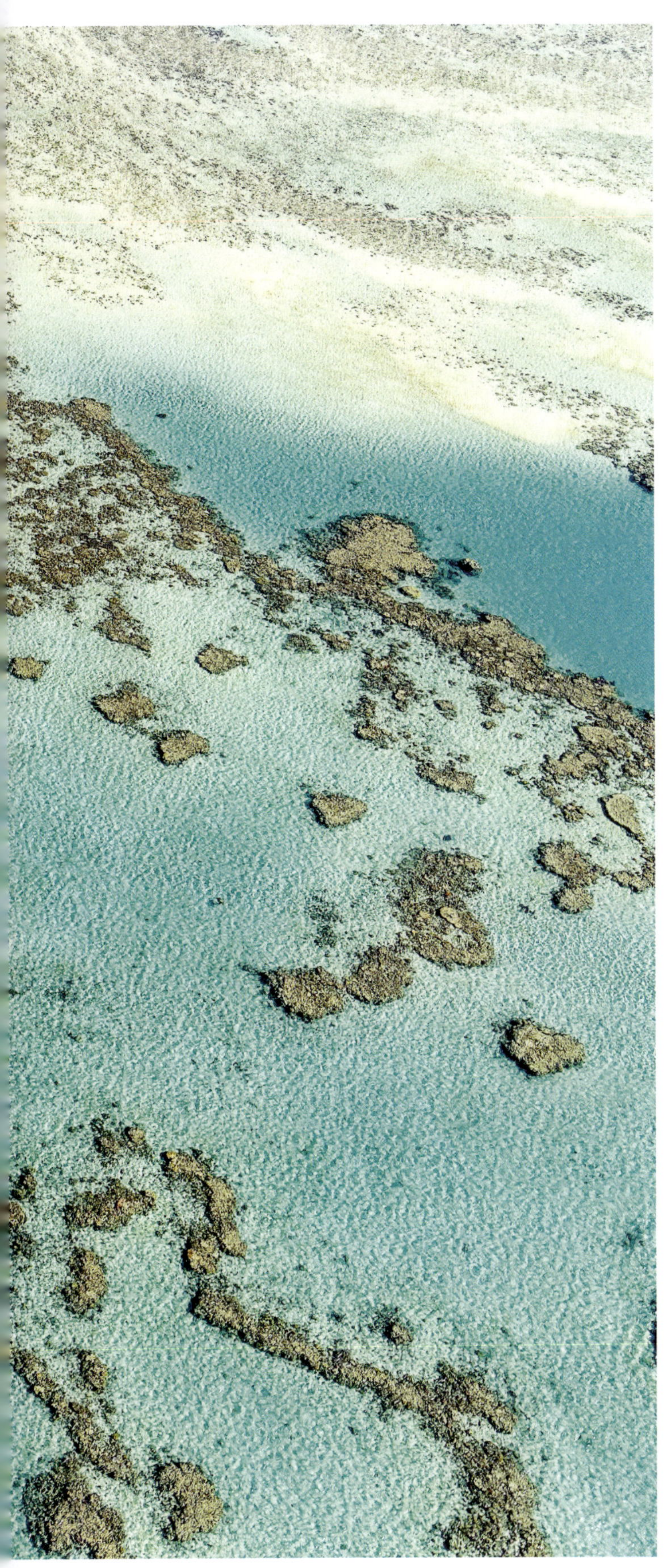

THERE ARE SEVENTY-FOUR Whitsunday Islands off the northeast coast of Queensland in the heart of the Great Barrier Reef. One of seven natural wonders of the world and the largest living structure on Earth, the Great Barrier Reef is home to more than 1,600 species of fish, 3,000 species of mollusks, 30 species of whales and dolphins, and 130 species of sharks and rays. Climate change (and the coral bleaching that goes with it) has unfortunately affected more than 90 percent of the reef. The local tourism commission makes an effort to educate visitors on reef do's and don'ts as well as how to reduce their personal carbon footprint. Additionally, all beaches and hospitality locations have visitor number caps to try to maintain equilibrium.

Whitehaven Beach on Whitsunday Island (the largest in the chain) is known for eye-popping turquoise waters over whorls of soft white silica sand. Since most of the Whitsunday Islands are uninhabited national parklands, visitors come to snorkel, scuba dive, and generally take in the beach beauty on day trips from the adjacent mainland town of Airlie Beach. Overnight sailing trips, scenic flights, and helicopter rides, as well as luxury accommodation options, are available on a number of islands in the chain, such as Hamilton Island.

The Whitsundays are in a tropical rain forest, so time of year is a major consideration when visiting. Many visitors peg September as peak visiting time for the high chance of cooler and drier days, and blue skies. September is also off-season for stinging jellyfish, which abound from October to May.

**Whitsunday Islands,
Queensland,
Australia**
Anita Brechbühl

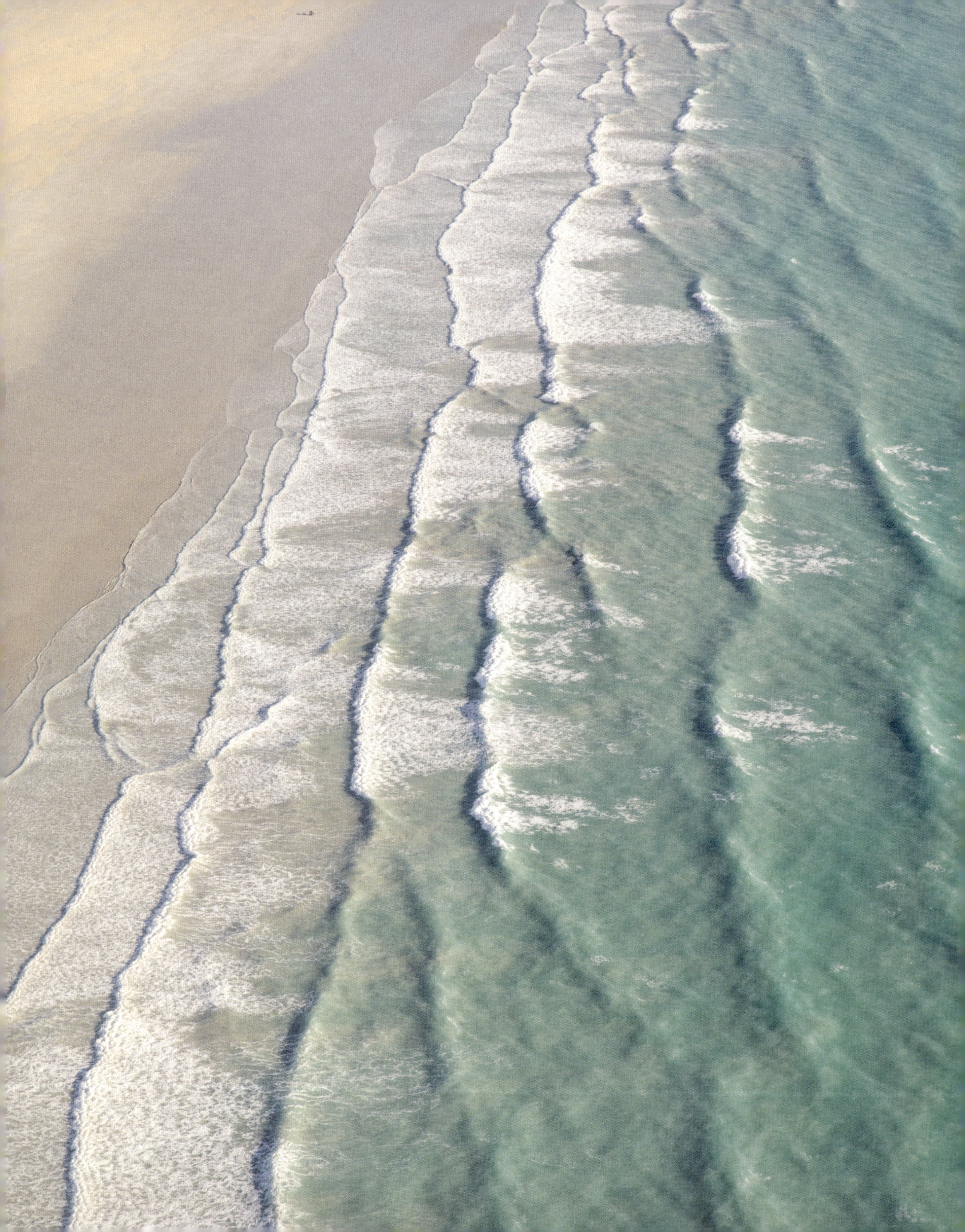

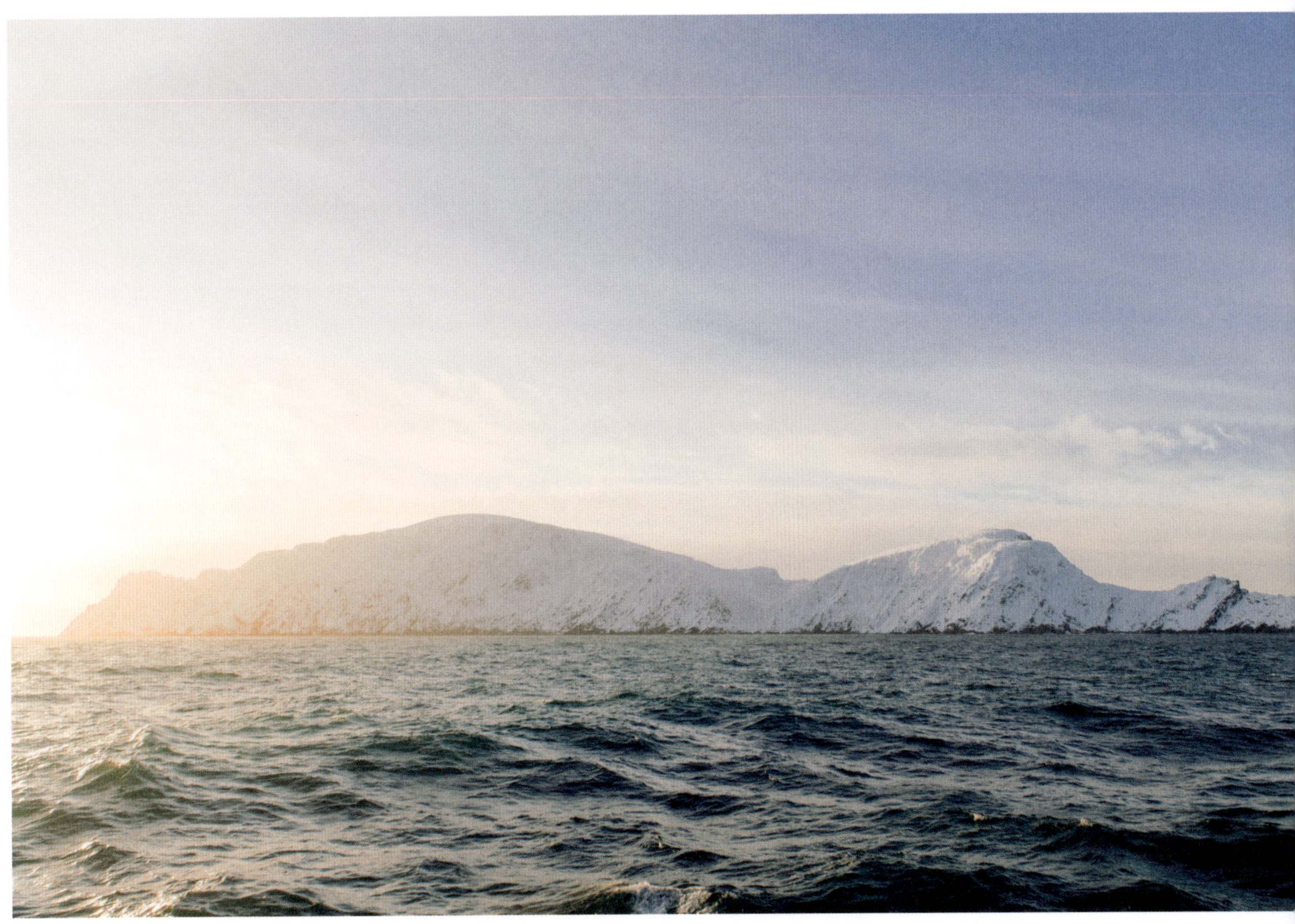

←
**Cable Beach,
Broome, Western
Australia**

Rhiannon Taylor

↑
**Bennett Island,
East Siberian
Sea, Russia**

Adrien de Bontin

The world has always known intense weather events, but it's becoming more clear that these are increasing in frequency and scale due to climate change. In 2019, the most devastating bushfires in history erupted across eastern Australia, propelled by the intense conditions in what was already Australia's hottest and driest year on record. The effects of the fires were devastating: entire communities disappeared, more than a billion animals were lost, and ecosystems have suffered immense damage. The 2018 wildfires in California released approximately sixty-eight million tons of carbon dioxide, roughly equivalent to the emissions from electricity to power the state for a year.

Momentous events like these are becoming even more common—floods, heat waves, powerful storms, droughts, and more are making increasingly frequent appearances in our lives. An overabundance of carbon in our environment, causing much of the damage to our world's coast, is a major contributor to the problem. Because of the warming climate, hurricanes and coastal storms have become more intense, threatening the environmental stability of our coastlines. While natural disasters might seem far off from our everyday actions, the choices we make as individuals and as a planet have a great collective impact.

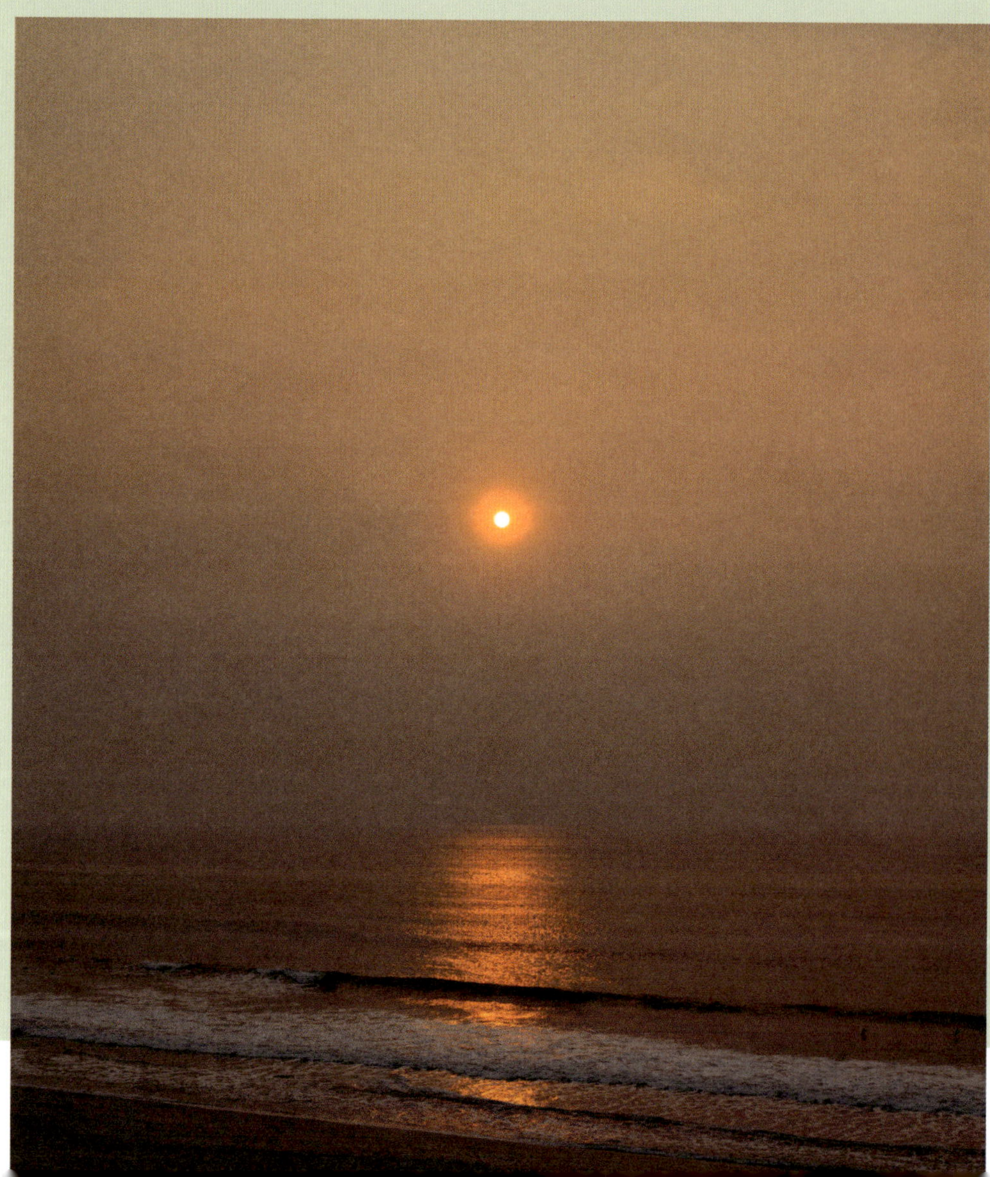

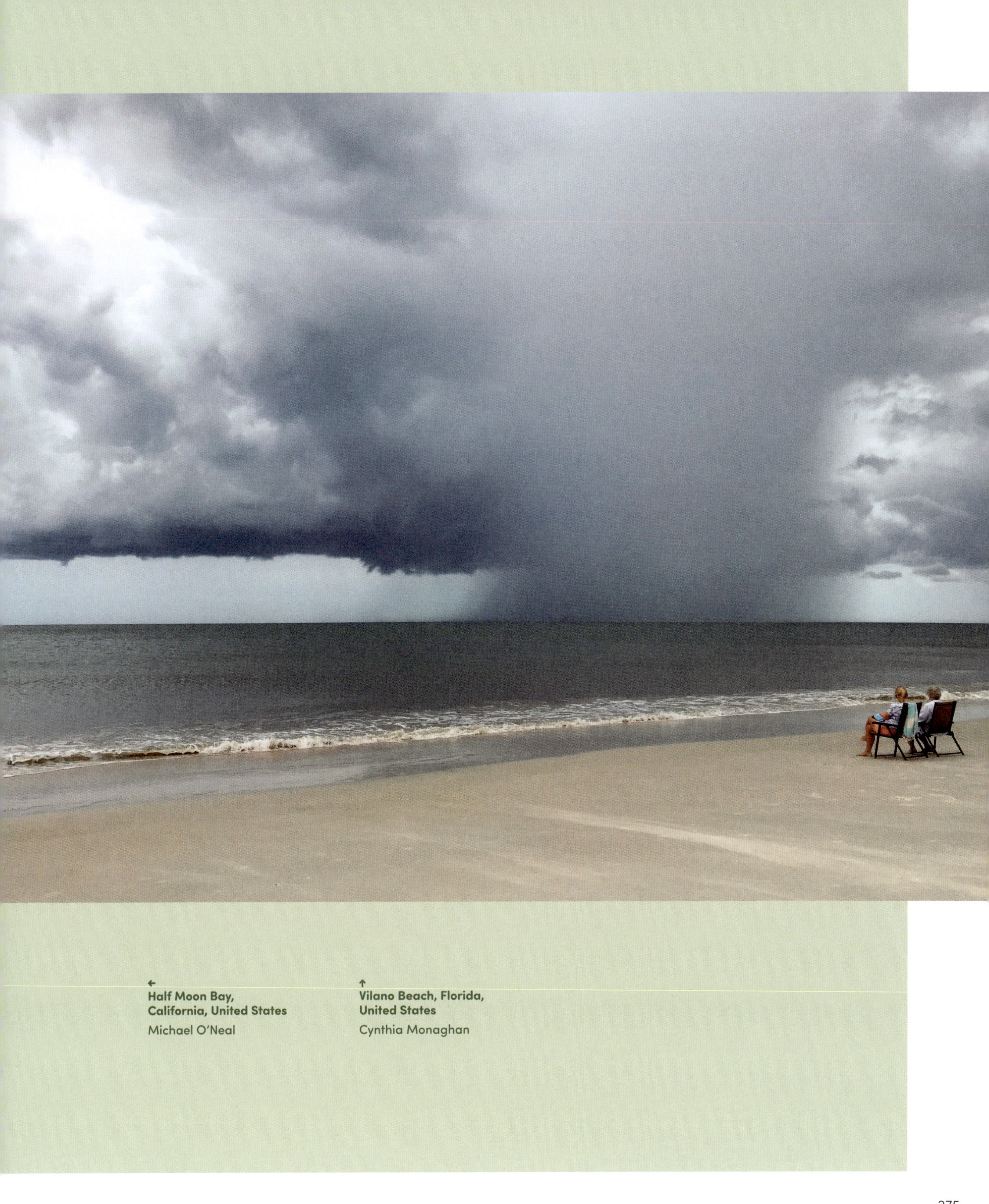

←
**Half Moon Bay,
California, United States**

Michael O'Neal

↑
**Vilano Beach, Florida,
United States**

Cynthia Monaghan

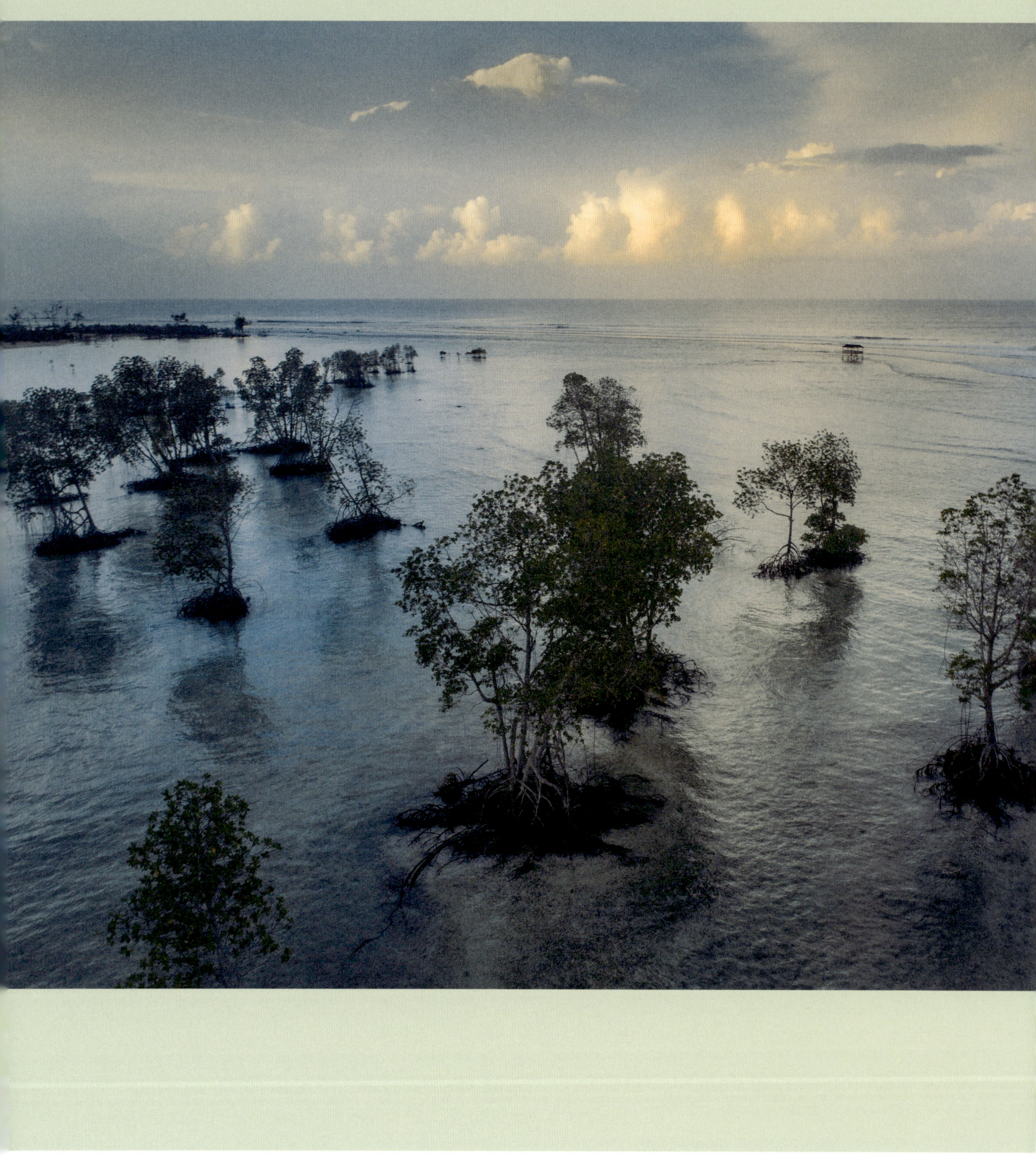

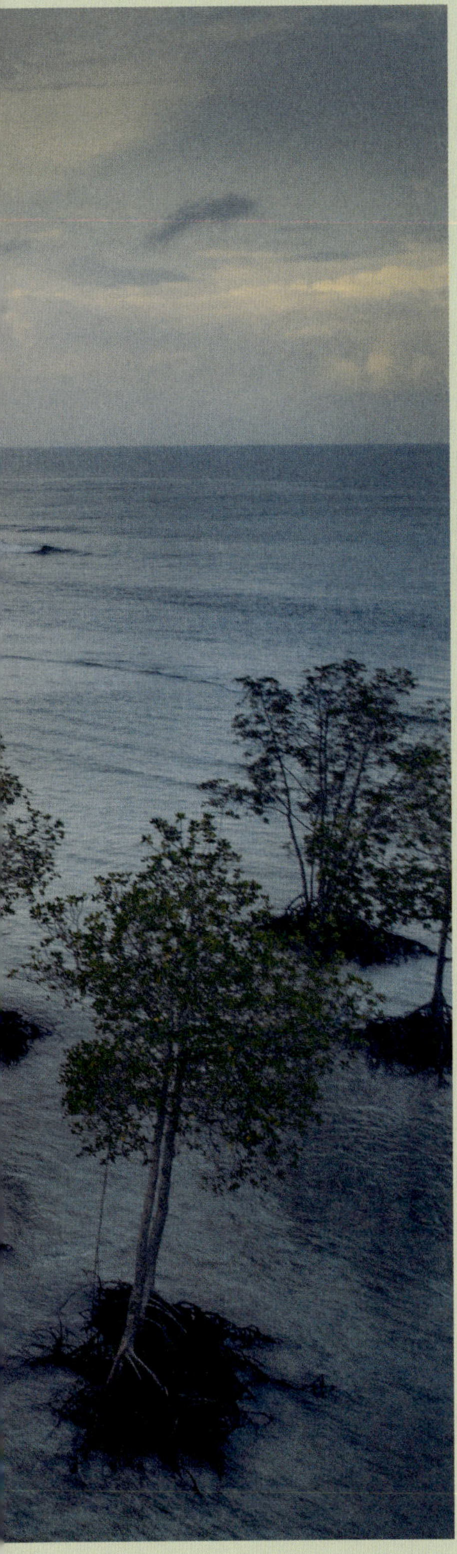

HOW YOU CAN HELP

- Whenever possible and especially when you're traveling, walk, bike, or use public transit instead of driving to reduce carbon dioxide air pollution.

- Use resources such as Regenerative Travel, an online booking tool where travelers can book stays in vetted locations dedicated to protecting the environment and considering their social impact.

- Use the power of your vote to elect local, state, and federal representatives who acknowledge global warming exists and cast a vote for low-emissions vehicles with your dollars when purchasing a new car.

Sumatra, Indonesia
Justin Bastien

acknowledgments

When putting together a book with contributions from over a hundred photographers, the first order of thanks must go to them. Images of our world's coastlines are constantly being captured and it was a delight to curate from such a talented group. Thank you photographers for seeking out the spectacular where sea and land meet and for sharing your work with me and with the world. Second, I would like to thank you, the reader and our Tiny Atlas community. I love connecting our global community of travelers, armchair travelers, and photographers with each other and in turn, sharing their vision with you.

My life in publishing is due in large part to my incredible literary agent Kate Woodrow and team Present Perfect Literature. I cannot imagine creating a book without Kate's support, insight, and advice. A massive thanks to my editor Kaitlin Ketchum and our team at Ten Speed, Kimmy Tejasindhu and Kelly Booth for making this book (and making it so beautiful) with me. A big thanks to our copyeditor Janet Silver Ghent for going all the extra miles to make sure the details we share are correct and clear in oh so many geographic locations.

One major part of the process in making a book is the development of a book pitch and I owe thanks on the pitch for Coastlines to a talented young designer, Tara Hadipour. Jennifer Rodrigue and Lindsey Adams made this entire book with me. Jennifer's help with writing and editing the ideas behind my thoughts was essential throughout as was Lindsey's organization and communication with all our contributors. As with my first book, Charlotte Boates' assistance with writing and research on sustainability issues was invaluable.

Many of the images in Coastlines come from projects Tiny Atlas worked on over the past few years in collaboration with others. I send very special thanks to Chiara Zonca who created a gorgeous set of images at Pelican Point Lodge in Namibia, and to Ben Ono who explored above and below water in Cuba. Thanks to Andrew Tyree from Coast to Costa for getting Ben to Cuba and being the best host. Thank you to Marianna Jamadi who explored the eastern seaboard of Canada and the US aboard a Seaborn ship. Thanks to Gabriel Flores who shared the beauty of Baja California with us, to Playa Viva, David Leventhal, and Amanda Ho from Regenerative Resorts for leading by example with truly exceptional sustainable travel work, to Jesse Evans for sharing her fantastic work and time in Greenland, to Jordan Dyck for her imagery in Greece, to Alex Krowiak for sharing his environmental photography from the Channel Islands, and to Elke Frotscher for her windswept images and dedication to going the distance in Scotland.

Some of the trips I created for clients and Tiny Atlas projects were wonderful reservoirs for contributions to this book. Thanks goes to

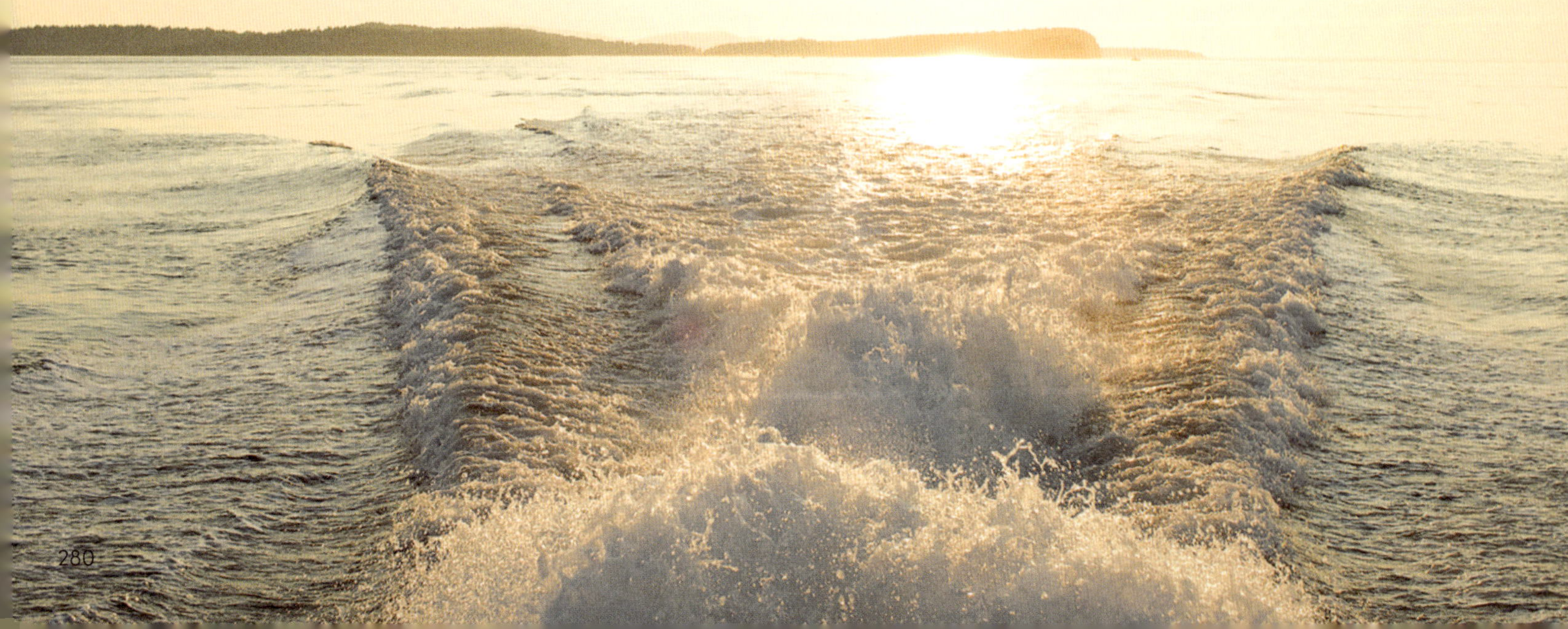

Stephanie Eburah for collaborating with me on retreats to Lummi Island, and to Molly Goodson's Assembly team, Anabel Paksoy and Nancy Lappetito, for collaborating on Lummi. Thanks to Pia Edenhog for taking me out to Tisvilde and Line Borella at the Audo for hosting me in Denmark, to Erik Warner and Stephanie Versin from Sightline Hospitality for the work that brought me to the Kauai coast and the North Fork of Long Island, to Emily Onkey when she was with team Soludos for working with Tiny Atlas on some great projects including one that brought me to Trancoso, Brazil, and to Tamara Siquiera in Trancoso for making all of my last minute production dreams there a reality. Thank you to Brian Pearson from Upscape Travel for bringing our team to Patagonia. Thanks to Megan Lyon from Wintec University for bringing me out to Hamilton, New Zealand to speak, and to Debbie Zampieri and Fiordland Discovery for the opportunity to explore the wonders of Milford Sound on the Fiordland Jewel.

Thanks to Meg Haywood Sulllivan for her contribution and ongoing inspiration to be a planet advocate and conscious traveler, to Liz Clark, and Tasha Van Zandt for the same.

Love and thanks to my husband, Jake, who is my rock at home when he and my son, Otto, can't join me on my travels. He has, along with my parents and sisters, offered endless emotional support and encouragement for my work.

And finally, thanks again to Laura Rubin for getting Tiny Atlas to take those first two trips in the real world with groups and clients many years ago. Our travels have brought so much more of the planet to our photographers, to me, and to all of you.

Thank you,
Emily

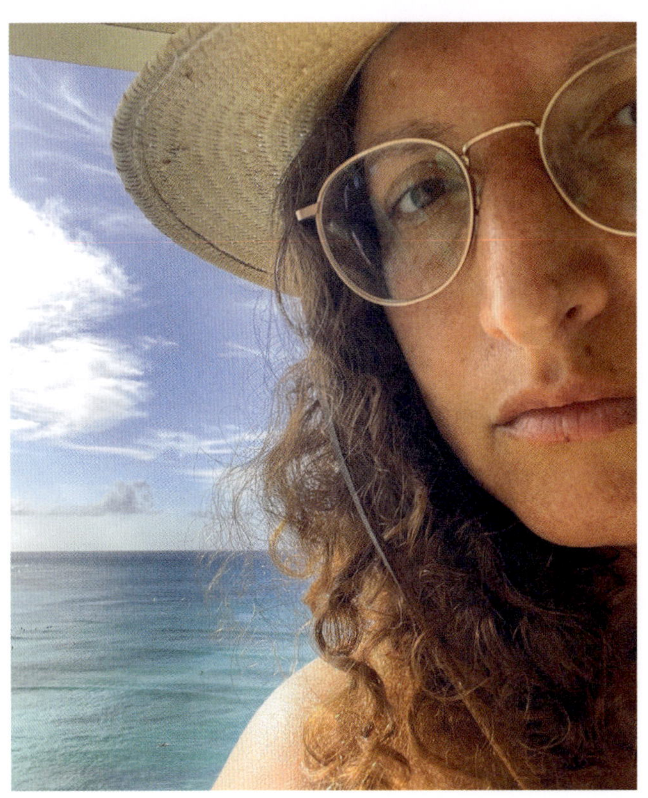

←
Lummi, Washington, United States
Emily Nathan

↗
Honolulu, Oʻahu, Hawaiʻi, United States
Emily Nathan

about the author

EMILY NATHAN founded *Tiny Atlas Quarterly* in 2012 to offer something that was missing from her work as a professional photographer shooting lifestyle and travel images for commercial and editorial clients: the photographer's experience, the intimate moments, and the everyday extraordinary. *Tiny Atlas Quarterly*, the Tiny Atlas Instagram account and accompanying hashtag #mytinyatlas came to be known for merging incredible imagery from some of the best travel photographers in the world with the personal narratives and helpful travel tips that one always brings home from any trip. Emily is based in Oakland, California, where she lives with her husband and son.

Library of Congress Cataloging-in-Publication Data
Names: Nathan, Emily, 1976- editor.
Title: Coastlines / Emily Nathan.
Other titles: Coastlines (Ten Speed Press)
Description: First edition. | California ; New York : Ten Speed Press, [2020] |
  Includes index.
Identifiers: LCCN 2020037047 (print) | LCCN 2020037048 (ebook) | ISBN
  9781984858344 (hardcover) | ISBN 9781984858351 (ebook)
Subjects: LCSH: Coasts—Pictorial works. | Seashore—Pictorial works.
Classification: LCC TR670 .C63 2020 (print) | LCC TR670 (ebook) |
  DDC 779/.37—dc23
LC record available at https://lccn.loc.gov/2020037047
LC ebook record available at https://lccn.loc.gov/2020037048

Hardcover ISBN: 978-1-9848-5834-4
eBook ISBN: 978-1-9848-5835-1

Printed in China

Acquiring editor: Kaitlin Ketchum | Project editor: Kimmy Tejasindhu
Designer: Kelly Booth | Production designers: Mari Gill and Faith Hague
Typefaces: Mostardesign's Sofia Pro Soft by Olivier Gourvat,
Sharp Type's Ogg, and SilkType's Silk Serif by Rakel Tómasdóttir
Production manager: Jane Chinn
Prepress color managers: Nick Patton and Zoe Tokushige
Copyeditor: Janet Silver Ghent | Proofreader: Mikayla Butchart
Publicist: Lauren Kretzchmar | Marketer: Chloe Aryeh

10 9 8 7 6 5 4 3

First Edition

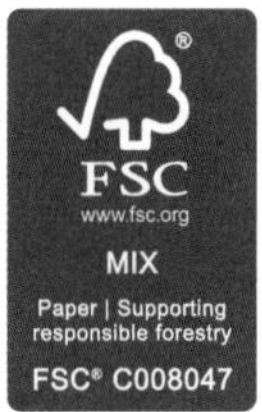

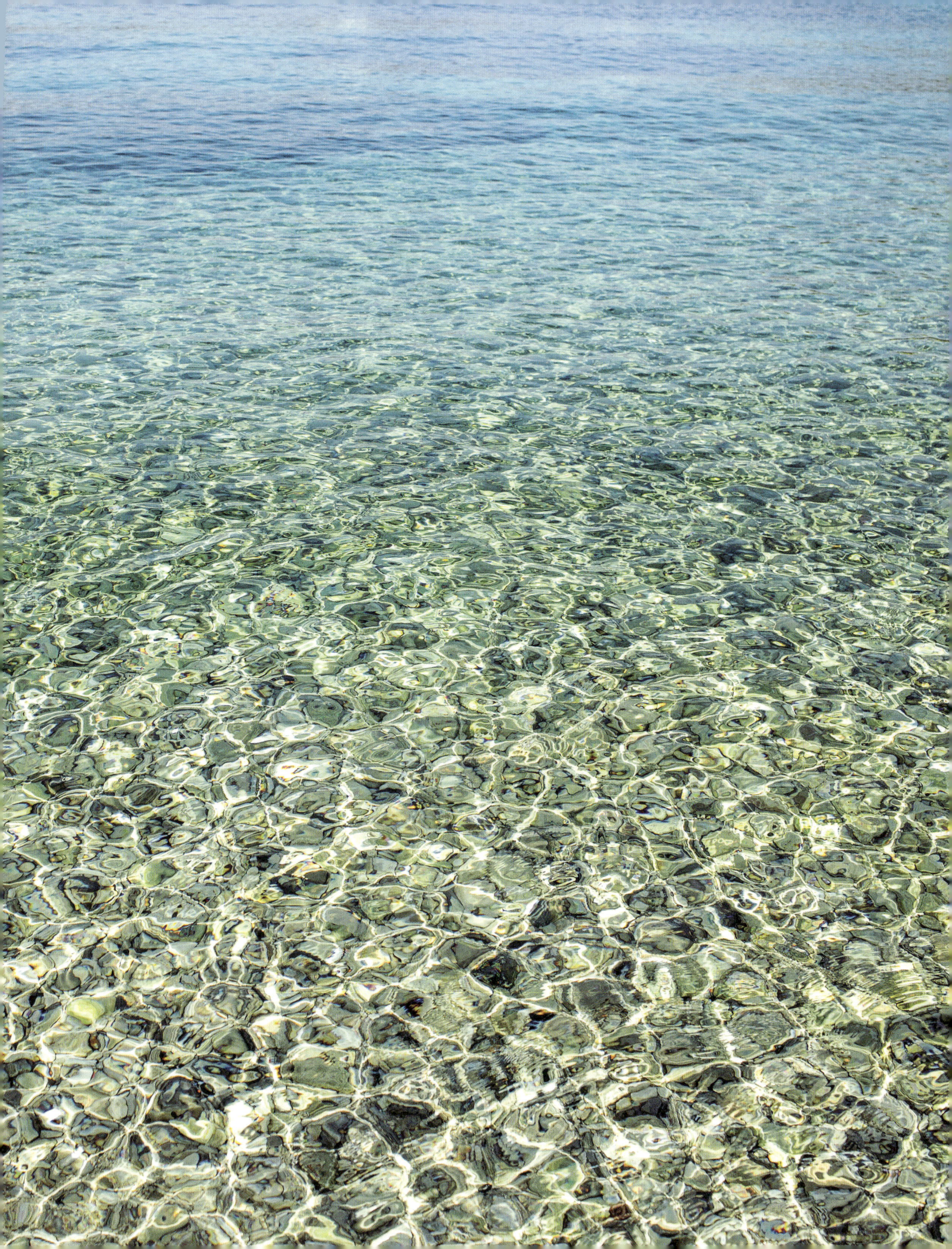